A Treatise
on the
Law of Liens

Common Law, Statutory, Equitable,

and Maritime.

By

Leonard A. Jones

Author of Treatise on Mortgages, Railroad Securities,

and Pledges.

Volume I

BeardBooks

Washington, D.C.

CONTENTS OF VOLUME I.

CHAPTER I.

LIENS AT COMMON LAW.

CHAPTER II.

EQUITABLE LIENS.

CHAPTER III.

CHAPTER IV.

AN ATTORNEY'S GENERAL OR RETAINING LIEN.

CHAPTER V.

AN ATTORNEY'S SPECIAL OR CHARGING LIEN ON JUDGMENTS.

CHAPTER VI.

BANKERS' LIENS.

CHAPTER VII.

CARRIERS' LIENS.

CHAPTER VIII.

LIENS OF CORPORATIONS ON THEIR MEMBERS' SHARES.

CHAPTER IX.

LIENS OF FACTORS, BROKERS, CONSIGNEES, AND MERCHANTS.

CHAPTER X.

CHAPTER XI.

INNKEEPERS' AND BOARDING–HOUSE KEEPERS' LIENS.

CHAPTER XII.

LANDLORDS' LIENS FOR RENT.

CHAPTER XIII.

LIENS OF LIVERY-STABLE KEEPERS AND AGISTORS.

CHAPTER XIV.

LUMBERMEN'S LIENS.

CHAPTER XV.

LIENS OF MECHANICS, ARTISANS, AND LABORERS, UPON PERSONAL PROPERTY.

CHAPTER XVI.

CHAPTER XVII.

SELLER'S LIEN FOR PURCHASE-MONEY.

CHAPTER XVIII.

THE SELLER'S RIGHT OF STOPPAGE IN TRANSITU.

CHAPTER XIX.

WAREHOUSEMEN AND WHARFINGERS' LIENS.

CHAPTER XX.

ASSIGNMENT OF LIENS.

CHAPTER XXI.

WAIVER OF LIENS.

CHAPTER XXII.

REMEDIES FOr THE ENFORCEMENT OF LIENS.

CONTENTS OF VOLUME II.

LIENS UPON REAL PROPERTY, AND MARITIME LIENS.

CHAPTER XXIII.

GRANTOR'S OR VENDOR'S IMPLIED LIEN FOR PURCHASE-MONEY.

CHAPTER XXIV.

CHAPTER XXV.

THE VENDOR'S LIEN BY CONTRACT OR RESERVATION.

CHAPTER XXVI.

IMPROVEMENT LIENS OF OCCUPANTS.

CHAPTER XXVII.

IMPROVEMENT LIENS OF JOINT TENANTS, TENANTS IN COMMON, AND TENANTS FOR LIFE OR FOR YEARS.

CHAPTER XXVIII.

CHAPTER XXIX.

CHAPTER XXX.

CHAPTER XXXI.

MECHANICS' LIENS : CONTRACT OR CONSENT OF OWNER.

CHAPTER XXXII.

MECHANICS' LIENS OF SUB-CONTRACTORS.

CHAPTER XXXIII.

MECHANICS' LIENS : FOR WHAT LABOR AND MATERIALS GIVEN.

CHAPTER XXXIV.

MECHANICS' LIENS : WHAT PROPERTY IS SUBJECT TO.

CHAPTER XXXV.

MECHANICS' LIENS : THE CLAIM, CERTIFICATE, OR NOTICE.

CHAPTER XXXVI.

MECHANICS' LIENS : PRIORITY AS REGARDS MORTGAGES AND OTHER INCUMBRANCES AND LIENS.

CHAPTER XXXVII

CHAPTER XXXVIII.

MECHANICS' LIENS : WAIVER AND LOSS OF.

CHAPTER XXXIX.

MECHANICS' LIENS : PROCEEDINGS TO ENFORCE.

THE LAW OF LIENS

AT COMMON LAW, BY STATUTE, EQUITABLE, AND MARITIME.

———•———

CHAPTER I.

LIENS AT COMMON LAW.

I. *Definition and Limitation of the Subject.*

1. Introductory. The present chapter is intended merely as an introduction to the general subject of common law liens. But liens at common law naturally introduce the other forms of liens treated of, namely, equitable liens, liens by statute, and maritime liens. The characteristics of these liens are generally described by stating how they differ from liens at common law.

The common law liens all relate to personal property, though there are also liens upon personal property in equity and by statute. The common law liens upon personal property are, in many instances, modified or enlarged by statute; while also equitable liens, upon both personal property and real property, are in many instances modified or enlarged by statute. By statute, moreover, maritime liens are in like manner affected. Finally, new liens have been created by statute which had never been asserted at law or in equity, or by maritime law. It is impossible therefore to treat of all common law liens by themselves; to treat of all equitable liens by themselves; and then to treat of all maritime liens by themselves. The subject must be divided by reference to the subject-matter of the liens: first, by reference to the kinds of property to be affected, and then by reference to the classes of

1

persons in whose favor the liens arise. As to the kinds of property, there are the two natural divisions of personal and real; and maritime property, being governed by peculiar laws, forms a third division. When we come to the consideration of the liens pertaining to the several trades and callings, such as the liens of attorneys, bankers, and others, within the division of liens upon personal property, it has seemed best to treat of them in separate chapters, because these liens generally differ from each other by marked peculiarities; and, moreover, as we find no natural order of arrangement, as indicated by the principles governing these liens, as a matter of practical convenience in referring to the book they are arranged alphabetically.

The introductory chapters upon Common Law Liens, Equitable Liens, and Statutory Liens treat of some of the principal characteristics of these liens in a general manner; but reference should be had to other parts of the work treating of particular liens for a fuller development and illustration of many points touched upon in these general chapters, and for others not referred to in them. As regards liens upon personal property, there are some principles and rules applicable to several different kinds of liens in respect to the assignment, waiver, and enforcement of these liens; and therefore the first volume, which is devoted to liens upon personal property, closes with general chapters relating to the Assignment of Liens, the Waiver of Liens, and Enforcement of Liens.

2. The word "Lien" is here used in its legal and technical sense.[1] Much confusion has arisen from using the word in a loose manner, at one time in its technical sense, and at another in its popular sense. It is often convenient and proper to speak of the lien of a mortgage, or of the lien of a pledge. Of course it will often happen, when the word is used in this sense, that the

---

[1] The word "lien" became a law term at a comparatively recent date. The right existed, under the name of a right of retainer, as early as the reign of Edward IV.; but the name "lien" does not seem to have been given to this right till about the beginning of the eighteenth century. The word is derived from the French, and farther back from the Latin, and primarily means to "tie," to "bind." The common law right of retainer implies possession; and a common law lien implies possession; but the term is sometimes used in a broader sense than the mere right to retain: it is often used to designate rights which do not depend upon possession, as in the case of statutory, equitable, and maritime liens.

description of the lien shows that the word is used merely to denote the charge or incumbrance of a mortgage, pledge, attachment, or judgment. And so in many other instances the word is used in a popular sense to denote a charge which is not in a strict sense a lien by law, custom, statute, or in equity. But in a treatise upon the subject it is imperative, not only to use the word in its proper sense, but also to distinguish between the proper and improper use of the word in the decisions that are used as authorities, or are commented upon.

3. Definitions. — A lien has been well defined to be " a right in one man to detain that, which is in his possession, belonging to another till certain demands of him, the person in possession, are satisfied." [1] The codes of California [2] and Dakota [3] declare that " a lien is a charge imposed in some mode, other than by a transfer in trust, upon specific property by which it is made security for the performance of an act."

" The term 'lien,'" says Chancellor Bland, [4] "is applied in various modes; but, in all cases, it signifies an obligation, tie, or claim annexed to or attaching upon property, without satisfying which such property cannot be demanded by its owner. Lien, in its proper sense, is a right which the law gives. But it is usual to speak of lien by contract, though that be more in the nature of an agreement for a pledge. And there are liens which exist only in equity, and of which equity alone can take cognizance. The existence of a lien, however, and the benefit which may be derived from it, as well as the mode in which that benefit may be obtained, depend upon principles of law and circumstances so various that it is always indispensably necessary carefully to attend to those particulars by which its very substance may be materially affected."

4. A lien at law is an implied obligation whereby real or personal property is bound for the discharge of some debt or engagement. It is not the result of an express contract; it is given by implication of law. [5] It is true that we often speak of

---

[1] Hammonds v. Barclay, 2 East, 227, 235, per Grose, J.; and see McCaffrey v. Wooden, 62 Barb. (N. Y.) 316, 323, per Johnson, J.

[2] 2 Codes and Stats. 1885, § 2872 of Civ. Code.

[3] Dak. Codes, 1883, § 1697 of Civ. Code.

[4] Ridgely v. Iglehart, 3 Bland (Md.) Ch. 540.

[5] Leith's Estate, in re, L. R. 1 P. C. 296, 305, per Lord Westbury;

a lien by contract; but such an obligation is rather in the nature of an agreement for a pledge or mortgage. In its strict and proper sense a lien is a right which the law gives, for, to make a lien at law, possession must be given, and possession under a contract for security generally constitutes a pledge or a mortgage, according to the terms of the contract. A lien by contract without possession is an equitable lien or charge. If a lien be given by express contract in a case where the law would otherwise imply a lien, the express stipulation excludes the implied lien, and limits the rights of the parties to the express contract.[1]

5. A lien by contract exists only where it is expressly agreed that a party may retain the property as security for the work done or expense incurred in respect of it. There must be something more than a contract for the payment of the price. The law implies no lien from such a contract, but the parties may so form their contract as to create a lien, if they choose.[2]

A lien by contract cannot, any more than an implied lien, exist without possession. The contract itself is not equivalent to possession, and it does not give possession. Thus a declaration at the end of a promissory note or other obligation, that it constitutes a lien upon certain property, does not amount to a contract for a lien, unless the creditor retains possession of the property.[3]

6. It was at one time doubted whether a lien could exist at common law where the parties had specially agreed as to the price;[4] but this doubt was removed by the judgment in Chase

---

Gladstone v. Birley, 2 Mer. 401, 404, per Grant, Master of the Rolls; Wilson v. Heather, 5 Taunt. 642, 646; Ridgely v. Iglehart, 3 Bland (Md.), 540; Cummings v. Harris, 3 Vt. 244. In the latter case Hutchinson (C. J.) said: "The usual cases in which the law creates a lien are, where the person performing services would have no other sure remedy, as a blacksmith shoeing a horse for a stranger; or a watchmaker cleaning a watch for a stranger; or an innkeeper furnishing entertainment for travellers; and, where the persons applying for these services are not strangers, the usage of their dealing may be such that the law will create a lien. For instance, the course of their dealing may be that payment for services is always made before the property is taken away."

[1] Leith's Estate, in re, supra.

[2] Cummings v. Harris, 3 Vt. 244.

[3] Roberts v. Jacks, 31 Ark. 597; Barnett v. Mason, 7 Ark. 253; Waddell v. Carlock, 41 Ark. 523.

[4] Brenan v. Currint, Sayer, 224; Case of an Hostler, Yelv. 67, note; Stevenson v. Blakelock, 1 M. & S. 535.

v. Westmore,[1] and the rule was there established that such agreement does not impair the right of lien unless a future time of payment is fixed by the parties, or some other stipulation be made which is inconsistent with the lien.   Lord Ellenborough, delivering the judgment of the court in this case, said: " We believe the practice of modern times has not proceeded upon any distinction between an agreement for a stipulated price and the implied contract to pay a reasonable price or sum ; and that the right of detainer has been practically acknowledged in both cases alike. In the case of Wolf *v.* Summers[2] Mr. J. Lawrence does not appear to have been aware of any such distinction.   It is impossible, indeed, to find any solid reason for saying that, if I contract with a miller to grind my wheat at 15*s.* a load, he shall be bound to deliver it to me, when ground, without receiving the price of his labor ; but that, if I merely deliver it to him to grind, without fixing the price, he may detain it until I pay him, though probably he would demand, and the law would give him, the very same sum.   Certainly, if the right of detainer, considered as a right at common law, exists only in those cases where there is no manner of contract between the parties, except such as the law implies, this court cannot extend the rule ; and authorities were quoted to establish this proposition ; but, upon consideration, we are of opinion that those authorities are contrary to reason, and to the principles of law, and ought not to govern our present decision."

The learned Chief Justice notices in detail some of the early authorities and *dicta* in which it was held that the fixing of a price beforehand defeats the exercise of the right of lien.[3]   But

---

[1] 5 M. & S. 180 (1816).

[2] 2 Campb. 631.

[3] In 2 Rol. Abr. 92, a *dictum* of Williams, J., is quoted in these words: " If I put my clothes to a tailor to make, he may keep them until satisfaction for the making.   But if I contract with a tailor that he shall have so much for making my apparel, he cannot keep them until satisfaction for the making."   See, also, *dictum* of Lord Holt in Collins *v.* Ougly, Selw. N. P. 1280 ; and the case of Brenan *v.* Currint, Sayer, 224.   There are expressions in other cases to the effect

that a lien is a right accompanying an implied contract, as by the Lord Chancellor in Cowell *v.* Simpson, 16 Ves. 275.   Chief Justice Ellenborough, however, in Chase *v.* Westmore, 5 M. & S. 180, suggests that Williams, J., above quoted, should be understood to speak of a contract for time, as well as the amount of payment, and that the authorities built upon his saying are founded on a mistake ; for the earliest authority on the subject makes no distinction between an implied contract and a contract for fixed price. This authority is in the Year Book,

all this is now chiefly interesting as showing the history of the doctrine, for since the judgment in Chase *v.* Westmore it is everywhere held to be immaterial as regards the lien whether the price be fixed by special agreement or not.[1]

7. A lien by express contract supersedes the lien implied at common law;[2] but upon a failure of the owner of the property to comply with the stipulations of the contract, so that a lien can arise within its terms, the common law lien may attach. Thus, where one agreed to supply to the owner of a sawmill a certain quantity of logs to be sawed into boards and transported to market at a stipulated price, to be paid upon the delivery of specified quantities, and the mill-owner was to have a lien for the price, the other party failed to furnish the specified quantity of logs, so that the mill-owner was unable to saw and deliver the specified quantity of boards and claim a lien within the terms of his contract; but it was held his common law lien attached to the boards in his hands, notwithstanding the special agreement.[3]

8. A lien which arises by operation of law generally over-

Easter Term, 5 Edw. 4, fol. 2, b. "Note, also by Haydon, that an hostler may detain a horse if the master will not pay him for his eating. The same law is, if a tailor make me a gown, he may keep the gown until he is paid for his labor. And the same law is, if I buy of you a horse for 20s., you may keep the horse until I pay you the 20s.; but if I am to pay you at Michaelmas next ensuing, then you shall not keep the horse until you are paid."

The distinction drawn is where a future time of payment is fixed. "If so material a distinction as that which depends upon fixing the amount of the price had been supposed to exist at that time, we think," says Lord Ellenborough, "it would have been noticed in this place ; and, not being noticed, we think it was not then supposed to exist."

In a case so late as 1809 Lord Eldon speaks of a lien, except in the case of a lien for purchase money, as *primâ facie* a right accompanying the implied contract; and says that if possession be commenced under an implied contract, and afterwards a special contract be made for payment, in the nature of the thing the one contract destroys the other. But, as Lord Ellenborough remarks in Chase *v.* Westmore, it is evident that the Lord Chancellor was speaking of a special contract for a particular mode of payment, — a contract inconsistent with the common law right.

[1] 2 Selwyn's N. P. 540; Crawshay *v.* Homfray, 4 B. & Ald. 50; Steinman *v.* Wilkins, 7 W. & S. (Pa.) 466 ; Mathias *v.* Sellers, 86 Pa. St. 486 ; Pinney *v.* Wells, 10 Conn. 104 ; Hanna *v.* Phelps, 7 Ind. 21.

[2] Leith's Estate, *in re*, L. R. 1 P. C. 296.

[3] Mount *v.* Williams, 11 Wend. (N. Y.) 77.

rides all other rights in the property to which it attaches, while
a lien which is created by contract or by statute is generally subordinate to all prior existing rights therein.   Thus the lien of a
workman who has repaired a chattel is superior to an existing
mortgage upon it.[1] But a farmer who, under a special contract
with the owner of horses, has kept and fed them during the winter, has no lien upon them for the price of keeping as against the
mortgagee.[2]

9. As a general rule, a person can create a lien on property only to the extent of his interest in it.   He need not be
the sole and absolute owner in order to give a lien upon property: but if he has an equitable title with possession, or some
legal interest with possession, he may create a lien upon such interest as he has; but this lien will not ordinarily affect rights of
other part owners, or of a mortgagee or other incumbrancer. One
who is merely a conditional purchaser, so long as the condition
on which title was to vest in him is not fulfilled, cannot create a
lien on the property so as to impair the title of the owner.[3] One
who has no title to property can confer no lien upon it, either by
his act or by express contract.[4]

10. A lien, whether implied or by contract, confers no
right of property upon the holder.   It is neither a *jus ad rem*,
nor a *jus in re*.   It is neither a right of property in the thing,
nor a right of action for the thing.   It is simply a right of detainer.[5] "Liens are not founded on property," says Mr. Justice
Buller;[6] "but they necessarily suppose the property to be in
some other person, and not in him who sets up the right."   Consequently the interest of the lien-holder is not attachable, either
as personal property or as a chose in action.[7]

---

[1] Williams *v.* Allsup, 10 C. B. N. S.
417; Hammond *v.* Danielson, 126
Mass. 294; Scott *v.* Delahunt, 5 Lans.
(N. Y.) 372.

[2] Bissell *v.* Pearce, 28 N. Y. 252.

[3] Walker *v.* Burt, 57 Ga. 20.

[4] Conrow *v.* Little, 41 Hun (N. Y),
395.

[5] Brace *v.* Marlborough, 2 P. W.
491 ; Hammonds *v.* Barclay, 2 East,
227, 235; Peck *v.* Jenness, 7 How. 612,
620, per Grier, J. ; Meany *v.* Head,
1 Mason. 319, per Story, J. ; Foster,

ex parte, 2 Story, 131, 147, per Story,
J.; Jacobs *v.* Knapp, 50 N. H. 71.

[6] Lickbarrow *v.* Mason, 6 East, 21,
24.

Notwithstanding an agreement to
the contrary, a lien, or a contract for
a lien, transfers no title to the property subject to the lien. 2 Codes
and Stats. of California, 1885, § 2888
of Civ. Code ; Dakota Codes, 1883,
§ 1706 of Civ. Code.

[7] Meany *v.* Head, *supra;* Jacobs *v.*
Knapp, 50 N. H. 71.

11. A mortgage is sometimes inaccurately called a lien.
"And so it certainly is," says Mr. Justice Story,[1] "and something more: it is a transfer of the property itself as security for
the debt. This must be admitted to be true at law; and it is
equally true in equity, for in this respect equity follows the law.
It does not consider the estate of the mortgagee as defeated and
reduced to a mere lien, but it treats it as a trust estate, and, according to the intention of the parties, as a qualified estate, and
security. When the debt is discharged, there is a resulting trust
for the mortgagor. It is therefore only in a loose and general
sense that it is sometimes called a lien, and then only by way of
contrast to an estate absolute and indefeasible."

In like manner we speak of the lien of a pledge. But a pledge
is also a lien and something more. It is a deposit by a debtor of
personal property by way of security, with an implied power in
the creditor to sell it upon default. But a lien-holder has no
power of sale, and except as authorized by statute he cannot
at law enforce his lien. He can only hold possession of the
property.[2]

12. An attachment on mesne process does not constitute a lien in any proper legal sense of the term. Though
an attachment is sometimes spoken of as a lien, the term is then
used only in a general sense, by way of analogy and illustration.
"An attachment," says Judge Story,[3] "does not come up to the
exact definition or meaning of a lien, either in the general sense
of the common law, or in that of the maritime law, or in that of
equity jurisprudence. Not in that of the common law, because
the creditor is not in possession of the property: but it is *in cus-
todiâ legis*, if personal property; if real property, it is not a fixed
and vested charge, but it is a contingent, conditional charge,
until the judgment and levy. Not in the sense of the maritime
law, which does not recognize or enforce any claim as a lien
until it has become absolute, fixed, and vested. Not in that of
equity jurisprudence, for there a lien is not a *jus in re*, or a *jus
ad rem*. It is but a charge upon the thing, and then only when
it has, in like manner, become absolute, fixed, and vested."

13. Even a judgment does not constitute a lien upon

[1] Conard *v.* Atlantic Ins. Co. 1 Pet.
386, 441.

[2] Jones on Pledges, §§ 1, 2.

[3] Foster, *ex parte*, 2 Story, 131, 145.

the real estate of the debtor. It is only a general charge upon all his real estate to be enforced by an execution and levy upon some part or the whole of it. It is not a common law lien, for it is not supported by possession. It had its origin in the statute of 2 Westminster, 13 Edw. 1,[1] giving the right to an *elegit*,[2] though a judgment charging the lands of the debtor is called a lien in the courts of equity in England, and in the courts of law of many of our states.[3] "Lien upon a judgment is a vague and inaccurate expression," said Mr. Justice Erle.[4]

II. *Specific and General Liens.*

14. A lien is either specific or general. The former attaches to specific property as security for some demand which the creditor has in respect to that property, such as a demand for the unpaid price of work done, or materials furnished in repairing or constructing a specific chattel. The codes of California[5] and Dakota[6] declare that a special lien is one which the holder thereof can enforce only as security for the performance of a particular act or obligation, and of such obligations as may be incidental thereto.

A specific lien may arise by implication of law, by usage of trade, by the contract of the parties, or by statute. The implied lien, or lien by common law, was doubtless the first in the order of development in English jurisprudence; and in this country it was adopted as a part of the common law. "It is not to be doubted," said Chief Justice Gibson of Pennsylvania,[7] "that the law of particular or specific lien on goods in the hands of a tradesman or artisan for the price of work done on them, though there is no trace of its recognition in our own books, was brought hither by our ancestors, and that it is a part of our common law. It was as proper for their condition and circumstances here as it had been in the parent land; and though a *general* lien for an entire balance of accounts was said by Lord Ellenborough[8] to be

---

[1] St. 1, ch. 18.

[2] Foster, *ex parte*, 2 Story, 131, 146.

[3] Peck *v.* Jenness, 7 How. 612, 620, per Grier, J.; Waller *v.* Best, 3 How. 111 ; Dunklee *v.* Fales, 5 N. H. 527; Kittredge *v.* Bellows, 7 N. H. 399, 428.

[4] Brunsdon *v.* Allard, 2 E. & E. 17.

[5] Civil Code, § 2875.

[6] Civil Code, § 1700.

[7] M'Intyre *v.* Carver, 2 Watts & S. (Pa.) 392, 395.

[8] Rushforth *v.* Hadfield, 7 East, 224, 229.

an encroachment on the common law, yet it has never been intimated that a particular lien on specific chattels for the price of
labor bestowed on them does not grow necessarily and naturally out of the transactions of mankind as a matter of public
policy. Originally the remedy by retainer seems to have been
only coextensive with the workman's obligation to receive the
goods; a limitation of it which would, perhaps, be inconsistent
with its existence here, for we have no instance of a mechanic
being compelled to do jobs for another. But even the more
recent British decisions have extended it to the case of every
bailee who has, by his labor or skill, conferred value on the
thing bailed to him."

The principal specific or particular liens upon personal property at common law are those of Mechanics and Artisans, of
Innkeepers, of Carriers, of Sellers or Vendors, and of Landlords
under the process of distress.[1]

15. A lien expressly or impliedly limited to a particular
debt will not be extended to cover another debt, except
by express agreement or plain intention of the parties.[2] Thus,
where certain dyers who had a lien on goods dyed by them
for the price of the dyeing of the same, also claimed a lien upon
them for other goods dyed and returned by them at a prior
time, it was held that the lien could not be thus extended,
because it was to be inferred from the manner of dealing between the parties that the dyers relied upon the personal credit
of the owners of the goods for the price of dyeing those which
had been returned.[3]

One who has a specific lien upon property cannot retain it for
the payment of other debts due him by the owner without a
special agreement to that effect.[4]

16. Specific liens have always been favored by the
courts. Lord Mansfield, in a case where he was obliged to decide against a general lien, said:[5] "The convenience of commerce, and natural justice, are on the side of liens; and therefore, of late years, courts lean that way." In a later case Chief

---

[1] See the chapters on these liens.

[2] Jarvis v. Rogers, 15 Mass. 389,
394, per Wilde, J.; Walker v. Birch,
6 T. R. 258.

[3] Green v. Farmer, 4 Burr. 2214.

[4] Nevan v. Roup, 8 Iowa, 207.

[5] Green v. Farmer, 4 Burr. 2214,
2221, S. C. 1 W. Black. R. 651.

Justice Best said:[1] " As between debtor and creditor, the doctrine of lien is so equitable that it cannot be favored too much."

Similar declarations have been made by the courts in this country. Thus, in the Court of Appeals of Maryland, Chief Justice Dorsey said:[2] " The doctrine of lien is more favored now than formerly; and it is now recognized as a general principle, that wherever the party has, by his labor or skill, improved the value of property placed in his possession, he has a lien upon it until paid. And liens have been implied when, from the nature of the transaction, the owner of the property is assumed as having designed to create them, or where it can be fairly inferred, from circumstances, that it was the understanding of the parties that they should exist. The existence of liens has also been sustained where they contributed to promote public policy and convenience."

17. A **general lien** is one which the holder thereof is entitled to enforce as a security for the performance of all the obligations, or all of a particular class of obligations, which exist in his favor against the owner of the property.[3] A general lien is one which does not necessarily arise from some demand which the creditor has in respect to the property upon which the lien is claimed, but is one for a general balance of accounts. A general lien may exist: 1, where there is an express contract; 2, where it is implied from the usage of trade; 3, from the manner of dealing between the parties in the particular case; 4, or where the defendant has acted as a factor.[4] Lord Mansfield made this statement of the general rule of law in a case where he decided that a dyer had no lien on goods delivered to him in the course of trade, except for the price of the dyeing, because there was no express contract to give a lien for a general balance, and none could be inferred from any usage of trade or manner of dealing between the parties; but on the contrary the manner of dealing showed that the dyer relied solely upon the personal credit of the owner.

The principal general liens are those of Factors and Brokers, of Bankers, of Attorneys upon their clients' papers and money, and of Warehousemen and Wharfingers.[5]

---

[1] Jacobs v. Latour, 5 Bing. 130.

[2] Wilson v. Guyton, 8 Gill (Md.), 213.

[3] California Civ. Code, § 2874; Dakota Civ. Code, § 1600.

[4] Green v. Farmer, 4 Burr. 2214, 2221.

[5] See the chapters on these several topics.

18. A lien for a general balance may arise by agreement of parties, or by a usage which implies an agreement. In 1788 certain dyers, bleachers, and others, in Manchester, at a public meeting, agreed not to receive goods to be dyed or bleached, except upon the condition that they should respectively have a lien upon them, not only for work done upon the particular goods, but also for a general balance of account. In trover, by the assignee of a bankrupt, for a quantity of yarn which the owner, with notice of this agreement, delivered to a bleacher, it was held that the latter had the right to hold the yarn for a general balance of account due him from the bankrupt.[1] It was contended that though one individual might impose such an agreement upon his customers, it was not competent for a class of men to do so. But Lord Kenyon said: " It seems to me that that is a distinction without a difference ; there is no reason why a body of persons should not make such an agreement as (it is admitted) the defendant himself might have made." And Lawrence, J., upon this point said: " The question here is whether an agreement, which is on the side of natural justice, be or be not illegal, it having been made by a number of persons. But I cannot say that it is illegal when it is supported on such a foundation ; and if it is not illegal, it must be binding upon the parties."

19. General liens are regarded by courts of law with jealousy. Lord Ellenborough, speaking of such liens in a case where it was sought to establish liens for carriers for a general balance of account by force of usage, said:[2] " They are encroachments upon the common law. If they are encouraged, the practice will be continually extending to other traders and other matters. The farrier will be claiming a lien upon a horse sent to him to be shod. Carriages and other things which require fre-

[1] Kirkman v. Shawcross, 6 T. R. 14. " We are now desired to abrogate an agreement which the parties themselves have made, and which the courts have said that justice requires ; and it is said that unless we do so, the innkeepers will enter into similar resolutions. But their case is widely different from the present ; for they are bound by law to receive guests who come to their inns, and are also bound to protect the property of those guests. They have no option either to receive or reject guests; therefore I said it was a material circumstance in the present case that these persons had an option either to work or not, as they pleased." Per Lord Kenyon.

[2] Rushforth v. Hadfield, 7 East, 224, 229 ; and see same case, 6 East, 519.

quent repair will be detained on the same claim; and there is no saying where it is to stop. It is not for the convenience of the public that these liens should be extended further than they are already established by law. But if any particular inconvenience arise in the course of trade, the parties may, if they think proper, stipulate with their customers for the introduction of such a lien into their dealings."

III. *Possession an Essential Element in Liens at Law.*

20. A lien in its proper legal sense imports that one is in possession of the property of another, and that he detains it as security for some demand which he has in respect of it. "The question always is whether there be a right to retain the goods till a given demand shall be satisfied."[1] A lien, therefore, implies: 1, possession by the creditor; 2, title in the debtor; 3, a debt arising out of the specific property.

A lien being a right to detain goods until a certain demand in respect to them is satisfied, possession is implied in the beginning of the lien; and, as a general rule, a continuance of possession is equally implied. Lord Kenyon[2] expressed the general rule when he declared that "the right of lien has never been carried farther than while the goods remained in possession of the parties claiming them." Mr. Justice Buller[3] observes that "liens at law exist only in cases where the party entitled to them has the possession of the goods; and if he once parts with the possession after the lien attaches, the lien is gone."

21. Possession is essential to create, and essential to preserve, a lien at common law.[4] "A lien," said Lord Ellenborough, "is a right to hold; and how can that be held which was never possessed?"[5] The right begins and ends with possession. It attaches only while the property actually remains in possession of the creditor. If he suffers it to go out of his possession, he cannot regain it by any judicial proceeding. A lien is only a mode of enforcing satisfaction by the mere passive hold-

---

[1] Gladstone v. Birley, 2 Mer. 401, 404, per Grant, M. R.

[2] Sweet v. Pym, 1 East, 4, approved by Lord Ellenborough in McCombie v. Davies, 7 East, 7.

[3] Lickbarrow v. Mason, 6 East, 21, 25, n.

[4] Reed v. Ash, 3 Nev. 116; Clemson v. Davidson, 5 Binn. (Pa.) 392; Stewart v. Flowers, 44 Miss. 513.

[5] Heywood v. Waring, 4 Camp. 291, 295. And see Wilson v. Balfour, 2 Ib. 579; Ridgely v. Iglehart, 3 Bland (Md.), 540, 543, per Bland, Ch.

ing of the creditor. He thus prevents the debtor from deriving any benefit from his own until he pays the debt he owes in respect to the property.

As illustrating the necessity of possession to sustain a lien may be instanced the case of a trainer of race-horses, who has the benefit of the general principle that the person exercising care and skill in the improvement of a chattel is entitled to a lien for his services. But to perfect a lien he must, in accordance with another general principle, retain exclusive and continuous possession of the horse. If by usage or agreement the owner may send the horse to run at any race he chooses, and may select the jockey, the trainer has no continuing right of possession, and consequently no lien. Coleridge, J., in a case involving the question of a trainer's lien under such usage or agreement, said: " Now a good test of the existence of such right of possession is to consider in whose possession the race-horse is when it is employed in doing that for which it has been trained. The evidence showed that the horse, during the race, was in the owner's possession, and in his possession rightfully and according to usage or contract. The horse, before the race, is placed for convenience in the stable of the trainer; but during the race it is in the care of the jockey nominated by the owner. It appears, too, that if on any occasion the jockey were selected by the trainer, the trainer, *pro hâc vice*, would have only the delegated authority of the owner. I think it is part of the understanding that the owner shall have the possession and control of the horse to run at any race. This is quite inconsistent with the trainer's continuing right of possession." [1]

22. As between the immediate parties a change of possession may not defeat the lien. It is only between the claimant and third persons that continued possession is essential. As between the claimant and the owner, possession is by no means essential, except when, by surrendering the possession, the claimant can be fairly understood to have surrendered his lien; and then the question is, not whether he has yielded his possession, but whether he has surrendered his lien. When the lien-holder has parted with possession, it is a question for the jury whether he has so far voluntarily parted with the possession as to warrant the conclusion that he intended to abandon his lien. If the owner of the property has obtained possession without the knowl-

[1] Forth *v.* Simpson, 13 Q. B. 680, 686.

edge or consent of the lien-holder, the latter is not divested of his lien. The lien would continue in such case after the change of possession.[1]

A lien-holder may so part with the possession as to lose his lien with respect to third persons, though not as against the owner of the property. Thus where the owners of a sawmill permitted boards, sawed by them at a stipulated price, to be removed from their mill-yard to the bank of a canal at the distance of half a mile from the mill, it was held that they lost their lien in respect to third persons, though not against the owner of the boards, it being expressly stipulated between the parties that the lien should continue notwithstanding the removal.[2]

23. The possession must be rightful. A lien cannot arise in favor of a person who has received possession of the property for a purpose inconsistent with the notion of a lien.[3] Thus, if he has received certificates of stock for the purpose of raising money upon them for the owner, he cannot retain them for an indebtedness to himself. His possession of the certificates in such case is in trust. " To create a lien on a chattel, the party claiming it must show the just possession of the thing claimed; and no person can acquire a lien founded upon his own illegal or fraudulent act, or breach of duty; nor can a lien arise where, from the nature of the contract between the parties, it would be inconsistent with the express terms or the clear intent of the contract." [4] The mere fact that a creditor has possession of his debtor's goods gives him no lien upon them.[5]

24. While possession is essential to a lien at law, the possession need not be the actual and direct possession of the creditor, but may be that of his agent, servant, or warehouse keeper, acting under his authority.[6] A lien may be protected by placing the property in the hands of a third person, with notice of the lien, although such person may not be expressly the agent of the lien-holder.

[1] Allen v. Spencer, 1 Edm. (N. Y.) Sel. Cas. 177.

[2] McFarland v. Wheeler, 26 Wend. (N. Y.) 467, reversing S. C. 10 Ib. 318.

[3] Randel v. Brown, 2 How. 406. Randel v. Brown, *supra*, per McKinley, J.

[5] Allen v. Megguire, 15 Mass. 490; Jarvis v. Rogers, 15 Mass. 389, 414, per Parker, C. J.

[6] Allen v. Spencer, 1 Edm. (N. Y.) Sel. Cas. 117; McFarland v. Wheeler, 26 Wend. (N. Y.) 467, 474.

25. A mechanic who works for another upon the premises of the latter acquires no lien upon the articles manufactured or repaired, because he has no sufficient possession to support a lien. One who makes and burns brick upon the land of another without a lease of the land, or other interest than a right to enter and make the brick for a stipulated price per thousand, has no such possession of the brick as to give him a lien for his labor. If the right exists in such case in the absence of any express contract, it must rest on the common law right of mechanics and artisans to retain property upon which they have bestowed labor. For the maintenance of such a lien possession is essential, and the possession must be actual, without relinquishment or abandonment. One who has merely a license to use the brickyard and materials of another for the purpose of making and burning brick, in the case mentioned, has no such possession of the yard as will support a lien. His possession of the brick manufactured is only a qualified and mixed possession, which can form no valid basis for a lien.[1]

26. A lien at common law belongs strictly to the bailee who by contract performs the service for which the lien is claimed, and who receives into his custody the thing upon which the skill and labor are to be expended. Inasmuch as an exclusive right to the possession of the thing is the basis of the lien, a servant, or laborer, or journeyman, or sub-contractor of such bailee, cannot claim to retain the thing for his own services, except as such a lien is provided for by statute; for the possession of the laborer, or other person employed by the bailee, is the possession of such bailee.[2] Thus, if the owner of a machine employ a mechanic to make repairs upon it, and the mechanic, without the owner's authority, employs another to perform the entire work, the latter cannot claim a lien for the work, although he has performed the entire work, and claims a lien in accordance with the contract with the owner.

[1] King v. Indian Orchard Co. 11 Cush. (Mass.) 231.
[2] Hollingsworth v. Dow, 19 Pick. (Mass.) 228; Jacobs v. Knapp, 50 N. H. 71; M'Intyre v. Carver, 2 W. & S. (Pa.) 392, 395, per Gibson, C. J.; Wright v. Terry (Fla.), 2 Southeast. Rep. 6.

CHAPTER II.

EQUITABLE LIENS.

I. *Arising by Express Contract.*

27. In general. An equitable lien arises either from a written contract which shows an intention to charge some particular property with a debt or obligation, or is declared by a court of equity out of general considerations of right and justice as applied to the relations of the parties and the circumstances of their dealings. Equitable liens by contract of the parties are as various as are the contracts which parties may make. Equitable liens by contract cannot be classified under any of the common divisions of equitable liens, and therefore are treated of in the present chapter. Of implied equitable liens, those arising by orders and assignments, those arising from advances made and money paid for others, those arising from agreements to give mortgages, and those arising in favor of creditors and stockholders of corporations, are also treated of in the present chapter. But this second division of equitable liens, that is, liens implied and declared by courts of equity from equitable considerations, is necessarily subdivided into several other distinct subjects, which are so well defined and so important that it has seemed best to treat of them in several separate chapters of this work. Whether an attorney's special lien upon a judgment recovered is purely an equitable lien seems to be a matter of dispute, and the nature and origin of this lien are discussed in the chapter devoted to it.[1] Partnership liens, which arise from general equitable principles applied to the relations of the

---

[1] See Chap. v.

parties, are treated in a separate chapter;[1] and so are liens of grantors of real property for purchase-money, and of vendees for purchase-money paid before obtaining title ; liens of joint owners of real property for repairs and improvements made by one for the joint benefit ; liens of trustees for improvements which permanently enhance the value of the trust property ; and liens of purchasers and others for improvements upon real estate under void contracts of purchase, or under parol gifts, or under the erroneous belief that they are the real owners of the property.[2]

28. **Equitable liens do not depend upon possession as do liens at law.** Possession by the creditor is not essential to his acquiring and enforcing a lien. But the other incidents of a lien at common law must exist to constitute an equitable lien. In courts of equity the term " lien " is used as synonymous with a charge or incumbrance upon a thing, where there is neither *jus in re*, nor *ad rem*, nor possession of the thing.[3] The term is applied as well to charges arising by express engagement of the owner of property, and to a duty or intention implied on his part to make the property answerable for a specific debt or engagement.[4]

Mr. Justice Erle once remarked that " the words *equitable lien* are intensely undefined."[5] It is necessarily the case that something of vagueness and uncertainty should attend a doctrine that is of such a wide and varied application as is this of equitable lien. And yet the principles are as well defined as other equitable principles, and their application to certain well established classes of liens is well settled. To apply them to that undefined class of liens which arises from the contracts of parties may be more difficult, because these liens are as various as are the contracts, and precedents which exactly apply may not be found. This wide application of the doctrine is one element of the importance of this branch of equity jurisprudence. " There is no doctrine," says Mr. Pomeroy,[6] " which more strikingly shows

---

[1] See chapter on Partnership Liens.

[2] See chapters on these subjects in Vol. II.

[3] Peck *v.* Jenness, 7 How. 612, 620, per Grier, J.; Donald *v.* Hewitt, 33 Ala. 534.

[4] Equitable liens arising from the equitable circumstances of the case are unknown to the jurisprudence of **Pennsylvania.** Cross's Appeal, 97 Pa. St. 471; Hepburn *v.* Snyder, 3 Pa. St. 72.

[5] Brunsdon *v.* Allard, 2 E. & E. 19 27.

[6] Pomeroy's Eq. Jur. § 1234.

the difference between the legal and the equitable conceptions of the juridical results which flow from the dealings of men with each other from their express or implied undertakings."

Equitable liens have commonly been regarded as having their origin in trusts. Perhaps they are better described as analogous to trusts. Remedies at law are for the recovery of money. Remedies in equity are specific. "Remedies in equity, as well as at law," says Mr. Pomeroy,[1] "require some primary right or interest of the plaintiff which shall be maintained, enforced, or redressed thereby. When equity has jurisdiction to enforce rights and obligations growing out of an executory contract, this equitable theory of remedies cannot be carried out, unless the notion is admitted that the contract creates some right or interest in or over specific property, which the decree of the court can lay hold of, and by means of which the equitable relief can be made efficient. The doctrine of 'equitable liens' supplies this necessary element; and it was introduced for the sole purpose of furnishing a ground for the specific remedies which equity confers, operating upon particular identified property, instead of the general pecuniary recoveries granted by courts of law. It follows, therefore, that in a large class of executory contracts, express and implied, which the law regards as creating no property right, nor interest analogous to property, but only a mere personal right and obligation, equity recognizes, in addition to the personal obligation, a peculiar right over the thing concerning which the contract deals, which it calls a 'lien,' and which, though not property, is analogous to property, and by means of which the plaintiff is enabled to follow the identical thing, and to enforce the defendant's obligation by a remedy which operates directly upon that thing. The theory of equitable liens has its ultimate foundation, therefore, in contracts, express or implied, which either deal with, or in some manner relate to, specific property, such as a tract of land, particular chattels, or securities, a certain fund, and the like."

29. **An agreement which creates a charge upon specific property is in equity an effectual lien as between the parties without a change of possession, even though void as against subsequent purchasers in good faith without notice, and creditors levying executions or attachments; and if the agreement be fol-**

[1] Pomeroy's Eq. Jur. § 1234.

lowed by a delivery of possession, before the rights of third persons have intervened, it is good absolutely.[1]

Thus the owner of a tannery, in consideration of money advanced by another for the purchase of skins, agreed to tan them and place the leather in the hands of his creditor for sale upon commission, and that the skins, whether tanned or not, should be considered as security for the payment of the money advanced. After several months the tanner became financially embarrassed, and was also disabled by illness from continuing his business. The parties then entered into a new contract whereby the creditor was to take possession of the tannery and use it with such materials as might be necessary to finish the skins and sell them as previously agreed. Four days afterwards the debtor filed his petition in bankruptcy. The creditor having taken possession of the tannery, the debtor's assignee in bankruptcy brought replevin for the skins. It was held that the creditor had an equitable lien upon them which was binding, not only upon the debtor but upon his assignee, and that the second contract, though made in contemplation of bankruptcy, was not fraudulent, inasmuch as it was made in good faith to secure the benefits of the first contract, which created a valid charge upon the property.[2]

The court, Mr. Justice Matthews delivering the opinion, said in substance that, while it is true that the creditor could not have compelled his debtor, by an action at law, to deliver to him the possession of his tannery and its contents, and could not have recovered possession of the skins, tanned or untanned, by force of a legal title; yet it is equally true that in equity he could, by injunction, have prevented the debtor from making any disposition of the property inconsistent with his obligations under the contract; and upon proof of his inability or unwillingness to complete the performance of his agreement, the court would not have hesitated, in the exercise of a familiar jurisdiction, to protect the interests of the creditor by placing the property in the custody of a receiver for preservation, with authority, if such a course seemed expedient, in its discretion, to finish the unfinished work, and ultimately, by a sale and distribution of its proceeds, to adjust the rights of the parties.

30. A charge in the nature of a lien upon real as well as personal estate may be created by the express agreement of

[1] Hauselt *v.* Harrison, 105 U. S. 401; Gregory *v.* Morris, 96 U. S. 619.

[2] Hauselt *v.* Harrison, *supra.*

the owner, and it will be enforced in equity, not only against such owner, but also against third persons who are either volunteers, or who take the estate on which the lien is given, with notice of the stipulation.[1] " Such an agreement raises a trust which binds the estate to which it relates; and all who take title thereto, with notice of such trust, can be compelled in equity to fulfil it. It is obvious that the law gives no remedy by which such a lien can be established, and the trust thereby created be declared and enforced. Equity furnishes the only means by which the property on which the charge is fastened can be reached and applied to the stipulated purpose." [2]

Thus, if the owner of land agrees, in writing, for a valuable consideration, to pay to another person a certain sum " out of the proceeds of the sale of said lands, if the same shall be sold, or, if the lands shall not be sold, and a company shall be formed for working the mines thereon," then to convey stock to that amount, it being understood and agreed that such amount is to be a charge on the estate of the owner, a charge in the nature of a lien upon the land is thereby created, which may be enforced in equity against all who take title to the lands with notice of the charge.[3]

31. To create an equitable lien by agreement, it must appear that the parties to it intended to create a charge upon the property. Thus a clause in a charter-party, whereby the freighter bound the goods to be taken on board for the performance of every covenant therein contained, does not give the ship-owner any lien in equity on the goods brought home in the ship, either for dead freight or for demurrage that became due by virtue of the provisions of the charter-party. The Court of King's Bench determined that there was no lien at law.[4] The ground of the judgment was, not that a lien might not have been contracted for, but that the clause of the charter-party did not contain a contract to that effect.

In the subsequent suit in equity, the Master of the Rolls, Sir William Grant, delivering the judgment, said: [5] " The plaintiffs, however, suppose that, although a court of law has said that the clause does not give them a lien, a court of equity may say

<hr>

[1] Clarke v. Southwick, 1 Curtis, 297.

[2] Pinch v. Anthony, 8 Allen (Mass.), 536, per Bigelow, C. J.

[3] Pinch v. Anthony, *supra*.

[4] Birley v. Gladstone, 3 M. & S. 205.

[5] Gladstone v. Birley, 2 Merivale, 401, 403.

that it gives them what is precisely tantamount to a lien, namely, a right to have their demand satisfied out of the produce of the goods in preference to any other creditors of the bankrupt freighter. Putting this clause out of the question, it was not contended that equity gives the ship-owner any lien for his freight beyond that which the law gives him. There are, to be sure, liens which exist only in equity, and of which equity alone can take cognizance, but it cannot be contended that a lien for freight is one of them. As to liens on the goods of one man in the possession of another, I know of no difference between the rules of decision in courts of law and in courts of equity. The question that so frequently occurs, whether a tradesman has a lien on the goods in his hands for the general balance due to him, or only for so much as relates to the particular goods, is decided in both courts in the same way, and on the same grounds. To extend the lien, the party claiming it must show an agreement to that effect, or something from which an agreement may be inferred, such as a course of dealing between the parties, or a general usage of the trade. Lien, in its proper sense, is a right which the law gives. But it is usual to speak of lien by contract, though that be more in the nature of an agreement for a pledge. Taken either way, however, the question always is, whether there be a right to detain the goods till a given demand shall be satisfied. That right must be derived from law or contract."

32. **The intention must be to create a lien upon the property, as distinguished from an agreement to apply the proceeds of a sale of it to the payment of a debt.** A debtor verbally agreed that his creditor should have a lien upon a certain stock of cattle, and that the cattle should be placed in charge of a third person to hold until they should be in a suitable condition to be sold. The debtor placed the cattle in charge of his sons, as herders, without declaring any lien or trust upon the property, and afterwards died. The creditor sought to charge the funds arising from a sale of the cattle by the executor with a lien. But the court held that the evidence merely showed an intention on the part of the debtor to apply the proceeds of the property to the payment of his debt to the plaintiff, but that there was no lien.[1]

A written agreement made by a son to his father, whereby the

[1] Cook v. Black, 54 Iowa, 693.

son undertook to pay a mortgage on the lands of his father, does not create a lien upon the son's interest in such lands as heir after his father's death, the agreement showing no intent that such a lien should be created.[1]

33. **The instrument creating the lien is not effectual unless it plainly designates the property to be charged.** By a marriage settlement, the husband provided for an annuity to his wife in case she should survive him, from and after his decease, for her natural life ; and for the payment of such annuity he did " promise, covenant, and agree, that the same shall be, and the same is hereby made and constitutes, a lien and charge upon all the property and estate, real and personal, of every name and nature, kind and description, which he may own and to which he may be entitled at the time of his decease." His estate, though ample at the date of the settlement, was insolvent at the time of his decease. In a suit by the widow to enforce the lien it was held that the settlement did not create an equitable lien, as against the husband's creditors, either upon the property which he owned at the time of making the agreement, or that which he owned at the time of his death, for the reason that it failed to designate, with sufficient certainty, the property to be charged therewith.[2] Mr. Justice Boardman, delivering the opinion of the court, said : " The charge or lien must have taken effect, if at all, at the date of the contract, and must plainly designate the property charged. In the present case that was impossible : the property to be charged was not known to the contracting parties. The intestate may not have owned it. It was utterly uncertain what property, if any, he would own at his death. The contract could not have been enforced specifically as to such property in his lifetime, because the court could not possibly ascertain the property to be bound by its decree. If the property had been then owned by him and described, the equitable lien would have attached. But it does not appear that the property owned by the intestate at his death was owned by him twelve years before, when the contract was made. It was wholly uncertain whether property owned by him then would remain his at his death. Between the parties to the contract there was no obligation to retain it. As to such property the intestate owed no duty to the plaintiff. We apprehend this does not constitute that degree of cer-

<hr>

[1] Rider v. Clark, 54 Iowa, 292.   [2] Mundy v. Munson, 40 Hun (N. Y.), 304.

tainty in designating the property to be charged which the law requires. It is not enough that at some future time the descriptions will become certain. It must not be forgotten that, as against the party himself, his heirs at law, and those claiming under him voluntarily, such an agreement may raise a trust which will be enforced in equity. But, as to purchasers and others acting in good faith and without notice, a different rule applies."

34. It is essential to an equitable lien that the property to be charged should be capable of identification, so that the claimant of the lien may say, with a reasonable degree of certainty, what property it is that is subject to his lien.[1] Though possession is not necessary to the existence of an equitable lien, it is necessary that the property or funds upon which the lien is claimed should be distinctly traced, so that the very thing which is subject to the special charge may be proceeded against in an equitable action, and sold under decree to satisfy the charge. A fund is not thus traced when it has gone into the general bank account of the recipient, or after it has been mixed with funds from other sources.[2] Money which has been intermixed with other money cannot be the subject of an equitable lien after the money itself, or a specific substitute for it, has become incapable of identification.[3]

A firm of merchants furnished to a firm of silk manufacturers raw materials for silk goods, and funds to purchase such materials under an agreement whereby the goods when manufactured were to be delivered to and sold by the merchants, who were authorized to deduct from the proceeds of the sales the amount due them for advances and insurance and for commissions. Some two years afterwards the manufacturers failed, and made a general assignment of their property. The assignee took possession of the debtors' stock, among which were nineteen pieces of silk finished, and about forty-five pieces unfinished. The merchants claimed an equitable lien upon these goods for a balance due them, and brought suit to enforce the lien ; but it was held they could not recover, because they did not trace their advances to these particular goods.[4]

35. An equitable lien is created by an agreement between

[1] Payne v. Wilson, 74 N. Y. 348.
[2] Grinnell v. Suydam, 3 Sandf. (N. Y.) 132.
[3] Drake v. Taylor, 6 Blatchf. 14.
[4] Person v. Oberteuffer, 59 How. (N. Y.) Pr. 339.

several persons that the cost of certain improvements shall be a lien on their respective estates, though these are not immediately connected with the improvements. Certain mill-owners associated themselves for the purpose of building reservoirs, and agreed that there should be a lien on their respective estates for the share of the expenses which each was to pay. This agreement was held to create an equitable lien which each member who had paid more than his proportion might enforce against the property of any other member who had paid less than his proportion.[1] Such an agreement is not executory merely, but executed. It creates a trust which a court of equity will work out so as to secure the payment of the obligations in the manner the parties intended they should be paid. The lien is created in behalf of each member of the association, and not in behalf of the association collectively, because such appears to be the intent of the agreement. The covenant is a several covenant of each with each member. The other members of the association need not be joined in a suit by one member against the purchaser of the property of another for contribution, because the others have no interest in the suit.[2] Mr. Justice Curtis, delivering judgment, said : —

" If there was any property of this association capable of being, applied, and which, equitably, ought to be applied, in payment of its debts, before resorting to the lien asserted by the bill, all the members would be necessary parties, because they would then have an interest both in the account of the debts and of the property, and in its application. But there is no such property. The works which the association has erected for the improvement of these mills cannot be sold without defeating the very object for which the association was formed. Every member has a right to have them preserved, and to have every other member pay his contributory share, in order that they may be preserved. So far from these works constituting a fund to be resorted to in relief of the contributors, they are the very object of the contribution, and equity requires it to be made in order that the original purposes of the parties may be fulfilled. It is objected that the defendant may hereafter, by other suits, have other debts of the association charged on his estates, so that he is exposed to pay more than his just share, and thus

[1] Clarke v. Southwick, 1 Curtis, 297. And see Campbell v. Mesier, 4 Johns. (N. Y.) Ch. 334.

[2] Clarke v. Southwick, supra, per Curtis, J.

be forced to seek for contribution himself in another suit. If this were so, it would be a fatal objection; but the defendant, not being a member of the association, and so not being personally liable, can never be forced to pay any more than three sixths of any debt, and so can never have any claim for contribution; for this proportion is what is justly and ultimately chargeable on his estates."

36. **An equitable lien may be imposed upon a changing stock of goods by agreement of the parties.** Persons who have been induced to execute a bond to release an attachment on a stock of goods belonging to a business firm, upon a promise that the goods so released shall be held for the obligors' indemnity and security, have an equitable lien on such stock of goods for the amount they have been compelled to pay by reason of having executed such bond; and such lien may be enforced as against the general assignee of the firm for the benefit of their creditors.[1] The fact that it was agreed that the owners of the stock of goods should keep it replenished up to its value at that time, and the further fact that, without the knowledge or consent of the obligors, the owners disposed of parts of the stock and put in other stock to supply its place, do not affect the lien; but this will attach to the mingled goods in the condition they are in at the time the lien is enforced.[2]

37. **An equitable lien is distinguished from a trust in this respect.** A bank which receives a draft for collection holds the proceeds when collected as trustee of the depositor, and upon the failure of the bank the depositor is entitled to have the amount paid by a receiver of the bank's property in preference to the general creditors. The receiver of the bank takes its assets subject to the same equities under which the bank held them. It is immaterial whether the identical moneys collected by the bank passed into the hands of the receiver or not, for in some shape they went to swell the assets which fell into the receiver's hands.[3] " It is not to be supposed the trust fund was dissipated and lost

---

[1] Arnold v. Morris, 7 Daly (N. Y.), 498.

[2] Arnold v. Morris, *supra.*

[3] People v. Bank of Dansville, 39 Hun (N. Y.), 187; People v. City Bank of Rochester, 96 N. Y. 32; Van Alen v. Am. Nat. Bank, 52 N. Y. 1; McLeod v. Evans, 66 Wis. 401; Peak v. Ellicott, 30 Kans. 156.

altogether, and did not fall into the mass of the assignor's property ; and the rule in equity is well established that, so long as the trust property can be traced and followed into other property into which it has been converted, that remains subject to the trust: . . . we do not understand that it is necessary to trace the trust fund into some specific property in order to enforce the trust. If it can be traced into the estate of the defaulting agent or trustee, this is sufficient." [1]

The discussion of this matter is not followed farther, because the principle involved is one of trust rather than lien. A lien is a charge on some specific thing, as lands, goods, or bonds ; but a trust may exist with reference to any funds or a mere credit.

38. An equitable lien under an agreement of the parties arises only when the terms and conditions contemplated by the agreement are fulfilled. A contractor about to furnish certain manufactured articles to the government agreed that advances to be made him by a bank, to enable him to carry out his contract, should be a lien on the drafts to be drawn by him on the government for the proceeds of the articles manufactured. The government afterwards annulled the contract, the contractor being at the time largely indebted to the bank for advances made. The contractor many years afterwards recovered a judgment in the Court of Claims against the government for damages for a violation of the contract. It was held that the bank had no lien on this judgment. The lien, by its terms, only attached to the proceeds of sales of the manufactured goods. There was no lien on the contract itself; and there could be none on the damages for a breach of the contract.[2]

39. It is sometimes declared to be a general doctrine of equity that a lien will be given when the plaintiff's rights can be secured in no other way. This doctrine was asserted in a recent case by the Court of Appeals of New York.[3] The plaintiff was chairman of a committee appointed by a con-

[1] Per Cole, C. J., in McLeod v. Evans, *supra.*

[2] Bank of Washington v. Nock, 9 Wall. 373; and see Kelly v. Kelly, 54 Mich. 30.

[3] Perry v. Board of Missions, 102 N. Y. 99.; *S. C.* 1 N. Y. St. Rep. 169.

vention of the Episcopal Church to procure a residence for the
bishop of the Diocese of Albany. With the advice of the
bishop and consent of the committee, he purchased certain premises, and, at the request of the bishop, commenced making necessary repairs and improvements. The committee reported to
the convention at its annual meeting, which adopted a resolution directing a transfer of the title to the defendant, and requiring the latter to execute a bond and mortgage to secure the payment of an existing mortgage and of the sum advanced for
repairs. At this time the repairs were in progress, and the
plaintiff went on and completed the work, advancing the money
required for the purpose. The premises were conveyed to the
defendant, which executed a mortgage, and applied the moneys
obtained upon it as directed, but they were insufficient to pay
the whole amount advanced by the plaintiff. The plaintiff,
having completed the repairs, demanded payment of the balance
due him, and, upon the defendants' refusal to reimburse him,
brought an action for equitable relief, asking to have a lien in
the nature of a mortgage declared upon the property, and that
he be allowed to foreclose the same. It was held that he was
entitled to this relief, as his rights could be secured in no other
way. Judge Danforth, delivering the judgment of the court,
said: " The advances were directly for the benefit of the real
estate; they were approved by the convention by whose directions the title was conveyed to the defendant: but neither the
convention nor the defendant have incurred any corporate liability; and, while it may be said that the advances were made
on the promise of, or in the just and natural expectation that, a
mortgage would be given, it is also true that they were made on
the credit of the property for the improvement of which they
were expended. The repairs and improvements were permanently beneficial to it, made in good faith, with the knowledge
and approbation of the parties interested, and accepted by them,
not as a gratuity, but as services for which compensation should
be given. The plaintiff's right to remuneration is clear; and,
unless the remedy sought for in this action is given, there will
be a total failure of justice."

40. Upon a sale of real and personal property together
for one price, a lien for the purchase-money reserved in
the conveyance will be enforced in a court of equity, both

upon the real and upon the personal property. Thus, where a lease of certain coal property, with all the personal property of the lessee upon the demised premises, was sold and transferred for a gross sum for both, and in the instrument of transfer a lien was reserved for the payment of the purchase-money, the lien was declared to be valid as between the parties and as against those having actual notice of it, and was enforced by a sale of both the real and personal property.[1] Of course there is no *implied* equitable lien for purchase-money in favor of a vendor of personal property;[2] but there is no reason why the lien should not exist by contract or reservation, or why a lien upon both real and personal property, reserved by the same contract, should not be enforced against all the property.

41. An equitable lien arises from a conditional delivery of goods upon a sale, the condition being that the goods shall be paid for before the title passes. Thus, where goods were sold at auction to be paid for in approved indorsed notes, and, in accordance with a usage, the goods were delivered to the buyer when called for, the notes being left for subsequent adjustment, and, before the notes were delivered, the purchaser stopped payment and assigned the goods so bought, with other property, for the benefit of his creditors, it was held that the vendee was a trustee for the goods until the notes should be delivered; that the vendor had an equitable lien upon them for the purchase-money, and a better right than the voluntary assignee.[3]

One may have an equitable lien upon a boat for work and material furnished under an agreement for such a lien. Thus, where one built and put up an engine in a boat under an express contract with the owner that he should have a lien upon the boat for the price of the engine, it was held that he had an equitable lien upon the boat, not dependent for its validity upon his retaining possession.[4]

42. There may be an equitable lien upon future prop-

[1] Cole v. Smith, 24 W. Va. 287, 290.

[2] Lupin v. Marie, 6 Wend. (N. Y.) 77; Cole v. Smith, *supra;* McCandlish v. Keen, 13 Gratt. (Va.) 615, 629, per Lee, J.; James v. Bird, 8 Leigh (Va.), 510; Beam v. Blanton, 3 Ired. (N. C.) Eq. 59.

[3] Haggerty v. Palmer, 6 Johns. (N. Y.) Ch. 437.

[4] Donald v. Hewitt, 33 Ala. 534.

erty.[1] Whenever a positive lien or charge is intended to be created upon real or personal property not in existence or not owned by the person who grants the lien, the contract attaches in equity as a lien or charge upon the particular property as soon as he acquires title and possession of the same.[2] An equitable lien upon future property may be even more effectual than such a lien upon property in existence, for the registration laws apply to liens upon property in existence, but not to liens upon future property. Therefore it happens that, while, as against creditors, a lien cannot be created by contract upon a personal chattel in existence at the time of such contract without registration, yet, as this rule does not apply to a contract in regard to future property, a lien effectual as against creditors may be created by agreement upon future property, such, for instance, as the products of a farm, or the profits of the farm, not then in existence.[3]

II. *Arising by Equitable Assignments.*

43. An equitable lien arises from an order given by a debtor to his creditor, to receive payment out of a particular fund, and this is effectual from the time the creditor receives the order or assignment, though the debtor become bankrupt before the order is received by the drawee. Thus, a merchant at Liverpool, having property in the hands of an agent at Bahia, agreed with a creditor to apply such property to the discharge of his indebtedness to him, and sent directions to his agent to convert the property and apply the proceeds to that purpose ; but, before such instructions could reach his agent, he became bankrupt.[4]

[1] Under the Codes of **California** and **Dakota** an agreement may be made to create a lien upon property not yet acquired by the party agreeing to give the lien, or not yet in existence. In such case the lien agreed for attaches from the time when the party agreeing to give it acquires an interest in the thing to the extent of such interest. California Civ. Code, § 2883 ; Dakota Civ. Code, § 1704.

A lien may be created by contract, to take immediate effect, as security for the performance of obligations then in existence. California Civ. Code, § 2884 ; Dakota Civ. Code, § 1705.

[2] Wisner v. Ocumpaugh, 71 N. Y. 113 ; Coates v. Donnell, 16 J. & S. (N. Y.) 46 ; Barnard v. Norwich & Worcester R. R. Co. 4 Cliff. 351 ; Coe v. Hart, 6 Am. L. Reg. 27 ; Kirksey v. Means, 42 Ala. 426 ; Bibend v. Liverpool & London F. & L. Ins. Co. 30 Cal. 78.

[3] Jones on Chattel Mortgages, § 157 ; Tedford v. Wilson, 3 Head (Tenn.), 311.

[4] Burn v. Carvalho, 4 Mylne & Cr. 690. In *Ex parte* South, 3 Swanst. 393, Lord Eldon says : " It has been decided in bankruptcy that, if a creditor gives an order on his debtor to pay a sum in discharge of his debt,

The chancellor, Lord Cottenham, held that, notwithstanding the assignment by the bankrupt, the creditor had an interest in the goods, in the nature of a lien, which equity would protect. He stated the rule to be that, in equity, an order given by a debtor to his creditor upon a third person having funds of the debtor, to pay the creditor out of such funds, is a binding, equitable assignment of so much of the fund.

A part of a particular fund may thus be assigned by an order, and the holder may enforce payment against the drawee. No particular form of words is necessary to effect an equitable assignment. Any words which show an intention of transferring or appropriating a chose in action to the use of the assignee, and which place him in control of the same, are sufficient.[1]

44. This rule applies to agreements made by attorneys with their clients, whereby they are to receive a share of the fund to be recovered as a contingent compensation for professional services, for such agreements, when made for the prosecution of certain classes of claims, of which may be instanced claims against a government, or in one of the executive departments of a government, are not in violation of public policy.[2] Such agreements, if they virtually assign a part of the claim, or an interest in it, create a lien upon the fund recovered.[3] Thus, where professional services were rendered by an attorney under such an agreement, in prosecuting a claim against the Republic of Mexico, and the claim was finally, through his efforts, allowed, it was held that he had a lien upon

and that order is shown to the debtor, it binds him. On the other hand, this doctrine has been brought into doubt by some decisions in the courts of law which require that the party receiving the order should, in some way, enter into a contract. That has been the course of their decisions, but is certainly not the doctrine of this court." See, also, Fitzgerald v. Stewart, 2 Sim. 333; *S. C.* 2 Russ. & Mylne, 457; Lett v. Morris, 4 Sim. 607; Watson v. The Duke of Wellington, 1 Russ. & Mylne, 602, 605; Malcolm v. Scott, 3 Hare, 39; Crowfoot v. Gurney, 2 Moo. & Scott, 473;

Row v. Dawson, 1 Ves. Sr. 332, per Lord Hardwicke; Yeates v. Groves, 1 Ves. Jr. 280, per Lord Thurlow; Trist v. Child, 21 Wall. 441, 447, per Swayne, J.; Field v. The Mayor, 6 N. Y. 179; Richardson v. Rus., 9 Paige (N. Y.), 243; Powell v. Jones, 72 Ala. 392.

[1] Row v. Dawson, 1 Ves. Sr. 332, per Lord Hardwicke.

[2] Stanton v. Embrey, 93 U. S. 548; Fairbanks v. Sargent, 39 Hun (N. Y.), 588; Williams v. Ingersoll, 23 Ib. 284; Brown v. Mayor, 11 Ib. 21.

[3] Stanton v. Embrey, *supra;* Dowell v. Cardwell, 4 Sawyer, 217.

the fund recovered, and that a court of equity would exercise jurisdiction to enforce the lien, if it appeared that equity would give him a more adequate remedy than he could obtain in a court of law.[1]

45. An order upon a specific fund, of which the drawee has notice, though he has not accepted it, or though he may have refused to accept it, is effectual, not only as between the parties, but also as against the drawer's assignee in bankruptcy, or his voluntary assignee, for the benefit of his creditors.[2] A debtor, being about to sell some leasehold property, gave to a creditor an order for the payment of the purchase-money. The order was not accepted, though the drawees had notice of it. Before the transaction was completed by payment of the order, the debtor became bankrupt. Lord Thurlow, in holding that the order was an equitable assignment of the purchase-money, said:[3] " This is nothing but a direction by a man to pay part of his money to another for a foregone valuable consideration. If he could transfer, he has done it; and, it being his own money, he could transfer. The transfer was actually made. They were right not to accept it, as it was not a bill of exchange. It is not an inchoate business. The order fixed the money the moment it was shown to the parties upon whom it was drawn."

The assignment of a mail contract, accompanied by an agreement that the assignee should receive all the moneys that might become payable under the contract for carrying the mail, constitutes an equitable lien on the funds which is superior to a subsequent order given by the assignor upon the same fund.[4]

46. But the assignment is not effectual until the creditor is notified of the assignment to himself. Though a consignment be made with directions to apply the proceeds to a creditor of the consignor, that is no effectual appropriation or lien in favor

---

[1] Wylie v. Coxe, 15 How. 415; Stanton v. Embrey, supra. Where the amount of compensation to be paid the attorney in such case is not fixed, evidence of what is ordinarily charged by attorneys in cases of the same character is admissible.

[2] Alderson, ex parte, 1 Mad. 53; S. C. affirmed, nom. Ex parte South, 3

Swanst. 392; Lett v. Morris, 4 Sim. 607; Burn v. Carvalho, 4 My. & Cr. 690; Yeates v. Groves, 1 Ves. Jr. 281; Clark v. Mauran, 3 Paige (N. Y.), 373.

[3] Yeates v. Groves, supra.

[4] Bradley v. Root, 5 Paige (N.Y.), 632.

of the creditor until the creditor is notified of the appropriation. Until such notice the directions amount to no more than a mandate revocable at the pleasure of the consignor, who may make any disposition of the property or of its proceeds that he may see fit to make.[1]

47. An order which amounts to an equitable assignment cannot be revoked. An order given by a landlord on his tenant to pay to another the rents to accrue during a certain time, and assented to by the tenant, operates as an equitable assignment of such rents, which is effectual not only as against third persons, but also against the landlord himself.[2] Although he revokes the order, the tenant is not only justified in paying the rents in accordance with the order, but may be compelled to do so. The order itself amounts to an assignment of the fund without any formal acceptance, whether written or verbal.[3] Such an order differs in this respect from a bill of exchange or check, inasmuch as these do not specify a particular fund, whereas the order mentioned does specify a particular fund.

48. A mere agreement, whether by parol or in writing, to pay a debt out of a designated fund, when received, does not give an equitable lien upon that fund, or operate as an equitable assignment of it.[4] The agreement is personal merely. There must be an order, or something that places the creditor in a position to demand and receive the amount of the debt from the holder of the fund without further action on the part of the debtor; something that would protect the holder of the fund in making the payment. A covenant by a debtor to pay certain debts out of a particular fund when the same should be received, is merely a personal covenant.[5] Thus, to create in favor of a contractor a lien upon particular funds of his employer, there must be not only an express promise of the employer upon which

---

[1] Scott *v.* Porcher, 3 Mer. 652.

[2] Morton *v.* Naylor, 1 Hill (N. Y.), 583; Bradley *v.* Root, 5 Paige (N. Y.), 632.

[3] Lett *v.* Morris, 4 Sim. 607; Yeates *v.* Groves. 1 Ves. Jr. 280; Alderson, *ex parte*, 1 Mad. 53.

[4] Wright *v.* Ellison, 1 Wall. 16; Christmas *v.* Russell, 14 Wall. 69;

Trist *v.* Child, 21 Wall. 441; Dillon *v.* Barnard, 21 Wall. 430; Williams *v.* Ingersoll, 89 N. Y. 508; Rogers *v.* Hosack, 18 Wend. (N. Y.) 319, reversing *S. C.* 6 Paige, 415; Morton *v.* Naylor, 1 Hill (N. Y.), 583.

[5] Rogers *v.* Hosack, *supra;* Hoyt *v.* Story, 3 Barb. (N. Y.) 262.

the contractor relies, to apply them in payment of such services,
but there must be some act of appropriation on the part of the
employer relinquishing control of the funds, and conferring upon
the contractor the right to have them thus applied when the services are rendered. A contractor entered into an agreement with
a railroad company to build a portion of its road, which had just
been mortgaged by the company to raise money to pay its existing debts and to complete and equip the road. The mortgage
provided, among other things, that the expenditure of all sums
of money realized from the sale of the bonds should be made
with the approval of at least one of the mortgage trustees, and
that his assent in writing should be necessary to all contracts
made by the company before the same should be a charge upon
any of the sums received from such sales. The contractor obtained the assent of two of the trustees to his contract; and, having completed the work, upon the bankruptcy of the company
claimed a lien upon the property in the hands of the assignees
in bankruptcy acquired or received from the mortgage bonds.
It was held, however, that he acquired no lien, because he was
never given control of the funds to be received from the bonds.[1]
Upon this point Mr. Justice Field said: "Before there can
arise any lien on the funds of the employer, there must be,
in addition to such express promise upon which the contractor
relies, some act of appropriation on the part of the employer
depriving himself of the control of the funds, and conferring
upon the contractor the right to have them applied to his payment when the services are rendered or the materials are furnished. There must be a relinquishment by the employer of the
right of dominion over the funds, so that without his aid or consent the contractor can enforce their application to his payment
when his contract is completed. In the case at bar there is no
circumstance impairing the dominion of the corporation over the
funds received from the bonds; there is only its covenant with
the trustees that the expenditure of those funds shall be made
with the approval of one of them, and that one of them shall
give his written assent to its contracts before they are paid out
of such funds. There is no covenant with the contractor of any
kind in the instrument, and no right is conferred upon him to interfere in any disposition which the corporation may see fit to
make of its moneys. The essential elements are wanting in the

[1] Dillon v. Barnard, 21 Wall. 430.

transaction between him and the corporation to give him any lien upon its funds. No right, therefore, exists in him to pursue such funds into other property upon which they have been expended. The case, as already intimated, is on his part one of simple disappointed expectation, against which misfortune equity furnishes no relief."

49. A creditor has no lien on money in the hands of the debtor's agent until the debtor has given an order upon the agent to pay it to the creditor. A tax was levied for the amount of the subscription of a county to a railroad company, and an agent was appointed in behalf of the county to receive the money when collected, and to pay it over when ordered. It was held that the railroad company had no specific or other lien on money collected and in the hands of the agent before he had been ordered to pay it over. The county could recall the money in the hands of its agent at any time before payment to the company.[1]

50. To constitute an equitable lien on a fund, there must be some distinct appropriation of the fund by the debtor, such as an assignment or order that the creditor should be paid out of it. It is not enough that the fund may have been created through the efforts and outlays of the party claiming the lien.[2] It is not enough that a debtor authorizes a third person to receive a fund and to pay it over to a creditor.[3] One who was largely indebted to his banker, being pressed for payment, wrote to the solicitor of a railroad company which was indebted to him, authorizing the solicitor to receive the money so due to him, and to pay it to the banker. The solicitor, by letter, promised the banker to pay him such money on receiving it. The solicitor received the amount, but paid it over to the debtor instead of the banker. It was held, that the transaction did not amount to an equitable assignment, because there was no order or assignment by the debtor placing the fund in the control of the creditor. There was nothing more than a promise or undertaking on the part of the solicitor, for the breach of which he may be responsible in law, but not in equity.[4] Lord Truro, delivering the judg-

---

[1] Henry County v. Allen, 50 Mo. 231.

[2] Wright v. Ellison, 1 Wall. 16; Hoyt v. Story, 3 Barb. (N. Y.) 262.

[3] Rodick v. Gandell, 12 Beav. 325. Affirmed 1 De G., M. & G. 763.

[4] Rodick v. Gandell, 12 Beav. 325.

ment upon appeal, said:[1] "I believe I have adverted to all the cases cited which can be considered as having any bearing upon the present case; and the extent of the principle to be deduced from them is, that an agreement between a debtor and creditor that the debt owing shall be paid out of a specific fund coming to the debtor, or an order given by a debtor to his creditor upon a person owing money or holding funds belonging to the giver of the order, directing such person to pay such funds to the creditor, will create a valid equitable charge upon such fund; in other words, will operate as an equitable assignment of the debts or fund to which the order refers." He then proceeds to examine the letters referred to, with reference to determining whether they come within the principle declared. He says that the debtor's letter to the solicitor does not come within the principle, because it was not an order upon one owing money to him, nor upon one having funds of his. It was not an order upon the railway company, nor upon any officer of the company, such as to make it available against the company. He concludes, after a full examination of all the circumstances, that the letter was not intended to be, and did not, according to the law applicable to the subject, operate as an equitable assignment to the banker of the debt due from the railway company. It was a mere authority to the solicitor to receive, which might or might not be acted upon.

51. The rule that an equitable assignment can be effected only by a surrender of control over the funds or property assigned is one that is strictly held to. A mere promise that the goods shall be held in trust for the benefit of another, and that the proceeds shall be paid to him, does not amount to an equitable assignment of the goods or specific lien upon them; for in such case the owner retains control of the goods, and may appropriate them or their proceeds to the payment of other creditors, and the holder of such promise cannot follow the goods any more than he could follow their proceeds. He has no lien either upon the goods or their proceeds. The owner has violated his promise, and for this he is personally responsible.[2]

52. The promise of a debtor to pay a debt out of a particular fund is not sufficient. There must be an appropria-

---

[1] Rodick v. Gandell, 1 De G., M. & G. 763, 777.

[2] Gibson v. Stone, 43 Barb. (N. Y.) 285.

tion of the fund *pro tanto*, either by giving an order on the specific fund, or by transferring the amount otherwise in such a manner that the holder of the fund is authorized to pay the amount directly to the creditor without the further intervention of the debtor.[1] Thus a mere personal agreement by a claimant against the United States, whereby he promises to pay an attorney a percentage of whatever sum may be appropriated by Congress through his efforts to secure the payment of the claim, does not constitute a lien on the fund to be appropriated; there being no order on the government to pay the percentage out of the fund so appropriated, nor any assignment to the attorney of such percentage.[2] The remedy for the breach of such an agreement is at law, and not in equity.

A sale of goods upon the mere promise of the purchaser to pay for them out of the avails of their sale, and of a stock of other goods then owned by the purchaser, does not give the seller a lien on the goods after their delivery, nor on the avails of their sale, that can be specifically enforced.[3] Such an agreement merely creates the relation of debtor and creditor, and does not effectually appropriate the funds to the payment of the specific debt.

53. Workmen have no lien on money retained by the owner of property out of sums due to a contractor, for the owner's own protection against claims for labor and materials. A provision in a contract for work and the furnishing of materials whereby the employer is authorized to retain, out of the moneys that may be due to the contractor, such amount as may be necessary to meet the claims of all persons who have done work or furnished materials, and who shall have given notice of their claims within a limited time, until such liability shall be discharged, creates no equitable lien upon the fund retained, and raises no equitable assignment of it in favor of laborers or material-men. The contract does not provide for any

---

[1] Trist *v.* Child, 21 Wall. 441; Wright *v.* Ellison, 1 Wall. 16; Hoyt *v.* Story, 3 Barb. (N. Y.) 262; Gibson *v.* Stone, 43 Barb. (N. Y.) 285, 291.

[2] Trist *v.* Child, *supra.* In this case, Congress having appropriated a sum for the payment of the claim,

the attorney obtained an injunction against the claimant from withdrawing this sum from the treasury until he had complied with his agreement about compensation; but the Supreme Court reversed the order.

[3] Stewart *v.* Hopkins, 30 Ohio St. 502.

application of the moneys retained to the payment of claims contained in the notice. The only benefit a laborer or material-man could secure by filing such notice would be that he would stop the payment of the amount to the contractor, and he would know where his debtor had funds wherewith to pay the claim ; but he could reach these funds only by trustee process, or some other form of attachment.[1]

54. **The designation of the particular fund must be clear and definite to give effect to an order as an equitable assign-ment,** in distinction from an order drawn against a general credit. The president of a company wrote a letter stating that, if a certain person in its employ would make an order on its treasurer for any portion of his salary, and the payee would file it with the treasurer, the sum would be paid monthly so long as the employee remained with the company and the order " re-mained unrevoked." The employee accordingly drew an order for three hundred dollars in monthly payments of fifty dollars, closing the order with the words, " and charge the same to my salary account." The order and letter were filed with the treas-urer, but before anything was paid upon the order the drawer wrote the treasurer countermanding the order. In a suit against the company to recover the amount of the order, it was held that the plaintiff could not recover ; that, treating the order as a bill of exchange, the company accepted it only conditionally that it " remained unrevoked ; " and that it did not operate as an equi-table assignment, inasmuch as the order was not a requirement to pay out of a designated fund or from a particular source. Upon this point the court said : " The order does not, in terms, direct the payment of the salary or wages, or any part thereof, to the payee. It is a request, or at most a direction by the drawer, to pay certain specific sums of money, generally, for a certain period and on particular days, without the designation therein of any claim for a debt due or to become due to him, unless it is contained in the further direction to charge the amounts paid to his salary account. This, it is true, recognizes the fact that there was a relation between the parties at the time which en-titled the drawer to a credit for services rendered by him, and for which a salary was payable ; but the direction would have been as proper if the sums to be charged were for moneys lent

[1] Quinlan v. Russell, 15 J. & S. (N. Y.) 212.

and advanced previous to the earning of the salary, as for a salary actually earned, and for which an indebtedness had accrued. It was not a requirement that the payment should be made out of a designated fund, or from a particular source, but it was a provision made for the reimbursement of what should be paid in compliance with the request or direction.[1]

55. A bill of exchange does not of itself constitute an equitable assignment of the sum named, unless it specifies a particular fund upon which the order or bill is drawn, and the drawer has divested himself of all right to control the fund.[2] A bill of exchange in the ordinary form does not specify any particular fund upon which it is drawn, and therefore does not constitute an equitable assignment of any sum in the hands of the drawee ; and an order which is payable out of a particular fund is not a negotiable bill of exchange, for such an instrument must be payable absolutely, and not contingently out of a particular fund. Even after an unconditional acceptance of a bill, it cannot in strictness be held to operate as an assignment to the payee of the drawer's funds in the hands of the drawee, since the latter becomes bound by the consent of acceptance, irrespective of the funds in his hands.[3]

56. If a bill of exchange drawn against a consignment does not itself refer to the consignment, and the consignee is not otherwise instructed to hold the consignment or the proceeds of it for the payment of the bill, there is no appropriation for the payment of the bill which will constitute a lien.[4]

A mere letter of advice from the consignor to the consignee that a bill of exchange has been drawn against the consignment does not, it seems, operate as a specific appropriation of the proceeds to the payment of the bill. Even if the letter of advice amounts to a specific direction to apply the proceeds of the consignment to the payment of such bill, it does not operate as a

[1] Shaver v. Western Union Telegraph Co. 57 N. Y. 459.

[2] Yeates v. Groves, 1 Ves. Jr. 280; Watson v. Wellington, 1 Russ. & M. 602, 605; Lett v. Morris, 4 Sim. 607; Burn v. Carvalho, 4 Mylne & C. 690; Malcolm v. Scott, 3 Hare, 39; Chapman v. White, 6 N. Y. 412; Marine & F. Ins. Bank v. Jauncey, 3 Sandf. (N. Y.) 257; Winter v. Drury, 5 N. Y. 525; Cowperthwaite, v. Sheffield, 1 Sandf. 416; affirmed, 3 N. Y. 243; Harris v. Clark, Ib. 93.

[3] Cowperthwaite v. Sheffield, *supra*.

[4] Frith v. Forbes, 4 De G., F. & J. 409, 421, per Turner, J.

specific appropriation of the proceeds to the payment of the bill, unless it be shown that the purchaser or holder of the bill took it on the faith that the proceeds of the shipment were to be applied to its payment.[1] But a draft or order made payable out of a particular fund is an assignment of the fund *pro tanto*.[2]

57. A check drawn upon a bank does not operate as an equitable assignment of the funds of the drawer to the amount of the check, nor does it create any lien upon such funds,[3] if it is drawn in the ordinary form. In such form it does not describe any particular fund, or use any words of transfer of the whole or a part of any particular amount standing to the credit of the drawer. Such a check is in legal effect like an unaccepted bill of exchange in the ordinary form. It does not operate as an equitable assignment of any part of the funds of the drawee in the hands of the drawer; and it is immaterial that the drawer is not a bank.[4] Accordingly, where an insurance com-

---

[1] Cowperthwaite *v.* Sheffield, 3 N. Y. 243, affirming *S. C.* 1 Sandf. 416.

[2] Yeates *v.* Groves, 1 Ves. Jr. 280; Hall *v.* City of Buffalo, 1 Keyes (N. Y.), 193; Vreeland *v.* Blunt, 6 Barb. (N. Y.) 182. The fund drawn upon in this case had been set apart for certain specified purposes, among which was the payment of the sum mentioned in the order, and the order itself specified the fund. It was of course an equitable appropriation of the amount so drawn.

[3] Hopkinson *v.* Forster, L. R. 19 Eq. 74; Christmas *v.* Russell, 14 Wall. 69; Thompson *v.* Riggs, 5 Wall. 663; Bank of Republic *v.* Millard, 10 Wall. 152; First National Bank *v.* Whitman, 94 U. S. 343.

New York: Chapman *v.* White, 6 N. Y. 412; People *v.* Merchants' & Mechanics' Bank, 78 N. Y. 269; Duncan *v.* Berlin, 60 N. Y. 151; Ætna Nat. Bank *v.* Fourth Nat. Bank, 46 N. Y. 82; Tyler *v.* Gould, 48 N. Y. 682.

Missouri: Dickinson *v.* Coates, 79 Mo. 250; Merchants' Nat. Bank *v.* Coates, Ib. 168; Coates *v.* Doran, 83 Mo. 337. The former case ex-

pressly dissents from McGrade *v.* German Savings Inst. 4 Mo. App. 330.

Pennsylvania: Loyd *v.* McCaffrey, 46 Pa. St. 410.

Maryland: Moses *v.* Franklin Bank, 34 Md. 574, 580.

Massachusetts: Carr *v.* Nat. Security Bank, 107 Mass. 45; *S. C.* 9 Am. Rep. 6; Dana *v.* Third Nat. Bank, 13 Allen (Mass.), 445; Bullard *v.* Randall, 1 Gray (Mass.), 605.

[4] Attorney-General *v.* Continental L. Ins. Co. *in re* Merrill, 71 N. Y. 325; Lunt *v.* Bank of North America, 49 Barb. (N. Y.) 221.

There are some authorities to the effect that a check in the usual form is an equitable assignment of so much of the drawer's deposit as the check calls for. Such is the rule adopted in the following states : —

Illinois: Munn *v.* Burch, 25 Ill. 35 : Chicago Marine & F. Ins. Co. 28 Ill. 168; Union Nat. Bank *v.* Oceana Co. Bank, 80 Ill. 212; *S. C.* 22 Am. Rep. 185.

Iowa: Roberts *v.* Austin, 26 Iowa, 315.

South Carolina: Fogarties *v.* State Bank, 12 Rich. 518.

pany gave its check in the ordinary form upon a trust company in payment of a loss, but before its presentation a receiver of the company was appointed, who withdrew all the funds on deposit, it was held that the payee was not entitled to have the amount of the check paid out of funds in the receiver's hands in preference to the claims of other creditors. The fact that there was a receipt upon the back of the check, intended to be signed by the payee, was held not to create a lien upon the fund drawn upon. A statement of the consideration for a draft or check, either generally or specifically, whether on the back or in the body of the instrument, does not create a lien or appropriation of the particular fund without some expression to that effect.[1]

58. The lien of the holder of a bill of exchange upon the fund in the hands of the drawee has its foundation in a special agreement or implied understanding of the parties, entered into at the time of discounting or purchasing the bill, that the fund in the hands of the drawee is appropriated to the payment of the bill.[2] In upholding the lien and devoting the fund to the payment of the bill, the court executes the agreement and carries out the understanding of the parties. Even a verbal understanding between the drawer and a person discounting the bill, that it is founded on a shipment of goods, and that their proceeds shall be applied to the payment of the bill, is sufficient to effect an equitable transfer or lien.[3] A merchant shipped a cargo of wheat to commission merchants in New York, and the next day drew a draft upon the consignees and

[1] Attorney-General v. Continental L. Ins. Co. supra.

[2] Burn v. Carvalho, 4 Mylne & C. 690; Flour City Nat. Bank v. Garfield, 30 Hun (N. Y.), 579.

[3] Flour City Nat. Bank v. Garfield, supra. This is contrary to some expressions to be found in earlier cases. Marine & Fire Ins. Bank v. Jauncey, 3 Sandf. (N. Y.) 257, is perhaps the case most directly in conflict with the above. It is there said that a bill of exchange, though understood to be drawn against certain goods or their proceeds, makes no special appropriation of either to the payment of the bill. The drawer has the same legal control of the goods or of their proceeds in the hands of the consignee that he had before negotiating the bill of exchange. If the goods or their proceeds afterwards come into the drawer's hands, the holder of the bill will have no equitable lien upon them. The consignee, moreover, has the right to apply the proceeds to the payment of any general balance due him from the consignor, or in any other way that the consignor and consignee might agree upon. This decision in effect overruled the same case before the equity court in 1 Barb. 486.

procured a discount of it at a bank, upon the representation that the cargo had been shipped to the drawees, and with the understanding that the draft was drawn against the proceeds of the shipment. The drawer at the same time wrote to the consignees that the draft had been drawn, and requested them to accept it. The next day the drawer, being insolvent, made a general assignment for the benefit of his creditors. The assignee seized the wheat before it reached the consignees and sold it. In an action by the bank, a lien was established in its favor as against the assignee. The court say that the evidence showed that the draft was discounted by the bank upon the credit of the wheat which had been shipped by the drawer, and relied upon the avails of the same for the acceptance and payment of the draft. The bank was told that the wheat had been shipped, and that the draft was drawn against the shipment, and this justified the conclusion that the draft was discounted upon the credit of the shipment.[1]

59. A brief reference in a draft against a consignment to an appropriation of the proceeds has, together with other evidence of the appropriation, been held to create a lien.[2] Thus, in a recent case, it appeared that the draft against a consignment of corn directed the amount to be charged "as advised," and the consignee was advised by letter of the drawing of the draft. This reference made in the draft was regarded by the court as extending the nature of the transaction beyond that of the mere discounting of a bill of exchange; for the bankers discounting the bill were justified in concluding that property had been shipped to the consignee, and that he had been directed to pay the draft out of the proceeds of the shipment. It was a fact found that the discount was made with the knowledge of, and in reliance upon, that arrangement. Direct evidence of this was not given, but circumstances were proved from which that conclusion was reasonably drawn, and they were sufficient to establish the fact that when the bill was discounted it was done on the understanding that its payment had been provided for from the proceeds of the shipment. The letter and the bill, and the understanding of the parties, so far qualified the nature of the direction and request made in the bill

[1] Flour City Nat. Bank *v.* Garfield, 30 Hun (N. Y.), 579.

[2] Parker *v.* Baxter, 19 Hun (N. Y.), 410.

as substantially to render it an order for a corresponding amount of the proceeds of the shipment. That created a charge or lien upon the corn and its proceeds in favor of the bankers discounting the bill under these circumstances. There was something more than a simple direction by the shipper to the consignee to apply the property to the payment of the bill, for the bill itself was negotiated and discounted on the distinct understanding that the proceeds of the corn should be applied to its payment.[1]

60. If a consignee receives goods under an express direction to apply the proceeds to the payment of a particular bill of exchange, an equitable lien is created in favor of the holder of the bill, if he took it relying upon such appropriation, and this will prevail against the general lien of the consignee.

In general it may said that if, at the time a consignment is made, the consignee be notified that a draft has been drawn against it, and the draft is discounted on the faith of the consignment and instructions, then the nature of the transaction is extended beyond the mere discounting of a bill of exchange drawn against a consignment.[2] The party discounting the bill has an equitable lien upon the goods or their proceeds to the extent of his advances.

61. The general lien of a consignee cannot be set up against the express directions of the consignor given at the time when the consignment is offered and accepted, whereby a lien is created in favor of the payee of a draft drawn against the consignment.[3] If a consignee thinks proper to accept a consignment, with express directions to apply it or the proceeds in a particular mode, he cannot set up his general lien in opposition to those directions. In such a case, only what remains after answering the particular directions becomes subject to the general lien.[4] If the consignee be notified that a bill of exchange in favor of a third person is to be paid out of the proceeds of the

[1] Per Daniels, J., in Parker v. Baxter, *supra*.

[2] **New York**: Parker v. Baxter, 19 Hun, 410; Morton v. Naylor, 1 Hill, 583; Hoyt v. Story, 3 Barb. 262; Marine & F. Ins. Bank v. Jauncey, 1 Ib. 486 ; Lowery v. Steward, 25 N. Y. 239.

[3] Frith v. Forbes, 4 De G., F. & J. 409; Cayuga Co. Nat. Bank v. Daniels, 47 N. Y. 631 ; Bailey v. Hudson River R. R. Co. 49 N. Y. 70.

[4] Frith v. Forbes, per Turner, J. See, however, Robey v. Ollier, L. R. 7 Ch. 477; Phelps v. Comber, 29 Ch. D. 813; Brown v. Kough, Ib. 848.

consignment, this direction, in connection with the bill of exchange, amounts to an appropriation of the consignment to the payment of the bill of exchange, and the holder of the bill has a lien upon the consignment or the proceeds of it. The lien exists whether the bill be accepted or not. If it be not accepted, the consignment is subject to the lien in favor of the holder of the bill; if it be accepted, the consignee becomes personally liable upon the acceptance, and the lien also attaches to the consignment or the proceeds of it, so long as the proceeds can be traced.

But a mere direction of " Advice of draft " on a bill does not operate as an appropriation of the consignment ; and the case of Frith v. Forbes, so far as it goes to establish a general principle of law to this effect, is impugned by the later English cases.[1]

62. **The delivery of a bill of lading to one who discounts a draft drawn against the shipment is a sufficient appropriation of the property** to give the holder of the draft an equitable lien upon the property. Ordinarily the question of an equitable lien does not arise in such a case, because the delivery of the bill of lading amounts to a pledge and delivery of the property itself. But an equitable lien might be declared in such a case.[2] The fact that the discount of the draft is obtained on the delivery of the bill of lading is conclusive that an assignment of the property, either legal or equitable, was made for the security of the draft.

There is no equitable lien upon moneys advanced to the drawer of a bill of exchange on the security of a bill of lading of goods against which the bill of exchange is drawn, upon the failure of the consignee and the sale of the goods for a sum insufficient to. repay the advances upon them. When the borrower receives the money upon such a bill of exchange and bill of lading, the money is his, and not the money of the lender ; nor is

[1] Phelps v. Comber, 29 Ch. D. 813; Brown v. Kough, Ib. 848; Robey v. Ollier, L. R. 7 Ch. 695; *In re* Entwistle, 3 Ch. D. 477.

[2] Bank of Rochester v. Jones, 4 N. Y. 497, 499. In this case, which was a discount of a draft on the security of a bill of lading delivered at the time, Paige, J., declared that, if the bank which discounted the draft had filed a bill in equity for relief, it was clear that the bank would have been entitled to a decree declaring its demand against the consignor who drew the draft an equitable lien on the goods consigned. And see Cayuga Co. Nat. Bank v. Daniels, 47 N. Y. 631.

it clothed with a trust, or subject to a lien in his favor. The lender has parted with his money, and has in place of it the security he bargained for.[1]

III. *Arising from Advances Made and Money Paid.*

63. Where in terms the parties agree that one making advances for the purchase of merchandise to be shipped to him, shall have a lien upon the same, the lien arises upon the purchase of the merchandise before it is consigned to the creditor. The lien in such case attaches to the merchandise purchased and in the hands of the debtor at the time of his bankruptcy, and may be asserted as against the debtor's assignee in bankruptcy. Judge Story said that the possession of the property by the debtor was not a badge of fraud, or against the policy of the law, or in any manner to be deemed inconsistent with the just rights of his general creditors ; and therefore the agreement to give a lien or equitable charge was binding upon the property in the hands of the assignee.[2]

64. Under an executory agreement to purchase and consign property, no lien arises until the property is actually acquired by the debtor, and perhaps not till it is actually consigned to the creditor in accordance with the agreement. A merchant accepted a draft under an agreement that the drawer would invest the proceeds in cotton and ship the same to the merchant for sale. The drawer obtained a discount of the draft at his bank, and the proceeds were placed to his credit. Two days afterwards, the money still standing to his credit, he died. In a contest between the acceptor and the creditors of the drawer it was held that at law the money raised on the bill became unconditionally the property of the drawer, and at his death passed to his administrator, and that in equity the acceptor had no lien upon the proceeds of the draft.[3] If there was any lien, it arose out of the agreement of the parties, — the agreement that the proceeds of the draft should be used for the purchase of cotton to be consigned to the acceptor. Until the cotton was purchased, the thing did not come into being upon which the lien could attach. Whether the agreement to consign created a lien

---

[1] Grinnell *v.* Suydam, 3 Sandf. (N. Y.) 132.

[2] Fletcher *v.* Morey, 2 Story, 555.

[3] Holt *v.* Bank of Augusta, 13 Ga. 341.

at all, or merely a personal covenant, might be a question of
doubt. But certainly no lien could attach to the money, because
there was no contract in regard to the money under which a
lien could arise. Any lien implied by the contract was upon the
cotton. While the drawer lived, a lien upon the cotton was a
possible thing; it would arise upon the purchase and consignment of it in accordance with the agreement. Whether the lien
would arise upon the purchase before the consignment, is a question which did not arise in this case, though the court incidentally discussed the question and expressed a doubt whether the
lien would attach upon the purchase of the cotton.

65. A lien by express contract upon a crop to be raised
prevails against the debtor's assignee in insolvency. The
creditor having the earliest lien by contract has an equity superior to that of the general creditors.[1] The maxim, *qui prior
est tempore, potior est in jure*, applies.

A farmer entered into a contract with a firm of traders by
which they were to become his agents for the sale of his crops,
advance him money, and accept his drafts, for the payment of
which he pledged his crops on hand, and the growing crops of
the year. Upon the faith of this agreement the traders made
large advances to the farmer, who died at the close of the year,
largely indebted to them. His executor took possession of the
crops, and resisted the claim of lien on the part of the traders,
upon the ground that they were in no better condition as to the
crops than the other creditors of the deceased. It was held,
however, that the agreement constituted a lien which a court of
equity would enforce.[2]

66. An equitable lien arises under a contract whereby a
creditor is to receive half the proceeds of a certain crop
upon which the contract gives a lien. Thus, where a mortgagor,
in consideration of the mortgagee's forbearance in foreclosing the
mortgage, agreed to cultivate the mortgaged land in cotton for
one year, and to give the mortgagee one half of the cotton raised,
the value of the same to be credited on the mortgage notes, and
gave a lien on the whole crop for the payment of the one half,
the debtor having died during the year, and his estate having
been declared insolvent, it was held that the mortgagee obtained

---

[1] Kirksey *v.* Means, 42 Ala. 426.   [2] Sullivan *v.* Tuck, 1 Md. Ch. 59.

an equitable lien on the cotton, which he could enforce in a court of equity, and that his lien was superior to the equity of the general creditors.[1]

67. Liens by contract for advances to manufacturers upon manufactured goods. — A firm of merchants entered into an agreement with a firm of silk manufacturers, whereby the former agreed to furnish the latter with raw materials for the manufacture of silk goods, and to advance funds for purchase thereof ; and the goods when manufactured were to be delivered to and sold by the merchants, and the balance of the proceeds of each sale, after deducting commissions, insurance, and advances, was to be paid to the manufacturers. After this arrangement had continued some years the manufacturers failed, and made a general assignment for the benefit of their creditors. The assignee took possession of all the stock and machinery of the debtors, and among the stock were many pieces of silk goods, finished and unfinished. The merchants who had made the advances claimed an equitable lien on these for the balance due them from the manufacturers, and brought suit to enforce the same. It was held, however, that the plaintiffs were not entitled to recover, for, assuming that a lien was created by the agreement, there was no sufficient evidence to identify the property or its proceeds as that which the plaintiffs had advanced.[2]

An agreement whereby a merchant was to advance money to a tanner, to enable him to buy hides for his tannery, provided that the advances should be charged to the tanner, and that the hides bought by him with such money should be bought in the merchant's name and should be his as security for all sums due him. The hides were in fact bought in the tanner's own name. It was held that, while the merchant had a lien on the hides, this lien was not valid against a *bonâ fide* purchaser from the tanner without notice of the merchant's lien.[3]

68. There is no implied lien upon personal property in favor of one who has advanced money for it, without having either the title or possession.[4] Thus, a merchant received from

---

[1] Kirksey v. Means, 42 Ala. 426.

[2] Person v. Oberteuffer, 59 How. (N. Y.) Pr. 339.

[3] Marsh v. Titus, 6 T. & C. (N. Y.) 29.

[4] Allen v. Shortridge, 1 Duv. (Ky). 34.

another merchant a sum of money, for which he gave a receipt stating that he received it as an advance on a shipment of flour then making on board a certain ship, to be consigned to the house of the merchant making the advances. The flour was afterwards purchased by the merchant who received the advances, and was delivered by the seller on board a ship freighted by this merchant. The latter, having stopped payment about the same time, agreed with the seller of the flour, who was ignorant of the agreement with the merchant who made the advances, to rescind the sale, and gave him back the bill of parcels. It was held that the merchant who made the advances had no lien on the flour that could prevent the merchant who received the advances from rescinding the contract with the seller of the flour, and re-delivering to him the flour. To constitute a lien upon a corporeal chattel at common law, possession is essential; and, while in equity a fund may be appropriated by an assignment without delivery of the fund itself, yet this is only where, from the nature of the fund, a transfer of possession is impossible. There can be no appropriation of a chattel susceptible of delivery which will prevail against third persons, without a delivery good at common law.[1] Chief Justice Tilghman upon this point said: " Any order, writing, or act which makes an appropriation of a fund, amounts to an equitable assignment of that fund. The reason is plain: the fund being neither assignable at law, nor capable of manual possession, an appropriation of it is all that the case admits. A court of equity will therefore protect such appropriation, and consider it as equal to an assignment. But very different is the case of a parcel of flour, which admits of actual delivery. Every man who purchases an interest in property of this kind ought to take immediate possession; if he does not, he is guilty of negligence, and can have no equity against a third person who contracts with the actual possessor without notice of a prior right." [2]

69. A contract whereby a planter agrees to ship his crop of cotton to his factor, to reimburse him for advances and supplies, does not create a lien upon the cotton raised.[3]

A merchant, in the spring of the year, made advances to a planter on his verbal promise to give a lien on his crop for the

---

[1] Clemson v. Davidson, 5 Binn. (Pa.) 392.

[2] Clemson v. Davidson, supra, 398.

[3] Allen v. Montgomery, 48 Miss. 101.

year to secure the advances. In June, the planter died suddenly without having given the lien, and his estate was insolvent. On a bill in equity by the merchant to marshal the assets of the estate, it was held that he had no equitable ground for relief. To entitle one to the benefit of an agricultural lien under the statute, he must comply strictly with the conditions of the statute. When one comes into a court of equity to compel specific performance of a contract, he must first show that all has been done that could be done to comply with the law. If he has been negligent in the matter, the court will not lend its aid to complete the contract, for this would be to encourage negligence in parties making contracts.[1]

In like manner an agreement between an owner and a builder that a balance of account due the builder should be paid out of the income of the building does not create a lien upon such income which can be enforced in equity.[2]

70. An equitable lien does not arise in favor of one who has made advances to another to enable him to make improvements upon his property, though there was an understanding at the time that a lien should be given upon the property improved. Thus, where one loaned money to a mill-owner to be used in rebuilding a certain mill which had been destroyed, and it was understood that the lender was to have a lien on the mill to secure him, but no writing was made except a note for the money, upon the death of the borrower and the insolvency of his estate, it was held that equity would not sustain a lien on the mill in favor of the lender, to the prejudice of other creditors of the borrower.[3]

Had there been a written agreement that a mortgage should be given, equity might have declared such agreement to be an equitable mortgage; or had there been an express oral agreement that a mortgage should be given, and it could be shown that the failure to execute the mortgage was by reason of some fraud or accident, there might be good ground for relief in equity. But mere neglect to execute the mortgage, or neglect to execute a written agreement for a mortgage, is not such an accident as equity will relieve against. " It does not come to the aid of the sleeper, but of him who, though awake, has been

---

[1] Cureton v. Gilmore, 3 S. C. 46.

[2] Alexander v. Berry, 54 Miss. 422.

[3] Printup v. Barrett, 46 Ga. 407.

entrapped by fraud, or been prevented from getting his agreement put into writing by inevitable accident."[1]

Money advanced by one person to enable another to make improvements upon his property, as for instance to erect upon his own land a steam mill with machinery, creates no lien upon the mill and machinery. The advances constitute merely a debt from the party to whom the money is advanced.[2]

71. A lien upon the property of another is not created by a voluntary payment of a liability of his, without request.[3] But a request might be inferred from circumstances.[4] Under special circumstances a joint owner of property may have a lien upon the interest of the other part owners for advances made for repairing and preserving the property, especially if such repairs were necessary, and their consent to make them was unreasonably withheld. But in such case the party asserting the lien must show the special circumstances which will give him such lien.[5] Constructive liens will not now be extended and applied to cases where by the rules of law they are not already clearly established ; for such liens are not now encouraged.[6]

72. One who voluntarily pays premiums of insurance for another, in the absence of any agreement or understanding that for such payments he should have a lien upon the policy or its proceeds, has no lien upon the proceeds collected by him as the agent of the insured.[7]

One who procures insurance for another in pursuance of a request to do so and to forward the policy, and not as a broker or general agent, has no lien on the policy. By undertaking to execute the order, he binds himself to comply with the terms and forward the policy, and this precludes the supposition that he was to have any lien upon it or interest in it. And though such person be the ship's husband for the general management of a

---

[1] Printup v. Barrett, 46 Ga. 407, per McCay, J.

[2] Weathersby v. Sleeper, 42 Miss. 732. To like effect see Garland v. Hull, 13 Sm. & M. (Miss.) 76.

[3] Taylor v. Baldwin, 10 Barb. (N. Y.) 626.

[4] Oatfield v. Waring, 14 Johns. (N. Y.) 188.

[5] Taylor v. Baldwin, supra. And see Doane v. Badger, 12 Mass. 65.

[6] Taylor v. Baldwin, supra, per Allen, J.

[7] Meier v. Meier, 15 Mo. App. 68 ; affirmed, 88 Mo. 566.

vessel which is the subject of the insurance, yet he has no lien on the policy for the balance of his account.[1]

73. There is no equitable subrogation in favor of one who pays a debt for which he is not personally bound, and which is not a charge upon his property, so as to entitle him to be subrogated to a lien which the creditor had upon the estate of the debtor.[2]

A stranger, by voluntarily paying the wages of workmen who are entitled to a lien, obtains no right in equity to a subrogation to their lien, in the absence of any assignment, or of an agreement that he should have the benefit of their lien. The superintendent of the work of constructing a railroad, without any obligation on his part, voluntarily, for the purpose of befriending the workmen, advanced his own money to pay them their wages, supposing the railroad company to be solvent. He had no assignment, legal or equitable, of the wages paid, and there was no understanding that he was to have the benefit of their lien. It was held that he was not entitled, by subrogation, to the workmen's statutory lien for such wages.[3] "The statutory lien given to workmen is to be confined within its legitimate limits. It is not to be extended, by a forced application of the principle of subrogation in equity, to cases not within the mischief which the law was designed to remedy. The object of the legislature was to secure to a very meritorious but helpless class of persons the payment of the wages of their toil, and to that end to give them personally a paramount lien on the assets of the employer. It did not contemplate giving to creditors from whom the company might borrow money on its own credit, with which to pay its workmen, such a lien on the assets for their reimbursement."[4]

74. But one who pays a debt of a railroad company for rolling-stock under a contract with the company for security

[1] Reed *v.* Pacific Ins. Co. 1 Met. (Mass.) 166.

[2] Jones on Mortgages, § 874 *a;* Wilkes *v.* Harper, 1 N. Y. 586.

[3] *In re* North River Construction Co. 38 N. J. Eq. 433, 437. "It has never been held that one who lends or advances money to a corporation to enable it to pay laborers, who, if their wages had remained unpaid, would have been entitled to the lien therefor, is, merely by virtue of such loan or advance, entitled to that lien by equitable subrogation."

[4] North River Construction Co., *in re, supra,* per Runyon, Chancellor.

by subrogation to the rights of the vendor, under his contract
with the company, is entitled to such subrogation to the vendor's
lien, and cannot be considered a mere volunteer in making the
payment.[1]

75. A mere loan of money to be used in the purchase of
land does not create a lien upon the land for its repayment.[2]

76. A surety as such has no lien on the estate of his
principal. The fact that his money has gone to increase his
principal's estate raises, perhaps, a natural equity that it should
be returned to the surety out of the estate. But this natural
equity yields to legal rights. Thus, if one accepts drafts for the
accommodation of another under an agreement that the drawer
shall use the proceeds of the drafts in the purchase of merchandise to be consigned to the acceptor, and the drawer dies before
using the proceeds in the purchase of such merchandise, the
acceptor cannot maintain a lien upon the money raised upon the
drafts, although this still stands to the credit of the drawer at his
banker's. The fact that the money was raised on the credit of
the acceptor, and that he accepted for accommodation, gives him
no lien on the money. The money is the property of the drawer,
and passes upon his death to his executor or administrator without charge.[3]

IV. *Arising from Agreements to give Mortgages or other Security.*

77. An agreement, on a sufficient consideration, to give a
mortgage on specific property, creates an equitable lien upon
such property, which takes precedence of the claims of the prom-
isor's general creditors, and of the claims of subsequent purchasers and incumbrancers with notice of the lien.[4]

---

[1] Coe v. New Jersey Midland Ry.
Co. 27 N. J. Eq. 110. And see Payne
v. Hathaway, 3 Vt. 212; New Jersey
Midland Ry. Co. v. Wortendyke, 27
N. J. Eq. 658.

[2] Collinson v. Owens, 6 G. & J.
(Md.) 4.

[3] Holt v. Bank of Augusta, 13 Ga.
341, per Nisbet, J.

[4] Jones on Mortgages, §§ 163–167.

New York: Husted v. Ingraham,
75 N. Y. 251; Payne v. Wilson, 74
N. Y. 348; Chase v. Peck, 21 N. Y.
581; Howe, *in re*, 1 Paige, 125;
Wood v. Lester, 29 Barb. 145; Seymour v. Canandaigua & Niagara Falls
R. R. Co. 25 Ib. 284.

South Carolina: Dow v. Ker,
Speers' Ch. 413; Massey v. McIlwain,
2 Hill's Ch. 421, 428.

If the written agreement shows a clear intention to make some particular property a security for a debt or obligation, equity will treat the instrument as an executory agreement to give security.[1] The agreement creates a specific lien upon the property which takes precedence of the claims of subsequent creditors and purchasers with notice.[2]

Where the agreement was that a mortgage should be given upon one building and lot out of several buildings and lots, which were together sufficiently identified, and afterwards a mechanic's lien was filed against all the houses and lots, the fact that the original agreement did not point out the particular premises to be mortgaged was held not to impair its effect as an equitable lien, at least as against the claimant of a mechanic's lien, who could not be affected by the application of the lien to any one of the houses and lots, his lien being upon all.[3]

78. An agreement to give any other security rests upon the same principle. If one borrows a promissory note from a friend to obtain a discount at a bank, and promises by letter to give his friend a bill of sale of a schooner as security, and the borrower dies without giving the bill of sale, and the lender of the note is obliged to take it up, he has an equitable lien on the schooner in preference to the general creditors of the deceased. The bill of sale must be considered as made at the time of the giving of the note.[4]

In like manner, if a person covenant that he will, on or before a certain day, secure an annuity by a charge upon freehold estates, or by investment in the funds, or by the best means in his power, such covenant will create a lien upon any property to which he becomes entitled between the date of the covenant and the day so limited for its performance.[5]

In Price v. Cutts, 29 Ga. 142, however, it is said that an agreement to execute a mortgage in præsenti, the actual execution of it failing through inadvertence or other cause, does not constitute such a lien as will prevail against subsequent judgment creditors.

[1] Pom. Eq. Jur. 1235 ; Seymour v. Canandaigua & Niagara Falls R. R. Co. 25 Barb (N. Y.) 284; Kelly v. Kelly, 54 Mich. 30.

[2] Lanning v. Tompkins, 45 Barb. (N. Y.) 308.

[3] Payne v. Wilson, 74 N. Y. 348.

[4] Read v. Gaillard, 2 Desaus. (S. C.) 552.

[5] Wellesley v. Wellesley, 4 Mylne & Cr. 561; Roundell v. Breary, 2 Vern. 482; Lyde v. Mynn, 4 Sim. 505; S. C. 1 Mylne & K. 683, 685.

79. In this way a debtor's agreement to insure for the benefit of a creditor may give the latter an equitable lien upon an insurance obtained in the debtor's name, to the extent of the creditor's interest.[1] Thus, where a mortgagor covenants to keep the premises insured for the benefit of the mortgagee, and obtains a policy of insurance in his own name, upon the happening of a loss the mortgagee has an equitable lien upon the fund payable under the policy.[2]

But the mere fact that one is a mortgagee of premises which the mortgagor has insured in his own name, gives him no lien upon the money payable upon the policy. The contract of insurance is a personal contract of indemnity between the insured and the underwriter. The mortgagor has an insurable interest, and he may insure for his own benefit; and the mere fact that he is personally liable to pay a debt which is a lien upon the property insured, does not affect his right to claim the full benefit of the insurance. A mortgagee's equitable right to claim the benefit of such insurance arises only where he has a contract with the mortgagor for insurance as a further security. The mortgagee's equitable lien in such case rests wholly upon contract.[3]

80. Agreement to build and convey a mill as security. — A written contract was made by the owners of timber land for the sale of the standing timber at an agreed price, the purchaser agreeing to build a sawmill worth nine thousand dollars upon a forty-acre tract, the title to which the vendors were to convey to him. It was also agreed that the purchaser might mortgage the mill site and mill to a third person for the sum of sixty-five hundred dollars, and should give a second mortgage to the vendors to secure the performance of the contract. The purchaser, by means of the contract, borrowed about ten thousand dollars, and, after the mill was built, conveyed the mill and mill site to the lender by way of mortgage to secure the advances, before the vendors had conveyed the title of the mill lot to the vendee. It was held that under the circumstances the mortgagee was equitably entitled to a lien upon the mill lot, but that the amount

---

[1] Vernon v. Smith, 5 B. & Ald. 1.

[2] Thomas v. Von Kapff, 6 Gill & J. 372; Carter v. Rockett, 8 Paige (N. Y.), 437, per Walworth, Ch.

[3] Neale v. Reid, 3 Dow. & Ry. 158; Carter v. Rockett, 8 Paige (N. Y.), 437; Jones on Mortgages, § 401.

of such lien could not exceed the sum mentioned in the contract.[1]

81. For debt omitted from mortgage by mistake. — An equitable lien cannot be claimed for a debt omitted by a debtor in securing his creditor by a chattel mortgage for the supposed amount of his indebtedness. Thus, where personal property was exchanged for land of less value, and the difference in value was secured by a chattel mortgage upon the personalty exchanged, and it was afterwards discovered that the land was subject to taxes for a considerable amount which the mortgagor should have included in the amount of his mortgage, it was held that the mortgagee was not entitled to an equitable lien upon the goods for the amount of such taxes. Certainly such a lien will not be established as against other creditors of the mortgagor after his insolvency.[2] The mortgagee might have ascertained at the time of the transaction whether the taxes had been paid, had he exercised ordinary care and diligence. The mortgagee having chosen to take, without examination, the statement of the mortgagor and his covenant in his deed of the land, a court of equity will not give him relief. Whether, in case the mortgage note had by fraud or mistake been made for an amount less than a certain liquidated sum which by agreement the mortgage was to secure, the mortgagee would have an equitable lien upon the proceeds of the goods in the hands of an assignee for the benefit of creditors, is a question which the court did not consider.

82. A covenant or agreement of a purchaser of land to pay a debt which is supposed to be a lien on the land binds the land with a trust for the payment of such lien. Thus, a debtor confessed judgment to his creditor, but by mistake the judgment was not docketed in the county where the debtor's land was situated. The debtor afterwards sold the land to one who agreed to pay the supposed judgment lien as a part of the consideration. Afterwards, on learning that the judgment had not been docketed so as to make it a lien on the land, the purchaser refused to pay it. On a bill filed by the creditor against the purchaser, it was held that the latter took the land charged with an equitable lien or trust for the payment of the judgment;

[1] Hubbard *v.* Bellew, 10 Fed. Rep. 849.　　[2] Chamberlin *v.* Peltz, 1 Mo. App. 183.

and the fact that the amount of the judgment was greater than the parties supposed, was held to constitute no defence.[1]

An agreement, not under seal, given by a grantor of land at the time of the conveyance, stipulating that he would support and maintain the grantor, and pledging for that purpose the product of the land, and, should that prove insufficient, appropriating the entire fee, is an equitable lien upon the land in the nature of a mortgage.[2]

83. A verbal contract by one person to pay the debts of another, who should thereupon convey to the former certain lands, is void under the statute of frauds, and can support no rights, either legal or equitable.[3] If a party pays money under such a void contract, he may, perhaps, recover it back in assumpsit; but a court of equity will not create a lien upon real estate in favor of the party paying, unless, from the nature of the transaction, rights have sprung up which ought to be held binding upon the specific property.[4] That the parties to such contract are father and son does not afford any equitable ground for declaring a lien.

V. *Arising in favor of Creditors and Stockholders of Corporations.*

84. The creditors of a corporation have an equitable lien upon its capital stock for the payment of its debts.[5] When debts are incurred a contract arises with the creditors that the capital stock shall not be withdrawn or applied, otherwise than upon their demands, until these are satisfied. " If diverted, they may follow it as far as it can be traced, and subject it to the payment of their claims, except as against holders who have taken it *bonâ fide* for a valuable consideration and without notice. It is publicly pledged to those who deal with the corporation, for their security."[6] Therefore a corporation is not allowed to injuriously affect the rights of a creditor by purchas-

[1] Haverly v. Becker, 4 N. Y. 169.

[2] Chase v. Peck, 21 N. Y. 581.

[3] Kelly v. Kelly, 54 Mich. 30.

[4] Per Champlin, J., in Kelly v. Kelly, *supra.*

[5] Sanger v. Upton, 91 U. S. 56; Sawyer v. Hoag, 17 Wall. 610; Bart-

lett v. Drew, 57 N. Y. 587; Hastings v. Drew, 76 N. Y. 9; Clapp v. Peterson, 104 Ill. 26; Heman v. Britton, 88 Mo. 549; Gill v. Balis, 72 Mo. 424.

[6] Sanger v. Upton, 91 U. S. 56, 60, per Swayne, J.

ing its own stock and retiring it. Every stockholder is conclusively charged with notice of the trust character which attaches to its capital stock; and, therefore, if a stockholder takes from the corporation other property in exchange for such stock, he takes such property subject to an equity in favor of a creditor of the corporation to have the property in place of the stock applied to the payment of the debt to himself.[1]

The creditor of a corporation has also an equitable lien upon its property and assets; and if the corporation distributes these among its stockholders, leaving a creditor unpaid, he may, after obtaining judgment against the corporation, and the execution has been returned unsatisfied, maintain a creditor's bill against a stockholder to reach whatsoever he has received in the distribution.[2]

A claim of the corporation against a stockholder for his unpaid subscription for shares is an asset of the company, and a creditor has the same right to look to it as to any other asset of the company, and the same right to insist upon its payment as upon the payment of any other debt due the company.[3]

85. Lien of creditors of a corporation upon its property transferred to another corporation. — A corporation to which all the property of another corporation is transferred, which is thereupon dissolved without providing for the payment of its debts, takes the property subject to a lien in favor of the creditors of the old corporation to the amount of the property transferred.[4] Any arrangement whereby one corporation takes from another all its property, so that the old corporation is deprived of the means of paying its debts, and is enabled to dissolve its corporate existence and place itself practically beyond the reach of creditors, is unconscionable unless the new corporation pays the debts of the old. It matters not whether the stockholders of the two corporations are the same or different, only that the equity is all the stronger where the stockholders of both are the same. Equity certainly cannot permit the owners of one corporation to organize another, and transfer from the former to

---

[1] Clapp v. Peterson, 104 Ill. 26.
[2] Bartlett v. Drew, 57 N. Y. 587; Hastings v. Drew, 76 N. Y. 9.
[3] Sanger v. Upton, 91 U. S. 56, 60.
[4] Brum v. Merchants' Mut. Ins.
Co. 16 Fed. Rep. 140; Hibernia Ins. Co. v. St. Louis & N. O. Transp. Co. 13 Fed. Rep. 516; Harrison v. Union Pacific Ry. Co. Ib. 522.

the latter all the corporate property without paying all the corporate debts.[1]

A life insurance company, being about to close up its business, reinsured its policies in another company, to which it assigned certain bonds for the protection of sureties upon an indemnifying bond, under a contract that, after the liability of the sureties should be at an end, such bonds should be apportioned among the stockholders of the company effecting the reinsurance. It was held that the bonds became the property of the stockholders as against all the world, except the creditors of the company ; but that in favor of such creditors they constituted a trust fund for the payment of the debts of the company, and in the hands of such stockholders, or of any depositary, such bonds were subject to an equitable lien in favor of the creditors, which might be enforced upon the failure of the company reinsuring to comply with its contract.[2]

86. Lien of creditors of a corporation upon its property transferred to another corporation (*continued*). And so where the stockholders of a corporation which is in debt transfer all its assets to another corporation in consideration of receiving stock of such other corporation, and of its assuming the liabilities of the old corporation, a creditor of such old corporation has a lien upon the property so transferred which is superior to that of a mortgagee of the property made by the new corporation, if the mortgagee had notice of the debt at the time of taking the mortgage.[3] Treat, J., delivering the opinion, said : " The transferred assets were greater than the assumed obligations by the new corporation. Hence all persons subsequent in interest, with notice of such equitable lien, take subordinate thereto. The evidence discloses that, although the transfer from the old to the new corporation was not formally recorded, all the parties were

[1] Hibernia Ins. Co. *v.* St. Louis & N. O. Transp. Co. *supra,* per McCrary, C. J.

[2] Heman *v.* Britton, 88 Mo. 549.

[3] Blair *v.* St. Louis &c. R. R. Co. 24 Fed. Rep. 148, affirming *S. C.* 22 Ib. 36; Fogg *v.* St. Louis &c. R. R. Co. 17 Ib. 871.

The case of Hervey *v.* Ill. Midland Ry. Co. 28 Fed. Rep. 169, is in contradiction of this view. It is there

held that, where a railroad company purchases the property of another railroad company and assumes its indebtedness, creditors of the selling company do not thereby acquire an equitable lien upon the property sold for the payment of their claims, but they merely acquire the right to look for payment to the purchasing company.

sufficiently informed with respect thereto. The equitable doctrine applies, namely, that they took subject to the prior equitable lien."

87. **The minority shareholders of a corporation have an equitable lien upon its property which the majority has sold to themselves, in breach of their fiduciary relation.** "The majority cannot sell the assets of the company, and keep the consideration, but must allow the minority to have their share of any consideration which may come to them."[1] There is an implied contract in the association together of the members of a corporation, that its powers shall be exercised only for the purpose of accomplishing the objects for which the corporation was formed.[2] The majority of the members are in fact the corporation, so far as its management is concerned : they can bind the whole body of the associates in all transactions within the scope of the corporate powers. But when they assume to control the corporation, they assume the trust relation occupied by the corporation towards its stockholders.[3] "Although stockholders are not partners, nor strictly tenants in common, they are the beneficial joint owners of the corporate property, having an interest and power of legal control in exact proportion to their respective amounts of stock. The corporation itself holds its property as a trust fund for the stockholders, who have a joint interest in all its property and effects, and the relation between it and its several members is, for all practical purposes, that of trustee and *cestui que trust.* When several persons have a common interest in property, equity will not allow one to appropriate it exclusively to himself, or to impair its value to the others. Community of interest involves mutual obligation. Persons occupying this relation towards each other are under an obligation to make the property or fund productive of the most that can be obtained from it for all who are interested in it ; and those who seek to make a profit out of it, at the expense of those whose rights in it are the same as their own, are unfaithful to the relation they have assumed, and are guilty at least of constructive

---

[1] Menier *v.* Hooper's Telegraph Works, 9 Ch. App. Cas. 350, 354, per Mellish, L. J.

[2] Abbot *v.* American Hard Rubber Co. 33 Barb. (N. Y.) 578.

[3] Ervin *v.* Oregon Ry. & Nav. Co. 27 Fed. Rep. 625 ; *S. C.* 23 Blatch. 517. See, also, Atkins *v.* Wabash, St. L. & P. Ry. Co. 29 Fed. Rep. 161 ; S. C. 21 Am. L. Rev. 104.

fraud. Among the disabilities imposed by courts of equity upon those who occupy a fiduciary relation towards others, respecting property which is to be administered for beneficiaries, is that which precludes the fiduciary from purchasing the property on his own account, without such a full and complete understanding in advance with the beneficiaries as will repel all inferences that the fiduciary intended to derive any peculiar advantage for himself. The fiduciary cannot retain his bargain by showing that the sale was public, or that the price was fair, or that there was no intention on his part to gain an unfair advantage. Where he has a duty to perform which is inconsistent with the character of a purchaser, he cannot divest himself of the equities of the beneficiaries to demand the profits that may arise from the transaction." [1]

An equitable lien may be decreed to exist in favor of such minority shareholders upon the property of the old corporation in the hands of the new corporation to the extent of the value of the property which they have been deprived of. Such lien is prior to the lien of the stockholders of the new corporation, but is subject to the lien of the holders of its mortgage bonds.

88. The shareholders of a corporation have an equitable lien upon a fund specially deposited for the payment of a dividend declared by the company. Each shareholder has a lien upon the fund to the extent of the dividend to which he is entitled. The Erie Railway Company having declared a dividend of one per cent. upon its stock, deposited the money to pay the same with Duncan, Sherman & Co., bankers. Some three months afterwards the money remaining with the bankers was withdrawn by the company, and subsequently passed, with its other property, to a receiver of the road. Upon the application of a stockholder entitled to such dividend, it was held that he had an equitable lien upon the fund deposited for its payment, and that this lien followed the fund into the hands of the receiver, who held it as trustee for the benefit of the stockholders who had not been paid.[2]

In like manner a lien was declared in a case where an insurance company had declared a dividend, and given notice of it to the stockholders, and had prepared checks upon a fund in bank

[1] Per Wallace, J., in Ervin v. Oregon Ry. & Nav. Co. 27 Fed. Rep. 625.

[2] Le Blanc, in re, 14 Hun, 8; S. C. affirmed, 75 N. Y. 598.

for delivery to the stockholders as they should call. A great fire occurred before all the stockholders had been paid, whereby the company was rendered insolvent and its property passed into the hands of a receiver. The dividend was regarded as so far appropriated to the stockholders that they were entitled to it as against the general creditors of the company.[1]

89. **Liens created through the assumption of a mortgage or other lien upon property.** — An equitable lien is created in behalf of a creditor by an agreement made with the debtor by a third person whereby the latter undertakes to pay the debt, or to secure the payment of it. A common instance of the creation of such a lien occurs where the consideration for the conveyance of property is the assumption of the payment by the vendee of an existing lien upon the property, or debt of the vendor in respect of the property.[2] Thus, where two or more railroad companies consolidate, and part of the consideration for the transfer of the property of one of the roads to the consolidated company is the payment by it of certain unsecured equipment bonds issued by the company making the transfer, and the consolidated company agrees to "protect" such bonds, the bondholders thereby acquire an equitable lien on the property of the consolidated company for the payment of their bonds.[3]

90. **A consolidated corporation subject to liens existing against original corporation.** — The holder of the bonds of a railroad corporation, which are a specific lien upon the income of property which has passed by consolidation from the hands of the original debtor corporation to another corporation, can enforce his lien against the latter corporation when it receives such income. He has a lien on the income of the property in whosesoever hands it may come with notice of the lien, and he has the right to enforce this lien independently of any proceeding he may have at law to reach other property in the hands of the debtor corporation. He has the right to pursue the debtor, or to enforce his lien against the income; or he may pursue all his

---

[1] Le Roy v. Globe Ins. Co. 2 Edw. (N. Y.) Ch. 657.

[2] Jones on Mortgages, § 162; Vanmeter v. Vanmeters, 3 Gratt. (Va.) 148; Clyde v. Simpson, 4 Ohio St. 445; Nichols v. Glover, 41 Ind. 24; Harris v. Fly, 7 Paige (N. Y.), 421; Hallett v. Hallett, 2 Paige (N. Y.), 15.

[3] Tysen v. Wabash Ry. Co. 11 Biss. 510.

remedies at the same time.[1] But the lien does not attach in
favor of a stockholder of a railroad company upon its consolidation with another company, though the consolidated company
gave him notes for his interest in the old company instead of
stock which the agreement of consolidation provided should be
issued to the stockholders in the old corporation. The stockholder had no interest in the lands of the old company. These
belonged to the corporation, and the stockholder merely had an
interest in the corporation. The corporation, and not the stockholders, sold and transferred the lands to the consolidated company. An individual stockholder had nothing to sell but his
stock.[2]

91. But if the bonds of the original corporation were
neither a lien upon its property or its income, though it is
agreed that they shall be protected " as to the principal and interest as they shall respectively fall due " by the consolidated
company, and the bonds were issued after the passage of statutes
authorizing the consolidation, the holders have no lien upon the
property of the consolidated company, or upon the proceeds of a
sale of such property made under a mortgage executed by the
consolidated company. The agreement to protect the bonds
created only a personal obligation to see that they should be
paid at maturity. It was claimed also that the payment of the
bonds was a part of the consideration of the transfer, and that
the case came within the principle of a vendor's lien for unpaid
purchase-money. But the court, by Mr. Justice Gray, upon this
point declared : " We are unable to perceive any analogy between the two cases. The doctrine of vendor's lien applies only
to sales of real estate. The consolidation of the stock and property of several corporations into one is not a sale ; and it did not
affect real estate only, but included franchises and personal property." [3]

92. An equitable lien cannot be declared against railroad
property in the hands of a receiver, to secure the payment
for necessary supplies furnished the company before the ap-

---

[1] Ritten v. Union Pacific Ry. Co.
16 Rep. 199.
[2] Cross v. B. & S. W. R. Co. 58
Iowa, 62.

[3] Wabash, St. Louis & Pac. Ry.
Co. v. Ham, 114 U. S. 587.

pointment of the receiver, as against a mortgage then subsisting upon the property.[1] The creditor in such case only holds the relation of a general creditor of the corporation, with no lien upon anything to secure his claim. The mere act of appointing a receiver to preserve the property *pendente lite* does not change the character of the debt from an unsecured to a secured claim. The court may require the receiver to pay the current expenses of the road out of the current earnings before anything is paid upon the mortgage. The current running expenses may include by order of court, expenses incurred within a certain time prior to the date of the appointment of the receiver. But if the current earnings are insufficient to pay the current debts incurred within the time specified, the court will not declare a debt not incurred within that limited time a lien upon property previously pledged to the payment of the mortgage.

VI. *The Enforcement of Equitable Liens.*

93. A court of equity is the appropriate tribunal for enforcing an equitable lien.[2] " In equity there is no difficulty in enforcing a lien, or any other equitable claim constituting a charge *in rem*, not only upon real estate, but also upon personal estate, or upon money in the hands of a third person, whenever the lien or other claim is a matter of agreement, against the party himself and his personal representatives, and against any persons claiming under him voluntarily or with notice, and against assignees in bankruptcy who are treated as volunteers; for every such agreement for a lien or charge *in rem* constitutes a trust, and is accordingly governed by the general doctrine applicable to trusts." [3]

A court of equity, whose powers are limited to certain matters strictly defined, may be without jurisdiction to enforce an equitable lien. Such was formerly the case in Massachusetts when there was only a very limited equity jurisdiction. But wherever there is full equity jurisdiction — that is, an equity jurisdiction coincident and coextensive with that exercised by the Court of Chancery in England — there is jurisdiction for the enforcement

---

[1] United States Trust Co. *v.* New York, W. S. & B. R. R. Co. 25 Fed. Rep. 800; Olyphant *v.* St. Louis Ore & Steel Co. 28 Fed. Rep. 729.

[2] Vallette *v.* Whitewater Valley Canal Co. 4 McLean, 192; Ridgely *v.* Iglehart, 3 Bland (Md.), 540.

[3] Fletcher *v.* Morey, 2 Story, 555, 565.

of any equitable lien or charge;[1] and, unless there be a special remedy provided by statute, this jurisdiction should be invoked for the enforcement of any equitable lien.

The usual mode of enforcing an equitable lien is by an order of sale of the property to which it is attached.[2]

94. A lien at law or by statute cannot be enforced in equity. Except as remedy in equity is expressly provided by statute, a court of equity can enforce an equitable lien, either upon a legal or equitable estate in lands; but a lien which is purely legal, which is created by statute and is dependent upon statutory provisions for its enforcement, cannot be aided in equity if the lien fails at law.[3] In the absence of statutory provisions no lien will be foreclosed in equity except in conformity with established rules of equitable jurisprudence. Thus, a general lien of a judgment will not be turned into the specific lien of a decree in equity and enforced by a sale under such decree. Equity will not interfere where there is a full and complete remedy by statute. The foreclosure of a lien is either a statutory or an equitable proceeding. At law there is no remedy beyond retaining possession.

95. If the owner of property subject to an equitable lien disposes of it, in hostility to the lien, to a *bonâ fide* purchaser without notice of the lien, so that the lien is destroyed, the lienor has a cause of action against the person so selling the property for the restoration of such equitable lien.[4] This right is important where the lienor has no personal claim against such owner, as where by contract one is to have a share of the property or funds recovered by another, and has by a contract a lien upon the property or funds so recovered. In such case the creditor's only claim is against the funds recovered, and, it being a lien by contract, its maintenance does not depend upon possession. It is an equitable charge enforcible only in a court of equity. The person who recovers the funds or property and holds it in his own name can

---

[1] Fletcher *v.* Morey, 2 Story, 555.

[2] Perry *v.* Board of Missions, 102 N. Y. 99, 106; *S. C.* 1 N. Y. St. Rep. 169; Price *v.* Palmer, 23 Hun (N. Y.), 504, 507.

[3] Buchan *v.* Sumner, 2 Barb. (N. Y.) Ch. 165; Douglass *v.* Huston, 6 Ohio, 162; Howe Machine Co. *v.* Miner, 28 Kans. 441.

[4] Husted *v.* Ingraham, 75 N. Y. 251; Hale *v.* Omaha Nat. Bank, 49 N. Y. 626; *S. C.* 64 N. Y. 550, 555; Hovey *v.* Elliot, 21 J. & S. (N. Y.) 331.

transfer it to a purchaser for value and in good faith without notice of the lien ; but in so doing he inflicts a special injury upon the lienor, for which an action lies for damages for the destruction of the lien, or, perhaps, an action in the nature of an action for money had and received for the proceeds of his interest. The cause of action in either case arises at the time of the wrongful sale of the property, and the statute of limitations commences to run from that time.[1]

96. **Priorities.** — A specific equitable lien upon land is preferred to a subsequent judgment lien.[2] If the equitable lien and the judgment lien come into existence at the same time, the former is not entitled to preference' in case it was created to secure an antecedent indebtedness, with no new consideration advanced at the time on the faith of it.[3]

A prior equitable lien is also preferred to a mechanic's lien upon the same property, though the claimant under the latter had no notice of the equitable lien at the time his lien took effect.[4]

---

[1] Hovey v. Elliot, *supra.* In this case the plaintiffs made an agreement with a person who had a large claim pending before the mixed commission on British and American claims, under the treaty of 1871, for the value of certain cotton, by which the plaintiffs were to aid the claimant, and he was to pay them for their services twenty-five per cent. of any amount allowed on the claim, and this amount was made a lien upon any money, draft, or evidence of indebtedness, which might be paid or issued thereon. A large sum was recovered, and a receiver was appointed for one half of the award, and he was directed to invest the money in certain bonds, and this he did. A suit to establish the lien was dismissed, and the receiver was directed to pay the funds to the claimant. The receiver, under instructions of the court, turned over the bonds to the claimant, who sold them to purchasers who were chargeable with notice of the plaintiff's claim to a lien; and these purchasers, in turn, sold them to *bonâ fide* purchasers who had no notice of the claim. Thereafter the judgment dismissing the action to establish the lien was, on appeal, reversed, and judgment was entered that the plaintiffs had a lien on the award, or the proceeds thereof. It was held that this last judgment created no lien, for there was then no property on which a lien could be established : but it established the fact that a lien had existed on the bonds before they were sold to *bonâ fide* purchasers without notice and the lien destroyed ; that the purchasers of the bonds with notice of the claim of lien were liable to action for their wrongful act in destroying the lien, but that the cause of action accrued at the time of such wrongful sale, and was barred by the six years' limitation under the statute of limitations.

[2] Stevens v. Watson, 4 Abb. (N. Y.) Dec. 302.

[3] Dwight v. Newell, 3 N. Y. 185.

[4] Payne v. Wilson, 74 N. Y. 348.

But a specific equitable lien upon lands is not preferred to a prior lien by judgment thereon ; and this is so although the lands be acquired by the debtor after the recovery of the judgment.[1]

A mechanic's lien is subject to an equitable lien existing at the time the claimant files his notice of claiming a lien. Until he files his notice he has no greater equities than other general creditors, and is affected by all equities existing at that time in favor of others dealing with his debtor. His lien attaches only to the estate and interest of the debtor as it then exists, which is the estate and interest left to the debtor after satisfying prior liens and equities.[2]

[1] Cook *v.* Banker, 50 N. Y. 655.
[2] Payne *v.* Wilson, 74 N. Y. 348, affirming *S. C.* 11 Hun, 302.

CHAPTER III.

97. Introductory. — By recent legislation many of the liens recognized by the common law, and many of those asserted in equity, have been materially enlarged in their scope, or made more effectual by provisions for their enforcement; while only in one instance, that of distress for rent, has the common law right been modified or restricted. But modern legislation has in many instances gone beyond the liens previously recognized at law or in equity, and has created a great number of new liens; and the tendency of legislation in this country is to extend still further this remedy for the protection of all persons who labor or supply materials for others, and for the protection of the state and of municipal corporations in the enforcement of taxes and other claims. Of the liens created for the protection of individuals, those known as "Mechanics' Liens" [1] are the most familiar; for statutes of this kind have been enacted in all, or nearly all, the states and territories. Laborers upon plantations are protected by agricultural liens upon the crops raised. Laborers and contractors upon railroads are protected by liens upon the roads. In the mining states liens are given to miners and others upon the mines and their products. In states where lumbering is an important industry, lumbermen are protected by liens upon logs. Livery-stable keepers and agisters of cattle are protected by liens. Corporations are giving liens upon the shares of their members for debts due from them. In many states liens have been given to landlords in place of the common law remedy of distress. In many states, also, attorneys have been given complete protection by effectual liens upon judgments obtained by them, and upon the causes of action, in place of the somewhat indefinite and restricted rights they had under the general equity jurisdiction of the courts.

For the details of legislation upon all these subjects, and its

[1] See the chapters on Mechanics' Liens.

application, reference may be had to the chapters treating of these particular matters.

In the different states many different liens have been created, which it is impossible to notice in detail in this treatise. The law governing them, so far as it is not declared by the statutes creating them, may generally be determined by analogy to the more common statutory liens, the construction and interpretation of which are settled by adjudications. Only a few of the statutory liens, other than those before referred to, which are made the subjects of separate chapters, will be briefly mentioned in this chapter.

98. **Taxes are generally made a lien upon the real estate assessed, but a right of prior payment does not constitute a lien.** A statute which provides that taxes shall be preferred to all payments and incumbrances, and shall be a lien upon the real estate of the person assessed, does not create a lien upon his personal property. A right of prior payment is a preference in the appropriation of the proceeds of the debtor's property. It is not a qualified right which may be exercised over his property. It does not attach to the specific article of property. Hence, if the personal property of the person assessed be attached or assigned before it is seized by the tax-collector, the right of prior payment given by the statute is lost.[1]

99. **A statutory lien in favor of the state upon the land of a collector of taxes attaches not only to the lands owned by him at the time of the approval and recording of his bond, but also to after-acquired lands, the same as in the case of a judgment.**[2] The lien of the state is not discharged upon lands sold by the collector after the approval of his bond, although the legislature has extended the time of payment of taxes to the collector. Sureties upon the collector's bond, who have given written consent to such extension, are not discharged thereby, and, upon answering for the collector's default, are subrogated in equity to the lien of the state upon his lands, the lands he has conveyed, and the lands he has acquired since the approval of his bond.[3]

[1] Anderson *v.* Mississippi, 23 Miss. 459.

[2] Crawford *v.* Richeson, 101 Ill. 351.

[3] Crawford *v.* Richeson, *supra.*

100. A lien is sometimes given to a state upon the property of a defendant in a criminal prosecution for the payment of the costs of the prosecution in case of conviction, from the time of the arrest or indictment found; and such lien cannot be divested by any subsequent assignment by the defendant, though this be an assignment to counsel to assist him in his defence.[1]

101. Statutes authorizing cities and towns to make improvements in streets, generally provide that the expense thereof, or some part of such expense, may be assessed upon the land fronting upon such streets, and such assessments are made a lien upon the property.[2]

102. Water rates are sometimes made a lien upon the premises where the water is used. An act which makes water rates a charge upon lands in a municipality, with a lien prior to all incumbrances, in the same manner as taxes are, gives them priority over mortgages on such lands made after the passage of the act, whether the water be introduced on the mortgaged land before or after the giving of the mortgage,[3] if the mortgage was made after the enactment of the statute making such rates a lien upon the property.[4] Such an act does not deprive the mortgagee of his property without due process of law. The mortgagee, in such case, takes the mortgage subject to the statute. He voluntarily consents to making the water rates a first lien upon the property in accordance with the statute.

A lien may be given for the expense of placing a water-meter in a building, and the charge for extra consumption of water over and above the quantity covered by the usual water rate for the building may be made a lien upon the land.[5] Such a lien is given by virtue of the taxing power of the state.

---

[1] M'Knight v. Spain, 13 Mo. 534.

[2] Fitch v. Creighton, 24 How. 159.

[3] Provident Inst. for Savings v. Jersey City, 113 U. S. 506. The court, by Bradley, J., even say that they are not prepared to assert that an act giving preference to municipal water rates over existing mortgages or other incumbrances, would be unconstitutional: for the providing of water for a city is one of the highest functions of municipal government, and tends to enhance the value of all real estate within its limits; and the charges for the use of the water may well be entitled to rank as a first lien, without regard to existing liens.

[4] Vreeland v. Jersey City, 37 N. J. Eq. 574.

[5] Laws of New York, 1870, ch. 383, § 13; 1873, ch. 335, § 73; Moffat v. Henderson, 18 J. & S. (N. Y.) 211.

103. **Liens upon animals damage feasant.** — By the common law, a person finding upon his land animals belonging to another, doing injury by treading down his grass or grain or the like, was entitled to distrain them until satisfaction should be made him for his loss.[1] In the American states this right has existed from a very early period in the history of the country. It is now generally conferred by statutes which also prescribe and regulate the remedies for enforcing the right. Such statutes, it has been judicially determined, are not in excess of the legislative power, or in violation of any principle of constitutional law. These statutes, in fact, create a lien in favor of the injured party upon the animals found trespassing, and provide remedies for enforcing the lien. Such remedies are clearly within the province of legislation. It is competent to provide that the owner of the lands shall be indemnified for the actual damages sustained, and shall be paid a reasonable compensation for keeping the animals and for making the seizure. The sums so awarded are not in the nature of a penalty for the trespass, but merely indemnity to the party injured. The temporary seizure and detention of the property, awaiting judicial action, is not in violation of the constitutional provision directing that no person shall be deprived of his property without due process of law.[2]

104. **Statutory liens generally differ from common law liens in not requiring possession to support them.** The protection afforded at common law by possession is, in case of statutory liens, afforded by notice to the owner, or by attachment of the property within a limited time.[3] A statutory lien without possession, has generally the same operation and efficacy that a common law lien has with possession.[4]

105. **The character, operation, and extent of the lien must be ascertained by the terms of the statute creating and defining it;** and the courts cannot extend the statute to meet cases for which the statute itself does not provide, though these may be of equal merit with those provided for.[5] Thus where

[1] 3 Black. Com. 7.

[2] Cook *v.* Gregg, 46 N. Y. 439; Rood *v.* McCargar, 49 Cal. 117.

[3] Quimby *v.* Hazen, 54 Vt. 132, per Powers, J.

[4] Beall *v.* White, 94 U. S. 382, per Clifford, J.; Grant *v.* Whitwell, 9 Iowa, 152.

[5] Copeland *v.* Kehoe, 67 Ala. 594; Rogers *v.* Currier, 13 Gray (Mass.), 129, 134, per Metcalf, J.

a lien for taxes is given by statute [1] to every agent, guardian, or executor who, being seised or having the care of lands, pays the taxes thereon for the benefit of the owner, in order to maintain such lien, he must show that he was seised of the land or had the care of it. It is not sufficient that he advanced the money for the payment of the taxes. A note given by the owner of land to his agent for money advanced for the payment of taxes, in which he declares that he recognizes the existence of the statutory lien, does not create a lien where none would exist by statute.[2]

It is, nevertheless, a sound rule of construction, that a statute giving a lien is regarded as a remedial statute, and is to be liberally construed so as to give full effect to the remedy, in view of the beneficial purpose contemplated by it.[3]

106. A statutory lien can exist only when it has been perfected in the manner prescribed by the statute authorizing it. Thus, under an act which created a building association, and provided that the shares of stock should, from the date thereof, be a lien on the real and personal estate of the corporation, it was held that the mere payment of the subscription for shares, without their being actually issued, did not create a lien on the property of the association.[4] The subscriber became entitled to the rights of a stockholder in the association by such payment, but the lien did not necessarily flow from the relation of stockholder to the association. It was necessary under the statute that the stock should be actually issued in order to create a lien which could be enforced against other incumbrancers, for the statute declared that the stock should be a lien only from the date of the certificate.

107. A lien created by statute may be taken away or modified by a subsequent statute.[5] Such a lien is no part of the contract, but merely an incidental accompaniment of it. It derives its validity from the positive enactment, and, therefore, a subsequent statute modifying or removing the lien cannot be considered as in any manner impairing the obligation of the con-

---

[1] Arkansas Dig. § 5233.

[2] Peay v. Feild, 30 Ark. 600.

[3] Eckhard v. Donohue, 9 Daly, 214; Hudler v. Golden, 36 N. Y. 447; Weed v. Tucker, 19 N. Y. 422, 433.

[4] Winston v. Kilpatrick, 5 Daly, 524; affirmed in the Court of Appeals, 1 N. Y. Week. Dig. 569.

[5] Frost v. Ilsley, 54 Me. 345. See chapter on *Mechanics' Liens.*

tract itself. " The lien is but a means of enforcing the contract, a remedy given by law; and, like all matters pertaining to the remedy, and not to the essence of the contract, until perfected by proceedings whereby rights in the property over which the lien is claimed have become vested, it is entirely within the control of the law-making power in whose edict it originated."[1] A repeal of a statute giving a lien is merely the taking away of a remedy afforded by the statute; it does not impair the obligation of the contract.

Thus, the lien of a judgment upon real estate is purely statutory, and it is within the power of the legislature to abolish the lien at any time before it has ripened into a title by a sale. A statute abolishing such a lien does not take away any property, or affect the obligation of contracts, but simply affects a legal remedy.[2]

108. The repeal of a statutory lien defeats the lien remedy, although at the time of the repeal the proceedings prescribed by the statute for enforcing the lien had been instituted and were pending in court.[3] The repeal of the lien remedy does not, however, impair any personal remedy the creditor may have by virtue of the obligation of the contract between the parties. The remedy which the law affords for the enforcement of contracts constitutes no part of the contract itself, and any change of the law which does not amount to a deprivation of all effectual remedy does not in any just sense impair the obligation of the contract. A lien is only a cumulative remedy to enforce a contract, and is as much within legislative control as any other remedy afforded by law.[4]

But if a lien be given by statute to be enforced as another statutory lien is enforced, the repeal of the remedy in the latter case does not repeal the remedy applicable to the former, if there be no words in the repealing act which include the former. It was so held where a statute gave a lien on animals for feeding and sheltering them, the lien "to be enforced in the same manner as liens on goods and personal baggage by innkeepers or

[1] Frost v. Ilsley, 54 Me. 345, 351, per Barrows, J.

[2] Watson v. N. Y. Central R. R. Co. 47 N. Y. 157.

[3] Bangor v. Goding, 35 Me. 73; Gray v. Carleton, 35 Me. 481; Woodbury v. Grimes, 1 Colo. 100; Templeton v. Horne, 82 Ill. 491; Smith v. Bryan, 34 Ill. 364; Williams v. Waldo, 3 Scam. (Ill.) 264; Hall v. Bunte, 20 Ind. 304; Martin v. Hewitt, 44 Ala. 418.

[4] Templeton v. Horne, supra, per Scott, J.

keepers of boarding-houses." [1] Chief Justice Peters, delivering the judgment of the court, said: "That meant enforcement in the manner then existing, not as it might be in the future by a new enactment. A reference was the readiest way to describe the process to be employed for enforcement. The repeal of the process in the one case does not repeal the process in the other, there being no words in the act of repeal including the latter. Suppose the innholder's lien had been wholly abrogated, would it be pretended that the lien on animals would fall with it ? There is no dependency between the two classes of liens, or their enforcement."

109. Other courts, however, hold that liens which have become fixed rights under the statutes creating them cannot be taken away by repealing the statutes. If the lien arises directly upon the performing of labor, or the doing of any other act, the lien cannot be defeated by subsequent repeal. If the lien arises upon the taking of some preliminary step to enforce it, then the lien cannot be defeated after such step has been taken.[2] Thus, a mechanic's lien which has attached through the giving of notice, or otherwise complying with the statute, cannot be destroyed by the legislature by a repeal of the statute. The lien in such case has become a part of the obligation of the contract between the parties, which the legislature cannot impair.[3] Whenever a mechanic's lien is created for material furnished under a contract for the erection of a building, the right to the lien becomes a vested right at the time the material is furnished, and it is not within the power of the legislature to afterwards destroy such right by repealing the statute under which the right has accrued.[4] In like manner, where by statute a lien is acquired by performing labor in carrying on a quartz mill, a repeal of the statute after the lien has attached by perform-

[1] Collins v. Blake (Me.) 9 Atl. Rep. 358; Lord v. Collins, 76 Me. 443.

[2] Wabash & Erie Canal Co. v. Beers, 2 Black, 448; Streubel v. Milwaukee & Miss. R. R. Co. 12 Wis. 67; Hallahan v. Herbert, 11 Abb. (N. Y.) Pr. N. S. 326; Chowning v. Barnett, 30 Ark. 560.

[3] Handel v. Elliott, 60 Tex. 145. The fact that the constitution of the state declared this lien, was deemed an additional reason why the statute providing for the enforcement of the lien should be regarded as entering into and forming part of the contract.

[4] Weaver v. Sells, 10 Kans. 609; Hoffman v. Walton, 36 Mo. 613.

ance of the work does not defeat the lien.[1] Upon this principle a lien is not affected by a homestead exemption created by a statute subsequently enacted, or by a state constitution subsequently adopted. To enforce such exemption as against an existing lien would be obnoxious to the objection of impairing the validity of contracts, and in violation of the Constitution of the United States.[2]

110. **Revival of a lien.** — A lien which has already expired by limitation is not revived by the enactment of a statute enlarging the time for perfecting such a lien. The legislature cannot create a cause of action out of an existing transaction, for which there was no remedy at the time of the enactment.[3]

111. **Statutory liens are regulated by the law of the forum,** and cannot be claimed by virtue of the law of another state.[4] Not only is the enforcement of the lien dependent upon the law of the forum, but its existence also.[5] The statute has no extra-territorial operation.[6] The lien has no binding operation in another state as against a purchaser of the property in that state in good faith for a valuable consideration.

112. **Statutory liens are in their nature legal rather than equitable,** and legal rather than equitable proceedings are generally provided for their enforcement. A common form of remedy is a legal attachment. Yet in some states the statutory remedy is by an equitable action similar to an equitable action for the foreclosure of a mortgage. The jurisdiction of a court of equity invoked to enforce a statutory lien rests upon the statute, and can extend no further. Thus, in some states, mechanics' liens are enforced by ordinary equitable proceedings, resulting in a decree for the sale of the property. The equitable jurisdiction is in such cases created by statute, and the remedy cannot be enlarged by the exercise of the general equity jurisdiction of the court.[7]

---

[1] *In re* Hope Mining Co. 1 Saw. 710.
[2] Townsend Savings Bank *v.* Epping, 3 Woods, 390; Gunn *v.* Barry, 15 Wall. 610.
[3] Steamboat Thompson *v.* Lewis, 31 Ala. 497.
[4] Swasey *v.* Steamer Montgomery,

12 La. Ann. 800; Lee *v.* Creditors, 2 Ib. 559, 600; Wickham *v.* Levistones, 11 Ib. 702; Gause *v.* Bullard, 16 Ib. 107.
[5] Gause *v.* Bullard, *supra.*
[6] Marsh *v.* Elsworth, 37 Ala. 85.
[7] Canal Co. *v.* Gordon, 6 Wall. 561.

CHAPTER IV.

I. *Introductory.*

113. An attorney's general lien is a common law lien founded upon possession, and is a right on the part of an attorney to retain papers or other property that may have come into his possession, or moneys that he, in the course of his professional employment, has collected, until all his costs and charges against his client are paid. Like other common law liens springing from possession, it is a passive lien, a mere right of retainer, without any power of enforcement by sale. For this reason it is frequently called the attorney's retaining lien.

An attorney's lien upon papers was enforced as early as 1734. In a case where an attorney had been employed by one who became bankrupt, the assignee petitioned that this attorney should be required to deliver up the papers, and come in and prove his demand *pari passu* with the other creditors. Lord Chancellor Talbot said : [1] " The attorney hath a lien upon the papers in the same manner against assignees as against the bankrupt, and though it does not arise by any express contract or agreement yet it is as effectual, being an implied contract by law ; but as to papers received after the bankruptcy, they cannot be retained, and therefore, if the assignees desire it, let the bill be taxed, and, upon payment, papers delivered up."

The practice of protecting an attorney by a lien upon the papers and moneys of the client in his hands was an established one in 1779. In that year, in a suit before Lord Mansfield, in which it was sought to establish a lien in favor of the captain against the ship for his wages, the counsel instanced the case of attorneys who cannot be compelled to deliver up their clients'

---

[1] Bush, *ex parte* , 7 Viner's Abr. 74.

papers until their fees are paid; whereupon Lord Mansfield, interrupting the argument, observed that " the practice, in that respect, was not very ancient, but that it was established on general principles of justice, and that courts, both of law and equity, have now carried it so far that an attorney or solicitor may obtain an order to stop his client from receiving money recovered in a suit in which he has been employed for him, till the bill is paid." [1]   Again, in the same year, in a case directly involving the question, the same judge said : " An attorney has a lien on the money recovered by his client for his bill of costs ; if the money come to his hands, he may retain to the amount of his bill.   He may stop it *in transitu* if he can lay hold of it.   If he apply to the court, they will prevent its being paid over until his demand is satisfied.   I am inclined to go still further, and to hold that, if the attorney gave notice to the defendant not to pay till his bill should be discharged, a payment by the defendant after such notice would be his own wrong, and like paying a debt which has been assigned after notice." [2]

114. In this country this general lien, in several states, is declared by statute.   Thus, in Colorado,[3] a lien is given to attorneys upon any money or property in their hands belonging to their clients for any fee or balance of fee due them.   In Iowa,[4] and in Dakota Territory,[5] an attorney has a lien for a general balance of compensation upon any papers belonging to his client which have come into his hands in the course of his professional employment, and upon money in his hands belonging to his client.   In Georgia, attorneys have a lien on all papers and moneys of their clients in their possession, for services rendered to them, and may retain such papers until said claims are satisfied, and may apply such money to the satisfaction of their claims.[6]   In Kansas,[7] an attorney has a lien for a general balance of compensation upon any papers of his client which have come into his possession in the course of his professional employment, and upon

[1] Wilkins v. Carmichael, 1 Dougl. 101, 104 (1779).

[2] Welsh v. Hole, 1 Dougl. 238.

[3] G. L. 1877, § 32; G. S. 1883, § 85.

[4] R. Code 1880, p. 49, § 215, 216. The lien may be released by bond.

[5] R. Code 1877, pp. 32, 33, §§ 9, 10. In **Dakota** the lien is limited to papers and moneys received in the case for which the lien is claimed.

[6] Code 1882, § 1989.

[7] Comp. Laws, p. 114, §§ 468, 469.

money in his hands belonging to his client. In Kentucky,[1] attorneys at law have a lien upon any choses in action, account, or other claim or demand put into their hands for suit or collection, for the amount of any fee which may have been agreed upon by the parties, or, in the absence of such agreement, for a fair and reasonable fee for their services. In Minnesota,[2] an attorney has a lien for his compensation, whether specially agreed upon or implied, upon the papers of his client which have come into his possession in the course of his professional employment, and also upon money in his bank belonging to his client. In Montana Territory,[3] attorneys have a lien upon moneys in their hands for any fees or balance of fees due or to become due for any professional services rendered by them in any court of the territory. In Nebraska[4] and Wyoming Territory,[5] an attorney has a lien for a general balance of compensation upon the papers of his client which have come into his possession in the course of his employment, and upon money in his hands belonging to his client.

II. *Upon Papers and Property.*

115. An attorney has a lien upon his client's papers for a general balance due him for services, not only in the suit or matter to which such papers relate, but for other professional matters.[6] Thus he has a lien upon a bond or mortgage delivered

---

[1] G. S. p. 149, § 15.

[2] G. S. 1878, p. 866, § 16.

[3] R. S. 1879, p. 414, ch. 3, § 54.

[4] Comp. Stat. 1881, p. 66, ch. 7, § 8.

[5] Comp. Laws 1876, p. 16, § 8; Act of Dec. 9, 1869, § 8.

[6] Hollis *v.* Claridge, 4 Taunt. 807, 809; Hughes *v.* Mayre, 3 T. R. 275; Howell *v.* Harding, 8 East, 362; Stevenson *v.* Blakelock, 1 M. & S. 535; McPherson *v.* Cox, 96 U. S. 404; Leszynsky *v.* Merritt, 9 Fed. Rep. 688; Jones *v.* Morgan, 39 Ga. 310; Howard *v.* Osceola, 22 Wis. 453; Chappell *v.* Cady, 10 Wis. 111; Wilson, *in re*, 12 Fed. Rep. 235, per Brown, J.; Dennett *v.* Cutts, 11 N. H. 163; Wright *v.* Cobleigh, 21 N. H. 339, 340; Knapp, *in re*, 85 N. Y. 284; Ward *v.* Craig, 87 N. Y. 550, 560; Prentiss *v.* Livingston, 60 How. Pr. 380; Hurlbert *v.* Brigham, 56 Vt. 368; Hooper *v.* Welch, 43 Vt. 169; Hutchinson *v.* Howard, 15 Vt. 544; Patrick *v.* Hazen, 10 Vt. 183; Longworth *v.* Handy, 2 Dis. (Ohio) 75; Able *v.* Lee, 6 Tex. 427, 431; Casey *v.* March, 30 Tex. 180; Gist *v.* Hanly, 33 Ark. 233; Stewart *v.* Flowers, 44 Miss. 513. In **Arkansas** the statute in relation to the attorney's lien upon judgments is merely declarative of the law as it stood at the time of its enactment. It does not have the effect to take away the lien upon papers and securities which the law previously gave. In **Pennsylvania** an attorney has no lien for professional compensation on papers in his hands. Walton *v.* Dickerson, 7 Pa. St. 376; Dubois' Appeal, 38 Pa. St. 231. It seems to

to him for the purpose of obtaining a foreclosure of the mortgage, not only for his costs and charges in that proceeding, but for any sum due him from the client for other professional business ; [1] and he has a lien upon a promissory note or other negotiable paper, or upon a town warrant, or other municipal obligation in his hands for collection.[2]

116. But although the documents in an attorney's hands be bonds or notes, payable to bearer, his lien does not amount to a pledge ; for the only right he has over them is a right to retain them till his reasonable charges against his client are paid. He has no right of sale as a pledgee has. His lien upon such documents is valuable in proportion to their value to the client. The more embarrassing the attorney's possession is to the client, the greater the leverage the possession gives the attorney. In the case of the ordinary papers in a suit, the attorney's lien is not of great value, because the papers are not of intrinsic value. A workman's lien upon a chattel upon which he has labored is a valuable and direct security, because the owner wants the chattel, and must pay the amount of the lien before he can get it from the workman. But in the case of an attorney, his lien is very frequently upon papers which have no intrinsic value, and are not even indispensable to the prosecution of the suit to which they relate.

117. Such a paper, however, as a life-insurance policy belonging to a client, would seem to be a valuable security in his attorney's hands. Thus, a solicitor acted for his client in obtaining a re-assignment to his client of a life policy which the client had mortgaged, and the policy and re-assignment came into the attorney's hands and remained there, his charges not being paid. The client afterward wished to borrow money upon the policy, but, as he stated, forgot where the policy was. Upon application to the insurance office a certified copy of the policy was issued, and the client executed an assignment to the person who loaned him the money. Due notice of the assignment was given to the insurance company, which had no notice of the attorney's lien.

be uncertain whether such a lien exists in **Massachusetts**. Simmons *v.* Almy, 103 Mass. 33, 35, per Colt, J.

[1] Bowling Green Sav. Bank *v.* Todd,

52 N. Y. 489; Newton *v.* Porter, 5 Lans. (N. Y.) 416.

[2] Howard *v.* Osceola, 22 Wis. 453, * 457.

The lender afterwards, apparently wanting to enforce his security, discovered that the policy was in the hands of the attorney and that he claimed a lien upon it.. The lender brought suit in equity to have the policy delivered up to him, claiming that the assignment to him constituted a first charge on the policy and had priority over the claim of the solicitor. But the court dismissed the suit. Mr. Justice Fry observed in the first place, that the assignee *primâ facie* took the policy subject to all the equities under the general rule applicable to every assignee of a *chose in action.* He disposed of the objection that the solicitor should have given notice to the insurance office of his lien by pointing out that the solicitor had no right to the fund represented by the policy, and no right to constitute the insurance office a trustee in his behalf ; that the solicitor had merely a passive right to hold the policy, the piece of paper constituting the instrument, until his claim should be paid ; and that this was in fact merely a right to embarrass the person who might claim the fund, by the non-production of this piece of paper.[1] Finally the learned judge commented upon the laches of the lender in not requiring the production of the policy at the time of the assignment, saying that he run the risk of its being in the hands of some person who might have a lien upon it.

118. This lien extends to an execution or a copy of a judgment in the attorney's hands, but it does not reach to the judgment itself.[2] This lien rests upon possession, and there can

[1] West of England Bank *v.* Batchelor, 51 L. J. (N. S.) Ch. 199.

[2] Wright *v.* Cobleigh, 21 N. H. 339. A clerk of court who has possession of the papers could not probably have any lien upon them, because the papers are public and part of a public record. In a note to King *v.* May, 1 Doug. 193 (1779), Lord Mansfield desired the bar would take a note of this, that it might be publicly known. " A case occurred in this term, when I happened not to be in court, but I have seen a very accurate note of it. It came on upon a rule to show cause why an attachment should not issue against the defendant, who was clerk of assize on the Norfolk circuit, for

not obeying a writ of *certiorari* to remove an indictment for murder, and a special verdict founded upon it. The defendant insisted that he had a right to retain the record till he should be paid his fees for drawing, engrossing, etc., which the attorney for the prisoner refused to do, on the ground of their being exorbitant. However, on the attorney's undertaking to pay as much as should, on a reference to the master, be reported to be due, the record was returned into court, upon which the rule was discharged." Lord Mansfield said he should be very unwilling to determine that a clerk of assize has a lien on the records of the court for his fees for that he foresaw

be no possession of a judgment.[1] "It is but a decision of a court upon a claim made by one party against another. It exists but in intendment of law. The records of the courts are the evidences of such judgments; but these are public, preserved in the custody of public officers, over which neither the attorney nor his client has any control, and for which neither has any rightful possession. The execution is no such representative of the judgment as to give to the holder any control over the judgment. Neither does the possession of the execution, or of a copy of the judgment, by the attorney or any third person, disable a creditor from exercising any of his rights as such. The indispensable requisite to any ordinary lien, possession, is wanting.[2]

119. This lien attaches only when the client's papers come into the attorney's hands,[3] and come to him, moreover, in the course of his professional business.[4] The lien must arise from professional employment.[5] Thus he has no lien on papers which he has received as mortgagee[6] or trustee;[7] but, if he receives the papers in his professional capacity, it does not matter that he sustains some other business relation to his client.[8]

Where an attorney has prosecuted a suit and recovered land for his client, and the latter has afterwards sold it and taken a deed of trust and bond for the purchase-money, and has made the attorney a trustee in the deed of trust and delivered the papers to him, the attorney has a lien upon the papers for his services in the suit; and if the client brings a bill in equity for the removal of such trustee and the delivery of the papers, it is the duty of the court to decide upon the existence and amount of the lien claimed by the attorney, and to decree such delivery on payment of the amount of the lien found to exist; and it is proper for the court to decree such delivery on the performance of this condition, though the attorney, by neglecting to file a cross bill, can have no decree for affirmative relief.[9]

great inconvenience from such a doctrine.

[1] Hough v. Edwards, 1 H. & N. 171, per Martin, B.; Patrick v. Leach, 2 McCrary, 635; S. C. 12 Fed. Rep. 661.

[2] Wright v. Cobleigh, 21 N. H. 339, per Bell.

[3] St. John v. Diefendorf, 12 Wend. (N. Y.) 261.

[4] Stevenson v. Blakelock, 1 Maule & S. 535.

[5] Worrall v. Johnson, 2 Jac. & W. 218.

[6] Pelly v. Wathen, 7 Hare, 351, 364; S. C. 18 L. J. Ch. 281.

[7] Newland, ex parte, L. R. 4 Ch. D. 515.

[8] King v. Sankey, 6 N. & M. 839.

[9] McPherson v. Cox, 96 U. S. 404.

120. The lien attaches not only to papers, but to other articles which come into the attorney's hands professionally, such as articles delivered to him to be exhibited to witnesses.[1]

121. An attorney has no lien on his client's will,[2] nor on original records of court.[3]

122. There is a presumption in every case that an attorney has a lien on the papers in his hands, for compensation for his services rendered. If he has given up his employment and withdrawn from the case, he will be entitled to such lien, unless it is shown that he has agreed to make no claim to compensation, or to claim no lien for his services.[4] The client has a right to change his attorney if he likes, but if he does so the law imposes certain terms in favor of the attorney ; namely, that the papers in the suit cannot be taken out of his hands until his reasonable charges are paid. The things upon which he claims a lien are things upon which he has expended his own labor or money ; and he should have a lien in the same way as any other workman who is entitled to retain the things upon which he has worked until he is paid for his work.[5]

123. This lien covers the attorney's general balance of

---

[1] Friswell v. King, 15 Sim. 191. In this case the lien was enforced upon certain copies of a very expensive book used in evidence.

[2] Redfearn v. Sowerby, 1 Swanst. 84 ; Balch v. Symes, 1 T. & R. 87.

[3] Clifford v. Turrill, 2 De G. & Sm. 1.

[4] Leszynsky v. Merritt, 9 Fed. Rep. 688. By the English authorities a distinction is made between the case of a solicitor withdrawing from a case and the case of the discharge of the solicitor by the client. In the former case it is said that the client is entitled to an order for the delivery of the necessary papers in the cause for the further prosecution of the action, subject to the solicitor's lien, and subject to re-delivery after the hearing. Colegrave v. Manley, T. & R. 400 ; Wilson v. Emmett, 19 Beav. 233 ; Cane v. Martin, 2 Beav. 584. But in case the client discharges the solicitor, the latter is under no obligation to produce the papers, or to allow the client to inspect them. " The discharged solicitor," said Lord Eldon, " ought to be able to make use of the non-production of the papers in order to get at what is due him."

In **Massachusetts** it is held that, if an attorney voluntarily withdraws from a suit, he is not entitled to withhold a paper in his possession and prevent it from being used in evidence until his fees are paid. White v. Harlow, 5 Gray (Mass.), 463.

[5] Yalden, ex parte, 4 Ch. D. 129, per James, L. J.; Mitchell v. Oldfield, 4 T. R. 123 ; Nesbitt, ex parte, 2 Scho. & Lef. 279 ; S. C. 1 Maule & S. 535.

account as against his client, and is not limited to the services rendered in the particular matter in which the papers were received. Upon a petition by an assignee in bankruptcy to have deeds and papers belonging to the bankrupt delivered up by an attorney who claimed a lien upon them for his general bill, it was objected that the bill should be limited to the services rendered in the particular matter in which the papers were received. But Eldon, Lord Chancellor, said:[1] " The general lien must prevail. Different papers are put into the hands of an attorney, as different occasions for furnishing them arise. In the ordinary case of lien I never heard of a question, upon what occasion a particular paper was put into his hands; but if in the general course of dealing the client from time to time hands papers to his attorney, and does not get them again when the occasion that required them is at an end, the conclusion is that they are left with the attorney upon the general account. If the intention is to deposit them for a particular purpose, and not to be subject to the general lien, that must be by special agreement ; otherwise they are subject to the general lien which the attorney has upon all papers in his hands."

124. But the attorney's lien is limited to debts due to him in the character of attorney. It does not extend to general debts.[2] Accordingly, the lien of the solicitor of a railway company for his costs does not include costs incurred in relation to the promotion of the company before incorporation, such costs, by the usual clause in the act, having been made a statutory debt to be paid by the company.[3]

125. No one who is not an attorney, solicitor, or barrister, can maintain this lien upon papers. A real estate broker has no lien on papers and plans placed in his hands for the purpose of effecting a sale of the property, though he has rendered services and incurred expenses in an ineffectual attempt to make a sale.[4] It was claimed that the position of a real estate broker in regard to papers placed in his hands is the same as that of an attorney or solictor or other bailee who expends time and money upon the property of a bailor. But it may be

[1] Sterling, *ex parte*, 16 Ves. 258.
[2] Worrall *v.* Johnson, 2 Jac. & W. 214, 218, per Plumer, M. R.
[3] Galland, *in re*, 31 Ch. D. 296.
[4] Arthur *v.* Sylvester, 105 Pa. St. 233.

said, in answer to this claim, that the lien of an attorney or solicitor is peculiar to his profession. It is, moreover, a general lien for his balance of account, and not a particular lien for his labor or expense upon that particular article, such as is given by the common law to any bailee who expends time and money upon the property of another at his request. The real estate broker does not perform any labor upon the papers themselves, such as would give a particular lien at common law. Every one, whether an attorney or not, has by the common law a lien on a specific deed or paper delivered to him to do any work or business thereon, but not on other muniments of the same party, unless the person claiming the lien be an attorney or solicitor.[1]

A conveyancer who has not been admitted as an attorney or solicitor cannot have the benefit of the law and custom which gives the latter a general lien; but such conveyancer, like any other person, may have a lien for services done upon any particular paper.

The case of a real estate broker is like that of an auctioneer to whom a mortgage was delivered for the purpose of obtaining the money due thereon, and he made several applications to the mortgagor, but received no money. The Court of Exchequer held that he had no lien on the deed in respect of the charges for making the applications. Baron Bolland said:[2] " The distinction is that, where any work is to be done on a chattel to improve it or to increase its value, the lien attaches; but where it is merely delivered, as in this case, to make a demand upon it, no such right can be supported. My opinion does not rest upon principle alone, but is illustrated by the cases cited of the trainer and the livery-stable keeper. A livery-stable keeper is easily contradistinguished from a trainer or a breaker. The breaker or trainer, by the exercise of his labor and skill, gives to the horse delivered to him to be broken or trained, qualities and powers which are not given by the livery-stable keeper."

The auctioneer or the real estate broker do not come within the rule of the common law giving a lien, unless they show work done upon the papers upon which they claim a lien; and they certainly do not come within the rule giving a lien to attorneys upon papers in their hands.

[1] Hollis v. Claridge, 4 Taunt. 807.   [2] Sanderson v. Bell, 2 Crompt. & M. 304, 313.

126. Under some circumstances the attorney's lien upon papers is special, instead of being general, as is ordinarily the case. The attorney has a lien only upon such papers as are delivered to him for use in his professional employment.[1] If he has received the papers for a specific purpose, not connected with his professional employment, he can have no lien on them for his general balance of account. If it be agreed or understood that the papers are delivered for a specific professional purpose, a specific instead of a general lien may arise for the specific service rendered.[2]

127. An attorney's general lien upon papers may be followed by a particular lien upon the judgment recovered by the use of them. The former lien is not, however, transferred or transmuted into the latter. The former passive lien remains, though it may be of no value after judgment, and a new active lien arises upon the judgment. Thus, if a solicitor, having in his possession a deed belonging to his client, who has ceased to employ him, produces the deed in a suit which is prosecuted by another solicitor, the former solicitor is not entitled to a lien upon the fund recovered in the suit for his general professional charges against the client, but at most only for his costs in that suit. So long as he held the deed, he had by means of it a lien for his general professional demands. The lien upon the deed he could never actively enforce; but, having possession of it, he might make advantageous terms with the client who wants to produce it in evidence. But if he voluntarily produces the deed, and a fund is secured by the use of it, the solicitor is not entitled to a lien upon the fund so obtained for his general professional demands, but only for his costs in the cause. If the doctrine were otherwise, the attorney's lien would in most cases extend to the general balance of his account against his client, and would not be confined to his costs in the particular cause in which he obtains judgment; for it generally happens that the solicitor has in his hands the documents necessary to establish his client's title.[3] The lien upon the fund is newly created and is a new lien. It

---

[1] Balch v. Symes, 1 T. & R. 87, 92 ; Lawson v. Dickinson, 8 Mod. 306.

[2] Ex parte Sterling, 16 Ves. 258. See, also, Ex parte Pemberton, 18 Ves. 282.

[3] Bozon v. Bolland, 4 Myl. & C. 354. Lord Chancellor Cottenham said he found no decision to the contrary except Worrall v. Johnson, 2 J. & W. 214, which he could not reconcile with any sound principle.

is a lien for the solicitor's costs in the cause only, but a lien which can be actively enforced. The passive lien upon the papers used in a cause may, perhaps, continue as before, but very likely may be of no value.[1]

128. An attorney's lien upon papers is discharged by his taking security for his whole demand, or by his agreeing to postpone payment for a definite time. A client, after having settled his solicitor's bill for services by giving notes payable in three years, applied to him before the notes were due for the papers in his hands, wishing to employ another solicitor. The solicitor declined to give up the papers unless the client would also pay for services the solicitor had rendered him in his capacity as executor, though the client had no assets with which to discharge the debt. It was decreed that the solicitor should give up the papers upon the client's paying for the services rendered after the time of the settlement and the taking of the notes. Lord Eldon said a lien on the papers in favor of the solicitor was inconsistent with the giving of credit for three years by means of the notes.[2] Looking at the general doctrine of lien, Lord Eldon said: " It may be described as *primâ facie* a right accompanying the implied contract." That there could be a lien when there is a special agreement to give credit upon security, would involve a contradiction of the agreement. " My opinion therefore is, that, where those special agreements are taken, the lien does not remain ; and whether the securities are due or not, makes no difference." [3]

But the attorney's lien upon papers is not extinguished by his taking a note or acceptance from his client for the amount due him, unless it appear that the note or acceptance was given or received in payment of such balance.[4]

This lien is lost by the attorney's voluntary surrender of the papers to his client; for possession is indispensable to this lien.[5] The lien is lost when the attorney has parted with the possession

---

[1] Bowling Green Sav. Bank *v.* Todd, 52 N. Y. 489, affirming 64 Barb. 146, seems at first view to sustain a contrary doctrine. This case is criticised in Wilson, *in re*, 12 Fed. Rep. 235, by Brown, J.

[2] Cowell *v.* Simpson, 16 Ves. 275.

[3] Cowell *v.* Simpson, *supra;* also Balch *v.* Symes, T. & R. 87, 92; Watson *v.* Lyon, 7 De G., M. & G. 288.

[4] Stevenson *v.* Blakelock, 1 Maule & S. 535; Dennett *v.* Cutts, 11 N. H. 163.

[5] Nichols *v.* Pool, 89 Ill. 491; Dubois' Appeal, 38 Pa. St. 231.

of the papers by his own act, even though this was a mistake on his part.[1] But it is not lost by a transfer of possession to an agent, for the possession of the agent is the possession of the principal ; and it is not lost by a transfer to another, subject to the lien.[2] If the papers are obtained from him wrongfully, his lien remains, and he may maintain trover for them.[3]

129. An attorney's agent or correspondent has no lien upon the papers of the client for the balance of his own account against the attorney, but he has a lien upon the papers in his hands in the particular case, for the amount due him by the attorney in that particular case only. To this extent the agent's lien is good against the client.[4]

130. One member of a firm of attorneys has no lien for an individual demand upon papers of a client in the hands of the firm. The firm alone has a right to hold and retain the papers, in such case, and the firm alone has a right of lien thereon.[5] And so a solicitor having a lien for his account upon papers which have come into his hands professionally from a client acting in his individual capacity, cannot retain them for a debt due him from a firm of which the client is a member.[6] An attorney cannot have a lien upon papers to a greater extent than his client's interest in them.

131. An attorney's lien upon papers is not affected by his client's assignment in bankruptcy or insolvency, or for the benefit of creditors. The assignee in either case takes subject to the attorney's equitable right at the date of the assignment.[7] The lien is good against all persons claiming under the client.[8] He must therefore satisfy an attorney's lien existing at that time either upon papers or moneys collected, before he can claim the papers or moneys then in the attorney's hands.[9]

---

[1] Dicas v. Stockley, 7 C. & P. 587.
[2] Watson v. Lyons, 7 De G., M. & G. 288, 298.
[3] Dicas v. Stockley, supra.
[4] Dicas v. Stockley, supra.
[5] Pelly v. Wathen, 7 Hare, 351, 362; S. C. 14 Jur. 9; In re Forshaw, 16 Sim. 121; Vaughan v. Vanderstegen, 2 Dr. 408; Bowling Green Savings Bank v. Todd, 52 N. Y. 489.
[6] Turner v. Deane, 18 L. J. Ex. 343.
[7] Bush, ex parte, 7 Vin. Abr. 74; Sterling, ex parte, 16 Ves. 258; Ward v. Craig, 87 N. Y. 550, 560.
[8] In re Gregson, 26 Beav. 87.
[9] 18 Alb. L. J. 214.

The lien is not lost because the debt in respect of which the lien is claimed is barred by the statute of limitations.[1]

132. This lien of the attorney upon his client's papers cannot be actively enforced. It is a passive lien. It amounts to a mere right to retain. the papers, as against the client, until he is fully paid.[2] The papers cannot be sold, neither can the possession of them be parted with, without loss of the lien. No active proceedings of any kind can be taken either at law or in equity to enforce the lien for which the papers are held.

The lien, however, continues till the debt for which the lien exists is paid.[3]

An attorney's lien upon a promissory note in his hands for collection gives him no right to a judgment against the defendant for the amount of his fees after the defendant has paid the note to the attorney's client.[4]

133. Indirectly an attorney's lien upon papers in a suit for his fees may, under some circumstances, be enforced by order and execution. Thus, where the plaintiff in a suit petitioned the court for an order substituting other attorneys in place of the attorney who had been conducting it, and directing him to turn over the papers in his hands pertaining to the action, and there being a dispute in regard to the amount of the compensation due the attorney, the court ordered the plaintiff to file a bond conditioned to pay the sum that should be found due him, and referred the question of the compensation to a referee. Upon the coming in of the referee's report the court confirmed it, and ordered that the attorney should have execution for the amount. Upon appeal it was held that the court had power to compel compliance with its own order in this manner, though it might also have proceeded to enforce the order by proceedings in the nature of contempt.[5]

Where the client offers to give security for the amount that

---

[1] *In re* Murray, 3 W. N. (1867) 190.

[2] Bozon *v.* Bolland, 4 Myl. & C. 354, 358, per Cottenham, L. C.; Heslop *v.* Metcalfe, 3 Ib. 183; Colegrave *v.* Manley, T. & R. 400 ; Brown *v.* Bigley, 3 Tenn. Ch. 618, per Cooper, C.; *In re* Wilson, 12 Fed. Rep. 235,

per Brown, J.; *S. C.* 26 Alb. L. J. 271.

[3] Warburton *v.* Edge, 9 Sim. 508; Young *v.* English, 7 Beav. 10.

[4] Tillman *v.* Reynolds, 48 Ala. 365.

[5] Greenfield *v.* Mayor, 28 Hun (N. Y.), 320.

may be found due to his attorney, the latter should be ordered to deliver up the papers on security being given, especially if there be any doubt in regard to the validity of his claim.[1]

134. It is sometimes proper for the court to determine the existence and amount of the lien, and to establish the condition upon which the attorney shall deliver up the property. Upon a bill in equity for the removal of a trustee in a deed of trust, and for the surrender of the bond secured by such deed where the trustee claimed a lien upon it for professional services, it is the duty of the court to decide on the existence an amount of the lien, and to decree such delivery on payment of the amount of the lien, if one be found to exist. If the attorney has neglected to file a cross bill, he can have no decree for affirmative relief ; but it is proper for the court to establish the condition on which the delivery of the bond to the complainant shall be made, and to require such delivery on the performance of that condition.[2]

A litigant is not debarred of his right to change his attorney by having agreed to pay a fee contingent upon the amount recovered. Such agreement is regarded as providing for the mode of compensation only. On a motion for a substitution the court will grant it upon the client's filing a stipulation, and the entry of an order declaring the attorney's claim a lien to the extent of the services rendered, the amount to be afterwards determined, should any moneys or judgment be recovered ; and that notice of the lien be given to the other party to the suit.[3]

135. Summary application to court for surrender of papers. — Where an attorney's lien is questioned by a client, upon a summary application to the court requiring the attorney to surrender papers intrusted to his care, the question of the existence and amount of the lien may be determined by the court or a referee upon a proper investigation. The court cannot, upon such application, disregard the attorney's claim of a lien, and without investigation order the surrender of the papers. The court will never disregard the right of the attorney or deny him the right of his lien where it has justly attached.[4]

---

[1] Cunningham v. Widing, 5 Abb. (N. Y.) Pr. 413.

[2] McPherson v. Cox, 96 U. S. 404.

[3] Ronald v. Mut. Reserve Fund Life Asso. 30 Fed. Rep. 228.

[4] Attorney, in re, 63 How. (N. Y.) Pr. 152; S. C. 87 N. Y. 521.

Where the client claims that, by contract with his attorney, the latter upon giving up his employment has no claim for compensation, and therefore should surrender the papers in his hands, the fact in controversy cannot, except by consent, be determined by the court in a summary way. It must be left to be determined in a suit to be brought by the attorney for his compensation ; the lien, if any, remaining in *statu quo* meanwhile. If such suit be nót brought within a time limited, or be not then diligently prosecuted, the court would order the papers to be given up.[1]

136. A court has jurisdiction to order a solicitor to deliver up his client's papers, upon the client's paying into court, or upon his giving security in a sum sufficient to answer the solicitor's demand, before this is adjusted, where his retention of the papers on which he claims a lien would embarrass the client in the prosecution or defence of pending actions.[2] There is a *dictum* of Lord Romilly, who as Master of the Rolls was very conversant with these matters, in these words : [3] " Where a solicitor sends in his bill, and claims a stated balance to be due to him, the client is entitled, as a matter almost of course, to have his papers delivered over to him on payment of the amount claimed into court." In another case Lord Romilly again states his practice : [4] " The course I adopt in all these cases is this : Where a sum is claimed by a solicitor to be due to him, and some delay occurs in the taxation imputable to the fault of no one, I order the papers to be delivered over on the amount being secured, and on an undertaking to produce them as required in the course of the taxation." Mr. Justice Chitty stated the result reached in the recent case before cited as follows : [5] " The court, in the exercise of its discretion, says that if the solicitor is completely secured, and it takes care not to enter upon a matter of controversy as to the amount, but to give him the amount which he claims and a sum to answer the costs of the taxation, it is inequitable that he should be allowed to embarrass the client further by holding the papers."

[1] Leszynsky *v.* Merritt, 9 Fed. Rep. 688.
[2] Galland, *in re*, 31 Ch. D. 296.
[3] Bevan, *in re*, 33 Beav. 439.
[4] Jewitt, *in re*, 34 Beav. 22.
[5] Galland, *in re*, *supra*.

III. *Upon Moneys Collected.*

137. An attorney also has a lien upon moneys collected by him on his client's behalf, in the course of his employment, whether upon any judgment or award or not.[1] It does not matter that there is no express agreement as to the rate or measure of compensation, or as to the source from which this should be paid. A lien upon the moneys collected may be implied from the facts and circumstances of the case. Where the client is insolvent and unable to contribute to the disbursements in the proceedings, it cannot be doubted that there is an understanding that the attorney is to look to the fund ultimately recovered for reimbursement of the money paid by him, and for compensation for his services.[2]

138. Such lien does not, however, attach to money delivered to the attorney by his client for a specific purpose, such as the payment of a mortgage, to which the attorney agrees to apply it.[3] So, if the money is delivered to him to apply to the settlement of a suit, he cannot retain his fees out of it. Thus, where a guardian for minors, being plaintiff in an ejectment suit, agreed with the defendant to discontinue the action, and, leave of the Probate Court being had, to convey to him the interest of his wards in the land, in consideration of the payment of one hundred and fifty dollars, and the costs of the petition to the Probate Court, and the defendant deposited with his attorney in the ejectment suit one hundred dollars, taking from him a paper acknowledging the receipt of the money as " towards the settlement," such deposit is a special one, for a special purpose, and the attorney cannot retain his fees out of it. The plaintiff hav-

---

[1] Welsh *v.* Hole, 1 Doug. 238; Paschal, *in re*, 10 Wall. 483; Knapp, *in re*, 85 N. Y. 284; Bowling Green Savings Bank *v.* Todd, 52 N. Y. 489; Longworth *v.* Handy, 2 Dis. (O.) 75; Diehl *v.* Friester, 37 Ohio St. 473, 477, per Okey, C. J.; Cooke *v.* Thresher, 51 Conn. 105; Burns *v.* Allen, 1 New Eng. Rep. 143; Dowling *v.* Eggemann, 47 Mich. 171; Read *v.* Bostick 6 Humph. (Tenn.) 321; Hurlbert *v.* Brigham, 56 Vt. 368; Casey *v.* March, 30 Tex. 180 ; Kinsey *v.* Stewart, 14 Tex. 457; Able *v.* Lea, 6 Tex. 427, 431; Stewart *v.* Flowers, 44 Miss. 513, 532; Lewis *v.* Kinealy, 2 Mo. App. 33. *Contra*, Lucas *v.* Campbell, 88 Ill. 447, 451.

It seems not to exist in **Pennsylvania** under the name of lien, but rather under the name of a right of defalcation. Walton *v.* Dickerson, 7 Pa. St. 376; Dubois' App. 38 Pa. St. 231.

[2] *In re* Knapp, 85 N. Y. 284.

[3] *In re* Larner, 20 Weekly Dig. 73.

ing petitioned the court in which the ejectment suit was pending for an order requiring the attorney to pay over this money, the order was made accordingly.[1] Chief Justice Durfee remarked that the money was left with the attorney and received by him for a special purpose. He could not therefore, consistently with his agreement or duty, apply it to any other purpose without leave of his client. The equity of this view was the stronger, because the attorney, by giving the receipt, put it in the power of his client to use it, in effecting the settlement, as so much money in the attorney's hands.

139. Such lien does not attach for professional services rendered to an executor, in the administration of the estate of the decedent, upon property belonging to the deceased which was in the attorney's hands at the time of the decease and upon which he then had no lien. The attorney's claim in such case is against the executor who employed him and not against the deceased or his estate.[2]

140. The lien of an attorney attaches to money recovered or collected by him upon a judgment.[3] Upon the judgment before it was collected, he had a lien for his costs ; but when he has actually collected the money upon the judgment, this lien is satisfied and a new lien attaches for any claim he may have against his client for his services or disbursements, either in the cause in which the judgment was obtained or any other.[4]

141. The attorney has no lien upon a judgment for damages until he has collected the money ;[5] and until such a collection his client may receive the money and give an effectual discharge of the judgment. The attorney's general lien is rendered effectual by his possession and only by possession.[6]

---

[1] Anderson v. Bosworth (R. I.), 8 Atl. Rep. 339.

[2] Delamater v. M'Caskie, 4 Dem. (N. Y.), 549. See In re Knapp, 85 N. Y. 284, reversing 8 Abb. N. C. 308; In re Lamberson, 63 Barb. (N. Y.) 297; Barnes v. Newcomb, 11 Weekly Dig. 505 ; Platt v. Platt, 42 Hun (N. Y.), 659; S. C. on appeal, 12 N. East. Rep. 22.

[3] Wells v. Hatch, 43 N. H. 246; Bowling Green Sav. Bank v. Todd, 52 N. Y. 489.

[4] Wells v. Hatch, supra.

[5] See Ch. v.

[6] St. John v. Diefendorf, 12 Wend. (N. Y.) 261; Casey v. March, 30 Tex. 180.

142. The lien of an attorney extends to money collected upon an award as well as that collected upon a judgment. Chief Justice Kenyon, so deciding, placed his decision upon " the convenience, good sense, and justice of these things." He further says, " The public have an interest that it should be so ; for otherwise no attorney will be forward to advise a reference." [1]

143. This lien prevails against one to whom the client has assigned the claim while suit is pending, if the consideration of the assignment be a preëxisting debt, and the assignment be made in a state where a preëxisting debt is not regarded as a valuable consideration, as, for instance, in New York.[2] It also prevails against the client's assignment for the benefit of his creditors.[3]

144. Associate counsel employed by the attorney in a suit also have a lien for their fees where the attorney has such a lien ; or, if the attorney collects the judgment, he may deduct not only his own fees, but is protected in the payment of like reasonable fees to other attorneys or counsel employed in the suit.[4] But counsel have no lien on a judgment recovered. This is confined to the attorney of record.[5]

145. Whether a lien or right of set-off. It is a matter in dispute whether the attorney's claim upon moneys collected for his client, for the payment of any indebtedness of the client to him, rests upon the law of lien or the law of set-off. The courts generally declare that the right results from the law of lien ; but some courts hold that it results from the law of set-off.[6] Thus, in a Pennsylvania case, it is said to be a right to defalcate, rather than a right of lien.[7]

146. Lien for general balance of account. — An attorney's lien upon moneys collected extends not only to his services and disbursements in the case wherein the moneys are collected, but

---

[1] Ormerod v. Tate, 1 East, 464.

[2] Schwartz v. Schwartz, 21 Hun, 33.

[3] Ward v. Craig, 87 N. Y. 550; S. C. 9 Daly, 182.

[4] Jackson v. Clopton, 66 Ala. 29 ; S. C. 12 Rep. 773.

[5] Brown v. Mayor, 9 Hun (N.Y.), 587.

[6] Wells v. Hatch, 43 N. H. 246.

[7] Dubois' App. 38 Pa. St. 231 ; Balsbaugh v. Frazer, 19 Pa. St. 95 ; McKelvy's App. 108 Pa. St. 615.

also to pay the general balance due him for professional services and disbursements.[1] He may retain money to a reasonable amount to cover a stipulated fee in another case, in which he has performed only a part of the services, if in good faith he intends to perform the remainder.[2]

In some cases, however, it has been held that the lien of an attorney upon moneys of his client secures only his services in the matter in which he collected the money, not his services about other business of his client,[3] unless, perhaps, in case such other business is covered by the same retainer.[4]

The lien which an attorney has upon his client's papers is commensurate with the client's right and title to them. If the client has taken to his attorney, for his opinion, papers which the client has received from another person for inspection pending negotiations for a sale of property or other business transaction, the attorney cannot, upon a claim of lien, retain the papers as against the person to whom they belong. Judge Gibbs, of the Court of Common Pleas, states a similar case:[5] "Suppose one having a diamond offers it to another for sale for £100, and gives it to him to examine, and he takes it to a jeweller, who weighs and values it; he refuses to purchase, and, being asked for it again, he says the jeweller must be first paid for the valuation: as between the jeweller and purchaser, the jeweller has a lien; but as against the lender he has no right to retain the jewel."

147. An attorney may have a special lien upon a fund

---

[1] Hurlbert v. Brigham, 56 Vt. 368; In re Attorney, 87 N. Y. 521 ; S. C. 63 How. Pr. 152 ; In re Knapp, 85 N. Y. 284 ; Ward v. Craig, 87 N. Y. 550; Cooke v. Thresher, 51 Conn. 105. In the latter case the client had orally agreed that the attorney should have a lien, not only for his services in that case, but for previous services. Contra, Pope v. Armstrong, 3 S. & M. (Miss.) 214.

[2] Randolph v. Randolph, 34 Tex. 181. In Paschal, in re, 10 Wall. 483, which was a case from the State of Texas, and was regarded as governed by the laws of that state on this subject, the lien of an attorney was conferred for his fees and disbursements in the cause in litigation and in proceedings brought to recover other moneys covered by the same retainer. But the court did not undertake to decide whether an attorney's lien extends to the whole balance of his account for professional services.

[3] Waters v. Grace, 23 Ark. 118 ; McDonald v. Napier, 14 Ga. 89 ; Pope v. Armstrong, 3 S. & M. (Miss.) 214; Sage v. Wilkinson, Ib. 223.

[4] Paschal, in re, 10 Wall. 483.

[5] Hollis v. Claridge, 4 Taunt. 807.

in court or in the hands of a receiver, recovered by him, and a court of equity, having such a fund in its possession, will protect the attorney in retaining out of it a reasonable compensation for his services.[1]

148. Even in Pennsylvania, where an attorney's lien upon moneys collected is hardly recognized under that name, but is called rather a right of defalcation, a court of equity will protect an attorney who is entitled to a compensation out of a fund within its control. Thus, where a fund was brought into a court of equity by the services of an attorney, who looked to that alone for his compensation, the court, though declaring his interest not to be a lien, yet regarded him as the equitable owner of the fund to the extent of the value of his services, and intervened for his protection, awarding him a reasonable compensation to be paid out of the fund.[2] What is a reasonable compensation the court may determine by itself, or through an auditor, without referring the matter to a jury.[3]

149. But an attorney has no general lien upon a fund in court recovered by him for his client. His lien in such case is a lien upon the judgment, and is a special lien confined to his costs or services in the particular proceeding which produced the fund.[4] His general lien depends upon possession, and does not attach to a fund recovered until he obtains actual possession of that fund. If the attorney collects the whole fund, then this becomes subject to his general lien; if, however, he collects only such part of the fund as is sufficient to pay his costs or services, for which he had a lien upon the judgment, then the amount he receives is applicable to such costs or services, and not to his general balance of account against the client.

---

[1] Olds v. Tucker, 35 Ohio St. 581; Longworth v. Handy, 2 Dis. (Ohio) 75; Spencer's Appeal (Pa.), 9 Atl. Rep. 523. As to the law in Georgia, see Morrison v. Ponder, 45 Ga. 167.

[2] Spencer's App. (Pa.) 9 Atl. Rep. 523; McKelvy's App. 108 Pa. St. 615; Freeman v. Shreve, 86 Pa. St. 135. In the latter case Mr. Justice Sharswood said: "It is true that a chancellor will, out of a fund for distribution, order compensation to the counsel engaged, in his sound discretion, according to his estimate of what they reasonably deserve to have." See, to same effect, Dubois' App. 38 Pa. St. 231; Irwin v. Workman, 3 Watts, 357. In the latter case the fund was in the hands of the sheriff.

[3] McKelvy's App. supra.

[4] Bozon v. Bolland, 4 Milne & C. 354; Lann v. Church, 4 Madd. 391.

150. A court has summary jurisdiction over attorneys to order the payment of money wrongfully withheld from clients. " The summary jurisdiction," said Chief Justice Durfee in a recent case,[1] " evidently originates in the disciplinary power which the court has over attorneys as officers of the court. The opinion seems to have been prevalent at one time that the jurisdiction extended only to attorneys employed as such in suits pending in court, to hold them to their duty in such suits ; but a more liberal view has obtained, and it is now well settled that the jurisdiction extends to any matter in which an attorney has been employed by reason of his professional character.[2] In general, the jurisdiction applies only between attorney and client ; but it is not confined strictly to that relation." [3] In the case in which the decision was rendered from which this quotation is taken, the petition was made, not by the client, but by the opposite party. The attorney had received money from his client, the defendant in a suit, to be applied "towards the settlement" of the suit, and the attorney had given a receipt for the money to this effect. This receipt the client passed over to the plaintiff as so much money in the client's hands applicable to the settlement. The client claimed the right to retain his fees out of this money ; and the plaintiff accordingly petitioned the court in which the suit was pending for an order requiring the attorney to pay over the money. The court held that a case was presented for the summary jurisdiction of the court, and that it had discretionary power to order the money paid into its registry by a day named.[4]

In an early case in New York, the plaintiff's attorney, in a *qui tam* action, claimed and received certain costs from the defendant in partial settlement of the same. The costs were taken in the mistaken supposition that the defendant was liable to pay them. Nearly four years afterwards, upon his petition, the court ordered the attorney to refund them.[5]

---

[1] Anderson *v.* Bosworth (R. I.), 8 Atl. Rep. 339.

[2] *In re* Aitkin, 4 Barn. & Ald. 47, 49 ; Grant's case, 8 Abb. Pr. 357 ; *Ex parte* Saats, 4 Cowen (N. Y.), 76 ; *Ex parte* Cripwell, 5 Dowl. Pr. Cas. 689 ; De Wolfe *v.* ——, 2 Chit. 68 ; *In re* Knight, 1 Bing. 91.

[3] *In re* Aitkin, *supra;* Tharratt *v.* Trevor, 7 Exch. 161.

[4] Anderson *v.* Bosworth (R. I.), 8 Atl. Rep. 339.

[5] Moulton *v.* Bennett, 18 Wend. (N. Y.) 586, cited in Anderson *v.* Bosworth, *supra.*

151. An attorney who has collected money for a client cannot hold the entire amount, and refuse to pay it over, because a small part is due to him as fees. He will be allowed to retain enough to cover these, but no more.[1]

If an attorney retains money collected for a client, upon a disagreement as to the amount due him for services, and the client obtains a judgment for a part of the amount retained, the client is not then entitled to an order of court requiring the attorney to pay over the amount of the judgment. He has by obtaining judgment waived the right to a summary process; for the parties, no longer stand in the relation of attorney and client, but in that of debtor and creditor.[2] The client's remedy is either by suit or by summary process. "If the client is dissatisfied with the sum retained," says Chief Justice Black, "he may either bring suit against the attorney, or take a rule upon him. In the latter case, the court will compel immediate justice, or inflict summary punishment on the attorney, if the sum retained be such as to show a fraudulent intent. But if the answer to the rule convinces the court that it was held back in good faith, and believed not to be more than an honest compensation, the rule will be dismissed, and the client remitted to a jury trial."[3]

152. **How lien may be pleaded in defence.** In a proceeding by a client to recover money collected by his attorney, the latter need not set up in his answer a technical counter-claim for the value of his services; but it is sufficient that he alleges the performance of the services and their value, and his right to retain this sum from the amount collected. If the value of the services is equal to or exceeds the sum collected, he may retain the whole amount.[4]

---

[1] Miller v. Atlee, 3 Ex. 799; S. C. 13 Jur. 431; Conyers v. Gray, 67 Ga. 329. Under the English practice, a solicitor having a lien upon deeds of property greatly exceeding in value the amount of his bill, was ordered to give up a portion of them. Du Boison v. Maxwell, W. N. (1876) 146; Charboneau v. Orton, 43 Wis. 96; Burns v. Allen, R. I. 1885, Index W. 31; S. C. 1 New Eng. Rep. 143.

[2] Windsor v. Brown (R. I.), 9 Atl. Rep. 135; See, also, In re Davies, 15 Weekly Rep. 46; Bohanan v. Peterson, 9 Wend. (N. Y.) 503; Cottrell v. Finlayson, 4 How. (N. Y.) Pr. 242.

[3] Balsbaugh v. Frazer, 19 Pa. St. 95. See, also, In re Harvey, 14 Phila. (Pa.) 287.

[4] Ward v. Craig, 87 N. Y. 550.

CHAPTER V.

1. *Definition and Origin of the Lien.*

153. The lien of an attorney upon a judgment is properly denominated a lien in the broad sense of the term, although it rests merely on the equity of the attorney to be paid his fees and disbursements out of the judgment which he has obtained. It is not a lien that depends upon possession, as liens ordinarily do. There can be no possession of a judgment, for this exists only in intendment of law. The execution issued upon a judgment does not represent the judgment, and the possession of the execution is not a possession of the judgment.[1] In regard to possession, this lien of an attorney resembles the maritime lien of a seaman upon the vessel for his wages. Both liens are exceptions to the general rule as respects the element of possession.

This lien, therefore, not arising from a right on the part of the attorney to retain something in his possession, but being a

[1] Wright *v.* Cobleigh, 21 N. H. 339; Ward *v.* Wordsworth, 1 E. D. Smith (N. Y.), 598.

right to recover for his services in obtaining a judgment for his client, is called the attorney's charging lien. It is so called because the costs and fees of the attorney are made a charge upon the judgment recovered, and this charge is enforced by the court. Some confusion has arisen in the decisions on this subject from a failure in many cases to observe the distinction between the retaining lien and the charging lien. The latter lien never extends beyond the costs and fees due the attorney in the suit in which the judgment is recovered; but a retaining lien extends to the general balance due the attorney from the client for professional services and his disbursements in connection therewith.[1] In other words, the charging lien is a special lien, and the retaining lien is a general lien.[2]

154. By agreement, however, the attorney's lien upon a judgment may be made a general lien in equity, and an oral agreement is sufficient for this purpose. Thus, where an attorney had rendered services and expended money in instituting and conducting several suits for a client, and it was orally agreed between them that the attorney might retain so much of the avails of a particular suit as should be sufficient to pay for all his services, not only in that suit but his previous services in other matters, and the attorney having conducted the suit to a favorable conclusion and obtained judgment, and after the client's insolvency collected the same upon execution, it was held that he had an equitable lien upon the avails, both for his services and expenses in the suit and for the previous services covered by the agreement.[3]

155. An attorney's lien for his costs is not recognized at common law, but only in equity, unless declared by statute.[4] The common law only recognizes liens acquired by possession.

---

[1] Weed v. Boutelle, 56 Vt. 570, 579; In re Wilson, 12 Fed. Rep. 235, per Brown, J.; Goodrich v. McDonald, 41 Hun (N. Y.), 235.

[2] Bozon v. Bolland, 4 Myl. & C. 354.

[3] Cooke v. Thresher, 51 Conn. 105.

[4] Simmons v. Almy, 103 Mass. 33; Baker v. Cook, 11 Mass. 236; Getchell v. Clark, 5 Mass. 309; Hill v. Brinkley, 10 Ind. 102; Potter v. Mayo, 3 Me. 34; Stone v. Hyde, 22 Me. 318; Hobson v. Watson, 34 Me. 20; Forsythe v. Beveridge, 52 Ill. 268; Compton v. State, 38 Ark. 601, 603; Patrick v. Leach, 2 McCrary, 635; S. C. 12 Fed. Rep. 661, per McCrary, J.

A lien at law is not in strictness either a *jus in re* or a *jus ad rem*, but simply a right to possess and retain property until some charge attaching to it is paid. The lien of an attorney upon a judgment is an equitable lien.

In a strict sense, there is no such thing as a lien upon a thing not in possession. Baron Parke says: [1] "The lien which an attorney is said to have on a judgment (which is, perhaps, an incorrect expression), is merely a claim to the equitable interference of the court to have that judgment held as a security for his debt." More recently Chief Justice Cockburn expressed the same view, saying: [2] "Although we talk of an attorney having a lien upon a judgment, it is, in fact, only a claim or right to ask for the intervention of the court for his protection, when, having obtained judgment for his client, he finds there is a probability of the client depriving him of his costs."

Again, Mr. Justice Erle said: "*Lien*, properly speaking, is a word which applies only to a chattel; *lien upon a judgment* is a vague and inaccurate expression; and the words *equitable lien* are intensely undefined." [3]

An attorney's lien upon a judgment, as by force of usage we are permitted to designate his claim upon the judgment recovered, is founded upon the same equity which gives to every person who uses his labor and skill upon the goods of another, at his request, the right to retain the goods till he is paid for his labor. [4] This equitable principle is derived from the civil law. It is considered reasonable and proper that an attorney, by whose labor and at whose expense a judgment has been obtained for his client, should have an interest in that judgment which the law will regard and protect. [5] Lord Kenyon declared "that the convenience, good sense, and justice of the thing required it."

156. The time and manner of the origin of this lien are not shown by any reported case. Probably it had been the practice of judges to aid attorneys in securing their costs out of

---

[1] Barker *v.* St. Quintin, 12 M. & W. 441, 451.

[2] Mercer *v.* Graves, L. R. 7 Q. B. 499, 503.

[3] Brunsdon *v.* Allard, 2 E. & E. 17, 27.

[4] Weed *v.* Boutelle, 56 Vt. 570, 579 ; Turno *v.* Parks, 2 How. (N.

Y.) Pr. N. S. 35 ; Shapley *v.* Bellows, 4 N. H. 347, per Richardson, C. J. The lien of an attorney upon a judgment was established in New Hampshire by the above decision. Wright *v.* Cobleigh, 21 N. H. 339.

[5] *In re* Knapp, 85 N. Y. 284.

judgments obtained for their clients before the right to the lien
had been formally adjudicated. It was doubtless recognized
upon the ground of justice that the attorney had contributed by
his labor and skill to the recovery of the judgment, and the court,
wishing to protect its own officers, exercised its power to that
end ; or, as Lord Kenyon puts it:[1] " The party should not run
away with the fruits of the cause without satisfying the legal
demands of his attorney, by whose industry, and in many instances at whose expense, those fruits are obtained." In the
argument of a case before the King's Bench in 1779, before Lord
Mansfield,[2] in which it was sought to establish a lien in favor of
a captain against the ship for his wages, the counsel instanced
the case of attorneys, who cannot be compelled to deliver up
their clients' papers until they are paid ; upon which Lord Mansfield said that the practice in this respect was not very ancient,
but that courts both of law and of equity had then carried it so
far that an attorney might obtain an order to stop his client
from receiving money recovered in a suit till his bill should be
paid. Sir James Burrough, who was present, mentioned to the
court that the first instance of such an order of court was in the
case of one Taylor of Evesham, about the time of a contested
election for that borough ; and Lord Mansfield said he himself
had argued the question in the Court of Chancery.

Doubtless the lien was first established in the courts of chancery. Lord Hardwicke, in a case before him, in 1749, said:[3]
" I am of opinion that a solicitor, in consideration of his trouble,
and the money in disburse for his client, has a right to be paid
out of the duty decreed for the plaintiff, and has a lien upon it,
. . . and it is constantly the rule of this court."

157. It must be confessed that the origin of this lien is
obscure and uncertain. The attempts to account for it are
many and diverse. It seems from Comyn's Digest[4] that it was
founded on an old rule of court, that a client should not discharge
his attorney without leave. Lord Kenyon said the lien depended
on the general jurisdiction of the court over the suitors.

---

[1] Read *v.* Dupper, 6 T. R. 361.

[2] Wilkins *v.* Carmichael, 1 Doug.
101, 104. Some years afterwards this
lien was recognized by Chief Justice

Wilmot in Schoole *v.* Noble, 1 H. Bl.
23 (1788).

[3] Turwin *v.* Gibson, 3 Atk. 720.

[4] Attorney, B. 11, 16 ; also, Bacon's Abr. Attorney, E.

Baron Parke refers to Welsh *v.* Hole,[1] as the case first establishing an attorney's lien on a judgment. This lien is declared to be merely a claim to the equitable interference of the court to have the judgment held for his debt.[2] Baron Martin, adopting and explaining this view, says the right of the attorney is merely this, that, if he gets the fruits of the judgment into his hands, the court will not deprive him of them until his costs are paid.[3] These definitions are adopted and further developed in a recent decision in Rhode Island, Chief Justice Durfee saying:[4] " Primarily, without doubt, the lien originates in the control which the attorney has by his retainer over the judgment, and the processes for its enforcement. This enables him to collect the judgment and reimburse himself out of the proceeds. It gives him no right, however, to exceed the authority conferred by his retainer. But inasmuch as the attorney has the right, or at least is induced to rely on his retainer to secure him in this way for his fees and disbursements, he thereby acquires a sort of equity, to the extent of his fees and disbursements, to control the judgment and its incidental process against his client and the adverse party colluding with his client, which the court will, in exercise of a reasonable discretion, protect and enforce. And on the same ground, the court will, when it can, protect the attorney in matters of equitable set-off. We think this is the full scope of the lien, if lien it can be called."

II. *In what States it Prevails.*

158. It may be stated as a general rule that an attorney has a lien upon a judgment obtained for his client for his costs in the suit. In most of the states this rule was first established by the courts. In some states the lien did not exist till it was declared by statute ; and in several states, in which the courts had established the lien, this has by statute been extended or modified so that it is quite a different thing from the lien which the courts established and enforced. A summary statement in a note hereto annexed shows in what states this lien prevails in some form ;[5] but it will be necessary hereafter to refer

[1] 1 Doug. 238 (1779).
[2] Barker *v.* St. Quintin, 12 M. & W. 441, 451.
[3] Hough *v.* Edwards, 1 H. & N. 171.
[4] Horton *v.* Champlin, 12 R. I. 550.

[5] The lien exists in : —
Alabama : see § **169.**
Arkansas : see § **170.**
Colorado : see § **171.**
Connecticut: Gager *v.* Watson, 11

in detail to the legislation and the adjudications in those states where the ordinary lien on a judgment has been materially changed.

159. In several states the lien does not exist.[1] In most of

Conn. 168, 173; Andrews v. Morse, 12 Conn. 444; Benjamin v. Benjamin, 17 Conn. 110; Cooke v. Thresher, 51 Conn. 105.

Dakota Ter. : see § 175.
Florida: see § 172.
Georgia: see § 173.
Indiana: see § 174.
Iowa: see § 175.
Kansas: see § 176.
Kentucky: see § 177.
Louisiana : A special privilege is granted in favor of attorneys at law for the amount of their professional fees on all judgments obtained by them, to take rank as first privilege thereon. Rev. Laws 1884, § 2897.

Maine : Hobson v. Watson, 34 Me. 20; Newbert v. Cunningham, 50 Me. 231 ; Stratton v. Hussey, 62 Me. 286. The lien extends to fees in suits incidental to the judgment obtained. Newbert v. Cunningham, *supra*.

Maryland : In Marshall v. Cooper, 43 Md. 46, 62 (1875), the court said that no case involving the question of the attorney's lien had arisen or been decided in the appellate court. In Stokes' case, 1 Bland, 98, the Chancellor said that contracts between solicitors and suitors must be decided like other contracts.

Massachusetts: see § 162.
Michigan : see § 178.
Minnesota : see § 179.
Mississippi : Stewart v. Flowers, 44 Miss. 513; S. C. 7 Am. R. 707; Pope v. Armstrong, 3 S. & M. 214; Cage v. Wilkinson, Ib. 223. See § 181.
Montana Ter.: see § 182.
Nebraska: see § 183.
New Hampshire: Young v. Dearborn, 27 N. H. 324 ; Currier v. Boston & M. R. R. Co. 37 N. H. 223; Wells v. Hatch, 43 N. H. 246.

New Jersey: Barnes v. Taylor, 30 N. J. Eq. 467; Braden v. Ward, 42 N. J. L. 518; Heister v. Mount, 17 N. J. L. 438.
New York: see §§ 184–189.
Oregon: see § 180.
Rhode Island: see § 164.
South Carolina : Scharlock v. Oland, 1 Rich. 207; Miller v. Newell, 20 S. C. 123, 128.
Tennessee: see § 190.
Vermont: see § 191.
Virginia: see § 192.
W. Virginia: see § 192.
Wyoming Ter. : see § 183.

[1] The lien does not exist in : —
California : see § 160.
Illinois : see § 161.
Missouri : Attorneys have no lien upon judgments for fees. Frissell v. Haile, 18 Mo. 18; Lewis v. Kinealy, 2 Mo. App. 33; Roberts v. Nelson, 22 Ib. 28, 31. See § 163.
Nevada: Apparently the lien does not exist.
North Carolina : Apparently the lien does not exist.
Ohio : Does not exist. Diehl v. Friester, 37 Ohio St. 473.
Pennsylvania: This lien does not exist.
Texas : An attorney has no lien for his services upon a judgment. Casey v. March, 30 Tex. 180; Able v. Lee, 6 Tex. 427, 431; Whittaker v. Clarke, 33 Tex. 647.
Wisconsin : Courtney v. McGavock, 23 Wis. 619.
United States Court of Claims: No lien is allowed to an attorney who has prosecuted a case to judgment against the United States. Brooke's case, 12 Opin. Atty.-Gen. 216.

these states an attorney is not entitled to any taxable costs, and, the lien being in general limited to such costs, it cannot exist except by force of special statutes where there are no such costs. Generally there can be no lien for unliquidated fees, or for fees agreed upon, unless the right be conferred by statute.[1]

160. In California there is no statute giving costs to the attorneys; and, inasmuch as the lien cannot be extended to cover a *quantum meruit* compensation, an attorney in this state has no lien on a judgment recovered by him.[2]

161. In Illinois an attorney has no lien upon a judgment for his fees in the litigation resulting in its recovery;[3] and he has none for taxable costs, for there is no statute or rule of court allowing specific[4] costs to attorneys.

But it seems that, where the employment is by a special contract, the attorney has an equitable lien upon the proceeds of the litigation. Thus, where an attorney undertook the collection of a debt secured upon land under a special contract whereby he was to receive one fifth of the proceeds whether the same might be in land or money, and the suit was prosecuted to a decree and sale of the land, and the client purchased the land at the sale, it was held that the attorney was entitled to an equitable lien under the contract, and a decree in his favor was entered accordingly.[5]

162. In Massachusetts[6] an attorney has no lien at common law on a judgment recovered by him;[7] but it is provided by statute that an attorney lawfully possessed of an execution, or who has prosecuted a suit to final judgment in favor of his client, shall have a lien thereon for the amount of his fees and disbursements in the cause ; but this does not prevent the payment of the execution or judgment to the judgment creditor without notice of the lien.

---

[1] Swanston *v.* Morning Star Mining Co. 4 McCrary, 241.

[2] Kyle, *ex parte*, 1 Cal. 331 ; Mansfield *v.* Dorland, 2 Cal. 507; Russell *v.* Conway, 11 Cal. 93; Hogan *v.* Black, 66 Cal. 41.

[3] Forsythe *v.* Beveridge, 52 Ill. 268; Nichols *v.* Pool, 89 Ill. 491.

[4] La Framboise *v.* Grow, 56 Ill. 197.

[5] Smith *v.* Young, 62 Ill. 210. And see Morgan *v.* Roberts, 38 Ill. 65.

[6] P. S. 1882, p. 913, sect. 42. This was evidently derived from the statute of 1810, ch. 84.

[7] Baker *v.* Cook, 11 Mass. 236, 238 ; Dunklee *v.* Locke, 13 Mass. 525.

This statutory lien covers only taxable costs, and does not extend to counsel fees.[1]

Under this statute an attorney has no lien before judgment which will prevent his client from settling with the opposite party without the attorney's knowledge or consent. Even after judgment, the attorney's lien does not prevent a settlement if this be made without notice of the lien.[2]

The attorney of the defendant having recovered a judgment for costs is entitled to them as against the plaintiff who has recovered a judgment against the defendant. The plaintiff's judgment should be for the balance after deducting the attorney's claim for costs.[3]

The attorney may enforce his lien upon a judgment by an action on the judgment in the name of the client.[4]

163. In Missouri it is held that attorneys have no lien for their fees upon judgments recovered by them. They are not allowed under the laws of this state any fees which are taxed as costs. They look merely to contracts made with their clients for remuneration for their services. If they recover money for their clients, they may retain their fees, just as any bailee may retain for any services rendered in the care of the subject of the bailment.[5]

164. In Rhode Island an attorney probably has a lien for his costs upon the judgment recovered, but it is regarded only as a sort of equity to control the judgment and its incidental processes, against his client and the adverse party colluding with his client. The court will, in the exercise of a reasonable discretion, protect and enforce this equity. Though the judgment be for costs only, it does not belong to the attorney absolutely, so that he is authorized to bring suit upon it without the client's consent.[6]

---

[1] Ocean Ins. Co. v. Rider, 22 Pick. 210; S. C. 20 Pick. 259; Thayer v. Daniels, 113 Mass. 129.

[2] Simmons v. Almy, 103 Mass. 33; Getchell v. Clark, 5 Mass. 309; Potter v. Mays, 3 Greenl. (Me.) 34.

[3] Little v. Rogers, 2 Met. 478.

[4] Wood v. Verry, 4 Gray, 357.

[5] Frissell v. Haile, 18 Mo. 18.

[6] Horton v. Champlin, 12 R. I. 550, per Durfee, C. J.: "We think this is the full scope of the lien, if lien it can be called." See § 157.

III. *Whether the Lien is Limited to Taxable Costs or Includes Fees.*

165 It is also a general rule that an attorney's lien upon a judgment for his fees is limited to the taxable costs in the case, in the absence of any statute extending the lien.[1] The costs for which he has a lien are the taxable costs in the suit in which the judgment is rendered. The lien does not extend to costs in any other suit.[2]

His lien is limited to the taxable costs included in the judgment, and does not extend to fees accruing, and advances made subsequently;[3] nor to commissions on the amount of the judgment collected, though a charge of such commissions might properly be allowed as between attorney and client;[4] nor to disbursements or incidental expenses not taxable as costs;[5] nor to costs in other suits.[6]

But this lien cannot be defeated by the discharge of the attorney by the client.[7] The lien exists equally whether the services rendered by one attorney or more; or whether the suit be commenced by one attorney, and prosecuted to final judgment by another.[8]

166. An attorney's lien upon an uncollected judgment is confined to the judgment in the very action in which the services were rendered.[9] The theory upon which the lien is founded

---

[1] Newbert v. Cunningham, 50 Me. 231; Hooper v. Brundage, 22 Me. 460; Ocean Ins. Co. v. Rider, 22 Pick. (Mass.) 210; Currier v. Boston & Me. R. R. 37 N. H. 223; Wright v. Cobleigh, 21 N. H. 339; Wells v. Hatch, 43 N. H. 246, 247; Weed v. Boutelle, 56 Vt. 570, 578; Phillips v. Stagg, 2 Edw. (N. Y.) 108; Kyle, ex parte, 1 Cal. 331; Mansfield v. Dorland, 2 Cal. 507, 509.

This was the rule in **New York**, until the Code of Procedure provided that the measure of the attorney's compensation, for which he should have a lien, should be left to the agreement, express or implied, of the attorney and his client. Coughlin v. N. Y. C. & Hud. Riv. R. R. Co. 71 N. Y. 443.

[2] Phillips v. Stagg, 2 Edw. (N. Y.) 108.

[3] In re Wilson, 12 Fed. Rep. 235; Newbert v. Cunningham, 50 Me. 231; Cooley v. Patterson, 52 Me. 472; Currier v. Boston & Me. R. R. 37 N. H. 223; Wells v. Hatch, 43 N. H. 246; Ex parte Kyle, 1 Cal. 331; Mansfield v. Dorland, 2 Cal. 507.

[4] Wright v. Cobleigh, 21 N. H. 337.

[5] Wells v. Hatch, 43 N. H. 246.

[6] St. John v. Diefendorf, 12 Wend. (N. Y.) 261.

[7] Gammon v. Chandler, 30 Me. 152.

[8] Stratton v. Hussey, 62 Me. 286.

[9] Lann v. Church, 4 Madd. 391; Bozon v. Bolland, 4 Myl. & C. 354; Lucas v. Peacock, 9 Beav. 177; Stephens v. Weston, 3 Barn. & Cress. 535,

is, that the attorney has, by his skill and labor, obtained the judgment, and hence should have a lien upon it for his compensation, in analogy to the lien which a mechanic has upon any article which he manufactures. When, therefore, an attorney has several actions for a client, and recovers judgment in but one of them, he cannot, in the absence of a special agreement, have a lien upon that judgment for his compensation in all the actions.[1] And so, where an attorney recovered three judgments for his clients, who afterwards became bankrupts, and their assignee solicited other attorneys, to whom the first attorney transferred all the papers upon an agreement that his lien should not be waived, but should be satisfied out of the first moneys coming into the assignee's hands out of the suits, it was held that his lien in each case was limited to the funds collected upon the particular judgment in obtaining which the services were rendered; and, money having been collected upon two of the judgments, there was no lien upon this for services rendered in recovering the third judgment, upon which nothing was collected.[2]

167. In several states, however, there are adjudications that an attorney's lien upon a judgment covers his services without regard to taxable costs in obtaining the judgment, though there be no agreement between the attorney and his client as to the amount which the attorney is entitled to charge for his services.[3] The lien exists for a reasonable compensation,

---

538; *In re* Wilson, 12 Fed. Rep. 235; S. C. 26 Alb. L. J. 271; Williams v. Ingersoll, 89 N. Y. 508, 517; St. John v. Diefendorf, 12 Wend. (N. Y.) 261 ; Adams v. Fox, 40 Barb. (N. Y.) 442; Phillips v. Stagg, 2 Edw. (N. Y.) Ch. 108; Shapley v. Bellows, 4 N. H. 347; Wright v. Cobleigh, 21 N. H. 339, 341; McWilliams v. Jenkins, 72 Ala. 480 ; Forbush v. Leonard, 8 Minn. 303; Weed v. Boutelle, 56 Vt. 570; Pope v Armstrong, 3 S. & M. (Miss.) 214; Cage v. Wilkinson, Ib. 223.

[1] Williams *v.* Ingersoll, *supra,* per Earl, J.; Johnson *v.* Story, 1 Lea (Tenn.), 114.

[2] *In re* Wilson, 12 Fed. Rep. 235, 244, a well-considered case. Brown, J.,

says : "Neither principle nor authority can sanction an increase in the amount of a lien upon an uncollected judgment through subsequent services in independent matters."

The same rule undoubtedly prevails under the provision of the new Code of Procedure of New York, 1879, § 66, which gives an attorney "a lien upon his client's cause of action" from its commencement. This refers, doubtless, to services and charges in the cause itself, and not to services in any other matter. Wilson, *in re, supra,* per Brown, J.

[3] Henchey *v.* Chicago, 41 Ill. 136 ; Humphrey *v.* Browning, 46 Ill. 476, 482, per Breese, C. J.; Hill *v.* Brink-

which may be determined by the court, or by a referee, upon a summary application. The extent of the lien is to be ascertained upon the basis of a *quantum meruit*. It is argued that the rule restricting the lien to the amount of the taxed costs arose from the fact that in England these costs are the only charges for which an action might be maintained; the services of barristers being in theory gratuitous, and their charges only an honorary obligation of *quiddam honorarium;* and, consequently, where the payment of the fees and charges of an attorney may be legally enforced, as is the case in this country, the reason for the restriction fails, and the lien should cover fees other than the taxed costs, and should include the charges of counsel. The taxed costs of the attorney in England had no merit or justice superior to the claim of counsel in this country for a reasonable compensation; and, therefore, the lien should here be extended so as to secure such compensation.[1]

168. In other states the lien has been extended by statute so as to cover not merely taxable costs, but a reasonable compensation to the attorney for his services in obtaining the judgment.

The adjudications and statutes whereby the lien has been made to cover fees and disbursements instead of costs, are so different in the several states that it is necessary to state the law for several of the states in detail.

169. In Alabama it is settled by adjudication that an attorney has a lien on a judgment for any reasonable fees due him from his client for services rendered in its recovery.[2] In support of his claim he may prove his retainer or original employment, or he may show the performance of the services within the

ley, 10 Ind. 102; Andrews *v.* Morse, 12 Conn. 444; Carter *v.* Davis, 8 Fla. 183; Carter *v.* Bennett, 6 Fla. 214; Warfield *v.* Campbell, 38 Ala. 527; Pope *v.* Armstrong, 5 S. & M. (Miss.) 214; McDonald *v.* Napier, 14 Ga. 89. In **Illinois** and **Georgia** there is no allowance of taxable costs.

[1] Warfield *v.* Campbell, 38 Ala. 527, per Walker, C. J.; McDonald *v.* Napier, 14 Ga. 89, per Nisbet, J.

[2] Central R. R. Co. *v.* Pettus, 113 U. S. 116; Jackson *v.* Clopton, 66 Ala. 29; Mosely *v.* Norman, 74 Ala. 422; Warfield *v.* Campbell, 38 Ala. 527. The lien seems to have been established in this state by the decision in the latter case. In McCaa *v.* Grant, 43 Ala. 262, it was suggested that the principle there stated needed limitation; but in *Ex parte* Lehman, 59 Ala. 631, this suggestion was disapproved, and the principle reaffirmed.

knowledge of his client.[1] From the date of the rendition of the judgment or decree, the attorney is to be regarded as the assignee of it to the extent of his fees.[2]

170. In Arkansas an attorney has a lien upon and an interest in a judgment which he may have recovered in a court of record for his client; and when the judgment is for the recovery of real or personal property, his lien amounts to an interest to the extent of it in the property so recovered.[3] His lien covers not only his costs, but compensation for his services to the amount agreed upon, if there be any agreement, otherwise to a reasonable amount. His lien for services does not prevail against one who, in good faith and without notice of his lien, has made payments on account of the judgment. The attorney may assert his lien, however, by filing a statement of it with the clerk of the court within ten days of the rendition of the judgment; whereupon the clerk makes upon the record a memorandum of the lien, which he also indorses upon the execution, and such memorandum is made actual notice of the lien to all persons. This is necessary, however, only for the protection of those who, in good faith and without notice, have made payments to the judgment creditor upon or in consequence of the judgment. The notice is not necessary to protect the attorney against a purchaser of the judgment.[4]

171. In Colorado it is provided by statute that all attorneys and counsellors at law shall have a lien upon any money or property in their hands, or upon any judgment they may have obtained, belonging to any client, for any fee or balance of fees due, or any professional services rendered by them in any court of this state, which lien may be enforced by the proper civil action.[5]

---

[1] Jackson v. Clopton, 66 Ala. 29; Ex parte Lehman, 59 Ala. 631.

[2] Central R. R. Co. v. Pettus, 113 U. S. 116.

[3] Gantt's Dig. of Stats. §§ 3622, 3626; Lane v. Hallum, 38 Ark. 385; Gist v. Hanly, 33 Ark. 233, 235. In the latter case, Harrison, J., said : " The attorney is virtually an assignee of a portion of the judgment, or of the debt or claim, equal to his fee and the ad-vances which he has made for his client. For the parties, then, to make any arrangement or settlement between themselves, without his consent, by which his right might be defeated, would be a fraud upon him, against which he is entitled to protection."

[4] McCain v. Portis, 42 Ark. 402; Porter v. Hanson, 36 Ark. 591.

[5] G. L. 1877, § 32; G. L. 1883, § 85.

172. In Florida a lien is allowed upon a judgment for the reasonable and fair remuneration of the attorney, the statutes not providing for any taxable costs.[1] This lien is superior to any equitable set-off of the judgment debtor.

173. In Georgia [2] it is provided that an attorney, upon suits, judgments, and decrees for money, shall have a lien superior to all liens, except tax liens, and no person shall be at liberty to satisfy the suit, judgment, or decree until the lien or claim of the attorney for his fees is fully satisfied. Attorneys at law have the same right and power over such suits, judgments, and decrees, to enforce their liens, as their clients had or may have for the amount due thereon to them. Upon all suits for the recovery of real or personal property, and upon all judgments or decrees for the recovery of the same, attorneys have a lien on the property recovered, for their fees, superior to all liens but liens for taxes, which may be enforced by such attorneys, or their representatives, as liens on personal and real estate, by mortgage and foreclosure; and the property recovered remains subject to such liens, unless transferred to *bonâ fide* purchasers without notice. If an attorney files his assertion claiming a lien on property recovered on a suit instituted by him, within thirty days after a recovery of the same, then his lien binds all persons. The same liens and modes of enforcement thereof, which are allowed to attorneys who are employed to sue for any property, upon the property recovered, are equally allowed to attorneys employed and serving in defence against such suits, in case the defence is successful.[3]

If no notice of the lien be given, a settlement by the parties can be set aside by the attorney only in case he shows that it was made with the intent to defeat his lien.[4] The lien, however, attaches as soon as the suit is commenced; and the client cannot defeat the lien by dismissing the action before trial against the attorney's objections.[5]

After judgment the attorney may proceed to enforce his lien upon it by levy, and the judgment debtor cannot arrest the levy

---

[1] Carter *v.* Bennett, 6 Fla. 214, 257; Carter *v.* Davis, 8 Fla. 183.

[2] Code 1882, § 1989. And see Morrison *v.* Ponder, 45 Ga. 167.

[3] Code 1882, § 1989.

[4] Hawkins *v.* Loyless, 39 Ga. 5; Green *v.* Southern Express Co. 39 Ga. 20.

[5] Twiggs *v.* Chambers, 56 Ga. 279.

on the ground that the judgment creditor has agreed with him for value to give indulgence ; nor can he set up the claim that the attorney has been paid, and that therefore he has no lien, unless he himself has made such payment.[1]

174. Indiana. — Any attorney is entitled to hold a lien, for his fees, on any judgment rendered in favor of any person or persons employing him, to obtain the same, provided he shall, at the time such judgment is rendered, enter, in writing, upon the docket or record wherein the same is recorded, his intention to hold a lien thereon, together with the amount of his claim.[2]

This lien extends to a judgment for alimony obtained by an attorney in proceedings for divorce on behalf of the wife. If she knows of the lien and assents to the amount of the fee claimed, she is bound for such amount.[3]

175. Iowa [4] and Dakota Territory.[5] — An attorney has a lien for a general balance of compensation on money due his client in the hands of the adverse party, or attorney of such party, in an action or proceeding in which the attorney claiming the lien was employed, from the time of giving notice in writing to such adverse party, or attorney of such party, if the money is in the possession or under the control of such attorney, which notice shall state the amount claimed, and, in general terms, for what services.

After judgment in any court of record, such notice may be

---

[1] Tarver v. Tarver, 53 Ga. 43.

[2] Rev. Stat. 1881, § 5276, enacted Dec. 20, 1865.

[3] Putnam v. Tennyson, 50 Ind. 456. Prior to this statute, attorneys had no lien on the judgment for their fees. Hill v. Brinkley, 10 Ind. 102.

Strictly speaking, a judgment is rendered when it is announced by the court ; yet under this statute, which is loosely drawn, it appears that it was intended that the judgment should be entered on the docket or court records before the entry of the attorney's intention to claim lien upon it ; and it follows that the entry of notice of such lien can be made at any time within a reasonable time after

the recording of the judgment; and the entry of such notice upon the day following the entry of the judgment is within a reasonable time. Blair v. Lanning, 61 Ind. 499; Day v. Bowman, 10 N. East. Rep. 126.

The lien of an attorney for his fees is incident to the judgment to which it is attached, and is necessarily as much assignable as is the judgment to which it is incident. Day v. Bowman, supra.

[4] Rev. Code 1880, p. 49, §§ 215, 216.

[5] Rev. Code 1877, pp. 32, 33, §§ 9, 10. In Dakota the statute restricts the lien to a general balance of compensation in the case in which the lien is claimed.

given and the lien made effective against the judgment debtor, by entering the same in the judgment docket opposite the entry of the judgment.[1]

Any person interested may release such lien by executing a bond in a sum double the amount claimed, or in such sum as may be fixed by a judge, payable to the attorney, with security to be approved by the clerk of the court, conditioned to pay the amount finally due the attorney for his services, which amount

---

[1] Where the plaintiff, in an action for damages for a personal injury, agrees in writing with his attorney to pay him one third of the amount that may be ultimately recovered, and a judgment is recovered for $2,000, and the attorney enters on the judgment docket notice of " an attorney's lien on this judgment for $2,000 for services rendered plaintiff in this cause," and the judgment is reversed, and the claim compromised by the parties for $1,650, the lien so entered is binding upon the defendant to the extent of one third the amount agreed upon in the settlement. Winslow v. Central Iowa R. Co. (Iowa) 32 N. W. Rep. 330. Rothrock, J., said : "Counsel for appellant contend that the lien entered of record was on the judgment, and not upon money in the possession of the adverse party due the plaintiff in action. It is true that the entry made upon the judgment docket states that a lien is claimed on the judgment. We think, however, that the plaintiffs had no right to make any claim other than that provided by statute, and the section of the code above cited does not provide for a lien on the judgment as such. It expressly provides for a lien on money in the hands of the adverse party or his attorney. It is further claimed that as the statute provides where notice of the lien is placed upon the judgment docket, and thus made effective against the judgment debtor, the notice ceased or expired when the judgment was reversed, because there was then no ' judgment debtor.' We think, however, that the words ' judgment debtor,' as used in the fourth subdivision of the section above quoted, are merely descriptive of the person against whom the lien may be enforced. It will be observed that notice of the lien upon money in the hands of the adverse party is not required to be personally served after judgment. The adverse party is charged with notice by the entry on the judgment docket. From the time of such entry he cannot prejudice the rights of the attorney claiming the lien by a settlement with his client ; and as the law does not place the lien upon the judgment, but upon the claim against the adverse party, or the money in his hands, we think the notice remained binding upon the defendant as long as the money remained in its hands. If the plaintiffs had merely stated in the entry upon the judgment docket their lien upon the money claimed of the railroad company, and in its hands, due to the defendant for the injury of which he complained, the notice would have been in strict conformity with the statute, and would have been binding on the railroad company through all the further progress of the case, and up to the actual payment of the demand. We do not think the fact that the word ' judgment ' was used in the entry instead of ' suit,' ' action,' or ' claim ' or some other equivalent word, was a matter of any consequence in fixing the rights of the parties."

may be ascertained by suit on the bond. Such lien will be released unless the attorney, within ten days after demand therefor, furnishes any party interested a full and complete bill of particulars of the services and amount claimed for each item, or written contract with the party for whom the services were rendered.[1]

Under these statutes the attorney's lien attaches before judgment. Even in case the suit is for damages in an action of tort, though the lien may not be enforcible until the damages are determined by judgment, yet the lien attaches from the time of the service of notice. This notice must be in writing.[2] It may be served at the commencement of the action; and such notice is sufficient to cover all services rendered in the action, whether before or after the service of the notice.[3] The lien attaches from the time of the notice, and has priority to any lien of attachment obtained by proceedings in garnishment subsequently commenced.[4] Before notice of the lien the parties may settle without reference to the claim of the attorney for his fees;[5] but not afterwards.[6] A right of set-off existing at the time the notice is given is superior to the attorney's lien; but the lien is superior to a right of set-off subsequently arising.[7] Before notice of the attorney's lien, it is competent for the parties, acting in good faith without collusion, to settle the suit without reference to the attorney's claim for his fees.[8]

176. In Kansas [9] an attorney has a lien for a general balance of compensation upon money due to his client, and in the hands of the adverse party, in an action or proceeding in which the attorney was employed, from the time of giving notice of the lien to that party.[10] Any person interested in such matter may release such lien by giving security in a penalty equal to the

---

[1] Cross v. Ackley, 40 Iowa, 493.

[2] Phillips v. Germon, 43 Iowa, 101.

[3] Smith v. Railroad Co. 56 Iowa, 720.

[4] Myers v. McHugh, 16 Iowa, 335.

[5] Casar v. Sargeant, 7 Iowa, 317.

[6] Fisher v. Oskaloosa, 28 Iowa, 381; Brainard v. Elwood, 53 Iowa, 30.

[7] Hurst v. Sheets, 21 Iowa, 501.

[8] Casar v. Sargeant, 7 Iowa, 317.

[9] Comp. Laws, p. 114, §§ 468, 469.

[10] Leavenson v. Lafontane, 3 Kans. 523. The notice must be in writing and must be served upon the party personally, or upon his attorney of record. If the party be a corporation, the service must be upon a general officer. Service upon a station agent of a railroad company is not sufficient. Kansas Pacific Ry. Co. v. Thatcher, 17 Kan. 92.

amount claimed by the attorney, and conditioned to pay the amount that may finally be found due for his services.

Under this statute the lien exists even when the only claim in suit is one for damages for personal injuries, unliquidated and undetermined by judgment or verdict.[1] The notice need not state all the amount for which a lien is claimed. The lien is given for the amount agreed to be paid by the client, or, in the absence of any agreement, for the reasonable value of the services.[2]

177. In Kentucky [3] attorneys employed by either plaintiff or defendant, in any action which is prosecuted to recovery, have a lien upon the judgment for money or property, either personal or real which may be recovered in such action — legal costs excepted — for the amount of any fee which may have been agreed upon by the parties, or, in the absence of such agreement, for a fair and reasonable fee for their services.

Under this statute an attorney has no lien before judgment on a claim for unliquidated damages in actions of tort; and such an action may be compromised and dismissed by agreement of the parties against the objection of the attorney.[4] If no judgment is recovered in a suit, there is nothing to which an attorney's lien can attach.[5]

178. In Michigan, in 1867, all laws restricting or controlling the right of parties to agree with their attorneys for compensation were repealed, and the taxable costs were made payable to the parties.[6] Since that date the taxable costs form no part of the attorney's compensation, but this is left wholly to agreement, express or implied. A lien for such compensation is in some sort recognized by the provision that, in setting off executions, one against another, the set-off shall not be allowed as to so much

[1] Kansas Pacific Ry. Co. v. Thacher, 17 Kans. 92.

[2] Kansas Pacific Ry. Co. v. Thacher, *supra*.

[3] G. S. p. 149, § 15. Under this statute the institution and prosecution of a suit to judgment is sufficient notice to the judgment debtor that the plaintiff's attorney has a lien upon it for his reasonable compensation. If the debtor, after such implied notice or after actual notice, pays the amount of the judgment to the plaintiff in person, he is still liable to the attorney for the amount of his lien. Stephens v. Farrar, 4 Bush, 13; and see Robertson v. Shutt, 9 Bush, 659.

[4] Wood v. Anders, 5 Bush, 601.

[5] Wilson v. House, 10 Bush, 406.

[6] Annotated Stats. 1882, § 9004.

of the first execution as may be due to the attorney in that suit for his taxable costs and disbursements.[1]   The result is that, although no lien is expressly given to attorneys by statute, the courts recognize their lien to the extent of their taxable costs, at least,[2] and probably to the extent of the compensation agreed upon,[3] or, in case there is no agreement, to the extent of a reasonable compensation.

179. Minnesota.[4] — An attorney has a lien for his compensation, whether specially agreed upon or implied, upon money in the hands of the adverse party, in an action or proceeding in which the attorney was employed, from the time of giving notice of the lien to that party ; and upon a judgment to the extent of the costs included therein, or, if there is a special agreement, to the extent of the compensation specially agreed on, from the time of giving notice to the party against whom the judgment is recovered.   This lien is, however, subordinate to the rights existing between the parties to the action or proceeding.

180. Oregon.[5] — The statute is the same as the above, with the exception that it is also provided that the original notice shall be filed with the clerk where the judgment is entered or docketed.   Under this statute the attorney cannot have a lien for his compensation, unless he has a special agreement as to the amount of it.[6]

Under such a statute giving a lien upon "money in the hands of the adverse party," something more is required in order to

[1] Annotated Stats. 1882, § 7710.

[2] Kinney v. Robinson (Mich.), 29 N. W. Rep. 86.

[3] Wells v. Elsam, 40 Mich. 218.

[4] G. S. 1878, p. 866, § 16. Under this statute the attorney has no lien until he gives notice of it to the judgment debtor. Dodd v. Brott, 1 Minn. 270. If the attorney's compensation has been agreed upon, the writ must specify the amount of the lien claimed. Forbush v. Leonard, 8 Minn. 303. Statutory costs having been abolished in Minnesota, by Laws of 1860, p. 244, the lien can exist only in case there has been a special agreement as to compensation. For-

bush v. Leonard, *supra*. The attorney has no lien upon a judgment for compensation, unless he has made a special agreement with his client as to the amount of it. *In re* Scoggin, 5 Sawyer, 549; *S. C.* 8 Rep. 330. But a different view was taken in a later case, and it was held that under an implied contract it is sufficient if the notice fairly inform the party that a lien is claimed, what it is for, and upon what it is to be indorsed. Crowley v. Le Duc, 21 Minn. 412.

[5] G. L. 1872, § 1012.

[6] *In re* Scoggin, 5 Sawyer, 549 ; *S. C.* 8 Rep. 330.

give a lien than a mere debt from such party to the client.
Money, in this connection, means some specific fund which has
actually come into the party's possession as custodian or trustee,
to obtain which the suit is brought. After judgment is obtained
on the demand, or for the money, the lien can be acquired upon
the judgment only by giving notice in the manner provided by
statute.[1]

181. Mississippi. — Doubt has been expressed whether an attorney has a lien for his fees on a fund collected under a judgment recovered by him, where the amount of his fees has not
been fixed by special contract, or by established professional
usage; and it seems that a lien would not exist for fees resting
wholly upon the principle of *quantum meruit*. But, however
this might be, it was held that such a lien could not be asserted
on the trial of a motion against the sheriff for failure to pay over
money collected on execution issued upon such a judgment.
The attorney's claim should be asserted directly, and not in this
collateral way.[2] It is clearly settled that the lien of the attorney
attaches upon judgments recovered by him, with their incidents
and fruits; but it is difficult to make out, from the decided cases,
the various limitations, conditions, and incidents of such lien.[3]

182. Montana Territory.[4] — All attorneys have a lien upon
moneys in their hands, and upon judgments obtained for any client for any fees or balance of fees, due or to become due, for any
professional services rendered by them in any court or courts of
the territory. Such lien is deemed to attach from the commencement of the action or the performance of such services, and extends to and includes reasonable fees therefor. Notice of the
lien claimed upon any judgment must be filed in the office of the
clerk of the court in which the judgment is obtained, or with
the probate judge or justice of the peace rendering judgment,
within three days after final judgment shall have been entered;
and it is the duty of the clerk of the court, probate judge, or
justice of the peace, with whom such notice may be filed, to indorse on such notice the date of filing, and to file the same with

---

[1] *In re* Scoggin, 5 Sawyer, 549;
S. C. 8 Rep. 330. This case arose
upon the statute of Oregon.

[2] Pugh *v.* Boyd, 38 Miss. 326; and

see Stewart *v.* Flowers, 44 Miss.
513.

[3] See Stewart *v.* Flowers, *supra*.

[4] R. S. 1879, p. 414, ch. 3, § 54.

the papers pertaining to the cause. In case notice of the lien be not filed as provided, the lien does not attach to such judgment.

183. In Nebraska[1] and Wyoming Territory[2] an attorney has a lien for a general balance of compensation upon money in the hands of the adverse party in an action or proceeding in which the attorney was employed, from the time of giving notice of the lien to that party.

Under the statute it was regarded as doubtful by the Circuit Court of the United States whether an attorney can enforce a lien upon a judgment obtained by him for his client against a third person; for a judgment is not money in the hands of the judgment debtor belonging to his client.[3]

There can be no lien before judgment upon a cause of action for tort which, in case of the death of either of the parties, would not survive.[4]

The notice required by this statute is a personal notice, and it should be in writing.[5]

This lien covers the attorney's reasonable fees and disbursements in the suit, and is paramount to the right of the parties in the suit. But the lien is restricted to the claim set forth in the notice.[6]

184. In New York, prior to the Code of 1848,[7] an attorney had a lien upon a judgment recovered by him, but the amount of his lien was limited to his taxable costs. By that code the taxation of costs was abolished, and the compensation of the attorney was left to be determined by the contract of the parties, either expressly or impliedly made. The implied equitable lien was consequently extended to cover the agreed compensation, whatever the amount, in all cases where the cause of action was assignable or judgment was obtained. To the extent of his compensation the attorney was deemed an equitable assignee of the judgment, and had a lien upon it when recovered.[8] In the

---

[1] Comp. Stat. 1881, p. 66, ch. 7, § 8.

[2] Comp. Laws 1876, p. 16, § 8; Act of December 9, 1869, § 8.

[3] Patrick v. Leach, 2 McCrary, 635; S. C. 12 Fed. Rep. 661.

[4] Abbott v. Abbott, 18 Neb. 503.

[5] Patrick v. Leach, *supra*.

[6] Griggs v. White, 5 Neb. 467; Boyer v. Clark, 3 Ib. 161, 168.

[7] § 303.

[8] Rooney v. Second Av. R. R. Co. 18 N. Y. 368; Marshall v. Meech, 51 N. Y. 140, 143; Wright v. Wright, 70

absence, however, of any agreement on the subject, it was at one time thought that the amount of the taxable costs continued to be the measure of compensation allowed to the attorney, and consequently the extent of his lien.[1] But the rule seems afterwards to have been well settled that the attorney might, in the absence of a definite agreement as to the amount of his fees, recover the reasonable value of his services ; and such value is a fact to be established, like any other fact, by evidence.[2]

185. Under the present Code of New York,[3] the compensation of an attorney or counsellor for his services is governed by agreement, express or implied, which is not restrained by law.[4] From the commencement of an action, or the service of an answer containing a counter-claim,[5] the attorney who appears for a party has a lien upon his client's cause of action or counter-claim, which attaches to a verdict, report, decision, or judgment in his client's favor, and the proceeds thereof, in whosesoever hands they may come, and cannot be affected by any settlement between the parties before or after judgment.

This provision gives full and complete protection to the attorney. His lien extends to both costs and services, and cannot be affected by a settlement between the parties, though no notice of the lien be given.[6]

N. Y. 100; Ward v. Syme, 9 How. Pr. 16; Coughlin v. N. Y. Cent. & Hud. R. R. Co. 71 N. Y. 443; Crotty v. Mackenzie, 52 How. Pr. 54; Tullis v. Bushnell, 65 Ib. 465; Hall v. Ayer, 9 Abb. Pr. 220; Smith v. Central Trust Co. 4 Dem. (N. Y.) 75, 77.

The case of Haight v. Holcomb, 16 How. Pr. 173, is overruled.

[1] Rooney v. Second Av. R. R. Co. *supra*, per Harris, J.; Adams v. Fox, 40 Barb. (N. Y.) 442. It was thought that, if a lien were allowed for an attorney's services where his compensation was not agreed upon, the effect might be to tie up the collection of the judgment until the attorney could go into court and recover another judgment against his client fixing the amount of his compensation in the original suit. This seemed to be an extraordinary proceeding, and one for which there was no precedent.

[2] Whitelegge v. De Witt, 12 Daly, 319; Garr v. Mairet, 1 Hilt. 498; Gallup v. Perue, 10 Hun, 525.

[3] Code Civ. Proc. 1879, § 66 (July 10, 1879).

[4] Turno v. Parks, 2 How. (N. Y.) Pr. N. S. 35.

[5] The defendant's attorney has no lien where the claim set up by the defendant does not constitute a cause of action, so as properly to constitute a counter-claim within the meaning of that term as used in the statute, but is a claim which could only be set up in reduction of the damages which the plaintiff might recover. Pierson v. Safford, 30 Hun, 521.

[6] Albert Palmer Co. v. Van Orden, 54 How. Pr. 79; *S. C.* 4 N. Y. Civ. Pro. 44;

186. In New York the lien is now upon the cause of action, and continues till a final judgment is reached. It is not in terms upon the judgment. It attaches to every verdict, report, decision, or judgment in the client's favor.[1] The lien, being upon the cause of action, continues until a judgment is rendered which is final. It does not cease upon the first judgment rendered if this be not final. If such a judgment be rendered against the plaintiff, this may be reversed, and the cause of action established in favor of the plaintiff by another judgment. If the first and erroneous judgment destroyed the lien, there could be no lien thereafter, for the lien is created by the commencement of the action. It follows that the lien must continue until the judgment is final, either for want of power to appeal, or for failure to appeal in time. A final judgment against the plaintiff determines that there was no cause of action, and, therefore, nothing to support a lien. It follows, also, that a client has no absolute right to stop the litigation after a judgment against the plaintiff upon the merits; but this right is subject to the attorney's lien for his costs and the attorney's approval. While that judgment remains the plaintiff has no cause of action, and the attorney has practically, by the judgment, lost the benefit of his lien. If the attorney is not content with the judgment, and wishes to remove the adverse judgment as an obstacle in the way of enforcing his lien, his only remedy is to appeal and prosecute the action to final judgment. And this he may do. He may, at his own expense, prosecute the appeal against the wishes of the client in order to obtain a reversal of the judgment, so that, upon a new trial and a favorable judgment, he may have the chance of collecting his costs from the opposite side by means of such judgment.[2]

187. Under the Code of New York the costs recovered in a suit belong to the party and not to the attorney.[3] He simply

McCabe v. Fogg, 60 N. Y. 488; Lansing v. Ensign, 62 Ib. 363; *In re* Bailey, 66 Ib. 64; Tullis v. Bushnell, 65 Ib. 465; Kehoe v. Miller, 10 Abb. (N. C.) 393; Murray v. Jibson, 22 Hun, 386; Coster v. Greenpoint Ferry Co. N. Y. Civ. Pro. 146; Dimick v. Cooley, 3 N.Y. Civ. Pro. 141; Lewis v. Day, 10 Week. Dig. 49 (affirmed by Court of Appeals, 31 Alb. L. J. 304); More v. Bowen, 9 Rep. 588; Goodrich v. McDonald, 41 Hun, 235.

[1] Goodrich v. McDonald, 2 N. Y. St. Rep. 144; Whitaker v. N. Y. & Harlem R. R. Co. 3 Ib. 537.

[2] Adsit v. Hall, 3 How. (N. Y.) Pr. N. S. 373.

[3] Wheaton v. Newcombe, 16 J. &

has a lien for his compensation, whether this exceeds in amount the costs taxed in the judgment, or falls short of the amount of such costs.[1] Thus the attorney may agree with his client to receive a share of the recovery in addition to his costs and disbursements, in lieu of all charges for his services, and his interest in the action cannot be affected by any compromise made between the parties.[2] But it seems that there can be no lien for compensation, beyond the taxed costs based upon an express agreement, unless the agreement be made before or pending the action. It cannot be based upon an agreement made after judgment.[3]

An attorney who appears and answers for the defendant after notice that the parties have settled, acquires no lien for costs.[4]

188. Under the code the amount of the attorney's compensation for which he has a lien is undefined, unless there be an express agreement of the parties.[5] When the right is clear and only the amount is in question, this may be determined upon a petition and reference, or by the judge, or by a jury passing upon an issue sent to it. Upon a summary application by a client to compel the attorney to pay over moneys collected, the court has jurisdiction to determine the question of the amount

S. 215 ; Stow v. Hamlin, 11 How. Pr. 452 ; Garr v. Mairet, 1 Hilt. 498 ; Easton v. Smith, 1 E. D. Smith, 318 ; Moore v. Westervelt, 3 Sandf. 762 ; Bartle v. Gilman, 18 N. Y. 260, 262 ; Van Every v. Adams, 10 J. & S. 126. The amendment in 1879 of § 66 of the Code of Civil Procedure does not state in words what the attorney's lien is for, but leaves this to be determined by the provision of the code as it previously stood, which declared that " the compensation of the attorney is governed by agreement, express or implied, which is not restrained by law." Smith v. Central Trust Co. 4 Dem. 75, 78.

[1] Wheaton v. Newcombe, *supra ;* Rooney v. Second Av. R. R. Co. 18 N. Y. 368 ; McGregor v. Comstock, 28 Ib. 237 ; Marshall v. Meech, 51 Ib. 140 ; Wright v. Wright, 70 Ib. 98, 100 ;

Pulver v. Harris, 52 Ib. 73 ; Crotty v. McKenzie, 10 J. & S. 192 ; Creighton v. Ingersoll, 20 Barb. 541 ; Brown v. New York, 11 Hun, 21.

[2] Fortsman v. Schulting, 35 Hun, 504.

[3] Smith v. Central Trust Co. *supra.*

[4] Howard v. Riker, 11 Abb. (N. C.) 113.

[5] *In re* Knapp, 85 N. Y. 284 ; Wright v. Wright, 70 N. Y. 96 ; Zogbaum v. Parker, 55 N. Y. 120 ; Marshall v. Meech, 51 N. Y. 140, 143 ; Coughlin v. N. Y. C. & H. R. Co. 71 N. Y. 443 ; Ackerman v. Ackerman, 14 Abb. Pr. 229 ; Brown v. New York, 11 Hun, 21 ; *S. C.* 9 Hun, 587 ; Rooney v. Second Av. R. R. Co. 18 N. Y. 368 ; McGregor v. Comstock, 28 N. Y. 237 ; Crotty v. McKenzie, 10 J. & S. 192.

of his compensation, where this is the only matter in dispute, although the items of his account are such as in ordinary cases would subject them to taxation.[1]

189. In New York the attorney must take the same steps to establish his lien upon the cause of action that he was previously required to take to establish it upon the judgment; that is, he must obtain leave of court to prosecute the action for the purpose of determining his right of recovery in the suit, and for the purpose of establishing his lien upon the subject-matter of the action; though it would seem that he is not required to show that the settlement was a fraud upon him, but only that it inequitably affected his lien upon the cause of action.[2]   After a settlement between the parties, the lien cannot be enforced upon a mere motion to compel the defendant to pay the plaintiff's attorney his taxable cost by awarding a judgment therefor.[3]

190. In Tennessee the attorney's lien attaches not only to the judgment but to the property, whether real or personal, which is the subject of the litigation.[4]   The attorney is entitled to an equitable lien on the property or thing in litigation for his just and reasonable fees, and the client cannot, while the suit is pending, so dispose of the subject-matter in dispute as to deprive the attorney of his lien.[5]   If property be attached in the suit, the attorney has a lien upon such property for his fees.[6] The lien dates from the commencement of the suit, and its pendency is, of itself, notice to all persons of the existence of the

---

[1] *In re* Knapp, 85 N. Y. 284.

[2] McCabe *v.* Fogg, 60 How. Pr. 488; Smith *v.* Baum, 67 How. Pr. 267; Tullis *v.* Bushnell, 65 How. Pr. 465; Albert Palmer Co. *v.* Van Orden, 64 Ib. 79; Goddard *v.* Trenbath, 24 Hun, 182; Wilber *v.* Barker, Ib. 24; Jenkins *v.* Adams, Ib. 22, 600; Dimick *v.* Cooley, 3 N. Y. Civ. Pro. 141; Ackerman *v.* Ackerman, 14 Abb. Pr. 229; Palmer *v.* Van Orden, 49 N. Y. Supr. 89; Thompkins *v.* Manner, 50 Ib. 511; Kehoe *v.* Miller, 10 Abb. (N. C.) 393; Deutsch *v.* Webb, Ib. 393;

Quinnan *v.* Clapp, Ib. 394; Russell *v.* Somerville, Ib. 395.

Under the present code it seems that the attorney may proceed without leave of court.

[3] Smith *v.* Baum, 67 How. Pr. 267.

[4] Hunt *v.* McClanahan, 1 Heisk. 503; Brown *v.* Bigley, 3 Tenn. Ch. 618; Garner *v.* Garner, 1 Lea, 29; Vaughn *v.* Vaughn, 12 Heisk. 472; Perkins *v.* Perkins, 9 Heisk. 95.

[5] Hunt *v.* McClanahan, *supra;* Pleasants *v.* Kortrecht, 5 Heisk. 694.

[6] Pleasants *v.* Kortrecht, *supra.*

lien. It may be preserved and extended by stating its existence in the judgment or decree. Notice from the pendency of the suit affects not only the client, but his creditors and purchasers.

191. In Vermont an attorney has a lien for his costs upon a judgment recovered by him in favor of his client; but this lien does not bind the opposite party so as to prevent his settling or discharging the suit and cause of action.[1] In the early decisions this lien was confined to the taxable costs in this suit.[2] But in a recent decision the rule was established that the lien extends to the attorney's reasonable fees and disbursements in the suit in which the judgment was recorded.

" No good reason can be given," say the court,[3] " for limiting an attorney's charging lien to what under our law are the taxable costs in favor of his client in the suit. If he is to be given a lien at all upon a judgment recovered by his services, it should be to the extent of the value of his services in the suit. His services are presumed to have been skilfully performed, and valuable because so performed. They enhance his client's claim presumably to the extent of the value of his services, the same as the tailor's services, in manufacturing a patron's cloth into a coat, enhance the value of the materials to the extent of the value of the services. We are aware that the decisions in this country are not uniform on the extent of an attorney's charging lien. In some states it is held to cover his reasonable charges and disbursements in the suit, while in others it is limited to the amount of costs taxable in favor of his client in the suit. But these are what the law allows to be recovered in favor of the prevailing party. They are taxed between party and party, and not between attorney and client, and are in no sense the measure of the value of the attorney's services and disbursements in the suit. They include frequently court, clerk, witness, and officer's fees, in the suit, which the client has advanced. I cannot help thinking that this class of decisions has its origin in not observing

---

[1] Hutchinson v. Pettes, 18 Vt. 614; Walker v. Sargeant, 14 Vt. 247; Beech v. Canaan, 14 Vt. 485; Smalley v. Clark, 22 Vt. 598; Fairbanks v. Devereux (Vt.), 3 Atl. Rep. 500.

[2] Heartt v. Chipman, 2 Aik. (Vt.) 162.

[3] Weed v. Boutelle, 56 Vt. 570, 580; Hooper v. Welch, 43 Vt. 169, 172; Hutchinson v. Howard, 15 Vt. 544.

the distinction between taxable costs which, at the common law, was a taxation between the attorney or solicitor and his client, and taxable costs under our statutes, which is a taxation in favor of the recovering party against the defeated party."

192. Virginia and West Virginia. — Formerly the attorney's lien was limited to his fees taxed in the costs.[1] But in the Virginia statute of 1840,[2] reënacted in West Virginia,[3] attorneys are authorized to make contracts with their clients for their fees, and their liens on judgments received cover not merely their taxable costs, but their services and disbursements.[4] While the lien is a special lien for services rendered in obtaining the particular judgment or decree, yet it extends to all services rendered in obtaining that judgment or decree, though the services may have been rendered in other suits, if these are so connected with the principal cause as to form the basis on which the judgment or decree is rendered, or is essential to the rendering of such judgment or decree.[5]

IV. *Rule that there is no Lien until Judgment has been Entered.*

193. An attorney has no lien for costs until a judgment is entered, or at least until after the verdict; unless it is given upon the cause of action by statute, as is now the case in New York under the present code;[6] and, until the lien attaches, the parties can settle the suit regardless of his claim for costs.[7] The

[1] Major v. Gibson, 1 Patt. & H. 48.

[2] Code 1873, ch. 160, § 11.

[3] Code 1868, ch. 119, § 11.

[4] Renick v. Ludington, 16 W. Va. 378.

[5] Renick v. Ludington, *supra.*

[6] Code of Civ. Proc. 1879, § 66. See § **186**, *supra.*

[7] **New York:** Coughlin v. N. Y. C. & Hud. Riv. R. Co. 71 N. Y. 443; Wright v. Wright, 70 N. Y. 93; S. C. 7 Daly, 62; Rooney v. Second Av. R. R. Co. 18 N. Y. 368; Marshall v. Meech, 51 N. Y. 140; Crotty v. MacKenzie, 52 How. Pr. 54; Shank v. Shoemaker, 18 N. Y. 489; Sweet v. Bartlett, 4 Sandf. 661; Tullis v. Bushnell, 65 How. Pr. 465; Brown v. New York, 11 Hun, 21; Sullivan v. O'Keeffe, 53 How. Pr. 426; Christy v. Perkins, 6 Daly, 237; Quincey v. Francis, 5 Abb. (N. C.) 286. **Vermont:** Foot v. Tewksbury, 2 Vt. 97; Walker v. Sargeant, 14 Vt. 247; Hutchinson v. Howard, 15 Vt. 544; Hooper v. Welch, 43 Vt. 169; Weed v. Boutelle, 56 Vt. 570, 578. **New Hampshire:** Wells v. Hatch, 43 N. H. 246; Young v. Dearborn, 27 N. H. 324. **Maine:** Potter v. Mayo, 3 Me. 34; Gammon v. Chandler, 30 Me. 152; Hobson v. Watson, 34 Me. 20; Averill v. Longfellow, 66 Me. 237. **Other States:** Lamont v. Railroad Co. 2 Mack. (D. C.) 502; Getchell v.

retaining of an attorney to prosecute an action, and the commencement of it by him, gives him no lien upon what may in the event of a trial be recovered therein ; [1] for otherwise it would not be in the power of the parties to settle their controversy until such lien should be satisfied, and it would be in the power of the attorney to continue the litigation for his own benefit in case of a favorable result, without incurring any liability should the result be adverse.[2] Accordingly, in a case where a judgment was recovered by a plaintiff in an action for assault and battery, and he assigned this to his attorney as security for costs, giving notice of the assignment to the defendant, but upon appeal the judgment was reversed and a new trial was granted, and before the new trial was had the parties settled, and the plaintiff executed a release to the defendant, it was held that, the assignment of the judgment having become a nullity by the reversal, the attorney had no lien, either legal or equitable, and could not proceed with the action and obtain a further judgment. The defendant, after the reversal of the judgment, had a right to settle with the plaintiff, and was not bound to take care of the interests of the attorney, though knowing that the attorney relied upon the fruits of the action as security for his services. The defendant owed no duty to the attorney, even so far as to inform him of the settlement, so as to save him from expending labor and money in preparing for a new trial.[3]

194. **The entry of a default does not constitute a perfected judgment,** and the parties may after that, and before an actual entry of judgment, make a *bonâ fide* settlement of the claim and costs of suit without reference to the attorney's fees. He has then no lien that can stand in the way of such a settlement.[4]

An order of court after verdict, that judgment be entered on

Clark, 5 Mass. 309; Brown v. Bigley, 3 Tenn. Ch. 618; Henchey v. Chicago, 41 Ill. 136; Mosely v. Norman, 74 Ala. 422. *Contra:* That an attorney's lien for compensation attaches to the cause of action. Keenan v. Dorflinger, 19 How. (N. Y.) Pr. 153.

In **New York,** since the Code of 1879, the lien attaches to the cause of action. So also in **Georgia** and in **Tennessee** the lien by statute dates from the commencement of the action. See §§ **173, 186, 190,** *supra.*

[1] Kirby v. Kirby, 1 Paige (N. Y.), 565.

[2] Pulver v. Harris, 52 N. Y. 73, per Grover, J. And see Henchey v. Chicago, *supra.*

[3] Pulver v. Harris, *supra,* affirming *S. C.* 62 Barb. 500.

[4] Hooper v. Welch, 43 Vt. 169.

the verdict, is deemed to be a judgment so far as to give the attorney his lien. Such order is a final determination of the case, and is the end of all litigation as to the merits of the case. The time when the judgment is entered up in form is immaterial.[1]

When exceptions are taken in the trial court, and these are overruled or sustained by the law court, the certificate of that court making a final disposition of the cause is the final judgment of the court, and the attorney's lien attaches when the certificate is received by the clerk of the court in which the suit is pending, and a subsequent settlement of the parties cannot be allowed to defeat it.[2]

Whether a final judgment has been rendered or not, depends upon the records of the court in which the trial was pending. Whether an appeal has been taken from the judgment must be shown from the records.[3]

When a judgment is nullified on a review, the attorney's lien for costs on such judgment is lost.[4]

195. While a suit is pending on a writ of error in the Supreme Court of the United States, the court will not prevent the parties from agreeing to dismiss the case, though in the court below there was a judgment for costs and the attorney claims a lien upon the judgment. To permit the attorney to control the proceedings, say the court, would, in effect, be compelling the client to carry on the litigation at his own expense, simply for the contingent benefit of the attorney.[5]

196. Therefore, until a judgment is entered, the client may settle or compromise the suit in any manner that he may think to be for his interest, without consulting his attorney; and the attorney has no right to interfere or power to prevent such settlement or compromise.[6] If, after such settlement, the attor-

---

[1] Young v. Dearborn, 27 N. H. 324.
[2] Cooley v. Patterson, 52 Me. 472.
[3] Gammon v. Chandler, 30 Me. 152.
[4] Dunlap v. Burnham, 38 Me. 112.
[5] Platt v. Jerome, 19 How. 384.
[6] Chapman v. Haw, 1 Taunt. 341; Nelson v. Wilson, 6 Bing. 568; Clark v. Smith, 6 M. & G. 1051; Francis v. Webb, 7 C. B. 731; Brunsdon v. Al-lard, 2 E. & E. 17; Emma Silver Mining Co. (limited) v. Emma Silver Mining Co. 12 Fed. Rep. 815; Peterson v. Watson, 1 Blatchf. & H. 487; Brooks v. Snell, 1 Sprague, 48; Purcell v. Lincoln, Ib. 230; Getchell v. Clark, 5 Mass. 309; Simmons v. Almy, 103 Mass. 33; Grant v. Hazeltine, 2 N. H. 541; Young v. Dear-

ney proceeds to enforce judgment, this will be set aside as irregular.[1]

Under statutes which give an attorney a lien upon the judgment and execution for his fees and disbursements in obtaining the same, he has no lien before judgment, for the lien is one that is expressly created upon the judgment and execution. Before judgment the client may settle the action and discharge the debtor without the consent of the attorney;[2] or the client may at any time before the entry of judgment assign his interest in the cause of action, and thus defeat the lien of the attorney.[3]

197. An action for unliquidated damages may always be settled by the parties, against the assent of the attorney, in the absence of a statute protecting him from the beginning of the litigation.[4] Thus, where a person having a claim against a railroad company, for damages resulting from negligence, agreed with an attorney that he should have half the amount that might be recovered for his services in prosecuting the suit, and while the suit was pending settled with the defendant and gave a release, it was held that the release was a bar to the further prosecution of the action, though the defendant had notice of the attorney's interest in the claim.[5] If the attorney has omitted to protect himself by giving notice of his lien, and the parties compromise before judgment, and with notice of such settlement he proceeds with the suit for his costs, he must show that the

born, 27 N. H. 324; Lamont v. Railroad Co. 2 Mack. (D. C.) 502; S. C. 47 Am. Rep. 268; Foote v. Tewksbury, 2 Vt. 97; Hutchinson v. Pettes, 18 Vt. 614; Tillman v. Reynolds, 48 Ala. 365; Parker v. Blighton, 32 Mich. 266; Swanston v. Morning Star Mining Co. 4 McCrary, 241; S. C. 13 Fed. Rep. 215; Wood v. Anders, 5 Bush (Ky.), 601; Connor v. Boyd, 73 Ala. 385. **New York**: Power v. Kent, 1 Cow. 172; McDowell v. Second Av. R. R. Co. 4 Bosw. 670; Shank v. Shoemaker, 18 N. Y, 489; Wade v. Orton, 12 Abb. Pr. (N. S.) 444; Coughlin v. N. Y. Cent. & Hud. Riv. R. R. Co. 71 N. Y. 443; Pulver v. Harris, 52 N. Y. 73; Wright v. Wright, 70 N. Y. 96; Roberts v. Doty, 31 Hun, 128; Reynolds v. Port Jervis Boot & Shoe Factory, 32 Ib. 64; Eberhardt v. Schuster, 10 Abb. (N. C.) 374, 391, note; otherwise since 1879.

[1] McDowell v. Second Av. R. R. Co. supra; Pinder v. Morris, 3 Caines (N. Y.), 165. See, however, Rasquin v. Knickerbocker Stage Co. 21 How. Pr. (N. Y.) 292.

[2] Simmons v. Almy, 103 Mass. 33; Getchell v. Clark, 5 Mass. 309; Coughlin v. N. Y. Cent. & Hud. Riv. R. R. Co. supra; Hawkins v. Loyless, 39 Ga. 5.

[3] Potter v. Mayo, 3 Me. 34.

[4] Kusterer v. City of Beaver Dam (Wis.) 14 N. W. Rep. 617.

[5] Coughlin v. N. Y. C. & Hud. Riv. R. R. Co. 71 N. Y. 443.

adverse party made the settlement collusively, with the design of defeating the attorney's demand for his costs or fees; and, failing to show this, his proceedings will be set aside.[1]

198. Where by statute the lien is upon the cause of action and attaches from the commencement of the suit, as is now the case in New York,[2] Georgia,[3] and Tennessee,[4] no settlement or compromise can be made between the parties which will affect the attorney's lien, unless made with his consent or by leave of court. The attorney may proceed with the action to final judgment. And, according to the practice in New York, he may do this without obtaining leave of court.[5]

But if the action be for unliquidated damages, such, for instance, as an action for personal injuries, the lien can hardly attach until it has been established by verdict, when it becomes for the first time certain and vested. Thus, in an action for damages arising from assault and battery, the plaintiff will be allowed to discontinue the action against the objection of his attorney who insists that the suit shall go on, so that he may get his taxable costs in case a recovery is had.[6]

And so where a lien is given upon a cause of action from the time of giving notice of it to the adverse party, there can be no lien before judgment upon a cause of action for tort which, in case of the death of the parties or of either of them, would not survive.[7]

Where the attorney has a lien upon the cause of action, a settlement made in good faith by the parties will not be set aside at the instance of the plaintiff's attorney, where it appears that the sum agreed to be paid to his client exceeds the amount necessary to satisfy his lien, and especially where the defendant has offered to pay this amount directly to the attorney.[8]

199. When an attorney withdraws from a case of his own motion before judgment, the court will impress no lien in his favor on any ultimate recovery, as a condition to the substitu-

[1] McDonald v. Second Av. R. R. Co. 4 Bosw. (N. Y.) 670.

[2] § 186, supra.

[3] § 173, supra.

[4] § 190, supra.

[5] Fortsman v. Schulting, 35 Hun, 504; Lewis v. Day, 10 Weekly Dig.

49; Coster v. Greenpoint Ferry Co. 5 N. Y. Civ. Pro. 146.

[6] Cahill v. Cahill, 9 N. Y. Civ. Pro. 241; Ward v. Orton, 12 Abb. (N.Y.) Pr. N. S. 444.

[7] Abbott v. Abbott, 18 Neb. 503.

[8] In re Tuttle, 21 Weekly Dig. 528.

tion of other attorneys, unless a special reason is shown for this.[1]

200. Only the attorney who is in charge of the suit at the time the judgment is entered is entitled to this lien ;[2] though of course a former attorney may be given a lien by special agreement between him and his client.[3]   Counsel employed to assist an attorney in the trial of a cause have no lien for their services upon the judgment recovered.[4]

Where the original attorney holds an irrevocable power of attorney coupled with an interest in the claim, in case a new attorney is substituted by motion of the party, the former attorney has rights which the court will protect.   Thus the United States Court of Claims held in such a case that, where an attorney's fees are fixed by statute, a substitution will not be ordered until the original attorney's fees are ascertained and paid. Where the attorney's fee is contingent, the court will assure him of a lien upon the ultimate judgment, and secure his immediate reimbursement of the expenses that have been incurred.[5]

201. This lien may be availed of by an agent who is not an attorney at law, if he renders services of the same character as those rendered by an attorney at law.   Thus, where one who was not an attorney was employed to prosecute a claim against the government, under a stipulation that he should receive for his services one half of the amount that might be recovered, and he employed attorneys and controlled the suit, and after many years recovered a judgment for a large sum, it was held that the plaintiff was not entitled to vacate the appearance of the agent's attorney, and to substitute his own attorney, without paying to the agent or his representative one half of the amount of the judgment, in accordance with the agreement.[6]

---

[1] Hektograph Co. v. Fourl, 11 Fed. Rep. 844.

[2] Wells v. Hatch, 43 N. H. 246.

[3] *In re* Wilson, 12 Fed. Rep. 235 ; Ronald v. Mut. Reserve Fund Life Asso. 30 Fed. Rep. 228.

[4] Brown v. New York, 9 Hun (N. Y.), 587 ; *S. C.* 11 Ib. 21.

[5] Carver v. United States, 7 Ct. Cl. 499.   In this case it was ordered that

the original attorney have and retain a lien upon the cause of action, and papers and effects of the client, and upon the judgment, for his contingent fees and costs.

To like effect, see Supervisors of Ulster County v. Brodhead, 44 How. (N. Y.) Pr. 411; *S. C.* Ib. 426.

[6] Dodge v. Schell, 20 Blatchf. 517; *S. C.* 10 Abb. (N. Y.) N. C. 465; *S. C.*

A party to a suit prosecuted for himself, and others having a like interest, is entitled to a lien for his reasonable costs, counsel fees, charges, and expenses incurred in the proper prosecution of the suit, and such lien may be enforced against the trust funds brought under the control of the court by the suit so instituted.[1]

202. No lien exists upon a judgment rendered in a court not of record for services performed in such court in obtaining the judgment. In such courts there are no attorneys, in the sense in which the term is used in courts of record; and it is said to be only in respect of the office of attorney or solicitor that the lien exists. Besides, courts not of record possess only limited jurisdiction, and have no such equitable control over their judgments as will enable them to adjudicate upon and enforce liens thereon.[2] Therefore no lien exists for services rendered by an attorney in a justice's court, nor in a probate court;[3] nor was there such a lien for services rendered in the Surrogate's Court of New York, before that court was made by statute a court of record;[4] and whether there is since that statute, seems to be a disputed question.

The attorney's lien extends to an award of arbitrators.[5]

---

12 Fed. Rep. 515. Wallace, J., said : "If the agent had been an attorney, the agreement and services would have created a lien. There is no magic in the name 'attorney' which conjures up a lien. It is the nature of the services, and the control, actual or potential, which the mechanical or professional laborer has over the object intrusted to him, which determines whether a lien is or is not conferred."

[1] Trustees v. Greenough, 105 U. S. 527; Central R. R. Co. v. Pettus, 113 U. S. 116.

[2] Flint v. Van Dusen, 26 Hun (N. Y.), 606; Fox v. Jackson, 8 Barb. (N. Y.) 355; Read v. Joselyn, 1 Sheld. (N. Y.) 60; Eisner v. Avery, 2 Dem. (N. Y.) 466. See In re Halsey, 13 Abb. (N. Y.) N. C. 116. See, however, § 201.

[3] McCaa v. Grant, 43 Ala. 262.

[4] Flint v. Van Dusen, 26 Hun (N. Y.) 606. Such a lien was said to exist in Eisner v. Avery, 2 Dem. (N. Y.) 466. But in a later case it was held that § 66 of the Code of Civil Procedure, as amended in 1879, does not apply to surrogates' courts, because in these tribunals actions are unknown. The lien established under that clause of the code is for services of the attorney in an action, and is confined to actions for the recovery of money, or actions wherein a demand for money is asserted by way of counter-claim. The surrogates' courts have no jurisdiction to try and determine such a cause. Smith v. Central Trust Co. 4 Dem. 75.

[5] Hutchinson v. Howard, 15 Vt. 544. See § 142.

V. *Settlement of the Suit by the Parties before Judgment, in Fraud of the Attorney.*

203. But a settlement made by the parties before judgment, in fraud of the attorney's rights, and with the intention to cheat him out of his costs, would be set aside so as to allow the suit to proceed for the purpose of collecting his costs.[1] Slight circumstances are often regarded as competent proof of collusion, — as that the party has a good cause of action for a larger sum than that received in settlement, and is irresponsible and unable to satisfy his attorney's costs ; or that there is an appearance of concealment in the settlement. But generally suspicious circumstances alone are not enough to authorize the court to interfere for the attorney's protection. There must be something to show

[1] Swain *v.* Senate, 5 Bos. & Pul. 99; Cole *v.* Bennett, 6 Price, 15; Morse *v.* Cooke, 13 Price, 473; Brunsdon *v.* Allard, 2 E. & E. 19. **New York :** Talcott *v.* Bronson, 4 Paige, 501; Tullis *v.* Bushnell, 65 How. Pr. 465 ; Rasquin *v.* Knickerbocker Stage Co. 12 Abb. Pr. 324; *S. C.* 21 How. Pr. 293; Sweet *v.* Bartlett, 4 Sandf. 661 ; Dimick *v.* Cooley, 3 N. Y. Civ. Proc. Rep. 141; Zogbaum *v.* Parker, 66 Barb. 341; Dietz *v.* McCallum, 44 How. Pr. 493 ; Keenan *v.* Dorflinger, 19 Ib. 153 ; Owen *v.* Mason, 18 Ib. 156. **Other States :** McDonald *v.* Napier, 14 Ga. 89; Jones *v.* Morgan, 39 Ga. 310 ; The Victory, Blatch. & H. 443, per Betts, J.; Hutchinson *v.* Pettes, 18 Vt. 614; Parker *v.* Blighton, 32 Mich. 266; *Ex parte* Lehman, 59 Ala. 631 ; Jackson *v.* Clopton, 66 Ala. 29 ; Mosely *v.* Norman, 74 Ala. 422.

In Coughlin *v.* N. Y. Cent. & Hud. Riv. R. R. Co. 71 N. Y. 443, 448, Earl, J., said : " There are many cases where this has been allowed to be done. It is impossible to ascertain precisely when this practice commenced, nor how it originated, nor upon what principle it was based. It was not upon the principle of a lien, because

an attorney has no lien upon the cause of action, before judgment, for his costs ; nor was it upon the principle that his services had produced the money paid his client upon the settlement, because that could not be known, and in fact no money may have been paid upon the settlement. So far as I can perceive, it was based upon no principle. It was a mere arbitrary exercise of power by the courts ; not arbitrary in the sense that it was unjust or improper, but in the sense that it was not based upon any right or principle recognized in other cases. The parties being in court, and a suit commenced and pending, for the purpose of protecting attorneys who were their officers and subject to their control, the courts invented this practice and assumed this extraordinary power to defeat attempts to cheat the attorneys out of their costs. The attorneys' fees were fixed and definite sums, easily determined by taxation, and this power was exercised to secure them their fees."

Under the present Code of **New York,** the attorney has complete protection from the beginning of the action. **§ 185.**

that the judgment debtor fraudulently colluded with the judgment creditor to defeat the attorney's lien.[1]

The mere fact that the parties to a suit make a settlement after verdict, but before entry of judgment and pending a stay of proceedings, is not conclusive that the parties acted collusively to defraud the attorney of his rights. Something more must be shown.[2] Baron Parke on this point justly said:[3] "It is quite competent to parties to settle actions behind the backs of the attorneys, for it is the client's action and not the attorney's. It must be shown affirmatively that the settlement was effected with the view of cheating the attorney of his costs." The burden of proving collusion or bad faith in the settlement rests with the attorney.

204. **Even after judgment, if the debtor acts in collusion with his creditor and pays him,** with the intention of cheating the attorney out of his lien, the debtor is not protected in making such payment, though he has received no actual notice of the lien.[4] If notice of the attorney's lien has been given to the adverse party, and the latter disregards the notice and pays the judgment, or compromises it with the client, such adverse party is liable to the attorney for the amount of his lien.[5]

A settlement of a judgment in an action for damages for a personal injury, effected by the defendant's attorney with the plaintiff, a married woman, without notice to her counsel, may be set aside as fraudulent and not binding, even without placing it upon the ground that the plaintiff's attorney has a lien for his fees, and that the settlement was made in fraud of his rights.[6]

[1] Francis v. Webb, 7 C. B. 731; Clark v. Smith, 6 M. & G. 1051; Nelson v. Wilson, 6 Bing. 568.

[2] Wright v. Burroughes, 3 C. B. 344; Frances v. Webb, 7 Ib. 731; Nelson v. Wilson, *supra;* Jones v. Bonner, 2 Exch. 230; Wade v. Orton, 12 Abb. Pr. (N. Y.) N. S. 444.

[3] Jordan v. Hunt, 3 Dowl. P. C. 666.

[4] Heartt v. Chipman, 2 Aik. (Vt.) 162; Heister v. Mount, 17 N. J. L. 438; Howard v. Osceola, 22 Wis. 453; Rasquin v. Knickerbocker Stage Co. 12 Abb. Pr. (N. Y.) 324; *S. C.* 21 How. Pr. 293.

[5] **New Jersey** : Barnes v. Taylor, 30 N. J. Eq. 467; Heister v. Mount, 17 N. J. L. 438; Braden v. Ward, 42 N. J. L. 518. In this state the attorney's right of lien exists only where he has received the money upon the judgment, or has arrested it *in transitu,* or where the defendant has paid the money after receiving notice of the attorney's lien. Braden v. Ward, *supra;* Campbell v. Terney, 7 N. J. L. J. 189.

[6] Voell v. Kelly (Wis.), 25 N. W. Rep. 536.

But even as regards a settlement before judgment without the attorney's consent, the courts so far take notice of and regard the equitable claim of the attorney to be paid for his services in the case, that, wherever the party is obliged to ask the aid of the court to enforce or carry into effect his settlement, the court will refuse its assistance if any want of good faith to the attorney be discovered in the transaction.[1] The fact that there was no consideration, or no adequate consideration, for the settlement and discharge of the suit, is evidence of bad faith.[2]

205. **A court of admiralty will not allow an out-door settlement of a suit by a seaman for wages,** made without the concurrence of his proctor, to bar his claim for costs. Notwithstanding the settlement, the court will retain the suit and allow the proctor to proceed for costs.[3] The court will consider a settlement so made, unless explained, to have been made for the purpose of depriving the proctor of his costs. Collusion to defeat the lien of an attorney is at law a ground for avoiding a settlement so far as the attorney is concerned. But a court of admiralty proceeds upon a broader principle in protecting the proctor. Costs are treated as his distinct and exclusive right, although nominally granted to the party. They are, moreover, granted or denied, according to the merits and equities of the party in relation to the subject-matter of the litigation. Accordingly, where a suit for wages had almost reached a hearing, and the proctor had incurred large expenses, when the libellant made a secret settlement and gave a release in full, and it appeared that he had a good cause of action for more than the amount paid in settlement, the court protected the proctor, and decreed the payment of costs to him, notwithstanding the settlement.[4]

In suits for personal torts, settlements made by seamen in the absence of the proctor are allowed when deliberately made for a consideration not shown to be inadequate, and the proctor is tendered his costs. The latter will not be allowed to proceed

[1] Young v. Dearborn, 27 N. H. 324.

[2] Young v. Dearborn, *supra*.

[3] Brig Planet, 1 Sprague, 11; Collins v. Nickerson, Ib. 126; Angell v. Bennett, Ib. 85; The Victory, Blatch. & H. 443 ; The Sarah Jane, Ib. 401; Collins v. Hathaway, Olc. 176; Ship Cabot, Newb. Adm. 348 ; Trask v. The Dido, 1 Haz. Pa. Reg. 9; Gaines v. Travis, Abb. Adm. 297.

[4] The Victory, Blatch. & H. 443.

with the suit merely because he objects to the settlement.[1] And even though the proctor is not protected in the settlement, if this be made in good faith, and the situation of the respondent was such that there was more danger of undue influence upon him than upon the libellant, the proctor will not be allowed to proceed with the suit to recover his costs.[2] In a suit for a tort the respondent is not bound to regard the costs of the libellant's proctor in the light of a lien on him or on any funds under his control; because no costs could exist until damages had been decreed against the respondent, and because a recovery in such a suit does not conclusively carry costs as an incident in admiralty.[3]

VI. *Lien upon the Cause of Action by Agreement or Assignment.*

206. Unless the cause of action be assignable in its nature, the client cannot give his attorney any lien upon it, which will prevent a settlement by the parties, even by agreement.[4] Although in such case there be a definite agreement for a lien in which the amount of the fees is fixed, and the defendant is notified of this at the commencement of the action, the attorney can have no lien before judgment is rendered. A claim against a town for personal injuries caused by a defective sidewalk is not an assignable cause of action, and, therefore, an agreement by the plaintiff to give his attorney for his fees half of the amount that he might recover in the action, creates no lien upon the cause of action, and does not prevent the defendant from making a settlement with the plaintiff and paying him a sum of money for a release and discontinuance of the action

[1] Brooks v. Snell, 1 Sprague, 48.
[2] Purcell v. Lincoln, Ib. 230; Peterson v. Watson, Blatch. & H. 487.
[3] Peterson v. Watson, *supra*.
[4] Swanston v. Morning Star Mining Co. 13 Fed. Rep. 215; *S. C.* 14 Rep. 321.
New York: Coughlin v. N. Y. Cent. & Hud. Riv. R. R. Co. 71 N. Y. 443 (reversing *S. C.* 8 Hun, 136); Eberhardt v. Schuster, 10 Abb. N. C. 374, 391, note; McBratney v. R. W. & O. R. R. Co. 17 Hun, 385; *S. C.* 87 N. Y. 467; Sullivan v. O'Keefe, 53

How. Pr. 426; Brooks v. Hanford, 15 Abb. Pr. 342; Quincey v. Francis, 5 Abb. N. C. 286; Pulver v. Harris, 52 N. Y. 73 (affirming *S. C.* 62 Barb. 500); Wright v. Wright, 70 N. Y. 96 (affirming 9 J. & S. 432).
Otherwise by statute since 1879. See § 185.
Wisconsin: Voell v. Kelly, 25 N. W. Rep. 536, per Cole, C. J.; Kusterer v. City of Beaver Dam, 56 Wis. 471; *S. C.* 43 Am. Rep. 725; 14 N. W. Rep. 617.

against the attorney's protest. The attorney had no vested interest in the claim, and no lien even for his taxable costs.[1]

Where, in an action to recover land which the plaintiff claimed was held under fraudulent sales and transfers, the plaintiff entered into an agreement with his attorney whereby he was to receive for his services a part of the property that might be recovered in the action, and, pending the litigation, the plaintiff settled with the defendant, it was held that the attorney, who had taken no steps to perfect a lien in accordance with the statute, could not intervene to continue the suit by virtue of the contract.[2]

207. An action for slander or libel, or for assault and battery, is not assignable ; and the attorney can have no lien on the cause of action before judgment. Though the client promised the attorney before the suit was begun that he should receive for his services the damages that might be recovered, the client may discontinue the suit at any time before judgment without the attorney's consent.[3] Even under the new Code of New York, the attorney's lien does not attach so as to prevent a discontinuance of the action without costs when the plaintiff has forgiven the defendant, and the parties want the further prosecution of the action stopped.[4] Whenever the cause of action is for tort, and would not survive the death of either of the parties, the attorney is not entitled to a lien upon it.[5]

In like manner a cause of action for personal injuries, incurred through the negligence of a person or corporation, is not assignable in its nature, and does not survive a settlement by the parties before judgment without consent of the attorney.[6]

208. Where, however, the action is founded upon a negotiable instrument, or a contract in writing, which is in the attorney's possession, his lien attaches to the contract before judgment, and his client can make no settlement or assignment

---

[1] Kusterer v. City of Beaver Dam, 56 Wis. 471.

[2] Lavender v. Atkins (Neb.), 29 N. W. Rep. 467.

[3] Quincey v. Francis, 5 Abb. (N. Y.) N. C. 286 ; Miller v. Newell, 20 S. C. 123 ; S. C. 47 Am. Rep. 833; Cahill v. Cahill, 9 N. Y. Civ. Pro. 241.

New York : Pulver v. Harris, 62 Barb. 500 ; affirmed 52 N. Y. 73.

[4] Cahill v. Cahill, 9 Civ. Pro. 241.

[5] Abbott v. Abbott, 26 (Neb.) N. W. Rep. 361.

[6] Kusterer v. City of Beaver Dam, supra.

of the action without discharging his attorney's fees.[1]   The lien
in such case attaches from the time the contract is delivered
to the attorney and he commences the action.   In such case the
lien attaches not only for his attorney's services rendered in that
suit, but also for his general account for professional services
rendered the client.   The settlement or assignment is subject
to the attorney's general lien.[2]   In such case, also, the rule that
a *bonâ fide* settlement, payment, or assignment of the cause of
action made before judgment, without notice of the attorney's
lien, prevails against the lien, has no application ; neither has
the rule that the attorney's lien upon a judgment yields to the
right of set-off of the opposite party.[3]

The attorney may be in effect an assignee of the judgment by
virtue of the law that gives him a lien upon it, so that his lien
will be effectual though he does not hold the contracts upon
which the judgment is based.   Thus, in a suit against a corporation to enforce payment of debts, if the attorney succeeds in
bringing a fund under the control of the court for the common
benefit of a class of creditors, he is entitled to reasonable costs
and counsel fees out of the fund, both as regards the claim of the
complainants who employed him, and as regards other creditors
who come in and secure the benefit of the proceedings.   If after
decree and pending the proof of claims, the corporation buys
up all the claims, the attorney's lien upon the fund is not defeated ;[4] provided the law of the state where the suit was pending entitles the attorney to a lien upon the decree, in such manner that he is regarded as an assignee of the decree to the extent
of his fees.   The right of the attorney in such case is superior
to any which the defendant corporation could acquire subsequent
to the decree, by the purchase of the claims of the creditors.[5]

VII. *When the Attorney is required to give Notice of his Lien
to the Judgment Debtor.*

209. Where the judgment is for damages as well as for
costs, the attorney should give notice of his lien to the judg-

[1] Coughlin *v.* N. Y. Cent. & Hud.
R. R. Co. 71 N. Y. 443, 449, per Earl,
J.; Courtney *v.* McGavock, 23 Wis.
619, 622; Kusterer *v.* City of Beaver
Dam, 56 Wis. 471; Howard *v.* Osceola,
22 Wis. 453; Dennett *v.* Cutts, 11 N.
H. 163.

[2] Schwartz *v.* Schwartz, 21 Hun
(N. Y.), 33.

[3] Schwartz *v.* Schwartz, *supra.*

[4] Trustees *v.* Greenough, 105 U. S.
527; Central Railroad *v.* Pettus, 113
U. S. 116.

[5] Central Railroad *v.* Pettus, *supra.*

ment debtor; otherwise he will not be protected against a settlement of the judgment with his client.[1] But the notice affords such protection, so that, if the debtor afterwards pays the judgment, he does so in his own wrong; for the attorney may proceed with the execution against the debtor, and enforce payment of it to the extent of his fees and disbursements.

210. **In several states there are statutory provisions in regard to giving notice of the lien.** Thus in Georgia the lien continues if the attorney files a claim of lien upon the property recovered within thirty days after the recovery. In Indiana the attorney has a lien on the judgment if he enters in writing upon the docket or records, at the time such judgment is rendered, his intention to claim a lien. In Iowa and Dakota Territory the lien attaches during the pendency of the suit, if the attorney gives notice of his claim to the adverse party. It attaches from the time of such notice. After judgment the notice may be given by entry in the judgment docket. In Kansas, also, the lien exists from the time of giving notice of the lien to the adverse party. In Minnesota and Oregon the lien exists from the time of giving notice of the lien to the adverse party. After judgment the lien exists in Minnesota from the time of giving notice to the judgment debtor; and in Oregon from the time of filing notice with the clerk where the judgment is entered. In Montana Territory the lien attaches from the commencement of the suit; but after judgment notice must be filed within

---

[1] Welsh v. Hole, 1 Doug. 238, per Lord Mansfield; Read v. Dupper, 6 T. R. 361; Mitchell v. Oldfield, 4 T. R. 123.

New York: Pulver v. Harris, 52 N. Y. 73; Marshall v. Meech, 51 N. Y. 140; Crotty v. Mackenzie, 52 How. Pr. 54; Owen v. Mason, 18 Ib. 156; Ackerman v. Ackerman, 14 Abb. Pr. 229; Bishop v. Garcia, 14 Abb. Pr. (N. S.) 69, 72; Lesher v. Roessner, 3 Hun, 217; Martin v. Hawks, 15 Johns. 405; St. John v. Diefendorf, 12 Wend. 261; Carpenter v. Sixth Av. R. R. Co. 1 Am. L. Reg. (N. S.) 410; Nicoll v. Nicoll, 16 Wend. 446; Pinder v. Morris, 3 Caines, 165; Power v. Kent, 1 Cow. 172; Ten Broeck v.

De Witt, 10 Wend. 617; Pearl v. Robitchek, 2 Daly, 138.

Georgia: Gray v. Lawson, 36 Ga. 629; Hawkins v. Loyless, 39 Ga. 5.

Vermont: Heartt v. Chipman, 2 Aik. 162; Hooper v. Welch, 43 Vt. 169.

Wisconsin: Courtney v. McGavock, 23 Wis. 619; Voell v. Kelly (Wis.), 25 N. W. Rep. 536, per Cole, C. J.

Other States: Andrews v. Morse, 12 Conn. 444; Barnes v. Taylor, 30 N. J. Eq. 467; Young v. Dearborn, 27 N. H. 324; Boston & Colorado Smelting Co. v. Pless (Col.), 10 Pac. Rep. 652.

three days in the office of the clerk in which the judgment is obtained. In Nebraska and Wyoming Territory, if any lien exists, it is from the time of filing notice of it with the adverse party.

In New York, under the present code, the lien exists from the commencement of the suit, and no notice of the lien need be given.[1] But notice of the lien is necessary where no lien is expressly given by statute.[2] In Tennessee, also, the lien dates from the commencement of the suit, the pending of which is of itself notice of the lien.

Where by statute the lien exists from the time of giving notice of it, the parties, acting in good faith, may make a valid settlement at any time before the notice is given in the manner prescribed.[3]

211. The notice should be given to the adverse party personally and not to his attorney. It would be inequitable to require a party to pay a judgment, or any part of it, a second time, when it appears that he has never received notice of any lien upon it, though such notice may have been given to his attorney.[4]

But notice to the attorney of record, or to the attorney in fact, may often be sufficient.[5] Where, however, one member of a law firm in a particular matter is individually the attorney of the party, and the other members have nothing to do with the case, a notice of an attorney's lien served upon either of the other members of the firm is not notice to the attorney actually engaged in the case, so as to bind him or his client.[6]

The placing of a paper upon the files of the court in which the judgment was rendered is not notice to the judgment debtor, in the absence of a statute making it so. If, without knowledge of such paper or other notice of the attorney's lien upon the judg-

[1] Coster v. Greenport Ferry Co. 5 Civ. Pro. 146; Dimick v. Cooley, 3 Ib. 141; Kehoe v. Miller, 10 Abb. N. C. 393; Tullis v. Bushnell, 65 How. Pr. 465; Albert Palmer Co. v. Van Orden, 64 How. Pr. 79; S. C. 4 Civ. Pro. 44. See, however, Jenkins v. Adams, 22 Hun, 600.

[2] Lablache v. Kirkpatrick, 8 N. Y. Civ. Pro. Rep. 256.

[3] Casar v. Sargeant, 7 Iowa, 317; Hawkins v. Loyless, 39 Ga. 5; Green v. Southern Express Co. 39 Ga. 20.

[4] Wright v. Wright, 7 Daly (N. Y.), 62; S. C. 70 N. Y. 96.

[5] Kansas Pacific Ry. Co. v. Thacher, 17 Kans. 92.

[6] St. Louis & San Francisco Ry. Co. v. Bennett, 35 Kans. 395; S. C. 11 Pac. Rep. 155.

ment, the debtor makes a *bonâ fide* settlement of the judgment with the creditor, by payment or otherwise, the attorney cannot look to the debtor for his unpaid fees.[1]

212. But actual notice of the attorney's claim to a lien is not in all cases necessary for the protection of his rights. If the judgment debtor acts in the face of circumstances which are sufficient to put him upon inquiry, he acts contrary to good faith, and at his peril; and a discharge of the judgment under such circumstances is, as to the attorney, void in the same manner as it would be after an actual notice of his claim to a lien.[2] But the mere fact that the attorney appears in a cause is not sufficient notice of his lien.[3]

Where a judgment debtor settled a judgment by offsetting claims against his creditor and agreeing to pay the costs of the plaintiff's attorney, it was held that the terms of the agreement imparted to the debtor notice of the attorney's lien and of the amount of it.[4]

213. An attorney has no lien upon the damages recovered in a suit before the money comes into his hands, although his demands against his client equal or exceed the amount of judgment. He has a lien for his costs out of a judgment for damages and costs; but he may lose this if he does not give notice to the judgment debtor before the latter discharges the judgment by payment to the plaintiff.[5]

214. When the judgment is for costs only, this is of itself a legal notice of the lien, which can be discharged only by payment to the attorney.[6] The judgment debtor pays such a judg-

---

[1] Boston & Colo. Smelting Co. v. Pless (Colo.), 10 Pac. Rep. 652; Wright v. Wright, 7 Daly (N. Y.), 62; *S. C.* 70 N. Y. 96.

[2] Abel v. Potts, 3 Esp. Cas. 242; Currier v. Boston & Me. R. R. Co. 37 N. H. 223; Young v. Dearborn, 27 Ib. 324; Sexton v. Pike, 13 Ark. 193.

Vermont: Weed v. Boutelle, 56 Vt. 570, 581; Lake v. Ingham, 3 Vt. 158; Hooper v. Welch, 43 Vt. 169, per Wilson, J.

New York: Wilkins v. Batterman, 4 Barb. 47; Martin v. Hawks, 15 Johns. 405; Ten Broeck v. De Witt, 10 Wend. 617.

[3] Gray v. Lawson, 36 Ga. 629.

[4] Hall v. Ayer, 19 How. (N. Y.) Pr. 91.

[5] St. John v. Diefendorf, 12 Wend. (N. Y.) 261.

[6] **New York**: Marshal v. Meech, 51 N. Y. 140; McGregor v. Comstock, 28 N. Y. 237, 240; Wilkins v. Batterman, 4 Barb. 48; Haight v. Holcomb,

ment to the creditor at his peril. His payment is equivalent to paying the assignor a debt which has been assigned after notice of the assignment.

Where a judgment was recovered for six cents damage and costs, and the plaintiff's attorney gave notice of his lien, and the sheriff to whom the execution was committed arrested the defendant, and afterwards voluntarily permitted his escape, the attorney was allowed to sue the sheriff in the name of his client; and the sheriff was not allowed to avail himself of a release afterwards obtained from the client, for this was a fraud upon the attorney.[1]

VIII. *Whether the Attorney's Lien is subject to a Right of Set-off in the Judgment Debtor.*

215. The rule in the Court of the King's Bench was that no set-off should be allowed to the prejudice of the attorney's lien for his costs.[2] The Courts of Common Pleas, however, did not follow the King's Bench in this practice, but allowed a set-off in all such cases, upon the ground that the lien of the attorney was subject to, and must give way to, the equitable rights of the parties.[3] The two courts thus stood in conflict until the adoption

16 How. Pr. 173; Lesher *v.* Roessner, 3 Hun, 217; Naylor *v.* Lane, 66 How. Pr. 400; Martin *v.* Hawks, 15 Johns. 405; Kipp *v.* Rapp, 7 Civ. Pro. 385 ; Ennis *v.* Currie, 2 Month. L. Bul. 66.

Maine: Hobson *v.* Watson, 34 Me. 20; Newbert *v.* Cunningham, 50 Me. 231; McKenzie *v.* Wardwell, 61 Me. 136; Stratton *v.* Hussey, 62 Me. 286.

There are a few decisions that are inconsistent with the view that a judgment for costs only belongs absolutely to the attorney. Thus in People *v.* Hardenburgh, 8 Johns. (N. Y.) 335, it was held that such a judgment might be settled between the parties, if the debtor acts in good faith and without notice from the judgment creditor's attorney of his claim of a lien. And in the recent case of Horton *v.* Champlin, 12 R. I. 550, it was held that an attorney who had obtained a judgment for his client for costs only had no authority to bring a suit on the judgment without his client's consent and direction.

[1] Martin *v.* Hawks, 15 Johns. (N. Y.) 405.

[2] Mitchell *v.* Oldfield, 4 T. R. 123 (1791); Randle *v.* Fuller, 6 T. R. 456, 457; Smith *v.* Brocklesby, 1 Anstr. 61 ; Middleton *v.* Hill, 1 M. & S. 240 ; Stephens *v.* Weston, 3 B. & C. 535 ; Holroyd *v.* Breare, 4 B. & A. 43 ; Simpson *v.* Lamb, 7 E. & B. 84.

[3] Schoole *v.* Noble, 1 H. Bl. 23; Vaughan *v.* Davies, 2 H. Bl. 440; George *v.* Elston, 1 Scott, 518; Emdin *v.* Darley, 4 B. & P. 22.

In Hall *v.* Ody, 2 B. & P. 28, before the Common Pleas of England, in which the lien was declared to be subject to set-off, Lord Eldon, then recently appointed chief justice of that court, expressed his surprise that by the settled practice of that court the attorney, by whose diligence the

of the new rules in 1853,[1] when the rule of the King's Bench was made applicable to all the courts. Now, however, under the Judicature Acts of 1873, it seems that the equitable rule prevails.[2]

216. In Equity it seems to have been long established that a solicitor's lien is not to interfere with the equities between the parties. In a case before Lord Langdale, M. R., in 1838,[3] it was held that a solicitor's lien upon a balance due to his client could not extend beyond the amount of the true balance as ultimately ascertained, and that the court would not allow the lien to interfere with the equities between the parties. As before remarked, the rule in equity seems now to have become the rule of all the courts since the Judicature Act.[4]

But even in equity a judgment for costs alone is not subject to set-off by another judgment for costs in a different matter so as to interfere with the attorney's lien for his costs.[5] Thus, if a plaintiff in an action obtains a judgment for costs against the defendant, and in a different matter he becomes liable to pay costs to the defendant, neither the plaintiff nor the defendant can have the costs set off to the detriment of the attorney having a lien for his costs. But if the judgments for costs have been rendered in the same manner, they may be set off. The principle is declared to be that, where a solicitor is employed in a suit or action, he must be considered as having adopted the proceeding from the beginning to the end, and acted for better or worse. His client may obtain costs in some matters in the suit or action and not in others, and the solicitor takes his chance

---

fund had been recovered, was not entitled to take his costs out of it, in preference to the right of the opposite party to the set-off; and emphatically declared that it was in direct contradiction to the practice of every other court, as well as to the principles of justice; and he acquiesced in the decision in that case only because the attorney who claimed the lien had acted with the knowledge of the settled practices of that court, and therefore had no right to claim the advantages of a more just principle.

[1] General Rules of Hilary Term, 1853, Rule 63.

[2] § 24.

[3] Bawtree v. Watson, 2 Keen, 713. See, also, Cattell v. Simons, 6 Beav. 304; Verity v. Wylde, 4 Drew. 427; Roberts v. Buèe, L. R., 8 Ch. D. 198.

[4] Mercer v. Graves, L. R. 7 Q. B. 499; Brandan v. Allard, 2 E. & E. 17.

[5] Roberts v. Buèe, supra; Cattell v. Simons, supra; Collett v. Preston, 15 Beav. 458. Explained, however, in Roberts v. Buèe, supra.

and may ultimately enforce his lien for any balance which may appear to be in favor of his client.[1]

217. In this country the rule of the Court of Common Pleas in England has been followed in the greater number of states. The lien of an attorney upon a judgment is upon the interest of his client in the judgment, and is subject to an existing right of set-off in the other party to the suit.[2] In other words, an attorney can have a lien for an amount no greater than what is actually found to be owing by the opposite party to his client. It is subject to the equitable claims of the parties in the cause, as well as to the rights of third persons, which cannot be varied or affected by it.

218. When a defendant has a right by statute to set off a judgment in his favor against a judgment against him, the

---

[1] Roberts v. Buèe, L. R. 8 Ch. D. 198, per Hall, V. C.

[2] National Bank v. Eyre, 3 McCrary, 175 ; S. C. 8 Fed. Rep. 733; Shirts v. Irons, 54 Ind. 13 ; Renick v. Ludington, 16 W. Va. 378.

Connecticut : Gager v. Watson, 11 Conn. 168; Rumrill v. Huntington, 5 Day, 163 ; Andrews v. Morse, 12 Conn. 444; Benjamin v. Benjamin, 17 Conn. 110.

Kansas : Turner v. Crawford, 14 Kans. 499, 500, overruling Leavenson v. Lafontane, 3 Kans. 523.

New York : Mohawk Bank v. Burrows, 6 Johns. Ch. 317 ; Porter v. Lane, 8 Johns. 357 ; Nicoll v. Nicoll, 16 Wend. 446 ; People v. N. Y. Com. Pleas, 13 Wend. 649 ; Cragin v. Travis, 1 How. Pr. 157; Nixon v. Gregory, 5 Ib. 339 ; Brooks v. Hanford, 15 Abb. Pr. 342 ; Hayden v. McDermott, 9 Abb. Pr. 14; Martin v. Kanouse, 17 How. Pr. 146 ; Davidson v. Alfaro, 16 Hun, 353 ; Sanders v. Gillett, 8 Daly, 183.

The practice in New York has been to allow the set-off since Porter v. Lane, supra, was decided, in 1811. In some earlier cases, as in Devoy v.

Boyer, 3 Johns. 247, and Cole v. Grant, 2 Caines, 105, the lien of the attorney for his costs was not allowed to be affected by the set-off. In equity the doctrine of these cases was followed at a later day in Dunkin v. Vandenbergh, 1 Paige, 622, and Gridley v. Garrison, 4 Paige, 647.

A set-off as against the attorney's lien for costs was refused in Smith v. Lowden, 1 Sandf. 696 ; Gihon v. Fryat, 2 Ib. 638 ; Purchase v. Bellows, 16 Abb. Pr. 105.

Since the passage of the act of 1879, § 66, no set-off is allowed as against the attorney's lien. Naylor v. Lane, 66 How. Pr. 400 ; S. C. 18 J. & S. 97 ; Ennis v. Curry, 22 Hun, 584 ; S. C. 61 How. Pr. 1 ; Hovey v. Rubber Tip Pencil Co. 14 Abb. Pr. (N. S.) 66. See § 185.

Iowa : Hurst v. Sheets, 21 Iowa, 501 ; Tiffany v. Stewart, 60 Iowa, 207; Watson v. Smith, 63 Iowa, 228.

Alabama : Mosely v. Norman, 74 Ala. 422 ; Ex parte Lehman, 59 Ala. 631. The statute gives a legal right to set off one judgment against another. Code 1876, § 2993.

court, in order to protect the attorney's costs, will not interfere.[1] An attorney's lien upon a payment is not equivalent to an equitable assignment to him of the judgment debt,[2] or to an equitable interest in the proceeds of the judgment. The protection the courts afford to the attorney stops very far short of putting him in the position of *cestui que trust* to his client, so as to compel the client to act as his trustee in collecting the judgment.[3] The attorney cannot maintain a bill in equity in such a case against a judgment debtor to restrain him from exercising his own legal rights under a statute allowing a set-off.[4]

219. When set-off good against the attorney's lien. — But when the set-off is one which would have been a good defence to the action wherein the judgment was recovered, the judgment debtor has a right of set-off against the attorney's lien.[5]

It is clear that a set-off acquired after the judgment should not be allowed to prevail against the attorney's lien.[6]

Texas: Wright *v.* Treadwell, 14 Tex. 255.

Maryland : Levy *v.* Steinbach, 43 Md. 212 ; Marshall *v.* Cooper, 43 Md. 46.

Vermont : McDonald *v.* Smith, 57 Vt. 502; Walker *v.* Sargeant, 14 Vt. 247 ; Hooper *v.* Welch, 43 Vt. 169, per Wilson, J. ; Fairbanks *v.* Devereaux, 58 Vt. 359 ; *S. C.* 3 Atl. Rep. 500.

Wisconsin : Bosworth *v.* Tallman, 66 Wis. 533 ; *S. C.* 29 N. W. Rep. 542; Yorton *v.* Milwaukee, Lake Shore & W. Ry. Co. 62 Wis. 367 ; *S. C.* 21 N. W. Rep. 516; Gano *v.* Chicago & N. W. Ry. Co. 60 Wis. 12 ; *S. C.* 17 N. W. Rep. 15.

[1] Mercer *v.* Graves, L. R. 7 Q. B. 499 ; Brunsdon *v.* Allard, 2 E. & E. 17 ; *Ex parte* Lehman, 59 Ala. 631 ; Mosely *v.* Norman, 74 Ala. 422; Fairbanks *v.* Devereaux, *supra;* McDonald *v.* Smith, 57 Vt. 502. See Walker *v.* Sargeant, *supra.* Royce, J., said : " We recognize nothing in this particular species of lien, which ought, in a case like this, to be interposed against a salutary provision of statute

law. We think it clear that the lien here asserted should be held subordinate to the defendant's right of set-off." In Fairbanks *v.* Devereaux, *supra,* Ross, J., referring to that decision, said : " The principles then announced have remained the unquestioned law of the subject from the time of its rendition in 1842 to the present time."

[2] Brunsdon *v.* Allard, *supra,* per Campbell, C. J., Erle and Crompton, JJ.

[3] Mercer *v.* Graves, *supra,* per Blackburn, J.

[4] Mercer *v.* Graves, *supra,* per Lush, J.

[5] Robertson *v.* Shutt, 9 Bush (Ky.), 659 ; Calvert *v.* Coxe, 1 Gill (Md.), 95 ; Carter *v.* Bennett, 6 Fla. 214. In Nicoll *v.* Nicoll, 16 Wend. (N. Y.) 446, 449, Justice Cowen said that no authority could be produced where the attorney's lien was ever recognized on a trial at law as barring a set-off, the right to which would otherwise be perfect.

[6] Bradt *v.* Koon, 4 Cow. (N. Y.) 416 ; Warfield *v.* Campbell, 38 Ala.

220. In other states, however, the rule of the King's Bench is followed,[1] and it is held that an attorney's lien upon a judgment for his costs is not subject to a right of set-off in the adverse party; and when by statute he is given a right of lien for his fees, the same rule applies. His lien for costs is paramount to the right of the debtor to set off a judgment he holds against the judgment creditor. So strong is the equity of the attorney to claim and maintain his lien, that even a statute which requires the officer to set off executions, held by the parties against each other, is construed as containing an implied condition that this should not be done in derogation of the attorney's right to claim the judgment as his own, by way of a lien upon it, to the extent of his costs.

The right to set off one judgment against another, in the absence of a statutory provision, is one of equitable discretion, and will not be allowed where the just rights of another party, such as an assignee, would be disturbed; and the court will not allow such a set-off to the detriment of the claim of an attorney for his fees in obtaining a judgment where it appears to be right that his claim should be respected.[2]

In Maine[3] and Michigan[4] it is provided by statute that execu-

527; Rumrill v. Huntington, 5 Day (Conn.), 163.

[1] **New Hampshire**: Shapley v. Bellows, 4 N. H. 347; Currier v. Boston & Me. R. R. 37 N. H. 223.

Maine: Stratton v. Hussey, 62 Me. 286; Hooper v. Brundage, 22 Me. 460.

New York: Since the act of 1879, § 66. See § **185**; Turno v. Parks, 2 How. (N. Y.) Pr. N. S. 35; Hilton v. Sinsheimer, Daily Reg. March 27, 1885; Naylor v. Lane, 5 Civ. Pro. 149, 150; S. C. 66 How. Pr. 400; Davidson v. Alfaro, 80 N. Y. 660; In re Bailey, 4 N. Y. Civ. Pro. 140, 143. Contra, Sanders v. Gillette, 8 Daly, 123, 184, and Garner v. Gladwin, 12 Weekly Dig. 9, 10, criticised in Turno v. Parks, supra.

An attorney has a lien on motion costs in favor of his client which attaches the instant the costs are due. Costs arising upon an appeal from an

order are motion costs. Such costs are the property of the attorney, and are not subject to any offset in favor of the plaintiff. Place v. Hayward, 3 How. Pr. (N. S.) 59; S. C. 8 N. Y. Civ. Pro. 352. And see Tunstall v. Winton, 31 Hun, 219; affirmed 92 N. Y. 646; Marshall v. Meech, 51 N. Y. 140; In re Knapp, 85 N. Y. 284; Turno v. Parks, 2 How. (N. Y.) Pr. N. S. 35.

Indiana: Puett v. Beard, 86 Ind. 172; S. C. 44 Am. Rep. 280; Adams v. Lee, 82 Ind. 587; Johnson v. Ballard, 44 Ind. 270.

Other States: Dunklee v. Locke, 13 Mass. 525; Boyer v. Clark, 3 Neb. 161; Robertson v. Shutt, 9 Bush (Ky.), 659; Carter v. Davis, 8 Fla. 183.

[2] Diehl v. Friester, 37 Ohio St. 473.

[3] Rev. Stat. 1883, p. 725, § 28.

[4] Annotated Stats. 1882, § 7710.

tions shall not be set off against each other as to so much of the execution as is due to the attorney in the suit for his fees and disbursements therein.

221. Delay in objecting to a set-off allowed by court. When a set-off has been allowed by order of court, the attorney cannot after delay interfere at a subsequent term of court. Thus, where judgments in two actions between the same parties were by order of court set off against each other, the court refused, at a subsequent term and after the lapse of two years, to rescind the order upon the motion of the attorney of one of the parties, upon the ground that his lien was affected by it, for it was then too late; though the court could not have made the order had the objection been interposed at the time.[1]

IX. *Effect of an Assignment of the Judgment to the Attorney or to Another.*

222. But an assignment of a judgment by the judgment creditor to his attorney, in payment or security for his fees in the suit, is effectual to prevent a set-off against such judgment of another judgment previously recovered by the judgment debtor against the judgment creditor.[2] If an attorney undertakes the defence of a suit for an insolvent client in consideration that the costs that might be recovered should belong to him, and he recovers a judgment for costs and assigns this to the attorney, a judgment against the defendant cannot be set off against such judgment for costs. The attorney's claim in such case is not one of lien, but of ownership.[3] If the assignment be made before the right of set-off attaches, the assignment of course prevails.[4] If the assignment be made after a right of set-off given

And see Wells *v.* Elsam, 40 Mich. 218; Kinney *v.* Robinson (Mich.), 29 N. W. Rep. 86.

[1] Holt *v.* Quimby, 6 N. H. 79.

[2] Benjamin *v.* Benjamin, 17 Conn. 110; Rumrill *v.* Huntington, 5 Day (Conn.), 163; Rice *v.* Garnhart, 35 Wis. 282.

Otherwise in **Iowa** and **Vermont**, where it is held that the judgment in such case passes subject to the equities against it in the hands of the as-

signor. Tiffany *v.* Stewart, 60 Iowa, 207; Ballinger *v.* Tarbell, 16 Iowa, 491; Fairbanks *v.* Devereaux (Vt.), 3 Atl. Rep. 500.

[3] Ely *v.* Cook, 9 Abb. (N. Y.) Pr. 366; affirmed 28 N. Y. 365; Perry *v.* Chester, 53 N. Y. 240; Naylor *v.* Lane, 18 J. & S. (N. Y.) 97; Newberg *v.* Schwab, 17 Ib. 232.

[4] Firmenich *v.* Bovee, 4 T. & C. (N. Y.) 98.

by statute has accrued, then the statutory right of set-off is paramount to the attorney's right under the assignment.[1]

The assignee, however, should give notice to the judgment debtor of the assignment, for otherwise the latter may make a settlement with the judgment creditor which will discharge the judgment and destroy the lien under the assignment.[2]

An attorney's lien is merged in an assignment to him as security for his costs, and his only title or claim to the judgment after that arises from his title as owner.[3]

223. **Equitable assignment of the judgment.** — An agreement between an attorney and his client that the attorney shall have a lien for his services to a certain amount upon a judgment to be recovered, constitutes a valid equitable assignment of the judgment *pro tanto* which attaches to the judgment as soon as entered.[4] Such an agreement is within the principle that an agreement between a debtor and creditor that the creditor shall have a claim upon a specific fund for payment of his debt is a binding equitable assignment of the fund *pro tanto*. This is a settled rule in equity. Sometimes it has been objected that if such an assignment embraces only a part of the fund, it is not obligatóry on the debtor without his assent, because his single obligation cannot be split up into several without his consent. This objection prevails only at law, but does not affect the remedy in equity.[5]

The equity of the attorney under such an agreement is superior to the claim of the judgment debtor to set off against the judgment a judgment against the plaintiff, which the debtor had purchased after the entry of the judgment against himself, and before he had notice of the assignment. Failure to give notice of the assignment does not subject the assignee to merely equitable claims of the debtor, which do not attach to the debt itself, and which accrue to him after the assignment. A claim of set-

---

[1] Fairbanks *v.* Devereaux, 58 Vt. 359; *S. C.* 3 Atl. Rep. 500.

[2] Boston & Colorado Smelting Co. *v.* Pless (Colo.), 10 Pac. Rep. 652; Stoddard *v.* Benton, 6 Col. 508; Bishop *v.* Garcia, 14 Abb. (N. Y.) Pr. N. S. 69.

[3] Bishop *v.* Garcia, *supra;* Dodd *v.* Brott, 1 Minn. 270.

[4] Terney *v.* Wilson, 45 N. J. L. 282; Middlesex Freeholders *v.* State Bank, 38 N. J. Eq. 36; *S. C.* 19 Cent. L. J. 393; Ely *v.* Cook, 28 N. Y. 365; Williams *v.* Ingersoll, 89 N. Y. 508.

[5] See §§ 43–62.

off against a judgment arising from a subsequent purchase of a judgment against the judgment creditor, is not a set-off which attaches to the debt. A prior assignment, whether legal or equitable, of the judgment, prevents the right of set-off from attaching. The assignee's equity, being prior in time, is superior.[1]

224. Where a client agrees that his attorney shall have a paramount lien upon the claim in suit for his fees, charges, and disbursements, and to secure this agreement executes a power of attorney to a third person giving him the control of the suit, such power of attorney with the agreement operates to vest in the attorney an interest in the claim, of which he cannot be divested by the client of his own motion without satisfying his part of the agreement. It is the duty and practice of courts to protect attorneys in rights so acquired against the hostile acts of those from whom they are acquired.[2]

225. A lien upon a chose in action may be created by parol. Thus, an oral agreement by a client with his attorney that the latter should have a lien for all sums that the client might become entitled to from any of the suits or proceedings conducted by the attorney, which lien should be superior to any right the client might have, was held to operate as an equitable lien upon an award to the client as damages for a malicious prosecution.[3]

226. The lien of an attorney for his fees is, like any chose in action, assignable. It is incident to the judgment to which it is attached, and is necessarily as much assignable as is the judgment to which it is incident.[4]

An attorney's lien is superior to the rights of a third person who is assignee of the judgment,[5] for the assignee has

---

[1] Terney v. Wilson, 45 N. J. L. 282; Bradt v. Koon, 46 Cow. (N. Y.) 416; Wright v. Wright, 70 N. Y. 96, affirming 9 J. & S. 432.

[2] Stewart v. Hilton, 19 Blatchf. 290.

[3] Williams v. Ingersoll, 89 N. Y. 508; Middlesex Freeholders v. State Bank, 38 N. J. Eq. 36; S. C. 19 Cent. L. J. 393.

[4] Day v. Bowman (Ind.), 10 N. East. Rep. 126; Sibley v. County of Pine, 31 Minn. 201; S. C. 17 N. W. Rep. 337.

[5] Cunningham v. McGrady, 2 Bax. (Tenn.) 141; Longworth v. Handy, 2 Dis. (Ohio) 75; Sexton v. Pike, 13 Ark. 193.

no greater equities than the assignor had; and though the assignee had no notice of the lien, this may be enforced as against him.

X. *An Attorney's Lien is not Defeated by Attachment, or by the Client's Bankruptcy.*

227. An attorney's lien on a judgment is superior to the lien of a subsequent attaching creditor.[1] It is immaterial whether the client be the plaintiff or defendant in the suit. In equity, especially, the position of the party is of no consequence, because a nominal defendant may be adjudged entitled to the whole or a part of the funds in controversy. In equity, also, an attorney may have a lien before judgment by virtue of a special agreement that he shall be compensated out of the fund recovered; and such lien prevails against an attaching creditor of the client.[2] It matters not that such agreement is by parol and not in writing; and it is not needful, in order to make such lien valid, that notice of it should be given to the debtors.[3]

228. An attorney's lien is not defeated by the insolvency or bankruptcy of the client, or by his general assignment for the benefit of his creditors, pending the action, if judgment is finally entered in his favor.[4] The assignee in insolvency or bankruptcy stands in the debtor's place, and takes the estate burdened by the equitable incumbrance of the lien. Thus, where a railroad company, pending an action against it, became insolvent and a receiver was appointed, and a judgment for costs was afterwards entered in its favor, it was held that the receiver had no title to such costs; and the other party to the action, having paid the judgment to the receiver with notice of the lien, was not protected from an execution issued to the attorney on such judgment.[5]

But as against the judgment debtor, if he obtains a discharge

---

[1] *Ex parte*, Moule, 5 Madd. 462; Damson *v.* Robertson, 12 Lea (Tenn.), 372; Miller *v.* Newell, 20 S. C. 123; *S. C.* 47 Am. Rep. 833; Hutchinson *v.* Howard, 15 Vt. 544; Weed *v.* Boutelle, 56 Vt. 570, 581.

[2] Williams *v.* Ingersoll, 23 Hun, 284; *S. C.* 89 N. Y. 508.

[3] Williams *v.* Ingersoll, *supra.*

[4] Cooke *v.* Thresher, 51 Conn. 105.

[5] *In re* Bailey, 66 How. (N. Y.) Pr. 64; *S. C.* 4 N. Y. Civ. Pro. 140; Russell *v.* Somerville, 10 Abb. (N.Y.) N. C. 395; Anderson *v.* Sessions, N. Y. Daily Reg. Mar. 4, 1884; Clark *v.* Binninger, 1 Abb. (N. Y.) N. C. 421.

in bankruptcy or insolvency after the rendition of the judgment, the attorney's lien upon the judgment is discharged with the judgment, like any other debt of the bankrupt.[1]

If a receiver of the client's property is appointed, and a judgment upon which an attorney has a lien passes into his hands, the attorney can obtain full protection in all proceedings taken by the receiver upon such judgment, and may, if need be, apply to the court for relief out of the assets or funds collected by the receiver.[2]

The receiver acquires no other or better title than the assignor had, but takes the property subject to the liens affecting it.

If an attorney takes from his client collateral security for professional services, and upon demand of a receiver of his client's property delivers the security to the receiver with a written notice of his lien thereon and takes a receipt therefor, he does not thereby waive his lien.[3]

The receiver of a corporation appointed pending an action against it, who collects costs arising from a successful defence, may be required to pay them over to the attorney who conducted the defence.[4]

In equity an attorney has a lien for his fees and disbursements upon a fund in court recovered by his services.[5] This lien cannot be defeated by the insolvency of the client, or by his assignment of the fund. His assignee in bankruptcy or his assignee by purchase takes the fund subject to the attorney's lien with which it was affected as against the client.

But a court of equity, before awarding any part of the fund in satisfaction of the attorney's lien, will inquire if the fee is reasonable.[6]

[1] Blumenthal v. Anderson, 91 N. Y. 171.

[2] Moore v. Taylor, 40 Hun (N. Y.), 56.

[3] Corey v. Harte, 21 Weekly Dig. 247.

[4] In re Bailey, 31 Hun (N. Y.), 608; S. C. 5 N. Y. Civ. Pro. 253, affirming 4 Ib. 140 ; S. C. 66 How. Pr. 64.

[5] Turwin v. Gibson, 3 Atk. 720; Ex parte Price, 2 Ves. 407 ; Skinner v. Sweet, 3 Madd. 244 ; Lann v. Church, 4 Madd. 391; Ex parte Moule, 5 Madd. 462 ; Jones v. Frost, L. R. 7 Ch. 773.

[6] McCain v. Portis, 42 Ark. 402.

XI. *An Attorney's Lien on Land which is the Subject-Matter of the Suit.*

229. An attorney has no lien on his client's lands for services rendered in defending them against an effort to charge them with the payment of the debt of another;[1] nor for services in prosecuting a suit in equity to establish the title of his client to the lands.[2] To extend the attorney's lien to lands recovered in a suit would be in effect creating an equitable mortgage in his favor, and would be subject, not only to the objections urged against such a lien in England, but in this country to the further objection that it would be contrary to the policy of our registry system.[3]

In Iowa it is held that an attorney's lien for his fee upon the

---

[1] Shaw v. Neale, 6 H. L. Cas. 581; Lee v. Winston, 68 Ala. 402; McWilliams v. Jenkins, 72 Ib. 480.

[2] McCullough v. Flournoy, 69 Ala. 189; Hinson v. Gamble, 65 Ib. 605; Hanger v. Fowler, 20 Ark. 667; Smalley v. Clark, 22 Vt. 598; Cozzens v. Whitney, 3 R. I. 79; Humphrey v. Browning, 46 Ill. 476; Stewart v. Flowers, 44 Miss. 513; Martin v. Harrington, 57 Miss. 208.

In some early cases in England a lien seems to have been given upon the land in favor of the solicitor; as where a solicitor had been employed by the committee of a lunatic, he was regarded as subrogated to the lien of the committee upon the lunatic's estate, both real and personal. Barnesley v. Powell, 1 Amb. 102; *Ex parte* Price, 2 Ves. 407, referred to by Chancellor Kent in Southwick, *in re*, 1 Johns. Ch. 22. In the cases first cited, there is a *dictum* by Lord Hardwicke to the effect that a solicitor has a lien on the estate recovered in the hands of his client.

But the House of Lords, in Shaw v. Neale, 6 H. L. Cas. 581, repudiated the doctrine that an attorney or solicitor has an implied lien on the estate recovered. Interrupting the argument, Lord Wensleydale said: "I

never heard such a proposition at law." Lord St. Leonards: "Nor I in equity."

In consequence of the decision in Shaw v. Neale, *supra*, it was enacted by 23 & 24 Vic. ch. 127, § 28, that in every case in which an attorney or solicitor shall be employed to prosecute or defend any suit, the court or judge before whom the suit has been heard may declare such attorney or solicitor entitled to a charge upon the property recovered or preserved through his instrumentality for the costs, charges, and expenses of or in reference to such suit. This statute has been the subject of construction or application in several cases. See 16 Ir. L. T. 331, 345.

Of course the lien under this statute is confined to the client's interest in the land. Thus, if a tenant in tail employs a solicitor to defend a suit, the latter gets a charge on the estate of his client, but not on that in the remainder. If the client bars the estate tail, and gets the fee, the solicitor gets a charge on the fee; but otherwise only on the interest of the client. Berrie v. Howitt, L. R. 9 Eq. 1.

[3] Hanger v. Fowler, *supra;* Humphrey v. Browning, *supra.*

judgment recovered does not attach to land which is sold in satisfaction of the judgment and purchased by the client.[1]

In Arkansas an attorney's lien has been extended by statute so as to charge lands recovered by the attorney. The lien is declared to be an interest in the property, whether real or personal, recovered by judgment, to the amount of such judgment.[2]

In Georgia the code gives a lien on all property, both real and personal, recovered by judgment, superior to all liens except those for taxes.[3]

One who purchases the land after the attorney has filed a bill to enforce his lien, purchases with notice of the lien and takes the property subject to such lien.[4]

230. In Tennessee, however, it is held that an attorney is entitled to an equitable lien on the property or thing in litigation, whether real or personal, for his just and reasonable fees, and the client cannot, while the suit is pending, so dispose of the subject-matter in dispute as to deprive him of his lien.[5]

There can be no lien, however, unless the suit be for specific land, or it impounds the property in litigation by some process which places it within the custody of the court.[6]

His lien upon land which is the subject of a decree is also entitled to priority of satisfaction over the lien of a judgment creditor of the client acquired subsequently to the decree.[7]   The

---

[1] Cowen v. Boone, 48 Iowa, 350. And see Wishard v. Biddle, 64 Iowa, 526, 528. Apparently the same rule prevails in **Mississippi**: Stewart v. Flowers, 44 Miss. 513. Otherwise in **Arkansas** : Porter v. Hanson, 36 Ark. 591.

[2] § **170**, *supra ;* Gantt's Dig. § 3622 ; Porter v. Hanson, 36 Ark. 591; Compton v. State, 38 Ib. 601. Such a lien had been previously denied in 20 Ib. 667.

[3] § **173**, *supra ;* Code 1882, § 1989; Wilson v. Wright, 72 Ga. 848.

[4] Wilson v. Wright, *supra.*

[5] First recognized in Hunt v. McClanahan, 1 Heisk. 503 ; Perkins v. Perkins, 9 Ib. 95 ; Brown v. Bigley, 3 Tenn. Ch. 618. But when the land in controversy is conveyed to the complainant partly in exchange for land conveyed to the defendant, the attorney of the latter has no lien for his fees on the land so conveyed to his client. Sharp v. Fields, 5 Lea, 326.

[6] Sharpe v. Allen, 11 Lea, 518 ; Brown v. Bigley, *supra.*

[7] Pleasants v. Kortrecht, 5 Heisk. 694, though the principle perhaps not properly applied to the facts. "The inclination of the courts of this country, and none more so than those of this state, has been to enlarge the doctrine of equitable liens and charges with a view to the attainment of the ends of justice, without much respect for the technical restrictions of the

creditor's right is against the property of the debtor, and not against the interest of a third person in such property, though this interest be a mere lien or equity.

Independent of the registration laws, the creditor's equity is equal and not superior to the equity of third persons, and therefore whichever is prior in time has the better right.[1]

But the defendant's solicitor is not entitled to a lien on his client's land for services rendered in defending a suit in which it was sought to establish a resulting trust in such lands, although the defence was successful. The lien exists only in case of the actual recovery of land by a suit instituted for that purpose. It cannot be extended to services which merely predict an existing title or right to property.[2]

common law. It was a logical result of this tendency that our Supreme Court should follow the lead of Lord Hardwicke, made before the Revolution, rather than the modern doctrine of the House of Lords. And it was both natural and wise that the lien of the lawyer on the fruits of his professional labor should be treated as equitable rather than legal. The proper administration of justice is essential to the well-being of the republic, and cannot be secured without an enlightened and prosperous bar." Brown v. Bigley, 3 Tenn. Ch. 618.

[1] Brown v. Bigley, supra.

[2] Garner v. Garner, 1 Lea, 29; Stanford v. Andrews, 12 Heisk. 664; Sharp v. Fields, 5 Lea, 326; Guild v. Borner, 7 Bax. 266; Winchester v. Heiskell, 16 Lea, 556. The language used in the first decision in which a lien on land was recognized (Hunt v. McClanahan, supra), seemed to imply that the lien existed in favor of counsel, whether retained by the plaintiff or the defendant, and to give a lien on the land in controversy to the lawyer of the successful party. "In consequence of this construction the practice of the courts was, for a time, very liberal, and the lien was declared in favor of the counsel of the defendant as well as of the plaintiff. Upon further consideration it was seen that

this extension of the doctrine could not be sustained upon the principles of the original decision, nor upon general principles. It operated as a restraint upon the free disposition of property, and created a new and secret trust, not only unknown to the common law, but not warranted by its principles, and in conflict with the policy of our registration laws. It was therefore held by this court that the lien exists only in the case of the actual recovery of land, by a suit instituted for the purpose, just as at common law the lien was on the money judgment recovered. The lien, it was said, is declared to exist from the commencement of the suit, — manifestly contemplating a suit for the specific property; and the doctrine, although an extension of the principle of the common law, may be sustained upon the ground that the *lis pendens* is notice to all the world of the plaintiff's right, and no great harm can result from carrying out of this right, a lien in favor of the attorney running *pari passu* with the lien of the *lis pendens*. But the *lis pendens* is no notice to any one of the defendant's rights, which stand precisely as if no suit were pending; and consequently a lien on that right, without contract, would be without any rule or analogy to support it, besides being in conflict

An attorney's lien on land for services in defending a suit affecting the land may be rendered binding upon the parties, and those claiming under them, pending the litigation, if declared by the court in which the services were rendered; but such lien does not affect third persons having prior liens upon the land.[1]

XII. *Waiver of an Attorney's Lien.*

231. This lien may be waived by an arrangement or transaction between the attorney and his client which shows the attorney's intention to rely upon some other security or mode of payment; but the lien will be regarded as existing, unless the intention that it shall not continue manifestly appears.[2] The taking of a promissory note by the attorney does not necessarily imply a waiver of his lien, for this may have been given merely for the purpose of fixing the amount of the debt. But the taking of a distinct and independent security will generally amount to a waiver of the lien, for the attorney in such case has carved out his own security and is presumed to have intended to waive his lien. It is true, however, that the waiver arising from the acceptance of collateral security is presumptive only, and may be rebutted by evidence of an intention not to rely exclusively upon it, but to retain the equitable lien.[3]

An attorney's lien upon a judgment is waived by his procuring a transfer to his client of land attached in the suit in satisfaction of the judgment. His lien upon the judgment does not follow the land when the title is perfected in the client. Subsequent purchasers of the land from the client have a right to suppose the lien has been waived or satisfied.[4]

An attorney's lien upon a judgment is not discharged by his delay in collecting it, though this delay be for several years.[5]

It is not lost though his claim against his client is barred by the statute of limitations.[6]

It is not divested by his allowing his claim to become dormant, so that it has to be revived by other attorneys.[7]

Neither is it lost by the attorney's receiving or collecting a

---

with the policy of our registration laws." Cooper, J., in Pierce v. Lawrence (Tenn.), 1 S. W. Rep. 204.

[1] Pierce v. Lawrence, 16 Lea (Tenn.), 572; *S. C.* 1 S. West. Rep. 204.

[2] Renick v. Ludington, 16 W. Va.

378; Goodrich v. McDonald, 41 Hun (N. Y.), 235.

[3] Renick v. Ludington, *supra*.

[4] Cowen v. Boone, 48 Iowa, 350.

[5] Stone v. Hyde, 22 Me. 318.

[6] Higgins v. Scott, 2 B. & Ad. 413.

[7] Jenkins v. Stephens, 60 Ga. 216.

part of the judgment, and paying over the part so collected to his client without deducting his fees. He can enforce his lien upon the balance of the judgment.[1]

There may be circumstances under which the attorney will not waive his lien by allowing the proceeds of the judgment to be paid over to his client.[2]

It would seem that an attorney's lien would not prevail against a state in whose favor he has obtained a judgment, in the absence of a special statute giving such a lien.[3]

XIII. *An Attorney's Remedies for Enforcing his Lien.*

232. In general it may be said that the attorney has the same remedial process as his client to obtain satisfaction to the extent of his lien, inasmuch as he is regarded to that extent as an equitable assignee of the judgment. Therefore, where a judgment has been rendered for the defendant in a replevin suit, the attorney has a right to enforce the replevin bond taken from the plaintiff for the return of the goods. And if the sheriff has taken an insufficient bond, the attorney has a right to the damages which may be recovered from the sheriff for his neglect in taking such bond. The judgment in such suit belongs to the attorney to the extent of his lien.[4]

An attorney who has prosecuted a bastardy process to final judgment and execution has a lien upon the bond given by the respondent in that process.[5]

When an attachment has been made, the lien of the attachment inures to the benefit of the attorney for his fees and costs, and this cannot be defeated by any settlement made by the client with the debtor, without his consent.[6]

Where a judgment is a lien upon real estate, and this is about to be sold under execution, an attorney's lien upon the judgment will not be protected by a stay of a sale under the execution, but the sheriff may be stayed from paying the proceeds of sale

---

[1] Hooper v. Brundage, 22 Me. 460.
[2] Goodrich v. McDonald, 41 Hun (N. Y.), 235; S. C. 2 N. Y. St. Rep. 144.
[3] Compton v. State, 38 Ark. 601, 604. At any rate, no decree of a lien could be taken against a state, though, in case the funds are within the control of the court, it may, in the exer-

cise of its equitable powers, have the fees paid out of the fund. State v. Edgefield & Ky. R. R. Co. 4 Bax. (Tenn.) 92.

[4] Newbert v. Cunningham, 50 Me. 231.
[5] Bickford v. Ellis, 50 Me. 121.
[6] Gist v. Hanly, 33 Ark. 233.

to the plaintiff or his assignee under the execution until the amount of the attorney's compensation can be ascertained.[1]

But the attorney can hardly be considered as the assignee of the judgment in such a sense as to entitle him to go into another court to enforce his lien by an action in his own name.[2]

The attorney may enforce his lien by an action on the judgment in the name of the creditor.[3]

The lien of an attorney upon a judgment is enforced according to the law of the state where the judgment was recovered and the lien attached, and not according to the law of another state where it is sought to collect the judgment.[4]

233. When the parties have collusively settled a suit before judgment, with the design of preventing the attorney from obtaining his costs or fees, the court may allow the attorney to go on with the suit and obtain a judgment for the amount of his costs or fees, notwithstanding the settlement.[5] If the settlement has been filed in the court, the attorney should first obtain an order setting it aside. His course then is to bring the case to trial and final judgment in the name of his client. He is not entitled to an order to enter judgment for the amount of his costs without bringing the cause to trial; and a judgment

---

[1] Loaners' Bank v. Nostrand, 21 J. & S. (N. Y.) 525.

[2] Adams v. Fox, 40 Barb. (N. Y.) 442.

[3] Stone v. Hyde, 22 Me. 318.

[4] Citizens' Nat. Bank v. Culver, 54 N. H. 327.

[5] Rasquin v. Knickerbocker Stage Co. 12 Abb. (N. Y.) Pr. 324; People v. Hardenbergh, 8 Johns. (N. Y.) 335; Talcott v. Bronson, 4 Paige (N. Y.), 501; Chase v. Chase, 65 How. (N. Y.) Pr. 306.

In some cases it is said that, before an attorney can proceed with an action after settlement and discontinuance by the client, the attorney should obtain leave of court to enforce his lien by supplementary proceedings. Dimick v. Cooley, 3 N. Y. Civ. Pro.

141. In this case the court say: "It would be an unwise and dangerous practice, extremely hazardous to the rights of both parties, to allow an attorney to continue the action, for the purpose of collecting his costs, without first obtaining consent of the court that he may proceed for that purpose. When such permission is given, it is the duty of the court to direct as to the time and manner, and watch the proceedings and doings of the attorney, so as to fully protect the rights of both parties, and not unnecessarily annoy and embarrass either." Per Barker, J.

In Moore v. Taylor, 2 How. (N. Y.) Pr. N. S. 343, it is said that leave of court to institute such proceedings is especially requisite where the affidavit says nothing about any lien.

so obtained is irregular.[1] In such cases the attorney must establish the collusion.[2]

In New York, according to the later and present practice, the attorney is entitled to proceed with the action without first obtaining leave of the court to do so.[3] He may prosecute the suit to trial and final judgment in the name of his client, with a view to the protection of his own rights.

In this state, however, if the attorney is the equitable owner of the entire judgment recovered, as is the case where the judgment is for costs only, he should prosecute in his own name an undertaking given to secure its payment, inasmuch as the code directs that every action shall be prosecuted in the name of the real party in interest, whether he be a legal or equitable assignee of the cause of action.[4] If he brings such action, even with leave of the court, in the name of his client, for the purpose of enforcing his lien, a previous assignment by his client of the cause of action and release of the judgment will bar the action. The order allowing the attorney to proceed does not determine that the attorney is entitled to recover the sum he claims, nor does it determine any of the issues between the parties.[5]

234. The English practice in such cases seems to have been for the attorney, whose lien has been destroyed by the conduct of the parties, to move the court to vacate the satisfaction of judgment, and to apply for a rule calling upon the opposite party to pay him his costs.[6] Although the parties to the suit have collusively settled the judgment, the attorney has no such authority over the execution in his hands as to enforce it against the judgment debtor of his own mere motion and with-

---

[1] Pickard v. Yencer, 21 Hun (N. Y.), 403; S. C. 10 Week. Dig. 271; Smith v. Baum, 67 How. (N. Y.) Pr. 267 ; Wilber v. Baker, 24 Hun, 24.

[2] Lang v. Buffalo Seamen's Union, 22 Alb. L. J. 114.

[3] Pickard v. Yencer, supra; Wilber v. Baker, supra; Forstman v. Schulting, 35 Hun, N. Y. 504 ; Merchant v. Sessions, 5 N. Y. Civ. Pro. 24.

The case of Goddard v. Trenbath,

24 Hun, 182, holding that leave of court must be obtained to prosecute the suit in such cases, is overruled.

[4] Kipp v. Rapp, 2 How. (N. Y.) Pr. N. S. 169 ; S. C. 7 Civ. Pro. 316, 317.

[5] Kipp v. Rapp, supra.

[6] Welsh v. Hole, 1 Doug. 238; Graves v. Eades, 5 Taunt. 429; Reid v. Dupper, 6 T. R. 361; Charlwood v. Berridge, 1 Esp. 345; Jones v. Bonner, 2 Exch. 230.

out his client's consent.   He must apply to the equitable jurisdiction of the court.[1]

A similar mode of practice prevails, or has prevailed, in some of our state courts.

The plaintiff's attorney may also be protected upon his application to the court for a rule restraining the judgment debtor from paying the money to the plaintiff until the attorney's lien is satisfied.

When a decree has been entered for the payment of money to a complainant, and his solicitor has given the defendant notice that he claims a lien on the moneys decreed to be paid, and this notice is disregarded by the defendant, the latter may, on an order of the court to show cause, be required to pay to the solicitor such amount as he should establish a lien for upon a reference made by the court.[2]

235. An application to the court by an attorney to protect his lien upon a judgment is addressed to the discretion of the court.[3]   The right of the attorney to claim the lien should be clear to justify the court's interference.   But it has the power to interfere, whether the lien be for the taxable costs or for compensation, when a lien for this is given by statute.   When the amount of compensation is in dispute, the court may direct that a sufficient sum to cover the claims be brought into court to await an action at law, or other procedure between the attorney and client to settle the amount.[4]

In Indiana a complaint by an attorney to set aside an entry of satisfaction of a judgment on the ground that it was fraudulently made, should allege the amount of fees due him, either by stating the contract with his client respecting his fees, or by averring the value of his services.[5]   The complaint should allege that the lien was taken, and notice of it filed at the time of the rendition of the judgment, for such entry and notice are required to make the lien effectual.[6]

In some cases the courts, after declaring the lien, have directed

[1] Barker v. St. Quintin, 12 M. & W. 441; Brunsdon v. Allard, 2 E. & E. 17, 25.

[2] Barnes v. Taylor, 30 N. J. Eq. 467.

[3] Adams v. Fox, 40 Barb. (N. Y.) 442.

[4] Adams v. Fox, supra; Fox v. Fox, 24 How. (N. Y.) Pr. 409, 417.

[5] Dunning v. Galloway, 47 Ind. 182; Adams v. Lee, 82 Ind. 587; Day v. Bowman (Ind.), 10 N. E. Rep. 126.

[6] Day v. Bowman, supra.

a reference to a master to determine the proper amount of the attorney's charges;[1] but perhaps the better practice is to declare the lien, and leave the attorney to enforce his claim by an appropriate proceeding against his client.[2]

236. Upon an application by a solicitor for money which has been paid into court under a decree, his claim cannot be passed upon without notice to his client and proof to maintain his claim, though the client has assigned to him the cause of action upon which the decree was founded as security for his services.[3]

237. But if the attorney waits for an unreasonable time after his client has settled with the opposite party, and discharged the judgment, the satisfaction will not be set aside in order to allow the attorney to obtain his costs.[4] Great and unreasonable delays and laches on his part in asserting his rights are fatal to his claim, as they would be to the claim of any ordinary suitor. Although proceedings by an attorney to enforce his claim do not constitute an action within the literal operation of the statute of limitations, yet in enforcing a remedy of this character, depending upon the equitable powers of the court, and, to a certain extent, upon its discretion, it will in general be governed by the analogy of the statute.[5]

After the litigation is ended and the client has possessed himself of the entire fund recovered by the litigation, the court has no power to give relief to the attorney.[6]

---

[1] Hunt v. McClanahan, 1 Heisk. (Tenn.) 503; Yourie v. Nelson, 1 Tenn. Ch. 614; Bowling v. Scales, Ib. 618; Barnes v. Taylor, 30 N. J. Eq. 467.

[2] Perkins v. Perkins, 9 Heisk. (Tenn.) 95.

[3] Black v. Black, 32 N. J. Eq. 74. When an attorney claims a lien upon money in the hands of an officer of the court, and the claim is controverted by the client, a rule is the proper remedy in Georgia to settle the question. To such rule the attorney need not attach a bill of particulars of the services rendered by him, nor need he upon trial go into proof of the same; but the services will be treated as a whole. Walker v. Floyd, 30 Ga. 237. But after the client has possessed himself of the entire fund recovered, the attorney cannot proceed by rule to collect his fees. The court has no jurisdiction to control its officers and the parties connected with a judicial proceeding after the litigation has ended. Whittle v. Newman, 34 Ga. 377.

[4] Winans v. Mason, 33 Barb. (N. Y.) 522.

[5] Richardson v. Brooklyn, C. & N. R. R. Co. 7 Hun (N. Y.), 69.

[6] Whittle v. Newman, supra.

238. An attorney is not bound to make himself a party to the record in order to enforce his lien for fees against a judgment obtained for his client. If he has given notice to the judgment debtor of his lien, he may enforce it notwithstanding a compromise and settlement between the judgment debtor and his client: the court may, however, allow the attorney to intervene, after judgment, and be made a party to the suit, when that course seems necessary for the protection of his rights.[1]

In Nebraska it is said that under some circumstances the attorney may properly be admitted as a party plaintiff in the action for the purpose of protecting and enforcing his lien. In such proceeding it would be the proper practice for the attorney, on being admitted as a party, to file a petition in his own name against both plaintiff and defendant, setting forth the particulars of his claim, so that if it be disputed answers could be filed, and issues made up as in other cases.[2]

239. In an action to dissolve a partnership the court will not appoint a receiver in order to secure the lien of the plaintiff's attorney; for a receiver is appointed in such an action only when it is absolutely necessary to do so for the protection of the property. If the attorney has given notice of his claim before the settlement, he may be allowed to go on with the suit and enter up judgment for his costs.[3]

240. In proceedings to wind up an insolvent life insurance company an attorney was retained by certain policy holders, and appeared in their behalf. A dividend to each of his clients was declared, whereupon he claimed a lien and moved that the receiver pay the dividends to him. It did not appear that these policy holders were formal parties to the proceedings, or that the attorney entered his appearance of record, nor that his services procured the dividends. The attorney's motion was denied, except upon his filing authority from his clients to receive such dividends. It was doubted whether he had any lien under the code; and, whether he had or not, the court could not make an order practically enforcing a lien without notice to the clients.[4]

[1] Patrick v. Leach, 3 McCrary, 555; S. C. 17 Fed. Rep. 476.
[2] Reynolds v. Reynolds, 10 Neb. 574; S. C. 7 N. W. Rep. 322.
[3] Anon. 2 Daly (N. Y.), 533.
[4] Attorney-General v. N. A. L. Ins. Co. 93 N. Y. 387.

CHAPTER VI.

BANKERS' LIENS.

I. *Nature and Extent and the Indebtedness Secured.*

241. A bank has a lien on all moneys, funds, and securities of a depositor for the general balance of his account.[1] Thus, if a bank discounts a note for a depositor, and this is not paid at maturity, all funds of the depositor held by the bank at the time of the maturity of the note, or afterwards acquired in the course of business with him, whether on general deposit or in the form of commercial paper placed by him in bank for collection, may be applied to the discharge of his indebtedness to the bank on such note.[2] And the rule is the same as regards any other indebtedness, such as an overdraft or an advance of any kind.

242. The lien of bankers is part of the law merchant, and the courts are bound to take judicial notice of it, just as

---

[1] Jourdaine *v.* Lefevre, 1 Esp. 66; Davis *v.* Bowsher, 5 T. R. 488; Scott *v.* Franklin, 15 East, 428; Bolton *v.* Puller, 1 B. & P. 539; Giles *v.* Perkins, 9 East, 12; Bolland *v.* Bygrave, R. & M. 271 ; *In re* Williams, 3 Ir. R. Eq. 346; Brandão *v.* Barnett, 12 Cl. & F. 787; Marsh *v.* Oneida Bank, 34 Barb. (N. Y.) 298; Beckwith *v.* Union Bank, 4 Sandf. (N. Y.) 604; Commercial Bank of Albany *v.* Hughes, 17 Wend. (N. Y.) 94; Van Allen, *in re,* 37 Barb. (N. Y.) 225; Ford *v.* Thornton, 3 Leigh (Va.), 695; State Bank *v.* Armstrong, 4 Dev. (N. C.) 519; Whittington *v.* Farmers' Bank, 5 Har. & J. (Md.) 489; McDowell *v.* Bank of Wilmington, 1 Harr. (Del.) 369.

It is declared, in the codes of **California** and **Dakota Territory**, that a banker has a general lien, dependent on possession, upon all property in his hands belonging to a customer, for the balance due to him from such customer in the course of the business. Cal. Civ. Code, § 3054; Dak. Civ. Code, § 1808.

In **Pennsylvania** the doctrine of bankers' liens does not prevail. It is regarded as opposed to well established legal principles, and as a custom it cannot therefore obtain. Liggett Spring and Axle Co.'s Appeal, 111 Pa. St. 291.

[2] Muench *v.* Valley Nat. Bank, 11 Mo. App. 144.

158

they are bound to recognize the negotiability of bills of exchange. Thus Lord Lyndhurst, in a case before the House of Lords, said:[1] "I think there is no question that, by the law merchant, a banker has a lien upon securities deposited with him for his general balance. I consider this as part of the established law of the country: the courts will take notice of it; it is not necessary to plead it; nor is it necessary that it should be given in evidence in the particular instance." Lord Campbell in the same case said: "The usage of trade by which bankers are entitled to a general lien, is not found by the special verdict; and, unless we are to take judicial notice of it, the plaintiff is at once entitled to judgment. But, my lords, I am of opinion that the general lien of bankers is part of the law merchant, and is to be judically noticed, like the negotiability of bills of exchange, or the days of grace allowed for their payment. When a general usage has been judicially ascertained and established, it becomes part of the law merchant, which courts of justice are bound to know and recognize. Such has been the invariable understanding and practice in Westminster Hall for a great many years; there is no decision or *dictum* to the contrary; and justice could not be administered if evidence were to be given, *toties quoties*, to support such usages, an issue being joined upon them in each particular case."

243. Courts will not, however, judicially take notice of the lien of bankers who are not strictly such. In the case of persons engaged in discounting, buying, advancing on, or selling bills or notes, a lien for a general balance will not be presumed to exist in the absence of an express agreement. If a usage exists to give such a lien, it should be proved.[2]

244. A banker has a lien on all securities of his debtor in his hands for the general balance of his account, unless such a lien is inconsistent with the actual or presumed intention of the parties.[3] The lien attaches to notes and bills and other business

[1] Brandão v. Barnett, 12 Cl. & Fin. 787; S. C. 3 C. B. 519, 535; S. C. 6 M. & Gr. 630; approved in Misa v. Currie, L. R. 1 App. Cas. 554, 569; Muench v. Valley Nat. Bank, 11 Mo. App. 144; Grant v. Taylor, 3 J. & S. (N. Y.) 338.

[2] Grant v. Taylor, *supra*.

[3] Davis v. Bowsher, 5 T. R. 488, 491, per Lord Kenyon; Kelly v. Phelan, 5 Dill. 228; Brandão v. Barnett, 6 Man. & Gr. 630, 670; S. C. 7 Scott N. R. 301, 332, per Lord Denman; S. C. 3 C. B. 519; 12 Cl. & F. 787; ap-

paper which the customer has intrusted to the bank for collection, as well as to his general deposit account.[1] Whether there is such a lien in a particular case, depends upon the circumstances attending it. If there is nothing in the transaction which repels the presumption that the banker gave credit on the strength of the debtor's securities in his hands, he has a lien upon them for the general balance due him from the debtor. And so if the securities be deposited after the credit was given, the banker has a lien for his general balance of account, unless there be an express contract or circumstances that show an implied contract inconsistent with such lien.

A banker has a lien for a general balance of account upon securities left with him by a customer without any special agreement;[2] and if a portion of the securities so left be afterwards pledged to secure a particular debt, the banker has a lien upon the securities not so pledged for his balance of account.[3]

245. A banker's lien secures only such debts as are due and payable to the banker at the time he claims to retain his customer's funds or securities.[4] If a bank discounts a note for a

proved in London Chartered Bank of Australia v. White, L. R. 4 App. Cas. 413, and in Misa v. Currie, L. R. 1 App. Cas. 554, 569 ; In re European Bank, L. R. 8 Ch. 41; Wyman v. Colorado Nat. Bank, 5 Colo. 30; In re Williams, 3 Ir. Eq. 346; S. C. 20 L. T. N. S. 282.

[1] Barnett v. Brandão, supra ; Pease, ex parte, 1 Rose, 232; Ex parte Wakefield Bank, 1 Ib. 243; Scott v. Franklin, 15 East, 428.

[2] Davis v. Bowsher, 5 T. R. 488, 491.

[3] Damont v. Fry, 13 Fed. Rep. 423.

[4] Jordan v. Nat. Shoe & Leather Bank, 74 N. Y. 467; Beckwirth v. Union Bank, 4 Sandf. (N. Y.) 604. In the latter case a depositor was an indorser on a bill held by the bank. He made a general assignment for the benefit of his creditors before the bill matured, and at that time there was a balance to his account at the bank nearly equal to the amount of the indorsed bill. The bill was protested

at maturity and charged to his account by the bank, before notice of the assignment was given to the bank. It was held, however, that the bank was entitled to recover the entire sum in deposit, the situation of the bank not being affected by want of notice of the assignment.

In a case in Illinois (Fourth Nat. Bank v. City Nat. Bank, 68 Ill. 398), where a customer obtained a discount of his note at a bank, and the money was placed to his credit, and he became insolvent before the maturity of the note, having at the time a deposit to his credit against a part of which he had drawn a check, it was held that the bank had no lien as against the check holder who presented this check for payment before the maturity of the note. The value of this decision as an authority elsewhere is impaired by the rule adopted in this state that a check is an appropriation of so much of the depositor's

customer and places the proceeds to his account, it has no right to retain the amount of his general deposit to apply upon an indebtedness of the customer not yet matured. To do this would be in complete hostility to the purpose contemplated in the contract of discount. " The purpose existing and understood by the parties in that act is, that the customer of the bank may draw out at his pleasure the avails of the discount. After the paper discounted falls due and payable and remains unpaid, unless other rights have intervened, the bank may hold a balance of deposits and apply it towards the payment of the paper. But these deposits in a bank create between it and the depositor the relation of debtor and creditor. Now a debtor in one sum has no lien upon it in his hands for the payment of a debt owned by him, which has not yet matured; nor has a bank, more than any other debtor. Both hold, as debtors, the moneys of their creditors, and may set up no claim to them not given by the law of set-off, counter-claim, recoupment, or kindred rules."[1]

246. In equity it has been held that the lien of a bank may attach before the indebtedness has matured. Thus, where a depositor, having obtained a discount at a bank, died before the note matured, upon evidence of danger that his estate and also the indorser's would prove to be insolvent, it was held that the bank should be allowed to retain enough of the funds of the depositor in the hands of the bank to meet the note when it should be due.[2]

Of course securities may by express agreement be pledged to cover debts not matured or contingent liabilities;[3] but such a lien is a different thing from a banker's implied general lien.

But ordinarily equity follows the statute and the law in regard to a set-off, unless there are peculiar circumstances presented. The insolvency of a debtor sometimes moves equity to grant a set-off which would not be allowed at law; and that consideration doubtless much moved the court in the Virginia case above cited.[4]

account, giving him a right of action for it against the bank.

See Bolland v. Bygrave, Ry. & M. 271.

[1] Per Folger, J., in Jordan v. Nat. Shoe & Leather Bank, 74 N. Y. 467.

[2] Ford v. Thornton, 3 Leigh (Va.), 695. See Fourth Nat. Bank v. City Nat. Bank, 68 Ill. 398.

[3] Merchants' Bank of London v. Maud, 19 W. R. 657.

[4] Jordan v. Nat. Shoe & Leather Bank, supra, per Folger, J.

247. If a customer keeps several deposit accounts with a bank, they are to be regarded as one account as regards the bank's right of lien. Thus, if a customer, as a matter of convenience, keeps with a bank three accounts, namely, a loan account, a discount account, and a general account, and becomes a debtor to the bank on one account, the bank has a lien for the debt upon the customer's balance upon another account.[1] "In truth," said Lord Justice James, "as between banker and customer, whatever number of accounts are kept in the books, the whole is really but one account, and it is not open to the customer, in the absence of some special contract, to say that the securities which he deposits are only applicable to one account." Of course this rule applies only where all the accounts belong to the depositor in the same capacity.

A bank discounted for a customer bills of exchange drawn against goods consigned to India upon the security of the bills of lading. As a further security against a fall in the price of the goods, the bank retained a sum from the full discount value of the bills, and carried this to a suspense account until it should receive advice of the payment of the bills, and gave to the customer accountable receipts for such margins or sums retained. This was the usual course of dealing between the parties; and it was also the habit of the bank, when it had been advised that the bills had been paid in full, to carry over the retained margin to the credit of the customer in his general banking account. The customer pledged three of such receipts with a party who gave notice to the bank of such assignment. On the same day the customer suspended payment, being largely indebted to the bank upon an overdrawn account and on suspended accounts. It was held that the bank was entitled to a lien on the receipts for such margins or suspended account for such sums as were actually due and payable to it at the times when the receipts became payable, in respect of liabilities contracted before notice was received by the bank of the pledge or assignment of the receipts.[2]

248. As a general rule the lien attaches only to securities belonging to the customer in his own right, unless

---

[1] *In re* European Bank, L. R. 8 Ch. 41.

[2] Jeffryes *v.* Agra & Masterman's Bank, L. R. 2 Eq. 674; *S. C.* 35 L. J. N. S. Ch. 686; 14 W. R. 889.

the securities be transferable by delivery, or have been intrusted to the customer by the owner in such a way that he appears to be the owner, and has the power of transferring them as if they were his own; in which case the banker receiving the securities in good faith may acquire a title which the customer did not have.[1] If the property is subject to a trust, of which the banker must necessarily have notice, or of which he actually has notice, the trust must prevail against the banker's lien.[2]

If a depositor keeps two accounts, one of which is a trust account, the bank can acquire no lien on the latter account for a deficiency in the individual account. If the banker has knowledge of this, he is liable for permitting the customer to transfer money from his trust account to his private account.[3] A banker has no lien on the deposit of a partner on his separate account for a balance due to the bank from the firm.[4]

249. One cannot create an effectual lien by an agreement to transfer to a bank securities which he holds in trust, though they stand in his own name and are within his control. The agreement to transfer does not amount to the same thing as an actual transfer, so far as the rights of the beneficial owner are concerned; for the bank will not have a lien by the agreement as against such owner. Thus, one holding shares in a banking company in his own name, though part of them were purchased with trust funds, and were in fact held in trust, agreed to transfer a certain number of shares to the banking company as security for advances; but no transfer was actually made, and he became bankrupt without having shares sufficient to satisfy the trust and his agreement to assign. It was held that the banking company had no lien on the shares held in trust.[5] Referring to the trustee's agreement to transfer, Lord Cottenham, Lord Chancellor, said : " All that he has done has been an attempt to commit a breach of trust, and a fraud, undoubtedly, on the bank, by saying, ' I will pledge these shares so standing in my name for the purpose of securing the debt which I owe to

---

[1] Barnett v. Brandão, 6 M. & G. 630, 668, per Lord Denman, C. J.; Collins v. Martin, 1 Bos. & Pul. 648.

[2] Manningford v. Toleman, 1 Coll. 670; Locke v. Prescott, 32 Beav. 261.

[3] Bodenham v. Hoskyns, 2 De G., M. & G. 903.

[4] Watts v. Christie, 11 Beav. 546; Ex parte City Bank Case, 3 De G., F. & J. 629.

[5] Murray v. Pinkett, 12 Cl. & F. 764, 785.

you.' Then here are two equities, that is to say, here is a trustee of the property, which he held for the benefit of the *cestuis que trust*, endeavoring to create an equity upon that property to secure his own debt. Which of those two equities is to prevail? Undoubtedly the former."

250. A bank receiving deposits to the account of a customer, as executor, administrator, trustee, or agent, is chargeable with notice of the trust, and cannot have a lien upon the deposits to secure his private debts to the bank.[1] If the bank officers have actual knowledge that the money deposited by a customer is held by him in a fiduciary capacity, the bank for stronger reasons is affected with equities of the beneficial owners of the fund. Thus, where a customer opened an account with a bank in his own name, as general agent, and it was known to the bank that he was the agent of an insurance company; that the conducting of this agency was his chief business; that the account was opened to facilitate that business, and was used as a means of accumulating the premiums on policies collected by him for the company, and of making payments to it by checks, the bank is chargeable with notice of the equitable rights of the company, though he deposited his own money to the same account and drew checks against it for his private use. Therefore, when such depositor borrowed money from the bank for his own use upon the security of his wife's name and property, and the loan not being paid it was charged to the depositor's account as general agent; it was held that the bank had no lien as against the insurance company on such deposits.[2] Mr. Justice

[1] Bailey *v.* Finch, L. R. 7 Q. B. 34, 41. Blackburn, J., said that the opening of an account as executor operated as a notice to the bank of the trust, it being a statement to the bank: "This account which I am opening is not my own unlimited property, but it is money which belongs to the estate which I am administering as executor; consequently, there may be persons who have equitable claims upon it." The bank would be bound by any equity which did exist in another. And see Jones on Pledges, § 474.

[2] National Bank *v.* Insurance Co. 104 U. S. 54. The existence of this account as a profitable one to the bank was alleged by the customer as a reason why he should have the accommodation; but it was not pledged for the payment of the loan, either in express terms, or by any acts or conduct from which such an intention could be inferred. But, as against the insurance company, it could have made no difference if the depositor had attempted to pledge his account; for the bank had notice that this did not belong to him.

Matthews, delivering the opinion of the court, said: "Evidently the bank has no better right than the depositor, unless it can obtain it through its banker's lien. Ordinarily that attaches in favor of the bank upon the securities and moneys of the customer deposited in the usual course of business, for advances which are supposed to be made upon their credit. It attaches to such securities and funds, not only against the depositor, but against the unknown equities of all others in interest, unless modified or waived by some agreement, express or implied, or by conduct inconsistent with its assertion. But it cannot be permitted to prevail against the equity of the beneficial owner, of which the bank has notice, either actual or constructive. In the present case, in addition to the circumstance that the account was opened and kept by the depositor in his name as general agent, and all the presumptions properly arising upon it, we have found that other facts proven on the hearing justify and require the conclusion that the bank had full knowledge of the sources of the deposits made by the depositor in this account, and of his duty to remit and account for them as agent for the insurance company. It is, consequently, chargeable with notice of the equities of the insurance company."

251. A banker or broker holding securities pledged for the payment of a particular debt has no lien upon them for a general balance of account or for the payment of other claims.[1] The general lien is limited and defined by the express contract. Thus, if a partnership and an individual member of the firm have accounts with the same bank, and the partner deposits certain railway shares as collateral security for a certain promissory note of his own discounted by the bank, or for any sums he may thereafter owe to the bank, the fact that the shares were the property of the firm, and that the discounts obtained by the use of them were employed for the purposes of the firm, does not entitle the bank to hold the shares as a security for a balance due him from the firm.[2]

[1] Vanderzee v. Willis, 3 Bro. Ch. 21; *In re* Medewe's Trust, 26 Beav. 588; *In re* Gross, 24 L. T. N. S. 198; Brown v. New Bedford Inst. for Savings, 137 Mass. 262; Hathaway v. Fall River Nat. Bank, 131 Mass. 14; Jarvis v. Rogers, 15 Mass. 389; Lane v. Bailey, 47 Barb. (N. Y.) 395; Wyckoff v. Anthony, 90 N. Y. 442, affirming *S. C.* 9 Daly, 417; Davenport v. Bank of Buffalo, 9 Paige (N. Y.), 12.

[2] *Ex parte* City Bank Case, 3 De G., F. & J. 629. Lord Campbell, L. C.: "It cannot be said that a contract was

A customer of a bank deposited with it as security for his current indebtedness on discounts the note of a third person secured by mortgage, and afterwards withdrew the same for the purpose of foreclosure and collection, under an agreement to return the proceeds or to furnish other securities. He purchased the mortgaged property at the foreclosure sale, and at the request of the bank deposited with it the deed of the property. His indebtedness to the bank was afterwards fully paid, and for a time he had no dealings with it. Afterwards he incurred other debts to it, and was largely indebted to it when he became a bankrupt. It was held that the bank had no equitable lien on the property mentioned in the deed.[1]

Thus, also, where a deposit was made in a bank for the express purpose of paying coupons which had been made payable at the bank, it was held that the bank having accepted the deposit, knowing the purpose for which it was made, could not retain the money and apply it to a prior indebtedness of the depositor on another account.[2]

252. Surplus of pledged securities. — Where, however, the bankers have the right to sell the security pledged for a specified debt, after they have exercised this right, and have in their hands a surplus of money remaining after satisfying the specific charge, they may set off this money against further sums due to them.[3]

But before a sale, and while the security is held with a mere power of sale, which the debtor or his assignee may defeat, and which the bankers had not even signified their election to exercise, the bankers are not in a position to set off the debts due

entered into by which the shares were not to be a security for the separate debt of the partner, and were to be a security for the joint debt of the partnership." Turner, L. J., referring to the argument that the shares having become the property of the partnership, the pledge must be taken to have been on the joint and not on the separate account, said that it was untenable : "First, that it disregards the fact that one of the parties to the contract, the bank, did not even know of the partnership title, and dealt with the transaction as a transaction on the separate account; and, secondly, that it disregards also the distinction between the right and liabilities of the parties to the contract, and the extent of the contract itself."

[1] Railroad Co. v. McKinley, 99 U. S. 147.

[2] Bank of the United States v. Macalester, 9 Pa. St. 475.

[3] Jones v. Peppercorne, Johns. Ch. 430.

them against the surplus proceeds of the securities which might arise in case they should sell them under the power.[1]

Where a customer deposited a life insurance policy with his bankers, accompanied by a memorandum of charge to secure overdrafts, not exceeding a specified amount, it was held that the bankers' general lien was displaced, and the charge was limited to the amount specified. The court regarded it as inconsistent with the terms of the agreement, that the bankers should claim a general lien under an implied contract, when by the express contract the charge was limited to a stipulated sum.[2]

253. If a lien is given to bankers by express contract, the nature and extent of the lien depend upon the terms of the contract. Thus, where an agreement was made by a contractor about to furnish certain manufactured articles to the government, that advances, to be made by a bank to enable him to fulfil his contract, should be a lien on the drafts to be drawn by him on the government for the proceeds of the articles manufactured, it was held that the bank had no lien on a judgment obtained against the government for damages for violation of the contract, all the drafts drawn upon the government for the articles manufactured and delivered having been paid in full to the bank.[3]

254. Bankers have no lien on a box containing securities deposited with them by a customer for safe keeping, he keeping the key and having access to the box, and the bankers not having access to the contents of it.[4] The same rule would apply to securities left with a banker for safe keeping in

[1] Brown v. New Bedford Inst. for Savings, 137 Mass. 262.

[2] Strathmore v. Vane, 33 L. R. Ch. D. 586. To like effect see Wylde v. Radford, 33 L. J. (Ch.) 51; S. C. 12 W. R. 38; 9 Jur. N. S. 1169, which cannot be distinguished, except that in the latter case the security was limited to a part of the property included in the deposited deeds, and in Strathmore v. Vane the security was limited to cover a part only of the debt. See, also, In re Medewe's Trust, 26 Beav. 588; S. C. 5 Jur. N. S. 421; 28 L. J. Ch. 891, where it was held that a security given by a customer to his bankers for the balance "which shall or may be found due on the balance of" the account, covered the existing account only, and not a floating balance.

[3] Bank of Washington v. Nock, 9 Wall. 373.

[4] Leese v. Martin, L. R. 17 Eq. 224.

a sealed-up parcel;[1] and to a box of plate deposited in the bank vaults for safe custody.[2]

255. There can be no lien where the securities have come into the banker's hands under circumstances inconsistent with the existence of a general lien. A Portuguese merchant residing in Lisbon employed his correspondent, a merchant in London, to invest money for him in exchequer bills. The latter purchased the bills and deposited them in a box that he kept at his bankers, the key of which he himself retained. Whenever it became necessary to receive the interest on the bills and to exchange them for new ones, the London merchant was in the habit of taking them out of the box and giving them to the bankers for that purpose; and when such purpose was accomplished, as soon as conveniently might be the bankers handed them or the new bills back to their customer, who locked them up in the box. The amount of interest received by the bankers was passed to the credit of the customer. The bills themselves were never entered to his account, nor had the bankers any notice or knowledge that they were not the customer's own property. Finally the customer delivered the exchequer bills to the bankers for the purpose of receiving the interest and exchanging them for new bills; but after the exchange, on account of the customer's illness, the new bills remained in the possession of the bankers for some two months, and until the customer's failure, he having in the mean time considerably overdrawn his account. In a suit by the true owner of the bills against the bankers, it was held in the House of Lords that they had no lien for the general balance of their account upon the securities, although these were transferable by delivery.[3] Lord Lyndhurst, Lord Chancellor, said: "It is impossible, considering how this business was carried on, that we can come to any other conclusion than this, that it was the understanding between the parties that the exchequer bills were to be returned after the interest was received, or after they were exchanged. If so, and that was the understanding,— the fair inference from the transaction,— it is quite clear that there could be no lien, and that the case does not come within the general rule. . . . Although,

[1] Per Hall, V. C., in Leese v. Martin, L. R. 17 Eq. 224.

[2] Ex parte Eyre, 1 Ph. 227, 235.

[3] Brandão v. Barnett, 3 Com. B. 519; S. C. 12 Cl. & F. 787, overruling S. C. 1 M. & G. 908; 2 Scott N. R. 96. See, also, Grant v. Taylor, 3 J. & S. (N. Y.) 338.

from the accidental circumstance of the illness of the customer, these exchequer bills happened to remain for a longer period in the hands of the bankers than was usual, that accidental circumstance alone will not vary the case, or give the bankers a lien, if, under other circumstances, that lien would not have attached." Lord Campbell concurring, on another point said : " No reliance, I think, can be placed on the circumstance of the interest received on the old exchequer bills going to the credit of the account of the customer; for, while he gives the bankers the interest to keep for him with one hand, he locks up the new exchequer bills in his tin box with the other."

256. A banker has no lien on securities casually left with him after he has refused to advance money on them. In a leading case on this point, a person went to a banker to raise a certain sum of money on the security of a lease. The banker considered the proposition and rejected it. But the lease, in the language of the report, was "casually left" in the possession of the bankers, and the bankruptcy of the owner of the lease having afterwards happened, the bankers claimed they were entitled to hold this lease by virtue of a banker's lien upon it. The court held that there was no lien upon the lease.[1]

II. *Application of the Lien as between Corresponding Banks.*

257. A bank has a lien on paper received for collection from a corresponding bank, although it is not the property of that bank, if there be nothing on the face of the paper and no notice in any way to the collecting bank that the paper does not belong to the bank that transmits it. In a leading case before the Supreme Court of the United States, it appeared that two banks were in the habit of transmitting to each other paper for collection. They had for several years an account current between them in which they mutually credited each other with the proceeds of all paper remitted for collection which appeared to be the property of the respective banks. One bank transmitted to the other certain paper, indorsed by the bank which sent it, and apparently belonging to it, for collection. The bank which received the paper collected it, and held the proceeds, when the

---

[1] Lucas *v.* Dorrien, 7 Taunt. 278; *v.* Brandão, 6 Man. & Gr. 630; Petrie S. C. 1 Moore, 29. See, also, Barnett *v.* Myers, 54 How. (N. Y.) Pr. 513.

bank which had transmitted it proved to be insolvent, and indebted to the other bank. The paper in fact belonged to a third bank which brought suit against the collecting bank for the proceeds of the paper. The Supreme Court held that the bank which had collected the paper, in the absence of knowledge or notice of facts to put it upon inquiry that the paper did not belong to its correspondent, had the same right of lien for a general balance of account upon the paper and its proceeds that it would have had if the paper had actually belonged to its correspondent.[1] The court said that the plaintiff bank contributed to give to the bank which proved insolvent credit with the defendant bank, by placing in its hands paper which was apparently the property of the insolvent bank; thus enabling this bank to deal with the paper as if it were the real owner of it. The defendant bank, on the other hand, was not in any way responsible for the confidence which the plaintiff bank reposed in its agent. The superior equity is on the side of the defendant bank, which is entitled to a lien for a general balance of account with its corresponding bank.

258. Same subject continued. — A similar case was decided in like manner by the supreme court of Colorado.[2] It appeared that a customer of a banker drew his draft on London, payable to the banker, to whom he delivered it to collect and place to the customer's account. The banker indorsed and transmitted the draft to a national bank for collection. At this time the banker was indebted to the national bank for over-drafts. The draft was paid, but before the proceeds came into the actual possession of the national bank, it received notice that the drawer of the draft had delivered it to his banker for collection, and that he claimed the proceeds. In a suit by the drawer against the national bank, it was held that he could not recover; but that this bank had a lien upon the proceeds for a balance of account against the banker from whom the bank received the draft. The

---

[1] Bank of Metropolis v. New England Bank, 1 How. 234; affirmed, 6 Ib. 212; S. C. 17 Pet. 174; followed in Russell v. Hadduck, 3 Gilm. (Ill.) 233; Gordon v. Kearney, 17 Ohio, 572; Miller v. Farmers' and Mechanics' Bank, 30 Md. 392. See, also, Hoffman v. Miller, 9 Bosw. (N. Y.) 334; Van Namee v. Bank of Troy, 5 How. (N. Y.) Pr. 161.

[2] Wyman v. Colorado Nat. Bank, 5 Colo. 30.

bank received the draft without notice of the equities between the original parties, and thus became a *bonâ fide* holder of the draft for value.[1]

The possession of the paper by the bank transmitting it is regarded as *primâ facie* evidence that it owned the paper ; and the bank receiving it having no notice to the contrary, is entitled so to treat it.

259. This doctrine does not apply in New York, because under the rule established in Coddington *v.* Bay,[2] the taking of paper as security for, or in payment of, an antecedent debt, is not a valuable consideration therefor, and therefore a collecting bank not making any present advance upon the paper, or giving any new credit, or assuming any new responsibility on the faith of such paper, has no lien upon it for a balance of account arising from previous dealings between the banks.[3]

Where two banks act as collecting agents for each other, keeping a running account and settling balances at stated intervals, the collections not being kept separate from other funds of the bank, the relation between the banks is simply that of debtor and creditor. The creditor bank acquires no lien upon any specific fund, and, upon the failure of the debtor bank, is not entitled to any preference over other creditors.[4]

260. If a bank receives paper "for collection" from a corresponding bank, or with other notice that the paper does not belong to the latter, but that it is sent for collection for the account of a third person, such banker cannot retain the paper or its proceeds to answer a balance owing by the corresponding banker. If the corresponding banker indorsed the paper " for collection," the negotiability is thereby limited to that purpose, and, notwithstanding the rule that one who has placed his name on negotiable paper shall not afterwards be allowed to impeach the instrument, the banker who has indorsed paper for collection

---

[1] In support of this rule see Clark *v.* Merchants' Bank, 2 N. Y. 380 ; Sweeny *v.* Easter, 1 Wall. 166.

[2] 20 Johns. 637.

[3] McBride *v.* Farmers' Bank, 26 N. Y. 450. And see Lindauer *v.*

Fourth Nat. Bank, 55 Barb. 75 ; Dod *v.* Fourth Nat. Bank, 59 Ib. 265.

As to the rule in Coddington *v.* Bay, see Jones on Pledges, §§ 117–123.

[4] People *v.* City Bank of Rochester, 93 N. Y. 582.

171

is competent to prove that he was not the owner of it, and did not mean to give title to it or to its proceeds when collected.[1]

The fact that a banker received the paper, with knowledge that it was indorsed for collection only, may appear otherwise than by an indorsement in terms for collection only. Such knowledge may be shown by any competent evidence. If the paper be indorsed in blank, and sent to a banker with a letter of instructions, in which it is stated that the paper is sent for collection, the banker is not an assignee of the paper, but merely an agent for its collection, and cannot hold the paper or its proceeds for a general balance of account due from the correspondent who sent it, and who was also an agent for collection.[2]

A banker's lien is sustained in such case upon the presumption that credit was given upon the faith of the securities, either in possession or in expectancy. If the banker has knowledge of circumstances which should put a prudent man upon inquiry as to the title of the securities, he is affected with notice of such facts as the inquiry would lead to.[3]

261. The collecting bank cannot, however, maintain a lien if it has made no advances and given no credit to the corresponding bank on account of the paper received and collected. Where a bank employed to collect paper transmits it to another bank, either by express authority or under authority implied from the usual course of trade, or from the nature of the transaction, the principal may treat the latter bank as his agent, and, when it has received the money, may recover it in an action for money had and received.[4] Where there is no mutual arrangement between corresponding banks, or previous course of dealing between them, whereby it is expressly or impliedly understood that remittances of paper are to be placed to the

[1] Sweeny v. Easter, 1 Wall. 166; Cecil Bank v. Farmers' Bank, 22 Md. 148. And see Bank of the Metropolis v. New Eng. Bank, 6 How. 212.

[2] Lawrence v. Stonington Bank, 6 Conn. 521. The authorities relied upon in this case are Barker v. Prentiss, 6 Mass. 430; Herrick v. Carman, 10 Johns. (N. Y.) 224. Chief Justice Hosmer, giving the opinion, said : "The custom of transmitting bills for collection from one bank to another,

and crediting in account the avails received, whatever effect it may have between themselves, cannot affect the claims of a third person, who has confided the collection of a bill to one of them, without assent, either express or implied, to the mode of transacting their business."

[3] Russell v. Hadduck, 3 Gilm. (Ill.) 233.

[4] Wilson v. Smith, 3 How. 763.

credit of the remitting bank, or, where there is no credit given
upon the faith of the particular paper remitted, or of the usual
course of dealing, the collecting bank has no lien upon the
money collected in ·that manner; and the owner of the bill or
note remitted for collection, through his banker, may recover
the amount, although the collecting bank has placed the amount
to the credit of the corresponding bank in payment of a subsisting indebtedness.[1]

[1] Millikin v. Shapleigh, 36 Mo. 596.   Bank, 59 Barb. (N. Y.) 265; Lindauer
And see, also, Dod v. Fourth Nat.   v. Fourth Nat. Bank, 55 Ib. 75.

CHAPTER VII. |

I. *Are Specific, not General.*

262. A common carrier has a specific lien upon the goods carried for his hire in carrying them.[1] He is invested with this peculiar privilege, it is said, on account of his obligation to receive and carry any goods offered, and his liability for their safety in the course of transportation.[2] He is necessarily in possession of the goods, and, at the end of the journey, he is allowed to retain possession until he receives a reasonable remuneration for his services. The carrier's right to retain the goods until he is paid for his services is his lien. This right is merely a right of possession. The property is necessarily supposed to be in some other person. One cannot have a lien upon his own property. The lien confers no right of property. It does not enable the carrier to sell the goods, except as he is authorized to do so by some modern statute, even though the keeping of them be attended with expense and inconvenience.[3] The lien merely confers a right of possession until the charges

---

[1] Skinner *v.* Upshaw, 2 Ld. Raym. 752; Gisbourn *v.* Hurst, 1 Salk. 249; Middleton *v.* Fowler, Ib. 282; The Bird of Paradise, 5 Wall. 545; Ames *v.* Palmer, 42 Me. 197; Wilson *v.* Grand Trunk Ry. Co. 56 Me. 60; Sullivan *v.* Park, 33 Me. 438; Hunt *v.* Haskell, 24 Me. 339; Pinney *v* Wells, 10 Conn. 104, 115; Galena & Chicago Union R. R. Co. *v.* Rae, 18 Ill. 488; Clarkson *v.* Edes, 4 Cow. (N. Y.) 470; Langworthy *v.* N. Y. & Harlem R. R. Co. 2 E. D. Smith, 195;

Barker *v.* Havens, 17 Johns. (N. Y.) 234; Rucker *v.* Donovan, 13 Kans. 251; Brown *v.* Clayton 12 Ga. 564, 566; Boggs *v.* Martin, 13 B. Mon. (Ky.) 239 ; Goodman *v.* Stewart, Wright (Ohio), 216; Bowman *v.* Hilton, 11 Ohio, 303.

[2] Per Holt, C. J., in Yorke *v.* Greenaugh, 2 Ld. Raym. 866; per Lord Ellenborough, in Rushforth *v.* Hadfield, 6 East, 519.

[3] See §§ **335–374.**

for carriage are paid. This right avails against the true owner of the goods, though some one else be liable for the freight, unless they have been shipped in fraud of the owner.[1]

263. As regards the origin of this lien and the reasons for its existence, it does not seem necessary to go beyond the common law principle that a bailee of goods who alters or improves their condition is entitled to a lien on them for his compensation. The reason assigned for the existence of the lien, that carriers are bound to carry for any persons who may require them to do so, does not apply to carriers by water, who, nevertheless, have a lien for carrying goods. This lien for the freight of goods carried by sea does not depend upon any peculiar maritime law or custom. It is a common law lien as much as is the lien given to carriers by land; and the common law principle which lies at the foundation of most common law liens is sufficient to justify the lien of carriers by land, and carriers by water as well.

264. In several states the carrier's lien is declared by statute. The statutes of these states differ much in the terms in which the lien is declared. Some of them materially change the common law rules, and therefore it seems important to give a synopsis of these statutes.

In California[2] and Dakota Territory[3] every person who, while lawfully in possession of an article of personal property, renders any service to the owner thereof, by labor or skill employed for the protection, improvement, safe keeping, or carriage thereof, has a special lien thereon, dependent on possession, for the compensation, if any, which is due to him from the owner for such service.

In Colorado[4] and Wyoming Territory[5] every common carrier of goods or passengers who shall, at the request of the owner of any personal goods, carry, convey, or transport the same from one place to another, and any warehouseman or other person, who shall safely keep or store any personal property, at the request of the owner or person lawfully in possession thereof,

---

[1] Robinson v. Baker, 5 Cush. (Mass.) 137.

[2] Civ. Code, § 3051. See, also, § 2144.

[3] Civ. Code, § 1806.

[4] Gen. Stats. 1883, § 2119.

[5] Comp. Laws 1876, p. 462; Act Dec. 13, 1873, § 2.

shall in like manner have a lien upon all such personal property, for his reasonable charges for the transportation, storage, or keeping thereof, and for all reasonable and proper advances made thereon by him in accordance with the usage and custom of common carriers and warehousemen.

In Georgia [1] a carrier has a lien for freight upon the goods carried, and may retain them until the freight is paid. But such lien does not arise until the carrier has complied with his contract as to transportation. He can, however, recover *pro rata* for the actual distance the goods are carried, when the consignee voluntarily receives the goods at an intermediate point.

In Iowa [2] personal property transported by, or stored or left with, any warehouseman, forwarding and commission merchant, or other depositary, express company, or carriers, is subject to a lien for the just and lawful charges on the same, and for the transportation, advances, and storage thereof.

In Louisiana, [3] carriers' charges and the accessory expenses are a privilege on the thing carried, including necessary charges and expenses paid by carriers, such as taxes, storage, and privileged claims required to be paid before moving the thing.

In New Mexico, [4] common carriers have a lien on the things carried for the freight due, if payment of freight was to have been made on delivery of the things carried. All persons carrying goods for hire or pay are deemed common carriers.

In Minnesota [5] and Oregon [6] any person who is a common carrier, and any person who, at the request of the owner or lawful possessor of any personal property, carries, conveys, or transports the same from one place to another, and any person who safely keeps or stores any personal property, at the request of the owner or lawful possessor thereof, shall have the same lien and the same power of sale for the satisfaction of his reasonable charges.

In Utah Territory, [7] all common carriers in this territory have a lien upon any goods, wares, merchandise, or other property in their possession, as such carrier, for freight or transportation thereof, including back charges paid by such carriers to connecting lines.

---

[1] Code 1882, §§ 2077, 1986.
[2] R. Code 1880, § 2177.
[3] Rev. Laws 1884, § 2873.

[4] Comp. Laws 1884, §§ 1547, 1548, 1543, 1544.
[5] Stats. 1878, p. 875, ch. 90, § 17.
[6] Laws 1878, p. 102, § 2.
[7] Comp. Laws 1876, p. 389, § 1190.

The liens of carriers are also in other states either expressly or incidentally recognized in the statutory provisions authorizing the sale of goods by carriers, and the satisfaction of their charges out of the proceeds.[1]

265. The carrier's lien is a particular or specific lien, attaching only to the specific goods in his possession, and in general secures only the unpaid price for the carriage of those specific goods.[2] It is only by express agreement, or by an agreement implied from the general usage of trade, or from previous dealings between the same parties, that his lien can be extended to cover his general balance of account.[3] Such usage must be proved by clear and satisfactory instances, sufficiently numerous and general to warrant a conclusion affecting the custom of the country. A few recent instances of such a usage will not serve to establish the requisite proof of it.[4] Thus, proof of instances of such a usage by carriers in a particular part of the country for ten or twelve years, and in one instance so far back as thirty years, though not opposed by other evidence, was regarded by the King's Bench as insufficient to establish a general usage. Lord Ellenborough, referring to the evidence in this case, said:[5] "In many cases it would happen that parties would

[1] **Alabama**: Code 1876, § 2142.
Arizona Territory: Comp. Laws 1877, ch. 86.
Delaware : Laws, 13, ch. 164.
Illinois: Annotated Stats. 1885, ch. 141, § 1.
Indiana: R. S. 1881, § 2900.
Kansas : Comp. Laws 1885, ch. 58, § 3.
Maryland: R. C. 1878, art. 67, ch. 20, § 1.
Massachusetts: P. S. 1882, ch. 96, § 3.
Missouri: R. S. 1879, § 6277.
Nevada : Laws 1875, ch. 42, § 1.
New Jersey: 1 Rev. p. 593, § 1.
New York: R. S. 7th ed.
Ohio : R. S. 1880, § 3221.
Pennsylvania : Brightly's Purdon's Dig. 1882.
Rhode Island: P. S. ch. 139, § 5.
South Carolina: G. S. 1882, § 1663.

Tennessee: Code 1884, § 2788.
Texas : R. S. 1879, § 285.
Virginia : Code 1873, ch. 61, § 33.
Washington Territory : Code 1881, § 1980.
Wisconsin: R. S. 1878, § 1637.

[2] Butler v. Woolcott, 2 B. & P. N. R. 64 ; Hartshorne v. Johnson, 7 N. J. L. (2 Halst.) 108 ; Leonard v. Winslow, 2 Grant (Pa.), 139.

[3] Rushforth v. Hadfield, 6 East, 519 ; S. C. 2 Smith, 634.

[4] Rushforth v. Hadfield, supra; Whitehead v. Vaughan, 6 East, 523, n.; Holderness v. Collinson, 7 B. & C. 212; Kirkman v. Shawcross, 6 T. R. 14.

[5] Rushforth v. Hadfield, 7 East, 224, S. C. 3 Smith, 221. The words of Lord Ellenborough seem to imply his opinion that notice of the usage to the party dealing with a carrier might create a general lien; but in the same

be glad to pay small sums due for the carriage of former goods, rather than incur the risk of a great loss by the detention of goods of value. Much of the evidence is of that description. Other instances again were in the case of solvent persons, who were at all events liable to answer for their general balance. And little or no stress could be laid on some of the more recent instances not brought home to the knowledge of the bankrupt at the time. Most of the evidence, therefore, is open to observation. If, indeed, there had been evidence of prior dealings between these parties upon the footing of such an extended lien, that would have furnished good evidence for the jury to have found that they continued to deal upon the same terms. But the question for the jury here was, whether the evidence of a usage for the carriers to retain for their balance were so general as that the bankrupt must be taken to have known and acted upon it ? And they have in effect found either that the bankrupt knew of no such usage as that which was given in evidence, or, knowing, did not adopt it."

No usage can enable the carrier to retain the goods as against a consignee to whom they belong, for debts due to him from the shipper.[1]

266. A condition or provision in a contract giving the carrier a general lien must be clearly brought home to the knowledge of the customer. It seems proper that the carrier's right to create a lien for his general balance should be restricted in the same way that his right to limit his common law liability is restricted; that is to say, it should be incumbent upon the carrier, in case he attempts to make any change from the usual mode of dealing, to bring home to his customers such notice or knowledge of the change as warrants the implication of a contract to that effect. An agreement by a trader with a railway company providing for a general lien does not apply, after the trader's failure, to goods sent to the company by a receiver and manager appointed to carry on the trader's business in liquidation; and if such receiver, in order to obtain a delivery of such goods pays under protest a prior indebtedness of the trader to the company,

case Gosse, J., said : "I take it to be sound law that no such lien can exist except by the contract of the parties express or implied."

[1] Wright v. Snell, 5 B. & Ald. 350 ; Leuckhart v. Cooper, 3 Bing. N. C. 99 ; Butler v. Woolcott, 2 B. & P. N. R. 64.

the company is liable in a proper action for the repayment of the amount so paid.[1]

If the carrier demands a further sum besides the freight, or any charge connected with the carriage of the goods, and refuses to deliver them unless such further sum is first paid, the consignee, who is ready to pay the freight, is not bound to tender this to the carrier before bringing trover. The carrier's refusal to give up the goods, except upon receiving a payment he had no right to demand, is evidence of a conversion.[2]

A common carrier cannot seize goods while in transit for a debt due himself wholly unconnected with the shipment. He cannot by his own act prevent himself from performing his contract, and then plead his own act as an excuse for not performing it.[3]

267. A consignor's right of stoppage in transitu is not affected by an agreement for a general lien, such as a contract, express or implied, between the consignee of goods and the carrier, that the latter shall have a lien for a general balance of account.[4] A usage for carriers to retain goods, as a lien for a general balance of account between them and the consignees, does not affect the right of the consignor to stop the goods *in transitu*.[5]

268. But the owner of goods who stops them in transitu is bound by the carrier's specific lien, and cannot take the goods from him without first paying or tendering the freight thereon.[6]

II. *In whose Favor they Attach.*

269. This lien attaches in favor of a carrier of passengers to the luggage of a passenger, either to secure the payment of

---

[1] *Ex parte* Great Western Ry. Co. L. R. 22 Ch. D. 470.

[2] Adams *v.* Clark, 9 Cush. (Mass.) 215. The further sum demanded by the carrier in this case was for the passage of a third party, the consignor's son, who accompanied the goods.

[3] Pharr *v.* Collins, 35 La. Ann. 939; *S. C.* 48 Am. R. 251.

[4] Wright *v.* Snell, 5 B. & Ald. 350; Potts *v.* N. Y. & N. E. R. R. Co. 131 Mass. 455.

[5] Oppenheim *v.* Russell, 3 Bos. & P. 42, 43; Jackson *v.* Nichol, 5 Bing. N. C. 508, 518; *S. C.* 7 Scott, 577, 591.

[6] Raymond *v.* Tyson, 17 How. 53; The Eddy, 5 Wall. 481; The Volunteer, 1 Sum. 551; Chandler *v.* Belden, 18 Johns. (N. Y.) 157; Potts *v.* N. Y. & N. E. R. R. Co. *supra;* Cowing *v.* Snow, 11 Mass. 415.

his fare, or charges for extra luggage.[1] Upon a railroad the lien attaches not only to luggage which the passenger delivers to the company's servants to be marked and carried as such, but also to whatever the passenger takes with him as luggage into the passenger coach ; for this is considered so far in the possession of the agents of the company as to authorize it to exercise the right of detainer for the passenger's fare, or for freight upon the article itself.[2]

If a person goes to a coach-office and has a place booked for him in a particular coach, and leaves his portmanteau, the carrier has a lien upon this for some part, but not the full amount, of the regular fare,[3] in case the passenger does not occupy his place. But if a person merely leaves his portmanteau at the coach-office while he goes to inquire if there is an earlier coach, and no place is actually booked for him, the coach proprietor has no lien at all.[4]

270. Carriers by water have a lien as well as carriers by land. A ship-owner has a lien for freight upon the goods carried, whether the vessels be chartered, or be general ships carrying goods for all persons for hire. The master is not bound to deliver possession of any part of his cargo until the freight and other charges due in respect of such part are paid.[5] This lien may be regarded as a maritime lien, because it is cognizable in the admiralty, and, under the usages of commerce, arises independently of the agreement of the parties. The ship-owner may

---

[1] Wolf v. Summers, 2 Camp. 631. "There is no reason why there should not be the same lien for the recovery of passage money as for the recovery of freight." Per Lawrence, J. Woods v. Devin, 13 Ill. 746, 749, per Treat, C. J.; Nordemeyer v. Loescher, 1 Hilt. (N. Y.) 499; Southwest R. R. Co. v. Bently, 51 Ga. 311; Hutchings v. Western & Atlantic R. R. 25 Ga. 61.
In **California** : so declared by the Code, 2 Deering's Codes and Stats. 1885, § 2191 of Civ. Code. Also in **Georgia** : Code 1882, § 2079.

[2] Hutchings v. Western & Atlantic R. R. supra.

[3] Higgins v. Bretherton, 5 C. & P. 2.

[4] Higgins v. Bretherton, supra.

[5] Kirchner v. Venus, 12 Moore P. C. 361 ; Phillips v. Rodie, 15 East, 547, 554; Bird of Paradise, 5 Wall. 545 ; The Volunteer, 1 Sum. 551; Lane v. Penniman, 4 Mass. 91, 92 ; Lewis v. Hancock, 11 Mass. 72 ; Cowing v. Snow, 11 Mass. 414, 415; Hunt v. Haskell, 24 Me. 339 ; Frothingham v. Jenkins, 1 Cal. 42; Green v. Campbell, 52 Cal. 586.
In **Illinois** it is provided by statute that there shall also be a lien upon "goods, wares, and merchandise shipped, taken in, and put aboard any water-craft for sums due for freight, advanced charges, and demurrage." 1 Annotated Stats. 1885, ch. 12, § 2.

retain the goods until the freight is paid, or he may enforce it by a proceeding *in rem* in the admiralty court.[1] But although the lien is maritime and cognizable in the admiralty, it stands upon the same ground with the common law lien of the carrier on land, is subject to the same principles except as regards enforcement, and may therefore be considered in connection with the liens of carriers by land.[2]

271. **There is ordinarily a lien for freight under a charter-party.** This lien arises independently of the express terms of the charter-party, unless these are inconsistent with it; and it exists even where the charter freight is a fixed sum, having no direct relation to the quantity of goods carried. Whatever be the contract, if the ship-owner undertakes to carry the goods and not merely to lease his ship, it seems that there is a lien for freight.[3] The substance of the charter-party is considered, and not the form of it. If the ship be clearly leased to the charterer, there can be no lien, because the hirer is in exclusive possession for the term.[4] But the nature of the service is to be considered, as well as the terms of the charter-party, in determining whether the ship-owner has parted with possession. Where there is no express demise of the ship, and the nature of the service does not show that the charterer was to have possession, he does not become the owner for the voyage; but the possession continues in the ship-owner, and he may have a lien on the cargo for his freight.[5]

272. **Under a charter-party for the voyage the ship-owner generally has no lien on goods shipped by the charterer**, because he is considered the owner for the voyage, and the ship-owner has no possession of the ship or goods sufficient to maintain a lien.[6] But where the charter-party expressly reserves to the ship-owner a lien on the lading of the ship, the charterer in

[1] Bird of Paradise, 5 Wall. 545, 555, per Clifford, J.; The Volunteer, 1 Sum. 551; Certain Logs of Mahogany, 2 Sum. 589.

[2] Bird of Paradise, *supra*, per Clifford, J.; Bags of Linseed, 1 Black, 108, 113, per Taney, C. J.

[3] Carver's Carriage of Goods by Sea, § 655; Tate *v.* Meek, 8 Taunt. 280.

[4] Hutton *v.* Bragg, 7 Taunt. 14; *S. C.* 2 Marsh. 339; and see Vallejo *v.* Wheeler, Cowp. 143; Trinity House *v.* Clark, 4 Maule & S. 288.

[5] Saville *v.* Campion, 2 B. & Ald. 503.

[6] Hutton *v.* Bragg, *supra;* Belcher *v.* Capper, 4 M. & G. 502.

effect covenants that, whatever may be the legal operation of the charter-party as between themselves, the charterer's possession of the ship shall be the owner's possession, so far as the right of the latter to a lien on the cargo is concerned, and he may assert his lien as against the cargo though this belongs to the charterer.[1] If the latter sells the cargo during the voyage, the purchaser, with notice of the charter-party, takes it subject to the lien in favor of the ship-owner to which it was subject before the sale. The lien remains good even against an indorsee of the bill of lading with notice.[2]

273. If the master, being the agent of the ship-owner, signs bills of lading for the goods of third persons, or bills of lading which are transferred to others, subject only to the freight specified therein, and not expressly reserving a lien to the ship-owner for the charter freight, the ship-owner is regarded as having waived his lien under the charter-party, and he is estopped from enforcing such lien beyond the freight specified in the bills of lading, though this may be less than the charter freight. Third persons are authorized to deal with the holder of such bills of lading on the basis of the freight therein specified.[3]

The goods of third persons shipped in a general ship are not affected by a claim in a charter-party, of which he has no notice or knowledge, giving the ship-owner a lien on all the cargo and freight for arrears of hire due to him under the charter-party.[4] A shipper is not bound to assume that there is a charter-party, and he is not bound by its contents until he is put upon inquiry.[5] But if the charterer of a ship, under a charter-party giving the owner a lien on any part of the cargo for all the freight, fraudulently issues a bill of lading for the goods of a third party, using the master's name without his knowledge or authority, who had no knowledge of the charter-party, the goods are subject to the lien given by the charter-party.[6]

And so if the master of a ship collusively issues bills of lading

---

[1] Small v. Moates, 9 Bing. 574.

[2] Small v. Moates, supra. Some passages in the judgment rendered by Tindal, C. J., in this case, are not qualified as in the text above, and are not in accord with the later decisions.

[3] Foster v. Colby, 28 L. J. Ex. 81; Gardner v. Trechmann, 15 Q. B. D.

154; Mitchell v. Scaife, 4 Camp. 298; Chappel v. Comfort, 31 L. J. C. P. 58; The Karo, 29 Fed. Rep. 652.

[4] The Stornoway, 46 L. T. 773.

[5] Per Lord Romilly, in Peek v. Larsen, 12 Eq. 378.

[6] The Karo, supra.

to shippers with the purpose of depriving the ship-owner of his lien, the latter may nevertheless detain the goods for the freight due under the charter-party.[1] And so, if the master acts without authority in issuing bills of lading which make the freight payable to third persons, the ship-owner may still have a lien on the goods for the balance of the charter freight.[2] It is not in the power of the master to change the charter-party so as to release the charterer from his contract with the owner, and deprive the latter of his lien on the cargo for his freight. All the power delegated to the master while the charter-party continues to operate, is to perform the undertakings of the owner in the fulfilment of the contract.[3]

274. The bill of lading may by its terms incorporate the charter-party, or a provision of it giving a lien for freight, so that the owner's lien for charter freight will be preserved.[4] A provision, however, that freight shall be paid *as per charter-party*, may mean only that freight is payable at the rate mentioned in the charter-party, so that the lien would be limited to such rate,[5] and further liens given by the charter-party would not be preserved.[6] Under such a general reference to the charter-party, a lien given by that for dead freight, or demurrage, does not attach as against holders of the bills of lading who have no other knowledge of the provisions of the charter-party.[7]

A charter-party expressly provided that the owner should have a lien on the cargo for freight, dead freight, and demurrage, and also provided that the captain should sign bills of lading at any rate of freight; "but, should the total freight, as per bills of lading, be under the amount estimated to be earned by this charter, the captain to demand payment of any difference in advance." Goods were shipped and a bill of lading issued whereby freight was made payable at a less rate than that provided for by the charter-party; the bill of lading also containing a clause providing that extra expenses should be borne by the receivers, and " other conditions as per charter-party." Upon the arrival of

---

[1] Faith *v.* East India Co. 4 B. & Ald. 630.

[2] Reynolds *v.* Jex, 34 L. J. Q. B. 251.

[3] Gracie *v.* Palmer, 8 Wheat. 605.

[4] Porteus *v.* Watney, 3 Q. B. D. 223; Wegener *v.* Smith, 24 L. J. C. P. 25; Gray *v.* Carr, L. R. 6 Q. B. 522, 523.

[5] Fry *v.* Chartered Mercantile Bank, L. R. 1 C. P. 689.

[6] Smith *v.* Sieveking, 5 E. & B. 589.

[7] McLean *v.* Fleming, L. R. 2 H. L. (Scotch) 128; Chappel *v.* Comfort, 31 L. J. C. P. 58.

the ship at the port of discharge, the owner claimed and compelled payment at the rate mentioned in the charter-party. In a suit by the consignees to recover the excess paid above the freight specified in the bill of lading, it was held[1] that the bill of lading did not incorporate the stipulation of the charter-party as to the payment of freight; that no right of lien existed for the difference between the freight under the charter-party and that payable under the bill of lading; and that the plaintiffs were entitled to delivery of the goods upon payment of the freight specified in the bill of lading. Brett, M. R., said : " In the first place, I am of opinion that the charter-party gave no right of lien for that difference ; the excess of the amount estimated to be earned by the charter-party over the freight payable under the bills of lading was to be paid immediately before the ship sailed; it was to be demanded by the captain; the ship-owner had no right of lien for that excess even against the charterer ; the stipulation was a mere reservation of a right which the ship-owner could not enforce by lien. Secondly, if the right of lien ever existed, it was ousted by the terms of the bill of lading. There are many cases as to what is brought into the bill of lading by this general reference to the charter-party. It brings in only those clauses of the charter-party which are applicable to the contract contained in the bill of lading; and those clauses of the charter-party cannot be brought in which would alter the express stipulations in the bill of lading."

275. A ship-owner has no lien for freight, before the commencement of the voyage, on goods taken on board the ship. If the owner of the goods sells them before the voyage begins, and gives an order for their delivery to the purchaser, the ship-owner cannot detain them for the freight under an agreement for a charter-party made with the vendor, the charter-party never having been executed in accordance with the agreement. The purchaser is entitled to the goods, and the ship-owner must look to the vendor for damages for violation of the contract.[2]

A carrier or other person who has undertaken to perform a definite service in the carriage of goods cannot claim a lien if he has failed to perform his contract. Thus, if he has undertaken to haul all the logs upon a certain lot within a certain time,

[1] Gardner v. Trechmann, 15 Q. B. D. 154.   [2] Burgess v. Gun, 3 Har. & J. (Md.) 225, 227.

and only partly performs the contract, he cannot hold the logs he has hauled on the ground of a lien for the service he has done.[1]

276. One who is not a public or common carrier, but specially undertakes to carry particular goods for hire, is said to have no lien for his services, unless he specially reserves it by agreement. But if he holds himself out to the public as a carrier for hire, he is as much a common carrier on his first trip as on any subsequent one, and is entitled to a lien for his services.[2]

Upon general principles, however, there seems to be no reason why a private carrier should not have a lien for performing services similar to those rendered by a public carrier. His services go to increase the value of the thing carried, in the same manner that a mechanic adds to the value of a chattel by his labor upon it. The old notion of the origin of the lien, that it is a privilege given to a carrier on account of his obligation to receive and carry any goods offered, necessarily confined the lien to public carriers. We have already suggested doubts whether this should be accounted the true foundation for this lien; and it is admitted that all carriers by water have the lien, whether they be public or private carriers. The usage, moreover, seems now to be common that private carriers by land may demand and receive the same lien that is given to common carriers. The statutes of several states recognizing or declaring carriers' liens make no distinction between public carriers and private carriers.

It seems that where logs have been transported by being towed through a canal or river, or rafted together and floated, the person performing the service has a lien upon the logs for his compensation, upon the same principle which gives a lien for the freight of goods forwarded by ordinary conveyances.[3] A lumberman who carries lumber for hire upon a river, though not a common carrier, has a lien in the same way that a carrier by water, who is not a common carrier, has a lien.

[1] Hodgdon v. Waldron, 9 N. H. 66.

[2] Fuller v. Bradley, 25 Pa. St. 120; Picquet v. M'Kay, 2 Blackf. (Ind.) 465.

[3] Wing v. Griffin, 1 E. D. Smith (N. Y.), 162 ; In re Coumbe, 24 Grant (Ont.) Ch. 519. See Hodgdon v. Waldron, supra.

277. One substituted in the carrier's right occupies his place, but can occupy no better position. An officer levied upon goods which the consignor had stopped *in transitu*, and paid the carrier's charges. The consignor thereupon took the goods from the officer upon a writ of replevin, and the officer neither demanded the freight charges paid by him, nor in any way placed his right to retain possession upon the ground of the carrier's lien. It was held that he could not afterwards set up a claim of lien for such charges in defence to the suit.[1]

278. A carrier acting solely for the bailee or lessee of goods has no lien upon them as against the owner. Thus, a carrier employed to move household goods, including a leased sewing-machine, cannot assert any lien for his services upon such sewing-machine as against the owner.[2]

A carrier received goods from commission merchants for transportation to Europe, knowing, or having reason to know, that the merchants were acting merely as agents for the owner, and, upon the failure of the commission house, the owner demanded the goods of the carrier, who claimed a lien upon them, and refused to deliver them. In an action of replevin to recover the goods, it appeared that the commission merchants had no authority to bind the owner by the contract of freight made by them, and that, inasmuch as the carrier was put upon inquiry as to the agency and authority of the commission merchants, the

---

[1] Keep Manufac. Co. *v.* Moore, 11 Lea (Tenn.), 285. The case of Rucker *v.* Donovan, 13 Kans. 251; *S. C.* 19 Am. R. 84, is criticised. In that case, the officer attached the goods under the same circumstances as stated in the text, and paid the carrier's charges. It was rightly declared by the court that the officer was justified in paying them, and was substituted to all the rights of the carrier. It was further held that, before the officer's possession could be disturbed, he must be reimbursed the money so advanced by him. But it does not appear, by the facts stated, whether the officer demanded repayment of such advances, or disclosed the fact that he had paid them. Under these cir-

cumstances, the court, in the Tennessee case, say that there may have been facts which justified the decision, but that the facts stated do not justify it.

[2] Gilson *v.* Gwinn, 107 Mass. 126. The same rule was applied to the lien of a pilot on a vessel for his pilotage, where persons not authorized by the owner took command of the vessel and carried her out of the regular course of the voyage. The Anne, 1 Mason, 508, 512.

The same rule is applied to the lien of a keeper of animals.

In like manner the mortgage of a vessel is superior to a subsequent lien for materials. The Great West *v.* Oberndorf, 57 Ill. 168.

owner was not bound by the contract they had made with the carrier, and that the owner could maintain the action without paying or tendering the carrier's charges.[1]

279. There can be no lien upon goods belonging to the United States, or any other sovereignty, for services rendered by a carrier in transporting such goods.[2]

280. An insurance against fire effected by carriers "on goods their own, and in trust as carriers," in a warehouse, covers the whole value of goods in their hands as carriers, and also any interest they have in them for their lien as carriers.[3]

In Louisiana[4] it is provided by statute that there shall be a privilege for money paid by the carrier for prior necessary charges and expenses, such as taxes, storage, and privileged claims required to be paid before moving goods; and in case the thing carried be lost or destroyed without the fault of the carrier, this privilege for money paid by the carrier shall attach to the insurance effected on the thing for the benefit of the owner; provided written notice of the amount so paid by the carrier, and for whose account, with a description of the property lost or destroyed, be given to the insurer or his agent within thirty days after the loss; or, if it be impracticable to give the notice in that time, it shall be sufficient to give the notice at any time before the money is paid over.

III. *For what they Attach.*

281. A carrier has no lien for charges not connected with the transportation of the goods, and not within the contemplation of the parties.[5] Thus, ordinarily, a carrier has no lien for the storage of goods which he has carried, unless there be a special contract allowing him to charge for storage.[6] Nor has he a lien upon goods for damages arising from the consignee's neglect to take them away within a reasonable time

[1] Hayes v. Campbell, 63 Cal. 143.
[2] Dufolt v. Gorman, 1 Minn. 301. And see The Siren, 7 Wall. 152; The Davis, 10 Wall. 15; United States v. Wilder, 3 Sum. 308; Briggs v. Light Boats, 11 Allen (Mass.), 157; *contra*, Union Pacific R. R. Co. v. United States, 2 Wy. T. 170.

[3] London & N. W. Ry. Co. v. Glyn, 1 El. & El. 652.
[4] Rev. Laws 1884, § 2873.
[5] Lambert v. Robinson, 1 Esp. 119; Adams v. Clark, 9 Cush. (Mass.) 215.
[6] Lambert v. Robinson, *supra*; Somes v. British Empire Shipping Co. 30 L. J. (Q. B.) 229.

after notice to him of their arrival. Thus, a railroad company cannot retain goods to satisfy a charge for the detention of cars by the failure of the consignee to remove the goods after notice; for the claim is in the nature of demurrage, and no lien exists for this. Such detention is a breach of contract simply, for which, as in case of a contract in reference to pilotage or port charges, the party must seek his redress in the ordinary manner. He cannot enforce it by detaining the goods.[1]

282. A lien for demurrage in favor of carriers by land is not implied by law, and cannot be asserted except by virtue of an express agreement, or of a custom so recognized as to have the force of a contract. The rules and regulations of a railroad company, providing for a lien for demurrage, though published, are not binding upon the consignor or consignee of goods without their consent, or the consent of one of them, when the contract for shipping the goods was made. Even the knowledge of such rules by the shipper or consignee, without assent thereto, does not bind him. The law does not presume assent to the rules of a railroad company, for damages caused by delay of the consignee in receiving goods shipped, from the publication of such rules.[2]

283. Expenses of keeping property which the consignee refuses to receive. — Although a carrier may have no lien for charges incurred in keeping goods which the consignee neglects or refuses to receive, yet he may recover of the owner the expenses so incurred. Thus, the owner of a horse sent it by

---

[1] Crommelin v. N. Y. & Harlem R. R. Co. 4 Keyes (N. Y.), 90.

[2] Burlington & Mo. River R. R. Co. v. Chicago Lumber Co. 15 Neb. 390; Crommelin v. N. Y. & Harlem R. R. Co. supra; Chicago & Northwestern Ry. Co. v. Jenkins, 103 Ill. 588, 599. Walker, J., said: "The right to demurrage, if it exists as a legal right, is confined to the maritime law, and only exists as to carriers by sea-going vessels. But it is believed to exist alone by force of contract. All such contracts of affreightment contain an agreement for demurrage in case of delay beyond the period allowed by the agreement, or the custom of the port allowed the consignee to receive and remove the goods. But the mode of doing business by the two kinds of carriers is essentially different. Railroad companies have warehouses in which to store freights. Owners of vessels have none. Railroads discharge cargoes carried by them. Carriers by ship do not, but it is done by the consignee. The masters of vessels provide in the contract for demurrage, while railroads do not."

railroad' consigned to himself, and, on the arrival of the horse at its destination, there being no one present to receive it, the station-master sent it to a livery-stable. The owner's servant soon arrived, and was referred to the livery-stable keeper, who refused to deliver the horse except on payment of charges stated to be 6*d*. The next day the owner demanded the horse, and the station-master finally offered to pay the charges and let the owner take away the horse; but he declined to take it and went away. The horse remained at the livery-stable for some months, until the charges for his keeping amounted to £17, when the railroad company paid the charges and sent the horse to the owner, who accepted it. It was held that the owner was liable for these charges.[1] Baron Pollock said: "As far as I am aware, there is no decided case in English law in which an ordinary carrier of goods by land has been held entitled to recover this sort of charge against the consignee or consignor of goods. But in my opinion he is so entitled. It had been long debated whether a ship-owner has such a right, and gradually, partly by custom and partly by some opinions of authority in this country, the right has come to be established." [2] Chief Baron Kelly and Barons Pigott and Amphlett delivered separate opinions to the same effect. The question whether a lien existed for the charges of keeping the horse did not arise, but Pollock, B., incidentally expressed the opinion that such a lien did not exist, while Amphlett, B., said that, as at present advised, he should not wish to be considered as holding that, in a case of this sort, the person who, in pursuance of a legal obligation, took care of a horse and expended money upon him, would not be entitled to a lien on the horse for the money so expended.

284. A railroad company may, however, assume the double character of carrier and warehouseman, and is entitled to reasonable compensation as warehouseman, and a lien as such, in the same manner as any other warehouseman.[3] A consignee who has notice of a rule or custom of the railroad company to charge for storage, where goods have not been

[1] Great Northern Ry. Co. *v.* Swaffield, L. R. 9 Ex. 132.

[2] Citing Notara *v.* Henderson, L. R. 7 Q. B. 225, 230–235, where all the authorities are reviewed with care; Cargo ex Argos, L. R. 5 P. C. 134.

[3] Miller *v.* Mansfield, 112 Mass. 260; Norway Plains Co. *v.* B. & M. R. R. 1 Gray (Mass.), 263; Barker *v.* Brown, 138 Mass. 340; Illinois Cent. R. R. Co. *v.* Alexander, 20 Ill. 23.

called for within a certain time after their arrival at their destination, is regarded as having impliedly promised to pay charges for storage in accordance with such custom or rule; and the company may retain the goods till its reasonable warehouse charges, as well as its freight charges, are paid.[1] If the consignee refuses to receive the goods, the contract for carriage having been performed, the carrier may store the goods for the use of the owner,[2] and retain a lien upon them.

285. A well-established local custom for carriers by water to deliver goods to a storage agent, when the consignee is not present to receive them, and to make an additional charge for storage, becomes a part of the implied contract under which the goods are shipped, and the goods may be detained for the payment of such storage as well as the freight. The carrier has the right, in the absence of an agreement, to make a charge for storage where this is necessary for the protection of the goods; and this charge may be included in the general charge for freight, or it may be a separate charge.[3] The fact that the agent of the carrier who stores the goods is allowed to retain the entire amount of the charge for storage, for his own compensation, does not affect the case.

286. A common carrier by water has no lien for transporting goods from a wharf, at their place of destination, to the consignee's place of business in the same city, in the absence of any authority from either the consignor or consignee. The fact that the goods are marked with the consignee's place of business does not impart such authority.[4]

287. A ship-owner has a lien at common law for extraordinary expenses incurred for the preservation of the cargo from damage arising from causes for which the ship-

---

[1] Culbreth v. Phila. W. & B. R. R. Co. 3 Houst. (Del.) 392; McHenry v. Phila. W. & B. R. R. Co. 4 Harr. (Del.) 448.

[2] Rankin v. Memphis & Cincinnati Packet Co. 9 Heisk. (Tenn.) 564; Kremer v. Southern Express Co. 6 Cold. (Tenn.) 356; Arthur v. Sch'r Cassius, 2 Story, 81, 97; Fisk v. New-

ton, 1 Denio (N. Y.), 45, 47; Briggs v. Boston & Lowell R. R. Co. 6 Allen (Mass.), 246, 248; The Eddy, 5 Wall. 481.

[3] Hurd v. Hartford & N. Y. Steamboat Co. 40 Conn. 48.

[4] Richardson v. Rich, 104 Mass. 156.

owner is not responsible.[1] Such are the expenses of unloading and drying the cargo to save it from the wreck of the ship. The inquiry in such cases is whether the expenditure was incurred in saving the property at risk, as distinguished from an expenditure in performing the contract to carry the cargo to its destination and to earn freight. It is not only the right of the ship-owner to incur expenses, where reasonably practicable under all the circumstances, to save the goods intrusted on board the ship, but it is his duty to do so, and he is liable for not doing so, where his agent, the master, has neglected this duty.[2] The master, if necessary, may raise money by a *respondentia* bond upon the goods, in order to do what is necessary for their safety.[3]

The authority of the master to incur extraordinary expenses for the preservation of the goods does not arise where the owner of the goods or his representative is at hand, or it is practicable to communicate with him.[4]

288. The ship-owner has also liens for general average contributions from the cargo where the expenditure has been for the purpose of saving the whole venture, the ship as well as the cargo.[5] In that case the owners of each part saved must contribute ratably, and the master may retain each part of the property saved till the amount of the contribution in respect of it is paid or secured. The ship-owner is the only person who can exercise this lien; and he is liable in damages to a part owner of the cargo for not exercising it and securing payment of the contributions.[6]

289. By well-settled commercial usage, a carrier may pay the freight charges of previous carriers and have a lien for such payment. Each independent carrier who pays such back freight may be said to become the agent of his predecessors to forward the goods and collect the freight. He may also be regarded as in a manner substituted or subrogated to their

---

[1] Hingston *v.* Wendt, 1 Q. B. D. 367; Cargo ex Argos, L. R. 5 P. C. 134.

[2] Notara *v.* Henderson, L. R. 7 Q. B. 225.

[3] Cargo ex Sultan, Swa. 504, 510; The Glenmanna, Lush. 115.

[4] Cargo ex Sultan, *supra;* Cargo ex Argos, *supra.*

[5] Crooks *v.* Allan, 5 Q. B. D. 38; Hingston *v.* Wendt, 1 Q. B. D. 367, 370, per Blackburn, J.

[6] Crooks *v.* Allen, *supra.* See Hallett *v.* Bousfield, 18 Ves. 187.

rights. But more properly the carrier is to be regarded as the agent of the owner or consignee to receive and forward the goods. But, whatever may be the theoretical foundation of the right, usage, growing out of the necessities of the case, has made the right a part of the common commercial law.[1] If, upon the delivery of the goods to the consignee, they are found to be damaged, and it appears that the last carrier was not associated with the preceding carriers, and that the damage did not occur while the goods were in the hands of such last carrier, his lien for his own freight charges and for those of the prior carriers paid by him cannot be defeated by a claim for damages. A carrier receiving goods from a prior carrier is not obliged to open the packages for examination as to the condition of the goods; but if they are apparently in good order he has a right to pay the back freight, and have a lien on the goods for the charges paid as well as his own charges.[2] If the consignee notifies the carrier before he receives the goods, and pays the back charges to a prior carrier, that the goods have been damaged, and that he is not to receive them, he does so at his own risk. He has no right to meddle with the goods against the express direction of the owner, or other person in legal control of them.

290. If a carrier pays the import duties on goods, he has a lien upon them for his reimbursement. The United States

---

[1] Bissel v. Price, 16 Ill. 408, 413. "The reason of this is founded in commercial convenience and necessity, from which has originated a universal custom, pervading the whole country,—indeed, it might be said, the whole commercial world, — which has been so long established and so universally known that the courts themselves have long taken notice of and recognized it, and hence it has become a part of the law itself. This commercial convenience and universal necessity is the true reason why this principle has been engrafted upon and become a part of the law itself, although, for the sake of harmony, and to avoid apparent contradictions in legal maxims, artificial reasons have been invented, and legal implications

raised, in order to support it." Per Caton, J.

[2] Knight v. Providence & Worcester R. R. Co. 13 R. I. 572; Monteith v. Kirkpatrick, 3 Blatch. 279; Bissel v. Price, supra; White v. Vann, 6 Humph. (Tenn.) 70; Bowman v. Hilton, 11 Ohio, 303. In this case Birchard, J., said in substance that the carrier receiving the goods from a previous carrier, in apparent good order, has a right to presume that the owner had duly authorized the consignment. To entitle him to claim his lien for his own charges and his advances, the law imposed upon him nothing beyond what a prudent man would, under like circumstances, have done in the management of his own business.

has a specific lien on all imported good s for the duties on them,[1] and, though this lien may not be preserved for the benefit of the carrier who has paid the duties, a new lien arises in his favor under his implied authority to advance all reasonable back charges which constitute a lien on the goods, and for which they could be detained.[2]

IV. *On Through Freight.*

291. **When a consignor delivers goods to a carrier to be carried over successive routes,** beyond the route of the first carrier, he makes the first carrier his forwarding agent; and the second carrier has a lien, not only for the freight over his own route, but also for the freight paid by him to the first carrier.[3] Even if the first carrier makes a mistake in directing the goods, or in taking bills of lading, by reason of which the goods are sent to a wrong destination, the last carrier has a lien upon the goods, not only for the freight earned by him, but also for the sums paid by him for the freight from the commencement of the transportation. The first carrier who receives the goods, and directs them over the route of the succeeding carrier, is the owner's agent, and the successive carriers afterwards carrying the goods act under the authority of the owner, and cannot be considered as wrong-doers, though they carry the goods to a place to which the owner did not intend they should be sent.[4]

The question whether the lien continues to the successive carriers, and may be exercised by the last carrier, is in every case to be answered in accordance with the fact whether the first carrier to whom the goods were delivered is made, either expressly or impliedly, the agent of the owner to forward the goods.[5] If there is no such agency, and the first carrier at the end of his own route forwards the goods, contrary to the instructions of the owner, by an unauthorized route, then the subsequent carriers do not become the agents of the owner, but simply the agents of

[1] Dennie *v.* Harris, 9 Pick. (Mass.) 364; *S. C. nom.* Harris *v.* Dennie, 3 Pet. 292.

[2] Guesnard *v.* Louisville & Nashville R. R. Co. 76 Ala. 453.

[3] Briggs *v.* Boston & Lowell R. R. Co. 6 Allen (Mass.), 246, 250; Pott *v.* N. Y. & N. E. R. R. Co. 131 Mass.

455; *S. C.* 41 Am. R. 247; Bird *v.* Georgia R. R. 72 Ga. 655; Vaughan *v.* Providence & Worcester R. R. Co. 13 R. I. 578.

[4] Briggs *v.* Boston & Lowell R. R. Co. *supra.*

[5] Robinson *v.* Baker, 5 Cush. (Mass.) 137.

the first carrier, and, although they may act in perfect good faith, they have no lien upon the goods for their freight, or the freight of other carriers advanced by them. If the owner had constituted the first carrier his forwarding agent, the owner's consent to the diversion of the goods from the intended route would have been implied, and the subsequent carriers would have become entitled to a lien for the freight.[1]

292. A railroad receiving goods consigned to a place beyond its own line is clothed with the apparent authority to forward the goods by any usual route; and although the route selected is not that by which the owner of the goods intended they should be carried, the charges for freight by such route will constitute a valid lien upon the property.[2] This rule was followed in a recent case in the Circuit Court of the United States.[3] It appeared that a car-load of lumber was shipped in Ohio for Denver, Colorado. It was delivered to the Baltimore and Ohio Railroad Company, with instructions to forward it from Chicago over a particular railroad with which the owners had contract arrangements for special rates. The Baltimore and Ohio Company disregarded these instructions, and in the usual course of business forwarded the car by a different route. On the arrival of the car at Denver the owners declined to pay the freight charges, and brought a writ of replevin. They claimed that the Baltimore and Ohio Company, in disregarding their instructions, had exceeded its authority, and that the carriage by the unauthorized route created no charge for freight and no right of lien. The court, however, adopted the rule above stated, and held that the last carrier was entitled to a lien for its own charges and for prior charges paid to other carriers. "Any other rule," said Mr. Justice Brewer, "would work a serious

---

[1] Briggs v. Boston & Lowell R. R. Co. 6 Allen (Mass.), 246.

[2] Whitney v. Beckford, 105 Mass. 267, 271; Bird v. Georgia R. R. 72 Ga. 655.

[3] Patten v. Union Pacific Ry. Co. 29 Fed. Rep. 590. The case of Fitch v. Newberry, 1 Doug. (Mich.) 1, is criticised and dissented from. In that case it was held that the forwarding company is only a special agent with limited powers; that whoever deals with such agent is bound to take notice of the extent of his authority; and that if such carrier, disregarding his instructions, delivers the goods to the wrong carrier, the latter, though he carries them to the place of destination, does so at his own risk, and has no claim for freight or lien upon the goods. See § 298.

hindrance to the immense transportation business of to-day, while this rule protects both carrier and owner. If the first carrier disobeys his instructions, by which loss results to the owner, such carrier is liable to an action of damages, and, as is proper, the wrong-doer suffers the loss. At the same time, the second and innocent carrier, having done the work of transportation, receives, as it ought, the just freight therefor. The first carrier is the agent of the owner. If he has done wrong, why should not the principal be remitted to his action against his wrong-doing agent, and why should the burden of litigation be cast upon the innocent second carrier? Plaintiffs say that, in this case, they would have to go to Ohio to maintain their action; but, if they select an agent in Ohio, and that agent does wrong, why should they not go to Ohio to punish him for his wrong. And why should the defendant, innocent of any wrong, be forced to go thither to litigate with their agent? And why should the owner, who has had his goods carried to the place of destination, be permitted to take them from the carrier without any payment for such transportation? Is the route by which the freight is transported a matter so vital to him that, carried over the wrong route, he is entitled equitably to the possession of his goods free from any burden of freight?"

293. A connecting carrier who receives goods, knowing at the time that they were directed to be sent by another route, has no lien upon them. In such case his receiving them is wrongful, and his transportation of them afterwards would be voluntary. He would have no lien upon them for freight charges, and consequently he could not detain them from the consignee, His refusal to deliver them in such case would be a conversion for which trover would lie. The question whether the carrier had knowledge of a direction that the goods should be transported by a different route, is a question for the jury, and it would be proper for them to take into consideration the marks on the packages of goods, though these alone might not be conclusive.[1]

The fact that when the connecting carrier received the goods from the first carrier, they were loaded in a car appropriately marked for the particular railroad over which the first carrier was

[1] Bird v. Georgia R. R. 72 Ga. 655.

instructed to forward them, does not of itself amount to an implied notice to the second carrier of such instruction.[1]

294. A guaranty that the through freight shall not exceed a certain sum is not binding upon other independent connecting carriers on the route having no knowledge or notice of the guaranty.[2] Each carrier after the first may charge, and pay back charges, at the usual rates; and the last carrier, or the warehouseman who receives the goods and pays the back charges, has a lien for the total amount of such charges, without regard to the guaranty. It is regarded as unreasonable that the subsequent carrier, who receives and forwards the goods in the usual way, should be bound by a secret contract between the owner and a prior carrier, which may prevent his receiving his ordinary rates. Whether the bill of lading in this case showed the special rate guarantied was immaterial, because on the trial the parties stipulated that the succeeding carriers had no knowledge of the guaranty.

295. The prepayment of freight negatives the carrier's right to the lien ordinarily implied by law if he has knowledge of such prepayment. Thus, if a railroad company make a contract for carrying goods to their place of destination at a point beyond its own line, and receives the price of transportation to such place in advance, another railroad company which receives the goods from the first company with knowledge that a through contract had been made, cannot assert a lien upon the goods upon the ground that the sum allowed by the first company was insufficient to pay the connecting company its full share of freight charges. A carrier who receives goods from another carrier with knowledge that a through contract for carrying them has been made, and the freight prepaid, is bound by that contract, and can assert no lien upon the goods.[3]

296. If a bill of lading or way-bill accompanying the goods shows that the freight has been paid wholly or in part for the through route, the succeeding carriers would be affected with knowledge of such prepayment; for if they consult the bill

---

[1] Patten v. Union Pacific Ry. Co. 29 Fed. Rep. 590.

[2] Schneider v. Evans, 25 Wis. 241.

[3] Marsh v. Union Pacific Ry. Co. 3 McCrary, 236; S. C. 9 Fed. R. 873.

of lading they will have actual knowledge, and if they do not consult it they may be regarded as guilty of negligence, and constructively affected with knowledge of what the bill of lading actually shows.[1]

297. Where the first carrier has received payment on a through contract not known to the succeeding independent carrier, the latter, coming into possession of the goods under a lawful authority, may have a right to charge for his own services at the ordinary rate of transportation, and assert a lien therefor.[2]

298. If a carrier employs another carrier in his place to forward the goods, the latter has a lien, unless payment has been made to the carrier who received the goods in advance, in which case the substituted carrier has no lien, but must look to the person who employed him. In such case there is no privity of contract between the shipper and the carrier who performs the service.[3] The carrier to whom the goods were delivered had the right to exact payment for his services in advance; and, having done so, he is not the owner's agent to employ any other carrier to perform the service for him and to collect payment of the freight again. Consequently, the substituted carrier, though acting in good faith and without knowledge of prepayment of the freight, cannot collect it again, or retain the goods for its payment to himself. He can act only in subordination to the original contract with the owner. Where there is no arrangement between connecting carriers, a subsequent carrier is not bound by a receipt given by the first carrier for the through carriage of the goods; so that, although the first carrier has given a receipt stating that the freight charges have been paid through to the place of destination, the last carrier, having received and trans-

---

[1] Schneider v. Evans, 25 Wis. 241, 267, per Paine, J.; Travis v. Thompson, 37 Barb. (N. Y.) 236, per Hogeboom, J.

[2] Travis v. Thompson, 37 Barb. (N. Y.) 236, 242. Judge Hogeboom suggests the distinction, that such carrier may have no lien for previous charges paid by him upon the goods, for the reason that he is not obliged to receive the goods charged with this burden, and, at any rate, was bound to inquire whether such previous charges had been prepaid. But this distinction does not seem to be sound, for, by general usage, the last carrier pays all prior freight charges, and business could not well be conducted unless he is protected in making such payment.

[3] Nordemeyer v. Loescher, 1 Hilt. (N. Y.) 499.

ported the goods without notice of such prepayment, has a lien upon the goods for his own unpaid charges.[1] It is said that, while the receipt is binding upon the carrier who gave it, yet, before the subsequent carrier could be held to its terms, it must appear either that he had given authority to the first carrier to make such a contract, or that he had undertaken the transportation with notice that such a contract had been made.

Although the prior carrier has agreed with the owner that his charges should be applied to the account of a prior indebtedness of his to the owner, a subsequent carrier who has in good faith, and in accordance with the usual custom of business, paid the freight charges of the prior carrier without knowledge of such contract, is entitled to retain the goods until such charges are repaid to him.[2]

299. If the last carrier has paid to a previous carrier an amount in excess of the usual and proper charges for transporting the goods, he can assert a lien for only the customary and reasonable rates of transportion.[3]

300. If the last carrier has not paid the prior charges, his lien is limited to the amount agreed upon with the first carrier.[4] Thus, where a railroad company makes a through contract for the carriage of goods, and delivers them to an independent connecting company to be delivered at the place of destination, the latter, on carrying them to such point, must deliver them to the consignee upon his tendering the sum agreed upon, if this sum equals the regular charges of the latter company,

---

[1] Wolf v. Hough, 22 Kans. 659. A decision to the contrary is Fitch v. Newberry, 1 Doug. (Mich.) 1, which has been discredited in all the later decisions. In that case it was held that, if the consignor has paid in advance to the original carrier a portion of the freight charges, the ultimate carrier can assert a lien for only the remainder of the proper charges after deducting the payment on account. If the freight has been wholly prepaid, but the ultimate carrier, without knowledge of such prepayment, has received the goods from another carrier, and paid him the full amount of the customary charges for he previous transportation of the goods, he can assert no lien against the consignee either for the charges he has paid to the prior carrier, or for his own services in carrying the goods. See § 292.

[2] White v. Vann, 6 Humph. (Tenn.) 70.

[3] Travis v. Thompson, 37 Barb. (N. Y.) 234, 236; Mallory v. Burrett, 1 E. D. Smith (N. Y.), 234, 247.

[4] Evansville & Crawfordsville R. R. Co. v. Marsh, 57 Ind. 505.

whether it includes any charges for the former company or not ; and if such company refuses, upon a tender of such sum, to deliver the goods, the consignee may replevy them. The first company assumed the burden of satisfying the charges of the roads over which the goods were to be carried ; and the last carrier, not having paid the prior charges, can assert a lien only for the amount agreed upon, and must settle as it can with the company that made the contract.

301. **The lien does not cover advances made for matters not connected with the carriage of the goods.** The lien extends only to the carrier's own charges for carrying the goods, and such charges of prior carriers as he may have paid. It does not extend to or cover advances made on claims against the owners or consignees wholly foreign to, and disconnected with, any cost or charge for transportation. It is the duty of the carrier to examine the charges that are made by a prior forwarding agent or carrier, and the fact that he has paid charges upon the goods does not enable him to retain them for a greater sum than the usual and proper charges previously incurred in their transportation. If the carrier has paid charges which include a prior debt due the forwarding agent or carrier from the shipper, he cannot hold the goods against the owner or consignee for the amount paid on account of such prior debt.[1]

302. **The fact that the goods have suffered damage before they reach the last carrier,** who has received them from a prior carrier, does not deprive the last carrier of his lien for freight and for charges paid.[2] The last carrier, in receiving the goods in good faith and in apparent good order, and paying the costs and charges upon them, is regarded as acting as the agent of the owner, and not as the agent of the prior carrier ; and the last carrier is not liable for any damage to the goods which took place while they were in the hands of a prior carrier.[3]

A similar rule applies where the first carrier expressly limits its liability to its own line, but undertakes to forward goods, and prepays the charges for such further carriage : the lien of the first carrier is not in such case impaired by damages incurred

---

[1] Steamboat Virginia v. Kroft, 25 Mo. 76.

[2] Bowman v. Hilton, 11 Ohio, 303.

[3] Hunt v. N. Y. & Erie R. R. Co. 1 Hilt. 228 ; Bissel v. Price, 16 Ill. 408.

by the fault of the second carrier. Thus, where an express company received a package of money to be carried to the terminus of its line, and to forward it by a stage company, and through the delay of the stage company it did not reach its destination until the consignee had left, and the consignor ordered its return, it was held that the express company had a lien on the package after its return for its own charges, and also for the advances it had made to the stage company.[1]

V. *Upon Stolen Goods.*

303. Whether a carrier has a lien upon goods which have been stolen, so that he can detain them for his charges against the true owner, is a question upon which the authorities are not in harmony. The English courts hold that he has a lien even upon such goods. In an early case, Chief Justice Holt declared that a common carrier might detain goods for his charges, although they were delivered to him by one who had stolen them.[2] He cited the case of the Exeter carrier, "where A. stole goods, and delivered them to the Exeter carrier, to be carried to Exeter: the right owner, finding the goods in possession of the carrier, demanded them of him, upon which the carrier refused to deliver without being paid for the carriage. The owner brought trover, and it was held that he might justify detaining against the right owner for the carriage: for when A. brought them to him, he was obliged to receive them and carry them; and therefore, since the law compelled him to carry them, it will give him remedy for the premium due for the carriage."

304. The American decisions upon this point generally discard the English doctrine, and hold that the carrier has no lien for the carriage of goods which he has received from a wrong-doer, without the consent of the owner, express or implied; for they say that the duty of the carrier to receive and carry goods arises only when they are offered by the owner, or by his authority.[3] The chattel does not generally in such

---

[1] United States Express Co. v. Haines, 67 Ill. 137. See The Thomas McManus, 24 Fed. Rep. 509.

[2] Yorke v. Genaugh, 2 Ld. Ray. 866, Powell, J., dissenting; Butler v. Woolcott, 2 Bos. & P. N. R. 64. This view was incidentally recognized in King v. Richards, 6 Whart. (Pa.) 418.

[3] Robinson v. Baker, 5 Cush. (Mass.) 137; Stevens v. Boston & W. R. R. Co. 8 Gray (Mass.), 262; Clark v. Lowell & L. R. R. Co. 9 Ib. 231;

case become more valuable to the owner by reason of such carriage ; on the contrary, he is quite as liable to be injured as benefited by its transportation after it is wrongfully taken out of his possession. And, moreover, it is a settled general principle that no man can be divested of his property without his consent, so that even an honest purchaser under a defective title cannot hold it against the true owner.[1]

The Supreme Court of Massachusetts, asserting this fundamental principle against the carrier, ask :[2] " Why should the carrier be exempt from the operation of this universal principle ? Why should not the principle of *caveat emptor* apply to him ? The reason, and the only reason given, is, that he is obliged to receive goods to carry, and should therefore have a right to detain the goods for his pay. But he is not bound to receive goods from a wrong-doer. He is bound only to receive goods from one who may rightfully deliver them to him, and he can look to the title, as well as persons in other pursuits and situations in life. Nor is a carrier bound to receive goods unless the freight or pay for the carriage is first paid to him ; and he may in all cases secure the payment of the carriage in advance."

305. **The same rule applies where the goods have merely been wrongfully diverted from the route authorized by the owner, and have come into the hands of the carrier without the consent of the owner, express or implied.** Though the carrier is ignorant of this fact, and supposes that the goods have been rightfully delivered to him, he cannot in such case detain them for the payment of his services, or the payment of the charges of the previous carrier. Having in fact obtained possession of the goods wrongfully, though innocently, he is bound to deliver them to the owner or consignee on demand, and, on refusal, such owner or consignee may take them by writ of replevin, or recover their value in an action of trover.[3] A carrier

Gilson *v.* Gwinn, 107 Mass. 126; Ames *v.* Palmer, 42 Me. 197; Fitch *v.* Newberry, 1 Doug. (Mich.) 1, the first direct adjudication ; Vaughan *v.* Providence & Worcester R. R. Co. 13 R. I. 578; Martin *v.* Smith, 58 N. Y. 672; Collman *v.* Collins, 2 Hall (N. Y.), 569; Buskirk *v.* Purinton, Ib. 561; Everett *v.* Saltus, 15 Wend. (N. Y.) 474; Travis *v.* Thompson, 37 Barb. (N. Y.) 236 ; King *v.* Richards, 6 Whart. (Pa.) 418.

[1] Saltus *v.* Everett, 20 Wend. (N. Y.) 267, 275.

[2] Robinson *v.* Baker, 5 Cush. (Mass.) 137, 145.

[3] Fitch *v.* Newberry, *supra;* Robinson *v.* Baker, 5 Cush. (Mass.) 137;

who receives goods from a wharfinger, with whom the owner
has deposited them without authority to forward them, has no
lien on them for freight against the owner.[1]

For a stronger reason, a carrier who receives goods from an
agent, with notice that the agent in contracting with the carrier
has exceeded his authority, cannot hold them for his charges as
against the principal, who may reclaim them without paying
such charges.[2]

306. But a carrier receiving goods from one who, by the
owner's act, has been clothed with an apparent authority,
has a lien on them as against such owner.[3]   Thus, if the carrier
receives goods from one to whom the owner has delivered them,
intending at the time to part with his property in them, though
he may have been induced to sell and deliver them by fraud or
false pretences, which would authorize him to disaffirm the contract and reclaim them from the person to whom he had delivered
them, the carrier stands in the position of a *bonâ fide* purchaser,
and has a valid lien upon them for his charges and advances.[4]

307. The carrier's lien cannot be set up by a wrong-doer.
The lien of a common carrier is a personal privilege which he

Stevens *v.* Boston & Worcester R. R.
Co. 8 Gray (Mass.), 262.   In Robinson *v.* Baker, 5 Cush. (Mass.) 137,
the owner of a parcel of flour delivered it to a canal-boat company to be
transported to Albany.   This company gave bills of lading wherein they
agreed to deliver it at Albany to a
person named, who was the agent of
the Western Railroad Company.   The
owner sent one of these bills to this
agent, and the other to the consignee
at Boston, thus reserving to himself
the right, and assuming the responsibility, of giving to the agent the directions for forwarding the goods.   The
canal company did not become the
owner's agent to forward the goods,
and had no right to exercise any control over them, except to deliver them
to the agent of the railroad company.
Yet, in violation of their duty, the
canal company shipped the flour to

New York, and thence by vessel to
Boston.   It was held that the owners
of the vessel had no lien upon the
flour for the freight.

These cases are distinguished from
such cases as Briggs *v.* Boston &
Lowell R. R. Co. 6 Allen (Mass.),
246, where the owner makes the first
carrier his agent to forward the goods,
and the owner thus becomes responsible for mistakes of this agent in forwarding them.

[1] Clark *v.* Lowell & Lawrence R.
R. Co. 9 Gray (Mass.), 231.

[2] Hayes *v.* Campbell, 63 Cal. 143.
In this case the carrier was put upon
inquiry as to the terms upon which
the agent could contract for the carriage of the goods.

[3] Vaughan *v.* Providence & Worcester R. R. Co. 13 R. I. 578.

[4] Caldwell *v.* Bartlett, 3 Duer (N.
Y.), 341.

alone can set up. It does not deprive the owner of the goods of his right to immediate possession as against a wrong-doer. The owner has constructive possession, and may sue any one in trover or trespass who forcibly or wrongfully takes them from the carrier. Such trespasser or wrong-doer cannot set up the carrier's right of possession to destroy the right of the general owner to maintain such action.[1] If such wrong-doer pays the freight and charges of the carrier, he does not thereby acquire the carrier's lien and a right to hold the goods.[2]

VI. *Their Waiver and Loss.*

308. Of course the carrier may waive his lien, and he does so by delivering the goods without first requiring payment of the freight.[3] By relinquishing possession he is deemed to yield up the security he has by means of it, and to trust wholly to the personal responsibility of the owner or consignee. Possession is the first requisite of a common law lien, and if this be parted with the lien is gone. He may hold possession by an agent, but, if such agent acts on his instructions in such a way as to give the possession to the owner or consignee, the lien is lost.

309. The placing of the goods in a warehouse is not a delivery that destroys the carrier's lien, if the carrier still retains exclusive control of the goods. If the warehouse be his own, he of course retains such control. So, if by law a ship-owner is required to land and store the goods in a particular place, or in a public warehouse, his lien is not thereby affected.[4]

But if the carrier stores them in the warehouse of an independent person who has a lien for warehousing charges, it seems that the carrier's lien will be lost.[5]

---

[1] Ames *v.* Palmer, 42 Me. 197, supported by similar cases between principal and agent : Daubigny *v.* Duval, 5 T. R. 604 ; McCombie *v.* Davies, 7 East, 5 ; Holly *v.* Huggeford, 8 Pick. (Mass.) 73 ; Jones *v.* Sinclair, 2 N. H. 319.

[2] Guilford *v.* Smith, 30 Vt. 49.

[3] Bigelow *v.* Heaton, 4 Den. (N. Y.) 496 ; Wingard *v.* Banning, 39 Cal. 543 ; Reineman *v.* C. C. & B. R. R. Co. 51 Iowa, 338 ; Terril *v.* Rogers, 3 Hayw. (Tenn.) 203.

[4] Wilson *v.* Kymer, 1 M. & S. 157, 163. Lord Ellenborough, C. J., interrupting the argument, asked : "Is not this point incontrovertible, that, when goods on board a ship are subject to lien, if they are taken out of the ship *in invitum* and by compulsion of law, that the lien shall be preserved in the place of safe custody where the goods are deposited by law?"

[5] Mors-le-Blanch *v.* Wilson, L. R. 8 C. P. 227, 240. Brett, J.: "I very much doubt whether, if the master

310. A carrier who has once parted with the possession of the goods with the intention of making delivery cannot revive his lien by a resumption of possession, nor has he any right by reason of his claim to stop the goods *in transitu*.[1]

If one who has a lien on goods ships them to the owner on his account and at his risk and expense, his lien is gone, for this is equivalent to a delivery to the owner. The lien cannot be recovered by stopping the goods *in transitu*, and procuring a redelivery by means of a bill of lading from the carrier issued after the commencement of the voyage.[2]

A ship-owner's lien for freight depends upon his possession of the goods, and is lost by delivering them to the consignee voluntarily, and without notice that he looks to him for the payment of his charges;[3] or when any agreement is entered into by the parties in regard to the payment of freight, which involves a prior surrender of the possession. This lien cannot, like some maritime liens, be enforced by a proceeding *in rem* without possession.[4]

311. Delivery to the consignee upon condition. — What acts on the part of a ship-owner amount to a waiver of his lien for freight, it is often difficult to determine. It is not divested by a delivery to the consignee or his agent if conditions are annexed to the delivery, or if there be an understanding, express or implied, that the lien shall continue.[5] The ship-owner, or the master as his agent, may agree with the consignee or owner that the goods shall be deposited in the warehouse of the consignee or owner, and that such deposit shall not be regarded as a waiver of the lien, and the courts, both at law and in admiralty, will uphold the agreement and support the lien.[6]

The mere manual delivery of an article by a carrier to the

---

were so to deposit the goods on shore as to give another person a lien upon them, he would not as a matter of course lose his own lien, even though such other person should undertake to the master not to deliver the goods to the consignee without being paid the master's claim for freight."

[1] Sweet *v.* Pym, 1 East, 4, per Buller, J. ; Artaza *v.* Smallpiece, 1 Esp. 23 ; Coombs *v.* Bristol & Exeter Ry.

Co. 27 L. J. Exch. 401 ; Hartley *v.* Hitchcock, 1 Stark. 408.

[2] Sweet *v.* Pym, *supra*.

[3] Cranston *v.* Cargo of Coal, 22 Fed. Rep. 614.

[4] Cutler *v.* Rae, 7 How. 729 ; Dupont *v.* Vance, 19 How. 162, 171 ; Bags of Linseed, 1 Black, 108, 113.

[5] Bags of Linseed, *supra*.

[6] The Eddy, 5 Wall. 481, 495, per Clifford, J.

consignee does not of itself operate necessarily to discharge the carrier's lien for the freight; the delivery must be made with the intent of parting with his interest in it, or under circumstances from which the law will infer such an intent. The act of the party is characterized by the intent with which it is performed, either expressly or by necessary implication. Therefore, a delivery made under the expectation that the freight will be paid at the time, is not such a delivery as parts with the lien, and the carrier may afterwards libel the article. *in rem*, in admiralty, for the freight.[1]

312. What delivery is effectual to terminate a carrier's lien is often an important and difficult question. Delivery of the goods and payment of the freight are, in the absence of any special contract, acts to be done at the same time. A delivery may be complete for one purpose, and not for another. Thus, a delivery may be complete so far as to terminate the liability of a carrier, and yet be upon an implied condition as to payment. If a railroad company carries coal to its place of destination, and the owner's servants deposit it in bins on the company's land adjoining the owner's land, the lien is not lost.[2]

313. The payment of the freight and the delivery of the goods are ordinarily to be concurrent acts. Even if the bill of lading of a cargo provides for the payment of the freight *on the right delivery of the cargo*, the delivery of the cargo is not a condition precedent to the right to demand the freight.[3] The delivery of the cargo and the payment of the freight are still to

[1] 151 Tons of Coal, 4 Blatchf. 368.

[2] Lane *v.* Old Colony & Fall River R. R. Co. 14 Gray (Mass.), 143, 148. Hoar, J., said: " Suppose the railroad company should allow a customer, for whom they had brought a lot of flour, to unload it from the cars on to his wagon, and, as he started with the load, should demand the freight, could it be supposed that they would have no right to retake the flour if he should refuse to pay? But suppose, instead of one load, there should be a hundred barrels, and the first load should be allowed to go without payment, the rest being taken from the cars and put upon the platform in the freight-house, the company knowing that enough was left to make them secure, and the demand should be made as the owner was about removing the last load, could this destroy the right to retain for their lien? "

[3] Tate *v.* Meek, 8 Taunt. 280, 293, per Gibbs, C. J.; Paynter *v.* James, L. R. 2 C. P. 348; Black *v.* Rose, 2 Moore P. C. (N. S.) 277; Rankin *v.* Memphis & Cincinnati Packet Co. 9 Heisk. (Tenn.) 564.

be concurrent acts, and the master is not bound to deliver the cargo unless the consignee stands ready to pay the freight at the same time. On the other hand, the master is not entitled to demand the freight unless he is ready to deliver the cargo. There must be a concurrent readiness on both sides, — on the one to deliver, and on the other to pay. The ship-owner or master may require a *pro rata* payment of the freight of goods as they are landed from day to day on the wharf, if the goods are at the same time delivered to the consignee.[1] But the master cannot properly demand payment of the freight upon the whole shipment, when he has landed and is ready to deliver only a part of it.[2] The consignee is entitled to an opportunity to examine the goods and see if the obligations of the bill of lading have been fulfilled by the ship-owner. When the landing of a cargo occupies several days, and the consignee does not receive the goods and make *pro rata* payments of freight, if such payments are demanded the master may deliver the goods on the wharf; and if they are not taken by the consignee after notice, the master may store the goods for safe keeping at the consignee's expense and risk, in the name of the ship-owner, to preserve his lien for the freight.[3]

A frequent and even general practice at a particular port for the owners to allow goods to be transported to the warehouse of the consignee, and there inspected before freight is paid, is not such a custom as will displace the ordinary maritime right of the ship-owner to demand payment of the freight upon the delivery of the goods upon the wharf.[4]

314. **The terms of the charter-party may be such, however, that the chartered freight will not be due until the cargo has been completely delivered.** Thus, a ship was chartered to go to Algoa Bay for a cargo, with which to proceed to London, where it was to be delivered on payment of freight at certain specified rates. The freight was to be paid " on unloading and right delivery of the cargo." The master was to sign bills of lading under which the freights were to be collected by the charterer. It was held that the charter-party freight was

---

[1] Black *v.* Rose, 2 Moore P. C. (N. S.) 277.

[2] Brittan *v.* Barnaby, 21 How. 527.

[3] Brittan *v.* Barnaby, *supra*, per Wayne, J.; The Eddy, 5 Wall. 481.

[4] The Eddy, *supra*.

not due till the objects of the voyage had been carried out.[1] "On principle," said Lord Justice Wood, "we conceive that the freight cannot be due from the charterers on a charter-party, such as the present, until they have had the full uses of the ship for the purposes for which they chartered it. It is, in fact, analogous to the demise of property until a given purpose is answered, the purpose in this case being, first, the outward voyage; second, the taking in of a complete cargo at such profit freight as the charterers might be able to obtain above the freights they have agreed to pay to the owner; and third, the delivering of the cargo to the consignees by the charterers. . . . Now it is not alleged that there was any undue delay on the part of the charterers in the unloading and delivering. Until, therefore, that was absolutely completed, it appears to us the freight was not due to the owner." The ship-owner's right of lien was not involved in this case. A lien was expressly given by the charter-party, and the decision was not inconsistent with such a lien. The question in the case arose between a mortgagee of the ship, who had taken possession while the cargo was being discharged, and an assignee of the freight from the ship-owner. But the decision has an important application, and would cut away the lien for freight in like cases where no lien is expressly reserved.[2]

315. If a cargo is placed in the hands of a consignee, with the understanding that the lien is to continue, a court of admiralty will regard the transaction as a deposit of the goods, for the time, in the warehouse, and not as an absolute delivery, and on that ground will consider the ship-owner as being still constructively in possession so far as to preserve his lien.[3] It is the duty of the consignee, and not of the ship-owner, to provide a suitable and safe place for the storage of the goods; and several days are often consumed in unloading and storing the cargo. If the cargo could not be unladen and placed in the warehouse of the consignee without waiving the lien, it would seriously interfere with the convenience both of the ship-owner and the merchant. In such a case it is frequently understood between the parties that such a transfer of the goods to the consignee's

---

[1] Brown v. Tanner, L. R. 3 Ch. 597, 603.

[2] Carver on Carriage of Goods by Sea, § 658.

[3] Bags of Linseed, 1 Black, 108.

warehouse shall not be regarded as a waiver of the ship-owner's lien, but that he reserves the right to proceed *in rem* to enforce it, if the freight be not paid. But such a transfer of the goods into the possession of the consignee will defeat the lien, unless an understanding that it shall not have this effect can be shown to have existed between the parties, or unless it be plainly inferable from the established local usage of the port.[1]

316. A promise to pay the amount of a carrier's lien upon goods is not necessarily presumed from the taking possession of such goods with knowledge that such a lien is claimed. Thus, where a railroad company, having delivered a portion of a cargo of coal on the order of the consignee to a purchaser of the whole cargo, on the arrival of the remainder of the coal notified the purchaser that it claimed a lien on such remainder for the freight of the entire cargo, and directed him not to unload it, but the purchaser did unload and take possession of the coal without paying the freight, it was held the purchaser could not be conclusively presumed as a matter of law to have promised to pay the freight.[2]

317. The carrier's lien is not lost in case the goods are obtained from him by fraud. He has not in such case voluntarily parted with the possession. His right of possession remains, and he may assert this right by replevying the goods, though they be in the hands of the consignee.[3] Thus, if the goods are delivered to the consignee in consequence of his false and fraudulent promise to pay the freight as soon as the delivery is complete, such delivery does not amount to a waiver of the lien, and the carrier may, notwithstanding, maintain replevin for the goods.[4]

But there must be some evidence of fraud or trick in obtaining possession, or the loss of possession will defeat the lien. In replevin by a railroad company to enforce a lien for freight upon a horse, it appeared that the car containing the horse arrived at

---

[1] Bags of Linseed, 1 Black, 108.

[2] New York & N. E. R. R. Co. *v.* Sanders, 134 Mass. 53.

The case of New Haven & Northampton R. R. Co. *v.* Campbell, 128 Mass. 104, is distinguished. The question whether the law implied a contract to pay the freight was not adjudicated.

[3] Wallace *v.* Woodgate, Ry. & M. 193.

[4] Bigelow *v.* Heaton, 6 Hill (N. Y.), 43; *S. C.* 4 Denio, 496.

the depot at about eleven o'clock in the morning; that the consignee, being notified by telephone, asked if the horse could remain in the car till the following morning, and gave directions about the care of the horse; that the horse was allowed to remain in the car; and that in the morning the consignee sent and got the horse without paying the freight. It was held that a verdict finding that the company voluntarily abandoned its lien upon parting with possession of the horse would not be reversed on appeal, and that the action of replevin could not be maintained.[1]

318. A carrier can have no relief in equity on the ground of a mistake in fact in delivering the goods to the consignee under the belief that he is solvent, when in fact his estate proves to be insolvent. It is no fraud on the part of the consignee that immediately after the delivery of the goods he dies, and his estate proves to be insolvent.[2]

319. The carrier has a lien upon all the goods carried. The consignee cannot insist upon a delivery of any part until the whole freight is paid.[3] The carrier may deliver by instalments, if the goods are in distinct parcels, and the freight charges are divisible; and he may require the freight on each instalment to be paid upon the delivery of it.[4]

320. A delivery of a part of the goods is not a waiver of the lien upon the remainder for the whole freight.[5] The lien is gone upon the part delivered, but remains good upon the part retained for the payment of the entire freight, that upon the goods delivered as well as that upon the goods still retained. Even if the goods were delivered to the carrier in separate parcels at different times, but all the parcels are carried under one

[1] Geneva, Ithaca, & Sayre R. R. Co. v. Sage, 35 Hun (N. Y.), 95. Hardin, P. J. said: "We see no evidence of trick, fraud, or overreaching on the part of the defendant to obtain possession."

[2] Sears v. Wills, 4 Allen (Mass.), 212.

[3] Perez v. Alsop, 3 F. & F. 188.

[4] Black v. Rose, 2 Moo. P. C. N. S. 277; S. C. 11 L. T. N. S. 31.

[5] Sodergren v. Flight, 6 East, 622;

Potts v. N. Y. & N. E. R. R. Co. 131 Mass. 455; New Haven & Northampton Co. v. Campbell, 128 Mass. 104; Lane v. Old Colony & Fall River R. R. Co. 14 Gray, 143; Boggs v. Martin, 13 B. Mon. (Ky.) 239; Frothingham v. Jenkins, 1 Cal. 42; Phila. & Reading R. R. Co. v. Dows, 15 Phila. (Pa.) 101; Steinman v. Wilkins, 7 W. & S. 466, 468; Fuller v. Bradley, 25 Pa. St. 120.

contract, the lien will attach in respect to the charges incurred in the carriage of the whole upon any one or more of the parcels ; or, in other words, if some of the parcels be delivered, the lien for the carriage of these will attach to those not delivered.[1] Moreover, in such case, the carrier may treat all the parcels as one lot of goods, for the purpose of the lien, but not if the goods were shipped under several contracts.[2]

The part of the goods remaining will be discharged from the lien for the freight upon the part delivered, if such was the intention of the parties.[3]

321. If separate contracts be made for the carriage of separate parcels of goods, a separate lien will attach to each parcel, and the lien is lost by the delivery of such parcel. If, in such case, several bills of lading have been given, and these have been consigned to different persons, the carrier cannot have a lien for the freight due under one bill of lading upon goods comprised in another which is not held by the same person.[4]

Separate liens upon separate lots of goods carried may, by the action of the parties, be changed into a general lien upon all the goods. Thus, if several cargoes of coal carried by a railroad company are so far distinct subjects of contract that the company may deliver and demand freight for one before delivering another, and the consignee may demand the delivery of one without waiting for the arrival of the whole, there is a separate lien upon each cargo for the freight of that cargo, and a lien for the freight of several cargoes delivered could not be asserted against one cargo not delivered. But if the several cargoes be mingled together in bins upon the company's land by direction of the consignee, so that they cannot be distinguished, then all the coal will be regarded as delivered together, and the separate lien upon each cargo will be merged in a general lien upon the whole quantity. If, then, portions of the coal be taken from the bins by the owner, and delivered to purchasers from time to time, the railroad company may at any time forbid the taking away of any more of the coal without payment of the unpaid

[1] Chase *v.* Westmore, 5 M. & S. 180.

[2] Bernal *v.* Pim, 1 Gale, 17; Sodergren *v.* Flight, 6 East, 622.

[3] New Haven & Northampton Co. *v.* Campbell, 128 Mass. 104, 107.

[4] Sodergren *v.* Flight, *supra.*

freight, and may assert a lien upon the coal remaining for the freight of all the cargoes.[1]

322. The lien is waived by a contract whereby the carrier gives credit for the freight extending beyond the time when the goods are to be delivered.[2] A charter-party which provides that a part of the freight shall be paid by the charterer's acceptance, payable three months after delivery to him of a certificate of the right delivery of the cargo, displaces the lien for such part of the freight, although the charterer had become bankrupt before the arrival of the vessel at the port of discharge. The subsequent bankruptcy of the charterer can neither operate to erase the clause of the charter-party giving credit for an instalment of the freight, nor to shorten the term of the credit.[3] There can be no lien on a cargo for freight where the charter-party provides for the payment of it two months after the delivery of it, or in thirty days after the return of the vessel to her home port.[4]

The taking of bills of exchange or promissory notes for the freight, payable at a future time after the time at which the goods should be delivered, is a waiver of the lien.[5] It seems, however, that, if the paper be dishonored before the goods have been delivered, the lien will revive.[6]

323. If the provision be that the freight shall be paid by bills on a specified time after delivery, then the ship-owner has a lien on the cargo until payment by bills in the manner provided, the delivery of the cargo and the payment of the freight bring concomitant acts.[7] If the delivery of the cargo be a work

---

[1] Lane v. Old Colony & Fall River R. R. Co. 14 Gray (Mass.), 143.

[2] Crawshay v. Homfray, 4 B. & Ald. 50; Alsager v. Dock Co. 14 M. & W. 794, 798; Foster v. Colby, 3 H. & N. 705, 715; Chase v. Westmore, 5 M. & S. 180; S. C. 28 L. J. (Ex.) 81; Chandler v. Belden, 18 Johns. (N. Y.) 157, 162; Pinney v. Wells, 10 Conn. 104, 115.

[3] Bird of Paradise, 5 Wall. 545; Pinney v. Wells, 10 Conn. 104, 114. And see Tamvaco v. Simpson, 19 C. B. N. S. 453; Alsager v. St. Kathe-

rine's Dock Co. *supra;* Thompson v. Small, 1 C. B. 328.

[4] Pickman v. Woods, 6 Pick. (Mass.) 248.

[5] Hewison v. Guthrie, 2 Bing. N. C. 755; Horncastle v. Farran, 3 B. & A. 497; Bunney v. Poyntz, 4 B. & Ad. 568.

[6] Gunn v. Bolckow, L. R. 10 Ch. 491.

[7] Tate v. Meek, 8 Taunt. 280; Yates v. Railston, Ib. 293; Bohtlingk v. Inglis, 3 East, 381, 384; Tamvaco v. Simpson, L. R. 1 C. P. 363.

of several days, the bills should bear date from the last delivery, and to avoid a waiver of the lien the master may in the first instance land the cargo in his own name.

A charter-party provided that freight at a certain rate per ton should be paid part in cash at a certain time before the voyage could be ended, and part in bills having specified times to run from the day on which the ship should arrive in the Thames on her return upon her homeward voyage. The charterers became bankrupt, and neither they nor their assignees tendered the bills for freight. In an action by the assignees for the goods, it was held that the ship-owner was entitled to retain them until payment. Abbot, C. J., delivering the judgment, said:[1] "Upon this instrument therefore, and between the parties to this suit, we think the defendant had the possession of the ship and goods for the voyage, and a lien on the goods for the stipulated hire of the ship, there being nothing to show that the delivery of the goods was to precede the payment of that hire in cash and bills, as provided for by the deed."

324. A promissory note or bill of exchange given for freight and falling due before the delivery of the goods does not discharge the lien, but the carrier may stand upon his lien as fully as if the note or bill had never been given.[2] By the general commercial laws, a bill or note given for a precedent debt does not extinguish the debt or operate as payment, unless such was the express agreement of the parties. The creditor may return the bill or note when it is dishonored, and proceed upon the original debt, the bill or note being regarded as accepted upon the condition of its payment. The rule is different in Massachusetts, the presumption of law there being that a promissory note extinguishes the debt for which it was given. Yet in Massachusetts this presumption may be repelled by evidence that such was not the intention of the parties. Upon this ground it was held that under the Massachusetts rule it is not to be presumed that a ship-owner, having a lien upon a cargo for the payment of the freight, intended to waive his lien by taking the notes of the charterer drawn so as to be payable at the time of the expected arrival of the ship in port.[3]

[1] Saville v. Campion, 2 B. & A. 503, 512. See, also, Faith v. East India Co. 4 B. & Ald. 630.

[2] Bird of Paradise, 5 Wall. 545.

[3] The Kimball, 3 Wall. 37. There was evidence that the notes were given

325. There can be no lien for freight when the contract for its payment is inconsistent with a lien. If the time, place, and manner of payment of the freight are regulated by the charter-party in such a manner as to be inconsistent with the existence of a lien, then the only way of compelling payment is by an action upon the charter-party. Thus, where a ship was chartered at New York for several voyages, partly at the option of the charterer, with the agreement that the time of the employment should be the full term of fifteen months, with a privilege to the charterer to extend it to twenty-four months, the charterer paying at the rate of two thousand dollars per month, payable semi-annually at New York, it was held that the circumstances indicated that the owner meant to waive his lien upon the cargo for freight, and to trust wholly to the personal responsibility of the charterer. A libel filed at San Francisco to hold the cargo responsible for the freight was accordingly dismissed.[1]

326. There is a waiver of the lien as against an indorsee for value of a bill of lading, when this holds out that the goods are to be delivered free of freight. Where a bill of

for the accommodation of the shipowner, and were to be held over or renewed in case they fell due before the arrival of the ship.

[1] Raymond v. Tyson, 17 How. 53.

In this case, not only the time but the place of payment was regarded as of importance in determining whether the lien was waived. "Place for the payment of money is a substantial part of any contract to pay it there. It can be insisted upon by him who is to receive it, and cannot be rightfully refused or omitted by him who has to pay it. A broken promise of that kind gives to the creditor a right of action against the debtor for its recovery. Why, upon principle, should a promise to pay freight at a particular time, and at a place other than that where the owner of the ship has undertaken to deliver the cargo, be required to be paid elsewhere? It is the payer's privilege to pay it there. And, should it not be paid, why should the owner have more than a right of action

for its recovery, or larger remedies, by suit, than are given in any other contract? We confess we do not see why. Place for the payment of freight, other than that for which the cargo is shipped and discharged, amounts to a stipulation that freight will not be demanded at the last, as a condition for the cargo's delivery. All the authorities concur in this, that place for the payment of freight is a waiver of a lien upon the cargo, unless there are already circumstances or stipulations to show that it could not have been meant. It is so because it is at variance with the enforcement of such a lien, according to the usage of trade; and it is so because, when parties to a charter-party depart from that usage by agreeing to pay and receive freight at another place than that where the common law gives to an owner of a ship a lien to enforce payment, it must be regarded that the owner had some sufficient reason for not insisting upon his right according to common law."

lading of goods shipped at Liverpool for Sydney provided for the payment of the freight in Liverpool by the shipper one month after the sailing of the vessel, and the bill of lading passed into the hands of indorsees for value, it was held that the representations of the bill of lading were such that no lien could be claimed against the consignee at the port of discharge, though the master had been advised by the ship-owner that the freight had not been paid, and directed not to deliver the goods unless the freight should be paid.[1]

The ship-owner cannot claim a lien for freight when this is inconsistent with a bill of lading given with his authority. If the bill of lading represents the freight to have been paid, when in fact it had not been paid, an indorsee for value of the bill of lading is entitled to claim that the representation is true; and no lien for freight can be claimed as against him.[2]   And so, if the bill of lading holds out that the goods are to be delivered free of freight to the consignee, there can be no lien for freight. Such is the effect of a representation in the bill of lading that the freight is payable by the shipper in advance, on sailing or at a fixed time afterwards ; and though the shipper fails to pay as agreed, no lien for freight can arise as against the consignee.[3]

---

[1] Kirchner v. Venus, 12 Moore P. C. 361, 391, following How v. Kirchner, 11 Ib. 21, and dissenting from Gilkison v. Middleton, 2 C. B. N. S. 134, and Neish v. Graham, 8 El. & Bl. 505.

In Kirchner v. Venus, *supra*, Lord Kingsdown, delivering the judgment, said : "No doubt parties who have superseded by a special contract the rights and obligations which the law attaches to freight in its legal sense, may, if they think fit, create a lien on the goods for the performance of the agreement into which they have entered, and they may do this either by express conditions contained in the contract itself, or by agreeing that, in case of failure of performance of that agreement, the right of lien for what is due shall subsist as if there had been an agreement for freight. But in such case the right of lien depends entirely on the agreement, and if the

parties have not, in fact, made such a contract, it is very difficult to understand upon what grounds it can be implied, or why, upon failure of performance of the agreement which they have made, the law is to substitute for it another and very different contract which they have not made."

[2] Howard v. Tucker, 1 Barn. & Ad. 712 ; Tamvaco v. Simpson, L. R. 1 C. P. 363.

[3] How v. Kirchner, *supra*; Kirchner v. Venus, *supra*. In the latter case there is a *dictum* of Lord Kingsdown that freight payable in advance is not freight. It is not money for carrying the goods, but for taking them on board. But this view is not affirmed in later cases. Carver's Carriers of Goods by Sea, 666. This *dictum* is commented upon and explained in Allison v. Bristol Marine Ins. Co. L. R. 1 App. Cas. 209.

But a mere provision that the freight shall be paid in advance does not seem to be inconsistent with a lien, especially if the consignee is himself liable for it. An agreement for prepayment of freight does not alter its legal character of freight.[1]

327. No waiver of the lien will be inferred, however, unless it is evident from the terms of the contract that it is contemplated that delivery is to precede the payment for freight.[2] Accordingly a stipulation in a charter-party that the freight shall be paid within ten days after the return of the vessel to the port of departure does not displace the lien on the return cargo, inasmuch as the delivery of the cargo might be rightfully postponed beyond the ten days after the returning of the ship.[3] And so a stipulation that the freight shall be paid in five days or in ten days after the discharge of the cargo is held not to displace the lien, inasmuch as the word *discharge*, in this connection, is construed to mean merely the unloading of the cargo from the ship, and not the delivery of it to the owner or consignee.[4]

328. An attachment by the carrier of the property on which a lien is claimed for freight is a waiver or forfeiture of the lien.[5]

329. A carrier may bring an action for his freight charges, and attach other goods to secure the demand, without discharging his lien, especially if the owner has wrongfully taken the goods from him by means of a writ of replevin.[6]

On the principal point decided, the cases of Gilkison v. Middleton, 2 C. B. N. S. 134, and Neish v. Graham, 8 El. & Bl. 505, are discussed and dissented from in the Privy Council cases.

[1] Allison v. Bristol Marine Ins. Co. L. R. 1 App. Cas. 209.

[2] Faith v. East India Co. 4 B. & A. 630; The Bird of Paradise, 5 Wall. 545; Certain Logs of Mahogany, 2 Sum. 589, 600; Howard v. Macondray, 7 Gray (Mass.), 516, 521. In this case Dewey, J., delivering the judgment of the court, said : " While it is conceded that the maritime lien for freight may be considered as waived when there are stipulations in the contract as to time and place of payment inconsistent with the existence of such lien, in the cases reported there seems manifested a strong disposition to limit this exclusion of such lien to cases plainly importing such exclusion." Ruggles v. Bucknor, 1 Paine, 358, 363, per Thompson, J., is to the same effect.

[3] The Volunteer, 1 Sum. 551, 571.

[4] The Kimball, 3 Wall. 37, 42; Certain Logs of Mahogany, *supra*.

[5] Wingard v. Banning, 39 Cal. 543.

[6] Barnard v. Wheeler, 24 Me. 412.

330. A lien is destroyed by the carrier's taking on execution the same goods upon which the lien is attached, for he thereby gives up possession to the sheriff.[1]

331. The carrier's lien may be defeated by an injury to the goods carried, happening by the carrier's fault, to an amount larger than his charge for freight.[2] His right to freight, and to detain the goods for its payment, results from his performance of the contract to carry the goods. If he fails to carry the goods and have them ready for delivery, he cannot claim his freight. If through his fault the goods sustain damage to an amount exceeding the amount of his charges for freight, he is not entitled to demand anything for the carriage of the goods; and if the damages be less than the freight charges, the amount he is entitled to demand is reduced to that extent. His lien is, of course, only coextensive with his right to claim and recover freight. If by reason of such injury to the goods he is not entitled to demand any freight, he has no right to retain the goods for the payment of the freight, and if he does so they may be taken from him by replevin.   There is no good reason why the carrier's liability for damages to the goods accruing through his fault should not be asserted and determined by way of defence to his claim for freight, as well as by a cross action. It would be contrary to the analogies of cases involving similar relations of subject-matter and parties, to say nothing of the hardship to the consignee, to require him to pay the freight upon the goods, and then to trust to the responsibility of the carrier at the end of a lawsuit for the recovery of the damages to the goods sustained through the fault of the carrier.[3]

332. The refusal of the consignee to accept the goods after they arrive at their destination does not in any way affect the carrier's lien, whether this is implied by law or arises under an express stipulation of contract.[4] But upon the refusal of the

---

[1] Jacobs v. Latour, 5 Bing. 130; Re Coumbe, 24 Grant (Ont.) Ch. 519.

[2] Dyer v. Grand Trunk Ry. Co. 42 Vt. 441; Humphreys v. Reed, 6 Whart. (Pa.) 435; Boggs v. Martin, 13 B. Mon. (Ky.) 239. See § 302.

[3] Dyer v. Grand Trunk Ry. Co. supra, per Barrett, J.

[4] Westfield v. Great Western Ry. Co. 52 L. J. Q. B. 276. In this case the contract provided for a general lien, with power of sale in satisfaction of it.

consignee to accept the goods and pay the freight, the carrier is not entitled to take the goods forthwith back to the place whence they were shipped. He is bound to keep them for a reasonable time at the place where they were to be delivered, so as to give the consignee an opportunity of obtaining the goods upon paying the carrier's demand.[1] If the goods are left in the carrier's hands without fault on his part, he is bound to take reasonable measures for their preservation, and may recover, and have a lien, for the expenses so incurred.[2]

333. The carrier's lien is lost when the performance of his contract becomes impossible. Thus, if a ship be lost on the voyage, and the ship-owner has no means of carrying the cargo on to its destination, he has no lien upon it for freight.[3] But if the ship-owner substantially performs the contract, as by trans-shipping the goods to another ship, he may still exercise his lien, or enable the owner of the other ship to do so.[4] And so if a ship-owner deliver the cargo at a port which is within the terms of the charter-party, though the charterer had ordered the vessel to discharge at a port to which it had become impossible for her to go, on account of the breaking out of a war, the ship-owner does not lose his lien for his chartered freight.[5]

334. Claiming a general lien, or a lien for other charges, is not generally a waiver of a specific lien for freight. If the carrier claims to detain the goods, not only on the ground that he has a lien for freight, but also a lien for other charges, and the consignee disputes the latter claim, he should tender payment of the freight, for he is not relieved from paying this, though the carrier improperly joins with it a further claim of lien.[6] The carrier's conduct may, however, be such as to do away with the necessity of a tender.[7] Where a carrier detained three pigs out of a lot carried, to satisfy a balance due on former shipments, and the owner was ready to pay the freight on the

---

[1] Great Western Ry. Co. v. Crouch, 3 H. & N. 183.

[2] Great Northern Ry. Co. v. Swaffield, L. R. 9 Ex. 132.

[3] Nelson v. Association for Protection of Wrecked Property, 43 L. J. C. P. 218; Nyholm, ex parte, 43 L. J. Bank. 21.

[4] Matthews v. Gibbs, 30 L. J. Q. B. 55, 63, per Cockburn, C. J.

[5] Duncan v. Köster, L. R. 4 P. C. 171, affirming 3 A. & E. 394.

[6] Scarfe v. Morgan, 4 M. & W. 270.

[7] Jones v. Tarleton, 9 M. & W. 675.

present shipment, but the carrier refused to deliver the pigs until payment of the old account should be made, it was held that he waived a tender of the freight for the last shipment.[1]

VII. *Remedies upon a Carrier's Lien.*

335. The carrier's lien, like all other common law liens founded upon possession, gives him no right to sell the property, but only a right to retain it until his charges are paid.[2] He can enforce his lien indirectly by obtaining judgment for his charges and levying the execution upon the goods. But a sale without process is a conversion; the measure of damages for which is the market value of the goods, deducting the amount of the lien.[3]

The right of possession under the lien continues although the debt itself be barred by the statute of limitations. The possession, however, even for that length of time, confers no title to the property upon the bailee. The owner may at any time demand the property, and is entitled to it upon tendering the amount due upon the property under the lien.

A ship-owner cannot, of his own motion, sell the goods in order to pay the freight, except by virtue of a statute. His usual and proper remedy is by libel *in rem* before an admiralty court, by whose decree his rights may be protected.[4]

336. In almost every state and territory there are statutes which enable carriers to sell goods upon which they have liens for freight, and by means of these statutes the passive common law lien is converted into an active lien. These statutes are of two classes. One class in terms provides a

---

[1] Jones *v.* Tarleton, 9 M. & W. 675, 677. Alderson, B.: "I think, if the defendant absolutely refused to deliver the pigs when they were demanded, until payment by the plaintiff, not only of the freight for that particular cargo, but also of the freight due on a former account, and which, as now appears by the finding of the jury, the defendant was not entitled to demand, that must be considered as a waiver of any tender of the present sum really due, and which the plaintiff was ready to pay: it was equiva-lent to saying to the plaintiff, 'Do what you will, tender what you will, it is of no use; I will not receive it unless you pay the old account also.'"

[2] Lickbarrow *v.* Mason, 6 East, 21; Jones *v.* Pearle, 1 Stra. 556; Hunt *v.* Haskell, 24 Me. 339; Fox *v.* McGregor, 11 Barb. (N. Y.) 41; Saltus *v.* Everett, 20 Wend. (N. Y.) 267.

[3] Briggs *v.* Boston & Lowell R. R. Co. 6 Allen (Mass.), 246; Staples *v.* Bradley, 23 Conn. 167.

[4] Sullivan *v.* Park, 33 Me. 438; Hunt *v.* Haskell, *supra.*

remedy by sale for the enforcement of the carrier's lien. The other class in terms provides for the sale of unclaimed goods, and for the payment of the carrier's charges and expenses out of the proceeds. The result is substantially the same in both cases; the carrier is enabled to dispose of the goods and to get the amount due him. The provisions of these statutes are, however, widely different in the several states, and therefore it is impossible to make an adequate statement of the remedies which carriers have for the enforcement of their liens without giving the statutes substantially in detail.

337. In making a sale under a statute of unclaimed goods, to pay the freight and charges, a carrier is held not only to good faith in making the sale, but to reasonable diligence in ascertaining and giving notice of the contents of the packages sold. But, while he is required to examine all external marks and indications of the contents, he is not required or authorized to open the packages for the purpose of ascertaining their contents. If, knowing, or having reason to know, the contents of the packages, he withholds his knowledge or belief, and sells valuable goods to a favorite having superior knowledge, at a nominal price, this is a fraud which vitiates the sale, and renders him and the purchaser liable in damages to the owner.[1]

338. If, however, the goods are of a perishable nature, in the absence of the consignee, it is a matter of necessity for the carrier to sell them. But in such case he sells, not by virtue of his lien, but by virtue of his trust relation to the owner, and in his interest. Out of the proceeds he may retain his freight and charges. To justify the sale, it must be shown that the goods were perishable, and that the sale is one of absolute necessity in the interest of the owner.[2]

339. Alabama.[3] — When any article of freight has been delivered at its point of destination by any common carrier, and remains for the space of sixty days without being taken out of the care of such common carrier, the same, if it be of a perish-

---

[1] Nathan v. Shivers, 71 Ala. 117; S. C. 46 Am. R. 303.

[2] Arthur v. Schooner Cassius, 2 Story, 81, 97; Rankin v. Memphis &

Cincinnati Packet Co. 9 Heisk. (Tenn.) 564.

[3] Code 1876, §§ 2140-2142.

able character, may be advertised and sold after giving thirty days' notice by publication once a week for three successive weeks in any newspaper published at such point of delivery, or, if no newspaper is published at such point, by posting the same at three public places or precincts nearest to such point.

If such freight is not of a perishable character, and remains ninety days after its delivery, it may be advertised and sold as above provided. Before a sale, such common carrier must, within thirty days after the delivery of the freight, or ten days prior to the sale, give notice to the owner or consignee, demanding payment of freight and charges due thereon, if they or either of them reside at such place of destination; but if neither of them so resides, it shall not operate to prevent the sale.

The common carrier may insure the freight, at the expense of the owner or consignee, from the date of its delivery to the time of the sale. Such sale must be at some public place named in the advertisement, and to the highest bidder for cash; and the proceeds thereof must be applied to the payment of the freight and charges, storage, insurance, and the other costs and charges incident to the sale, and the residue, if any, must be paid over to the owner or consignee.

340. Arizona Territory.[1] — Common carriers having unclaimed articles, not perishable in nature, remaining for a period of ninety days in their possession after carrying the same, upon which their charges for freight and storage remain unpaid, may sell the same at public auction after notice to the consignee and publication of notice.

In all cases where the owner or consignee and his place of residence is known, the common carrier shall first cause notice to be given him personally, or by mail, of the fact of such unclaimed property remaining on hand; and, after the expiration of ninety days, if such article or package remains unclaimed, and the charges thereon unpaid, the common carrier shall cause notice, together with a description of the property, as near as may be, to be published for a period of twenty days in some newspaper published in the county, or, if there be no newspaper published within the county, then by posting such notice for a like period in at least three of the most public places in the county. Such notice shall contain the name of the consignee

---

[1] Comp. Laws 1877, ch. 86.

and of the consignor, if possible to obtain them, the amount of charges due thereon, and such further description of the property as may be practicable or necessary to identify the same; also the time and place at which such property will be disposed of to pay the charges due thereon. At the expiration of the twenty days' notification by publication or posting, such carrier may, at the time and place thereby appointed, proceed to sell such unclaimed property at public auction to the highest bidder.

Whenever any common carrier shall have remaining in his possession, unclaimed, any property, package, or article, perishable in nature, after having carried the same to its proper destination, as marked or directed, he may proceed to dispose of the same to the best advantage practicable for the payment of his charges thereon. No sale of perishable property shall be made by any common carrier without first giving at least one hour's notice thereof at the place of sale, and without first giving notice to the owner or consignee thereof for at least twenty-four hours before such sale, provided such owner or consignee is known and can be so notified without loss or danger to such property.

After the sale of either class of property, the common carrier may deduct from the money received thereat his reasonable charges for freight, storage, etc., and the costs of sale, and if any money remain over, it shall be paid to the owner or consignee of such property, if he be known and can be found. If not to be found, such remaining money shall be paid, as soon as practicable, to the county treasurer of the county in which the sale took place. There shall also be filed with the treasurer, at the time of paying over the money, a copy of the notice required to be given as above provided; which shall be sworn to as correct and as having been given for the time required; and, in cases of the sale of perishable property, there shall be filed with the treasurer, at the time of paying over such remaining money, a verified statement showing the character of the property sold, the time and place of sale, the amount received therefor, and the amount of charges for which the same was sold, and the amount of costs of sale. The treasurer shall give notice of the amount of money received, and on what account received, by posting the same for a period of six months outside of his office door. If at the expiration of six months' notice, as herein required, the money remains unclaimed, the treasurer is authorized and directed to carry and apply such money to the school fund of his county, as having escheated thereto.

341. California.[1] — If, from any cause other than want of ordinary care and diligence on his part, a common carrier is unable to deliver perishable property transported by him, and collect his charges thereon, he may cause the property to be sold in open market to satisfy his lien for freightage.

342. Colorado.[2] — When any goods have been received by any railroad or express company, or other common carrier, commission merchant, or warehouseman, and shall not be received by the owner, consignee, or other authorized person, until the expiration of thirty days, it shall be lawful for the said carrier, commission merchant, or warehouseman to hold the same, or the same may be stored with some responsible person, and be retained until the freight and storage and all just and reasonable charges be paid by the owner or consignee, or by some person for him, who shall be notified of the receipt of such goods within three days from the receipt thereof.

If no person within ninety days from the receipt thereof shall pay freight and charges thereon, it shall be lawful for such carrier, commisssion merchant, or warehouseman to sell such goods, merchandise, or other property, or so much thereof, at auction, to the highest bidder, as will pay said freight and charges, first having given twenty days' notice of the time and place of sale to the owner, consignee, or consignor, if known, and by advertisement in a daily paper (or if in a weekly paper four weeks) published where such sale is to take place; and, if any surplus be left after paying freight, storage, cost of advertising, and all other just and reasonable charges, the same shall be paid over to the rightful owner of said property at any time thereafter, upon demand being made therefor, within ninety days.

After the storage of goods, merchandise, or property, as herein provided, the responsibility of the carrier shall cease, nor shall the person with whom the same may be stored be liable for any loss or damage on account thereof, unless the same shall result from his negligence or want of proper care.

[1] 2 Codes and Stats. 1885, § 2204 of Civ. Code.

[2] G. S. 1883, ch. 91, §§ 3432, 3433, 3435, 3437.

In case the goods shall consist of articles which will perish, or become greatly damaged, by delay in disposing of the same, then it shall be lawful for such carrier, commission merchant, or warehouseman, unless the charges on such goods are paid, and they are claimed and taken away, to sell all of the same, either at auction or at private sale, for the best price that may reasonably be obtained therefor, and to dispose of the proceeds of such sale as above provided. Before any such sale is made, notice shall be given to the owner or consignee, or the agent of him, of the intent to so sell and dispose of such goods, merchandise, or other property, and the time and place of such sale, either by personal notice or by letter addressed and properly mailed to him, which said notice shall be given at least twenty-four hours before said sale, if the consignee, or owner, or agent of him so notified, shall reside at the place where such goods are : but if the person to be so notified of such sale reside at a distance, then the time of such sale shall be so appointed in said notice as to allow him, in addition to the twenty-four hours above mentioned, a reasonable length of time to claim said goods, or to attend such sale ; and if, upon reasonable inquiry, the residence of such consignee, owner, or agent cannot be learned, then, upon the affidavit of such carrier, commission merchant, or warehouseman, or some person in his or their behalf, to be filed and preserved by the carrier, commission merchant, or warehouseman, and by them to be produced and exhibited to any person claiming an interest in the goods sold or to be sold as aforesaid, such goods, merchandise, and other property may be sold as aforesaid without notice.

343. Connecticut.[1] — All goods of a perishable nature left with any person, the owner of which is unknown, or neglects to take them away after reasonable notice, shall be advertised at least one week in a newspaper published in the county where they were left ; and, if not then claimed and taken away, may be sold at public auction, under the inspection of the sheriff or a deputy sheriff of such county, and the proceeds of the sale, after deducting the expenses thereof and the charges for which they may be liable, shall be deposited with the treasurer of the town where they were left, who shall hold the same subject to the order of the owner thereof.

[1] G. S. 1875, p. 365.

All goods of a nature not perishable, left with any person, or upon any public wharf or highway, and all goods, other than personal baggage of passengers, left at any railroad station, or in any railroad car or carriage, the owner of which goods is unknown, or neglects to take them away for six months from the time when they were left, shall be advertised one month in a newspaper published in the county where such goods were left ; and if the owners thereof shall not take them away within said month, may be sold and the proceeds disposed of in the manner above provided, except that such proceeds, not claimed by the owner within one year, shall escheat to the state.

Every person engaged in the express business who shall have in his possession for six months any unclaimed article not perishable may sell it at auction, under the inspection of the sheriff, or a deputy sheriff, of the county where the same is held, and out of the proceeds retain the charges of transportation and storage, and of advertising and sale ; but no such sale shall be made until four weeks after the first publication, in a newspaper published in the place where the sale is to take place, of a notice thereof, containing a description of such article and the name of the person to whom it was directed ; and the expense of advertising shall be a lien upon the articles advertised in a ratable proportion according to the value of each article.

If such unclaimed article be in its nature perishable, it may be sold as soon as its condition makes it necessary without the notice required in the preceding section.

Such person engaged in the express business shall make an entry of the balance of the proceeds of such sales, credited to the person to whom such article was directed, as near as can be ascertained, and, at any time within five years thereafter, shall refund such balance to the owner of such article.

If such balance shall not be claimed by the owner within five years, it shall escheat to the state.

344. Dakota Territory[1] and Illinois.[2] — Whenever any article of property transported or coming into the possession of any railroad or express company, or any other common carrier, in the course of his or its business as common carrier, shall remain unclaimed and the legal charges thereon unpaid during the space

[1] 2 Codes 1883, §§ 1228 a, b, c, of Civil Code.　　　[2] Annotated Stats. 1885, ch. 141, §§ 1, 2.

of six months after its arrival at the point to which it shall have been directed, and the owner or person to whom the same is consigned cannot be found upon diligent inquiry, or, being found and notified of the arrival of such article, shall refuse or neglect to receive the same and pay the legal charges thereon for the space of three months, it shall be lawful for such common carrier to sell such article at public auction, after giving the owner or consignee fifteen days' notice of time and place of sale, through the post-office, and by advertising in a newspaper published in the county where such sale is made, and out of the proceeds of such sale to pay all legal charges on such articles, and the amount over, if any, shall be paid to the owner or consignee upon demand.

Perishable property which has been transported to its destination, and the owner or consignee, after being notified of its arrival, refuses orn eglects to receive the same and pay the legal charges thereon, or if upon diligent inquiry the consignee cannot be found, such carrier may, in the exercise of a reasonable discretion, sell the same at public or private sale without advertising, and the proceeds, after deducting the freight and charges and expenses of sale, shall be paid to the owner or consignee upon demand.

345. Delaware.[1] — In all cases in which commission merchants, factors, and all common carriers, or other persons, have a lien upon any goods, for or on account of the costs or expenses of carriage, storage, or labor bestowed thereon, if the owner or consignee shall fail or neglect or refuse to pay the charges upon the same within sixty days after demand thereof, made personally, or at his last known place of residence, it shall be lawful for the person having such lien to expose such goods, wares, merchandise, or other personal property to sale at public auction, and to sell the same, or so much thereof as shall be sufficient to discharge said lien, together with costs of sale and advertising. Notice of such sale, together with the name of the person or persons to whom such goods shall have been consigned, shall first be published for three successive weeks in a newspaper published in the county, and by six written or printed hand-bills, put up in the most public and conspicuous places in the vicinity of the depot where said goods may be.

[1] R. Code 1874, p. 667, §§ 1-3.

Upon the application of any of the persons or corporations having such lien, verified by affidavit to any judge of the Superior Court of this state, or to the chancellor, setting forth that the place of residence of the owner or consignee is unknown, or that such goods are of a perishable nature or damaged, or showing any other cause that shall render it impracticable to give the notice as required, it shall be lawful for the judge or chancellor hearing such application to make an order authorizing the sale of such goods, upon such terms as to notice as the nature of the case may admit of; provided that, in cases of perishable property, the affidavit and proceedings required by this section may be had before a justice of the peace.

The residue of moneys arising from any such sales, after deducting the amount of the lien as aforesaid, together with costs of advertising and sales, shall be held subject to the order of the owner of such property.

346. Georgia.[1] — Whenever any person, natural or artificial, exercising the right of transportation for hire in this state, shall transport to the place designated for its delivery any property, and the same cannot be delivered according to the terms upon which said carrier has agreed to carry it within six months from and after the time of arrival of such property at the place of delivery, then and in that case it shall be lawful for such carrier to sell for cash said property at public auction at such place as may be designated by such carrier, after having duly advertised the time, place, and terms of sale once a week for four weeks in some newspaper published, or having a general circulation, in the county wherein such sale is proposed to be made; and the proceeds of the sale shall be applied in the first place to the payment of all charges of carriage due to such carrier, together with all expenses incident to such sale and the advertisement thereof; and then the residue, if any, of the proceeds be deposited in some convenient state or national bank located in this state, to be selected by the carrier.

Whenever the property so transported and not delivered is live freight, the same may be sold as hereinbefore provided, on five days' notice; and whenever the property is fruit, vegetables, fresh meat, or other articles of an immediately perishable nature, the same may be sold as hereinbefore provided, on

[1] Code 1882, §§ 2084 a–2084 d.

twenty-four hours' notice. In any case so provided for the carrier may give the notice in such manner as in the exercise of good faith, and with a view to making the best sale, he shall determine; but in every such case, notice in a newspaper circulating or published at the place of sale, or personal notice to either the consignor or consignee of such freight, for the time for which such notice is required to be given, shall be deemed and held sufficient.

Upon the deposit in bank of the net proceeds of sale, the entry of such deposit shall show the names of both consignor and consignee, and the deposit shall not be drawn out except by the consent of both, or on the judgment or order of a court having jurisdiction in the premises.

On compliance with these provisions, such carriers shall be relieved from all liability as to the safe keeping of such freight after transportation, and also as to the proceeds of sale.

347. Indiana.[1]—When any freight, or any baggage of passengers, has been conveyed by a common carrier to any point in this state, and shall remain unclaimed for the space of three months at the place to which it is consigned or checked, and the owner, whether known or unknown, fails, within that time, to claim such freight or baggage, and to pay the proper charges, if any there be against it, then it shall be lawful for such common carrier to sell such freight or baggage at public auction, offering each box, bale, trunk, valise, or other article separately as consigned or checked.

Sixty days' notice of the time and place of sale, and a descriptive list of the articles to be sold, with the names, numbers, or other marks found thereon, shall be posted up in three public places of the county where the sale is to be made, and one on the door of the depot or warehouse, if any, where the goods are; and notice shall also be given in at least one paper in the county for sixty days before sale; and out of the proceeds of such sale the carrier shall pay the proper charges on such freight or baggage, including costs for storage for the previous three months, and hold the overplus, if any, subject to the order of the owner at any time within five years, on proof of ownership made by the affidavit of the claimant, or his duly authorized agent or attorney. After five years, all sums of money remaining unclaimed to be

[1] R. S. 1881, §§ 2900–2903.

paid into the county treasury, to be placed to the account of common schools.

The carrier shall keep a copy of the notice, a copy of the sale-bill, and the expenses thereof proportioned to each article sold, and also the oath of the claimant of the residue of the proceeds as aforesaid ; and shall furnish an inspection of the same, and, if required, copies thereof, to any one, on payment of the proper charges therefor.

If any perishable property or live-stock shall be so conveyed, either as freight or baggage as aforesaid, and remain unclaimed until in danger of great depreciation, or such live-stock be falling away because the carrier has not facilities to feed and water the same, then the carrier may, after the expiration of five days from the time said property is conveyed to the place to which it is consigned or checked, sell, at private sale or auction, without giving the ten days' notice, for the best price it will bring, and apply the proceeds as aforesaid.

348. Iowa.[1] — Personal property transported by, or stored or left with, any warehouseman, forwarding and commission merchant, express company, or carrier, is subject to a lien for transportation, advances, and storage.

If any such property shall for six months remain in his possession, unclaimed, with the just and legal charges unpaid thereon, the person having the same in charge or possession shall first give notice to the owner or consignee, if his whereabouts is known, and, if not known, shall go before the nearest justice of the peace and make affidavit stating the time and place where such property was received, the marks or brands by which the same is designated, if any, and, if not, then such other description as may best answer the purpose of indicating what the property is, and shall also state the probable value of the same, and to whom consigned ; also the charges paid thereon, accompanied by the original receipt for such charges and by the bill of lading ; also the other charges, if any, due and unpaid; and whether the whereabouts of the owner or consignee of such goods is known to the affiant, and, if so, whether notice was first given to him as hereinbefore provided : which affidavit shall be filed by the said justice of the peace in his office, for the inspection of any one interested in the same, and he shall also enter in his estray-book a

_____
[1] R. Code 1880, §§ 2177–2182.

statement of the contents of the affidavit, and time and place where and by whom the same was made.

If such property still remain unclaimed, and the charges are not paid thereon, then the person in possession of the same, either by himself or his agent, where the probable value does not exceed one hundred dollars, shall advertise the same for sale for the period of fourteen days, by posting five notices in five of the most public places in the city or locality where said property is held, giving such description as will indicate what is to be sold ; but when the goods exceed the probable value of one hundred dollars, then the length of notice shall be four weeks, and, in addition to the five notices posted, there shall be a publication of the notice of sale for the same length of time in some newspaper of general circulation in the locality where the property is held, if there be one, and, if not, then in the next nearest newspaper published in that neighborhood, at the end of which period, if the property is still unclaimed, or charges unpaid, the agent or party in charge shall sell the same at public auction, between the hours of ten o'clock A. M. and four o'clock P. M., for the highest price the same will bring in cash, which sale may be continued from day to day, by public announcement to that effect at the time of adjournment, until all the property is sold ; and from the proceeds of such sale the said party who held the same shall take and appropriate a sufficient sum to pay all charges thereon, and all costs and expenses of sale.

Fruit, fresh fish, oysters, game, and other perishable property shall be retained twenty-four hours, and if not claimed within that time and charges paid, after the proper affidavit is made as required by the section above, may be sold either at public or private sale, in the discretion of the party holding the property, for the highest price that the same will bring, and the proceeds of the sale disposed of as above provided. But in both cases, if the owner or consignee of said unclaimed property shall reside in the same city, town, or locality in which the same shall be, and shall be known to the agent or party having the same in charge, then personal notice shall be given to said owner or consignee, in writing, that said goods are held subject to his order, on payment of charges, and that unless he pays said charges, and removes the property, the same will be sold as provided by law.

After the charges due and unpaid on the property, and the expenses and costs of sale, have been taken out of the proceeds, the excess in the hands of the agent or person who was in charge thereof shall be by him forthwith deposited with the county treasurer of the county where the goods were sold, subject to the order of the owner, said ownership being properly authenticated under oath, and such person shall take from such treasurer a receipt for such money, and deposit the same with the county auditor. He shall also file with the county treasurer a schedule of the property, with the name of the consignee or owner, if known, of each piece of property sold, the sum realized from the sale of each separate package, describing the same, together with a copy of the advertisement as hereinbefore provided, and a full statement of the receipts of the sale, and the amount disbursed to pay charges, costs, and expenses of sale, all of which shall be under the oath of the party or his agent, which schedule, statement, oath, and advertisement shall all be filed and preserved in the treasurer's office, for the inspection of any one interested in the same.

Should the owner of the property sold not make a demand upon the county treasurer for any money that may be in the treasury to his credit, according to the above provisions, the sum so unclaimed shall be accounted for by the county treasurer, and placed to the credit of the county in the next subsequent settlement made by the treasurer with the county; and should the money, or any part thereof, remain unclaimed during the period of one year, it shall then be paid into the school fund, to be distributed as other funds may be by law which may be raised by tax on other property of the county. But nothing herein contained shall be a bar to any legal claimant from prosecuting and proving his claim for such money at any time within ten years, and, the claim being within that period prosecuted and proved, it shall be paid out of the county treasury in which it was originally placed, without interest.

349. Kansas.[1]— Any forwarding merchant, warehouse-keeper, stage, express, or railway company, hotel-keeper, carrier, or other bailee, having a lien upon goods which may have remained in store, or in the possession of such bailee, for six months or more, may proceed to sell such goods, or so much thereof as may be

[1] Comp. Laws 1885, §§ 3260-3266.

230

necessary to pay the amount of the lien and expenses ; and such sale may be advertised and made by any carrier, in any city of the first, second, or third class through which its line runs, where, in the judgment of such carrier, the best price can be obtained for the property to be sold.

If the property bailed or kept be horses, cattle, hogs, or other live-stock, or is of a perishable nature, and will be greatly injured by delay, or be insufficient to pay such charges for any further keeping, the person to whom such charges may be due may, after the expiration of thirty days from the time when such charges shall have become due, proceed to dispose of so much of such property as may be necessary to pay such charges and expenses. Additional compensation for keeping and taking care of such property, necessarily incurred, may be taken from the proceeds of the sale as part of the charges.

Before any such property shall be sold, if the name and residence of the owner thereof be known, at least twenty days' notice of such sale shall be given him in writing, either personally or by mail, or by leaving a notice in writing at his residence or place of doing business : but if the name and residence be not known, the person having the possession of such property shall cause a notice of the time and place of sale, containing a description of the property, to be published at least once a week, for the space of three weeks successively, in a newspaper, if there be one, published in the county where such sale is advertised to take place; if there be no newspaper published in such county, then said notice shall be published in some newspaper of general circulation in such county. If the value of the property does not exceed twenty dollars, such notice may be given by written or printed handbills posted up in at least five public places in the township or city where the bailee resides, or the sale is to take place, one of which shall be in a conspicuous part of the bailee's place of business.

All sales shall be at public auction for cash. The proceeds of such sale, after payment of charges and the expenses of publication and sale, shall, if the owner be absent, be deposited with the treasurer of the county where the sale takes place by the person making such sale, he taking the treasurer's receipt therefor, and shall be subject to the order of the person legally entitled thereto.

Copies of the notices required by this act, and proof of the publication, posting, or giving thereof, and an affidavit of the mechanic, artisan, tradesman, carrier, or other bailee, or some competent agent or witness in his behalf, setting forth his claim, and the actual expense of the publication and sale, shall be filed and kept in the county clerk's office of the county where the sale takes place, and the same, or copies thereof, duly certified by such clerk, shall be received as presumptive evidence of the matters therein contained.

350. Maine.[1] — Whenever goods, merchandise, packages, or parcels transported by any railroad, steamboat, express, or stage company, remain unclaimed for six months; or goods, merchandise, or other personal property remain in a public warehouse for six months after the charges thereon have been rightfully demanded and left unpaid, — the same may be sold at auction to pay the charges thereon and the expense of advertising and selling.

Before selling any such articles, the company holding the same shall give thirty days' notice of the time and place of sale, in a newspaper at the place where said articles are held, if any, otherwise in a newspaper published at a place nearest thereto; said notice shall describe said articles by all such marks thereon as serve to identify them, and the proceeds of sale, after deducting all charges and expense of advertising and sale, shall be held for the persons entitled thereto.

All sales under these provisions shall be recorded in a suitable book open to the inspection of claimants, in which the articles sold shall be correctly described, and the charges and expense thereon, and the price at which they were sold, shall be entered.

351. Maryland.[2] — Whenever freight, forwarded upon any railroad to any point in this state, shall remain unclaimed, and the legal charges thereon unpaid, for the space of three months after its arrival at the point to which it shall have been directed, and the owner, or person to whom the same is consigned, cannot be found upon diligent inquiry, or, being found and notified of the arrival of such freight, shall neglect to receive the same, and pay the legal charges thereon, for the space of three months,

---

[1] R. S. 1883, ch. 62, §§ 8–10.   [2] R. Code 1878, art. 67, ch. 20, §§ 1–3.

then it shall be lawful for such railroad company to sell such freight at public auction, after giving ten days' notice of the time and place of said sale, by posting up notices thereof in three public places in the county or city where such sale shall be made, and out of the proceeds of such sale to pay the legal charges, including the costs of storage, on said freight, and to pay the overplus, if any, to the owner or consignee of such freight on demand.

Whenever personal baggage, sample packages, bundles of baggage transported by any railroad company, doing business as common carriers, to any point in this state, shall remain at the place to which the same is or shall be directed for the space of three months, or any lost or stray baggage, sample package, bundles, or luggage shall remain unclaimed by the owner or consignee for the space of three months, at the place to which the same shall be or shall have been transported, and the said owner, or person to whom the same shall be directed, cannot upon diligent inquiry be found, or, being found and notified of the arrival of such property, shall neglect to receive the same and pay the reasonable charges thereon, then it shall be lawful for such railroad company to sell such property at public auction, after giving ten days' notice of the time and place of said sale, by posting up notices thereof in three public places in the county or city where such sale shall be made, and out of the proceeds of such sale to pay the legal charges, including cost of storage, on said property, and to pay the overplus, if any, to the owner or consignee of any such property on demand.

These provisions apply to all steamboat and transportation or forwarding companies, or other corporations or companies, who act as common carriers or forwarders in this state.

352. Massachusetts.[1] — Every railroad corporation, and the proprietors of every steamboat engaged in the transportation of passengers, shall, on the first Monday of January and July in each year, publish, in one newspaper at least, in every county of this state in which such railroad corporation or steamboat proprietors have a passenger station or office, a descriptive list of trunks, carpet-bags, valises, parcels, and passengers' effects, left and then remaining unclaimed at any passenger station or office, or in the possession of such corporation or proprietors or

[1] Pub. Stats. 1882, ch. 96, §§ 1-9.

their agents, and the list shall indicate all such specific marks as may serve to identify the same.

If, at the expiration of six months after such advertisement, any of the articles so advertised still remain unclaimed, the railroad corporation or steamboat proprietors in whose possession they are shall give notice to the mayor and aldermen of the city or selectmen of the town in which the articles may be, and said mayor and aldermen or selectmen shall cause the articles to be examined, and may order them to be sold at public auction upon notice given of the time and place of sale, by publishing as aforesaid, or may order any of them to be again advertised and to remain another six months before being sold. The proceeds of all articles thus sold, after deducting costs of storage, advertising, and other expenses due to such railroad corporation or steamboat proprietors, and the costs of said examination and sale, shall be paid over to the treasurer of the commonwealth for the use of the commonwealth.

If any railroad corporation or steamboat proprietors neglect or omit so to advertise and cause to be examined any such effects, such corporation or proprietors shall be liable for all damages on account thereof, to be recovered by the person injured in an action of tort; and shall also forfeit one hundred dollars for each case of neglect or omission.

When a common carrier has transported property consisting of fresh meats, fresh fish, shell fish, fruits, or vegetables to their place of destination, and has notified the owner or consignee of the arrival of the same, and the owner or consignee after such notice has refused or omitted to receive and take away the same and pay the freight and proper charges thereon, said carrier may, in the exercise of a reasonable discretion, sell the same at public or private sale without advertising, and the proceeds, after deducting the amount of said freight and charges and expenses of sale, shall be paid to the owner or consignee; and if the owner or consignee cannot be found, on reasonable inquiry, the sale may be made without such notice.

If goods carried by a railroad company or in a steam or sailing vessel are not called for by the owner or consignee within one year from the date of their receipt at the city or town to which they are consigned, they may be sold at public auction for the charges of transportation due thereon, notice of the time and place of sale being first given by publishing the same three days in each week for three weeks successively in some newspaper printed in such city or town, if there is any such paper, and, if not, then in the newspaper printed nearest thereto. The proceeds of all goods sold, after deducting costs of transportation, storage, advertising, and sale, shall be placed to the credit of the owner in the books of the company or owner of the vessels making the sale, and shall be paid to the owner of the goods on demand.

If goods carried by express are not called for by the owner or consignee, and such owner or consignee cannot be found for one year after the carriage, they may be sold at public auction, notice of the time and place of sale being first given by publishing the same four weeks successively in some newspaper printed in the city or town where such sale is to take place, and also in the city or town to which they were consigned, if there is any such paper, and, if not, then in the newspaper printed nearest thereto. Such notice shall contain a descriptive list of all such property, with all such specific marks as may serve to identify the same. The proceeds of all goods sold, after deducting costs of transportation, storage, advertising, and sale, shall be paid to the owner of said goods, if he claims the same and furnishes satisfactory proof of ownership within three years after the sale; otherwise to the treasurer of the commonwealth for the use of the commonwealth.

353. Michigan.[1]—Whenever any personal property shall be consigned to or deposited with any forwarding merchant, wharf-keeper, warehouse-keeper, tavern-keeper, or the keeper of any depot for the reception and storage of trunks, baggage, and other personal property, such consignee or bailee shall immediately cause to be entered, in a book to be provided and kept by him for that purpose, a description of such property, with the date of the reception thereof.

If such property shall not have been left with such consignee or bailee for the purpose of being forwarded or otherwise disposed of according to directions received by such consignee or bailee, at or before the time of the reception thereof, and the name and residence of the owner of such property be known or ascertained, the person having such property in his custody shall immediately notify such owner by letter, to be directed to him,

[1] Annot. Stats. 1882, ch. 58, §§ 2075-2086.

and deposited in a post-office, to be transmitted by mail, of the reception of such property.

In case any such property shall remain unclaimed for three months after its reception, as aforesaid, the person having possession thereof shall cause a notice to be published once in each week for four successive weeks in a newspaper published in the same county, if there be one, and, if not, then in some paper published at the seat of government, describing such property, and specifying the time when it was so received, and stating that unless such property shall be claimed within three months from the first publication of such notice, and the lawful charges thereon paid, the same will be sold according to the statute in such case made and provided.

In case the owner or person entitled to such property shall not, within three months after the first publication of such notice, claim such property and pay the lawful charges thereon, including the expense of such publication, the person having possession of the property, his agent or attorney, may make and deliver to any justice of the peace of the same county an affidavit setting forth a description of the property remaining unclaimed, the time of its reception, the publication of the notice, and whether the owner of such property be known or unknown. Upon the delivery to him of such affidavit, the justice shall cause such property to be opened and examined in his presence, and a true inventory thereof to be made, and shall make and annex to such inventory an order under his hand that the property therein described be sold, by any constable of the city or township where the same shall be, at public auction, upon due notice.

It shall be the duty of the constable receiving such inventory and order to give ten days' notice of the sale, by posting up written notices thereof in three public places in the city or township, and to sell such property at public auction for the highest price he can obtain therefor.

Upon completing the sale, the constable making the same shall indorse upon the order aforesaid a return of his proceedings upon such order, and deliver the same to such justice, together with the inventory and the proceeds of the sale, after deducting his fees, which shall be the same as upon an execution.

From the proceeds of such sale, the justice shall pay the charges and expenses legally incurred in respect to such property, or a ratable proportion to each claimant, if there be not sufficient for the payment of the whole; and such justice shall ascertain and determine the amount of such charges in a summary manner, and shall be entitled to one dollar for each day's services rendered by him in such proceedings.

Such justice shall deliver to the treasurer of the county in which the property was sold the affidavit, inventory, and order of sale, and return hereinbefore mentioned, together with a statement of the charges and expenses incurred in respect to such property, as ascertained and paid by him, with a statement of his own fees, and shall at the same time pay over to such treasurer any balance of the proceeds of the sale remaining after payment of such charges, expenses, and fees.

The treasurer shall file in the office, and safely keep, all the papers so delivered to him, and make a proper entry of the payment to him of all moneys arising from such sale in the books of his office.

If the owner of the property sold, or his legal representatives, shall, at any time within five years after such moneys shall be deposited in the county treasury, furnish satisfactory evidence to the treasurer of the ownership of such property, he or they shall be entitled to receive from such treasurer the amount so deposited with him.

If the amount so deposited with any county treasurer shall not be paid to such owner or his legal representatives within the said five years, such county treasurer shall pay such amount into the state treasury, to the credit of the general fund.

354. Minnesota.[1] — A common carrier and any person who, at the request of the owner or lawful possessor of any personal property, carries, conveys, or transports the same from one place to another, and any person who safely keeps or stores any personal property, shall have a lien for all his charges for caring for such property, and a right to hold and retain the possession thereof, and a power of sale for the satisfaction of his reasonable charges and expenses. If such charges are not paid within three months, a person having such lien may sell the property at public auction, on giving public notice by advertisement for three weeks in some newspaper printed or published in the county, or, if there is none, then by posting up notice of such sale in three

[1] Laws 1885, ch. 81; G. S. 1878, ch. 90, §§ 16, 17.

of the most public places in the county three weeks before the time of sale; and the proceeds of such sale shall be applied to the discharge of such lien, and the costs and expenses of keeping and selling such property, and the remainder, if any, shall be paid over to the owner.

355. Mississippi.[1] — When the consignee or owner of any goods or articles, transported on any railroad, and which remain in the possession of the company, cannot be found, or refuses to receive the same, or pay the charges, or neglects to do so, for an unreasonable time, application may be made by the company, or its agent, to any justice of the peace, or to the mayor or chief magistrate of any incorporated town, for an order of sale; and if it shall be made to appear to such justice or mayor that the goods have been transported by the company, and that the consignee or owner cannot be found, or refuses or neglects to pay the costs and charges of transportation, or to receive the goods, such justice or mayor shall issue an order, under his hand, directed to the sheriff, or any constable or marshal of a town, directing the sale of the goods at public vendue, at such time as the justice or mayor may direct, and out of the proceeds of sale to pay the charges on such goods, and all costs which have accrued in procuring the order and making the sale; and should there be a balance left, it shall be paid into the county treasury; and the owner of such goods may receive the same out of the treasury, on the order of the board of supervisors, if applied for within one year, but not afterwards. Perishable goods may be sold as herein provided, according to the exigency, if not immediately called for and taken.

356. Missouri.[2] — When any goods, merchandise, or other property shall have been received by any railroad or express company, or other common carrier, commission merchant, or warehouseman, and shall not be received by the owner, consignee, or other authorized person, it shall be lawful to hold the same by said carrier, commission merchant, or warehouseman, or the same may be stored with some responsible person, and be retained until the freight and all just and reasonable charges be paid.

If no person call for said goods, merchandise, or other prop-

[1] R. Code 1880, ch. 38, § 1055.   [2] 2 R. S. 1879, §§ 6277–6279.

erty within sixty days from the receipt thereof, and pay freight and charges thereon, it shall be lawful for such carrier, commission merchant, or warehouseman to sell such goods, merchandise, or other property, or so much thereof, at auction, to the highest bidder, as will pay said freight and charges, first having given twenty days' notice of the time and place of sale to the owner, consignee, or consignor, when known, and by advertisement in a daily paper, or if in a weekly paper, four weeks, published where such sale is to take place; and if any surplus be left after paying freight, storage, cost of advertising, and all other just and reasonable charges, the same shall be paid over to the rightful owner of said property at any time thereafter, upon demand being made therefor within sixty days. If the rightful owner or his agent fail to demand such surplus within sixty days of the time of such sale, then said surplus shall be paid into the county treasury, subject to the order of the owner.

357. Nebraska.[1]— Whenever any personal property shall be consigned to, or deposited with, any forwarding merchant, wharf-keeper, warehouse-keeper, tavern-keeper, or the keeper of any depot for the reception and storage of trunks, baggage, and other personal property, such consignee or bailee shall immediately cause to be entered, in a book to be provided and kept by him for that purpose, a description of such property, with the date of the reception thereof.

If such property shall not have been left with such consignee or bailee for the purpose of being forwarded or otherwise disposed of, according to directions received by such consignee or bailee at or before the time of the reception thereof, and the name and residence of the owner of such property be known or ascertained, the person having such property in his custody shall immediately notify such owner by letter, to be directed to him and deposited in a post-office, to be transmitted by mail, of the reception of such property.

In case any such property shall remain unclaimed for three months after its reception as aforesaid, the person having possession thereof shall cause a notice to be published once in each week for four successive weeks, in a newspaper published in the same county, if there be one, and if not, then in some paper published at the seat of government, describing such property

[1] Comp. Stats. 1885, ch. 92, §§ 1–12.

and specifying the time when it was so received, and stating that, unless such property shall be claimed within three months from the first publication of such notice, and the lawful charges thereon paid, the same will be sold.

In case the owner or person entitled to such property shall not, within three months after the publication of such notice, claim such property and pay the lawful charges thereon, including the expenses of such publication, the person having possession of the property, his agent or attorney, may make and deliver to any justice of the peace of the same county an affidavit setting forth a description of the property remaining unclaimed, the time of its reception, the publication of the notice, and whether the owner of such property is known or unknown.

Upon the delivery to him of such affidavit, the justice shall cause such property to be opened and examined in his presence, and a true inventory thereof to be made, and shall make and annex to such inventory an order under his hand that the property therein described be sold by the sheriff of the county where the same shall be, at public auction, upon due notice.

It shall be the duty of the sheriff receiving such inventory and order to give ten days' notice of the sale by posting up written notices thereof in three public places in the county or city, and to sell such property at public auction for the highest price he can obtain therefor. Upon completing the sale, the sheriff making the same shall indorse upon the order aforesaid a return of his proceedings upon such order, and the proceeds of the sale, after deducting his fees, which shall be the same as upon an execution.

From the proceeds of such sale the justice shall pay the charges and expenses legally incurred in respect to such property, or a ratable proportion, to each claimant, if there be not sufficient to pay the whole; and such justice shall ascertain and determine the amount of such charges in a summary manner, and shall be entitled to three dollars for each day's services rendered by him in such proceeding.

Such justice shall deliver to the treasurer of the county in which the property was sold the affidavit, inventory, and order of sale and return hereinbefore mentioned, together with a statement of the charges and expenses incurred in respect to such property as ascertained and paid by him, with a statement of his own fees, and shall at the same time pay over to such treasurer any balance of the proceeds of the sale remaining after payment of such charges, expenses, and fees. The treasurer shall file in his office and safely keep all the papers so delivered to him, and make a proper entry of the payment to him of any moneys arising from such sale in the books of his office.

If the owner of the property sold, or his legal representatives, shall, at any time within five years after such moneys shall have been deposited in the county treasury, furnish satisfactory evidence of the ownership of such property, he or they shall be entitled to receive from such treasurer the amount deposited with him. If the amount so deposited with any county treasurer shall not be paid to such owner, or his legal representatives, within the said five years, such county treasurer shall pay such amount into the school fund of the proper county, to be appropriated for the support of schools.

358. Nevada.[1]—When any goods, merchandise, or other property has been received by any railroad or express company, or other common carrier, commission or forwarding merchant, or warehouseman, for transportation or safe keeping, and are not delivered to the owner, consignee, or other authorized person, the carrier, commission or forwarding merchant, or warehouseman may hold or store the same with some responsible person until the freight and all just and reasonable charges on same are paid.

If a consignee does not accept and remove freight within twenty-four hours after notice has been served on him by the carrier, the carrier is released from further liability by placing the freight in a suitable warehouse on storage, or the carrier may hold the same upon his responsibility as a warehouseman.

If the consignee's place of residence or business be unknown, notice may be served on him through the post-office, and the carrier may place the freight in a suitable warehouse on storage, and give notice thereof to the consignor.

If, from any cause other than want of ordinary care and diligence on his part, a common carrier is unable to deliver perishable property transported by him, and collect his charges thereon, he may cause the property to be sold in open market to satisfy his lien of freightage.

If no person call for the freight or other property received by

[1] G. S. 1885, §§ 4964-4969.

such railroad, express company, or other common carrier, commission or forwarding merchant, or warehouseman, within sixty days from the receipt thereof, the carrier, forwarding or commission merchant, or warehouseman may sell such property, or so much thereof, at auction, to the highest bidders, as will pay freight and other just and reasonable charges, first having given notice of the time and place of sale to the owner, consignee, or consignor, when known, and by advertisement in a daily paper ten days, or, if a weekly paper, four weeks, published where such sale is to take place, or, if there is no paper published at the place where such sale is to take place, by posting a notice of the sale conspicuously in at least three public places; and if any surplus is left after paying freight, storage, cost of advertising, and other reasonable charges, the same must be paid over to the owner of such property, at any time thereafter, on demand being made therefor within six months after the sale : provided, that any trunk or valise, with the contents, shall be held six months before being advertised for sale.

If the owner, or his agent, fails to demand such surplus within six months from the time of such sale, then it shall be paid over to the county treasurer of the county in which the sale is made, to be held by him for a period of twelve months, subject to the order of the owner, after which time, if the same is not paid to the owner, or his authorized agent, or some person legally authorized to receive the same, it shall be paid over to the treasurer of the county where such sale is made, who shall pay the same over to the state treasurer for the benefit of the state school fund.

359. New Jersey.[1] — In all cases where the consignees or owners of any goods, wares, or merchandise transported by any railroad, canal, or express company in this state, or chartered by the laws of this state or any other state to any designated station or point in this state, are unknown, cannot be found, refuse to receive or to pay the costs or expenses of transportation of such goods, wares, and merchandise, it shall be lawful for any justice of the supreme court, supreme court commissioner, or any judge of the court of common pleas residing in the county where such goods, wares, or merchandise are consigned or directed, upon satisfactory proof made to him by such railroad,

---

[1] 1 Rev. Stats. 1877, pp. 591, 592, §§ 1, 3.

canal, or express company that such goods have been in their possession four months or over, and that the owners or consignees are unknown, cannot be found, have refused to receive or pay the costs and expenses of transportation, to issue an order under his hand, commanding the sheriff or one of the constables of said county to sell said goods, wares, and merchandise by public vendue, at the time, place, and in the manner in such order named: provided, that before such sale shall be made, public notice shall be given by such sheriff or constable of the time and place of such sale and the articles to be sold, and the person or persons to whom directed, by five notices, set up in five of the most public places in the neighborhood in which such goods, wares, and merchandise were consigned or directed to be left, at least five days before the time of sale, and by three successive insertions, within one week before the day of sale, in some daily newspaper, if any there be, published in the neighborhood of such place of sale: provided, further, that when it shall be made to appear to the satisfaction of such justice, supreme court commissioner, or judge, by due proof, by any railroad, canal, or express company or their agents, that any goods, wares, or merchandise by them transported and in their possession as aforesaid are perishable, and that they would depreciate in value and loss be occasioned by being longer kept, such justice, supreme court commissioner, or judge shall issue an order, directed as aforesaid, commanding sale of said goods, wares, and merchandise, in such manner as he shall deem most expedient: a copy of either of which said orders and notice of sale shall be served personally, or be left at the place of residence or business, or sent by mail to the owner or consignee of said goods, by said sheriff or constable, if the residence of such owner or consignee to whom such goods are directed can be ascertained.

The proceeds of said sale shall first be applied to defray the expenses of such sale, then to the account of transportation and storage of such railroad, canal, or express company upon such goods; the balance, if any there be, shall be paid to the clerk of the county, immediately, in which such goods were sold, who shall pay the same to the legal owner or consignee, upon order of said justice, supreme court commissioner, or judge, made upon due proof of such claim; and if no such claim is made in two years, then said clerk shall pay the same into the school fund of this state.

360. New Mexico Territory.[1] — Carriers have a lien on the things carried for the freight due, if payment is to be made on delivery of such things. In order to enforce said lien, those who are entitled to the same, as provided by this act, may, after the debt for which the lien is claimed becomes due and payable, serve the party or parties, against whom the lien is sought to be enforced, with a written notice, setting forth the amount of the indebtedness, upon what account or cause the same accrued, and that, if the same is not paid within ten days after the service of said notice, the property will be advertised and sold to satisfy said indebtedness.

If default be made in the payment of the debt, after notice as provided above, then it shall be lawful for the lien claimant or creditor, as herein provided, to advertise and sell such property at public auction to the highest bidder for cash, after giving twenty days' notice of such sale by at least six handbills posted up in public places in the county in which such sale is to be made ; such notices of sale shall set forth the time and place of sale and a description of the property to be sold.

After sale, the proceeds of such sale shall be applied to the payment of the costs of advertising and making the sale and satisfaction of the demand of the lien claimant, and the residue, if any, shall be refunded to the lien debtor : provided, that the lien claimant shall not be precluded from bidding on or purchasing the property at such sale.

361. New York.[2] — The proprietors of the several lines of stages, and the proprietors of the several canal-boat lines, and the proprietors of the several steamboats, and several incorporated railroad companies, and the keepers of the several inns and taverns within this state, who shall have any unclaimed trunks, boxes, or baggage within his, their, or either of their custody, shall immediately enter the time the same was left, with a proper description thereof, in a book to be by them provided and kept for that purpose. In case the name and residence of the owner shall be ascertained, it shall be the duty of such person, who shall have any such property as above specified, to immediately notify the owner thereof by mail.

In case there shall not be any information obtained as to the

---

[1] Comp. Laws 1884, p. 740, §§   [2] 3 R. S. 7th ed. p. 2260, §§ 1–5.
1543–1545.

owner, it shall be the duty of the person having the possession thereof to make out a correct written description of all such property as shall have been unclaimed for thirty days, stating the time the same came into his possession, and forward said description to the editor of the state paper, whose duty it shall be, on the first Mondays of July, October, January, and April in each year, to publish the same in the state paper once a week for three weeks successively.

In case the said property shall remain unclaimed for sixty days after the said publication, it shall be the duty of the person or company having possession thereof to apply to a magistrate of the town or city in which said property is retained, in whose presence and under whose direction said property shall be opened and examined, and an inventory thereof taken by said magistrate ; and if the name and residence of the owner is ascertained by such examination, it shall be the duty of the magistrate forthwith to direct a notice thereof to such owner by mail ; and if said property shall remain unclaimed for three months after such examination, it shall be the further duty of the person or company having possession thereof to apply to a magistrate as aforesaid ; and if said magistrate shall deem such property of sufficient value, he shall cause the same to be sold at public auction, giving six days' previous notice of the time and place of such sale ; and from the proceeds of such sale he shall pay the charges and expenses legally incurred in respect to said property, or a ratable proportion thereof to each claimant, if insufficient for the payment of the whole amount ; and the balance of the proceeds of such sale, if any, the said magistrate shall immediately pay to the overseers of the poor of said town or city, for the use of the poor thereof ; and the said overseers shall make an entry of such amount, and the time of receiving the same, upon their official records, and it shall be subject, at any time within seven years thereafter, to be reclaimed by, and refunded to, the owner of such property, his heirs or assigns, on satisfactory proof of such ownership.

362. Ohio.[1] — All express companies, transportation companies, forwarding and commission merchants, common carriers, warehousemen, wharfingers, and railroad companies, doing business in this state, shall, within thirty days after the receipt of any

[1] R. S. 1880, §§ 3221–3231.

property, when such property is plainly marked with the owner's name and place of residence, or be otherwise known, notify the owner that such property is held by them subject to charges, either by leaving such notice at the usual residence or place of business of the owner, or by depositing the same, postage prepaid, in the proper post-office, duly addressed to such owner.

When any such property has been conveyed to any point in this state, and remains unclaimed for the space of six months at the place to which it is consigned, and the owner fails within that time to claim the same, and to pay the proper charges, if there be any against it, such person, association, or company may sell such freight or other property at public auction, offering each parcel separately.

Such property may be offered for sale either in the place where the office, station, depot, or warehouse in which the same has been deposited for safe keeping is located, or at any other place where such person, association, or company may deem best to insure a prompt sale thereof. At least thirty days' notice of the time and place of sale, containing a descriptive list of the several articles to be sold, with names, numbers, and marks thereon, shall be given, by posting such notice at the office, station, or depot of such person, association, or company in the county where the place to which such property was consigned is situated, or, if there be no such office, station, or depot, by posting such notice in three public places in such county ; and, in addition to the posting at the place of consignment, such descriptive list must be posted at the place where the property is to be sold, and thirty days' notice of the time and place of the sale must be published in a newspaper of general circulation in the county where the property is to be sold.

Such person, association, or company, from the proceeds of the sale of such property, shall pay all the necessary costs and expenses of the sale and all proper charges for freight and storage of the property sold, apportioning such expenses and charges, as near as may be, among the articles sold, to the amount received for each, and hold the overplus, if any, subject to the order of the owner thereof at any time within one year after such sale, upon proof of ownership by affidavit of the claimant or his attorney ; and after the expiration of one year, all such sums unclaimed shall be paid into the state treasury, to be placed to the credit of the common schools ; but any such article remaining unsold may be again offered, as above provided, until sold.

Such person, association, or company may bring suit before any court of competent jurisdiction for the amount of the freight, storage, and legal charges thereon, and subject such freight to the payment thereof, after ten days from the giving of the notice first above provided for, unless such costs and charges are paid, if the owner or consignee is known or can be found in the county ; but if such owner or consignee is unknown, a non-resident of the county, or his place of residence is unknown, then such notice shall be published for not less than ten days in a newspaper of general circulation in such county, and in such case the suit may be brought after ten days from the first publication ; and the judgment obtained shall be a lien upon the freight, to satisfy which, with costs of suit, the same shall be sold.

Such person, association, or company, after the expiration of ten days from the receipt of goods at the place to which they are consigned, may, upon giving or depositing the notice first above provided, and the expiration of ten days, charge a fair and reasonable cost for storage, which shall be a lien upon the goods so stored; and such person, association, or company may, after the expiration of said ten days, deliver such goods to any warehouseman or storage merchant at the point of destination of such goods or merchandise, or, in case there be no responsible warehouseman or storage merchant at such point willing to receive the goods, then at the most convenient point where storage can be effected, and receive from such warehouseman the freight and charges due such railroad or other company upon the same, notifying the owner or consignee of such storage, when known, in the manner first above provided ; and the advances made, and all reasonable charges for storage, shall be a lien upon the goods so stored.

Such person, association, or company shall keep a copy of the notice, a copy of the sale bill, and the expenses thereof, proportional to each article sold, and also the oath of the claimant of the residue of the proceeds as aforesaid, and shall furnish an inspection of the same, and, if required, copies thereof, to any one, on payment of the proper charges therefor.

If any perishable property be so conveyed as freight, and remain unclaimed until in danger of great depreciation, or the same be refused, or the owner thereof cannot be found, then such person, association, or company may sell the same at private sale or auction, without giving notice, for the best price it will bring, and apply the proceeds as aforesaid.

If the owner of any such property, at any time within five years, reclaim the same, and produce satisfactory evidence to the auditor of state of his ownership thereof, the auditor shall draw his warrant in favor of such person upon the treasurer of the state for the amount paid into the state treasury.

Any such person, association, or company who refuses or neglects to perform any of the duties required by this chapter, with the intent to avoid the provisions thereof, shall forfeit and pay a sum not less than one hundred dollars, nor more than five hundred dollars, at the discretion of the court, to be recovered for the use of common schools in the county in which the principal office of such person, association, or company is located; and shall, moreover, be liable to any person injured thereby in double the value of the property.

363. Oregon.[1] — Whenever any personal property shall be consigned to, or deposited with, any forwarding merchant, wharfinger, warehouseman, or tavern-keeper, or the keeper of any depot for the reception and storage of trunks, baggage, merchandise, or other personal property, such consignee or bailee shall immediately cause to be entered in a book kept by him a description of such property, with the date of reception thereof.

If such property shall not have been left with such consignee or bailee for the purpose of being forwarded or disposed of, according to directions received by such consignee or bailee, at or before the time of the reception thereof, and if the name and residence of the owner of such property be known to the person having such property in his possession, he shall immediately notify the owner by letter, directed to him and deposited in the post-office, of the reception of such property.

If any such property shall not be claimed and taken away within one year after the time it shall have been so received, the person having possession thereof may at any time thereafter proceed to sell the same in the manner provided in this title. Before any such property shall be sold, if the name and residence of the owner thereof be known, at least sixty days' notice of such sale shall be given him, either personally or by mail, or

---

[1] Gen. Laws 1872, ch. 18, §§ 15–27.

by leaving a notice at his residence or place of doing business; but if the name and residence of the owner be unknown, the person having the possession of such property shall cause a notice to be published containing a description of the property, for the space of six weeks successively, in a newspaper, if there be one, published in the same county: if there be no newspaper published in the same county, then said notice shall be published in a newspaper nearest thereto in the state; the last publication of such notice shall be at least eighteen days previous to the time of sale.

If the owner or person entitled to such property shall not take the same away, and pay the charges thereon, after sixty days' notice shall have been given, it shall be the duty of the person having possession thereof, his agent or attorney, to make and deliver to a justice of the peace of the same county an affidavit setting forth a description of the property remaining unclaimed, the time of its reception, the publication of the notice, and whether the owner of such property·be known or unknown.

Upon the delivery to him of such affidavit, the justice shall cause such property to be opened and examined in his presence, and a true inventory thereof to be made, and shall annex to such inventory an order under his hand, that the property therein described be sold, by any constable of the precinct where the same shall be, at public auction.

It shall be the duty of such constable receiving such inventory and order to give ten days' notice of the sale, by posting up written notices thereof in three or more places in such precinct, and to sell such property at public auction to the highest bidder, in the same manner as provided by law for sales under execution from justices' courts.

Upon completing the sale, the constable making the same shall indorse upon the order aforesaid a return of his proceedings thereon, and return the same to the justice, together with the inventory and the proceeds of sale, after deducting his fees. From the proceeds of such sale the justice shall pay all legal charges that have been incurred in relation to such property, or a ratable proportion of each charge, if the proceeds of said sale shall not be sufficient to pay all the charges; and the balance, if any there be, he shall immediately pay over to the treasurer of the county in which the same shall be sold, and deliver a statement therewith containing a description of the property sold, the gross amount of such sale, and the amount of costs, charges, and expenses paid to each person. The county treasurer shall make an entry of the amount received by him, and the time when received, and shall file in his office such statement so delivered to him by the justice.

If the owner of the property sold, or his legal representatives, shall, at any time within five years after such money shall have been deposited in the county treasury, furnish satisfactory evidence to the treasurer of the ownership of such property, he or they shall be entitled to receive from such treasurer the amount so deposited with him. If the amount so deposited with any county treasurer shall not be claimed by the owner thereof, or his legal representatives, within the said five years, the same shall belong to the county, and may be disposed of as the county court may direct.

Property of a perishable kind and subject to decay by keeping, consigned or left in manner before mentioned, if not taken away within thirty days after it shall have been left, may be sold by giving ten days' notice thereof, the sale to be conducted, and the proceeds of the same to be applied, in the manner before provided : provided that any property in a state of decay, or that is manifestly liable immediately to become decayed, may be summarily sold by order of a justice of the peace, after inspection thereof.

364. Pennsylvania.[1] — In all cases in which commission merchants, factors, and all common carriers or other persons shall have a lien, under existing laws, upon any goods, wares, merchandise, or other property, for or on account of the costs or expenses of carriage, storage, or labor bestowed on such goods, wares, merchandise, if the owner or consignee of the same shall fail or neglect or refuse to pay the amount of charges upon any such property, goods, wares, or merchandise within sixty days after demand thereof, made personally upon such owner or consignee, then and in such case it shall and may be lawful for any such commission merchant, factor, common carrier, or other person having such lien as aforesaid, after the expiration of said period of sixty days, to expose such goods, wares, merchandise, or other property to sale at public auction, and to sell the same, or so much thereof as shall be sufficient to discharge said lien,

---

[1] Brightly's Pur. Dig. 1883, p. 266, §§ 6–8; also p. 1059, §§ 1–3.

together with costs of sale and advertising : provided, that notice of such sale, together with the name of the person or persons to whom such goods shall have been consigned, shall have been first published for three successive weeks in a newspaper published in the county, and by six written or printed handbills put up in the most public and conspicuous places in the vicinity of the depot where the said goods may be.

Upon the application of any of the persons or corporations having a lien upon goods, wares, merchandise, or other property, as mentioned in the first section of this act, verified by affidavit, to any of the judges of the courts of common pleas of this commonwealth, setting forth that the places of residence of the owner and consignee of any such goods, wares, merchandise, or other property are unknown, or that such goods, wares, merchandise, or other property are of such perishable nature, or so damaged, or showing any other cause that shall render it impracticable to give the notice as provided for in the first section of this act, then and in such case it shall and may be lawful for a judge of the city or county in which the goods may be to make an order, to be by him signed, authorizing the sale of such goods, wares, merchandise, or other property, upon such terms as to notice as the nature of the case may admit of, and to such judge shall seem meet : provided, that in cases of perishable property, the affidavit and proceedings required by this section may be had before a justice of the peace.

The residue of moneys arising from any such sales, either under the first or second sections of this act, after deducting the amount of the lien as aforesaid, together with costs of advertising and sales, shall be held subject to the order of the owner or owners of such property.

365. Rhode Island.[1] — Every common carrier who shall have had any unclaimed article, not perishable, in his possession for a period of one year, may sell the same at public auction, and out of the proceeds may retain the charges of transportation, storage, and advertising, and expense of sale thereof : but no sale shall be made until the expiration of four weeks from the publication of notice of such sale in a newspaper published at the place where such sale is to take place, if one is there published; if not, in the one published nearest to said place of sale ; and such notice

[1] P. S. 1882, ch. 139, §§ 5-7.

shall contain a description of such article, together with the name of the person to whom it is addressed.

Whenever any common carrier has transported property consisting of either fresh meats, fresh fish, shell fish, fruit, vegetables, or other perishable property to their place of destination, and has notified the owner or consignee thereof of the arrival of the same, and the owner or consignee, after such notice, has refused or omitted to receive and take away the same and pay the freight and proper charges thereon, said carrier may sell the same at public or private sale, without advertising; and the proceeds, after deducting the amount of said freight and charges and expenses of sale, shall be paid to the owner or consignee: provided that, if the owner or consignee cannot be found on reasonable inquiry, the sale may be made without such notice.

The proceeds of all property thus sold, after deducting costs of transportation, storage, advertising, and expense of sale, in case the owner or consignee does not appear within six months after said sale, shall be paid to the general treasurer for the use of the state; and the person making such payment shall at the time thereof file with the general treasurer a particular account in writing, verified by his oath or the oath of some other competent person, of the property sold, and of said cost of transportation, storage, advertising, and expense of sale.

366. South Carolina.[1] — Every railroad corporation, express company, and the proprietors of every steamboat engaged in the transportation of passengers and freight, or either, which shall have had unclaimed freight or baggage not perishable in its possession for the period of at least one year, may proceed and sell the same at public auction, after giving notice to that effect in one or more newspapers published in the state, or at the place where such goods are to be sold, once a week for not less than four weeks, and shall also keep a notice of such sale posted for the same time in a conspicuous place in the principal office of said company.

Said notice shall contain, as near as practicable, a description of such freight or baggage, the place and time when and where left, together with the name and residence of the owner of the freight or baggage, or person to whom it is consigned, if the same be known.

---

[1] G. S. 1882, ch. 51, §§ 1663–1666.

All moneys arising from the sale of freight or baggage as aforesaid, after deducting therefrom charges and expenses for the transportation, storage, advertising, commissions for selling the property, and any amount previously paid for advances on such freight and baggage, shall be paid by the company to the persons entitled to receive the same.

The said company shall keep books of record of all such sales as aforesaid, containing copies of such notices, proofs of advertisements and posting, affidavit of sale, with the amount for which each parcel was sold, the total amount of charges against such parcel, and the amount held in trust for the owner; which books shall be opened for inspection by claimants, at the principal office of the said company, and at the office where the sale was made.

367. Tennessee.[1] — All common carriers and express companies doing business within the limits of this state shall, after the receipt of freight or merchandise for delivery at their warehouse, depot, or station, notify the consignee by written or printed notice, to be delivered to the consignee in person at his place of business, if in the city or town where received, or, if not residing or doing business in the city or town, then through the post-office, within three days after the arrival of said goods.

After said freight or merchandise has been held at the said warehouse, depot, or station, uncalled for and not taken by the consignee, for the period of six months and one day from the date of the arrival of said goods at said warehouse, depot, or station, it shall be lawful for said common carrier and express company to send said goods to one of the principal offices in the state, to be sold for charges.

After said freight or merchandise has been held by said express company for the period of six months and one day, and giving notice to the consignor, if known, by written or printed notice, to be transmitted through the mail, placed in the post-office at least thirty days before the day of sale, it shall be lawful for said express company to advertise said goods that have not been taken by the consignees in one or more of the daily papers in such principal city, the said advertisment to be inserted on each Wednesday of the month preceding the sale,

[1] Code 1884, ch. 2788–2791.

specifying each article to be sold, and stating date of sale and place of sale.

After the sale has been made, the money received for the sale of such articles of merchandise, after deducting charges, shall be sent to the principal office in the state, there to be held for the benefit of the owners of the goods sold, — a sworn copy to be kept at the office where the sale has been made, and a sworn copy, certified to by the auctioneer, to be sent to the principal office where the money is to be deposited; and they shall also notify the person or persons, if known, who shipped the goods or packages, after being in the warehouse six months, as they are required to notify the person to whom the same was sent.

368. Texas.[1] — When any freight or baggage has been conveyed by a common carrier to any point in this state, and shall remain unclaimed for the space of three months at the office or depot nearest or most convenient to destination, and the owner, whether known or unknown, fails within that time to claim such freight or baggage, or to pay the proper charges, if any there be, against it, then it shall be lawful for such common carrier to sell such freight or baggage at public auction, offering each box, bale, trunk, valise, or other article separately, as consigned or checked.

Thirty days' notice of the time and place of sale, and a descriptive list of the packages to be sold, with names and numbers or marks found thereon, shall be posted up in three public places in the county where the sale is to be made, and on the door of the depot or warehouse, if any, where the goods are, and shall also give notice in at least one newspaper in the county, if any be published therein, for thirty days before sale; and out of the proceeds of such sale the carrier shall deduct the proper charges on such freight or baggage, including costs of storing and costs of sale, and hold the overplus, if any, to the order of the owner at any time within five years, on proof of ownership made by the claimant or his duly authorized agent or attorney.

The carrier shall keep an account of sales, copy of the notice, a copy of the sale bill, and the expense thereof proportioned to each article sold.

Should any live-stock remain unclaimed for the space of forty-eight hours after its arrival at the place of its destination, the

---

[1] R. S. 1879, ch. 2, arts. 285–289.

carrier may sell the same at public auction after giving five days' notice of the time and place of such sale, as hereinbefore prescribed, and apply the proceeds as above prescribed, after deducting reasonable expenses for keeping, feeding, and watering live-stock from the time of its arrival at the place of its destination until disposed of as herein provided; and such carrier shall also keep an account of any such sale, copy of the notice, copy of the sale bill, and an account of all expenses.

Should any perishable property remain unclaimed after arrival at its place of destination until in danger of depreciation, it shall be the duty of the carrier to sell the same at public auction, after giving five days' notice of the time and place of sale, as prescribed in preceding article, and apply the proceeds as prescribed in said article, and keep an account of such sale, copy of the notice, copy of the sale bill, and an account of all expenses.

369. Utah Territory.[1] — All common carriers have a lien upon goods in their possession for freight, and back charges paid by them.

Any railroad company or common carrier transporting freight may, if any property transported by such carrier be not accepted and taken away by the consignee thereof within six months from the time it shall have been received at the point on such carrier's line or route where the same is to be delivered, sell the same in the manner hereinafter prescribed, and out of the proceeds of such sale retain the amount due such carrier from the consignee for freight or carriage, and a reasonable compensation for the storage and care of such property during said time, together with reasonable and necessary costs of such sale; and the surplus, if any, shall be paid to the owner, consignee, or agent.

Whenever any goods, wares, merchandise, or other property shall remain in the possession of any carrier at the end of six months from the time of arrival at the place of delivery, it shall be lawful for such carrier to sell such property at public auction, by first publishing a notice thereof, in some newspaper published and having a general circulation in the county where such property is to be exposed for sale, for a period of thirty days prior to such sale; or if there is no paper published in such county, then in some newspaper published in this territory, and having a general circulation in such county. Said notice shall

[1] Comp. Laws 1876, ch. 6, §§ 2, 3.

contain the name and address, if known, of the consignee, the name of the consignor, from what place shipped, with a general description of the property to be sold, if the nature thereof be known; if not, then of the box, cask, or other covering of the same.

370. Vermont.[1] — If the personal property stored in a depot or other building of a railroad or steamboat corporation, or with a wharfinger, public storehouse-keeper, or express company, without a special contract for keeping the same, is not claimed by the owner or consignee within six months from the time it was so deposited, the persons or corporation with whom it is stored shall notify the owner or consignee by letter where the property is. If the owner or consignee is unknown, such persons or corporation at the expiration of such time may cause the property to be opened and examined by the sheriff of the county in which it remains; and if, upon such examination, the name and residence of the owner or consignee is ascertained, he shall be notified as aforesaid.

If such owner or consignee does not, within one month after such notice, claim such property, pay the charges thereon, and take it away, or if the owner or consignee is not ascertained or his residence known, the property may be sold by the sheriff.

The sheriff shall sell such property at public auction, giving notice of such sale in a newspaper printed in the town or county three weeks successively, the last of which publications shall be not less than four weeks previous to such sale. Such advertisement shall state the time and place of sale, the place where and the time when the property was received, a description of the same, the marks upon the articles to be sold, the place whence sent when known, and the names of the owners or consignees when known.

If the owner or consignee does not claim the property, and pay the legal charges thereon, and for advertising the same, before the day of sale, the sheriff shall sell the same and make return of the sale, with a list of the property sold, and a copy of the advertisement describing such property, within twenty days after such sale, to the treasurer of the state, with his affidavit to the truth of such return. The sheriff shall also return to the treasurer of the state the papers, notes, drafts, moneys, or other

[1] Rev. Laws 1880, ch. 184, §§ 4063–4067.

valuables of similar nature, found with such property, which, with the moneys arising from the sale, after deducting the legal charges thereon, and the charges and expenses of the sale, shall be kept by said treasurer for the benefit of the owner or consignee of such property, and shall be paid to him on producing satisfactory evidence of his right.

The treasurer of the state shall keep a record of the time when such moneys, notes, drafts, or other valuables, and the avails of such sale, are received ; and if the same remain in his office unclaimed by the owner or consignee thereof for two years, they shall become the property of the state, and shall be disposed of by the treasurer for the benefit of the state.

371. **Virginia.**[1] — Any express or railroad company, or persons engaged in the express business, or in any way in the transportation of goods or articles of any kind from one part of the country to another, as freight or baggage, and having an office or place of business in the state, who shall have had any unclaimed articles, goods, or things not perishable in its, his, or their possession for a period of sixty days at least, may, at the expiration of that time, proceed to sell the same at public auction ; and out of the proceeds may retain the charges of transportation and storage of such articles, goods, or things, which expense and charges shall be a lien upon such articles : provided, that said company, person, or persons shall first give public notice of such sale, in one or more newspapers, once a week for four successive weeks, published at the place nearest the said place of sale, which notice shall set forth the time and place of sale, the character of each unclaimed package distinctly, and the name of the person or persons to whom it is directed, if known.

Such company or persons engaged in the express or transportation business shall make an entry of the balance of the proceeds of sale of such articles, goods, or things directed to the same person or persons, as near as can be ascertained, and at any time within three years thereafter shall refund any surplus so retained to the owners of such articles, goods, or things, or to their personal representatives, upon satisfactory proof of such ownership ; and shall, if no claim is made for such retained balances, accompanied by satisfactory proof, within three years, pay the same into the treasury of the state, with a correct list

[1] Code 1873, ch. 61, §§ 33, 34.

of all and every article sold by said company, with the name or names of the person or persons to whom said packages originally belonged. The treasurer shall receipt to said companies or agents for the same, and shall keep a correct list thereof, and the sum or sums so paid in shall be applied to the support of public schools.

372. Washington Territory.[1] — Whenever property upon which charges for advances, freight, transportation, wharfage, or storage are due and unpaid, and there is a lien, shall remain and be held in store by the person or persons in whose favor such lien exists uncalled for, it shall be lawful for such person or persons to cause such property to be sold as is herein provided.

If said property consists of live-stock, the maintenance of which at the place where kept is wasteful and expensive in proportion to the value of the animals, or of other perishable property liable, if kept, to destruction, waste, or great depreciation, the person or persons having such lien may sell the same upon giving ten days' notice.

All other property upon which such charges may be unpaid, due, and there is a lien, after the same shall have remained in store, uncalled for, for a period of thirty days after such charges shall have become due, may be sold by the person or persons having a lien for the payment of such charges upon giving ten days' notice : provided, that where the property can be conveniently divided into separate lots or parcels, no more lots or parcels shall be sold than shall be sufficient to pay the charges due on the day of sale, and the expenses of sale.

The moneys arising from sales made under the provisions of this chapter shall first be applied to the payment of the costs and expenses of the sale, and then to the payment of the lawful charges of the person or persons having a lien thereon for advances, freight, transportation, wharfage, or storage, for whose benefit the sale shall have been made ; the surplus, if any, shall be retained subject to the future lawful charge of the person or persons for whose benefit the sale was made, upon the property of the same owner still remaining in store uncalled for, if any there be, and to the demand of the owner of the property, who shall have paid such charges or otherwise satisfied such lien; and all moneys remaining uncalled for, for the period of three

[1] Code 1881, ch. 140, §§ 1980–1983.

258

months, shall be paid to the county treasurer, and shall remain in his hands a special fund for the benefit of the lawful claimant thereof.

373. Wisconsin.[1] — Whenever any personal property shall be consigned or deposited with any common carrier, forwarding merchant, wharfinger, warehouseman, innkeeper, or the keeper of any depot for the storage of baggage, merchandise, or other personal property, such consignee or bailee shall immediately cause to be entered, in a proper book kept by him, a description of such property, with the date of the reception thereof ; and if the same shall not have been so consigned or deposited for the purpose of being forwarded or disposed of according to directions received by such consignee or bailee, at or before his reception thereof, he shall immediately notify the owner by mail thereof, if his name and residence be known, or can, with reasonable diligence, be ascertained.

If any such property shall not be claimed and taken away within one year after it shall have been so received, the same may be sold as hereinafter directed ; but when such property shall be perishable, or subject to decay by keeping, it may be sold if not claimed and taken within thirty days ; and if any such property be in a state of decay, or manifestly liable to immediate decay, it may be summarily sold without notice, by order of a justice of the peace, after inspection, as provided in the following section.

Before any such property, except as aforesaid, shall be sold, ten days' notice of such sale, if the property be perishable, or subject to decay by keeping, and sixty days' notice in other cases, shall be given the owner thereof by the person in possession of such property, either personally or by mail, or by leaving a written notice at his residence or place of business ; but if the name and residence of such owner be not known, and cannot with reasonable diligence be ascertained, such notice shall be given by publication thereof for the periods aforesaid respectively, dating from the first publication, at least once in each week, in a newspaper published in the county, if there be one ; and if there be none, then in a newspaper published in an adjoining county.

If the owner or person entitled to such property shall not take

[1] R. S. 1878, ch. 74, §§ 1637–1645.

the same away and pay the charges thereon, after notice as aforesaid shall have been given, the person having possession thereof, his agent or attorney, shall make and deliver to a justice of the peace of the same town an affidavit, setting forth a description of the property remaining unclaimed, the time of its reception, the publication of the notice, and whether the owner of such property be known or unknown.

Upon the delivery to him of such affidavit, the justice shall cause such property to be opened and examined in his presence, and a true inventory thereof to be made, and shall annex to such inventory an order under his hand that the property therein described be sold by any constable of the city or town where the same shall be, at auction.

The constable receiving such inventory and order shall give ten days' notice of the sale, by posting up written notices thereof in three or more public places in such city or town, and sell such property at public auction to the highest bidder, in the same manner as provided by law for sales under execution from justices' courts. Upon completing the sale, the constable making the same shall indorse upon the order aforesaid a return of his proceedings thereon, and return the same to the justice, together with the inventory and the proceeds of the sale, after deducting his fees.

From the proceeds of such sale the justice shall pay all legal charges that have been incurred in relation to such property, or a ratable proportion of each charge, if the proceeds of such sale shall not be sufficient to pay all charges; and the balance, if any there be, he shall immediately pay over to the treasurer of his county, and deliver a statement therewith, containing a description of the property sold, the gross amount of such sale, and the amount of costs, charges, and expenses paid to each person. The county treasurer shall file such statement, give a receipt for the money, and properly enter in his books the amount thereof and the date.

If the owner of the property sold, or his legal representatives, shall, at any time within five years after such money shall have been deposited in the county treasury, furnish satisfactory evidence to the treasurer of the ownership of such property, he or they shall be entitled to receive from such treasurer the amount so deposited with him. If not claimed within said time by the

260

owner or his legal representatives, the same shall belong to the county.

It is also provided in Wisconsin [1] that a mechanic, innkeeper, livery-stable keeper, consignee, factor, warehouseman, or carrier having a lien by common law or otherwise on personal property may, in case the debt remain unpaid for three months, and the value of the property affected thereby does not exceed one hundred dollars, sell such property at public auction, and apply the proceeds of such sale to the payment of the amount due him, and the expenses of such sale. Notice, in writing, of the time and place of such sale, and of the amount claimed to be due, shall be given to the owner of such property personally, or by leaving the same at his place of abode, if a resident of this state, and if not, by publication thereof, once in each week, for three weeks successively, next before the time of sale, in some newspaper published in the county in which such lien accrues, if there be one, and if not, by posting such notice in three public places in such county. If such property exceed in value one hundred dollars, then such lien may be enforced against the same by action in any court having jurisdiction.

374. Wyoming Territory.[2]—Agisters, innkeepers, livery-stable keepers, common carriers of goods or passengers, and mechanics who have bestowed labor upon personal property, whose charges are not paid after the same become due and payable, may apply to any justice of the peace of the county wherein he resides to appoint appraisers to appraise the several articles of personal property whereon such lien is claimed. Such justice shall thereupon appoint by warrant, under his hand and seal, three reputable householders of the county, not interested in the matter, to appraise such personal property.

The appraisers so appointed shall be sworn by the justice to well and faithfully appraise and value all such personal property, and shall thereupon proceed to view and appraise the same, and shall return their appraisement, wherein shall be set down each article separately, to the justice by whom they were appointed within ten days after their appointment.

After such appraisement is made, the person to whom such lien is given may, after giving ten days' prior notice of the time, place, and terms of such sale, with a description of the property

[1] Rev. Stats. 1878, p. 855, § 3347.   [2] Comp. Laws 1876, ch. 77, §§ 4-9.

to be sold, by the publication in some newspaper published in the county wherein he resides, or if there be no such newspaper, then by posting in three public places within such county, and delivering to the owner of such personal property, or, if he do not reside in the county, transmitting by mail to him at his usual place of abode, if known, a copy of such notice, proceed to sell all such personal property, or so much thereof as may be necessary, at public auction, for cash in hand, at any public place within such county, between the hours of ten A. M. and four P. M. of the day appointed, and, from the proceeds thereof, may pay the reasonable costs of such appraisement, notice, and sale, and his reasonable charges for which he has his lien. The residue of the proceeds of such property unsold he shall render unto the owner.

No such sale shall be made for less than two thirds of the appraised value of the article sold, nor except upon due notice, as required by the preceding section: every such sale made in violation of these provisions shall be absolutely void.

At any such sale, the person to whom such lien is given may become the purchaser.

In any case where the property to be sold cannot conveniently be sold in one day, the sale may be continued from day to day by public outcry at the place of sale. Upon the completion of such sale, the person to whom the lien is given hereby shall cause a sale bill thereof to be filed with the justice of the peace before whom the appraisement was had, in which shall be set down the sum for each separate article of property sold, and the name of the purchaser. The justice shall record such sale bill in his docket, and preserve the original thereof, together with the appraisement.

262

CHAPTER VIII.

LIENS OF CORPORATIONS ON THEIR MEMBERS' SHARES.

I. *How Created.*

375. A corporation has no lien at common law upon the shares of its members for any indebtedness to the company.[1] The reason sometimes given for this rule is that secret liens are repugnant to the general policy of the common law. But there is in fact no sufficient ground in law upon which to rest a claim to such a lien. Such possession as a corporation has of its members' shares does not give it a possessory lien for their debts.[2] The corporation really has no possession of stock that it has issued to its members except in case they transfer it to the corporation. The corporation is not a debtor to its members for the stock it

[1] Neale *v.* Janney, 2 Cr. C. C. 188; Driscoll *v.* West Bradley & Cary Manuf. Co. 59 N. Y. 96, per Folger, J.; McMurrich *v.* Bond Head Harbor Co. 9 U. C. Q. B. 333.

Kentucky: Dana *v.* Brown, 1 J. J. Marsh. 304; Frankfort Turnpike Co. *v.* Churchill, 6 Mon. 427; Fitzhugh *v.* Bank of Shepherdsville, 3 Mon. 126.

Louisiana: New Orleans Nat. Banking Asso. *v.* Wiltz, 10 Fed. Rep. 330; Bryon *v.* Carter, 22 La. Ann. 98; Byrne *v.* Union Bank, 9 Rob. (La.) 433.

Massachusetts: Mass. Iron Co. *v.* Hooper, 7 Cush. 183; Sargent *v.* Franklin Ins. Co. 8 Pick. 90; Nesmith *v.* Washington Bank, 6 Ib. 324; Hussey *v.* Manufacturers' & Mechanics'

Bank, 10 Ib. 414, 421, per Shaw, C. J.

Pennsylvania: Steamship Dock Co. *v.* Heron, 52 St. 280; Merchants' Bank *v.* Shouse, 102 Pa. St. 488; *S. C.* 16 Rep. 442.

Other States: Hagar *v.* Union Nat. Bank, 63 Me. 509; Vansands *v.* Middlesex Co. Bank, 26 Conn. 144; Farmers' & Merchants' Bank *v.* Wasson, 48 Iowa, 336; Mobile Mut. Ins. Co. *v.* Cullom, 49 Ala. 558; Bank of Holly Springs *v.* Pinson, 58 Miss. 421, per George, J.; Heart *v.* State Bank, 2 Dev. (N. C.) Eq. 111; People *v.* Crockett, 9 Cal. 112; Williams *v.* Lowe, 4 Neb. 382, 398, per Gantt, J.

[2] Fitzhugh *v.* Bank of Shepherdsville, *supra.*

263

has issued to them, so that no right can arise against them by way of set-off.

A further reason against such a lien is that it would operate as a restraint upon the transfer of stock, in the nature of a restraint of trade, and such a restraint is not allowed except by force of an express provision of statute.[1]

The lien of a corporation upon its members' shares prevents a transfer by the shareholder, but it gives the corporation no right of sale.[2]

376. Lien of corporation by statute.

376. Lien of corporation by statute.—Inasmuch as the common law implies no lien in favor of a corporation upon its shares for the debts of its shareholders, and inasmuch as it is not only reasonable but desirable that there should be such a lien, it has become usual in statutes or charters creating moneyed or commercial companies to provide expressly for such a lien.

In some states there are general laws declaring this lien, and in some instances prescribing the mode of enforcing the lien.[3]

[1] Farmers' & Merchants' Bank v. Wasson, 48 Iowa, 336.

[2] Tete v. Farmers' & Merchants' Bank, 4 Brew. (Pa.) 308.

[3] In **Alabama** a corporation having a lien by its charter or by-laws, or by contract, upon the stock standing in the name of a debtor, may enforce it after thirty days' notice to the debtor, or, if he is a non-resident, after publication once a week for three weeks, by selling the same at public auction. Code 1876, § 2040.

A mortgage, pledge, or other lien upon stock is void as to bonâ fide creditors and purchasers unless a transfer is registered within fifteen days. Code 1876, § 2044.

Colorado: Banks organized under the statutes of the state have a lien upon the stock and dividends of shareholders for their debts. G. S. 1883, §§ 271, 274.

Connecticut: Every corporation has at all times a lien upon all the stock owned by any person therein for all debts due to it from him. G. S. 1875, p. 279, § 8.

The stock of every joint-stock corporation shall be transferred only on its books in such form as the by-laws shall prescribe, and the corporation shall have a lien upon all the stock owned by any person or estate therein for all individual, joint, and partnership debts due it from him or such estate, and for any contingent liability to it as indorser, acceptor, guarantor, or surety upon any negotiable or commercial paper; and any corporation desiring to enforce such lien may give notice to such stockholder, his executor, or administrator, and, if there be none, his heir at law, that, unless he shall pay his indebtedness to said corporation within three months, it will sell said stock; and such corporation may prescribe by its by-laws the manner of giving notice required by this section, but the notice of sale shall in no case be given until the liability has become fixed. Acts 1882, ch. 82.

Florida: No shares of a private corporation shall be transferred until all previous assessments thereon shall

These statutes provide that the transferees of stock shall take it subject to all the liabilities of the stockholders who make the transfers ; or forbid transfers so long as the holder of the shares is indebted to the company ; or declare that the corporation shall have a paramount lien upon all shares to secure the debts of the shareholders to the corporation.[1]

377. By virtue of the general authority to regulate the transfer of shares conferred upon corporations by statute or special charter, many authorities hold that corporations may enact by-laws creating liens upon the shares of their members ; and that it matters not that this statutory authority is conferred in the most general terms.[2]

have been fully paid in. Laws 1881, p. 231, § 15.

Georgia : The by-laws of a corporation may create a lien upon the shares of other property of the stockholders in favor of the company; such lien is binding upon the corporators themselves, and upon all creditors given credit with notice, or purchasers at public or private sale purchasing with notice. Code 1873, § 1999.

Minnesota : A corporation has at all times a lien upon the stock or property of its members invested therein for all the debts due from them to such corporation, which may be enforced by advertisement and sale in the manner provided for selling delinquent stock. G. S. 1878, p. 395, § 114.

New York : Railroad corporations have a lien upon the shares of subscribers to stock for the amount of the unpaid calls. Laws 1881, ch. 468, § 12.

In **Utah** a private corporation has a lien on the amount paid in by a stockholder upon his subscription, and the dividends thereon for any balance due for the stock. Laws 1884, ch. 45, § 10.

Vermont : A private corporation has a lien upon the stock of its members, and their property invested therein, for debts due from them to the corporation. R. Laws 1880, § 3296.

West Virginia : No share shall be transferred without the consent of the board of directors, until the same is fully paid up, or security given to the satisfaction of the board for the residue remaining unpaid. R. S. 1878, ch. 25, § 22.

[1] Mechanics' Bank v. Seton, 1 Pet. 299, 309 ; Brent v. Bank of Washington, 10 Pet. 596, 614 ; National Bank v. Watsontown Bank, 105 U. S. 217, 220 ; Union Bank v. Laird, 2 Wheat. 390 ; Mount Holly Paper Co.'s App. 99 Pa. St. 513 ; Stebbins v. Phœnix F. Ins. Co. 3 Paige (N. Y.), 350 ; Conant v. Seneca Co. Bank, 1 Ohio St. 298 ; Bank of America v. McNeil, 10 Bush (Ky.), 54 ; Kenton Ins. Co. v. Bowman (Ky.), 15 Am. & Eng. Corp. Cas. 578 ; Hodges v. Planters' Bank, 7 G. & J. (Md.) 306 ; Reese v. Bank of Commerce, 14 Md. 271 ; Arnold v. Suffolk Bank, 27 Barb. (N. Y.) 424 ; Leggett v. Bank of Sing Sing, 24 N. Y. 283.

[2] Child v. Hudson's Bay Co. 2 P. Wms. 207. The decision of this case as reported, 1 Str. 645, was upon the ground that the corporation had a sort of set - off. Brent v. Bank of Washington, 10 Pet. 596, 616 ; Pendergast v. Bank of Stockton, 2 Sawyer,

The stockholders are regarded as having an implied power to enact by-laws giving the corporation a lien upon its members'

108 ; *In re* Bachman, 12 N. Bank. Reg. 223.

In Child *v.* Hudson's Bay Co. 2 P. Wms. 207; power was given to the Hudson's Bay Company by their charter to make by-laws for the better government of the company, and for the management of their trade, and they made a by-law that, if any of their members should be indebted to the company, his company stock should be liable in the first place for the payment of such debts as he might owe to the company, and that the company might seize and detain the stock as security for such indebtedness. In a contest between the assignees in bankruptcy of the shareholder and the company, the by-law was adjudged good upon the ground that the legal interest in all the stock was in the company.

Alabama : Cunningham *v.* Ala. L. Ins. Co. 4 Ala. 652. The charter gave the directors power " to make rules concerning the transfer of stock."

Delaware : McDowell *v.* Bank of Wilmington, 1 Harr. (Del.) 27; *S. C.* 2 Del. Ch. 1. In the latter report, however, it appears that the by-law was authorized expressly by the act of incorporation.

Louisiana : Bryon *v.* Carter, 22 La. Ann. 98. See New Orleans Nat. Banking Asso. *v.* Wiltz, 4 Woods, 43; *S. C.* 10 Fed. Rep. 330.

Missouri: Mechanics' Bank *v.* Merchants' Bank, 45 Mo. 513; St. Louis Perpetual Ins. Co. *v.* Goodfellow, 9 Mo. 149; Spurlock *v.* Pacific R. R. Co. 61 Mo. 319, 326.

New York : Leggett *v.* Bank of Sing Sing, 24 N. Y. 283; McCready *v.* Rumsey, 6 Duer, 574; Stebbins *v.* Phœnix Ins. Co. 3 Paige, 350, 361; Rosenback *v.* Salt Springs Nat. Bank, 53 Barb. 495; Arnold *v.* Suffolk Bank, 27 Ib. 424.

Pennsylvania : Tete *v.* Farmers'

& Merchants' Bank, 4 Brew. 308; Morgan *v.* Bank of North America, 8 S. & R. 73; Geyer *v.* Western Ins. Co. 3 Pitts. 41, 45. In this case the charter declared the stock assignable " subject to such restrictions and limitations as the stockholders, at a general and regular meeting, may adopt."

Rhode Island : Lockwood *v.* Mechanics' Nat. Bank, 9 R. I. 308, 335. This is one of the latest and ablest decisions sustaining this view. After an elaborate examination of the authorities, Potter, J., said : " We consider, therefore, that it is well settled by reason and authority, that the power to make by-laws to regulate the management of the business of the association, is sufficient to justify a by-law creating a lien on the stock ; that the power to regulate the transferring or manner of transferring stock is sufficient to authorize a by-law creating such a lien ; that the power to regulate the transferring or manner of transferring of stock, is sufficient to authorize 'a by-law that the stock shall be transferable only at the bank, or on the books ; and, in that case, until such transfer, the purchaser would take only an equitable, not a legal, title, and subject to any claim of the bank, by charter or by-law, or valid usage, or agreement ; that a majority, at a regular or legally called meeting, when a quorum is present, is sufficient to enact by-laws ; that a by-law informally adopted may be subsequently ratified, and, without any record of adoption, may be proved by the usage and acts of the bank, and parties dealing with it."

Other States : Bank of Holly Springs *v.* Pinson, 58 Miss. 421; Tuttle *v.* Walton, 1 Kelly (Ga.), 43; Vansands *v.* Middlesex Co. Bank, 26 Conn. 144.

shares, either by providing in express terms that the company shall have a paramount lien for any indebtedness of its members, or by prohibiting a transfer of shares upon its books while the holder is indebted to it.

But it is conceded in some of these decisions that a by-law made upon such authority does not bind others than the members of the corporation whose privilege and duty it is to know its rules and regulations, so far as these affect their interests ; [1] or purchasers and creditors having notice of such lien.[2]

Under a statute which provides that shares shall be transferable in such manner as may be agreed upon in the articles of association, the directors have no power to adopt a by-law prohibiting a transfer of shares by one indebted to the corporation, although the corporation in its articles of association delegated to the board of directors the power to make by-laws for the management of its business.[3]

378. Notice where by-law rests upon inferential authority. — If, however, such a lien is not created or authorized in special terms, but only by inference, notice of the lien by recital in the certificate may be essential to make the lien effectual. Thus, where the charter of a corporation provided in general terms that the mode and manner of transferring stock might be regulated by by-laws, and a by-law was enacted that no transfer of stock should be made while the stockholder was indebted to the company, and that the certificate should contain notice of the lien, it was held that a purchaser of stock without actual notice of the lien was not bound by the by-law, and took the stock free of the lien.[4] The purchaser in such case was not affected with

[1] M'Dowell v. Bank of Wilmington, 1 Harr. (Del.) 27.

[2] Steamship Dock Co. v. Heron, 52 Pa. St. 280, per Thompson, J.; Lockwood v. Mechanics' Nat. Bank, 9 R. I. 308, 330; Morgan v. Bank of North America, 8 S. & R. (Pa.) 73; Tuttle v. Walton, 1 Kelly (Ga.), 43. The question whether a *bonâ fide* purchaser without notice of such by-law would be protected against the lien, was left undecided.

[3] Bank of Attica v. Manufacturers' & Traders' Bank, 20 N. Y. 501. The question, whether a statutory power to determine the manner in which a transfer on the books may be made, includes a power to forbid it in case the shareholder is indebted to the corporation, was not determined in this case.

[4] Bank of Holly Springs v. Pinson, 58 Miss. 421, 435.

"By-laws of private corporations are not in the nature of legislative enactments, so far as third persons are concerned. They are mere regulations of the corporation for the con-

constructive notice through the charter that there would be any by-law preventing a stockholder indebted to the corporation from disposing of his stock, but only with notice that there might be some regulation of the mode and manner of the transfer; and the purchaser had a right to presume that the regulation referred to was one announced in the certificate that it was transferable at the company's office, in person or by attorney, and was not bound to inquire further.

379. But a statute conferring or authorizing such a lien is constructive notice of the lien to all persons affected by it. When a lien in favor of a corporation is created by statute, either general or special, it is not necessary for the corporation to make any claim to such lien, or to give any notice of it in its certificates of stock, in order to maintain the lien either as against the shareholder or his pledgee or purchaser.[1]

380. In a few cases it has been said that a usage of a corporation to claim a lien upon its members' stock for any indebtedness to it, or an informal regulation to that effect, made known to a purchaser of stock at the time of his taking a transfer, may have the effect of giving the corporation such a lien.[2] Thus, in a case in Connecticut where neither the charter nor the by-laws of a bank contained any provision in regard to such a lien, but the bank had from its organization, a period of fifteen years, used a form of certificate which provided that it was transferable at the bank, subject to the indebtedness and liabil-

trol and management of its own affairs. They are self-imposed rules, resulting from an agreement or contract between the corporation and its members to conduct the corporate business in a particular way. They are not intended to interfere in the least with the rights and privileges of others who do not subject themselves to their influence. It may be said with truth, therefore, that no person not a member of the corporation can be affected in any of his rights by a corporate by-law of which he has no notice." Per George, J.   And see Lee v. Citizens' Nat. Bank of Piqua, 2 Cin. Sup. (Ohio) 298.

[1] First Nat. Bank v. Hartford Life & An. Ins. Co. 45 Conn. 22 ; Rogers v. Huntingdon Bank, 12 S. & R. (Pa.) 77; Grant v. Mechanics' Bank, 15 Ib. 140 ; Sewall v. Lancaster Bank, 17 Ib. 285; Stebbins v. Phœnix Ins. Co. 3 Paige Ch. (N. Y.) 350, 361; McCready v. Rumsey, 6 Duer (N. Y.), 574; Downer v. Zanesville Bank, Wright (O.), 477; Farmers' Bank v. Iglehart, 6 Gill (Md.), 50 ; Bohmer v. City Bank of Richmond, 77 Va. 445.

[2] Morgan v. Bank of North America, 8 S. & R. (Pa.) 73; S. C. 11 Am. Dec. 575.

ity of the holder to the bank, the holder of such a certificate, having obtained discounts at the bank, afterwards made an assignment for the benefit of his creditors, and his assignee claimed the right to have the stock transferred to himself; and, in a suit against the bank upon its refusal to allow such transfer, it was held that the provision in the certificate was binding upon the shareholder by reason of his acceptance of the certificate in that form, such acceptance being equivalent to an agreement that the stock should be subject to the lien.[1] His assignee also was regarded as estopped to deny that the stock was held subject to the lien created by such assent.

It is even declared that a by-law, though unauthorized by statute or charter, is as binding on all the members of the corporation, and others acquainted with their mode of doing business, as is the charter itself, or any public law of the state.[2]

But of course such a by-law, though established by usage and binding upon the members of the corporation, can have no force or effect as against others, unless knowledge of the by-law be brought home to them. It is not binding upon a purchaser or pledgee without notice,[3] nor upon a judgment creditor of the stockholder.[4]

381. That such a lien can only be created or authorized by statute is the conclusion in which the latest and best authorities on this point generally concur, although there is still some conflict of opinion. A corporation cannot, under the authority given to it to regulate transfers of stock, create or declare by by-law a secret lien in its favor upon its stockholders' shares to secure their debts to the corporation.[5] Such a by-law can be made only in pursuance of a general statute, or of some provision in its special charter.[6] A by-law made simply in pur-

---

[1] Vansands v. Middlesex Co. Bank, 26 Conn. 144.

[2] Geyer v. Western Ins. Co. 3 Pitts. (Pa.) 41, 46, per Williams, J.

[3] People v. Crockett, 9 Cal. 112.

[4] Bryon v. Carter, 22 La. Ann. 98.

[5] Anglo-California Bank v. Grangers' Bank, 16 Rep. 70; S. C. 6 Am. & Eng. Corp. Cas. 543; Moore v. Bank of Commerce, 52 Mo. 377; Bryon v. Carter, supra.

[6] New Orleans Nat. Banking Asso-ciation v. Wiltz, 10 Fed. Rep. 330; Driscoll v. West Bradley & Cary Manuf. Co. 59 N. Y. 96; Carroll v. Mullanphy Sav. Bank, 8 Mo. App. 249; Chouteau Spring Co. v. Harris, 20 Mo. 382; Merchants' Bank v. Shouse, 16 Rep. 442; In re Long Island R. R. Co. 19 Wend. (N. Y.) 37; Byrne v. Union Bank, 9 Rob. (La.) 433; Steamship Dock Co. v. Heron, 52 Pa. St. 280.

suance of an incidental authority must be a reasonable one, and a by-law which interferes with the common rights of property, and the dealings of third persons with reference to it, is not considered a reasonable one.[1] A by-law creating a lien upon its members' stock is certainly a very serious hindrance to dealings in such stocks, for there would be no safety in a transfer of the certificate only, without an actual transfer upon the books; and, unless the right of the corporation is declared upon the face of its certificates of stock, the lien would also be a secret one, and as such objectionable.[2]

Moreover, the natural and obvious purpose of a power given to a corporation to regulate the transfer of its stock is simply to enable the corporation to determine who are its members, who is entitled to take part in its meetings and vote, and who are entitled to receive its dividends.

382. Such a lien may be conferred by statute upon a corporation already organized in respect of shares already issued for debts already incurred. In such case the lien is created by the statute immediately upon its going into effect, so that an indebtedness to the corporation from a shareholder existing at the time will be secured in preference to a pledgee to whom the shareholder has delivered the certificate with a power of attorney for its transfer, provided the corporation has received no notice of such pledge of the certificate.[3]

383. An option given by statute to a corporation to prohibit a transfer by a member indebted to the corporation does not of itself create a lien. There is no lien in such case until

---

[1] Driscoll v. West Bradley & Cary Manuf. Co. 59 N. Y. 96; Moore v. Bank of Commerce, 52 Mo. 377, 379.

[2] Chouteau Spring Co. v. Harris, 20 Mo. 382. "This power, however, of regulating transfers of stock, confers no corporate authority to control its transferability by prescribing to whom the owner may sell, and to whom not, or upon what terms. The truth is, the provision is considered as being intended exclusively for the benefit of the company, in order that they may, by proper regulations, provide themselves with the means of knowing who they are bound to treat as members liable to assessment and entitled to vote at corporate meetings and to receive dividends, and it is construed accordingly, the corporation being left to exercise the power or not, at its own pleasure, as being alone interested in the matter." Per Leonard, J.

[3] First Nat. Bank v. Hartford Life & An. Ins. Co. 45 Conn. 22.

the company or its directors have exercised the option conferred by the statute and declared a lien.[1]

It would seem that a corporation having authority to enact such a by-law could not enact one which should have a retrospective effect.[2]

384. Under the National Banking Act of 1864, a bank cannot have a lien on its own stock held by a debtor, although its articles of association and its by-laws are framed with a direct view to giving it such a lien ; for, aside from the fact that the act of the preceding year contained an express provision for such a lien, which was omitted in the substituted act of 1864, it was considered that such a lien would be inconsistent with the general policy of the act which prohibits loans upon the security of shares of its own capital stock.[3]

385. Under some circumstances this lien may cover the liability of one who is merely an equitable shareholder. The by-laws of an incorporated savings bank, enacted under statutory authority, declared a lien in favor of the bank on the stock of any shareholder who might be indebted to it in any manner. On the dissolution of a partnership owning stock in the bank, the continuing members of the firm bought all the interest of the retiring members and assumed all the partnership debts. The new firm became the equitable owners of the stock. It was held that the lien of the bank might be enforced upon

---

[1] Perrine *v.* Fireman's Ins. Co. 22 Ala. 575.

[2] People *v.* Crockett, 9 Cal. 112.

[3] Bank *v.* Lanier, 11 Wall. 369 ; Bullard *v.* Bank, 18 Wall. 589; National Bank of Xenia *v.* Stewart, 107 U. S. 676; New Orleans Nat. Banking Association *v.* Wiltz, 4 Woods, 43 ; *S. C.* 10 Fed. Rep. 330; Evansville Nat. Bank *v.* Metropolitan Nat. Bank, 2 Biss. 527; *S. C.* 10 Am. Law Reg. (N. S.) 774; Louisville Bank *v.* Newark Bank, 11 N. Bank. R. 49, 52; Delaware L. & W. R. R. Co. *v.* Oxford Iron Co. 38 N. J. Eq. 340. The earlier cases in this state, Young *v.* Vough, 23 N. J. Eq. 325, and Mattison *v.* Young, 24 Ib. 535, overruled. Second Nat. Bank of Louisville *v.* Nat. State Bank, 10 Bush (Ky.), 367; *S. C.* 14 Am. L. Reg. (N. S.) 281; Rosenback *v.* National Bank, 53 Barb. (N. Y.) 495; Conklin *v.* Second Nat. Bank, 45 N. Y. 655; Hagar *v.* Union Nat. Bank, 63 Me. 509; *S. C.* Thompson's Nat. Bank Cases, 523, per Virgin, J.; Lee *v.* Citizens' Nat. Bank, 2 Sup. Ct. Cin. (Ohio) 298, 306 ; *Contra*, see Vansands *v.* Middlesex Co. Bank, 26 Conn. 144; *In re* Bigelow, 9 Ben. 468; *S. C.* 1 N. Bank. R. 667; Knight *v.* Old Nat. Bank, 3 Cliff. 429; *In re* Dunkerson, 4 Biss. 227; Evansville Nat. Bank *v.* Metropolitan Nat. Bank, 2 Biss. 527.

such stock for the liabilities of the new firm incurred in subsequent transactions with the bank.[1]

386. **Shares which equitably belong to a debtor of the corporation, as well as those standing in his own name, are subject to the lien in its favor.** But if the officers of a corporation knowingly permit shares to be transferred to a mere nominal holder, it seems that a *bonâ fide* purchaser from him, even without a transfer on the books of the company, will be entitled to relief against the lien of the company for a debt due from the real owner.[2] If a certificate of stock be assigned with a power of attorney to complete the transfer upon the books, while the corporation might have a lien against the stockholder in whose name the shares were standing, or against the equitable owner, if the rights of others dealing with the equitable owner in good faith are not interfered with, yet the corporation cannot assert its lien against an equitable owner after he has transferred the certificate to a purchaser in good faith.

387. **Though the shareholder be only the holder of the legal title, the equitable ownership being in another, the lien may be enforced for the debt of the shareholder of record.**[3]

388. **As a general rule the equitable assignee of a certificate of stock can have no other or greater rights than his assignor had;** and, therefore, if the corporation had a lien as against the assignor, the assignee cannot obtain a transfer of the legal title upon the books without paying the amount for which the stock is affected with a lien.[4]

[1] Planters' & Merchants' Mut. Ins. Co. *v.* Selma Savings Bank, 63 Ala. 585, 594. "We can perceive no good reason, and we are not aware of any authority, requiring it to limit the lien to debts owing the bank by the holder of the legal title only, excluding such as may be due from the owner of the complete equitable title." Per Brickell, C. J.

[2] Stebbins *v.* Phœnix F. Ins. Co. 3 Paige (N. Y.), 350; Planters' & Merchants' Mut. Ins. Co. *v.* Selma Sav. Bank, *supra.*

The language of some decisions would imply that the lien could only be asserted against the stockholder of record. Helm *v.* Swiggett, 12 Ind. 194.

[3] New London & Brazilian Bank *v.* Brocklebank, L. R. 21 Ch. D. 302; Burford *v.* Crandall, 2 Cr. C. C. 86; Young *v.* Vough, 23 N. J. Eq. 325.

[4] Union Bank *v.* Laird, 2 Wheat. 390, 393; Brent *v.* Bank of Washington, 10 Pet. 596, 616; McCready *v.* Rumsey, 6 Duer (N. Y.), 574; Bank of Utica *v.* Smalley, 2 Cow. (N. Y.) 770; Bohmer *v.* City Bank of Richmond, 77 Va. 445; Farmers' Bank *v.*

The corporation can assert its lien against the stockholder of record, although he had already pledged the certificate before incurring the debt for which the corporation claims the lien, provided the corporation had no knowledge of the pledge at the time the stockholder became indebted to it.[1]

389. **Even if the corporation has notice of an equitable pledge of the shares, it may have priority by reason of provisions of the articles of association,** the terms of which are known to the pledgee. The articles of association of a company provided that it should have a first and paramount lien on every share for àll debts due from the shareholder to the company. A shareholder deposited his shares with his banker as security for a balance due him on current account, and notice of the deposit was given to the company.[2] The certificates stated that the shares were held subject to the articles of association. It was held that the company had priority over the bankers in respect of a debt due from the shareholder to the company, although the debt became due after notice of the deposit of the shares with the banker. The decision was placed upon the ground that, by the articles of association, a contract had been entered into between the company and the shareholder whereby the company was to have a first lien on his shares for any debt due him; and that by this contract a priority was conferred upon the company as against all persons claiming only an equitable interest in the shares, and having notice of the articles of association; the deposit of the shares without a transfer creating only an equitable interest.[3]

Iglehart, 6 Gill (Md.), 50; Reese v. Bank of Commerce, 14 Md. 271; Bishop v. Globe Co. 135 Mass. 132.

[1] *In re* Peebles, 2 Hughes, 394; Platt v. Birmingham Axle Co. 41 Conn. 255, 268. "In contemplation of law, the statute was known to petitioner when he accepted the certificate; it was to him as if it had been embodied therein; it was in the nature of a qualification or restriction of his equitable interest; it was notice to him that if, after a reasonable time had elapsed, he refrained from giving any notice of his interest in the stock to the corporation, a statute lien might come into existence at any moment." Per Pardee, J.

[2] Bradford Banking Co. v. Briggs, 31 Ch. D. 19; affirmed in Miles v. New Zealand Alford Estate Co. 32 Ch. D. 266. The former case overruled *S. C.* 29 Ch. D. 149, where it was held that the company could not claim priority after notice of the advance by the banker.

[3] Société Générale de Paris v. Tramways Union Co. 14 Q. B. D. 424.

390. The lien of a corporation, when conferred by general law or charter may be availed of in a state other than that in which the corporation was organized, when a suit is brought against the corporation in such other state by a person claiming to be an equitable assignee of shares of its stock, to recover damages for refusing to make a transfer upon the books. The rights and obligations of the stockholders of a corporation as between them and the corporation are to be determined by the laws of the state under which the corporation was organized.[1]

391. Corporations have an equitable lien upon the dividends of their shareholders to secure their debts. The rule against an implied lien in favor of corporations upon the shares of their members does not apply in respect to dividends declared upon such shares. Dividends are considered as so much money in possession of the bank belonging to the stockholder; and it is not inconsistent with any provision of the National Banking Act, or in conflict with any principle of public policy, that the bank should have an equitable lien upon such dividends.[2] The dividends, when payable, are a debt owing by the corporation to the shareholder, and in a suit by the shareholder for such debt the corporation could set off any debt owing to the corporation by the shareholder.[3]

392. The lien is not confined to stock owned by the stockholder at the time the debt was incurred,[4] unless the language of the statute or charter giving the lien suggests such a restriction. If the charter provides that the corporation shall "at all times have a lien upon the stock or property of its members invested therein, for all debts due from them to such corporation," the lien attaches to stock of members whenever afterwards ac-

---

[1] Bishop v. Globe Co. 135 Mass. 132.

[2] Hague v. Dandeson, 2 Ex. 741; Hagar v. Union Nat. Bank, 63 Me. 509; S. C. Thompson's Nat. Bank Cas. 523; Sargent v. Franklin Ins. Co. 8 Pick. (Mass.) 90; Stebbins v. Phœnix F. Ins. Co. 3 Paige (N. Y.), 350; Bates v. N. Y. Ins. Co. 3 Johns. Cas. (N. Y.) 238; St. Louis Perpetual Ins. Co. v. Goodfellow, 9 Mo. 149; Grant v. Mechanics' Bank, 15 S. & R. (Pa.)

140; Farmers' Bank v. Iglehart, 6 Gill (Md.), 50; McDowell v. Wilmington Bank, 1 Harr. (Del.) 27.

[3] St. Louis Perpetual Ins. Co. v. Goodfellow, supra; Hagar v. Union Nat. Bank, supra; Merchants' Bank v. Shouse, 102 Pa. St. 488; S. C. 16 Rep. 442.

[4] Schmidt v. Hennepin Co. Barrel Co. (Minn.) 29 N. West Rep. 200; S. C. 15 Am. & Eng. Corp. Cas. 576.

quired during the indebtedness. There is a lien whenever the indebtedness and the ownership of the stock concur.

II. *What Debts are Secured.*

393. The word "indebted," in statutory provisions for liens in favor of corporations, applies as well to debts to become due as to those actually due and payable.[1] Thus the lien applies in favor of a bank that has discounted a note or bill on which a shareholder is liable, though the note or bill has not matured.[2] So the liability of a shareholder for an unpaid balance of his subscription for the shares is a debt within the meaning of such provision for a lien, even before such balance of the subscription has been called.

A provision that shares of a bank shall not be transferable unless the shareholder shall discharge *all debts due by him* to the company, was held to embrace all debts of the shareholder, whether payable presently or in the future. The object of the provision was to protect and secure the bank, and to accomplish this the lien must cover debts not matured.[3]

There is an English case, not to be relied upon, however, where, under articles of association which provided that the company should have a lien upon all shares of any member for any money due the company, Master of the Rolls Jessel held that the lien was limited to moneys due and payable from a shareholder to the company, and was not applicable where the indebtedness was a mere acceptance of a bill of exchange.[4]

---

[1] Grant *v.* Mechanics' Bank, 15 S. & R. (Pa.) 140; Geyer *v.* Western Ins. Co. 3 Pitts. (Pa.) 41 ; St. Louis Perpetual Ins. Co. *v.* Goodfellow, 9 Mo. 149.

In Grant *v.* Mechanics' Bank, *supra*, Tilghman, C. J., said : " Where words are not technical, their meaning is, in general, best ascertained by common parlances. Laws are made for the people, and should be expressed in language which they understand. Now the word ' indebted ' has not acquired a technical signification, and, in common understanding, means a sum of money which one has contracted to pay another, whether the day of payment be come or not.

Even in law language we speak of *debitum in præsenti, solvendum in futuro*, — a present debt, to be paid in a future time. So, in act of assembly language, a debt signifies money payable at a future time."

[2] Brent *v.* Bank of Washington, 10 Pet. 596, 616 ; *In re* Bachman, 12 Nat. Bank. Reg. 223 ; Rogers *v.* Huntingdon Bank, 12 S. & R. (Pa.) 77 ; Sewall *v.* Lancaster Bank, 17 S. & R. (Pa.) 285 ; Leggett *v.* Bank of Sing Sing, 24 N. Y. 283, 284.

[3] Leggett *v.* Bank of Sing Sing, *supra*.

[4] *In re* Stockton Malleable Iron Co. 2 Ch. D. 101.

But if the words used to describe the debts for which there may be a lien imply more than a mere indebtedness, as where the words used are " debts actually due and payable to the corporation," the debts contemplated are such as are due at the time the lien attaches, and not to those payable in future, such as notes and bills afterwards to mature.[1]

394. Where the statute authorizing a lien is general in its terms and applies to all debts due the corporation, the lien will not be restricted to a particular debt or a particular class of debts. Thus, under the Companies Act of England, the provision that " the company may decline to register any transfer of shares made by a member who is indebted to them," is not limited to cases where the member is indebted for calls or otherwise indebted in respect of the particular shares proposed to be transferred, but enables the company to decline to register the transfer, if the member is indebted on any account whatever.[2]

But a provision of statute or charter, giving a corporation a lien to secure any indebtedness to it from a shareholder, does not authorize the corporation to make an accommodation loan to a shareholder, where it is not within the power of the corporation to make such a loan. The lien is in aid of the legitimate powers of the corporation, and cannot be held to imply a sanction to a diversion of the corporate assets to accommodation loans to a stockholder.[3]

395. Where the language of the statute declaring the lien is broad enough to embrace every form of indebtedness to the company which a member may incur, the courts will not confine the lien to debts due for the shares, or for calls upon them, but will extend it to debts due generally from the shareholder. The object in creating the lien is the security of the corporation, and there is no good reason for limiting general words embracing an indebtedness of any kind to an indebtedness of a special kind, namely, that for shares, or calls upon them.[4]

[1] Reesé v. Bank of Commerce, 14 Md. 271.

[2] Ex parte Stringer, 9 Q. B. D. 436.

[3] Webster v. Home Machine Co. (Conn.) 8 Atl. Rep. 482.

[4] Rogers v. Huntingdon Bank, 12 S. & R. (Pa.) 77 ; Mobile Mut. Ins.

396. If the by-law of a corporation creating a lien upon its stock is broader in terms than the statute authorizing it, the by-law will be restricted in its operation to the terms of the statute.[1]   Thus, where a statute gives a lien upon the shares of a stockholder for the balance due the corporation upon his subscription to the stock, the company has no lien upon the stock for any other debts due the company, though such a lien be declared by a by-law to that effect.[2]   Even if such a by-law has any effect, it can only apply to the interest of the debtor stockholder after the lien of the stock debt is satisfied.[3]

397. A lien for calls upon shares applies only to the shares upon which the calls are made, and not to other paid up shares of the shareholder.   Under a statute which provided that no shareholder should be entitled to transfer any share, after a call had been made in respect thereof, until he should have paid the call, and should have paid all calls for the time being due on every share held by him, the court of Queen's Bench held that the company had no power to hold paid up shares as a security for the amount of a call on other shares.[4] A like decision was made in Virginia under a statute providing that stock should not be transferred without the consent of the company until all moneys payable to the company on such stock should have been paid.[5]

398. Debt of partnership or of a surety. — A by-law prohibiting a transfer of shares by a member indebted to the corporation applies where the only indebtedness is by a partnership in which the shareholder is a copartner.[6]

Co. v. Cullom, 49 Ala. 558; Cunningham v. Ala. Life Ins. & Trust Co. 4 Ala. 652.

[1] Kahn v. Bank of St. Joseph, 70 Mo. 262; and see Presbyterian Congregation v. Carlisle Bank, 5 Pa. St. 345.

[2] Petersburg Savings & Ins. Co. v. Lumsden, 75 Va. 327.

[3] Petersburg Savings & Ins. Co. v. Lumsden, *supra.*

[4] Hubbersty v. Manchester, Sheffield & Lincolnshire Ry. Co. L. R. 2 Q. B. 59.

Otherwise, however, in Stebbins v. Phœnix F. Ins. Co. 3 Paige (N. Y.), 350.

[5] Shenandoah Valley R. R. Co. v. Griffith, 76 Va. 913; Code 1873, ch. 57, § 26.

[6] Geyer v. Western Ins. Co. 3 Pitts. (Pa.) 41, per Williams, J.; Mechanics' Bank v. Earp, 4 Rawle (Pa.), 384; Arnold v. Suffolk Bank, 27 Barb. (N. Y.) 424; *In re* Bigelow, 2 Ben. 469; German Security Bank v. Jefferson, 10 Bush (Ky.), 326.

It applies as well where the liability of the shareholder is that of a surety or indorser, as where his liability is that of a principal debtor.[1]

399. Debt of joint trustee.—Where the articles of association of a banking company provided that it should have a paramount lien on the shares of any shareholders for all moneys owing the company from him alone or jointly with any other person, and trustees invested in shares of the company which were transferred into their joint names, and one of the trustees was a partner in a firm which was indebted to the company, it was held that the bank had a lien on the shares for this debt which must prevail over the title of the *cestui que trust;* for the lien was within the express terms imposed by the articles of association as a condition upon which one might become a member of the company.[2]

400. Upon the bankruptcy of a stockholder whose shares are subject to a lien to the corporation, the corporation is entitled to appropriate the proceeds of such shares to the payment of the debt, and to prove against the bankrupt's estate for any balance of the debt not paid. This is the general rule; though under the insolvent laws of some of the states it is held that, after the corporation has applied the proceeds of the shares under its lien, it is postponed until the general creditors have been made equal out of the general estate by receiving an equal percentage, and then the residue is distributed *pro rata* among all the creditors.[3]

III. *Subrogation of Sureties to such Liens.*

401. A surety upon a debt of a stockholder, secured by a lien upon his stock, upon paying the debt is subrogated to the creditor's lien.[4] The debt to the corporation is the object

---

[1] St. Louis Perpetual Ins. Co. v. Goodfellow, 9 Mo. 149; Leggett v. Bank of Sing Sing, 24 N. Y. 283, Allen, J., dissenting; West Branch Bank v. Armstrong, 40 Pa. St. 278; Schmidt v. Hennepin Co. Barrel, &c. Co. (Minn.) 29 N. W. Rep. 200; McLean v. Lafayette Bank, 3 McLean, 587; McDowell v. Bank of Wilmington, 1 Harr. (Del.) 27.

[2] New London & Brazilian Bank v. Brocklebank, 21 Ch. D. 302.

[3] German Security Bank v. Jefferson, 10 Bush (Ky.), 326; Northern Bank v. Keizer, 2 Duv. (Ky.) 169.

[4] Klopp v. Lebanon Bank, 46 Pa. St. 88; Petersburg Savings & Ins. Co. v. Lumsden, 75 Va. 327, 340; Young v. Vough, 23 N. J. Eq. 325; Kuhns v. Westmoreland Bank, 2 Watts (Pa.), 136.

of the lien, and for which it is security, and equity lays hold of this security for the benefit of the surety. The equitable right of the surety in such case attaches at the time the lien of the corporation commences, although the corporation may not know of the existence of his suretyship. The surety's right of subrogation does not depend upon his giving any notice to the corporation, but upon the fact of his suretyship and his payment of the debt. Notice is important only for the purpose of preventing the corporation from allowing a transfer of the stock upon payment of the debt in ignorance of the surety's claim.[1]

If a corporation having a lien upon stock to secure a debt upon which there is a surety allows the stockholder to transfer his shares to secure another debt, or permits the stock to be sold and the proceeds applied to the payment of another debt, the surety is discharged.[2]

Where a corporation, though having the power to declare a lien, has neglected to do so, and consequently has no lien, it loses no right against the surety by allowing the debtor to make a transfer. There is nothing in such case to which the surety can be subrogated.[3]

402. In case a corporation has a lien to secure several debts, upon one of which there is a surety, the question arises whether the surety upon that debt, upon paying it, is subrogated to the lien, so as to be entitled in equity to have the shares applied to the discharge of that debt in priority to the other debts afterwards incurred. In a case in Rhode Island, where the charter of a bank provided that the stockholders should at all times be liable for the payment of debts due the bank, it was declared that this provision was not adopted with the view of securing an indorser, and it was held that the corporation could not be compelled to apply the shares to the payment of such indorsed debt in preference to any other debt due to it, although such other debt might be of later date.[4] This decision would seem to be

---

[1] Klopp v. Lebanon Bank, 46 Pa. St. 88.

[2] Kuhns v. Westmoreland Bank, 2 Watts (Pa.), 136.

[3] Perrine v. Fireman's Ins. Co. 22 Ala. 575.

[4] Cross v. Phœnix Bank, 1 R. I. 39, 41. "It was intended to secure the payment of such debts of each stockholder as became insecure, whether by the failure of principal or surety, or by the failure of both; and such intent is inconsistent with an application of the pledge regulated by a priority of date. Such a rule would make the provision operate only for

correct in case the corporation had no notice at the time the subsequent debt was incurred that there was a surety upon the prior debt. But, in case the corporation should allow the stockholder to incur a further debt after a surety had paid a prior debt and had claimed the right of subrogation, it would seem that the corporation should not be allowed to avail itself of its lien to the detriment of the surety ; and it would also seem that, if the corporation knew of the relation of suretyship at the time the obligation was incurred, it could not afterwards allow the stockholder to incur a further indebtedness to the detriment of the surety. The surety has an interest in the lien from the time the obligation is incurred, and it may reasonably be presumed that he incurred the obligation on the strength of the lien.[1]

IV. *How Waived or Lost.*

403. This lien, though declared by statute, may be waived by the corporation entitled to it, and the waiver may be made by an officer having the general management of its daily business: thus the cashier of a bank may waive the lien in behalf of the bank ;[2] and he does this by entering a transfer upon the books of the bank. Mr. Justice Matthews, delivering the opinion of the court,[3] said : " A complete transfer of the title to the stock upon the books of the bank, it is not doubted, would have the effect to vest it in the transferee free from any claim or lien of the bank. The consent of the bank, made necessary to such transfer, is the waiver of its rights, as its refusal would be the assertion of it. The transfer, when thus consummated, destroys the relation of membership between the corporation and the old stockholder, with all its incidents, and creates an original relation with the new member, free from all antecedent obliga-

the benefit of the surety, where security would not be needed until the indebtedness exceeded the amount of the stock ; and if in all such cases the surety was sufficient, the pledge would be of no value to the bank, whilst as to all debts exceeding the amount of stock, and for which its additional security would be needed, the pledge would be wholly inapplicable. This never could have been the understanding, either of the legislature, or of the stockholders, on becoming such; nor could the surety of an indebted stockholder indulge the expectation, with any degree of confidence, that such could be the construction of such a provision."

[1] See Rogers *v.* Huntingdon Bank, 12 S. & R. (Pa.) 77.

[2] National Bank *v.* Watsontown Bank, 105 U. S. 217 ; Case *v.* Bank, 100 U. S. 446.

[3] National Bank *v.* Watsontown Bank, *supra.*

tions. This legal relation and proprietary interest, on which it is based, are quite independent of the certificate of ownership, which is mere evidence of title. The complete fact of title may well exist without it. All that is necessary, when the transfer is required by law to be made upon the books of the corporation, is, that the fact should be appropriately recorded in some suitable register or stock list, or otherwise formally entered upon its books. For this purpose, the account in a stock ledger showing the names of the stockholders, the number and amount of the shares belonging to each, and the sources of their title, whether by original subscription and payment or by derivation from others, is quite suitable, and fully meets the requirements of the law."

404. Whether, after notice to a corporation of the equitable transfer of the shares, it can acquire a lien upon them as against the equitable assignee, is a question which has already been considered.[1] But it is certain that a corporation cannot claim a lien after it has permitted its debtor to transfer the shares upon its books, so as to give the assignee not merely the equitable but the legal title, unless the corporation in express terms, known and assented to by the assignee, reserves a lien at the time of the transfer.[2] But the assent of a corporation to a general assignment of a debtor for the benefit of his creditors, subject to preferences authorized by law, does not amount to a waiver of a lien by the corporation on the debtor's shares, for the lien is a preference authorized by law; and, moreover, the assignee in a voluntary assignment for the benefit of creditors stands in no better situation than the assignor.[3]

405. Notice to an officer of a corporation who has a general charge and management of its business is notice to the corporation. Thus, notice to the cashier of a bank of an outstanding equity is notice to the bank.[4] His knowledge that a stock-

---

[1] Bradford Banking Co. v. Briggs, 29 Ch. D. 149 ; S. C. 10 Am. & Eng. Corp. Cas. 120, overruled in S. C. 31 Ch. D. 19; and see Nesmith v. Washington Bank, 6 Pick. (Mass.) 324 ; Bank of America v. McNeil, 10 Bush (Ky.), 54 ; Conant v. Seneca County Bank, 1 Ohio St. 298 ; Newberry v. Detroit & Lake Superior Iron Co. 17 Mich. 141.

[2] Hill v. Pine River Bank, 45 N. H. 300 ; Hodges v. Planters' Bank, 7 G. & J. (Md.) 306.

[3] Dobbins v. Walton, 37 Ga. 614.

[4] Bank of America v. McNeil, supra; Connecticut Mut. Life Ins. Co. v. Scott, 81 Ky. 540, 549.

holder's shares had been pledged by delivery of the certificate to secure his note to a third person should put him upon inquiry, even after the maturity of that note, to ascertain whether the note had been renewed; for a renewed note would be secured by the original pledge, and if the bank under such circumstances should make a loan to the stockholder, even after the maturity of the original note for which the shares were pledged, the lien of the bank would be subject to the pledge to secure the renewed note.[1]

But notice to an employee of a corporation who has no power to transact its general business with third persons, and who is well known to have no such power, does not affect the corporation; and a waiver of a lien by such an employee does not bind the corporation.[2] A corporation is not estopped to assert a lien by the fact that, on a stockholder's presenting a certificate for transfer, the person in charge of the transfer-book promised to make a transfer and issue a new certificate as soon as an officer whose signature was necessary should return, when it does not appear that such person had any general authority, or any knowledge of the stockholder's indebtedness.[3]

406. A corporation is estopped to claim a lien as against one who has been induced to make a loan upon a pledge of its stock to a shareholder by representations of the officers of the company that the stock was unincumbered, and that he could safely make a loan upon it.[4]

407. Waived by taking a transfer of the shares. — A corporation having a lien by its charter upon the shares of a stockholder for his indebtedness to the corporation waives this lien by taking a transfer for the stock as collateral security for such indebtedness. The taking of the transfer shows that the corporation did not rely upon the lien.[5]

408. A corporation does not waive its lien by taking

[1] Bank of America v. McNeil, 10 Bush (Ky.), 54.

The pledgee was under no obligation to the bank to notify it of the renewal of the note.

[2] Kenton Insurance Co. v. Bowman (Ky.), 1 So. West. Rep. 717; S. C. 15 Am. & Eng. Corp. Cas. 578.

[3] Bishop v. Globe Co. 135 Mass. 132; S. C. 5 Am. & Eng. Corp. Cas. 161.

[4] Moore v. Bank of Commerce, 52 Mo. 377.

[5] McLean v. Lafayette Bank, 3 McLean, 587.

other security for the debt, as, for instance, by taking sureties upon it; for a creditor may lawfully take and hold several securities for the same debt, and he cannot be compelled to surrender either until the debt is paid.[1]

409. A lien acquired by a corporation for an indebtedness incurred after a stockholder's shares have been attached or levied upon by a creditor, and service of such attachment or levy has been made upon the company, is subject to the lien of such attachment or levy.[2] If the liability of the shareholder was incurred before, though the debt does not become payable till after, the attachment or levy by the creditor, the lien of the corporation is superior to that of the creditor.[3] Moreover, if the debt secured by the lien be renewed, the lien attaches to the renewed debt, though the debtor's shares be attached before or after the renewal.[4]

410. Where a bank waived its charter-right of lien upon a stockholder's shares for a period of six months, and within that time the stockholder pledged his shares for a debt, the right of the bank does not attach again immediately upon the expiration of that period, unless the debt for which the pledge was made has been paid, but is subordinate to the right of the pledgee until the debt is paid or the pledge released.[5]

411. The lien is not waived by permitting a transfer of a part of the shares. Though the debt be for a less sum than the value of the debtor's stock which the corporation holds a lien upon, it may hold all his shares till the debt is paid. It is not bound to appropriate part of the shares as security for the debt and transfer the rest.[6] Of course the corporation may permit the debtor to transfer part of his stock, and by such action it will not waive its lien upon the shares still remaining in his name.[7]

[1] Union Bank v. Laird, 2 Wheat. 390 ; In re Morrison, 10 N. Bank. Reg. 105 ; Mechanics' Bank v. Earp, 4 Rawle, 384; Kenton Insurance Co. v. Bowman (Ky.), 1 So. West Rep. 717; S. C. 15 Am. & Eng. Corp. Cas. 578.

[2] Geyer v. Western Ins. Co. 3 Pitts. (Pa.) 41.

[3] Sewall v. Lancaster Bank, 17 S. & R. (Pa.) 285; West Branch Bank v. Armstrong, 40 Pa. St. 278.

[4] Sewall v. Lancaster Bank, supra.

[5] Bank of America v. McNeil, 10 Bush (Ky.), 54.

[6] Sewall v. Lancaster Bank, supra; and see Union Bank v. Laird, supra.

[7] First Nat. Bank v. Hartford Life

412. A usage may operate against a lien which the by-laws of a corporation enact in its behalf. Thus, where by the by-law the consent of the directors of a corporation was required to a transfer of stock by a stockholder indebted to it, but in practice such cases were never brought before the board, it was held that a transfer made without such consent, but according to the usage of the company, was effectual, and passed the title to the stock unincumbered by a lien.[1]

413. The fact that the corporation allows its debtor's certificate of stock to remain outstanding does not amount to a waiver of its lien. When the lien is created by proper statutory authority, the corporation may assert the lien, although the shareholder has pledged his certificate to secure a prior loan. If the pledgee chooses to hold this certificate, and not obtain a transfer to himself upon the books of the company, he does so at his own risk. The corporation is not bound to call for a surrender of the certificate when it makes a loan to a shareholder. It does not waive its lien by leaving the certificate outstanding.[2]

414. The issuing of a certificate of shares upon which a corporation has a possible right of lien does not amount to a waiver or abandonment of that right,[3] though the certificate makes no reference to the lien, but declares that the shares are transferable only at the corporation's office, personally or by attorney, on surrender of the certificate.[4]

& Annuity Ins. Co. 45 Conn. 22. In Presbyterian Congregation *v.* Carlisle Bank, 5 Pa. St. 345, 351, the fact that the bank consented to a transfer of part of the shares was apparently one ground of the court's refusal to permit the bank to assert a lien to the remainder; but the blind prejudice of the court against all banks deprives the decision of any value it might otherwise have. This for a curiosity: "Since the days of Lord Bacon, who promulgated the idea, banks, then in their infancy, have been odious to the common mind, and, by pursuing with steadiness the law of their existence and individuality, they exposed them-

selves to the keen and deep sarcasm of Burke. The present case is a pregnant instance of the facility with which they bring themselves within the condemnation of whatever is magnanimous, just, and manly in our nature."

[1] Chambersburg Ins. Co. *v.* Smith, 11 Pa. St. 120.

[2] Bohmer *v.* City Bank, 77 Va. 445; and see Platt *v.* Birmingham Axle Co. 41 Conn. 255.

[3] Petersburg Savings & Ins. Co. *v.* Lumsden, 75 Va. 327, 340; Hussey *v.* Manufacturers' & Mechanics' Bank, 10 Pick. (Mass.) 415.

[4] Reese *v.* Bank of Commerce, 14 Md. 271.

415. If the transaction in which a corporation seeks to enforce a lien was unauthorized by its charter, and was a perversion of its corporate powers, it confers no right upon the corporation to enforce the lien.[1]

416. Of course, if the debt is discharged, the lien is gone.[2]

417. The lien is not lost though the right of action for the debt be barred by the statute of limitations, for the statute does not cancel the debt, but merely takes away the right of action for it; just as, in the case of a mortgage or pledge securing such a debt, the mortgage or pledge remains valid, and may be enforced, although the right of action upon the debt is barred.[3]

[1] White's Bank v. Toledo Ins. Co. 12 Ohio St. 601.

[2] Farmers' Bank v. Iglehart, 6 Gill (Md.), 50.

[3] Geyer v. Western Ins. Co. 3 Pitts. (Pa.), 41; Farmers' Bank v. Iglehart, supra; Brent v. Bank of Washington, 10 Pet. 596; Jones on Mortgages, § 1203; Jones on Chattel Mortgages, § 772; Jones on Pledges, § 581.

CHAPTER IX.

LIENS OF FACTORS, BROKERS, CONSIGNEES, AND MERCHANTS.

I. *In General.*

418. It is a general common law rule that a factor has, in the absence of any express agreement, a lien upon the goods in his hands as his security for all advances made, or acceptances given to his principal in the business of his agency, or connected with the goods consigned to him. The law implies or infers the lien from the relation between the parties.[1] The

---

[1] Kruger *v.* Wilcox, 1 Ambler, 252, 254 (1755). " Before this case it was certainly very doubtful whether a factor had a lien and could retain for the balance of his general account," remarked Lord Mansfield in Green *v.* Farmer, 4 Burr. 2214, 2218 (1768). The case of Kruger *v.* Wilcox was decided by Lord Hardwicke, Chancellor. He examined four merchants upon the custom and usage of merchants in regard to such a lien. " All the four merchants, both in their examination in the cause and now in court, agree that, if there is a course of dealings and general account between the merchant and factor, and a balance is due to the factor, he may retain the ship and goods, or produce, for such balance of the general account, as well as for the charges, customs, &c., paid on account of the particular cargo."

Lord Hardwicke gave his opinion that a factor has a lien for his general

balance, which was afterwards confirmed by Lord Mansfield in Godin *v.* London Assurance Co. 1 Burr. 489, and Foxcroft *v.* Devonshire, 2 Ib. 931, 936; by Lord Kenyon and Mr. Justice Ashurst, in Walker *v.* Birch, 6 T. R. 258, 262; and by Mr. Justice Buller in Lickbarrow *v.* Mason, 6 East, 21, 28.

Alabama: Barnett *v.* Warren, 2 So. Rep. 457.

Missouri: Archer *v.* McMechan, 21 Mo. 43.

New York: Nagle *v.* McFeeters, 97 N. Y. 196, 202; Williams *v.* Tilt, 36 N.Y. 319. See Holbrook *v.* Wight, 24 Wend. 169; Bank *v.* Jones, 4 N. Y. 497; Ohio & Miss. R. R. *v.* Kasson, 37 N. Y. 218; Myer *v.* Jacobs, 1 Daly, 32.

Ohio: Jordan *v.* James, 5 Ohio, 89, 99; Grieff *v.* Cowguill, 2 Dis. 58; Matthews *v.* Menedger, 2 McLean, 145.

Pennsylvania: Steinman *v.* Wilkins, 7 W. & S. 466.

factor's lien is a general lien covering the balance of account due him from his principal. He has a general lien, because he is an agent for a continuous service. An agent employed to perform services upon a particular thing has a lien for such services upon the thing upon which he has bestowed his labor. It is a lien for that particular service, and not for any other service or for any other debt.

Lord Kenyon in an early case said : " There is no doubt, and, indeed, the point has been so long settled that it ought not now to be brought into dispute, but that, in general, a factor has a lien for his general balance on the property of his principal coming into his hands." [1]

At first the factor's right by custom to a general lien appears to have been made the subject of proof in the cause.[2] Afterwards the right was regarded as fully established ; [3] and in modern practice no proof is ever required that such a general lien exists, as a matter of fact. Judicial notice is taken of the factor's right to a general lien.[4]

419. One who has no authority to make sales is not a factor. A warehouseman to whom goods are intrusted for the purpose of sale, but with authority merely to receive offers and to negotiate sales to be reported to the owner and concluded by him, is not a factor or other agent intrusted with the possession of merchandise for sale within the meaning of a factor's act.[5]

One who carries on the business of slaughtering hogs, and curing, storing, and selling the product, as well for himself as for others, and who makes advances to others on receiving their hogs and holds the product until he sells it, is a factor, and has a lien on the property so received and held, for his services and advances.[6]

420. A merchandise broker, like any other agent, may have a specific lien, when he has such possession of the prop-

---

[1] Walker v. Birch, 6 T. R. 258, 262.

[2] As in Kruger v. Wilcox, 1 Ambler, 252, cited as Kruger v. Wilcox in 1 Burr. 494.

[3] Green v. Farmer, 4 Burr. 2214, 2218; Drinkwater v. Goodwin, 1 Cowp. 251, 255.

[4] Barnett v. Brandão, 6 M. & G. 630, 665, per Lord Denman, C. J.

[5] Thacher v. Moors, 134 Mass. 156. See, also, Stollenwerck v. Thacher, 115 Mass. 224.

[6] Shaw v. Ferguson, 78 Ind. 547; Hanna v. Phelps, 7 Ib. 21. See East v. Ferguson, 59 Ib. 169.

erty that he can exercise the right. If the property does not come into his hands, or into the hands of some one who holds it in his interest, he can exercise no right of lien. Generally he is not intrusted with the possession of the property which he is employed to sell ; but his business is merely that of a negotiator between the contracting parties, and ordinarily he has no property in his hands on which the right of lien can attach. He must generally contract in the name of his principal, while a factor may buy and sell in his own name. A broker ordinarily has no possession of the goods he is employed to sell, nor has he any right to obtain possession. When in any case he has possession, his lien is a specific lien upon the goods for his services in negotiating a sale of the same, and not a general lien for a balance of account due from his principal.[1]

Moreover, when a broker claims a right of lien for brokerage as against property coming into his hands, he cannot enforce it unless he was employed by the owner. If he knew or had reason to believe that the person by whom he was employed was himself merely an agent, he was bound to inquire as to his authority, and to know that he could not retain the property for a debt due from the agent to himself.[2]

421. A stock-broker holding stocks and bonds of a customer upon which he has made advances, is a pledgee of the securities rather than the holder of a lien upon them,[3] though his interest is sometimes spoken of as a lien.[4] If stocks are placed in the hands of a broker for sale, and he makes advances upon them, he may be regarded as a factor for that purpose, and he would have a lien upon them or upon their proceeds for his advances and commissions. There is an important distinction between the rights of a broker having a lien, and those of a factor who has a lien. In the case of a factor there is an exception to the rule that no sale can be made under a lien except in pursuance of statutory authority, or by decree of a court of equity. A factor may sell to reimburse himself for advances made and liabilities incurred on account of the consignment. It is important for a stock-broker that he should be regarded as a factor, if his special interest in his customer's stocks is to be regarded as a lien ; and inasmuch as he ordinarily holds the customer's securities, which

---

[1] Barry v. Boninger, 46 Md. 59, 65.

[2] Barry v. Boninger, *supra*.

[3] Jones on Pledges, §§ 151–154, 722.

[4] Jones v. Gallagher, 3 Utah, 54.

are generally regarded as merchandise, he may properly be considered as a factor governed by the general law regulating factors.[1] He has such a special interest in stocks upon which he has made advances, that he may properly refuse to sell the stocks if the customer's order to sell is expressly given for the purpose of reinvesting in other stocks which the broker would be obliged to hold as security for his advances.[2] The broker in such case is entitled to the management and control of the stocks.

422. A broker or agent employed upon a commission to obtain a loan has a lien on the fund, and may retain out of it the amount of his commission.[3] He is not, however, a factor, and therefore is not entitled to a lien for his general balance of account. His lien is specific; though having in his hands money of his principal, he may, in an action for the money by his principal, have a right of set-off in respect of his principal's existing indebtedness to him.

423. An insurance broker, however, who is intrusted with his principal's policies, is a factor rather than a broker, and, like a factor, he has a lien on such policies, and the money collected by him for losses under the policies, for his general balance.[4] It is customary to intrust an insurance broker with the policies which he has effected, particularly marine policies, so that he may be able to adjust any losses which may occur. It is the broker's right to retain the policies so long as the principal is indebted to him. He has a lien on the policies for premiums paid and for his commissions.[5] If the broker acts for his principal continuously, or has an open insurance account with him, he has a lien upon the policies for the general balance of his insurance account.[6] Even if the broker has knowledge that the person who employs him is merely an agent for the insured, he is entitled to his special lien; and if it is not known to him

---

[1] Biddle's Law of Stockbrokers, pp. 118–120.

[2] Jones v. Gallagher, 3 Utah, 54.

[3] Vinton v. Baldwin, 95 Ind. 433; Hanna v. Phelps, 7 Ind. 21.

[4] Levy v. Barnard, 8 Taunt. 149; Snook v. Davidson, 2 Camp. 218; Mann v. Forrester, 4 Ib. 60.

[5] Levy v. Barnard, supra; Mann v. Forrester, supra; Sharp v. Whipple, 1 Bosw. (N. Y.) 557.

[6] Mann v. Forrester, supra, per Lord Ellenborough; per Woodruff, J., in Sharp v. Whipple, supra; Man v. Shiffner, 2 East, 523; Moody v. Webster, 3 Pick. (Mass.) 424.

that his employer is merely an agent, he has a lien for his general balance against his employer in the same way as if he had acted directly for the insured.[1]

An insurance broker may assert his general lien even against an assignee of the policy. Thus, where the owner of goods sells them after directing his broker to effect insurance upon them, and the broker retains the policy and collects money for a loss, he can hold the money for his general balance as against the purchaser.[2]

424. If one acts both as an insurance broker and as a factor for the sale of goods, his lien extends to a general balance of both accounts; he may retain a sum received for a loss on a policy, not only for a balance due him upon his insurance account, but also for a balance due him for advances and commissions upon goods.[3] But if the principal has remitted the premiums payable in respect of the insurance, so that he has no longer any lien as a broker upon the policy, he is not entitled to hold it for the general balance due from his principal to him as a factor.[4]

425. An agent, who is not a broker or general agent, who effects insurance for his principal, and pays or becomes bound for the premium, has a specific lien on the policy so long as he retains it. If he surrenders the policy to his principal, his lien is gone. Although the insurers are entitled to deduct the premium, if unpaid, from the amount payable upon a loss, yet, if the agent has paid the premium to the insurers, he has no equity to stand in their place, and to claim payment out of the sum due for the loss.[5]

---

[1] Mann v. Forrester, 4 Camp. 60; Sharp v. Whipple, 1 Bosw. (N. Y.) 557; Westwood v. Bell, 4 Camp. 349, 352. "I hold that, if a policy of insurance is effected by a broker, in ignorance that it does not belong to the persons by whom he is employed, he has a lien upon it for the amount of the balance which they owe him. . . . The only question is, whether he knew or had reason to believe that the person by whom he was employed was only an agent; and the party who seeks to deprive him of his lien must make out the affirmative. The employer is to be taken to be the principal till the contrary is proved." Per Gibbs, C. J. In Snook v. Davidson, 2 Camp. 218; and in Lanyon v. Blanchard, Ib. 596, 597, the broker must be taken to have had notice that the person who employed him was not the principal.

[2] Man v. Shiffner, 2 East, 523.

[3] Olive v. Smith, 5 Taunt. 56.

[4] Dixon v. Stansfield, 10 C. B. 398.

[5] Cranston v. Philadelphia Ins. Co. 5 Binn. (Pa.) 538.

But such an agent who procures a policy in pursuance of a specific order, and under directions to forward the policy to his principal, has no lien on the policy. " By undertaking to execute the order," said Chief Justice Shaw,[1] " he bound himself to comply with the terms and forward the policy; and this precludes the supposition that he was to have any lien upon it or interest in it."

A ship's husband, for the general management of the vessel insured, has no lien on a policy for the balance of his account, where he has procured the insurance under specific directions to forward the policy to the owner.[2]

If the broker knew at the time of effecting a policy that the person who employed him was acting for another, he has no lien upon the policy for the general balance due him from such agent,[3] but only a special lien for the premium and commissions due on that policy.[3]

II. *To what Property they Attach.*

426. A factor's lien for his general balance attaches only to goods received by him in his general capacity as factor: it does not attach to goods received by him under a special agreement for a particular purpose. " The lien which a factor has on the goods of his principal arises upon an agreement which the law implies; but when there is an express stipulation to the contrary, it puts an end to the general rule of law." [4] Thus, where the owner of certain cotton deposited it with a broker for sale, under a special agreement that the latter should pay the proceeds to the owner, it was held that the broker had no lien on this cotton for the balance of his general account arising upon other articles; for the express stipulation of the parties excluded the idea of such a lien. The goods not having been sold, the owner, or his assignee in bankruptcy, was entitled to have them returned.[5]

The special agreement may, however, be consistent with the implied lien. Wool merchants in Ohio, in consideration of further advances by their factors in New York, agreed to ship them wool enough to balance their account for such advances and a

---

[1] Reed *v.* Pacific Ins. Co. 1 Met. 166.

[2] Reed *v.* Pacific Ins. Co. *supra.*

[3] Man *v.* Shiffner, 2 East, 523.

[4] Walker *v.* Birch, 6 T. R. 258, 262, per Lord Kenyon.

[5] Walker *v.* Birch, *supra.* See Hall *v.* Jackson, 20 Pick. (Mass.) 194.

large indebtedness already existing, and any indebtedness that might subsequently accrue. It was held that the lien of the factors upon the wool received was not limited to their advances on each shipment, but was available for the satisfaction of the general balance due them.[1]

If a factor receives goods in the general course of business without notice of the fact that they were consigned to him for a special purpose, he has a lien upon them for his general balance.[2]

427. A general lien is not implied when there is a special agreement which is inconsistent with such a lien.[3] If a transaction between two houses having many dealings between them is shown to be an isolated dealing on a particular footing, and to have been intended to be brought to a point and settled by itself, it does not enter into the general account between the parties and become subject to a lien for a general balance. A firm of merchants in Hamburgh directed their correspondents in London, a firm of merchants, to purchase Mexican bonds upon certain terms, and to hold them in safe custody at the disposal of the Hamburgh firm. The bonds were accordingly purchased July 2, and the next day the London firm drew upon the Hamburgh firm for the amount, which, they said, balanced the transaction. The bills were accepted and paid. On the 19th of November the Hamburgh firm requested that the bonds be sent to them by post; but on the same day the London firm wrote that they had stopped payment, but that the bonds had not been jeopardized. The Hamburgh firm afterwards stopped payment. In a suit by the representatives of this firm for the delivery of the bonds, it was held that the bonds were not subject to the general balance of account between the two firms.[4]

Under an agreement that certain advances shall be paid out of the proceeds of a certain consignment, the factor is bound to apply the proceeds of such consignment to the payment of the specific advances, and cannot apply them to a debt due him not contracted under the agreement, and for which he had no lien.[5]

---

[1] Chapman v. Kent, 3 Duer (N. Y.), 224.

[2] Archer v. McMechan, 21 Mo. 43.

[3] Brandão v. Barnett, 3 C. B. 519, 531.

[4] Bock v. Gorrissen, 30 L. J. Ch. 39.

[5] Owen v. Iglanor, 4 Cold. (Tenn.) 15.

428. A factor has no general lien on goods which he has received under express directions to apply the proceeds in a particular way. He must first carry out the instructions of the consignor as to the application, and then, if there is a surplus, his general lien may attach to this.[1]

He has no lien on goods which are delivered to him as agent for the use of his principal. Such a delivery is considered as a delivery to the principal, and the possession is considered to be in the principal.[2]

No lien arises in favor of an agent with whom goods or a policy of insurance is deposited for safe keeping.[3] And so if he is intrusted with property for a particular purpose, he cannot retain it under a claim of a general lien.[4] An agent employed merely to purchase certain goods is entitled to a lien for his advances in making the purchase, but he is not entitled to a lien for a general balance due him from his principal.[5]

429. A third person to whom a factor has intrusted his principal's goods for sale, has no lien on them as against the principal.[6] The relation of a factor to his principal is one of trust, and he cannot delegate his authority to another, or substitute another in his place, without the sanction of his principal, express or implied. A transfer of the goods by the factor to another whom he authorizes to act in his place, is a conversion of the goods by the factor. The principal may thereupon sue the factor in trover for the conversion, or, waiving the tort, he may sue him in assumpsit for the value of the goods.[7]

The lien of a factor is a personal privilege, and cannot be set up by any other person in defence to an action by the principal. He may avail himself of it or not, as he pleases.[8]

430. If a factor or consignee makes a general assignment for the benefit of his creditors, the assignee has no right to sell the goods, for the factor or consignee cannot delegate his authority to another without the consent of the principal. All that passes by the assignment is the lien on the goods. The

---

[1] Frith v. Forbes, 32 L. J. Ch. 10.
[2] Gurney v. Sharp, 4 Taunt. 242.
[3] Muir v. Fleming, 1 D. & R. 29.
[4] Burn v. Brown, 2 Stark. 272.
[5] De Wolf v. Howland, 2 Paine, 356, 365.

[6] Phelps v. Sinclair, 2 N. H. 554.
[7] Campbell v. Reeves, 3 Head (Tenn.), 226.
[8] Holly v. Huggeford, 8 Pick. (Mass.) 73.

assignee has lawful possession of the goods under the assignment, but this gives him no right to assume to himself the entire property, or right of disposing of the goods. A sale of the goods by him is a tortious conversion of them. His legal right extends no further than to hold the goods by virtue of the lien, or to foreclose the lien in the manner provided by statute.[1]

431. Goods received after death of principal. — Although the death of the principal is a revocation of the agent's authority, yet the possession of goods acquired by a factor after the death of his principal, where he has made advances upon the goods, may entitle him to a lien.[2]

But if the factor does not obtain actual or constructive possession of the goods till after the death of the principal, he has no lien for an existing debt, or general balance of account. Thus, a manufacturer wrote to commission merchants to whom he was indebted, and enclosed an invoice of goods which he was about to ship to them, but died before the letter was mailed or the goods had left his possession. His son the next day forwarded the letter and the goods, and the merchant sold the goods, and gave credit for the proceeds in reduction of their balance of account against the manufacturer. In a suit against them by the administrator of the deceased, it was held that they must pay over the proceeds of these goods to the administrator.[3]

432. A factor has no general lien on goods which the consignor has informed him belong to another person to whose credit he is directed to place the proceeds.[4] Dealers in live-stock shipped to brokers in Chicago certain car-loads of stock, which had been purchased with the money of a banker at the place of shipment, and the dealers so informed the broker,

---

[1] Terry v. Bamberger, 44 Conn. 558; S. C. 14 Blatchf. 234.

[2] Hammonds v. Barclay, 2 East, 227; Lempriere v. Pasley, 2 T. R. 485.

[3] Farnum v. Boutelle, 13 Met. (Mass.) 159, 165. Per Shaw, C. J. "But before such lien attaches, the goods must have been delivered or sent to the consignee, or at least put upon their transit to him; and an intention so to consign them, and an intimation of such intention by letter, whilst they remain in the actual possession and custody of the consignor, is not sufficient to create a lien. In the present case, it appears that the goods remained on the premises of the intestate at the time of his decease, and were subsequently forwarded by his son."

[4] Weymouth v. Boyer, 1 Ves. Jr. 416, 425; Darlington v. Chamberlain (Ill.), 12 N. East. Rep. 78.

and directed him to place the proceeds of sale to the credit of the banker in a certain bank in Chicago, in accordance with their custom in previous transactions. The stock really belonged to the banker, though the dealers had shipped it in their own names without consulting him, in order to get better rates of freight. The brokers applied the proceeds of the sale, less their commissions, to an old account against the dealers for advances made to them for which they claimed a factor's lien. It was held that their claim was inadmissible as against the owner of the stock.[1]

433. And so if the agent has notice of the bankruptcy of his principal, or of his assignment for the benefit of his creditors, before he gets possession of the property, he cannot hold it under a claim of a general lien.[2] But if he has received a bill of lading or other insignia of property in the goods before notice of his principal's bankruptcy, he is not divested of his right of lien, though he has such notice before the goods actually arrive, for the bill of lading confers title and constructive possession. The bankruptcy of the principal after the factor has received the goods, does not divest him of his lien.[3]

After a factor has obtained possession of the goods, his lien is not divested by an attachment of them by a creditor of his principal.[4]

434. Whether a consignee has a lien upon goods which have been wrongfully consigned to him depends very much upon the manner in which the consignment is made.[5] A carrier has no lien on such goods for freight as against the rightful owner,[6] and the consignee could acquire no lien as against such owner by paying the freight. As regards the duties upon goods

[1] Darlington v. Chamberlain (Ill.), 12 N. East Rep. 78.

[2] Copland v. Stein, 8 T. R. 199; Robson v. Kemp, 4 Esp. 233, 236. Per Lord Ellenborough, C. J.

[3] Hudson v. Granger, 5 B. & Ald. 27.

[4] Maxon v. Landrum, 21 La. Ann. 366.

In **Indiana**: Goods attached in the hands of a consignee shall be subject to a lien for any debt due him from the consignor. R. S. 1881, § 927.

In **Kansas**: When property is attached in the hands of a consignee or other person having a prior lien, his lien thereon shall not be affected by the attachment. Comp. Laws 1885, § 4602.

Louisiana: see § **437**.

[5] Fowler v. Parsons (Mass.), 9 N. East. Rep. 799, per Field, J.

[6] § **304**.

imported by one who has come wrongfully into possession of the goods, the United States would have a lien, and the duties must be paid if the goods are entered, and withdrawn from the custody of the United States ; but this lien would not ordinarily be transferred to the consignee under the wrongful consignment, who has paid the duties and received the goods, for no lien can be implied in favor of one who acts adversely to the rights of the owner.[1]

But the owner may be estopped by his conduct from denying that such consignee paid the duties for his use and at his request. Thus, if the owner intending to replevy the goods, stands by and knowingly allows the consignee, who honestly believes the goods were properly consigned to him, to pay the customs duties, the owner cannot maintain his action of replevin without tendering the amount so paid. Under such circumstances the consignee obtains an equitable lien upon the goods by reason of such payment.[2]

It is held, however, that, although the consignor has obtained the goods by means of fraudulent representations, a factor who has in good faith received the goods for sale, and made advances upon them to the consignor, acquires a valid lien, and the original vendor cannot obtain them from him without paying the advances.[3]

But a factor who has obtained possession of the property on which he claims a lien by means of misrepresentations, or in any manner which makes his possession unauthorized or tortious, is not entitled to a lien.[4]

435. A consignee who has insured the goods on which he has made advances, has a lien upon the insurance money collected by him for a loss by fire without his fault, though the insurance was effected for the benefit of the consignor. He had a lien upon the goods, and when these were destroyed the amount recovered by him upon their loss was substituted in their place, and was held subject to the same lien.[5]

---

[1] Fowler v. Parsons (Mass.), 9 N. East. Rep. 799.

[2] Fowler v. Parsons, supra.

[3] Williams v. Birch, 6 Bosw. (N. Y.) 299.

[4] Madden v. Kempster, 1 Camp. 12 ; Taylor v. Robinson, 8 Taunt. 648.

[5] Johnson v. Campbell, 120 Mass. 449.

436. In several states there are statutes which protect factors in their dealings with consignors. These statutes are generally made a part of the Factors' Acts of these states. The general purpose of the factors' acts is to enable third persons to deal with agents intrusted with goods, or with the documents of title to goods, for sale, as though they were the absolute owners of the goods.[1] The same acts also generally afford a similar protection to factors who make advances to consignors upon goods consigned.

437. Louisiana.[2] — Every consignee or commission agent who has made advances on goods consigned to him, or placed in his hands to be sold for account of the consignor, has a privilege for the amount of these advances, with interest and charges, on the value of the goods, if they are at his disposal in his store, or in a public warehouse, or if, before their arrival, he can show by a bill of lading or letter of advice that they have been dispatched to him. Such privilege is preferred to that of any attaching creditor on the goods consigned to him, for any balance due to him, whether specially advanced on said goods or not: provided they, or an invoice or bill of lading, have been received by him previous to the attachment. This privilege shall not have a preference over a privilege preëxisting in behalf of a resident creditor of this state.[3]

Under this statute giving a consignee a lien by way of pledge upon goods consigned to him for his advances upon them, if he has control of the goods, or if before their arrival he can show by a bill of lading, or letter of advice, that they have been dispatched to him,[4] the consignee, after receiving such letter of advice, or a bill of lading, has a lien which cannot be defeated by the consignor's drawing a draft against the goods, obtaining a discount of it, and using the proceeds for the purchase of the goods so consigned.[5]

438. Maine.[6] — Every person in whose name merchandise is forwarded, every factor or agent intrusted with the possession

---

[1] Jones on Pledges, § 333.

[2] R. Civ. Code 1870, art. 3247.

[3] Rev. Laws 1884, § 2887. See Buddecke v. Spence, 23 La. Ann. 367; Maxen v. Landrum, 21 Ib. 366.

[4] R. Civ. Code 1870, art. 3247.

[5] Helm v. Meyer, 30 La. Ann. 943.

[6] R. S. 1883, ch. 31, §§ 1-3.

of any bill of lading, custom-house permit, or warehouse-keeper's receipt for the delivery of such merchandise, and every such factor or agent not having the documentary evidence of title, who is intrusted with the possession of merchandise for the purpose of sale, or as security for advances to be made thereon, shall be deemed the true owner thereof, so far as to give validity to any lien or contract made by such shipper or agent with any other person for the sale or disposal of the whole or any part of such merchandise, money advanced, or negotiable instrument, or other obligation in writing, given by such person upon the faith thereof.

No person, taking such merchandise in deposit from such agent as security for an antecedent demand, shall thereby acquire or enforce any right or interest therein other than such agent could then enforce. But the true owner of such merchandise, upon repayment of the money so advanced, restoration of the security so given, or satisfaction of all legal liens, may demand and receive his property, or recover the balance remaining as the produce of the legal sale thereof, after deducting all proper claims and expenses thereon.

439. Maryland.[1] — Any person intrusted with and in possession of any bills of lading, storekeeper's or inspector's certificates, order for the delivery of goods, or other document showing possession, shall be deemed the true owner of the goods, wares, or merchandise described therein, so far as to give validity to any contract thereafter to be made by such person with any other person or body corporate for the sale or disposal of the said goods, wares, or merchandise, or for the pledge or deposit thereof as a security for any money or negotiable instrument advanced or given on faith of such documents, or either of them : provided, that such person or body corporate shall not have notice, by such document or otherwise, that the person so intrusted is not the actual and *bonâ fide* owner of such goods, wares, and merchandise.

If any person or body corporate shall take any goods, wares, or merchandise, or any document mentioned in the foregoing clause, in deposit or pledge from any person so intrusted with the same, or to whom the same may be consigned, or who may be intrusted with and in possession of any such bill of lading, storekeeper's

---

[1] R. Code 1878, pp. 291, 292, §§ 3, 5, 6; p. 294, § 14.

or inspector's certificate, order for the delivery of goods, or other such document showing possession, without notice, as a security for any debt or demand existing before the time of such deposit or pledge, then such person shall acquire such right, title, or interest as was possessed and might have been enforced by the person from whom he received the same, and no more.

440. Massachusetts.[1] — Every person in whose name merchandise is shipped for sale by a person in the lawful possession thereof at the time of the shipment, shall be deemed to be the true owner 'thereof so far as to entitle the consignee to a lien thereon for money advanced, or securities given to the shipper for one on account of such consignment unless the consignee, at or before the time when he made the advances or gave the securities, had notice, by the bill of lading or otherwise, that the shipper was not the actual and *bonâ fide* owner.

When a person intrusted with merchandise, and having authority to sell or consign the same, ships or otherwise transmits or delivers it to any other person, such other person shall have a lien thereon for any money or merchandise advanced, or negotiable security given by him, on the faith of such consignment, to or for the use of the person in whose name such consignment or delivery was made ; and for any money, negotiable security, or merchandise, received for the use of the consignee by the person in whose name such consignment or delivery was made, if such consignee had, at the time of such advance or receipt, probable cause to believe that the person in whose name the merchandise was shipped, transmitted, or delivered, was the actual owner thereof, or had a legal interest therein to the amount of said lien.

441. New York[2] and Ohio.[3] — Every person in whose name any merchandise shall be shipped shall be deemed the true owner thereof, so far as to entitle the consignee of such merchandise to a lien thereon : 1. For any money advanced or negotiable security given by such consignee, to or for the use of the person in whose name such shipment shall have been made ; and, 2. For any money or negotiable security received by the person in whose

---

[1] P. S. 1882, ch. 71, §§ 1, 2.

[2] 2 R. S. 7th ed. p. 1168, § 1; 3 R. S. 1882, p. 2257.

[3] 1 R. S. 1880, § 3214.

name such shipment shall have been made to or for the use of such consignee. The lien so provided for shall not exist where such consignee shall have notice, by the bill of lading or otherwise, at or before the advancing of any money or security by him, or at or before the receiving of such money or security by the person in whose name the shipment shall have been made, that such person is not the actual and *bonâ fide* owner thereof.

442. Pennsylvania.[1] — Whenever any person intrusted with merchandise, and having authority to sell or consign the same, shall ship or otherwise transmit the same to any other person, such other person shall have a lien thereon : 1st. For any money advanced or negotiable security given by him on the faith of such consignment to or for the use of the person in whose name such merchandise was shipped or transmitted ; 2d. For any money or negotiable security received for the use of such consignee by the person in whose name such merchandise was shipped or transmitted. But such lien shall not exist for any of the purposes aforesaid, if such consignee shall have notice, by the bill of lading or otherwise, before the time of such advance or receipt, that the person in whose name such merchandise was shipped or transmitted is not the actual owner thereof.

443. Rhode Island.[2] — The consignee of merchandise shipped shall have a lien thereon for any money or negotiable security by him advanced upon the faith of such shipment to, or for the use of, the person in whose name the shipment shall have been made, in the same manner, and to the same extent, as if such person were the true owner thereof : provided, at the time of the advance, the consignee shall have had no notice or knowledge that the shipper was not the true owner of such merchandise.

444. Wisconsin.[3] — Every consignee of property shall have a lien thereon for any money advanced or negotiable security given by him to or for the use of the person in whose name the shipment of such property is made, and for any money or negotiable security received by such person for his use, unless he shall, before advancing any such money, or giving such security, or

---

[1] Brightly's Purdon's Dig. 1883, p. 772.

[2] G. S. 1872, ch. 123, § 1; P. S. 1882, ch. 136, § 1.

[3] R. S. 1878, §§ 3345–3347.

before it is so received for his use, have notice that such person is not the actual owner thereof.

Every factor, broker, or other agent intrusted by the owner with the possession of any bill of lading, custom-house permit, warehouse receipt, or other evidence of the title to personal property, or with the possession of personal property for the purpose of sale, or as security for any advances made or liability by him incurred in reference to such property, shall have a lien upon such personal property for all such advances, liability incurred, or commissions or other moneys due him for services as such factor, broker, or agent, and may retain the possession of such property until such advances, commissions, or moneys are paid or such liability is discharged.[1]

III. *What Indebtedness is Secured.*

445. A debt due from the principal to the agent is the foundation of the agent's lien. The debt must be certain and liquidated. A liability of an agent as surety for his principal does not entitle him to a lien, in the absence of an express contract,[2] unless this liability is connected with the agency.

The debt must be one contracted in the agent's business. It is usually limited to advances, expenses, and commissions incurred in this business. The debt which is covered by the lien is not limited to the advances and charges pertaining to a particular consignment; but the lien covers the grand balance of account between the parties in their relation of principal and factor.

446. The lien covers interest upon the debt as well as the debt itself, though this be payable immediately, but the factor is permitted or requested to defer the sale of the goods in his possession.[3]

---

[1] This statute applies to receipts given by private warehouses, and not merely to bonded warehouses. In this respect the statute is construed differently from the New York statute, from which that of Wisconsin was taken; for in the latter state there are no bonded warehouses. Price *v.* Wisconsin Marine & Fire Ins. Co. 43 Wis. 267.

[2] Drinkwater *v.* Goodwin, 1 Cowp. 251 ; Hammond *v.* Barclay, 2 East, 227.

[3] *Ex parte* Kensington, 1 Deac. 58 ; Heins *v.* Peine, 6 Rob. (N. Y.) 420.

447. The debt must be due from the owner of the goods which the factor retains by virtue of his lien,[1] unless the debt be in the form of negotiable paper of a third person, transferred to the factor by the owner of the goods, or the factor is employed by an agent for an undisclosed principal. If a broker effects insurance in ignorance that the person who employs him is not the owner of the property insured, but is acting for another, he has a lien for the balance of account due him from the person who employs him. He is supposed to have made advances on the credit of the policy which is allowed to remain in his hands.[2] If the broker receives notice that a third person is interested in the policy, his lien upon it is limited to the amount of his general balance at that time.[3]

A merchant, after advising his factor of an intended consignment of oats, and drawing upon him in anticipation, indorsed the bill of lading to a third person. The latter sent the bill of lading to the factor first mentioned, who took possession of the cargo and paid the freight. It was held that the factor had no lien on the cargo for his advances, because he held the goods, not as agent of the person to whom he made the advances, but as the agent of the person from whom he received the bill of lading.[4]

And so if an insurance broker effects a policy in the name of an agent employed by the master of a vessel, the agency being known to the broker, he cannot, upon collecting the amount of a loss under the policy, retain it for a debt due to him from the agent.[5] The employer is to be taken as the principal until the contrary is proved, and knowledge of the agency is brought home to the insurance broker.[6]

448. A factor cannot claim a lien for debts not due, to himself, but to his principal. Thus, a factor sold goods of his principal in his own name to a purchaser who did not pay for them at the time, but sent other goods to the factor to be sold for him, never having employed him as a factor before. This

---

[1] Barry v. Longmore, 12 Ad. & El. 639.

[2] Westwood v. Bell, 4 Camp. 349 ; Mann v. Forrester, Ib. 60, per Ellenborough, C. J.

[3] Mann v. Forrester, *supra.* See Levy v. Bernard, 8 Taunt. 149.

[4] Bruce v. Wait, 3 M. & W. 15.

[5] Foster v. Hoyt, 2 Johns. Cas. (N. Y.) 327. See § **432.**

[6] Westwood v. Bell, 4 Camp. 352; S. C. 1 Holt, 122, per Gibbs, C. J. ; Maanss v. Henderson, 1 East, 335.

purchaser then became bankrupt, and his assignees claimed the goods sent by him to the factor, and which remained unsold, tendering the charges upon them. The factor refused to deliver the goods, claiming a lien upon them for the price of the goods sold by him to the bankrupt. There was then a balance due the factor from his first principal.[1] It was held that the assignees of the bankrupt were entitled to recover.

449. A factor has no lien for a debt due from his principal before he became his factor, unless it was contracted in anticipation of the relation of principal and factor. "I do not find," said Chambre, Justice,[2] "any authority for saying that a factor has any general lien in respect of debts which arise prior to the time at which his character of factor commences; and if a right to such a lien is not established by express authority, it does not appear to me to fall within the general principle upon which the liens of factors have been allowed. It seems to me that the liens of factors have been allowed for the convenience of trade, and with a view to encourage factors to advance money upon goods in their possession, or which must come to their hands as factors; but debts which are incurred prior to the existence of the relation of principal and factor, are not contracted upon this principle." To give a lien for such debts would, he says, operate the contrary way, since it would tend to prevent insolvent persons from employing their creditors as factors, lest the goods intrusted to them should be retained in satisfaction of former debts.

A factor's lien for a general balance rests on the custom of trade, and nothing can fall within the custom of trade but what concerns the trade. Therefore collateral obligations, such as money due for rent, are not within the custom which authorizes a factor to retain for a general balance.[3]

The factor's lien does not cover the price of goods sold by

---

[1] Houghton *v.* Matthews, 3 Bos. & Pul. 485. Lord Alvanley, C. J., dissented, being of opinion that the moment the goods were sent, the relation of principal and factor arose, and when that relation commenced, the right to a general lien attached.

[2] Houghton *v.* Matthews, 3 Bos. & Pul. 485, 488; Mann *v.* Forrester, 4

Camp. 60, 61, per Ellenborough, C. J.; Olive *v.* Smith, 5 Taunt. 56; Walker *v.* Birch, 6 T. R. 258; Stevens *v.* Robbins, 12 Mass. 180, 182; Sturgis *v.* Slacum, 18 Pick. (Mass.) 36, 40, per Wilde, J.

[3] Houghton *v.* Matthews, 3 Bos. & Pul. 485, 494, per Heath, J.; *Ex parte Deese*, 1 Atk. 229.

the factor to his principal. It does not cover any debt not connected with the general purposes of the relation of principal and agent.[1]

450. The lien covers acceptances as well as advances in money. An agent or consignee to whom goods are consigned for sale under an agreement that he will accept bills drawn upon him for the amount, has a lien on the goods for the amount of his acceptances, and is entitled to retain the goods until the acceptances are paid. It is a necessary inference in such case that the drafts are to be drawn on the credit of the goods, and that the consignee is to have a lien on the goods to secure him against his acceptances. If the consignee had upon the request of the consignor advanced money upon the goods, he would clearly have had a lien upon the goods to secure his advances; and his acceptances amount in fact to advances.[2] The debt need not be payable immediately. The factor may retain goods to meet his liability upon an acceptance payable at a future time.[3]

451. Lien for duties paid. — There is a lien in favor of the government upon goods in its possession for the duties due thereon; but the lien is restricted to the duties upon the particular goods.[4] The consignee cannot take the goods until he has paid the duties. Neither can the creditor of the owner by any attachment or other process take the goods out of the possession of the officer of customs by attachment or other process until the lien for duties be actually discharged.[5]

The owner's property in the goods is not divested by the pos-

---

[1] Thacher v. Hannahs, 4 Rob. (N. Y.) 407.

[2] Nagle v. McFeeters, 97 N. Y. 196, 202. "Here was the principal consigning goods to his agents to sell, under an agreement that he should be permitted to draw upon them drafts which they were to accept for his accommodation, to the amount of the goods thus consigned. What is the legal inference from such a state of facts? What other inference can there be, except that the drafts were drawn on the credit of the goods, and that the goods were to be held as an indemnity against the drafts? There could have been no other understanding, and no other legal effect can be given to the arrangement." Per Earl, J. See, also, Eaton v. Truesdail, 52 Ill. 307.

[3] Hammonds v. Barclay, 2 East, 227.

[4] Dennie v. Harris, 9 Pick. (Mass.) 364; Meeker v. Wilson, 1 Gall. 419; Dias v. Bouchaud, 10 Paige (N. Y.), 445; Guesnard v. Louisville & Nashville R. R. Co. 76 Ala. 453, 457.

[5] Harris v. Dennie, 3 Pet. 292.

session of the United States for the purpose of maintaining the lien for duties. That possession is not adverse to the title of the owner, and, indeed, may be properly deemed not so much an exclusive as a concurrent and mixed possession for the joint benefit of the owner and of the United States. It leaves the owner's right to the immediate possession perfect the moment the lien for the duties is discharged. And if he tenders the duties, or the proper security therefor, and the collector refuses the delivery of the goods, it is a tortious conversion of the property for which an action of trespass or trover will lie.[1]

452. Though the debt has been barred by the statute of limitations, a lien for such debt attaches to goods of the principal which afterwards come into the agent's hands, for the debt is not discharged by the statute, but only the remedy by action; he has a subsisting demand, and therefore if goods come into his possession he has the remedy in his own hands, and has no occasion for an action.[2]

IV. *For Advances on Crops.*

453. By common law, one who advances money or supplies to a farmer or planter to enable him to make a crop acquires no lien upon the crop for such advances.[3] Such a lien may, however, be created by express agreement,[4] and in some states it is given by statute. Such a lien is commonly called an agricultural lien.

454. Alabama.[5] — Whenever advances in horses, mules, oxen, or necessary provisions, farming tools and implements, or money to purchase the same, shall be made by any person to any other person in this state, and such advance shall be obtained by the

---

[1] Conard *v.* Pacific Ins. Co. 6 Pet. 262; Conard *v.* Atlantic Ins. Co. 1 Pet. 386; Conard *v.* Nicoll, 4 Pet. 291.

[2] Spears *v.* Hartly, 3 Esp. 81, 82, per Lord Elden; Higgins *v.* Scott, 2 B. & Ad. 413, 414.

[3] Franklin *v.* Meyer, 36 Ark. 96.

[4] Bell *v.* Radcliff, 32 Ark. 645.

[5] Code 1876, §§ 3286–3288. Re-enacted as to certain counties, Acts 1886–1887, p. 164.

An instrument which does not contain words essential to constitute a statutory lien, if in the form of a mortgage of personal property conveying crops to be grown, with other property, is valid and operative as a mortgage, and takes effect, as against purchasers, from the time of its admission to record as a mortgage. Dawson *v.* Higgins, 50 Ala. 49; Ellis *v.* Martin, 60 Ala. 394; Hamilton *v.* Maas, 77 Ala. 283.

latter, to enable him to make a crop,[1] and it shall be declared in a written note or obligation for the same, given by the person to whom such advance is made, that the same was obtained by him *bonâ fide*[2] for the purpose of making a crop,[3] and that without such advance it would not be in the power of such person to procure the necessary team, provisions, and farming implements to make a crop, the advance so made, or the amount thereof, shall be a lien on such crop, and on the stock bought or furnished with the money so advanced; and such lien shall have preference of all other liens, except that for the rent of the land on which such crop may be made, and that for advances by the landlord to make the crop.[4]

The lien must be recorded in the office of the judge of probate of the county within sixty days from the making of the same.

[1] The statutory lien extends only to the crops of the current year, although the instrument may purport to give a lien for that year and the next ensuing year. Boswell v. Carlisle, 55 Ala. 554.

[2] The language of the statute must be strictly pursued, and therefore a recital that the " advances were made me to enable me to make a crop the present year " is not sufficient. Dawson v. Higgins, 50 Ala. 49.

[3] It is essential to a valid lien for such advances that they should actually be made in good faith, for the specified purpose. A stranger to the contract, not being bound by its recitals, may show that they are untrue, and that the instrument was in fact given to secure an antecedent debt. Boswell v. Carlisle, *supra*.

The person making the advances is not, however, required to see to their proper application, nor is he responsible for any misapplication made without his knowledge or consent. Boswell v. Carlisle, *supra*.

If the note or obligation be intentionally made to include a debt not contracted for the purpose of making a crop, but for a separate and distinct purpose, and the debt so included

constitutes a material portion of the consideration, the statutory lien on the crop is vitiated. Comer v. Daniel, 69 Ala. 434; Pearson v. Evans, 61 Ala. 416; Collier v. Faulk, 69 Ala. 58; Carter v. Wilson, 61 Ala. 434; Schuessler v. Gains, 68 Ala. 556; Bell v. Hurst, 75 Ala. 44.

[4] This lien is superior to a prior mortgage of the crop given only for an antecedent debt. Hamilton v. Maas, 77 Ala. 283.

If a merchant sues out an attachment to enforce his lien for advances, and the landlord becomes surety for his tenant on a replevin bond, he is estopped to deny the liability of the property to the attachment. Brown v. Hamil, 76 Ala. 506.

This lien is enforced by attachment. This remedy is subject to the same limitations and restrictions that are imposed on the landlord (see ch. xii.), and can only be issued upon an affidavit which, upon a fair construction, discloses the existence of a particular contract within the terms of the statute, and a state of facts which authorizes the issue of the writ upon that contract. Flexner v. Dickerson, 65 Ala. 129.

Any person having such lien has the same rights and remedies to enforce it as landlords have for the collection of rents.

455. Georgia.[1] — A lien is established in favor of merchants, factors, and others who furnish clothing, medicines, supplies, or provisions for the support of families, or medical services, tuition, or school-books. They have the right to secure themselves, from the crops of the year in which such things are furnished, upon such terms as may be agreed upon by the parties. The contract must be in writing.[2]

The lien of the landlord has priority;[3] but if the crop be delivered into the possession of a factor or of his agent, he has a lien upon it at common law. In such case his lien is superior to that of a landlord for the rent of the land upon which the cotton is raised, if the landlord's lien has not been foreclosed and the factor has no notice of it.[4]

The lien given to merchants and factors upon growing crops does not cover money advanced with which the planter is to purchase provisions and supplies; and a note given for money, which upon its face recites that the money is to be used to purchase provisions, does not create a debt which is secured by the lien.[5]

The affidavit to foreclose such lien must state that the deponent is either a factor or a merchant, and that, as such, he has furnished either provisions or commercial manures, or both, to the defendant; and it must also state the terms upon which such supplies were furnished.[6] It must also aver a demand of payment of the debt, and a refusal to pay, and that the lien is prosecuted within one year after the debt became due.[7]

456. In Louisiana[8] a privilege is given for debts incurred for

---

[1] R. Code 1882, §§ 1972, 1978. This statute, which also applies to landlords furnishing supplies, is stated fully in ch. xii. *infra.*

[2] Inasmuch as it is one of the conditions of a valid crop lien that it should be created by a special contract in writing, that fact should be alleged in the plaintiff's affidavit to foreclose the lien. The affidavit must state all the facts necessary to constitute a valid lien. Powell *v.* Weaver, 56 Ga. 288.

[3] Code, § 1977.

[4] Clark *v.* Dobbins, 52 Ga. 656.

[5] Saulsbury *v.* Eason, 47 Ga. 617. See Speer *v.* Hart, 45 Ga. 113. See, also, Dart *v.* Mayhew, 60 Ga. 104.

[6] Toole *v.* Jowers, 49 Ga. 299.

[7] Callaway *v.* Walls, 54 Ga. 167; Anderson *v.* Beard, 54 Ga. 137.

[8] Civ. Code, art. 3184; Wood *v.* Calloway, 21 La. Ann. 471.

The constitution provides that "no mortgage or privilege shall affect third

necessary supplies furnished to any farm or plantation on the product of the last crop and the crop in the ground.　This privilege must be confined to the crop cultivated, standing or being gathered and taken off at the time the supplies were furnished. It cannot be extended to the crop subsequently planted, and sold with the plantation to a third party.[1]

A privilege in favor of one who furnishes supplies to a plantation springs only from the law that confers it.　It cannot be the subject of contract.　An acknowledgment that a creditor has a privilege on a crop cannot, therefore, be recognized as conferring a lien on it, unless it be shown that he, the creditor, has furnished the supplies to make it.[2]

It is also provided [3] that the appointments or salaries for the overseer for the current year are a privilege on the crops of the year and the proceeds thereof ; debts due for necessary supplies furnished to any farm or plantation, not including articles furnished and which were sold to laborers ; and debts due for money actually advanced and used for the purchase of necessary supplies ; and the payment of necessary expenses for any farm or plantation, are privileges on the crops of the year and the proceeds thereof.

The privileges granted to the overseer, the laborers, the furnishers of supplies, and the party advancing money necessary to carry on any farm or plantation, shall be concurrent, and shall not be divested by any prior mortgage, whether conventional, legal, or judicial, or by any seizure and sale of the land while the crop is on it.

All the privileges on the growing crop in favor of the class of persons mentioned shall be concurrent, except that in favor of the laborer, which shall be ranked as the first privilege on the crop.

persons, unless recorded in the parish where the property to be affected is situated."

Consequently a privilege in favor of a merchant for supplies furnished a planter must be recorded in the book of mortgages and privileges in order to have effect against third persons. White v. Bird, 23 La. Ann. 270.

The recording of a privilege too late is equivalent to not recording it at all, so far as seizing creditors are concerned. Lapene v. Meegel, 26 La. Ann. 80.

[1] McCutchon v. Wilkinson, 12 La. Ann. 483 ; Given v. Alexander, 25 La. Ann. 71.

[2] Payne v. Spiller, 23 La. Ann. 248.

[3] Rev. Laws 1884, §§ 2873, 2874, 2875.

457. North Carolina.[1] — If any person shall make any advance, either in money or supplies, to any person who is engaged in, or about to engage in, the cultivation of the soil, the person so making such advance shall be entitled to a lien on the crops which may be made during the year upon the land in the cultivation of which the advances so made have been expended, in preference to all other liens existing or otherwise, to the extent of such advances:[2] provided an agreement in writing shall be entered into before any such advance is made to this effect, in which shall be specified the amount to be advanced, or in which a limit shall be fixed beyond which the advance, if made from time to time during the year, shall not go; which agreement shall be recorded, in the office of the register of the county in which the person to whom the advances are made resides, within thirty days after its date.[3]

The lien for work on crops or farms or materials shall be preferred to every other lien or incumbrance which attached upon the property subsequent to the time at which the work was commenced or the materials were furnished.

---

[1] Code 1883, vol. i. §§ 1799, 1782.

[2] The advances must be made in money or supplies to a person about to engage in the cultivation of the crops, and after the agreement for such advances has been made, or simultaneously with the making and delivery of the agreement. The advances must be expended in the cultivation of the crop of that year, and the lien must be on the crop of that year, made by reason of the advances. Clark *v.* Farrar, 74 N. C. 686; Reese *v.* Cole, 93 N. C. 87.

One who makes advances of agricultural supplies to a tenant or cropper, does so with notice of the rights of the landlord, and takes the risk of the tenant or cropper abandoning or otherwise violating his contract. If the cropper abandons his contract, this being special and entire, he cannot recover of the landlord for a partial performance, and his interest becomes vested in the landlord, divested of any lien which may have attached

to it for advances while the cropper was in possession. Thigpen *v.* Leigh, 93 N. C. 47.

A mortgagee of a cotton crop has no lien for further advances made to enable the mortgagor to secure the crop, which will take precedence of a second mortgage duly recorded. The fact that the advances were essential to the gathering of the crop, which might otherwise have been lost, does not aid the claim. The doctrine contended for is a principle of maritime law, which applies in favor of those who, by personal efforts and at great peril, save vessels and cargoes from loss at sea; but it is not a principle of the common law, nor can it be recognized when in conflict with statutory regulations in reference to liens. Weathersbee *v.* Farrar (N. C.), 1 S. East Rep. 616.

[3] The lien is valid as between the parties, although not registered within the time limited. Gay *v.* Nash, 78 N. C. 100; Reese *v.* Cole, 93 N. C. 87.

458. South Carolina.[1] — If any person or persons shall make any advance or advances,[2] either in money or supplies, to any person or persons who are employed or about to engage in the cultivation[3] of the soil, the person or persons so making such advance or advances shall be entitled to a lien on the crops which may be made during the year upon the land in the cultivation of which the advances so made have been expended, in preference to all other liens, existing or otherwise, to the extent of such advance or advances : provided an agreement in writing shall be entered into before such advance is made to this effect, in which shall be specified the amount to be advanced, or in which a limit shall be fixed beyond which the advances, if made from time to time during the year, shall not go.[4]

Any person who shall make advances in provisions, supplies, and other articles for agricultural purposes, shall have a lien in preference to all other liens, existing or otherwise, upon such provisions, supplies, and other articles, until the same shall be consumed in the use.

459. Virginia.[5] — If any person or persons shall make any advance or advances, either in money or supplies, to any person or persons who are engaged in, or who are about to engage in, the cultivation of the soil, the person or persons so making such advance or advances shall be entitled to a lien on the crops which may be made during the year upon the land in the cultivation of which the advances so made have been, or were in-

---

[1] G. S. 1882, §§ 2397, 2402.

[2] A mule cannot be considered an "advance" to be "expended" upon the land. McCullough v. Kibler, 5 S. C. 468.

[3] Richey v. Du Pre, 20 S. C. 6; Kennedy v. Reames, 15 S. C. 548. A mere employee, who cultivates the crop of another for hire, either in money or a part of the crop, is not, in the sense of the agricultural acts, "a cultivator of the soil," and entitled to incumber it with liens. But a contract by the owner of land, whereby he gives to another the possession of land for a year for the purpose of planting cotton, and the owner is to receive all of the crop above a certain quantity, is substantially a lease for a year, and gives the lessee such an interest in the crops as enables him to incumber them with liens for advances, subject to the landlord's lien by statute for rent to the extent of one third of the crop. Whaley v. Jacobson, 21 S. C. 51; Kennedy v. Reames, supra.

[4] On proof of an attempt of the person to whom the advances have been made to dispose of the crop or to defeat the lien, a warrant may be issued for a seizure and sale of the crop by the sheriff. G. S. § 2398.

[5] Code 1873, ch. 115, §§ 12, 13.

tended to have been, expended, to the extent of such advance or advances: provided, however, that an agreement in writing shall be entered into before any such advance is made to that effect, in which shall be specified the amount to be advanced, or in which a limit shall be fixed beyond which the advance or advances made from time to time during the year shall not go; which agreement shall be recorded in the clerk's office of the county in which the land lies, in the manner in which deeds are required by law to be recorded.

Any person about to dispose of the crops, or in any way to defeat the lien, may be restrained by a decree in equity.

V. *When the Lien Attaches.*

460. On general principles a delivery of goods by the owner to a third person, with the intention of passing a special property to a factor as security for advances, should be sufficient to confer a lien from the time of such delivery, though the factor might not obtain the actual possession of the goods till long afterward.[1] The delivery of possession to an agent or servant of the factor is a delivery to the factor himself, and his lien attaches from the time of such delivery.[2] It is immaterial whether the depositary be a common carrier, a shipmaster, or warehouseman, or any other bailee, provided only such bailee receives the goods on account of the factor who is to have a special property in them. It is material, however, whether the bailee's receipt of the goods for the factor be evidenced by some document, for the document is evidence of a change of property. In this respect a bill of lading or shipping receipt issued by a carrier is important; for in the absence of this or other sufficient evidence of an intention on the part of the consignor to vest the specific property in the consignee, the consignor may change the destination of the goods at any time before they come into the actual possession of the consignee.[3]

But unless the consignment be made in pursuance of an express agreement, or one implied from the dealings between the

---

[1] Gibson *v.* Stevens, 8 How. 384; Grove *v.* Brien, Ib. 429; Nesmith *v.* Dyeing Co. 1 Curtis, 130.

[2] M'Combie *v.* Davies, 7 East, 5, 8, per Lord Ellenborough; Clemson *v.* Davidson, 5 Binn. (Pa.) 392; Ganseford *v.* Dutillet, 13 Mart. (La.) 284;

Sumner *v.* Hamlet, 12 Pick. (Mass.) 76 ; Nesmith *v.* Dyeing Co. *supra.*

[3] Mitchel *v.* Ede, 11 Ad. & El. 888; Lewis *v.* Galena & C. U. R. R. Co. 40 Ill. 281; Strahorn *v.* Union Stock Yards & Transit Co. 43 Ill. 424.

parties, no lien attaches until the factor has accepted it upon the terms of the letter of consignment.[1]

461. The delivery of goods to a common carrier consigned to a factor under a contract made before that time, is such a delivery to the factor as will cause his lien to attach for advances made.[2]   Thus, if a planter deliver cotton to a carrier for a consignee in pursuance of an agreement that he should have the selling of the crop, and should reimburse himself from the proceeds of the sales for advances made by him to the planter to enable him to make the crop, such delivery is a delivery to the factor, whose lien immediately attaches to the cotton.

It is essential to the acquisition of a lien by a factor that he should have and retain possession of the property upon which he claims a lien. "A man cannot have a lien on goods unless he have in some sort the possession of the goods."[3]   But the possession may be constructive as well as actual.   It is only necessary that the goods should be so appropriated to the factor that they are essentially under his control.[4]

462. But a factor's lien cannot attach while the goods remain under the consignor's control.   A delivery of goods to a carrier is undoubtedly a delivery to the factor to whom they are consigned, if the delivery is made with the intention of passing a special property in the goods, and the consignor wholly parts with control of the goods.   But the rule is otherwise when goods are sent by a consignor on his own account without any previous arrangement, and they remain while in transit under the consignor's control.   Thus, a manufacturer put goods into the hands of a carrier at Providence, to be carried to Boston and left at a tavern where the carrier's wagon usually stopped.   The manufacturer then went to Boston and presented an invoice of the goods to his factor, stating that they were on the way, and obtained an advance on them.   While the goods were on their

[1] Winter v. Coit, 7 N. Y. 288.
[2] Nesmith v. Dyeing Co. 1 Curtis, 130; Holbrook v. Wight, 24 Wend. (N. Y.) 169; Grosvenor v. Phillips, 2 Hill (N. Y.) 147; Elliott v. Cox, 48 Ga. 39; Wade v. Hamilton, 30 Ga. 450; Hardeman v. De Vaughn, 49 Ga. 596.
[3] Hutton v. Bragg, 7 Taunt. 14, 15, 26, per Gibbs, C. J.   See, also, Hallett v. Bousfield, 18 Ves. 187, 188.
[4] Nesmith v. Dyeing Co. supra.

way they were attached at the suit of a creditor of the manufacturer. It was held that the factor had no lien.[1] Chief Justice Shaw, delivering the opinion, said: " Authorities were cited by the defendants to show that, when goods are consigned, a delivery to a common carrier is in law a delivery to the consignee. This is no doubt so where the goods are sent in pursuance of a previous order by the consignee. But in this case, so far from a previous order from the consignees, they were sent by the consignors for their own account, subject to their own order, and there would be no change of legal possession till some further act done or destination given to the goods by them; and before any such act done, the goods were attached. The new advance created no such lien, because no actual or constructive possession was obtained before the attachment."

463. A delivery of the bill of lading, or some authorized appropriation of the goods, is essential. While a delivery of a bill of lading amounts to a transfer of the property, the making of a bill of lading in the name of an agent, by direction of the principal, does not effect a transfer to such agent without delivery to him. A firm of merchants in Philadelphia, being indebted to their agent in Boston, without previous arrangement delivered on board a ship bound for Boston certain flour, taking bills of lading in three parts, by which the ship-owner agreed to deliver the flour to the agent. The ship-owner retained one of the bills of lading, and the merchants retained the others. The latter, finding themselves in a failing condition, and not having paid for the flour, delivered the bills of lading to their vendor, and returned to him the bill of the flour. The ship-owner refused to deliver possession to the vendor, who obtained possession by replevin. The ship-owner delivered his part of the bill of lading to the agent in Boston. It was held that the latter obtained no title to the flour.

There was no authorized delivery of a bill of lading to the consignee, and there was no possession or right of possession conferred upon him. The consignors, not having delivered the bills of lading, could countermand the shipment.[2]

[1] Baker v. Fuller, 21 Pick. (Mass.) 318, 321. See Farnum v. Boutelle, 13 Met. (Mass.) 159, 165, per Shaw, C. J.

[2] Walter v. Ross, 2 Wash. 283.

464. Of course, if a factor makes advances upon a mere executory agreement of his principal to make a consignment, he acquires no lien until there is some sort of a delivery to him, either actual or constructive. A factor's lien at common law is a right to retain a thing of which the factor has the actual or constructive possession. It cannot apply to property which the owner has merely agreed to send to his factor to secure and reimburse him for advances made upon it.[1] In equity, perhaps, a specific performance of the contract might be enforced, in case this should be indispensable to justice.[2] But at law the factor would have only a right of action for the non-performance of the agreement.

465. If the consignee has made advances upon the faith of a bill of lading, or shipping-receipt, a delivery to the carrier is a sufficient delivery to the consignee to enable him to maintain a lien upon the goods for his advances. A factor can claim a lien on goods in his possession either actual or constructive.[3]

A bill of lading is now regarded as a document of title, conferring the right of possession and constructively possession itself. Therefore a factor, upon receiving a bill of lading, has the right to take possession of the goods, and his lien attaches immediately.[4] The transaction is no longer an intended consignment, but it has become an actual consignment by the transmission and delivery of the bill of lading.[5]

But a consignment under a bill of lading is not essential to the vesting of a lien in the factor. That document may itself confer a title: it certainly manifests the intent of the consignor to have the carrier hold the property and deliver it to the factor; but this intent may be manifested in other ways. Any other competent evidence of such intent is admissible, and may be equally conclusive.[6]

[1] Kinloch v. Craig, 3 T. R. 783, 786; Bruce v. Wait, 3 M. & W. 15; Kinloch v. Craig, 3 T. R. 119; Farnum v. Boutelle, 13 Met. (Mass.) 159.

[2] Sullivan v. Tuck, 1 Md. Ch. 59.

[3] Davis v. Bradley, 28 Vt. 118; Dows v. Greene, 16 Barb. (N. Y.) 72; Holbrook v. Wight, 24 Wend. (N. Y.) 169; Grosvenor v. Phillips, 2 Hill (N. Y.) 147; Jordan v. James, 5 Ohio, 89,

101. See Rice v. Austin, 17 Mass. 197; Vallé v. Cerré, 36 Mo. 575.

[4] Haille v. Smith, 1 Bos. & Pul. 563; see, also, Bryans v. Nix, 4 M. & W. 775, 791; Vertue v. Jewell, 4 Camp. 31; Patten v. Thompson, 5 M. & S. 350, 356.

[5] Desha v. Pope, 6 Ala. 690.

[6] Nesmith v. Dyeing Co. 1 Curtis, 130, 135, per Curtis, J.; Bryans v. Nix, 4 M. & W. 775, 791, per Parke, B.

Yet it has been held in some cases that a delivery to a carrier is not sufficient to give a lien to a consignee who has made advances under an agreement that he should receive and sell the goods, and apply the proceeds towards the advances made, in preference to a creditor who has levied an attachment upon the goods before the shipping-receipts have been forwarded to the consignee, provided no bill of lading or shipping-receipt has been delivered to the consignee.[1]

Some authorities even go to the extent of holding that the factor must have actual possession before he can have a lien. Although the factor has a bill of lading of a consignment to him, and has made advances upon it and paid the freight, he has no lien without possession of the goods. The lien does not attach to goods in transit to the factor, or to goods of which the factor has only the right of possession.[2]

VI. *Waiver and Loss of the Liens.*

466. The lien of a factor is lost by parting with the possession of the goods on which the lien is claimed, so that neither the goods nor their proceeds are within his control.[3] If he reships them to his principal, he cannot afterwards stop them *in transitu.*[4] If in any way he allows his principal to have control of the goods, he waives his lien. But if he sells the goods to a third person, who is accountable to him for the price, his lien upon the goods is transferred to a lien on the price.[5] " Where a factor is in advance for goods by actual payment, or where he sells under a *del credere* commission, whereby he becomes responsible for the price, there is as little doubt that he has a lien on the price, though he has parted with the possession of the goods. If he acts under a *del credere* commission, he is to be considered, as between himself and the vendee, as the sole

[1] Elliot *v.* Bradley, 23 Vt. 217; Bank of Rochester *v.* Jones, 4 N. Y. 497; Desha *v.* Pope, 6 Ala. 690; Hodges *v.* Kimball, 49 Iowa, 577.

See Davis *v.* Bradley, 28 Vt. 118, in connection with Elliott *v.* Bradley, *supra.*

[2] Oliver *v.* Moore, 12 Heisk. (Tenn.) 482; Woodruff *v.* N. & C. R. R. Co. 2 Head. (Tenn.) 87.

[3] Kruger *v.* Wilcox, 1 Ambler, 252; Godin *v.* London Assurance Co. 1 Burr. 489, 494; Lickbarrow *v.* Mason, 6 East 21, 27 *n.*, per Buller, J.; Sharp *v.* Whipple, 1 Bosw. (N. Y.) 557; Bligh *v.* Davies, 28 Beav. 211; Matthews *v.* Menedger, 2 McLean, 145.

[4] Sweet *v.* Pym, 1 East, 4; Kruger *v.* Wilcox, *supra.*

[5] Houghton *v.* Matthews, 3 Bos. & Pul. 485, 494.

owner of the goods. There is no doubt of the authority of a factor to sell upon credit, though not particularly authorized by the terms of his commission so to do: but if he sell without a *del credere* commission, it is well established that he does not become a surety; the debt is due to the owner of the goods only." [1]

467. A broker who has not had possession of the merchandise sold by him, cannot maintain a lien against the proceeds of the sales, if these come into his hands after the principal has assigned such proceeds with notice to the broker of the assignment. An iron-master employed brokers to sell iron and collect the proceeds for a stipulated commission. A large contract of sale was made and several shipments made under it, the brokers making the collections. Upon a further shipment the iron-master assigned the bill for it with notice to the brokers, who collected the amount of the bill and claimed the right to deduct this from their commissions for the entire contract, both for the iron delivered and that which had not been delivered. It was held that they had no lien.[2] The court said: " They were simply brokers for the sale of the iron, and agents for the collection of the proceeds of the sale. They were not factors or commission merchants to whom the iron was consigned for sale. They had no possession of it, or right of possession of it, and therefore had no lien on it or its proceeds for their commissions. Their claim was a mere personal claim for the services rendered and to be rendered by them as brokers and agents for collection. They therefore could not retain this money as against the assignee whose claim, it had become before the money came into their hands."

468. The agent, however, may allow his principal to have temporary possession of the goods under an agreement reserving the right of lien, and still retain his lien. The possession of the principal is in such case regarded as the possession of the agent.[3]

Possession obtained by the principal by means of fraud or

---

[1] Houghton *v.* Matthews, 3 Bos. & Pul. 485, 489, per Chambre, J.

[2] Shoener *v.* Cabeen, 15 Phila. 65, affirmed by the Supreme Court.

[3] Reeves *v.* Capper, 6 Scott, 877, 884.

misrepresentation,[1] or by compulsion, does not destroy the factor's lien.[2]

If a factor at the request of his principal reships goods upon which he has made advances to the place from which they were consigned, he has the right to retain them in the hands of his agent at that place, until his advances are paid; and the principal cannot obtain the possession of them until he has paid or tendered the amount of such advances.[3]

469. Revival of the lien. — An insurance broker who has a lien, whether special or general, upon policies taken out for his principal, waives it by delivering them to his principal or his agent.[4] But if the policies are returned to the broker after a loss has occurred, to enable him to collect the insurance, his lien will revive. Such revival is not in strictness a revival of a pre-existing lien; but when the policies come back into the broker's possession a lien attaches, as it would upon new policies coming into his hands. But his lien for a general balance will not attach again if, at the time the policies come again into his hands, circumstances have occurred which would prevent the attaching of a general lien if they then for the first time came into his hands. If, for instance, the policies are not, at the time of their return to the broker, the property of the principal for whom the broker took them out, he can have no lien upon them.[5]

470. Disclosure of his principal does not defeat the factor's lien. A factor having a lien on goods does not preclude himself from insisting on his lien, by holding out his principal as the owner of the goods.[6]

Upon a sale by a factor to a purchaser to whom the principal is disclosed, the purchaser cannot offset a debt due to him from the principal so as to defeat the factor's lien.[7]

If a purchaser from a factor, having knowledge of the factor's lien, pays over the purchase-money to the principal, he renders

[1] Wallace v. Woodgate, 1 Car. & P. 575.

[2] Ex parte Good, 2 Deac. Bky. R. 389.

[3] Grieff v. Cowguill, 2 Dis. (O.) 58.

[4] Levy v. Barnard, 8 Taunt. 149; Sharp v. Whipple, 1 Bosw. (N. Y.) 557; Cranston v. Philadelphia Ins. Co. 5 Binn. (Pa.) 538.

[5] Levy v. Barnard, supra; Sharp v. Whipple, supra; Spring v. S. C. Ins. Co. 8 Wheat. 268.

[6] Seymour v. Hoadley, 9 Conn. 418.

[7] Alkyns v. Amber, 2 Esp. Cas. 493.

himself liable to the factor for the amount of his lien.[1] It is said that in order to charge the purchaser, the factor should, in addition to giving notice of his lien, offer to indemnify him from the consequences of an adverse suit by the principal;[2] but this is regarded by Judge Story as a questionable point.[3]

471. The lien ceases to exist upon the payment of the debt due him from his principal.[4] But a factor does not lose his lien by drawing a draft on his principal for the amount of his advances and charges, especially if the draft has not been paid, and the principal has become insolvent before the draft has become due.[5]

VII. *Enforcement of the Liens.*

472. As regards the enforcement of his lien a factor has an advantage over other persons having liens at common law or by custom ; for he is intrusted with the goods for the purpose of selling them, and ordinarily it is right to sell them and apply the proceeds to the payment of his principal's indebtedness to him.   He has a lien, therefore, not only upon the goods while he holds them, but when he has sold them his lien attaches to the proceeds.[6]

Moreover, by virtue of the Factors' Acts and recent statutes giving bills of lading a negotiable character, a factor may take advantage of his lien by pledging the goods received for sale, for these statutes enable third persons to deal with a factor for sale as though he were the absolute owner of the goods.

473. The case of a factor employed to purchase goods is different from that of one employed to sell them ; for while the latter has by the very nature of his employment the implied consent of his principal to sell the property and satisfy his lien from the proceeds, the former has no such implied consent; and therefore, while the factor for purchase has a lien on the goods purchased for advances made on the purchase, the additional right

---

[1] Drinkwater *v.* Goodwin, 1 Cowp. 251.

[2] Lord Mansfield in Drinkwater *v.* Goodwin, *supra.*

[3] Story, Agency, § 409.

[4] Woodruff *v.* N. & C. R. R. Co. 2

Head (Tenn.) 87 ; The Ship Packet, 3 Mason, 334.

[5] De Wolf *v.* Howland, 2 Paine, 356, 361.

[6] Hudson *v.* Granger, 5 B. & Ald. 27, 31, per Bayley, J. ; Jones on Pledges, §§ 333–353.

of selling the goods in order to reimburse himself for his advances is not conferred upon him.[1]

Moreover, a factor for purchase has no advantages under the Factors' Acts.[2]

474. A factor has a special property in the goods intrusted to him for sale. He has the right to manage the property and to sell it at his discretion, unless expressly restricted by instructions from his principal. He is not, however, the owner of the goods, and unless he sells them in the usual course of his business, or forecloses his lien as authorized by statute in some states, he has no right except to detain the goods until his demands against his principal are satisfied. He has no general property in the goods. " No doubt a factor who has made advances upon goods consigned to him may be regarded, in a limited sense and to the extent of his advances, as an owner. Yet, in reality, he has but a lien, with a right of possession of the goods for its security. He may protect that possession by suit against a trespasser upon it, and he may sell the property to reimburse advances, remaining, however, accountable to his consignor for any surplus. But, after all, he is not the real owner. He is only an agent of the owner for certain purposes. The owner may, at any time before his factor has sold the goods, reclaim the possession upon paying the advances made with interest and expenses. He has not lost his ownership by committing the custody of the goods to a factor and by receiving advances upon them. He is still entitled to the proceeds of any sale which may be made, even by his agent, the factor, subject to a charge of the advances and expenses. A factor, therefore, notwithstanding he may have made advances upon the property consigned to him, has but a limited right. That right is sometimes called a special property, but it is never regarded as a general ownership. At most it is no more than ownership of a lien or charge upon the property." [3]

475. A factor who has made advances, or incurred liabilities, on a consignment, has a right to sell so much of the consignment as may be necessary to reimburse such advances, unless there is some agreement between him and the consignor

---

[1] Lienard v. Dresslar, 3 Fost. Fin. 212.

[2] Jones on Pledges, §§ 344, 345.

[3] United States v. Villalonga, 23 Wall. 35, 41, per Strong, J.

which varies the right.[1] " Thus, for example, if, contemporaneous with the consignment and advances or liabilities, there are orders given by the consignor, which are assented to by the factor, that the goods shall not be sold until a fixed time, in such a case the consignment is presumed to be received by the factor subject to such orders ; and he is not at liberty to sell the goods to reimburse his advances or liabilities until after that time has elapsed.   The same rule will apply to orders not to sell below a fixed price ; unless, indeed, the consignor shall, after due notice and request, refuse to provide any other means to reimburse the factor.   And in no case will the factor be at liberty to sell the consignment contrary to the orders of the consignor, although he has made advances or incurred liabilities thereon, if the consignor stands ready and offers to reimburse and discharge such advances and liabilities.   On the other hand, where the consignment is made generally, without any specific orders as to the time or mode of sale, and the factor makes advances or incurs liabilities on the footing of such consignment, there the legal presumption is, that the factor is intended to be clothed with the ordinary rights of factors to sell, in the exercise of a sound discretion, at such time and in such mode as the usage of trade and his general duty require ; and to reimburse himself for his advances and liabilities out of the proceeds of the sale ; and the consignor has no right, by any subsequent orders given after advances have been made or liabilities incurred by the factor, to suspend or control this right of sale, except so far as respects the surplus of the consignment not necessary for the reimbursement of such advances or liabilities.   Of course, this right of the factor to sell to reimburse himself for his advances and liabilities, applies with stronger force to cases where the consignor is insolvent, and where, therefore, the consignment constitutes the only fund for indemnity." [2]

476. A factor may sell the goods at a fair market price and reimburse himself for advances, after a reasonable notice to his principal, although the latter has limited him to a higher price, or given express instructions not to sell.[3]

---

[1] Brown v. M'Gran, 14 Pet. 479 ; Brander v. Phillips, 16 Pet. 121 ; Beadles v. Hartmus, 7 Bax. (Tenn.) 476 ; Mooney v. Musser, 45 Ind. 115.

[2] Brown v. M'Gran, 14 Pet. 479, 495, per Story, J.

[3] Brander v. Phillips, supra ; Landis v. Gooch, 1 Dis. (O.) 176 ; Hallowell

The English rule is otherwise ; the factor there having no right
to sell against his principal's consent in order to satisfy his advances, after giving notice of his intention to do so.[1]

If a consignor, after advances have been made, instructs his

Fawcett, 30 Iowa, 491 ; Parker v.
Brancker, 22 Pick. (Mass.) 40, 46, per
Wilde, J. " But after such a reasonable time had elapsed, and a demand
had been made upon the principal to
repay the money advanced, and he
had refused so to do, he had no further power, by any principle of law
or justice, to control the factor's right
of sale to his prejudice. Such a
power would be inconsistent with the
understanding of the parties as it must
be presumed to have been when the
advances were made ; and it would
enable the principal to impair the factor's security at his own will and
pleasure for an unlimited time, if he
were disposed so to do. To sanction
such a right, would operate injuriously on the interests of consignees,
and would check the continuance of
those large advances by the aid of
which a flourishing trade has been carried on, for years past, to the great
profit of the mercantile community.
For although such advances may sometimes lead to over-trading, and may induce individuals to venture upon rash
speculations, yet it cannot be doubted
that on the whole they have contributed to the increase of the wealth and
prosperity of the country. The principle, therefore, involved in this case
is of great importance, and has been
considered by the court with great
care."

[1] Smart v. Sandars, 5 C. B. 895,
914. Chief Justice Wilde, delivering
the opinion of the court, said : " The
substantial question in this case is,
whether a factor who has made advances on account of his principal has
a right to sell the goods in his hands,
contrary to the orders of his principal,
on the principal's making default in
repaying those advances. It is now

settled law, that a factor has a lien
for his advances. But the defendant
claims more than a lien : he claims a
right, if the principal, when called on
to repay the advances, makes a default
in doing so, to sell the goods at such
prices and times as, in the exercise of
a sound discretion, he thinks best for
his principal. No case in an English
court can be produced in support of
this doctrine ; yet it is a right which
one would expect to find enforced
every day, if it existed. The silence
of our law-books is a strong argument
against the existence of such a right.
. . . But, it is said, a factor for sale
has an authority as such (in the absence of all special orders) to sell;
and when he afterwards comes under
advances, he thereby acquires an interest ; and, having thus an authority
and an interest, the authority becomes
thereby irrevocable.   The doctrine
here implied, that whenever there is
in the same power an authority and
an interest, the authority is irrevocable, is not to be admitted without
qualification. In the case of Raleigh
v. Atkinson, 6 M. & W. 676, goods
had been consigned to a factor for
sale, with a limit as to price. The
factor had a lien on the goods for advances ; and the principal, in consideration of those advances, agreed with
the factor that he should sell the goods
at the best market prices, and realize
thereon against his advances : the
court held that this authority was revocable, on the ground that there was
no consideration for the agreement.
Now in that case there was an authority given, and one which the principal was fully at liberty to give ; the
party to whom it was given had an interest in it, yet the authority was held
to be revocable."

factor not to sell for less than a certain price, and the factor replies that it is doubtful whether the goods could be sold at the price fixed, and that he would await further instructions, and that he would return the goods and remit an account if desired, after the lapse of a reasonable time without receiving any response from the consignor, the factor may sell the goods for the best price he can get in the market.[1]

477. In two or three states the right of the factor to reimburse himself by sales is declared by statute. Thus, in California,[2] a factor has a general lien, dependent on possession, for all that is due to him as such, upon all articles of commercial value that are intrusted to him by the same principal. A factor must obey the instructions of his principal to the same extent as any other employee, notwithstanding any advances he may have made to his principal upon the property consigned to him, except that, if the principal forbids him to sell at the market price, he may nevertheless sell for his reimbursement, after giving to his principal reasonable notice of his intention to do so, and of the time and place of sale, and proceeding in all respects as a pledgee.

In Georgia,[3] a factor's lien extends to all balances on general account, and attaches to the proceeds of the sale of goods consigned, as well as to the goods themselves. Peculiar confidence being reposed in the factor, he may, in the absence of instructions, exercise his discretion according to the general usages of the trade. In return, greater and more skilful diligence is required of him, and the most active good faith.

478. The factor's lien attaches to the proceeds of all sales made by him, whether these be in money or securities, so long as he retains them in his possession. The factor sells the goods, and thereby parts with the lien on the goods; but at the same moment he takes the proceeds, whether the money or security, which he may take in his own name, and thus, as between him and his principal, the lien is immediately transferred to the proceeds.[4]

[1] Mooney v. Musser, 45 Ind. 115.
[2] Codes & Stats. 1885, §§ 2027 and 3053 of Civ. Code; 2 Dakota Codes, 1883, § 1807 of Civ. Code.
[3] Code 1882, § 2111.
[4] Brander v. Phillips, 16 Pet. 121.

But the fact that the factor has a lien on the proceeds of a sale of goods on which he had a lien, does not authorize him to sell them in payment of his own debt, or in an unusual and irregular manner;[1] unless the principal's indebtedness to him equals or exceeds the value of the goods, so that the factor is substantially the owner.[2]

479. A factor who sells his principal's property, on which he has a lien for his services and advances, may retain the amount of his lien out of the proceeds, whether the sale was authorized or not. Thus, if the factor sell the goods after the death of his principal, without waiting for the appointment and consent of an administrator, in an action against him for the value of the goods, the measure of damages is the value of the property, less the amount of his lien; and if no question is made in regard to the price obtained, the damages would be such price less the amount of his lien.[3] Though the sale be a conversion, he may insist upon his lien in defence to an action for the conversion.

480. Bill of sale from principal to agent. — An agent under a *del credere* commission has a lien for his advances and commissions, and a bill of sale to him by his principal of the goods in his possession is in effect a foreclosure of his lien upon them. Even if his principal be insolvent at the time, the bill of sale, though perhaps technically illegal, will be sustained as a foreclosure of the lien. In such a case, when the agent has used large acceptances of his principal for his own benefit, he is not obliged, for the benefit of creditors of his principal, to set off these against his principal's indebtedness to him, and release the security of his lien to that extent. It was not unlawful for him to retain, with his principal's consent, his lien for the entire indebtedness.[4]

481. A factor may maintain an action for the debt, although he has a lien on the goods in his possession for the debt; and in an action by trustee process, or process of garnishment, by a third person against the factor, the principal may be

[1] Benny v. Rhodes, 18 Mo. 147.
[2] Eaton v. Bell, 5 B. & Ald. 34.
[3] Shaw v. Ferguson, 78 Ind. 547.
[4] Fourth Nat. Bank v. American Mills Co. 29 Fed. Rep. 611; S. C. 30 Ib. 420.

charged as trustee or garnishee, and judgment entered against the principal.[1]

482. In a few states there are statutory provisions for the foreclosure of factors' liens.[2] In Colorado,[3] when any commission merchant or warehouseman shall receive on consignment, or on storage, produce, merchandise, or other property, and shall make advances thereon, either to the owner or for freight and charges, and no time be agreed upon for the repayment of the same, it shall be lawful for the person who makes such advances, if the same be not paid to him within ninety days from the date of such advances, to cause the produce, merchandise, or property on which the advances were made to be advertised and sold ; and if a time for the repayment of such charges be agreed upon, then such notice of sale may be made immediately upon default of such payment. Twenty days' notice of the time and place of sale must be given to the consignor, and advertisement made for the same time in a daily paper (or, if in a weekly paper, for four weeks), published where such sale is to take place ; and if any surplus be left after paying the debt and charges, the same shall be paid to the rightful owner upon demand made within ninety days.

In Missouri,[4] when any commission merchant or warehouseman shall receive on consignment produce, merchandise, or other property, and shall make advances thereon, either to the owner or for freight and charges, it shall be lawful for the person who may make such advances, if the same be not paid to him within sixty days from the date of such advances, to cause the produce, merchandise, or property on which the advances were made to be advertised and sold at auction, or so much thereof as will pay the debt, first having given twenty days' notice of the time and place of sale to the consignor, and by advertisement in a daily paper (or, if in a weekly paper, four weeks) published where such sale is to take place ; and if any surplus be left after paying the debt, the same shall be paid to the rightful owner upon demand made within sixty days.

---

[1] Mobile & Ohio R. R. Co. v. Whitney, 39 Ala. 468.

[2] In some states the statutes authorizing common carriers to sell goods in satisfaction of their liens apply also to commission merchants and factors ; as in **Pennsylvania**, § 364, and **Delaware**, § **345**; G. S. 1883, §§ 3432–3436.

[3] R. S. 1870, §§ 6278–6281.

[4] R. S. 1878, § 3347.

In Wisconsin,[4] every person having a lien as a consignee by statute, or by common law, may, in case such debt remain unpaid for three months, and the value of the property affected thereby does not exceed one hundred dollars, sell such property at public auction, and apply the proceeds of such sale to the payment of the amount due him, and the expenses of such sale. Notice, in writing, of the time and place of such sale, and of the amount claimed to be due, shall be given to the owner of such property personally, or by leaving the same at his place of abode, if a resident of this state, and if not, by publication thereof once in each week for three weeks successively next before the time of sale in some newspaper published in the county in which such lien accrues, if there be one, and if not, by posting such notice in three public places in such county. If such property exceed in value one hundred dollars, then such lien may be enforced against the same by action in any court having jurisdiction.

CHAPTER X.

483. The finder of a chattel has at common law no lien upon it for the labor and expenses he may have been at in securing it, and in taking care of it for the owner. A quantity of timber belonging to one Nicholson was accidentally loosened from a dock in which it was placed on the bank of the Thames, and was carried a considerable distance by the tide and left at low water upon a towing-path. Chapman, finding it there, placed it in a safe place beyond the reach of the tide at high water. The owner then demanded the timber of Chapman, who refused to deliver it up unless a certain sum should be paid to him for his trouble in securing and taking care of the timber. In an action of trover by the owner against Chapman, the court held that he had no lien on the timber.[1] Lord Chief Justice Eyre, delivering the opinion, said: "This is a case of mere finding and taking care of the thing found for the owner. This is a good office and meritorious, at least in the moral sense of the word, and certainly entitles the party to some reasonable recompense from the bounty, if not from the justice, of the owner; and of which, if it were refused, a court of justice would go as far as it could go toward enforcing the payment. . . . So it would be if a horse had strayed, and was taken up by some good-natured man, and taken care of by him till, at some trouble and perhaps at some expense, he had found out the owner. So it would be in every case of finding that can be stated, — the claim to recompense differing in degree, but not in principle; which, therefore, reduces the merits of this case to this short question, whether every man who finds the property of another, which happens to have been lost or mislaid, and voluntarily puts himself to some trouble and expense to preserve the thing and to find out the owner, has a lien upon it for the casual, fluctuating, and uncertain amount of the recompense which he may reason-

---

[1] Nicholson v. Chapman, 2 H. Black. 254, 258.

ably deserve. It is enough to say that there is no instance of
such a lien having been claimed and allowed; the case of the
pointer dog [1] was a case in which it was claimed and disallowed,
and it was thought too clear a case to bear an argument. Principles of public policy and commercial necessity support the
lien in the case of salvage. Not only public policy and commercial necessity do not require that it should be established in
this case, but very great inconvenience may be apprehended
from it if it were to be established. . . . I mentioned, in the
course of the cause, another great inconvenience, namely, the
situation in which an owner seeking to recover his property in
an action of trover will be placed, if he is at his peril to make
a tender of a sufficient recompense before he brings his action :
such an owner must always pay too much, because he has no
means of knowing exactly how much he ought to pay, and because he must tender enough. I know there are cases in which
the owner of property must submit to this inconvenience, but
the number of them ought not to be increased. Perhaps it is
better for the public that these voluntary acts of benevolence
from one man to another, which are charities and moral duties,
but not legal duties, should depend altogether for their reward
upon the moral duty of gratitude. But at any rate it is fitting
that he who claims the reward in such case should take upon
himself the burden of proving the nature of the service which
he has performed, and the *quantum* of the recompense which he
demands, instead of throwing it upon the owner to estimate it
for him at the hazard of being nonsuited in an action of trover."

484. **A riparian owner has no lien on property cast adrift
on his land.**[2] If a bridge be swept away by a flood, and parts
of it lodge upon the land of a riparian owner who removes them
at his own expense after the owner of the bridge had refused
to do so, the land-owner is liable in trover for a conversion of the
fragments of the bridge.[3] A riparian owner cannot even claim
a lien for preserving a raft cast upon his land.[4] The claim in
these cases is very unlike that of salvage of goods at sea. The

[1] Binstead *v.* Buck, 2 W. Bl.
1117.

[2] Nicholson *v.* Chapman, 2 H. Bl.
254; Baker *v.* Hoag, 3 Barb. (N. Y.)
203; *S. C.* 7 Ib. 113.

[3] Foster *v.* Juniata Bridge Co. 16
Pa. St. 393.

[4] Etter *v.* Edwards, 4 Watts (Pa.),
63, 65.

distinction between salvage, properly so called, and the taking care of goods found upon the banks of rivers, is fully pointed out by Chief Justice Eyre, in the leading case already noticed:[1] "The only difficulty that remained with any of us, after we had heard this case argued, was upon the question whether this transaction could be assimilated to salvage. The taking care of goods left by the tide upon the banks of a navigable river, communicating with the sea, may in a vulgar sense be said to be salvage; but it has none of the qualities of salvage, in respect of which the laws of all civilized nations, the laws of Oleron, and our own laws in particular, have provided that a recompense should be a lien upon the goods which have been saved. Goods carried by sea are necessarily and unavoidably exposed to the perils which storms, tempests, and accidents far beyond the reach of human foresight to prevent, are hourly creating, and against which it too often happens that the greatest diligence and the most strenuous exertions of the mariner cannot protect them. When goods are thus in imminent danger of being lost, it is most frequently at the hazard of the lives of those who save them that they are saved. Principles of public policy dictate to civilized and commercial countries, not only the propriety, but even the absolute necessity, of establishing a liberal recompense for the encouragement of those who engage in so dangerous a service. Such are the grounds upon which salvage stands. . . . But see how very unlike this salvage is to the case now under consideration. In a navigable river, within the flux and reflux of the tide, but at a great distance from the sea, pieces of timber lie moored together in convenient places; carelessness, a slight accident, perhaps a mischievous boy, casts off the mooring-rope, and the timber floats from the place where it was deposited, till the tide falls, and leaves it again somewhere upon the banks of the river. . . . The timber is found lying upon the banks of the river, and is taken into the possession and under the care of the defendant, without any extraordinary exertions, without the least personal risk, and in truth with very little trouble. It is, therefore, a case of mere finding, and taking care of the thing found for the owner."

485. Whether a finder can recover compensation for his services in respect of the property found seems to have been

[1] Nicholson v. Chapman, 2 H. Bl. 254.

an unsettled question at the time of the decision of Nicholson *v.* Chapman,[1] in 1793. But in a Kentucky case, in 1836[2] it was held that the finder may recover for his time and expenses, on the ground that there is an implied request on the part of one who has lost a chattel to every one else to aid him in recovering it. It now seems to be an established doctrine that the finder is entitled to be paid his reasonable expenses incurred in respect of the thing found.[3] Thus, the owner of a boat, who has taken it from a person who found it adrift on tidewater and brought it to shore, is liable for the necessary expense of preserving the boat while it remained in his possession. " His claim is for the reasonable expenses of keeping and repairing the boat after he had brought it to the shore ; and the single question is, whether a promise is to be implied by law from the owner of a boat, upon taking it from a person who has found it adrift on tidewater and brought it ashore, to pay him for the necessary expenses of preserving the boat while in his possession. We are of opinion that such a promise is to be implied. The plaintiff, as the finder of the boat, had the lawful possession of it, and the right to do what was necessary for its preservation. Whatever might have been the liability of the owner if he had chosen to let the finder retain the boat, by taking it from him he made himself liable to pay the reasonable expenses incurred in keeping and repairing it."[4]

486. In the absence of an agreement, a landlord has no lien, unless he is an innkeeper, on chattels left on his premises by an outgoing tenant.[5] The law applicable to cases of deposits by the finding of goods lost on land, and deposits of property made by the force of winds or floods, which are termed involuntary deposits, is applicable to the case of goods left by the outgoing tenant. The law in those cases gives no lien for the care and expense of the finder in keeping and preserving the property.[6] It is only in case that the loser offers a reward

---

[1] 2 H. Bl. 254.

[2] Reeder *v.* Anderson, 4 Dana (Ky.), 193.

[3] Chase. *v.* Corcoran, 106 Mass. 286; Amory *v.* Flyn, 10 Johns. (N. Y.) 102; *S. C.* 6 Am. Dec. 316; Tome *v.* Four Cribs of Lumber, Taney, 533, 547; *contra*, Watts *v.* Ward, 1 Oregon, 86.

[4] Chase *v.* Corcoran, 106 Mass. 286, 288, per Gray, J.

[5] Preston *v.* Neale, 12 Gray (Mass.), 222.

[6] Preston *v.* Neale, *supra*, per Metcalf, J.

for the restoration of the property that the finder has a lien upon it to the extent of the reward so offered.

487. Reward offered. — Though the finder of lost property has no lien upon it at common law for his services in recovering and restoring it to the owner, yet, if the owner has offered a reward for the return of the property, or has entered into an agreement to pay for its discovery and restoration, the finder has a lien upon the property for the payment of the reward,[1] or of the labor and expense of rescuing it under the agreement.[2] The finder in such case is entitled to receive his compensation before he parts with the possession of the property. He stands in the same position as a mechanic or artisan who performs services upon property at the request of the owner; and, like a mechanic or artisan, he has a lien upon the property itself for the amount of his compensation.[3]

488. An offer of a reward becomes a contract with any one who complies with the terms of the offer. Thus, where one offered a reward of twenty dollars for the return of a watch which he had lost, but refused to pay the reward, and the finder refused to deliver the watch, in an action of trover by the owner

---

[1] Wentworth v. Day, 3 Met. (Mass.) 352; Preston v. Neale, 12 Gray (Mass.), 222; Cummings v. Gann, 52 Pa. St. 484; Wood v. Pierson, 45 Mich. 313, 314; Harson v. Pike, 16 Ind. 140; Wilson v. Guyton, 8 Gill (Md.), 213, 215. In the latter case Dorsey, C. J., said: "If any article of personal property has been lost, or strayed away, or escaped from its owner, and he offers a certain reward, payable to him who shall recover and deliver it back to his possession, it is but a just exposition of his offer, that he did not expect that he who had expended his time and money in the pursuit and recovery of the lost or escaped property would restore it to him but upon the payment of the proffered reward, and that, as security for this, he was to remain in possession of the same until its restoration to its owner, and then the payment of the reward was to be a simultaneous act. It is no forced construction of his act to say that he designed to be so understood by him who should become entitled to the reward. It is, consequently, a lien created by contract. It is for the interest of property-holders so to regard it. It doubles their prospect of a restoration to their property. To strangers it is everything; the few, indeed, would spend their time and money, and incur the risks incident to bailment, but from a belief in the existence of such a lien. Public convenience, sound policy, and all the analogies of the law, lend their aid in support of such a principle."

[2] Baker v. Hoag, 7 Barb. (N. Y.) 113.

[3] Baker v. Hoag, supra.

against the finder, judgment was given for the defendant.[1] Chief
Justice Shaw, delivering the opinion in the leading case of Wentworth *v.* Day, said : " The duty of the plaintiff to pay the stipulated reward arises from the promise contained in his advertisement.   That promise was, that whoever should return his watch
to the printing-office should receive twenty dollars.   No other
time or place of payment was fixed.   The natural, if not the
necessary, implication is that the acts of performance were to be
mutual and simultaneous, the one to give up the watch on payment of the reward, the other to pay the reward on receiving
the watch.   Such being, in our judgment, the nature and legal
effect of this contract, we are of opinion that the defendant, on
being ready to deliver up the watch, had a right to receive the
reward, and was not bound to surrender the actual possession of
it till the reward was paid ; and therefore a refusal to deliver
it without such payment was not a conversion.   It was competent for the loser of the watch to propose his own terms.   He
might have promised to pay the reward at a given time after the
watch should have been restored, or in any other manner inconsistent with a lien for the reward on the article restored ; in
which case, no such lien would exist.   The person restoring the
watch would look only to the personal responsibility of the ad-
vertiser.   It was for the latter to consider whether such an offer
would be equally efficacious in bringing back his lost property
as an offer of a reward secured by a pledge of the property
itself, or whether, on the contrary, it would not afford to the
finder a strong temptation to conceal it.   With these motives
before him, he made an offer to pay the reward on the restoration of the watch ; and his subsequent attempt to get the watch
without performing his promise is equally inconsistent with the
rules of law and the dictates of justice."

489. A telegram to a sheriff offering a reward for the recovery of a stolen horse is a general offer, and binds the
sender to any person who recovers the horse, and gives a lien on
it till the reward is paid.   The reward in this case was claimed
by one Cummings, an innkeeper, who had previously detained
the horses of two men who had stopped at his inn, suspecting
that the horses had been stolen.   He sent for the sheriff and had
one of the men arrested.   When the sheriff received the telegram,

---

[1] Wentworth *v.* Day, 3 Met. (Mass.) 352, 356 ; Harson *v.* Pike, 16 Ind. 140.

he showed it to Cummings, who had the horse in his possession. The sheriff claimed the reward, and it was paid to him; and the owner of the horse took it by replevin from Cummings. Judge Thompson, delivering the opinion of the court,[1] said: "The recovery of the property was the object, and the hands by which the result should be accomplished were nothing to the owner. It was as much an offer to Cummings as to the sheriff or anybody. It amounted to nothing unless to a successful party. It was but an offer until its terms were complied with. When that was done, it thenceforth became a binding contract, which the offerer was bound to perform his share of. . . . The service is to be performed for a reward offered, not especially to any one, but to any one who may undertake and perform the request. It is valuable toward both the owner and his property, and why should there not be a lien? The owner may live at a distance, and if the finder is required to yield up the property and then look to the owner, it might be great injustice to him; whereas it is no injury to the owner who constitutes the finder his bailee by his advertisement to perform the services of seizure and taking care of the property."

490. To entitle a person to a reward he must show a rendition of services with a view of obtaining the reward. The finding of property lost, and advertising it without knowledge of the offer of a reward, does not entitle the finder to a reward offered. If a finder has any claim, it is in fact a claim upon a contract. Where a contract is proposed to all the world, in the form of an offer of a reward for the recovery, or for information leading to the recovery, of property lost, any one may assent to it, and it is binding if he complies with the terms of the offer; but he cannot assent without knowledge of the proposition.[2] But it is not necessary that notice should be given to the party offering the reward that his proposal is being acted upon.[3]

---

[1] Cummings v. Gann, 52 Pa. St. 484, 490. See, also, Wentworth v. Day, 3 Met. (Mass.) 352, 354, per Shaw, C. J.

[2] Howland v. Lounds, 51 N. Y. 604. And see Fitch v. Snedaker, 38 N. Y. 248; Lee v. Flemingsburg, 7 Dana (Ky.), 28. The Court of Appeals of Kentucky departed from this authority in Auditor v. Ballard, 9 Bush. 572. Williams v. Carwardine, 4 B. & Ad. 621, is sometimes cited to the contrary of the proposition stated in the text, but the case is not in point.

[3] Harson v. Pike, 16 Ind. 140.

491. A finder must comply with all the conditions of an offer of reward. If this be payable at a certain place, it must be demanded at that place. But a demand at a place named may be waived.[1]

492. But no lien is implied by an offer of "a liberal reward." Under such an offer it may well be asked, as it was by the Court of Appeals of Maryland,[2] "Who was to be the arbiter of the liberality of the offered reward? It cannot be supposed that the owner, by his offer, designed to constitute the recoverer of his property the exclusive judge of the amount to be paid him as a reward. And it is equally unreasonable and unjust to say that the owner should be such exclusive judge. In the event of a difference between them upon the subject, the amount to be paid must be ascertained by the judgment of the appropriate judicial tribunal. This would involve the delays incident to litigation, and it would be a gross perversion of the intention of the owner to infer, from his offered reward, an agreement on his part that he was to be kept out of the possession of his property till all the delays of litigation were exhausted. To the bailee thus in possession of property, such a lien would rarely be valuable except as a means of oppression and extortion; and therefore the law will never infer its existence either from the agreement of the parties, or in furtherance of public convenience or policy."

493. An offer of a reward for lost property may be withdrawn at any time, until something is accomplished in pursuance of the offer. Services afterwards rendered by one who was ignorant of the withdrawal of the offer do not entitle him to the reward.[3] "Until something is done in pursuance of it, it is a mere offer, and may be revoked. But if, before it is retracted, one so far complies with it as to perform the labor for which the reward is stipulated, it is the ordinary case of labor done on request, and becomes a contract to pay the stipulated compensation. It is not a gratuitous service, because something is done

---

[1] Wood v. Pierson, 45 Mich. 313, 317. And see Wentworth v. Day, 3 Met. (Mass.) 352.

[2] Wilson v. Guyton, 8 Gill (Md.), 213, 215, per Dorsey, C. J. See Shuey v. United States, 92 U. S. 73.

[3] Wentworth v. Day, *supra*; Shuey v. United States, *supra*.

which the party was not bound to do, and without such offer might not have done." [1]

494. A finder may be entitled to a portion of a reward offered proportioned to the value of the property returned. Thus, where a person had lost from his pocket a number of bank-bills, contained in a paper wrapper, amounting to more than fifteen hundred dollars, he published an advertisement, in which he described the money lost, and offered a reward of two hundred dollars to any person who would find and restore the same. The plaintiff having seen the advertisement, and having observed an unusual number of bank-bills in the possession of a man whom he suspected of having stolen or found them, gave notice to the defendant, who in consequence recovered a large part of the sum lost. It was held that the finder was entitled to be paid a *pro rata* proportion of the reward offered.[2] "An offer of a reward might undoubtedly be so expressed as to exclude any apportionment; for the owner of the property might prescribe his terms for the restoration of it, he having a right to reclaim it wherever it might be found. But where a compensation is offered in general terms, like those in the present case, it is consistent with honesty and fair dealing, and with the interest of the loser himself, and not inconsistent with any principle of law, that a proportion of the reward should be recovered, according to the sum actually restored." [3]

495. A detective officer may have a lien upon property recovered from the wrongful possession of another, under an agreement that he shall be paid for his services; but he has no lien in case the wrongful holder has already sent the property to the owner, and the officer compels him by arrest to recall it before it was delivered to the owner.[4]

496. A reward for lost property is not waived by insisting on its identification.[5] It is a question of fact for the jury whether the finder of a chattel has given a fair and reasonable

---

[1] Wentworth v. Day, 3 Met. (Mass.) 352, per Shaw, C. J.; and see Symmes v. Frazier, 6 Mass. 344, per Parker, J.

[2] Symmes v. Frazier, *supra;* S. C. 4 Am. Dec. 142.

[3] Per Parker, J., in Symmes v. Frazier, *supra.*

[4] Hoffman v. Barthelmess, 63 Ga. 759; S. C. 36 Am. Rep. 129.

[5] Wood v. Pierson, 45 Mich. 313.

opportunity for its identification before restoring it, and whether
the claimant should have been given an opportunity to inspect
it in order to decide whether it belonged to him. Lord Coke
states the duties of a finder thus : [1] " If a man therefore which
findes goods, if he be wise, he will then search out the right
owner of them, and so deliver them unto him; if the owner
comes unto him and demands them and he answers him, that it is
not known unto him whether he be the true owner of the goods,
or not, and for this cause he refuseth to deliver them, this refusal is no conversion, if he keep them for him." In a recent
decision in Michigan on this point, Mr. Justice Graves, after
quoting this passage, says : [2] " Lord Coke very clearly enforces
the right and duty of the finder to be certain of the true owner
before he makes delivery. As he is bound to hold for the true
owner, and is liable in case of misdelivery, the law makes it his
duty as well as his right, even when there is no reward, to
' search out,' or, in other language, find the ' right owner,' or see
to it that he submits to no other than the ' right owner.' Undoubtedly, if the finder's conduct was such that a jury would,
under the circumstances of the case, feel satisfied that he was
actually perverse and unreasonable, and pursued a course which
was adapted to baffle fair investigation, instead of maintaining
the attitude of a man whose duty it was, in the quaint terms of
Lord Coke, to ' search out the right owner,' it would be just to
regard him as having detained the property unlawfully."

497. In several states there are statutes which confer a
lien upon the finder of a chattel for his services and expenses
in recovering it and taking care of it. Some of these statutes
are confined wholly to estrays, others apply to goods, and still
others to both estrays and goods.[3]

It is not practicable to give a statement of the provisions of
these statutes, and therefore only a reference is made to them,
with the exception only of the statute in force in California and
Dakota Territory, which is given on account of its comprehen-
siveness and brevity as well.

[1] Isaack v. Clark, 2 Bulst. 306, 312.
[2] Wood v. Pierson, 45 Mich. 313, 320.
[3] Connecticut : R. S. 1875, ch. 9, §§ 7–9.
Illinois : Annotated Stats. 1885, ch. 50.

Indiana : R. S. 1881, §§ 4803–4833.
Iowa : R. Code 1880, §§ 1509–1522.
Maine : R. S. 1883, ch. 98.
Oregon : G. L. ch. 18.

In California[1] and Dakota Territory[2] it is provided that —

The finder of a thing is entitled to compensation for all expenses necessarily incurred by him in its preservation, and for any other service necessarily performed by him about it, and to a reasonable reward for keeping it.

The finder of a thing may exonerate himself from liability at any time by placing it on storage with any responsible person of good character, at a reasonable expense.

The finder of a thing may sell it if it is a thing which is commonly the subject of sale, when the owner cannot, with reasonable diligence, be found, or, being found, refuses upon demand to pay the lawful charges of the finder, in the following cases : 1. When the thing is in danger of perishing or of losing the greater part of its value ; or, 2, When the lawful charges of the finder amount to two thirds of its value.

A sale under the provisions of the last section must be made in the same manner as the sale of a thing pledged. The owner of a thing may exonerate himself from the claims of the finder by surrendering it to him in satisfaction thereof.

[1] Civ. Code, 1864–1872.   [2] Ib. 1064–1072.

CHAPTER XI.

I. *To what Property it Attaches.*

498. An innkeeper has a particular lien, for the reason that he is under an obligation to serve the public. He is bound to receive a guest and his ordinary luggage, and is liable for the value of this if stolen. His liability for the goods of his guest is a special and extraordinary one, and is founded upon grounds of public policy. In this respect his lien is similar to that of a common carrier, though the two liens are distinct, and are not to be confounded. The innkeeper, in return for the obligation imposed upon him to entertain any guest who may come to his house, and the liability incurred for the safe keeping of his goods, is invested with a lien upon the property of his guest; and this lien has some exceptional characteristics. Perhaps the most noteworthy of these characteristics is that the lien is not confined to property owned by the guest, but attaches to all property brought with him, and in good faith received by the innkeeper as the property of the guest.[1]

499. An innkeeper has a lien upon the goods of a third person brought to the inn by a guest. At first the judges were equally divided on the question whether an innkeeper had a lien upon a horse brought to the inn by a stranger.[2] In the next case they were divided three to one in favor of the lien.[3] In Johnson v. Hill[4] it was stated by counsel to have been held

---

[1] Cook v. Prentice, 13 Oregon, 482; S. C. 25 Am. L. Reg. (N. S.) 700; Black v. Brennan, 5 Dana (Ky.), 310. See, also, Mowers v. Fethers, 61 N. Y. 34 ; Shaw v. Berry, 31 Me. 478.

[2] Skipwith v. ———, 1 Bulst. 170 ; S. C. 3 Ib. 271.

[3] Robinson v. Walter, 3 Bulst. 269 ; S. C. 1 Roll. R. 449 ; Poph. 127.

[4] 3 Stark. 172 (1822).

by all the judges, that even in the case where a robber had brought a horse, which he had stolen, to an inn, the innkeeper was entitled to receive compensation from the owner before the latter could insist on a redelivery to himself.   Chief Justice Abbot said he had no doubt as to the law as stated.

Thus it has become the settled law with reference to this lien, that there is no distinction between the goods of a guest and those of a third person brought by a guest, and in good faith received by the innkeeper as the property of the guest.[1]   The innkeeper cannot investigate the title of property brought by his guests, and is bound, unless there is something to excite suspicion, to receive, not only the guest, but his horse or other property brought by him, as belonging to him because it is in his possession.   Therefore, if a guest departs leaving his horse, and after many months it appears that the guest had stolen the horse, and the owner demands possession, the innkeeper may retain him for his charges in keeping him.[2]   Of course there is no personal obligation on the part of the owner to pay the charges for keep-

---

[1] Robinson v. Waller, 3 Bulst. 269; S. C. 1 Roll. Rep. 449 n.; Johnson v. Hill, 3 Stark. 172; Yorke v. Grenaugh, 2 Ld. Raym. 866; S. C. 1 Salk. 388; Snead v. Watkins, 1 C. B. N. S. 267; Turrill v. Crawley, 13 Q. B. 197; Threfall v. Borwick, L. R. 7 Q. B. 711; Manning v. Hollenbeck, 27 Wis. 202; Fox v. McGregor, 11 Barb. (N. Y.) 41; Grinnell v. Cook, 3 Hill (N. Y.), 485; Black v. Brennan, 5 Dana (Ky.), 310; Woodworth v. Morse, 18 La. Ann. 156; Peet v. McGraw, 25 Wend. (N. Y.) 653. In Waugh v. Denham, 16 Irish C. L. 405, 410, Pigot C. B., said, as to the reason of this rule: "When an innkeeper receives a guest, with the horse on which he travels, or when, in the ordinary course of business, a carrier receives goods from the possession of the sender, he deals with a person having all the *indicia* of property.   Possession is, in itself, *primâ facie* evidence of ownership To encumber an innkeeper or a carrier with the obligation of inquiring and determining the relation in which the guest or the sender of the goods stands in reference to his possession of what he brings, would be totally inconsistent with the relations in which both the innkeeper and the carrier stand towards the public, for whose benefit they profess to act, and do act, in their respective callings. The business of either could not be carried on if, in the one case, the doors of the inn were closed against a traveller, or, in the other, if the carrier's conveyance were delayed at each stopping-place on his journey until such inquiry should be made. But no such mischief can result from the qualification which Lord Tenterden applied to the rights and obligations of an innkeeper.   There can, I apprehend, be no room for doubt that a similar qualification applies to the rights and liabilities of a carrier, and that if a carrier knows (for example) that a thief gives him the goods of the true owner to carry, he cannot charge the owner for the service which he has knowingly rendered to the thief in the carrying of the goods."

[2] Black v. Brennan, *supra*.

ing the horse ; and if, upon a sale by virtue of the lien, the proceeds are insufficient to pay the innkeeper's charges, he has no claim, and can have no judgment or decree against the owner for, the balance.[1]

An innkeeper has a lien on a carriage brought to the inn by a guest for its standing-room, though the carriage does not belong to the guest himself.[2]

500. It has sometimes been attempted to limit this principle, that the lien of an innkeeper attaches to goods of a third person brought to an inn by a guest, to such articles and property as a guest may ordinarily travel with.

This claim was set up in a case where an attorney's clerk had put up at a public house and had departed without paying his bill, but leaving the lawyer's blue bag and his letter-book behind him. The innkeeper wrote to the lawyer stating that the clerk had left his bill unpaid, and that he held the letter-book, which he would forward on receiving the amount of the bill. The attorney's counsel contended that the innkeeper's lien extends only to those things with which a man ordinarily travels ; but the court were of opinion that there was a clear case of lien.[3] The bag, they said, was brought by the guest to the inn, with some things of his own in it, in the ordinary way. The innkeeper could have no suspicion that it contained property belonging to a third person. They regarded the case as very distinguishable from Broadwood v. Granara,[4] in which case there are *dicta* to the effect that an innkeeper is not bound to receive and protect as the property of a guest such an article as a piano.[5]

501. It is now settled, however, that the lien is not limited to such things as a guest ordinarily takes with him. An innkeeper who receives a piano in his character as innkeeper, believing it to be the property of his guest, is entitled to a lien

---

[1] Black v. Brennan, 5 Dana (Ky.), 310.

[2] Turrill v. Crawley, 13 Q. B. 197.

[3] Snead v. Watkins, 1 C. B. N. S. 267. The bill seems to have been somewhat after the style of Falstaff's — but one halfpennyworth of bread to this intolerable deal of sack. (*King Henry* IV., Part I. Act ii. Sc. 4.)

[4] 10 Ex. 417.

[5] Broadwood v. Granara, 10 Ex. 417. The real ground of the decision in this case was that the innkeeper knew that the piano was the property of the manufacturer, who had loaned it to the guest.

upon it for his guest's board and lodging, although in fact the piano is the property of another person, who had consigned it to the guest to sell on commission.[1]   In a case before the Queen's Bench,[2] where an innkeeper had received in good faith a piano as part of the goods of his guest, it was held that he had a lien upon it.   Mr. Justice Lush said : " The innkeeper's lien is not restricted to such things as a travelling guest brings with him in journeying ; the contrary has been laid down long ago.   It extends to all goods the guest brings with him, and the innkeeper receives as his. . . . If he has this lien as against the guest, the cases have established beyond all doubt that he has the same right as against the real owner of the article, if it has been brought to the inn by the guest as owner." And in the same case Mr. Justice Quain said : " There is no authority for the proposition that the lien of the innkeeper only extends to goods which a traveller may be ordinarily expected to bring with him. . . . The liability, as shown by the old cases, extends to all things brought to the inn as the property of the guest, and so received, even a chest of charters or obligations ; and why not a pianoforte ? If, therefore, the innkeeper be liable for the loss, it seems to follow he must also have a lien upon them. And if he has a lien upon them as against the guest, the two cases cited (and there are more) show that if the thing be brought by the guest as owner, and the landlord takes it in, thinking it is the guest's own, he has the same rights against the stranger — the real owner — as against the guest."

502. **If the innkeeper knows that the goods brought to the inn by a guest belong to another person, he can have no lien upon them for the guest's personal expenses.**[3]   Thus, if a manufacturer sends a piano to a guest at a hotel for his temporary use, and the hotel-keeper knows that it does not belong to the guest, he acquires no lien upon it.[4]

503. **The innkeeper's lien can only attach to goods received by one in his capacity as innkeeper.**[5]   Neither the lia-

---

[1] Cook v. Prentice, 13 Oregon, 482 ; S. C. 25 Am. L. Reg. 700 ; and see note to same, p. 704, by C. A. Robbins ; Jones v. Morrill, 42 Barb. (N. Y.) 623.

[2] Threfall v. Boswick, L. R. 7 Q. B. 711 ; affirmed, 10 Ib. 210.

[3] Johnson v. Hill, 3 Stark. 172 ; Broadwood v. Granara, 10 Ex. 417, 425.

[4] Broadwood v. Granara, *supra.*

[5] Binns v. Pigot, 9 Car. & P. 208 ; Orchard v. Rackstraw, 9 C. B. 698 ;

bility nor the privileges of an innkeeper attach to one who is not the keeper of a public house. The owner of a steamship carrying passengers for hire is not an innkeeper, although the passenger pays a round sum for transportation, board, and lodging.[1] An innkeeper may also be a stable-keeper ; but as an innkeeper he cannot claim a lien for stabling the horses of one who is not a guest,[2] but, for instance, a mail contractor.[3] Where an innkeeper receives horses and a carriage to stand at livery, the circumstance that the owner, at a subsequent time, occasionally took refreshment at the inn, and sent a friend to be lodged there at his charge, was held not to entitle the innkeeper to a lien in respect of any part of the demand.[4]

504. An innkeeper has no lien on a horse placed in his stable, unless placed there by a guest, or by his authority.[5] Thus, if a person is stopped upon suspicion, and his horse is placed at an inn by the police, the innkeeper has no lien on the horse, and if he sells him for his keeping he is liable in trover to the owner.[6]

But if one sends his horse or his trunk in advance to an inn, saying he will soon be there himself, it may be that he should be deemed a guest from the time the property is taken in charge by the host.[7]

If one leaves a horse and carriage in the care of an innkeeper, the latter has a lien upon them for such care, though the guest lodges elsewhere.[8]

Fox v. McGregor, 11 Barb. (N. Y.) 41; Ingallsbee v. Wood, 33 N. Y. 577; Miller v. Marston, 35 Me. 153.

[1] Clark v. Burns, 118 Mass. 275.

[2] Binns v. Pigot, 9 C. & P. 208; Ingallsbee v. Wood, supra; Grinnell v. Cook, 3 Hill (N. Y.), 485. A different view was taken in Mason v. Thompson, 9 Pick. (Mass.) 280, 284, which related to the liability of an innkeeper for a harness belonging to one who was not himself a guest. Wilde, J., said : " To constitute a guest, in legal contemplation, it is not essential that he should be a lodger or have any refreshment at the inn. If he leaves his horse there, the keeper is chargeable on account of the benefit he is to receive for the keeping of the horse. Lord Holt held a different opinion in the case of Yorke v. Grenaugh, 2 Ld. Raym. 866 ; but the opinion of the majority of the court has ever since been considered as well settled law." See, also, McDaniels v. Robinson, 26 Vt. 316.

[3] Hickman v. Thomas, 16 Ala. 666.

[4] Smith v. Dearlove, 6 C. B. 132.

[5] Binns v. Pigot, supra; Fox v. McGregor, supra.

[6] Binns v. Pigot, supra.

[7] Grinnell v. Cook, 3 Hill (N. Y.), 485, 490.

[8] Yorke v. Grenaugh, supra ; S. C. 1 Salk. 388; McDaniels v. Rob-

The innkeeper is bound to provide for his guest's horse as well as for the guest himself, and he has a lien upon the horse, and may refuse to deliver him to the guest until the charges against the guest are paid. If the guest goes away and leaves the horse, the innkeeper is not bound to turn the horse loose, and give up his lien, but may still keep the horse and look to his lien for remuneration.[1]

If an innkeeper is also a keeper of a livery-stable, and he receives a horse in the latter capacity, and the owner afterwards becomes a guest at his house, no lien upon the horse arises in favor of the innkeeper for the entertainment of the guest.[2]

505. An innkeeper is defined to be one who keeps a house where a traveller is furnished with everything which he has occasion for whilst upon his way;[3] or one who holds out that he will receive all travellers and sojourners who are willing to pay a price adequate to the sort of accommodation provided.[4] A house of public entertainment in London, where beds and provisions were furnished, but which was called a tavern and coffee-house, and was not frequented by stage-coaches, and had no stable, was held to be an inn. The keeper of the house did not charge, as a mere lodging-house keeper, by the week or month, but for the number of nights. He did not, like a lodging-house keeper, make a special contract with every man who came; but held himself ready, without making a special contract, to provide lodging and entertainment for all, at a reasonable price.[5]

One may be at the same time an innkeeper and a boarding-house keeper, and in such case it may be difficult to determine

inson, 26 Vt. 316; Peet v. McGraw, 25 Wend. (N. Y.) 653. In the latter case Chief Justice Nelson said : "It is not necessary, in point of fact, that the owner or person putting the horses to be kept at a public inn should be a guest at the time, in order to charge the innkeeper for any loss that may happen, or to entitle him to the right of lien. . . . If the horses be left with the innkeeper, though the owner may put up at a different place, the former is answerable for the safe keeping, and should, of course, be entitled to the summary remedy for his reasonable charges."

[1] Black v. Brennan, 5 Dana (Ky.), 310.

[2] Smith v. Dearlove, 6 C. B. 132. In Mason v. Thompson, 9 Pick. (Mass.) 280, 285, it was held in effect, that if an innkeeper, who is also a keeper of a livery-stable, receives a horse to be fed, without giving notice that he receives it as a keeper of a livery-stable, he is answerable as an innkeeper. It was found by the jury, as a matter of fact, that he received the horse as an innkeeper.

[3] Thompson v. Lacy, 3 B. & Ald. 283, 286, per Bayley, J.

[4] Ib. per Best, J.

[5] Thompson v. Lacy, supra.

whether a person entertained at the house is a guest of the inn-keeper or a boarder. Perhaps the more prominent occupation might control, and afford a presumption in a case where there is no other evidence. But if there is any evidence in the matter, the question is one for the jury, and not a matter of law for the court. The duration of the stay of the guest or boarder, the price paid, the amount of accommodation afforded, the transient or permanent character of his residence and occupation, his knowledge or want of knowledge of any difference of accommo-dation afforded to, or price paid by, boarders and guests, are all to be regarded in settling the question.[1]

It is not necessary that one should be licensed as an innkeeper in order to subject him to the liabilities or entitle him to the privileges of an innkeeper.

506. To constitute one a guest it is not necessary that he should be at the inn in person. It is enough that his property is there in charge of his wife, or servant, or any agent who is there in his employment, or as a member of his family, provided such person is there in such a way that the law will imply that the property is in the possession of the owner, and not merely in the possession of his agent.[2]

507. Where a husband and wife board at a hotel, the hus-band is presumptively liable for the bill. It is competent, how-ever, for the hotel-keeper to show that the husband was impecu-nious, and that credit was given to the wife so as to justify the detention of her property for their bill.[3]

If board is furnished to a man and his wife under a contract with the husband, the innkeeper or boarding-house keeper has no lien upon the wife's effects, which are her separate property, brought with her to the house; for no lien can exist against a guest who does not become liable to the keeper of the house.[4]

Where a father and his two daughters boarded at a hotel, and the board of the three was charged to the father, it was held that

[1] Hall v. Pike, 100 Mass. 495, per Colt, J.; Danforth v. Pratt, 42 Me. 50; Norcross v. Norcross, 53 Me. 163.

[2] Coykendall v. Eaton, 37 How. (N. Y.) Pr. 438; Smith v. Keyes, 2 T. & C. (N. Y.) 650.

[3] Birney v. Wheaton, 2 How. (N. Y.) Pr. (N. S.) 519. So decided in-dependently of the statute of 1884, ch. 381, providing that married women may make contracts in the same manner as if single.

[4] McIlvane v. Hilton, 7 Hun (N. Y.), 594.

the hotel-keeper could not detain the trunks of one of the daughters for the board of the three, but only for that of such daughter alone ; and not for her board if this was charged to the father.[1]

508. An innkeeper has a lien on the baggage of an infant guest for the price of his entertainment, and also for money furnished him and expended by him in procuring necessaries. The innkeeper is legally bound to receive and entertain an infant as well as an adult applicant. The price of his entertainment is recoverable from him or his guardian on the ground that the entertainment is necessary.[2]

509. An innkeeper cannot detain the guest's person, or the clothes or ornaments on his person, as security for his bill,[3] although there are some *dicta* by early authorities to the effect that he had this right.[4] There has, however, been no claim of such a right since the case of Sunbolf v. Alford in the Court of the Exchequer.[5] In that case Sunbolf sued his innkeeper in trespass for assaulting and beating him, shaking and pulling him about, stripping off his coat, carrying it away and converting it to his own use. The innkeeper pleaded his lien. Lord Abinger, chief baron, giving an opinion against the innkeeper, said : " If an innkeeper has a right to detain the person of his guest for the non-payment of his bill, he has a right to detain him until the bill is paid, which may be for life ; so that this defence supposes that, by the common law, a man who owes a small debt, for which he could not be imprisoned by legal process, may yet be detained by an innkeeper for life. The proposition is monstrous. Again, if he have any right to detain the person, surely he is a judge in his own cause ; for he is then the party to determine whether the amount of his bill is reasonable, and he must detain him till the man brings an action against him for false imprisonment, and then, if it were determined that the charge was not reasonable, and it appeared that the party had made an offer of a reasonable sum, the detainer would be unlawful. But

---

[1] Clayton v. Butterfield, 10 Rich. (S. C.) 300.

[2] Watson v. Cross, 2 Duv. (Ky.) 147 ; and see Read v. Amidon, 41 Vt. 15.

[3] Sunbolf v. Alford, 3 Mees. & W.

248 ; *S. C.* 1 H. & H. 13 ; Wolf v. Summers, 2 Camp. 631.

[4] Bacon's Abr. Inns, D ; Newton v. Trigg, 1 Shower, 269 ; Dunlap v. Thorne, 1 Rich. (S. C.) 213 ; Grinnell v. Cook, 3 Hill (N. Y.), 485.

[5] 3 Mees. & W. 248, 254.

where is the law that says a man shall detain another for his debt without process of law? As to a lien upon the goods, there are undoubtedly cases of exception to the general law in favor of particular claims; and if an innkeeper has the possession of the goods, and his debt is not paid, he has a right to detain them by virtue of that possession; but I do not agree that he has any right to take a parcel or other property out of the possession of the guest. If the guest is robbed of goods while they are in his own hands, the innkeeper is not liable. It appears to me, therefore, being without any authorities on the subject, that the plea is in principle utterly bad, and that there is no ground for the attempt to justify an assault, under the pretence of detaining a man for a debt due to an innkeeper. It is also bad under the pretence of justifying the stripping the plaintiff's coat off his back, and thereby inviting a breach of the peace, and making an assault necessary in order to exercise the right to the lien on the coat."

510. **Property exempt from execution.** — Property of a guest is not exempt from an innkeeper's lien by reason of the fact that it is property which would be exempt from general execution. Thus, the lien may attach to the coat of a guest notwithstanding his claim that it is a part of his ordinary wearing apparel, and is exempt from execution.[1] " An innkeeper's lien exists by common law, and we see nothing in the statute exempting certain property from execution to indicate an intention to abrogate the common law in this respect. The statute exempts only from general execution. It was never designed to prevent persons from giving a lien upon whatever property they see fit. Where a lien is given, it may of course be enforced. Had the plaintiff given a chattel mortgage upon his coat to secure his hotel bill, no one would doubt the right of the defendant to foreclose it, notwithstanding the coat might have been a part of the plaintiff's ordinary wearing apparel. When the plaintiff became defendant's guest at his hotel he gave the defendant a lien upon his coat as effectually as if he had given him a mortgage upon it. The law implied that from the act of becoming the defendant's guest and taking his coat with him. The rule is too well established to require support from authorities."

[1] Swan v. Bournes, 47 Iowa, 501, 503.

511. The distinction between a guest and a boarder is that the former comes without any bargain as to the length of time he is to stay, and therefore may go when he pleases. A guest may remain a long time at an inn without becoming a boarder. He may contract to pay by the week or month without losing his character as a guest and assuming that of a boarder.[1] If one goes to a hotel as a wayfaring man and a traveller, and the relation of innkeeper and guest is once established, the presumption is that this relation continues so long as the traveller remains, and the length of his stay is immaterial so long as he retains his character as a traveller. The simple fact of his agreeing to pay a certain price by the week does not take away his character as a traveller and guest. "A guest for a single night might make a special contract as to the price to be paid for his lodging ; and, whether it were more or less than the usual price, it would not affect his character as a guest. The character of guest does not depend upon the payment of any particular price, but upon other facts. If an inhabitant of a place makes a special contract with an innkeeper there for board at his inn, he is a boarder, and not a traveller or a guest, in the sense of the law." [2]

512. One who keeps a lodging-house, in which no provision is made by him for supplying his lodgers with meals, is not an innkeeper. That there is a restaurant in the basement of the house which is leased to and managed by another person, and that this is connected by passageways and doors with the upper part of the house to facilitate access to the restaurant from the lodging-rooms, does not make the keeper of the lodgings an innkeeper.[3]

513. The innkeeper's lien does not at common law apply to goods of a boarder,[4] or to the goods of a person received

---

[1] Berkshire Woollen Co. v. Proctor, 7 Cush. (Mass.) 417; Shoecraft v. Bailey, 25 Iowa, 553; Norcross v. Norcross, 53 Me. 163; Chamberlain v. Masterson, 26 Ala. 371; Pinkerton v. Woodward, 33 Cal. 557; Jalie v. Cardinal, 35 Wis. 118.

[2] Berkshire Woollen Co. v. Proctor, 7 Cush. (Mass.) 417, 424, per Fletcher, J.

[3] Cochrane v. Schryver, 17 N. Y. Week. Dig. 442.

[4] Drope v. Thaire, Latch. 127; Grinnell v. Cook, 3 Hill (N.Y.), 485 ; Bayley v. Merrill, 10 Allen (Mass.), 360; Brooks v. Harrison, 41 Conn. 184; Ewart v. Stark, 8 Rich. (S. C.) 423; Hursh v. Byers, 29 Mo. 469; Manning v. Wells, 9 Humph. (Tenn.) 746; Nichols v. Halliday, 27 Wis. 406 ; Pollock v. Landis, 36 Iowa, 651.

under a special agreement,[1] for in such case the innkeeper does not assume an innkeeper's responsibility, nor is he obliged to receive the boarder or other person under a special agreement. By statute, however, in several states, boarding-house keepers are given the same lien that innkeepers have.

A boarding-house keeper has no lien except by virtue of a statute upon the property of his boarders ; and a lodging-house keeper has no lien except by virtue of a statute on the property of his lodgers for rent due. The latter can neither be regarded as an innkeeper nor as a boarding-house keeper.[2]

514. A boarding-house keeper's lien under a statute attaches as and when the board is furnished. Thus, if a guest of a boarding-house keeper pays board by the week, though by his contract nothing is due until the end of the week, the lien nevertheless attaches in the mean time.[3] Otherwise, a guest who had obtained credit upon the strength of the lien, might destroy the security by selling or removing the goods before the bill for board had become payable by the contract. Such a result would be inconsistent with the nature and purpose of the lien. A sale of such property by the boarder is ineffectual as against the lien, except from the time that notice of the sale is given to the boarding-house keeper, or the property is actually removed ;[4] and in the case of a notice of a sale to a third person, the lien is effectual to secure the amount due up to the time of such notice.[5]

515. By statute in several states, boarding-house keepers and others have a lien similar to that of an innkeeper. These statutes generally apply to innkeepers as well, and these common law rights are sometimes modified. These statutes are, therefore, important not only as conferring a lien similar to that of an innkeeper upon other persons, but also in determining the extent of the innkeeper's lien.

In California,[6] hotel, inn, boarding-house, and lodging-house

---

[1] Wintermute v. Clarke, 5 Sandf. (N. Y.) 242; Hursh v. Byers, 29 Mo. 469.

[2] Cochrane v. Schryver, 17 N. Y. Week. Dig. 442.

[3] Smith v. Colcord, 115 Mass. 70; Bayley v. Merrill, 10 Allen, 360.

[4] Bayley v. Merrill, *supra*.

[5] Bayley v. Merrill, *supra*.

[6] Codes and Stats. 1885, § 1861 of Civ. Code.

keepers have a lien upon the baggage and other property of value of their guests, or boarders, or lodgers, brought into such hotel, inn, or boarding or lodging - house, by such guests, boarders, or lodgers, for the proper charges due from such guests, boarders, or lodgers, for their accommodation, board and lodging, and room rent, and such extras as are furnished at their request, with the right to the possession of such baggage, or other property of value, until all such charges are paid.

In Colorado,[1] every hotel, tavern, boarding-house keeper, and person who rents furnished rooms, has a lien upon the baggage of his or her patrons, boarders, and guests for the amount that may be due from such patrons, boarders, guests, or tenants for such boarding, lodging, or rent, and may hold and retain possession of such baggage until the amount so due for boarding, lodging, or rent, or either, is paid.

In Connecticut,[2] when a special agreement shall have been made between the keeper of any boarding or lodging-house, and any person boarding or lodging at such house, regarding the price of such board or lodging, all the baggage and effects kept by such person at such house shall be subject to a lien in favor of the keeper of such house for all such sums as shall be at any time due him from such person for board or lodging ; and such boarding-house or lodging-house keeper may detain such baggage and effects until such debts shall be paid.

In Dakota,[3] an innkeeper, or keeper of a boarding-house, has a lien upon personal property placed by his guests or boarders under his care, for the payment of such amount as may be due him for lodging, fare, boarding, or other necessaries, by such guest or boarder.

In Florida,[4] the proprietor or manager of a hotel in this state has a lien of superior dignity to all others upon all the goods and chattels and personal property of every lodger, boarder, guest, or person staying in or at said hotel, for all sums of money due by him, her, or them to such proprietor or manager for board or lodging, advances of money or loans thereof, or things furnished.

In Georgia,[5] innkeepers and boarding-house keepers have a lien for their dues on the baggage of their guests, which is

---

[1] G. S. 1883, § 2118.
[2] R. S. 1875, p. 363, § 23.
[3] Code 1883, § 1062 of Civ. Code.

[4] Dig. of Laws 1881, ch. 114, § 6.
[5] Code 1882, §§ 1986, 2122.

superior to other liens, except liens for taxes, special liens of landlords for rent, liens of laborers, and all general liens of which they had actual notice before the property claimed to be subject to lien came into their control, to which excepted liens they are inferior.

The innkeeper has a lien on the goods of all his guests for all his reasonable charges, and may retain possession until they are paid; his lien attaches though the guest has no title, or even stole the property, and the true owner must pay the charges upon that specific article before receiving the same.[1]

In Illinois,[2] hotel, inn, and boarding-house keepers have a lien upon the baggage and other valuables of their guests or boarders brought into such hotel, inn, or boarding-house by such guests or boarders, for the proper charges due from such guests or boarders for their accommodation, board and lodging, and such extras as are furnished at their request.

In Louisiana,[3] innkeepers have a privilege, or more properly a right of pledge, on the property of travellers who take their board or lodging with them, by virtue of which they may retain the property and have it sold, to obtain payment of what such travellers may owe them, on either of the accounts above mentioned. Innkeepers enjoy this privilege on all the property which the traveller has brought to the inn, whether it belongs to him or not, because this property has become their pledge by the fact of its introduction into the inn. This privilege extends even to coined money which may be found in the apartment of the traveller who has died in their house.

The term " travellers " applies to strangers and such as, being transiently in a place where they have no domicile, take their board and lodging at an inn.

In Maine,[4] innholders or keepers of boarding-houses have a lien on the goods and personal baggage of their guests and boarders, to secure the payment of any money due from them for · board or lodging.

In Massachusetts,[5] boarding-house keepers have, for all proper

---

[1] An innkeeper has no lien on the goods in possession of his guest, as against the true owner, unless there be charges upon the specific article on which the lien is claimed. *Domestic Sewing-Machine Co. v. Watters*, 50 Ga. 573.

[2] Annotated Stats. 1885, ch. 82, § 48.

[3] R. Civ. Code 1870, arts. 3232–3236. And see Rev. Laws 1884, § 2873.

[4] R. S. 1883, ch. 91, § 46.

[5] Pub. Stats. 1882, ch. 192, § 31.

charges due for fare and board, a lien on the baggage and effects brought to their houses and belonging to their guests or boarders, except when such guests or boarders are mariners.[1]

In Missouri,[2] hotel, inn, and boarding-house keepers have a lien upon the baggage and other valuables of their guests or boarders, brought into such hotel, inn, or boarding-house by such guests or boarders, and upon the wages [3] of such guests or boarders, for their proper charges due from such guests or boarders for their accommodation, boarding and lodging, and such extras as are furnished at their request.

In New Hampshire,[4] all boarding-house keepers have a lien upon the baggage and effects of their guests and boarders, except seamen and mariners, brought to their respective boarding-houses, until all the proper charges due to such keepers for the fare and board of such guests and boarders shall be paid or tendered.

In New Jersey,[5] all hotel, inn, and boarding-house keepers have a lien on all baggage and property belonging to boarders and lodgers at said hotel, inn, or boarding-house, for the amount of their bill or bills due to the proprietor thereof for the hire of rooms or board in said hotel, inn, or boarding-house, and have the right, without the process of law, to retain the same until the said amount of indebtedness is discharged.

In New Mexico Territory,[6] innkeepers and those who board

---

[1] This lien is not so broad in some respects as the common law lien of an innkeeper. It attaches only to property belonging to the guests or boarders. It does not attach to the property of a husband brought to a boarding-house by his wife, for board furnished to his wife and child, who had been driven from home by the husband's cruelty and neglect. Mills v. Shirley, 110 Mass. 158.

[2] R. S. 1879, § 3198.

[3] A lien for wages cannot be enforced in the manner provided by the statute for the enforcement of the innkeeper's lien. The mode provided is by sale, and this is not apt for the enforcement of a lien upon wages. In a process by garnishment the last thirty days' wages are exempt. Hodo v. Benecke, 11 Mo. App. 393.

Where the plaintiff fails to establish his lien, he is entitled to a general judgment for the debt for board shown to be due. Hodo v. Benecke, *supra.*

[4] G. L. 1878, ch. 139, § 1.

The statute embraces innkeepers who, in addition to their business as innkeepers strictly, also take boarders. Such keepers of boarders are entitled to a lien upon the baggage and effects of their boarders for their fare and board. They have a lien upon the horse of a boarder for his own fare and board, but not for the keeping of the horse. The terms of the statute limit the lien to the fare and board of the guest. It does not include the fare and board of his horse. Cross v. Wilkins, 43 N. H. 332.

[5] Rev. 1877, p. 495, § 68.

[6] Comp'd Laws 1884, § 1542.

others for pay have a lien on the property of their guests, while the same is in their possession, and until the same is paid.

In New York,[1] the keeper of a boarding-house has the same lien upon and right to detain the baggage and effects of any boarder to the same extent and in the same manner as inn-keepers have such lien and right of detention; but nothing herein shall be deemed to give to any boarding-house keeper any lien upon or right to detain any property the title to which shall not be in such boarder.

In Pennsylvania,[2] all proprietors of hotels, inns, and boarding-houses have a lien upon the goods and baggage belonging to any sojourner, boarder, or boarders, for any amount of indebtedness contracted for boarding and lodging, for any period of time not exceeding two weeks, and have the right to detain said goods and baggage until the amount of said indebtedness is paid.

In Tennessee,[3] keepers of hotels, boarding-houses, and lodging-houses, whether licensed or not, have a lien on all furniture, baggage, wearing apparel, or other goods and chattels brought into any such hotel, boarding or lodging-house, by any guest or patron of the same, to secure the payment by such guest of all sums due for board or lodging.

In Texas,[4] proprietors of hotels and boarding-houses have a special lien upon all property or baggage deposited with them

---

[1] 2 R. S. 7th ed. p. 1282; Act of 1860, ch. 446, as amended by Laws 1876, ch. 319. A subsequent statute (1879, ch. 530) enumerates lodging-house keepers among those entitled to the benefits of the act; but it has been held that a mere lodging-house keeper has no lien upon the effects of the lodger by force of the latter statute, and certainly had none before. Cochrane v. Schryver, 17 N. Y. Week. Dig. 442. No lien can be acquired under this act upon the goods of a third person brought to the house by a boarder. Misch v. O'Hara, 9 Daly, N. Y. 361. Under this statute it is only the baggage and effects of the boarder that are affected by the lien, and the lien is given only for the amount that may be due for board by such boarder. McIlvane v. Hilton, 7 Hun (N. Y.), 594.

This statute applies to cases of special contracts for board at a fixed rate by the week or month, although an innkeeper, under such circumstances, would have no lien. Misch v. O'Hara, supra.

The statute applies only to those who make a business, in whole or in part, of keeping boarders. Cady v. McDowell, 1 Lans. 484.

The lien exists with reference to permanent as well as transient boarders. Stewart v. McCready, 24 How. Pr. 62.

[2] Brightly's Purdon's Dig. 1883, p. 890, § 17.

[3] Code 1882, § 2784.

[4] R. S. 1879, p. 461, art. 3182.

for the amount of the charges against them or their owners, if guests at such hotel and boarding-house.

In Utah Territory [1] and Virginia,[2] where an agreement shall have been made between the keeper of any ordinary house of private entertainment or boarding-house, and any person boarding or lodging at such house, regarding the price of board or lodging, all the baggage and effects kept by such person at such ordinary house of private entertainment or boarding-house shall be subject to a lien in favor of the keeper of such ordinary house of private entertainment or boarding-house for all such sums as shall be at any time due from such persons for such board or lodging, and the keeper of any such ordinary house of private entertainment or boarding-house may retain such baggage and effects until such debt shall be paid.

In Wisconsin,[3] every innkeeper, and every keeper of a boarding-house, has a lien upon, and may retain the possession of, the baggage and effects of any guest or boarder for the amount which may be due him for board from such guest or boarder, until such amount is paid.[4]

In Wyoming Territory,[5] any keeper of a hotel or boarding-house or lodging-house has a lien upon the baggage or other personal property of any person who shall obtain board, or lodging, or both, from such keeper, for the amount due for such board or lodging, and is hereby authorized to retain the possession of such baggage or personal property until the said amount is paid.

II. *What Charges are Secured.*

516. The landlord has a lien for his reasonable charges, whatever may be the amount of his bill, provided the guest be possessed of his reason and be not an infant. If the goods of a guest be seized upon execution, or be attached, they can only be taken subject to the landlord's reasonable charges, and not merely subject to a lien for a reasonable quantity of wines.[6] Lord Abinger, in his summing up to the jury, said: "It has been

[1] Acts 1879, ch. 84, § 1.
[2] Comp'd Laws 1877, § 1193.
[3] R. S. 1878, § 3344.
[4] This statute is changed in form, though apparently not in substance, from that of 1863, ch. 89, § 1. That was held to give to a boarding-house keeper the same lien upon the effects

of a boarder for his charges which an innkeeper had at common law upon the goods of his guest for the price of his board and lodging. Nichols *v.* Halliday, 27 Wis. 406.

[5] Laws 1882, ch. 50, § 1.
[6] Proctor *v.* Nicholson, 7 C. & P. 67.

urged that the plaintiff was asked not to allow his guest more than a certain quantity of brandy and water, and that the guest's mother sent to him to that effect; however, I must say, that I never heard that the landlord of an inn was bound to investigate the nature of the articles which were ordered by a guest before he supplied them. The landlord of an inn may supply whatever things the guest orders, and the guest is bound to pay for them, provided that the guest be possessed of his reason, and is not an infant. In either of these latter cases the landlord must look to himself."

517. **The lien covers advances of money** made to a guest on the credit of his effects.[1]

518. **The lien of an innkeeper is a general one for the whole amount of his bill.** The lien covers the charges for the guest's personal entertainment, and the charges made specially against the property brought by the guest, such as horses and a carriage.[2] In a case before the Queen's Bench Division, Lord Justice Bramwell fully and clearly stated the law, saying:[3] "The first question for our decision is, What was the innkeeper's lien? Was it a lien on the horses for the charges in respect of the horses, and on the carriage in respect of the charges of the carriage, and no lien on them for the guest's reasonable expenses; or was it a general lien on the horses and carriage and guest's goods conjointly for the whole amount of the defendant's claim as innkeeper? I am of opinion that the latter was the true view as to his lien, and for this reason, that the debt in respect of

[1] Proctor *v.* Nicholson, 7 Car. & P. 67. Lord Abinger instructed the jury that they were to consider whether it was understood between the innkeeper and the guest, at the time of the advances, that the goods in question were to be considered as security for these sums. Watson *v.* Cross, 2 Duvall (Ky.), 147.

[2] Thompson *v.* Lacy, 3 B. & Ald. 283; Pollock *v.* Landis, 36 Iowa, 651; Mason *v.* Thompson, 9 Pick. (Mass.) 280; McDaniels *v.* Robinson, 26 Vt. 316; Fox *v.* McGregor, 11 Barb. (N. Y.) 41.

In some early cases it was said that the horse of a guest might be detained for his own meals, and not for the guest's personal entertainment. Bac. Abr. Inns, D, citing Rosse *v.* Bramsteed, 2 Roll. 438 and 2 Roll. Abr. 85; but these cases do not support the doctrine. The reason for the doctrine is said to be, that chattels are in the custody of the law for the debt which arises from the thing itself, and not for any other debt due from the same party. Story Bailm. § 476. As remarked in effect by Story, this doctrine is without substantial support.

[3] Mulliner *v.* Florence, 3 Q. B. D. 484, 488.

which the lien was claimed was one debt, although that debt was made up of several items.   An innkeeper may demand the expenses before he receives the guest, but if he does not, and takes him in and finds him in all things that the guest requires, it is one contract, and the lien that he has is a lien in respect of the whole contract to pay for the things that are supplied to him while he is a guest.   If this was not the case, a man might go to a hotel with his wife, and then it might be said that the innkeeper's lien was on the guest's luggage for what he had consumed, and on the wife's luggage for what she had had.   The contract was, that the guest and his horses and carriage shall be received and provided for : there was one contract, one debt, and one lien in respect of the whole of the charges."   Lord Justice Colton, in the same case, to like effect said : " The innkeeper has a general lien for the whole amount of his bill.   As to the horses, harness, and carriage, there would be a lien for any special expenditure, and there is no reason for exempting the horses, harness, and carriage from the general lien an innkeeper has in the guest's goods by the general law.   The innkeeper is bound to receive the horses, harness, and carriage with the guest as much as he is bound to receive the guest himself ; the liability of the innkeeper with respect to them is the same as his liability with respect to the other goods of the guest, and there is no reason for excluding the claim of the innkeeper, although the horses, harness, and carriage are not received in the dwelling-house, but in adjoining buildings.   There is no authority for saying that the innkeeper's lien does not extend to the horses, harness, and carriage the guest brings with him as much as to other things of the guest."

If one who is already a guest at a hotel brings his horses and carriages there, a lien attaches to them for the charges then existing against the guest, as well as for the subsequent entertainment of the guest and his horses.[1]

The lien does not cover board to become due in the future, but only that which is due at the time of the detention.[2]

A lien for charges for the entertainment of a servant who is a' guest at a hotel alone without his master, may be enforced against the master's horse and wagon which the servant brought with him and used in his master's business.[3]

---

[1] Mulliner v. Florence, 3 Q. B. D. 484.

[2] Shafer v. Guest, 35 How. (N. Y.) Pr. 184 ; S. C. 6 Robt. 264, 268.

[3] Smith v. Keyes, 2 T. & C. (N. Y.) 650.

III. *Waiver and Loss of the Lien.*

519. Possession is essential to the preservation of this lien. If the guest be allowed to take his goods away with him, the innkeeper cannot retake the goods and assert his lien ; and even if the guest returns again with the same goods, the innkeeper cannot hold them for a prior debt.[1]

But a boarding-house keeper, having a valid lien under the laws of Massachusetts upon the trunk of a boarder, does not lose it by sending it by an express company to New Hampshire, with instructions not to deliver it until the amount of the claim for which the trunk was detained should be paid.[2]

520. If the guest fraudulently removes his goods, or even through fraudulent representations obtains the consent of the innkeeper to their removal, the right of lien remains.[3] Thus, if the guest pays his bill with a fraudulent draft, which he represents to be good, the lien is not released.[3]

521. The lien is not defeated by the occasional absence of the guest, if he has the intention of returning.[4] For example, if a traveller leave his horse at the inn, and then go out to dine or lodge with a friend, he does not thereby cease to be a guest, and the rights and liabilities of the parties remain the same as though the traveller had not left the inn. And if the owner leave the inn and go to another town, intending to be absent two or three days, it seems that the same rule holds good.[5] And so if one goes to an inn with two race-horses and a groom, in the character of a guest, and remains there for several months, taking the horses out every day for exercise and training, though he is occasionally absent for several days, but always with the intention of returning to the inn, the innkeeper's lien is not destroyed. In the absence of any alteration in the relation of the parties, that of innkeeper and guest is presumed to continue.[6]

[1] Jones *v.* Pearle, 1 Strange, 556; Jones *v.* Thurloe, 8 Mod. 172.

[2] Jaquith *v.* American Express Co. 60 N. H. 61.

[3] Manning *v.* Hollenbeck, 27 Wis. 202.

[4] Allen *v.* Smith, 12 C. B N. S.

638; Grinnell *v.* Cook, 3 Hill (N. Y.), 485 ; Caldwell *v.* Tutt, 10 Lea (Tenn.), 258.

[5] Grinnell *v.* Cook, *supra*, per Bronson, J.

[6] Allen *v.* Smith, *supra*.

522. An innkeeper who accepts security from a guest for the payment of hotel charges does not waive his lien at common law upon the goods of his guest for the amount of such charges, unless there is something in the nature of the security, or in the circumstances under which it was taken, which is inconsistent with the existence or continuance of the lien, and therefore destructive of it.[1]

This lien, like other liens, is waived by an arrangement for payment at a future day.

IV. *Enforcement of the Lien.*

523. An innkeeper who sells the goods of a guest without judicial or statutory authority waives his lien, and renders himself liable in trover for the value of the property, and it is no excuse for such a sale that the retention of the chattel is attended with expense.[2] In an action by the owner of the property for the conversion, the innkeeper might set off his charges if the owner was his guest and liable for the debt; but if the property detained belonged to a third person, there could be no set-off in a suit by him for a conversion of the property. Thus, if the property be horses, which had been stolen or obtained by fraud from the owner, the damages to which the owner would be entitled in an action against the innkeeper, for an unlawful sale of them, would be the full value of the horses at the time of sale. In a leading case on this subject before the Queen's Bench Division, Lord Justice Bramwell said:[3] "The defendant, who had only a lien on the horses, was not justified in selling them, and he has therefore been guilty of a conversion, and that enables the plaintiff to maintain this action for the proceeds of the sale. The very notion of a lien is, that if the person who is entitled to the lien, for his own benefit parts with the chattel over which he claims to exercise it, he is guilty of a tortious act. He must not dispose of the chattel so as to give some one else a right of possession as against himself. The lien

---

[1] Angus *v.* McLachlan, 23 Ch. D. 330.

[2] Jones *v.* Pearle, 1 Strange, 556; Mulliner *v.* Florence, 3 Q. B. D. 484; Doane *v.* Russell, 3 Gray (Mass.), 382; Carr *v.* Fogg, 46 Mo. 44. In Jones *v.* Thurloe, 8 Mod. 172, Chief Justice Pratt is reported as saying, "that, though the innkeeper might detain a horse for his meat for one night, yet he could not sell the horse and pay himself; if he did it was a conversion, for he is not to be his own carver."

[3] Mulliner *v.* Florence, 3 Q. B. D. 484, 489, 491.

is the right of the creditor to retain the goods until the debt is paid. . . . If the plaintiff, after the sale of the horses, had thought fit to go to the vendee and say to him, ' Those horses are mine,' and the vendee had refused to give them up, he could have maintained an action against the vendee for the full value of the horses; but, instead of acting in this manner, he has treated the sale by the defendant as a conversion. He is not to be worse off because he has brought his action against the defendant instead of against the vendee. It is said, if the plaintiff succeeds, that the defendant's lien would be useless to him, and that the plaintiff would be better off than he was before the sale of the horses by the defendant. I do not think there is anything unreasonable in holding the defendant liable if the defendant was not bound to feed the horses."

524. Care and use of the property detained. — An innkeeper retaining the goods of his guest by virtue of a lien, is not bound to use greater care as to their custody than he uses as to his own goods of a similar description.[1]

Whether the innkeeper has the right to use the property may depend in some degree upon circumstances. It seems that he may do so if the property is of a nature that involves expense to keep it, such as a horse. Where, soon after a horse and wagon and other articles were left with an innkeeper to be kept for a few days, he had good reason to believe that the person leaving the property did not own it, and had abandoned it and was acting in bad faith towards the owner, and the innkeeper did not know who or where the owner was, and the owner, as the innkeeper had reason to believe, did not know where the property was, it was held that the innkeeper had the right to use the property moderately and prudently to the extent of compensating him for his charges for keeping; and such use, being lawful, was not a conversion.[2]

525. The innkeeper's lien, like other liens at common law, confers no right of sale in satisfaction of the debt. It is a right to retain and nothing more.[3] By statute, however, a

---

[1] Angus v. McLachlan, 23 Ch. D. 330.
[2] Alvord v. Davenport, 43 Vt. 30.
[3] Mulliner v. Florence, 3 Q. B. D. 84; Thames Iron W. Co. v. Patent Derrick Co. 1 Johns. & H. 93, 97; Carr v. Fogg, 46 Mo. 44; People v. Husband, 36 Mich. 306; Fox v. McGregor, 11 Barb. (N. Y.) 41.

remedy by sale is quite generally provided. In several states the statutes which authorize carriers to sell property on which they have a lien apply also to innkeepers.[1] In a few states there are general statutes applicable to all holders of liens, which authorize the sale of any property for the satisfaction of the lien debt in the manner prescribed.[2]

526. **California.**[3] — Whenever any trunk, carpet-bag, valise, box, bundle, or other baggage has heretofore come, or shall hereafter come, into the possession of the keeper of any hotel, inn, boarding or lodging house, as such, and has remained, or shall remain, unclaimed for the period of six months, such keeper may proceed to sell the same at public auction, and out of the proceeds of such sale may retain the charges for storage, if any, and the expenses of advertising and sale thereof ; but no such sale shall be made until the expiration of four weeks from the first publication of notice of such sale, in a newspaper published in or nearest the city, town, village, or place in which said hotel, inn, boarding or lodging house is situated. Said notice shall be published once a week, for four successive weeks, in some newspaper, daily or weekly, of general circulation, and shall contain a description of each trunk, carpet-bag, valise, box, bundle, or other baggage, as near as may be, the name of the owner, if known, the name of such keeper, and the time and place of such sale ; and the expenses incurred for advertising shall be a lien upon such trunk, carpet-bag, valise, box, bundle, or other baggage, in a ratable proportion, according to the value of such piece of property, or thing, or article sold ; and in case any balance arising from such sale shall not be claimed by the rightful owner within one week from the day of said sale, the same shall be paid into the treasury of the county in which such sale took place ; and if the same be not claimed by the owner thereof, or

---

[1] Such is the case in —
Illinois : See § 344.
Kansas : See § 349.
Michigan : See § 353.
Nebraska: See § 359.
New Mexico : See § 360.
New York : See § 361.
Oregon : See § 363.
Wisconsin : See § 373.
Wyoming Territory : See § 374.

[2] **Colorado** : G. S. 1883, §§ 2121–2126. See chapter 23, *infra.*
Georgia : Code 1882, § 1991.
New Hampshire: G. S. 1878, ch. 139, §§ 3–8. See chapter 23, *infra.*
Massachusetts : ch. 192, §§ 24–30, 33. See chapter 23.
Texas : R. S. 1879, §§ 3186–3189.
[3] 2 Codes and Stats. 1885, § 1862 of Civ. Code.

his legal representatives, within one year thereafter, the same shall be paid into the general fund of said county.

527. Connecticut.[1] — If any sum due to the keeper of any boarding or lodging-house, under a special agreement, from any person, for the price of his board or lodging, be not paid within sixty days after it is due, such boarding-house or lodging-house keeper may sell the baggage and effects kept by such person at such house, or such part thereof as shall be necessary, and apply the proceeds thereof to the payment of such debt.

528. Dakota Territory.[2] — Any innkeeper's lien may be enforced by sale in the manner prescribed for the sale of pledged property; that is to say,[3] a demand of payment must first be made of the debtor. Then actual notice must be given him of the time and place of sale, at such reasonable time before the sale as will enable him to attend. Notice of sale may be waived, but it is not waived by a mere waiver of demand of performance. He may waive a demand of performance as a condition precedent to a sale, by a positive refusal to perform, after performance is due, but cannot waive it in any other manner, except by contract. The sale must be at public auction, in the manner and upon the notice to the public usual at the place of sale, in respect to auction sales of similar property, and must be for the highest obtainable price. After sale, the creditor may deduct from the proceeds the amount due him and the necessary expenses of sale and collection, and must pay the surplus to the debtor on demand.

Instead of selling in the manner prescribed, the creditor may foreclose the right of redemption by a judicial sale under direction of a competent court, and in that case he may be authorized by the court to purchase at the sale.

529. Florida.[4] — In case of the non-payment on demand of any sum due to the proprietor of a hotel from any lodger,

---

[1] R. S. 1875, p. 363, § 23. Under this statute no special notice of the time and place of sale is necessary. The attachment of the lien, coupled with the right to sell on the expiration of a definite limitation, is, in legal effect, if not in express terms, no-tice to the debtor that, at the termination of the time fixed, a sale may be made at the option of the creditor. Brooks *v.* Harrison, 41 Conn. 184.

[2] Code 1883, § 1062 of Civ. Code.

[3] §§ 1772–1782.

[4] Dig. of Laws 1881, ch. 114, § 6.

boarder, or guest, his goods, chattels, or personal property, being in the hotel, may be sold at public auction by said proprietor or manager of said hotel, at some public place, to satisfy the amount due as aforesaid, together with the costs of sale, upon notice being given of the time and place of said sale, by advertisement in some newspaper published in the county where such hotel may be located, for at least once a week for the term of four weeks prior to said sale.

530. In Louisiana,[1] the innkeeper who retains the property of a traveller for tavern expenses due to him cannot sell it of his own authority; he must apply to a tribunal to have his debt ascertained, and the property seized and sold for the payment of it.

531. In Maine,[2] innkeepers and keepers of boarding-houses, having a lien on the goods and personal baggage of their guests and boarders, may enforce the same by a sale of such goods or baggage, in the manner following: After such goods or personal baggage have remained in the possession of such innholder or boarding-house keeper for six months unredeemed, they may be sold at auction to pay the sum due for board or lodging, and the expense of advertising and selling the same. Thirty days' notice of the time and place of sale must be given in a newspaper published in the town where such articles are held, if any, otherwise by posting in three conspicuous places therein; with a description of such articles, and the name of the owner; and the proceeds of sale, after deducting charges and expenses, shall be applied in satisfaction of the claim, and the balance, if any, shall be held for the benefit of the person entitled thereto. All such sales shall be recorded in the office of the town clerk where the sale took place, with a description of the articles sold, the charges and expenses, and the prices at which they were sold.

532. Minnesota.[3] — All goods or property taken by any hotel, inn, or boarding-house keeper, and by him held for non-payment of any bill for board, lodging, or accommodation, may be sold after the expiration of ninety days, and default being made in the payment of such bill, upon a notice of ten days, at public auction, upon notice as in cases of constables' sales.

---

[1] R. Civ. Code 1870, art. 3236.
[2] R. S. 1883, ch. 91, § 46.
[3] Stats. 1878, ch. 124, § 25.

533. Missouri.[1] — Keepers of hotels, inns, and boarding-houses having a lien upon the baggage and other valuables of their guests or boarders, may enforce them as follows: The person claiming the lien shall file with a justice of the peace of the ward, district, or township in which he resides, a statement duly verified by himself, his agent or attorney, setting forth his account and a description of the property on which the lien is claimed; and thereupon the justice shall issue a summons as in ordinary civil actions, returnable forthwith; and upon the return of the summons duly served, shall set the cause for hearing at any time after the lapse of one day. If summons be returned " defendant not found," and if it be proven to the satisfaction of the justice that the defendant is not a resident of the county, the justice shall order a notice of the proceedings to be published for three successive days in a daily newspaper, if one be published in the county; and if there be none, then once in a weekly, if such be published in the county; and if no paper be published in the county, then by six handbills put up in six public places in the county, notifying the defendant of the filing and the particulars of the account, the description of the property on which the lien is claimed, its whereabouts, and the day and place set for the hearing of the cause, which shall be at least ten days from the day of the last publication of the notice; and the proof of such publication shall be filed in the justice's office on or before the day of trial. When the defendant shall have been summoned or notified as aforesaid, the cause shall, on the day fixed for trial, be tried as any ordinary case in a justice's court. If the judgment be for the plaintiff, the justice shall order the property upon which the lien shall have been found to exist to be sold to satisfy the same. If the lien be not established, and the defendant shall not have been summoned, or shall not have voluntarily appeared to the action, the cause shall be dismissed at the cost of the plaintiff; if the defendant shall have been summoned, or shall have appeared to the action, and the plaintiff shall have established an indebtedness on the account sued on, but shall have failed to establish the lien claimed, the judgment shall be for the plaintiff for such indebtedness, but the costs of the suit, or any part thereof, may be taxed against him.

534. Nevada.[2] — Whenever any person shall leave a hotel

[1] 1 R. S. 1879, §§ 3197–3199.　　　　[2] G. S. 1885, §§ 4960–4962.

or lodging-house indebted to the proprietor or proprietors thereof, and shall remain absent for the period of six months, it shall be lawful for such proprietor or proprietors to sell, or cause to be sold, at public auction, any baggage or property of such person so indebted, or so much thereof as may be necessary to pay such indebtedness, expenses, and charges of sale, which may have been left at such hotel or lodging-house by such person.

All baggage or property, of whatever description, left at a hotel or lodging-house for the period of twelve months, may be sold at public auction by the proprietor or proprietors thereof, and the proceeds arising from such sale, after deducting the expenses and charges of sale and storage, shall be paid over to the county treasurer of the county in which such baggage or property is left, to be held by him for the period of six months for the benefit of the owner thereof, at which time, if the same is not paid to the owner, or some person legally entitled to the same, it shall be transferred to the school fund of the county.

All sales made under the preceding provisions shall be made by a licensed auctioneer, or by some constable of the township in which such baggage or property may be left; provided that no sale shall be valid unless a notice of such sale shall be posted up in three public places in such township for the period of twenty days immediately preceding the day of sale, giving a particular description of the property to be sold, the time and place of such sale, the name of the hotel or lodging-house at which such baggage or property may be left, the name of the owner or owners of such baggage or property, when known, and signed by such auctioneer or constable.

535. New Jersey.[1] — All baggage and property so held by any hotel, inn, and boarding-house keeper shall, after the expiration of six months from the date of such detention, be sold at public auction, upon a notice published for three days in a public newspaper published in the city or town where said hotel, inn, or boarding-house shall be kept, and the proceeds thereof shall be applied to the payment of such lien, and the proceeds of such sale and the balance, if any remaining, shall be paid over to the owner of such property or his representatives; and if said

---

[1] Rev. 1877, p. 495, § 69.

balance is not claimed by such owners within thirty days, then the said balance to be paid over to the overseer of poor-house of said city or town for the support of the poor.

536. New York.[1] — Any hotel-keeper, innkeeper, boarding-house or lodging-house keeper who shall have a lien for fare, accommodation, or board, upon any goods, baggage, or other chattel property, and in his possession for a period of three months at least after the departure of the guest or boarder leaving the same, or who for a period of six months shall have in custody any unclaimed trunk, box, valise, package, parcel, or other chattel property whatever, may proceed to sell the same at public auction, and out of the proceeds of such sale may, in case of lien, retain the amount thereof and the expense of advertisement and sale; and, in cases of unclaimed property, the expense of storage, advertisement, and sale thereof; provided, in all instances, the notice specified in the next section be first given as therein directed.

Fifteen days at least prior to the time of the sale a notice of the time and place of holding the sale, and containing a brief description of the goods, baggage, and articles to be sold, shall be published in a newspaper of general circulation, published in the city or town in which such hotel, inn, or boarding-house is situated; but if there be none, then in such newspaper published nearest said city or town; and shall also be served upon said guest, boarder, or owner of such chattel articles and property, if he reside or can be found within the county where said hotel, inn, boarding-house, or lodging is situated, by delivering the same to him personally, or leaving it at his place of residence with a person of suitable age in charge thereof. But if such guest, boarder, or owner does not reside or cannot be found in said county, then said notice shall be deposited in the post-office of said city or town, with the postage prepaid thereon, fifteen days prior to said sale, and addressed to said guest, boarder, or owner at his place of residence, if he left his address, or it be otherwise known to said hotel, inn, boarding-house keeper, or lodging-house keeper. The sale shall take place between the hours of ten o'clock in the forenoon and four o'clock in the afternoon, and all articles sold shall be to the highest bidder for cash.

Such hotel-keeper, innkeeper, boarding-house keeper, or lodg-

[1] 2 R. S. 1882, p. 1283, §§ 1–5.

ing-house keeper shall make an entry of the articles sold, and the balance of the proceeds of the sale, if any, and within ten days from such sale, shall, upon demand, refund such balance and surplus to such guest, boarder, or person leaving the articles sold.

In case such balance shall not be demanded and paid as specified in the last section, within said ten days, then within five days thereafter said hotel-keeper, innkeeper, boarding-house keeper, or lodging-house keeper shall pay said balance to the treasurer of the county, or chamberlain of said city, as the case may be, and shall at the same time file with said treasurer or chamberlain an affidavit made by him, in which shall be stated the name and place of residence, as far as they are known to him, of the guest, boarder, or person whose goods, baggage, or chattel articles were sold; the articles sold, and the price at which they were sold; the name and residence of the auctioneer making the sale; and a copy of the notice published, and how served, whether by personal service or by mailing, and if not so served, the reason thereof.

Said treasurer or chamberlain shall keep said surplus moneys for, and credit the same to, the person named in said affidavit as said guest, boarder, or person leaving the articles sold, and shall pay the same to said person, his or her executors or administrators, upon demand, and evidence satisfactory to said treasurer or chamberlain furnished of their identity.

537. Pennsylvania.[1] — Proprietors of hotels, inns, and boarding-houses have a lien upon the goods and baggage belonging to any sojourner, boarder or boarders, for any amount of indebtedness contracted for boarding and lodging, for any period of time not exceeding two weeks, and shall have the right to detain said goods and baggage until the amount of said indebtedness is paid; and at the expiration of three months, the said proprietor or proprietors may make application to any alderman or justice of the peace of the proper city, borough, or county, who is hereby authorized to issue his warrant to any constable within said city, borough, or county, and cause him to expose the said goods and baggage to public sale, after giving at least ten days' notice, by public written or printed notices put up in three or more public places in the ward of said city or

---

[1] Brightly's Purdon's Dig. 1883, p. 890, § 17.

borough, or in the township, where said inn, hotel, or boarding-house is located; and after he shall have sold the same, he shall make return thereof to the said justice or alderman, who shall, after the payment of all costs and the said amount of indebtedness, pay over the balance, if any there be, to the owner or owners of said goods and baggage: provided that the owner or owners of said goods and baggage shall have the right to redeem said goods and baggage, at any time within the said three months, upon paying the amount of said indebtedness, and at any time previous to the sale as aforesaid, upon paying also the additional cost established by law for like services.

538. Utah Territory.[1] — In case of the non-payment of a debt for which any hotel-keeper, innkeeper, or boarding-house keeper has a lien, for the period of sixty days after it is due, such hotel-keeper, innkeeper, or boarding-house keeper shall have the right to sell said baggage, goods, and effects, or such part thereof as shall be necessary, and apply the proceeds of such sale to the payment of such debt.

The sale shall be at public auction for cash. Before any such baggage, goods, and effects shall be sold, at least ten days' notice of such sale shall be given, by advertising the same at least five times in some newspaper published and having general circulation in the city, village, or town in which the hotel, inn, or boarding-house is situated; or, where no such paper is so published or circulated, then by written or printed handbills posted up in at least five public places, one of which shall be in the hotel, inn, or boarding-house where the baggage, goods, and effects are detained.

539. Virginia.[2] — In case any sum due to an innkeeper or boarding-house keeper from a boarder or lodger be not paid within thirty days after it is due, he may, after due notice, sell the baggage and effects of such boarder or lodger, or such part thereof as may be necessary, at public auction, and apply the proceeds of sale to the payment of such debt.

[1] Comp. Laws 1877, §§ 1194–1195.　　[2] Acts 1879, ch. 84, § 1.

CHAPTER XII.

LANDLORDS' LIENS FOR RENT.

I. *Liens by Reservation or Contract.*

540. In general. — The right of a landlord to a first lien upon his tenant's goods for his rent has always been regarded as just and proper. It is a right greatly to the interest of tenants, especially those of the poorer class, for it gives them credit, and enables them to hire property which they otherwise could not. This lien has been regarded with such favor that at common law the landlord was allowed to take the enforcement of it into his own hands, and by the hands of a bailiff of his own appointment to seize and sell his tenant's chattels found on the premises for the rent in arrear.[1] At common law, however, the landlord had no lien for rent upon his tenant's goods; but he had a right to seize or distrain the goods found upon the leased premises for rent due and unpaid. This right of distraint may in some sense be called a lien, though it differs essentially from the landlord's lien created by statute. One essential difference is, that by the common-law process no fixed lien upon the property existed until the property was actually seized or levied upon; while by statute a lien is ordinarily imposed upon the property from the beginning of the tenancy.

The process of distraint, modified more or less by statute, is still in use in several states,[2] and in many others a lien is given

---

[1] Gibson *v.* Gautier, 1 Mack. (D. C.) 35.

[2] The right of distress exists in some form in **Delaware**, § 608; **Florida**, for the enforcement of liens, § 610; **Illinois**, and there is also a lien on crops, §§ 613, 614; **Kentucky**, and there is also a lien, §§ 618, 619; **Mary-

to landlords by statute;[1] but aside from the one or the other, it is competent for the landlord and tenant to create a lien upon the tenant's property by contract. This contract is usually in the form of a mortgage clause in the lease. This creates a lien as against the tenant, and those having notice of the contract, and the lien can be made effectual against all the world by giving notice of it by recording.

541. To create a present lien by agreement, the words used should indicate that the lien is created and attaches at the time of the execution of the instrument; and it is not sufficient that they indicate that the lien is to be created at a future time. Thus a lease of a hotel, stipulating for the payment of a certain rent, contained these words: "And a lien to be given by said lessees to said lessors, to secure the payment thereof, . . . on all the furniture which shall be placed in said hotel by said lessees." It was held that these words indicated a covenant on the part of the lessees to create a lien by future action; and that no present lien was created upon the furniture then in the hotel, or upon such as should afterwards be placed in it.[2] It was a covenant, however, of which a court of equity would decree specific performance; for while a contract for the sale of chattels will not ordinarily be specifically performed, for the reason that a party can have adequate compensation at law, this reason does not apply to an agreement for a lien or security upon personal property when there can be no remedy at law.[3] Where in such case a mortgagee of the tenant, with full notice of the equities of the lessor, seized the furniture and sold it, so that a specific performance was rendered impossible, it was held that the lessor could have a lien declared upon the proceeds of such sale, and in this way obtain the benefit of the lien contracted for.[4] If, however, the mortgagee took his

land, §§ 622, 623; Mississippi, in the nature of an attachment, § 625; New Jersey, §§ 627, 628; Pennsylvania, §§ 632, 633; South Carolina, also a lien, §§ 634, 635; Texas, lien enforced by distress, § 638; Virginia and West Virginia, § 639.

[1] Liens in favor of landlords exist in some form in Alabama, §§ 602–604; Arizona, § 605; Arkansas, §§ 606, 607; District of Columbia, § 609; Florida, though enforced by distress, § 610; Georgia, §§ 611, 612;

Illinois, §§ 613, 614; Indiana, § 615; Iowa, § 616; Kansas, § 617; Louisiana, § 620; Maine, § 621; Missouri, § 626; New Mexico, § 630; North Carolina, § 631; South Carolina, §§ 634, 635; Tennessee, §§ 636, 637; Texas, § 638.

[2] Hale v. Omaha Nat. Bank, 1 J. & S. (N. Y.) 40; *S. C.* 49 N. Y. 626.

[3] Hale v. Omaha Nat. Bk. 49 N. Y. 626, 633, per Allen, J.

[4] Hale v. Omaha Nat. Bank, *supra.*

mortgage and made a loan in good faith without notice of the provision in the lease in respect to a lien to be given the lessor, no equitable lien is raised in favor of the latter as against the proceeds of the furniture in the mortgagee's hands.[1]

A lien in favor of the landlord as against his tenant may be created by a verbal agreement that the landlord shall have a lien upon the tenant's crop for rent, or for supplies furnished him ; and it will be operative against all persons except *bonâ fide* purchasers without notice.[2] Such an agreement does not contravene any provision of the statute of frauds.[3] The landlord may take possession of the crop under such verbal agreement whenever by its terms he is entitled to do so, and he may defend the possession as against the tenant or any claiming under him who is not a *bonâ fide* purchaser for value without notice.[4]

542. A lien may be imposed by contract upon property not then in existence, but which the parties contemplate will be in existence during the time the lien is to operate: the lien will take effect and be rated in equity when the property is acquired and used as contemplated.[5]

Thus a clause in a lease which mortgages all the crops to be raised on the leased premises for the current year, is valid in equity, and the lien attaches to the crops as they come into existence.[6]

A lease of a hotel contained a stipulation that all fixtures, furniture, and other improvements should be bound for the rent. At the date of the lease the house was unfurnished. It was held that the stipulation created a lien, valid at least in equity ; that this lien was for the full amount of the rent reserved for the whole term, and not simply for any portion that might from time become delinquent, and that it had priority of a mortgage given after the lease took effect, but before any rent became

[1] Hale v. Omaha Nat. Bank, 7 J. & S. 207.

[2] Gafford v. Stearns, 51 Ala. 434 ; Beck v. Venable, 59 Ind. 408.

[3] Morrow v. Turney, 35 Ala. 131.

[4] Gafford v. Stearns, *supra ;* Driver v. Jenkins, 30 Ark. 120 ; Roberts v. Jacks, 31 Ark. 597, 602.

[5] See Jones on Chattel Mortgages,

§ 170 ; Wright v. Bircher, 72 Mo. 179 ; Webster v. Nichols, 104 Ill. 160 ; Everman v. Robb, 52 Miss. 653; Wisner v. Ocumpaugh, 71 N. Y. 113 ; McCaffrey v. Woodin, 65 N. Y. 459; Coates v. Donnell, 16 J. & S. (N. Y.) 46.

[6] Butt v. Ellett, 19 Wall. 544.

delinquent, to a person having knowledge of the stipulation in the lease.[1]

Inasmuch as the essence of the right of lien at law is possession, there can be in law no lien by contract upon a future or an unplanted crop,[2] at least until possession is taken after the crop has been raised;[3] but such a lien may be created by statute,[4] and, as already noticed, it is valid in equity. But such a lien not being good at law, it cannot avail against exemption rights in favor of the tenant's family.[5]

Under a contract whereby a tenant undertakes to secure his landlord by a lien upon a crop to be raised, a mortgage or other incumbrance given by the tenant upon the crop to another, who takes it in good faith and without knowledge of such contract before the landlord takes possession of crop, takes precedence.[6]

An agreement by a lessee to deliver wool to his lessor in payment or security for rent, creates no lien upon wool not shipped to the lessor, as against the lessee's assignee in insolvency.[7]

543. Chattel mortgage clause. — A clause in a lease making the lease a charge upon property upon which it is not a lien by statute, is in effect a chattel mortgage, and is valid and enforcible as such.[8] Thus a clause making rent a charge on the crops and farming stock upon the leased premises, " whether exempt from execution or not," is in effect a chattel mortgage.[9] It is immaterial that the instrument does not contain any words of grant or conveyance. If it creates a lien or equitable charge, its validity and the rights of the parties depend upon the same principles as in case of a chattel mortgage executed in technical terms.[10] But an instrument without words of grant or conveyance is not a legal mortgage vesting the title and giving the right to seize and sell.[11]

---

[1] Wright v. Bircher, 72 Mo. 179.

[2] Hamlett v. Tallman, 30 Ark. 505; Alexander v. Pardue, Ib. 359; Roberts v. Jacks, 31 Ark. 597.

[3] Gittings v. Nelson, 86 Ill. 591.

[4] Abraham v. Carter, 53 Ala. 8.

[5] Vinson v. Hallowell, 10 Bush (Ky.), 538.

[6] Person v. Wright, 35 Ark, 169.

[7] Hitchcock v. Hassett, 12 Pac. Rep. (Cal.) 228. In **California** the landlord has no lien for rent reserved.

[8] Merrill v. Ressler (Minn.), 33 N. W. Rep. 117; Wisner v. Ocumpaugh, 71 N. Y. 113.

[9] Fejavary v. Brœsch, 52 Iowa, 88.

[10] McLean v. Klein, 3 Dill. 113; Fejavary v. Brœsch, supra; Atwater v. Mower, 10 Vt. 75 ; Merrill v. Ressler, supra; Harris v. Jones, 83 N. C. 317; Whiting v. Eichelbèrger, 16 Iowa, 422.

[11] Kennedy v. Reames, 15 S. C. 548, 552; Green v. Jacobs, 5 S. C. 280. In

It creates merely an equitable mortgage which should be enforced in equity.

If the mortgage clause contains a provision which in a chattel mortgage would render it fraudulent as to creditors, the mortgage clause, though valid between the parties, will be void as against the lessee's assignee under a general assignment for the benefit of his creditors. Thus, where, in a lien clause of a lease made in New York, a lessor agreed with the lessee, a retail merchant, that in default of paying the rent, or in case of seizure of his goods under legal process, the lien should be enforced against all the goods and personal property on the demised premises in the same manner as if it were a chattel mortgage, and it was further stipulated that the lessee should remain in possession of the mortgaged goods, and might continue to deal with them in the prosecution of his business, the lien clause, though valid between the parties, both as to property in existence and on the demised premises when the lease was executed, and as to that afterwards acquired, is, under the rule established in New York, fraudulent on its face as to creditors, and therefore void as to an assignee of the lessee.[1]

544. A lease, or a provision of a lease, which is in legal effect a chattel mortgage of the lessee's goods, must be recorded or filed as such a mortgage, in the absence of any statute giving effect to the lien, in order to make the stipulated lien effectual against purchasers and creditors.[2] Thus, a lease which provides that the lessor shall have a lien for the rent upon all goods and property that may be upon the demised premises, belonging to the lessee or to any one claiming the whole or any part of the premises under him as assignee, under-tenant, or otherwise, and that the lien might be enforced by taking possession of the property and selling the same, in the same manner as in the case of a chattel mortgage, is in legal effect a chattel mortgage, and is void as to the lessee's creditors if not filed or recorded. In such case, the only way to give effect to the intention of the parties is to treat the transaction as a chattel mortgage.

this case at the bottom of an agricultural lien were added the words: "I consider the above instrument of writing a mortgage of all my personal property, such as," &c.

[1] Reynolds v. Ellis (N. Y.), 8 N.

East. Rep. 392 ; S. C. 7 Eastern Rep. 342.

[2] McCaffrey v. Woodin, 65 N. Y. 459, reversing S. C. 62 Barb. 316; Reynolds v. Ellis, 34 Hun (N. Y.), 47; Weed v. Standley, 12 Fla. 166.

A stipulation in the lease, that the rent shall be a first lien on the buildings and improvements that may be put upon the premises by the lessee, and upon his interest in the lease and premises, is a security in the nature of a mortgage. It is enforcible against the lessee and all persons claiming under him, except creditors and purchasers without notice, although it be not acknowledged or recorded. It attaches as a lien or charge upon the property named as soon as the lessee acquires title to it, not only as against him, but as against all persons claiming under him, either voluntarily or with notice, or in bankruptcy.[1]

A lien given by a lease containing a mortgage clause can only be enforced by the landlord or his assignee. It is inseparable from the lease. A purchaser from the lessor of the leased property, subject to the lease, stands in place of the lessor, and may enforce the lien.[2]

545. A lease of a farm to be worked on shares, which provides that the lessor shall have a lien on the growing crops, and that the lessee would execute a chattel mortgage of the same when requested, must be filed or recorded as a chattel mortgage, in order to preserve the lien as against that of a mortgage by the lessee, duly filed or recorded, of his interest in the crops, when the mortgagee has taken the mortgage in good faith and without notice of the terms of the lease.[3]

The possession of the lessor in such case, though he resided upon the farm with the lessee, is not such a possession as would relieve him from the necessity of filing or recording his lease, in order to preserve the lien as against a subsequent purchaser or mortgagee of the lessee.[4] The possession of one tenant in common is regarded in law as the possession of both, as between themselves, but it is not notice to subsequent purchasers or mortgagees of any lien he may have in the share of his co-tenant who is in actual possession of his share.

546. In a recent case in Missouri, the court regarded a landlord having a lien reserved by his lease as a pledgee, rather than a mortgagee, of the property subject to the lien. The lease in this case provided that the landlord should have a lien

---

[1] Webster v. Nichols, 104 Ill. 160; Wright v. Bircher, 72 Mo. 179.
Hansen v. Prince, 45 Mich. 519.

[3] Thomas v. Bacon, 34 Hun (N. Y.), 88.

[4] Thomas v. Bacon, *supra*.

on the furniture which the lessee should place in the leased building. Afterwards the lessee gave a deed of trust on the same furniture to secure a loan. The landlord subsequently entered for non-payment of rent, took possession of the furniture, used it for a time, and then sold it for less than the amount of his claim. In a suit by the mortgagee against the landlord, to obtain payment for the use of the furniture while it was in his possession, it was held that the landlord was merely a pledgee of the property; and that, while he might retain possession of it, he could not use it without accounting for the value of its use.[1] The lien did not confer upon the landlord the title to the property. The mortgagee in the chattel mortgage, however, became invested with the title of ownership of such property after breach of the condition; and though the landlord, by virtue of his lien, was entitled to the immediate possession, he had not the title, and could not use the property without liability to the mortgagee, in whom the title was vested.

In an earlier case in this state it was held, that the lien of a landlord reserved in a lease of land rented for the purpose of cutting timber and wood, is not equivalent to a chattel mortgage, so as to preclude the lessee of disposing of the timber and wood cut before the landlord's reëntry for condition broken. The lien attaches to whatever property, upon which the lien was reserved, that may be found upon the premises or in the tenant's possession at the time of the reëntry.[2]

547. There may, however, be a sufficient delivery to a third person to protect the lien. Under a lease of a farm, the lessor was to have half of the products of the farm for rent, and a lien upon the other half for advances to be made. Among the products of the farm there was a quantity of cheese, which the parties carried to a railroad depot, and left with the agent for shipment to New York for sale, with the understanding that the lessor should receive the entire proceeds, and should account to the lessee for his share after payment of the advances made on a general settlement. Afterwards, on the same day, the lessee sold his interest in the cheese, which he pointed out to the purchaser at the depot, and verbally delivered to him, without the knowledge of the lessor, and with the intention to embarrass or defeat his enforcement of his lien. It was held that

---

[1] State v. Adams, 76 Mo. 605.   [2] Burgess v. Kattleman, 41 Mo. 480.

the sale was void as to the lessor ; and that, even if the sale was made in good faith, there was no change of possession sufficient to affect the lessor.[1]

If a lessor, having an equitable lien under a provision of the lease, does not take possession before the property passes into the hands of an assignee of the lessee for the benefit of his creditors, the equities of the other creditors are as great as his, and the court will not interfere to give his lien preference.[2]

A provision in a lease, that the lessor shall hold the crop to be raised as security for the rent, is inoperative as a lien against a purchaser in good faith, but is good as against a mere wrongdoer, who has no claim but possession, derived through the wrongful act.[3]

A provision in a lease of a farm, that whenever any of the products shall be sold the proceeds shall be paid to the lessor until he shall receive the full rent of it, is a mere personal covenant, and gives the lessor no lien upon such proceeds.[4]

The mere fact that the landlord agrees for a rent to be paid in a share of the crop to be raised by the tenant, gives the landlord no lien upon the crop.[5]

No lien attaches to a promissory note given for rent of land. The fact that it is given for rent adds nothing to its legal effect.[6]

548. A provision which in effect gives the lessor the ownership and control of a crop to be raised on the leased premises, makes his lien effectual against the lessee and all persons claiming under him. Such is the effect of a provision in a lease of a farm that the crops to be raised should be and remain the sole property of the lessor as a lien and security for the payment of the rent.[7] A provision in a lease of a farm that the lessor retains a full lien on all the crops as security for the payment of the rent, was held to constitute him the sole owner of the crops, and to entitle him to the control of them.[8] Such a

---

[1] Shepard v. Briggs, 26 Vt. 149.

[2] Reynolds v. Ellis, 34 Hun (N. Y.), 47.

[3] Fowler v. Hawkins, 17 Ind. 211.

[4] Barber v. Marble, 2 T. & C. (N. Y.) 114. See Brown v. Thomas, 14 Bradw. (Ill.) 428.

[5] Deaver v. Rice, 4 Dev. & B. (N. C.) 431.

[6] Roberts v. Jacks, 31 Ark. 597.

[7] Paris v. Vail, 18 Vt. 277; Smith v. Atkins, Ib. 461 ; virtually overruling Brainard v. Burton, 5 Vt. 97, which held that a lessor could acquire no property in crops before they are grown and delivered to him.

[8] Baxter v. Bush, 29 Vt. 465. See McCombs v. Becker, 3 Hun (N. Y.), 342; S. C. 5 T. & C. 550.

provision was regarded as the same in principle as that in the cases cited above where the lessor was to have the sole property in the crops as a lien. The provision that the lessor should have a lien on the crops is a legal implication of the control and ownership which were expressed in the other cases.

In a perpetual lease of real estate with fixtures and machinery, the lessor reserved a lien upon the property for the purchase-money and rents, but giving the lessee liberty to remove at his pleasure any portion of the machinery upon condition of substituting other machinery equally good. It was held that this reservation of a lien was not in legal effect a chattel mortgage, which the law required to be filed to make it valid, but that to the extent of the reservation the property never passed to the lessee; and therefore that the lien in favor of the lessor was superior to that of creditors of the lessee who had attached the property.[1]

If a lease be wholly inoperative, or operative only between the parties as an agreement, so that no legal title or estate passes to the lessee, then the title to crops raised upon the leased premises is in the landlord and not in the lessee, and a lien given by the lease may be enforced, not only as between the parties, but also as against attaching creditors of the lessee. Such creditors would acquire under the attachment only such title to the crops raised upon the leased premises as the lessee had; and the lessee in such case has no attachable interest.[2]

549. A lease which reserves a right of re-entry upon nonpayment of rent, is in effect a lien for the rent. And so, for a stronger reason, a conveyance of land in fee, subject to the payment of annual rents by the grantee to the grantor, with a reservation to the grantor of the right to enter and avoid the conveyance upon default of payment, gives the grantor a lien upon the premises for the rent, superior to that of a mortgagee of the grantee.[3]

550. Re-entry. — A provision in a lease that the lessor may enter upon the leased land and hold or sell the crops for the payment of the rent due him, gives him no priority until he

---

[1] Metcalfe v. Fosdick, 23 Ohio St. 114.

[2] Buswell v. Marshall, 51 Vt. 87.

[3] Stephenson v. Haines, 16 Ohio St. 478.

takes possession over subsequent purchasers and creditors of the lessee. Until the lessor takes possession the crops remain the property of the lessee, who may sell them, or his creditors may attach or levy executions upon them.[1] But where a lessor was to have part of a grain crop as rent, and was to have possession of the whole crop until the rent should be paid, a sale of the crop by the lessee was held not to pass the title as against the lessor. The purchaser took possession of the crop in the field, and placed it in charge of an agent, but the lessor took the grain from the agent and removed it to his warehouse. The court declared that so far as the crop was in possession of the lessee, he held it simply as a servant of the lessor, and that the lessee could give no right to the possession as against the lessor.[2]

II. *Statutory Liens and their Priority.*

551. At common law the landlord's right under a distraint attached only from the time of seizure for rent then due and payable, while a landlord's statutory lien attaches from the commencement of the tenancy.[3] " At common law the landlord could distrain any goods found upon the premises at the time of the taking, but he had no lien until he had made his right active by actual seizure. A statutory lien implies security upon the thing before the warrant to seize it is levied. It ties itself to the property from the time it attaches to it, and the levy and sale of the property are only means of enforcing it. In other words, if the lien is given by statute, proceedings are not necessary to fix the status of the property. But in the absence of this statutory lien, it is necessary to take proceedings to acquire a lien upon the property of the tenant for the benefit of the landlord. This the landlord is entitled to do in a summary way to satisfy the rent which is due him, and in this he has an advantage as creditor over creditors at large of the tenant."[4]

552. The lien of a distress warrant dates from the time of

---

[1] Butterfield v. Baker, 5 Pick. (Mass.) 522; Lewis v. Lyman, 22 Ib. 437 ; Munsell v. Carew, 2 Cush. (Mass.) 50; Wilkinson v. Ketler, 69 Ala. 435.

[2] Wentworth v. Miller, 53 Cal. 9.

[3] Morgan v. Campbell, 22 Wall. 381 ; Woodside v. Adams, 40 N. J. L.

417; Gibson v. Gautier, 1 Mack. (D. C.) 35 ; Stamps v. Gilman, 43 Miss. 456; Marye v. Dyche, 42 Miss. 347.

[4] Morgan v. Campbell, *supra*, per Davis, J. See, also, Hobbs v. Davis, 50 Ga. 213; Johnson v. Emanuel, 50 Ga. 590.

its levy.[1] Consequently a prior levy of a general execution or attachment takes priority of the landlord's lien under the distress warrant.[2] This was the common law before the passage of the English statute of 8 Anne,[3] which provided that after the first day of May, 1710, no goods upon leased lands should be liable to be taken on execution, unless the party at whose suit the execution is sued out shall, before the removal of such goods, pay to the landlord all sums due for the rent of the premises at the time of the taking of such goods, provided the arrears do not amount to more than one year's rent. This statute was always in force in Maryland,[4] and, being in force when the District of Columbia was set off in 1801, it became a part of the law of that District,[5] and continues in force to the present day. That statute does not, however, form a part of the common law as generally adopted in this country, and therefore the old common-law rule would prevail here when not modified by statute, and a creditor's execution, levied on the tenant's goods prior to a distraint, would take precedence of the landlord's claim for rent.[6] But statutes similar to the English statute have been generally adopted in this country in states where the right of distress exists.

553. The landlord's statutory lien for rent attaches from the beginning of the tenancy.[7] The lien exists independently of the prescribed methods for enforcing it. The lien attaches to

---

[1] Pierce v. Scott, 4 W. & S. (Pa.) 344; Hamilton v. Reedy, 3 McCord (S. C.), 38; Leopold v. Godfrey, 11 Biss. 158; Woodside v. Adams, 40 N. J. L. 417; Herron v. Gill, 112 Ill. 247, 252.

[2] Levy v. Twiname, 42 Ga. 249; Rowland v. Hewitt, 19 Bradw. (Ill.) 450; Hamilton v. Reedy, supra. Where a distress warrant for rent and an attachment for an ordinary debt are levied at the same time, and on the same property, the distress has priority. Canterberry v. Jordan, 27 Miss. 96.

[3] Ch. 14.

[4] Washington v. Williamson, 23 Md. 252. Also in force in South Carolina, Margart v. Swift, 3 McCord, 378.

[5] Gibson v. Gautier, 1 Mack. (D. C.) 35.

[6] Rowland v. Hewitt, supra; Herron v. Gill, supra; Ege v. Ege, 5 Watts (Pa.), 134, 139; Pierce v. Scott, supra; Hamilton v. Reedy, supra; Grant v. Whitwell, 9 Iowa, 152, 156; Doane v. Garretson, 24 Iowa, 351; Craddock v. Riddlesbarger, 2 Dana (Ky.), 205, 208.

[7] Morgan v. Campbell, 22 Wall. 381; Martin v. Stearns, 52 Iowa, 345; Garner v. Cutting, 32 Iowa, 547; Grant v. Whitwell, supra; Carpenter v. Gillespie, 10 Ib. 592; Doane v. Garretson, 24 Ib. 351, 355; Bryan v. Sanderson, 3 McArthur (D. C.), 431; Gibson v. Gautier, supra.

the property from the commencement of the tenancy, and the levy upon the property and the sale of it in the manner prescribed by the statute are only the means of enforcing the lien. The lien is given by the statute, and not by the proceedings to enforce the lien. A subsequent mortgage of the property or levy of execution upon it is subject to the lien for rent, and upon a sale of the property under such mortgage or execution the landlord may intervene, and is entitled to payment of his rent in arrear out of the proceeds before any payment is made on account of the mortgage or judgment, although he has taken no steps to enforce his lien.[1] And so, if the property subject to such lien comes into the possession of a court of equity, or of its officers, it comes into such possession subject to the lien created by the statute in favor of the landlord.[2]

554. A statutory lien takes precedence of a subsequent lien by attachment or execution levied upon the tenant's property.[3] This is so even as regards crops which are raised by a tenant upon shares; for while the right of property as between him and his landlord is in the tenant until a division of the crop takes place, yet a creditor of the tenant cannot seize the whole crop by execution or attachment regardless of the landlord's lien.[4]

A landlord's lien upon a crop of cotton raised upon the leased premises, and surrendered to him by the tenant in payment of rent and supplies furnished, is paramount to a judgment lien operative against the cotton before it was delivered to the landlord.[5]

555. Priority of lien to tenant's mortgage. — The lien of a landlord for rent attaches to the tenant's chattels upon the premises at the commencement of the tenancy, and to such chattels of his as he may afterwards bring upon the premises at any time during the continuance of the tenancy, from the time he brings them upon the premises.[6] The lien of the landlord has priority,

[1] Bryan v. Sanderson, 3 McArthur (D. C.), 431; Fox v. Davidson, 1 Mack. (D. C.) 102.

[2] Bryan v. Sanderson, supra; Fox v. Davidson, supra.

[3] Miles v. James, 36 Ill. 399; Cunnea v. Williams, 11 Bradw. (Ill.) 72; O'Hara v. Jones, 46 Ill. 288; Atkins v. Womeldorf, 53 Iowa, 150; Sullivan v. Cleveland, 62 Tex. 677.

[4] Atkins v. Womeldorf, supra.

[5] Okolona Savings Inst. v. Trice, 60 Miss. 262.

[6] Beall v. White, 94 U. S. 382; Fowler v. Rapley, 15 Wall. 328;

therefore, over a deed of trust or mortgage made by the tenant after the commencement of the tenancy, whether the chattels covered by the deed were upon the premises when it was executed or were subsequently acquired and placed upon them by the tenant.[1] It is immaterial that the mortgage purports to cover chattels to be acquired and placed upon the premises in the future; for in such case the terms of the deed are inconsistent with the statutory rights of the landlord, and must give place to them. Effect will not be given to a mortgage of after-acquired property to the prejudice of the rights of third persons.

When the landlord's lien is created by statute and attaches from the beginning of the tenancy, or from the time the property subject to it is placed upon the demised premises, the lien necessarily attaches before the mortgage, unless the mortgage was made before the tenancy commenced, or before the property was placed upon the premises. The landlord's lien does not prevail against the tenant's mortgagee whose mortgage is delivered and recorded before the lien attaches. When the lien attaches only upon the levy of a distress warrant, a mortgage executed and made an effectual lien before such levy must prevail as against the landlord.[2]

556. A landlord's statutory lien upon his tenant's crop is paramount to a mortgage of the crop executed by the tenant.[3] The landlord's lien accrues as soon as there is any crop upon which it may attach, and though the mortgage lien may attach at the same time, inasmuch as the statutory lien was created and was ready to attach from the beginning of the tenancy, it takes priority of a mortgage lien subsequently created by the tenant.

Although the owner of land has given a bond to convey it which does not provide for possession, but does provide that the obligee shall pay rent if he fails to pay the purchase-money, he has a lien for the rent which is superior to a chattel mortgage

Webb v. Sharp, 13 Wall. 14; Hadden v. Knickerbocker, 70 Ill. 677.

[1] Beall v. White, 94 U. S. 382.

[2] Woodside v. Adams, 40 N. J. L. 417; Hood v. Hanning, 4 Dana (Ky.), 21; Snyder v. Hitt, 2 Ib. 204.

[3] Tomlinson v. Greenfield, 31 Ark. 557; Meyer v. Bloom, 37 Ark. 43; Smith v. Meyer, 25 Ark. 609; Buck v. Lee, 36 Ark. 525; Lambeth v. Ponder, 33 Ark. 707; Watson v. Johnson, 33 Ark. 737; Roth v. Williams, 45 Ark. 447; Adams v. Hobbs, 27 Ark. 1; McGee v. Fitzer, 37 Tex. 27.

executed by the obligee upon the crop to be grown upon the land. The mortgagee relies on the title bond at his peril. He is bound to take notice of the limitation of the obligee's rights under the contract of sale.[1]

The assignment by a landlord of his lease carries with it a statutory lien on the crop, and the assignee is protected against a subsequent mortgage of the crop given by the landlord.[2]

557. A landlord's lien does not take precedence of a chattel mortgage existing when the lien attaches.[3] There are some statutory liens that are given precedence over existing mortgages, such as the lien for repairing vessels, or that of an agister for keeping and feeding cattle.[4] Such preference is given upon the principle that the mortgagee is as much benefited by the repairs of the vessel, or by the feeding of the cattle, as is the mortgagor. There may also be in many cases an implied authority in the mortgagor left in possession to incur upon the faith of the property whatever expense is necessary for its preservation.[5] But no such reason exists in the case of a landlord's lien. The mortgagee is not benefited by the renting of the premises to the mortgagor, out of which act the landlord's lien has its origin, nor is the mortgaged property thereby preserved or enhanced in value. The lien of a mortgage of chattels executed before a lease is prior to the landlord's lien under the lease, although the mortgagee has actual knowledge that such chattels are being used upon the leased premises.[6]

558. A fraudulent cancellation of the prior chattel mortgage does not give the landlord's lien priority. Thus, if the mortgage note be assigned after the landlord's lien has attached, without an assignment of the mortgage, and the mortgagee fraudulently enters satisfaction on the margin of the record, and after this a third person is substituted for one of the original

---

[1] Bacon v. Howell, 60 Miss. 362.

[2] Taylor v. Nelson, 54 Miss. 524.

[3] Rand v. Barrett, 66 Iowa, 731; Perry v. Waggoner, 68 Iowa, 403; Jarchow v. Pickens, 51 Iowa, 381; Hempstead Ass'n v. Cochran, 60 Tex. 620; Souders v. Vansickle, 3 Halst. (N. J.) 313.

[4] Provost v. Wilcox, 17 Ohio, 359; Case v. Allen, 21 Kans. 217.

[5] Jones on Chattel Mortgages, § 474; Hempstead Ass'n v. Cochran, supra.

[6] Jarchow v. Pickens, supra.

lessees without making a new lease, the mortgage is still entitled to priority.[1]

559. The tenant's assignee in bankruptcy or insolvency, or for the benefit of creditors, takes the property subject to the landlord's lien. If the lien is created by the lease or by statute, the assignee takes the property subject to the lien, whether the assignment took place before or after a distraint or attachment upon the property by the landlord. His right is not affected by the assignment.[2] At common law the right of distraint would be cut off by a prior assignment in insolvency or for the benefit of creditors.[3] Where at the present time a lien is given by statute, but a distress warrant is one of the remedies for enforcing it, the lien does not depend upon a levy of the distress warrant, but exists independently of that,[4] and therefore takes precedence of an assignment in insolvency or for the benefit of creditors.

560. An assignment in bankruptcy of a tenant's property takes precedence of a distress warrant levied after the commencement of the proceedings in bankruptcy. The assignment relates back to the commencement of the proceedings, and by operation of law vests the title of the estate of the bankrupt in the assignee. No lien attaches under a distress warrant until the property is actually seized under it. If the lien attached before the filing of the petition, it could be enforced in the bankrupt court; but if it did not exist then, it could not be brought into existence afterwards.[5]

In Pennsylvania, a landlord having a right to distrain for rent in arrear, at the date of the issuing of a warrant in bankruptcy, is entitled to be paid in full by the assignee in bankruptcy, be-

---

[1] Rand v. Barrett, 66 Iowa, 731.

[2] Eames v. Mayo, 6 Bradw. (Ill.) 334; Hoskins v. Paul, 4 Halst. (N. J.) 110; Rosenberg v. Shaper, 51 Tex. 134; In re Wynne, Chase, Dec. 227, 256, per C. J. Chase.

[3] In re Wynne, supra, per C. J. Chase.

[4] Hunter v. Whitfield, 89 Ill. 229; In re Wynne, supra; Rosenberg v.

Shaper, supra; Dutcher v. Culver, 24 Minn. 584. Though the landlord himself be the assignee, his acceptance of the trust is not a waiver of his right.

In Pennsylvania, whenever an execution will carry a valid sale over the assignee, it carries with it a claim for rent. Barnes' App. 76 Pa. St. 50.

[5] Morgan v. Campbell, 22 Wall. 381.

fore the removal of the goods, rent in arrear not exceeding one year, in preference to all other creditors.[1]

Whether the lien of a distress warrant, which has already been levied upon the tenant's property at the time of the filing of a petition in bankruptcy against him, is dissolved by the assignment in bankruptcy, in the same manner as an attachment upon mesne process is dissolved, is a question that has occasioned some discussion.[2]

III. *To what Property the Liens Attach.*

561. At common law all chattels found upon the demised premises were prima facie distrainable, whether they belonged to the tenant or not. The landlord's prerogative of distraint is an ancient one, having its origin in feudal tenures. It seems to have originated from two remedies of the common law still more ancient. By the processes of *gavelet* and *cessavit* the landlord could seize the land itself for rent in arrear, and hold it until payment was made. These processes fell into disuse long ago, and in their place the landlord's right of distress arose, whereby, instead of seizing the land, he seized all movables upon the land, and held them until he received payment. In process of time he was authorized by statute to sell the property seized, and in this way we have the modern process of distraint.[3]

562. The general rule still is, that all chattels found upon the demised premises are prima facie liable to distress for rent. Certain property may be exempt upon grounds of public policy, or by force of express statute ; but it is incumbent upon the claimant of such property to show that it falls within such exemption. The fact that the chattels belong to a stranger was no ground for exemption at common law, and is not now except when so declared by statute.[4] The goods of a married

---

[1] Longstreth *v.* Pennock, 20 Wall. 575, 576; Gibson *v.* Gautier, 1 Mack. (D. C.) 35.

[2] Morgan *v.* Campbell, 22 Wall. 381, 393. The case was decided on another point.

[3] Emig *v.* Cunningham, 62 Md. 458, per Bryan, J.

[4] Kleber *v.* Ward, 88 Pa. St. 93; Spencer *v.* M'Gowen, 13 Wend. (N. Y.) 256; Ratcliff *v.* Daniel, 6 H. & J. (Md.) 498 ; Cromwell *v.* Owings, 7 Ib. 55, 58; Kennedy *v.* Lange, 50 Md. 91; Giles *v.* Ebsworth, 10 Md. 333; Trieber *v.* Knabe, 12 Md. 491 (1858). In the latter case a distress for the rent of a hotel was levied upon a piano-forte belonging to a stranger, and leased to a music-teacher who boarded in the hotel; and not being

woman found upon the demised premises may be distrained for rent due by her husband.[1] So the goods of an under-tenant.[2]

This common-law rule has generally been modified by statute in America, so that the goods of a stranger on the premises are not liable to distress, but only the goods of the tenant, or of some other person who is liable for the rent.[3]

563. Exemptions from distress on the ground of public policy. — The landlord's prerogative of distress authorized the seizure of any chattels found upon the premises, though they might not belong to the tenant, on the ground that the landlord may be supposed to have given credit to all the visible property upon the premises. Upon considerations of public policy certain property was exempt from seizure. Chief Justice Willes in 1744 stated clearly the exemptions then established, saying:[4] —

"There are five sorts of things which at common law were not distrainable : —

"1. Things annexed to the freehold.

"2. Things delivered to a person exercising a public trade, to be carried, wrought, worked up, or managed in the way of his trade or employ.

"3. Cocks or sheaves of corn.

"4. Beasts of the plough and instruments of husbandry.

in use as an instrument of trade or profession, and there not being a sufficiency of other goods on the premises, the piano-forte was held liable to distraint. See, also, Reeves v. McKenzie, 1 Bailey (S. C.), 497 ; Kessler v. M'Conachy, 1 Rawle (Pa.), 435; Price v. M'Callister, 3 Grant (Pa.), 248 ; Karns v. McKinney, 74 Pa. St. 387; Whiting v. Lake, 91 Ib. 349; Stevens v. Lodge, 7 Blackf. (Ind.) 594; Himely v. Wyatt, 1 Bay (S. C.), 102.

[1] Emig v. Cunningham, 62 Md. 458 (1884); Blanche v. Bradford, 38 Pa. St. 344.

[2] Lane v. Steinmetz, 9 Weekly N. C. (Pa.) 574. A sub-tenant cannot compel the lessor to sell the goods of the original lessee, in satisfaction of the rent in arrear, before having recourse

to his own. Jimison v. Reifsneider, 97 Pa. St. 136, reversing S. C. 37 Leg. Int. 273. If the landlord distrain upon a sub-tenant, he must show affirmatively that a former distress upon his immediate tenant was unproductive. Quinn v. Wallace, 6 Whart. (Pa.) 452.

[3] **Mississippi** : Stamps v. Gilman, 43 Miss. 456; Marye v. Dyche, 42 Miss. 347.

Kentucky: Hall v. Amos, 5 T. B. Mon. 89.

Virginia : By Act of 1818; Davis v. Payne, 4 Rand. 332.

[4] Simpson v. Hartopp, Willes, 512. And see, in support, Muspratt v. Gregory, 3 M. & W. 677, per Lord Denman; Joule v. Jackson, 7 Ib. 450, 454, per Baron Parke ; Fenton v. Logan, 9 Bing. 676, per Tindal, C. J.

" 5. The instruments of a man's trade or profession.

" The first three sorts were absolutely free from distress, and could not be distrained, even though there were no other goods besides.

" The two last are only exempt *sub modo*, that is, upon a supposition that there is sufficient distress besides.

" Things annexed to the freehold, as furnaces, mill-stones, chimney-pieces, and the like, cannot be distrained, because they cannot be taken away without doing damage to the freehold, which the law will not allow.

" Things sent or delivered to a person exercising a trade, to be carried, wrought, or manufactured in the way of his trade, as a horse in a smith's shop, materials sent to a weaver, or cloth to a tailor to be made up, are privileged for the sake of trade and commerce, which could not be carried on if such things under these circumstances could be distrained for rent due from the person in whose custody they are." [1]

564. Upon the ground of the privilege of trade,[2] it is well settled that all goods delivered to tradesmen,[3] artificers, manu-

---

[1] In further explanation of, and comment upon, these exemptions, Chief Justice Willes continues : —

" Cocks and sheaves of corn were not distrainable before the statute 2 W. & M. ch. 5 (which was made in favor of landlords), because they could not be restored again in the same plight and condition that they were before upon a replevin, but must necessarily be damaged by being removed.

" Beasts of the plough, etc., were not distrainable, in favor of husbandry (which is of so great advantage to the nation), and likewise because a man should not be left quite destitute of getting a living for himself and his family. And the same reasons hold in the case of the instruments of a man's trade or profession.

" But these two last are not privileged in case there is distress enough besides; otherwise they may be distrained.

" These rules are laid down and fully explained in Co. Lit. 47 *a, b,* and many other books which are there cited ; and there are many subsequent cases in which the same doctrine is established, and which I do not mention because I do not know any one case to the contrary."

[2] Muspratt *v.* Gregory, 3 M. & W. 677, 678; Gilman *v.* Elton, 3 Brod. & B. 75; Findon *v.* McLaren, 6 Q. B. 891; Matthias *v.* Mesnard, 2 Car. & P. 353; Brown *v.* Sims, 17 S. & R. (Pa.) 138; Connah *v.* Hale, 23 Wend. (N. Y.) 462; Walker *v.* Johnson, 4 McCord (S. C.), 552; horse at livery-stable, Youngblood *v.* Lowry, 2 McCord (S. C.) 39; cattle reserved for agistment, Cadwalader *v.* Tindall, 20 Pa. St. 422; a merchant's books of account, Davis *v.* Arledge, 3 Hill (S. C.), 170.

[3] For an exceptional case see Goodrich *v.* Bodley, 35 La. Ann. 525.

facturers,[1] carriers, factors,[2] auctioneers,[3] and the like, are exempt from distress for rent.

Upon a like principle are exempt the goods of a traveller at an inn,[4] and goods of a boarder in his own use.[5] Otherwise, if the boarder's goods are with his consent in the tenant's use.[6]

The goods of others, in the hands of tenants who are such bailees, are exempt from distress, not on account of a special privilege to the tenant, but for the benefit of trade and commerce, and for the purpose of protecting the owner of the goods, who has confided them to the tenant for sale, storage, transportation, manufacture, repair, or the like purpose.[7]

The fact that the goods belong to a bailee must be proved in order to establish the exemption on this ground.[8]

565. General exemption laws do not apply as against a distress. A distress is not an execution for debt, and therefore the goods of a tenant have never been held to be protected by any of the exemption laws which put the property of a debtor beyond the reach of his creditors. In like manner, although the constitution of a state declares that the property of a wife shall be protected from the debt of her husband, this declaration has no effect upon the right of distress. If the goods of the wife were upon the premises of any other tenant, they would be liable to distraint, and in such case the goods of an unmarried woman could be seized. It was not intended to give any greater immunity to a married woman's property than was extended to it before marriage.[9]

566. A landlord's statutory lien for rent does not gen-

---

[1] Knowles v. Pierce, 5 Houst. (Del.) 178; Hoskins v. Paul, 4 Halst. (N. J.) 110.

[2] Howe Machine Co. v. Sloan, 87 Pa. St. 438; Walker v. Johnson, 4 McCord (S. C.), 552; Brown v. Sims, 17 S. & R. (Pa.) 138; Briggs v. Large, 30 Pa. St. 287; McCreery v. Clafflin, 37 Md. 435; Trieber v. Knabe, 12 Md. 491.

[3] Himely v. Wyatt, 1 Bay (S. C.), 102; Brown v. Arundell, 10 C. B. 54; Williams v. Holmes, 8 Exch. 861.

[4] Harris v. Boggs, 5 Blackf. (Ind.) 489.

[5] Riddle v. Welden, 5 Whart. (Pa.) 9; Jones v. Goldbeck, 8 Weekly N. C. (Pa.) 533; S. C. 14 Phila. 173; Lane v. Steinmetz, 9 Weekly N. C. (Pa.) 574.

[6] Matthews v. Stone, 1 Hill (N. Y.), 565.

[7] McCreery v. Clafflin, 37 Md. 435, 442.

[8] Bevan v. Crooks, 7 W. & S. (Pa.) 452.

[9] Emig v. Cunningham, 62 Md. 458, per Bryan, J.

erally attach to goods of other persons which happen to be upon the demised premises.[1] It does not attach to the goods of a sub-tenant of a part of the demised premises,[2] unless specially so provided by statute, as is the case in Louisiana.[3] The terms of the statutes in the different states are, however, quite dissimilar, and reference must be had to these statutes to determine the extent of the lien.

Thus, in Iowa, the statute gives a lien upon property used upon the premises. The lien, therefore, attaches to all personal property kept by the tenant upon the premises for the prosecution of the business for which the tenancy was created. Therefore the lien attaches to merchandise kept for sale upon the leased premises. The lien is given not merely in case of leases of farms and agricultural lands, but also in case of leases of houses and store-rooms. The property *used* upon the premises is made subject to the lien. The word is employed in a large and liberal sense, and the only limitation intended is that incident to the nature and purposes of the occupation of the premises. Thus, the cloths and goods of a merchant tailor, when *used* for the purposes of sale, and for making into garments for customers, upon premises hired for such purposes, are subject to the statutory lien of the landlord.[4]

567. **The lien attaches only to personal property.** If it be sought to enforce the lien or to levy a distress warrant upon a dwelling-house, some agreement changing the character of the property must be shown, for the presumption is that it is part of the realty.[5] The lessee may, however, by stipulation in the lease, give the lessor a lien on buildings to be erected by the lessee, and such a lien, like the landlord's ordinary lien by statute, will prevail against the lessee's assignee in insolvency, or for the benefit of his creditors.[6]

Things fixed to the realty are not, as a general rule, subject to distress or to a lien; but a tenant's trade fixtures, when separated from the realty by the tenant, may be distrained for rent.[7]

---

[1] Johnson v. Douglass, 2 Mack. (D. C.) 36; Wells v. Sequin, 14 Iowa, 143.

[2] Gray v. Rawson, 11 Ill. 527.

[3] See § 620.

[4] Grant v. Whitwell, 9 Iowa, 152.

[5] Kassing v. Keohane, 4 Bradw.

(Ill.) 460; Hamilton v. Reedy, 3 M'C. (S. C.) 38.

[6] Webster v. Nichols, 104 Ill. 160.

[7] Reynolds v. Shuler, 5 Cow. (N. Y.) 323; Vausse v. Russel, 2 M'C. (S. C.) 329.

A fixture which is removable at the tenant's pleasure, it being only slightly attached to the realty, so that it may be removed without destroying its character, such, for instance, as a spinning-mule fastened to the floor of a mill with screws, is distrainable.[1]

568. A landlord's lien upon crops covers the entire crops raised upon the demised premises. Therefore, where land is rented for a share of the crops, and the tenant delivers to the landlord his share of the oats raised upon the land, but makes default in paying the rent upon the land planted in corn, the landlord has a lien on the remainder of the oats for the payment of the rent of the land planted with corn. The lien is not confined to any particular crop, but embraces all the crops, or any portion of them, and extends to crops on every part of the premises for the whole rent.[2] If, however, the different tracts are not all rented by one demise, but there is a distinct rent for each, the crops on one tract are not subject to lien for rent of another tract.[3]

569. The landlord's lien is not made to attach to property not on the demised premises, unless he is authorized by statute to follow it after removal, as in case he can show that the removal was fraudulent.[4] A purchaser from a tenant, in good faith, of property not on the demised premises, is not affected by a landlord's lien afterwards established. A distress at common law for rent must be made upon the demised premises,[5] and the right terminates with removal, unless the right be expressly extended by statute. Even where the tenant assigns the goods to a receiver, under a creditor's bill, and the receiver removes them from the demised premises into the public street, they are not then liable to distraint, though the creditor has notice that the tenant's rent is in arrear.[6] Goods removed from the premises by assignees for the benefit of creditors are not liable to distress.[7]

Goods of a stranger can only be distrained for rent while they are on the demised premises.[8]

[1] Furbush v. Chappell, 105 Pa. St. 187.

[2] Prettyman v. Unland, 77 Ill. 206; Thompson v. Mead, 67 Ill. 395.

[3] Gittings v. Nelson, 86 Ill. 591.

[4] Nesbitt v. Bartlett, 14 Iowa, 485.

[5] Bradley v. Piggot, Walk. (Miss.) 348.

[6] Martin v. Black, 9 Paige (N. Y.), 641.

[7] Hastings v. Belknap, 1 Den. (N. Y.) 190; Martin v. Black, 3 Edw. Ch. 580.

[8] Adams v. La Comb, 1 Dall. (Pa.

570. A landlord's lien attaches to property which is already subject to a mortgage or other incumbrance, when it is placed upon the demised premises, but the lien attaches in such case subject to the prior mortgage or incumbrance.[1] Care must be taken, however, that no substantial injury be done to the interest of the mortgagee in seizing and selling the equity of redemption.[2]

A distress at common law could not, however, be levied upon an equity of redemption.[3] But this may generally be done under the modern statutes modifying the common law remedy.[4]

IV. What Rent is Secured by the Liens.

571. The right of distress at common law cannot arise until there has been an actual demise at a fixed rent, payable either in money, services, or a share of the crops. Unless there is rent due, there can be no distress. The first requisite to support the proceeding is proof of a demise under which rent is payable.[5] The right is incident to the reservation of rent where the reversionary interest remains in the lessor.[6] The rent need not be reserved *eo nomine*, if it appear that it is really payable.[7]

440; Scott *v.* McEwen, 2 Phila. (Pa.) 176; Sleeper *v.* Parrish, 7 Ib. 247.

[1] Johnson *v.* Douglass, 2 Mack. (D C.) 36; Woodside *v.* Adams, 40 N. J. L. 417; Holladay *v.* Bartholomae, 11 Bradw. (Ill.) 206; Johnson *v.* Douglass, *supra;* Fisher *v.* Kollerts, 16 B. Mon. (Ky.) 398, 408; Williams *v.* Wood, 2 Met. (Ky.) 41, 42.

[2] Woodside *v.* Adams, *supra.* In this case Mr. Justice Depue said : "The property mortgaged may be a single chattel of considerable value, or the machinery in a factory, or the stock of goods in a store, which may be sold in entirety or in parcels, subject to the lien of the mortgage, without any appreciable injury to the right of the mortgagor. To permit the officer to take such possession only as will enable him to make a legal sale under his execution, would be consonant with public policy, and consistent with sound legal principles, provided that, in doing so, no substantial injury be done to the interests of the mortgagee."

[3] Snyder *v.* Hitt, 2 Dana (Ky.), 204 ; Trescott *v.* Smyth, 1 McCord (S. C.), Ch. 486.

[4] Prewett *v.* Dobbs, 13 S. & M. (Miss.) 431.

[5] Cohen *v.* Broughton, 54 Ga. 296; Moulton *v.* Norton, 5 Barb. (N. Y.) 286; Grier *v.* Cowan, Add. (Pa.) 347; Wells *v.* Hornish, 3 P. & W. (Pa.) 30; Helser *v.* Pott, 3 Pa. St. 179; Johnson *v.* Prussing, 4 Bradw. (Ill.) 575; Jacks *v.* Smith, 1 Bay (S. C.), 315; Marshall *v.* Giles, 3 Brev. (S. C.) 488; Reeves *v.* McKenzie, 1 Bail. (S. C.) 497; Hale *v.* Burton, Dud. (Ga.) 105.

[6] Cornell *v.* Lamb, 2 Cow. (N. Y.) 652; Schuyler *v.* Leggett, Ib. 660; Wells *v.* Hornish, *supra.*

[7] Price *v.* Limehouse, 4 McCord (S. C.), 544.

The rent must be due and payable;[1] but rent payable in advance may be distrained for as soon as it is payable by the terms of the demise.[2]

572. For the purpose of a distress the rent must be fixed and certain, but it is sufficiently fixed and certain if it is capable of being reduced to a certainty by computation.[3] If, for instance, the rent be payable in cotton, as this has a certain commercial value from day to day throughout the country, the exact money value of the rent is capable of exact calculation.[4] If the rent be payable in grain or other produce, or in a share of the crops, or in merchandise, and the price of these be stipulated in the contract, or can be determined by a market price, the remedy will lie.[5] But if there be no fixed price for the rent, or this be payable in services and no price has been agreed upon for the services, there can be no distress for the rent.[6]

A share of the profits of a business reserved as rent may be distrained for, if the amount can be determined from the books of account.[7] If the rent be payable in goods upon the order or demand of the lessor, a prior demand is necessary to sustain a distress.[8] Under a lease for a fixed rent in money, and an additional rent of thirty dollars for each five hundred dollars of improvements made on premises by the lessor, the additional rent

[1] Anders v. Blount, 67 Ga. 41; Fry v. Breckinridge, 7 B. Mon. (Ky.) 31; Evans v. Herring, 27 N. J. L. 243; Burchard v. Rees, 1 Whart. (Pa.) 377.

[2] Conway v. Starkweather, 1 Den. (N. Y.) 113; Russell v. Doty, 4 Cow. (N. Y.) 576; Peters v. Newkirk, 6 Ib. 103; Giles v. Comstock, 4 N. Y. 270, 272; Bailey v. Wright, 3 McCord (S. C.), 484; O'Farrell v. Nance, 2 Hill (S. C.), 484; Collins' App. 35 Pa. St. 83; Beye v. Fenstermacher, 2 Whart. (Pa.) 95; Anderson's App. 3 Pa. St. 218.

[3] Smith v. Colson, 10 Johns. (N. Y.) 91; Valentine v. Jackson, 9 Wend. (N. Y.) 302; Smith v. Fyler, 2 Hill (N. Y.), 648; Dutcher v. Culver, 24 Minn. 584; Brooks v. Cunningham, 49 Miss. 108; Tifft v. Verden, 11 S. & M. (Miss.) 153; Smith v. Sheriff,

1 Bay (S. C.), 443; Fraser v. Davie, 5 Rich (S. C.), 59; Ege v. Ege, 5 Watts (Pa.), 134; Detwiler v. Cox, 75 Pa. St. 200.

[4] Brooks v. Cunningham, supra; Fraser v. Davie, supra.

[5] Briscoe v. McElween, 43 Miss. 556; Jones v. Gundrim, 3 W. & S. (Pa.) 531; Fry v. Jones, 2 Rawle (Pa.), 11. See McCray v. Samuel, 65 Ga. 739. See, however, Bowser v. Scott, 8 Blackf. (Ind.) 86; Clark v. Fraley, 3 Ib. 264; Poer v. Peebles, 1 B. Mon. (Ky.) 1.

[6] Briscoe v. McElween, supra. See, however, Wilkins v. Taliafero, 52 Ga. 208; Dailey v. Grimes, 27 Md. 440; Wells v. Hornish, 3 P. & W. (Pa.) 30; Marshall v. Giles, 2 Treadw. (S. C.) Const. 637.

[7] Melick v. Benedict, 43 N. J. L. 425.

[8] Helser v. Potts, 3 Pa. St. 179.

may be distrained for, for the amount of the rent can be determined.[1]

Under a covenant to pay rent in Indiana scrip, distress was held not to lie. Presumably the value was too uncertain.[2]

573. At common law, the landlord could distrain his tenant's goods for rent only after the rent was due and payable;[3] and if, in the mean while, and before the rent was due, a judgment creditor issued an execution and levied upon the same goods, he had priority over the landlord. By the statute of 8 Anne[4] it was provided, that whenever execution was levied upon the tenant's goods on the premises, the judgment creditor should be bound to pay to the landlord the rent due at the time of the levy to the extent of one year's rent, and the sheriff might include this in the levy against the tenant. Under this statute it seems to be settled that the landlord had a claim only to the rent which had actually accrued prior to the levy of an execution upon the tenant's goods, and no claim for an instalment of rent then accruing.[5]

But generally, under the statutes in this country modifying the right of distress, the landlord may claim the accruing rent up to the time of the levy of the execution. When an execution is levied upon a tenant's goods after a periodical instalment of rent has begun to accrue, the landlord is entitled to be paid not only the rent then in arrear, but the amount for the periodical instalment then accruing. Thus, where the tenancy is from month to month, and one month has commenced, we may assume that the landlord's lien for the rent of that month commences with the month. It commences before the rent is due, and has priority over a lien acquired by execution issued during the month. The landlord is entitled to the whole of the accruing rent for that month.[6]

[1] Detwiler v. Cox, 75 Pa. St. 200.

[2] Purcell v. Thomas, 7 Blackf. (Ind.) 306.

[3] 3 Bl. Com. 6, 7; Evans v. Herring, 27 N. J. L. 243; Weiss v. Jahn, 37 N. J. L. 93.

[4] Ch. 14.

[5] Hoskins v. Knight, 1 Maule & S. 245, 247; Trappan v. Morie, 18 Johns. (N. Y.) 1; Washington v. Williamson, 23 Md. 244; Harris v. Dammann, 3 Mack. (D. C.) 90, per Cox, J.; Denham v. Harris, 13 Ala. 465; Whidden v. Toulnim, 6 Ala. 104.

[6] Joyce v. Wilkenning, 1 MacArthur (D. C.), 567; Gibson v. Gautier, 1 Mack. (D. C.) 35; Harris v. Dammann, supra.

574. But the landlord's lien does not extend beyond the accruing rent of the period in which the execution is levied, although the officer, instead of removing the goods, keeps them upon the premises for a longer period.[1] The landlord may have his remedy against the sheriff, but not against the tenant's goods.

575. The statutory lien for rent does not depend upon the maturity of the rent. Even before the rent falls due, it takes precedence of a lien by attachment.[2] The lien attaches at the commencement of the tenancy for the entire term, although it is not enforcible as to rent which has not accrued, so long as the property is dealt with in the usual course of business, as contemplated by the lease.[3] The lien may be enforced for rent not due whenever this is necessary to prevent such a disposition of the property by the tenant as would make the security worthless.[4] Therefore, where a building was leased as a store-room, and occupied with a stock of merchandise, it was held that the execution of an absolute sale or of a mortgage of the stock by the tenant rendered the lien enforcible for the rent of the entire unexpired term of the lease.[5]

576. Expenses, costs, and the like. — Where the rent is payable in a share of the crops grown on the demised premises, and by the terms of the lease the lessee is to gather and deliver to the landlord his share, and he fails to do so, and the landlord is obliged to gather it himself, he has a lien for the value of such labor as a part of t he rent which the tenant agreed to pay, or in addition thereto.[6]

The lien for rent includes also the costs of the action brought to enforce the lien by attachment.[7]

[1] Harris v. Dammann, 3 Mack. (D. C.) 90, 94. "If we should go any further and hold that the rent which accrued for the next period afterwards should be paid, there would be no limit in case of leases running for a term of years. We should have to yold that, at the commencement of the term, the landlord's lien attached for the whole term, giving him a preference for the whole over an execution creditor who levied pending the term. This would effectually cover up the tenant's property from his other creditors." Per Cox, J.

[2] Sevier v. Shaw, 25 Ark. 417; Martin v. Stearns, 52 Iowa, 345.

[3] Martin v. Stearns, supra.

[4] Martin v. Stearns, supra.

[5] Gilbert v. Greenbaum, 56 Iowa, 211.

[6] Decrist v. Stivers, 35 Iowa, 580.

[7] Conwell v. Kuykendall, 29 Kans. 707.

Under a covenant to pay for gas used upon the premises, a sum due for gas is to be regarded as rent in arrear, and may be distrained for.[1]

A landlord can only distrain for rent in arrear. He cannot distrain for interest,[2] nor for a claim on any other account.[3]

V. *How the Liens may be Waived or Lost.*

577. A landlord's statutory lien upon his tenant's goods is lost by a sale made by the tenant to a purchaser in good faith for a valuable consideration. If the property was not upon the leased premises at the time of the purchase, and there is no evidence that it had been fraudulently removed, there is strong ground to believe that the purchaser took the property in good faith, and therefore free of the landlord's lien.[4] A purchaser of a crop of cotton, who buys after it has been removed by the tenant to a gin, and without notice, takes it discharged of the landlord's lien.[5] And so a factor who, without notice of any lien, makes advances on cotton raised upon rented land and stored with him by the tenant, has a lien on the cotton in preference to the landlord's lien for rent.[6] In like manner a landlord's lien does not prevail against any *bonâ fide* purchaser from the tenant.[7] Whether the purchaser buys the goods upon the leased premises and himself removes them, or whether he buys them of the tenant after they have been removed by the latter, is chiefly of importance with reference to the question whether the purchaser bought in good faith without notice of the lien, for a lien is not lost by a sale to a purchaser with notice of the lien.[8]

578. A landlord's statutory lien on a crop is lost by a sale by the tenant to a purchaser without notice after its

---

[1] Fernwood Masonic Hall Asso. v. Jones, 102 Pa. St. 307.

[2] Lansing v. Rattoone, 6 Johns. (N. Y.) 43; Vecht v. Brownell, 8 Paige (N. Y.), 212.

[3] Sketoe v. Ellis, 14 Ill. 75.

[4] Nesbitt v. Bartlett, 14 Iowa, 485; Grant v. Whitwell, 9 Iowa, 152.

[5] Puckett v. Reed, 31 Ark. 131.

[6] Clark v. Dobbins, 52 Ga. 656; Wilson v. Walker, 46 Ga. 319; Frazer v. Jackson, 46 Ga. 621; Rose v. Gray, 40 Ga. 156.

[7] Webb v. Sharp, 13 Wall. 14; Slocum v. Clark, 2 Hill (N. Y.), 475; Coles v. Marquand, Ib. 447; Frisbey v. Thayer, 25 Wend. (N. Y.), 396; Martin v. Black, 9 Paige, 641; Hastings v. Belknap, 1 Den. 190; Davis v. Payne, 4 Rand. (Va.) 332, 333; Stone v. Bohm, 79 Ky. 141; Herron v. Gill, 112 Ill. 247; Hadden v. Knickerbocker, 70 Ill. 677; Lamotte v. Wisner, 51 Md. 543.

[8] Volmer v. Wharton, 34 Ark. 691.

removal from the leased premises.[1]   The lien does not change
the ownership of the crop, nor put any restraint upon the incidents of ownership, except as against persons dealing with the
tenant with notice of the lien.   The lien of course prevails
against the tenant himself so long as he has possession, and
against volunteers and purchasers from him with notice, though
upon a valuable consideration.   The statute itself may be a sufficient notice of the lien so long as the tenant remains in possession upon the rented land.   But when the crop is removed
from the rented land by the tenant, he then has a separate possession of the crop only, distinct from the land, and such possession must furnish security to all who deal with him in good faith
and for value; otherwise there would be no safety in dealing in
agricultural products.   Statutes are always to be construed in
accordance with the common law, and are not regarded as in-
fringing upon its rules and principles, except so far as may be
expressed, or fairly implied to give them full operation.   When
a charge merely is created by statute, it cannot be supposed, unless the intention is clearly expressed or may be justly inferred,
that the charge is to have a superiority which the common law
does not attach to such a charge.   The common law protects
purchasers in good faith from secret liens of which they have no
notice.[2]

579. The mere consent of a landlord to a removal of a
crop from the rented premises is not necessarily a waiver
of his lien on the crop.   Much must depend upon the purposes
for which the consent was given.   If the landlord consents to a
removal and sale of the crop, a sale to a *bonâ fide* purchaser
would operate a destruction of the lien.   But if he should consent to a removal in order that the crop might be better prepared for market, or more safely stored, it would be unjust to
infer that he waived, or intended to waive, the lien.   All the
attendant circumstances should be considered, and from these
the intention of the landlord should be inferred; and from these
also it should be determined whether one dealing with the tenant in good faith, and finding the crop in the possession of the

---

[1] Scaife *v.* Stovall, 67 Ala. 237.   [2] Scaife   *v.*   Stovall, *supra*, per
Brickell, C. J.

tenant separated from the possession of the rented premises, has been misled.[1]

580. There are, however, some decisions that go to the extent of charging the purchaser of a crop from a tenant with notice of the statutory lien, in the same way that a purchaser from a mortgagor is chargeable with notice of a duly recorded mortgage of the property.   In such case the purchaser can acquire no better title than the vendor had, and the removal of the crop by the purchaser amounts to a conversion, which renders the purchaser liable for the value of the crop converted, to the extent of the rent due or to become due from the tenant.[2]

The purchaser may be chargeable with such notice from a knowledge of circumstances from which he should infer the existence of the lien.   Thus, if one purchasing corn knows that the seller had been living, during the year in which the corn was raised, upon the farm of another, where the corn was then stored, and that the owner of the land was living there at the time of the sale, the purchaser is chargeable with notice of the landlord's lien.[3]   The purchaser's knowledge of the fact of the tenancy, and of the fact that the corn was raised on the demised premises, has been held to imply notice to him of any lien the landlord may have for unpaid rent;[4] but the better opinion seems to be that mere knowledge by the purchaser of the fact that rent is due and owing from the tenant is not sufficient to invalidate his purchase as against the landlord.[5]

581. A lien upon a stock of goods kept as merchandise upon the leased premises is displaced by sales in the usual course of trade, if the goods are delivered to the purchasers and they remove them from the leased premises.   The lien in such case is upon the chattels in bulk, or upon the stock in mass, and not in detail.[6]   Business could not be safely carried on unless goods sold and delivered in the usual course of business became discharged of the lien.

[1] Tuttle v. Walker, 69 Ala. 172; Coleman v. Siler, 74 Ala. 435.

[2] Kennard v. Harvey, 80 Ind. 37; Watt v. Scofield, 76 Ill. 261; Volmer v. Wharton, 34 Ark. 691; Lamotte v. Wisner, 51 Md. 543.

[3] Hunter v. Whitfield, 89 Ill. 229; Prettyman v. Unland, 77 Ill. 206.

[4] Watt v. Scofield, supra.

[5] Herron v. Gill, 112 Ill. 247, 251.

[6] Fowler v. Rapley, 15 Wall. 328, 336, per Clifford, J.; Webb v. Sharp, 13 Wall. 14, 15; Holden v. Cox, 60 Iowa, 449; Knox v. Hunt, 18 Mo. 243.

In the case of goods kept for sale, it would seem that the lien would not attach to goods sold in good faith and for a valuable consideration before proceedings are commenced to enforce the lien.[1] In case the leased property is a farm or agricultural land, the stock of the tenant, such as cows, horses, and hogs, are not kept for sale to the same extent as goods in a store ; and yet the landlord knows that they are legitimate and very common subjects of traffic and trade ; and such property, equally with goods kept for sale, should not be affected by a lien established after a sale made in good faith for a valuable consideration.[2]

582. A sale by a tenant of his entire stock of merchandise upon which a landlord's lien has attached, does not displace the lien, in case the sale is made to a person who knows that the premises are leased, and who continues to occupy them, and to sell the goods in the ordinary way.[3] Even a second sale of this sort does not displace the lien. Purchasers of goods and chattels take them at common law, subject to the liens which existed against the vendor, and the same rule applies in case of a sale by a tenant of chattels which are subject to a landlord's statutory lien, where the sale is of the stock in mass, which is not removed from the premises, or with knowledge of the lien,[4] and not in the usual course of trade. The lien, when it has once attached, continues to attach to the chattels into whosesoever hands they may come during the time allowed for instituting proceedings to enforce the lien, unless the lien is displaced by the removal of the goods, or by a sale of them in the ordinary course of trade.

583. The landlord may estop himself by his declarations and conduct from claiming his lien as against a purchaser who has knowledge of his lien. Thus, a tenant sold a part of a crop of corn raised upon the leased premises, and the purchaser before he paid for the corn informed the landlord of his purchase, who said it was all right, that he was satisfied, that

---

[1] Grant v. Whitwell, 9 Iowa, 152.

[2] Nesbitt v. Bartlett, 14 Iowa, 485.

[3] Man v. Shiffner, 2 East, 523 ; Godin v. London Assurance Co. 1 Burrow, 489; Burton v. Smith, 13 Peters, 464, 483 ; Fowler v. Rapley, 15 Wall. 328.

[4] Grant v. Whitwell, *supra ;* Carpenter v. Gillespie, 10 Iowa, 592; Doane v. Garretson, 24 Iowa, 351 ; Nesbitt v. Bartlett, *supra.*

he had settled with the tenant, and that nothing was due except a part of the crop which remained, and which he was to gather at his own expense.   After this the purchaser sold the corn to a second purchaser, and paid the tenant for the corn.   It was held that the landlord had waived his lien by his declarations and conduct.[1]

Where a landlord has a lien for advances as well as for rent upon his tenant's crop, and he agrees with a merchant not to make any advances if the latter will furnish his tenant with supplies, and the merchant, on the faith of such agreement, makes advances, the landlord's lien for any advances subsequently made is necessarily postponed to the merchant's lien for his advances ; and the landlord cannot claim to appropriate any part of the proceeds of sale of the tenant's crop to his lien for such advances, until the merchant's lien is fully paid.[2]

584. On the other hand, the purchaser may by his declarations or acts make himself liable to the landlord for the rent.   Thus, where a factor received cotton from a tenant with full knowledge of the landlord's special lien for the rent of the premises, and, as the landlord was about to seize the cotton upon a distress warrant, the factor informed him that there was cotton enough to pay his advances and the rent, and thereby prevented the landlord from asserting his lien by distress, it was held that an implied promise to pay the rent arose from these facts, and that the landlord could recover the rent from the factor.[3]

585. A landlord's lien on his tenant's property for rent is not waived by his taking his tenant's note or bond with personal security, though a vendor's lien would be waived by his taking such note and security.[4]   The distinction is that the right or lien of a landlord is a legal right, not a mere equitable

---

[1] Goeing v. Outhouse, 95 Ill. 346.

[2] Coleman v. Siler, 74 Ala. 435.

[3] Saulsbury v. McKellar, 59 Ga. 301.

[4] Rollins v. Proctor, 56 Iowa, 326 ; Giles v. Ebsworth, 10 Md. 333 ; Snyder v. Kunkleman, 3 P. & W. (Pa.) 487; Coleman v. Siler, supra; Lewis v. Lozee, 3 Wend. (N. Y.) 79 ; Story

v. Flournoy, 55 Ga. 56 ; Sullivan v. Ellison, 20 S. C. 481; Bailey v. Wright, 3 McCord (S. C.), 484 ; Smith v. Wells, 4 Bush (Ky.), 92 ; Atkins v. Byrnes, 71 Ill. 326 ; Cunnea v. Williams, 11 Bradw. (Ill.) 72 ; Franklin v. Meyer, 36 Ark. 96; Gordon v. Correy, 5 Binn. (Pa.) 552 ; Paulding v. Ketty, 9 Martin (La.), 186, 187.

lien ; and before the court can say that the landlord has waived this legal right, there must be some plain evidence to show it.[1] The taking of the note of course suspends the remedy by distress or by suit to foreclose the lien until the note becomes due.[2] But after this he may proceed, although he has previously negotiated the note, provided he has taken it up before commencing proceedings.[3]

The landlord's lien is not lost by his assigning the tenant's promissory note for the rent, and afterwards taking it up upon non-payment by the maker.[4] And so, if he has transferred the note under an agreement that he would collect the rents and pay them to the transferee, the landlord, still retaining possession of the note, may maintain a distress warrant against the tenant for the rent represented by the note.[5]

586. A landlord's lien upon goods for rent is not displaced by his taking a mortgage upon the same goods for the rent. The mortgage is regarded as a cumulative security, and he may enforce either security.[6] The acceptance of an obligation, of an inferior or even of an equal degree, does not extinguish a prior obligation, unless such is the express agree-

Otherwise where tenant's note for a share of the produce reserved as rent is taken. Warren *v.* Forney, 13 S. & R. (Pa.) 52.

[1] Denham *v.* Harris, 13 Ala. 465 ; Smith *v.* Wells, 4 Bush (Ky.), 92.

[2] Fiske *v.* Judge, 2 Speers (S. C.), 436; Fife *v.* Irving, 1 Rich. (S. C.) 226 ; Hornbrooks *v.* Lucas, 24 W. Va. 493. In the English case of Davis *v.* Gyde, 2 Ad. & El. 623, it is held the taking of a note does not suspend the right of distress, unless there be a special agreement that the note shall have this effect. This case and the South Carolina case are fully and ably discussed by Judge Green in Hornbrooks *v.* Lucas, *supra*, and the position taken by the South Carolina case is sustained. This position seems to be clearly right. The decision of the English court seems to be based upon the peculiar favor in which the right of distress is held in England.

But in this country no such favor is extended to the right of distress.

[3] Giles *v.* Ebsworth, 10 Md. 333.

[4] Farwell *v.* Grier, 38 Iowa, 83.

[5] Bolton *v.* Duncan, 61 Ga. 103.

[6] Franklin *v.* Meyer, 36 Ark. 96. The rule in this case is distinguished from that which applies to a vendor's lien for purchase - money. The vendor's lien is the mere creation of courts of equity, independent of common law or statute. Courts of equity apply to this lien such equitable qualifications as they see fit; and one of these qualifications is that this lien cannot co-exist with an express lien, or with other security, unless there be shown a manifest intention to retain it. The landlord's lien, however, is a legal right, and it remains unless it be expressly renounced, or there be some contract between the parties inconsistent with it. Per Eakin, J.

ment of the parties. Rent is regarded as an obligation of a higher degree than any simple contract, and therefore the execution of a promissory note for rent, secured also by a chattel mortgage, does not operate as a waiver of the right to enforce payment by distress,[1] without an express understanding to that effect, even if by such an understanding it would so operate; for this has been questioned.[2]

There are authorities which hold that the lien must be regarded as waived whenever, from the circumstances, it can be inferred that the lien was not relied upon. But this inference cannot be drawn from the taking of a security which is not enforcible against third persons, such for instance as a chattel mortgage which is not recorded.[3]

If a landlord receives from his tenant his draft upon a third person, accepted by such person, and thereupon gives his tenant a receipt for the rent, he waives his lien though the draft is never paid.[4]

587. A landlord's lien is not released by a voluntary obligation executed by a third person upon purchasing the tenant's goods upon the demised premises, not in the ordinary course of business, whereby the obligor binds himself to pay for the tenant the rent due from him to the landlord at that time, if the consideration for such obligation moves from the tenant and not from the landlord.[5] In such case the landlord, who has seized the goods on the premises for the rent, cannot be compelled by other attaching creditors, who attach the purchase of the goods as fraudulent, to resort first to the voluntary promise of the purchaser to pay the rent, before seeking satisfaction out of the goods themselves under the lien.[6]

588. A landlord who has taken collateral security for his rent may pursue all his remedies at the same time. He may sue the tenant personally, may seize his goods by distress where this remedy is given, or may foreclose his statutory lien

---

[1] Davis v. Gyde, 2 Ad. & El. 623; Atkins v. Byrnes, 71 Ill. 326 ; O'Hara v. Jones, 46 Ill. 288, 291; Hornbrooks v. Lucas, 24 W. Va. 493, 497, per Green, J.; Cornell v. Lamb, 20 Johns. (N. Y.) 407.

[2] Hornbrooks v. Lucas, supra.
[3] Pitkin v. Fletcher, 47 Iowa, 53.
[4] Cambria Iron Co.'s Appeal (Pa.), 6 Atl. Rep. 563.
[5] Block v. Latham, 63 Tex. 414.
[6] Block v. Latham, supra.

for the rent in the manner provided, and he may at the same time proceed to enforce the collateral security.[1]

A landlord may distrain although he has recovered a personal judgment for the rent, and special bail has been entered for a stay of execution.[2]

A landlord waives his lien on property seized under a distress warrant, when he proceeds to take a personal judgment without foreclosing his lien on the property.[3]

The reservation of a lien by the terms of the lease is not a waiver of the right to distrain, although the lien reserved is more extensive than that given by statute.[4]

A stipulation in a lease that the landlord· may reënter if the rent remain unpaid for a certain period after it becomes due, does not take away or suspend his immediate right of distress.[5]

589. A tender of the rent due does not release or discharge a landlord's lien, unless the tender be kept good by payment of the money into court.[6] And so a distress for rent after a tender of the rent and charges due is unlawful, unless the tenant fails to make the tender good on demand.[7]

A tender made after costs have been properly incurred is not effectual unless such costs are included in the tender.[8]

590. As against a distress warrant at common law, a landlord's lien is destroyed by the levy of an execution upon the tenant's goods, for an execution takes precedence of all debts except specific liens.[9] But to place the tenant's goods *in custodia legis* by an execution and levy, the sheriff must not only take, but must keep the actual possession of the goods. The landlord's right to distrain is not suspended unless the sheriff takes possession of the goods, and his right revives if the

---

[1] Cunnea v. Williams, 11 Bradw. (Ill.) 72; King v. Blackmore, 72 Pa. St. 347; S. C. 13 Am. Rep. 684.

[2] Shetsline v. Keemle, 1 Ash. (Pa.) 29.

[3] Wise v. Old, 57 Tex. 514.

[4] O'Hara v. Jones,, 46 Ill. 288.

[5] Smith v. Meanor, 16 S. & R. (Pa.) 375.

[6] Bloom v. McGehee, 38 Ark. 329; Hamlett v. Tallman, 30 Ark. 505.

[7] Smith v. Goodwin, 4 B. & Ad. 413; Davis v. Henry, 63 Miss. 110.

[8] Hunder v. Le Conte, 6 Cow. (N. Y.) 728.

[9] Harris v. Dammann, 3 Mack. (D. C.) 90; Gibson v. Gautier, 1 Ib. 35; Pierce v. Scott, 4 W. & S. (Pa.) 344; Kelly v. Davenport, 1 Bro. (Pa.) 231; Dawson v. Dewan, 12 Rich. (S. C.) L. 499.

officer withdraws from the premises without leaving a bailiff in charge.[1]

Goods which have previously been levied upon by foreign attachment are in the custody of the law and cannot be distrained.[2]   And so are goods taken on replevin.[3]

If the landlord consents to a sale of his tenant's goods taken in execution, upon the promise of the officer made before the sale that he would pay the rent claimed, he waives his right to sue the sheriff under the statute.[4]   To render such waiver effectual, it is not necessary that the jury should believe that the landlord actually waived his right under the statute and relied upon the promise of the sheriff, and it is error to submit such an inquiry to them.'

591. But property rightfully in the hands of a receiver is in the custody of the court, and cannot be distrained upon without permission of the court by which the receiver was appointed.[6]   In such case the landlord should apply for an order on the receiver to pay the rent, or for leave to proceed by distress or otherwise.[7]

A receiver of the tenant's goods does not ordinarily become liable for the rent of the leased premises by entering upon them in order to take possession of the goods and to dispose of them under the order of court.   Therefore, for rent becoming due after a sale by the receiver and the removal of the goods by the purchaser, the landlord has no lien upon the proceeds of the sale, notwithstanding a statutory provision allowing the landlord to follow and distrain goods for rent due after their removal

---

[1] Beekman v. Lansing, 3 Wend. (N. Y.) 446; Newell v. Clark, 46 N. J. L. 363.   In **New Jersey**, however, a levy is valid without an actual seizure and continued possession.   A distress for rent of property already seized upon execution may be made in the same manner as the levy of a second execution.

[2] Pierce v. Scott, 4 W. & S. (Pa.) 344.

[3] Commonwealth v. Lelar, 1 Phila. (Pa.) 173.   But goods replevied may be distrained for subsequent arrears of rent.   Woglam v. Cowperthwaite, 2 Dall. (Pa.) 68; Gray v. Wilson, 4 Watts (Pa.), 39, 42.

[4] Rotherey v. Wood, 3 Camp. 24; Cloud v. Needles, 6 Md. 501.

[5] Cloud v. Needles, *supra.*

[6] Noe v. Gibson, 7 Paige (N. Y.), 513; Riggs v. Whitney, 15 Abb. (N. Y.) Pr. 388; Martin v. Black, 3 Edw. (N. Y.) 580; Garther v. Stockbridge (Md.), 9 Atl. Rep. 632; S. C. 9 Paige, 641.

[7] Everett v. Neff, 28 Md. 176.

from the premises, in case they have not been sold to a *bonâ fide* purchaser without notice.[1]

A landlord's statutory lien is not defeated by the conversion of the tenant's property into money by a receiver, under an order of court, but will attach to the proceeds in the receiver's hands. The money in such case takes the place of the property, and is distributed to the persons who establish their claims to it.[2]

592. Of course a landlord's lien for rent is lost by his acceptance of a surrender of the leasehold estate by the lessee. But such a surrender can be effected only by express words, by which the lessee manifests his intention of yielding up his interest in the premises, or by operation of law, where the parties, without express surrender, do some act which implies that they have both agreed to consider the surrender as made.[3] But when acts are relied upon as evincing such agreement, they should be such as are not easily referable to a different motive. Even the delivery by the tenant to the landlord of the keys of a leased building, and the leasing of the same by the latter to another tenant, is not conclusive evidence that a surrender has been accepted.[4]

But a surrender and acceptance of a part of the demised premises does not destroy the landlord's right of distress as to the residue.[5]

As between the landlord and tenant, the execution of a new lease during the term of an existing lease is a surrender of the old lease. But as against the holder of a chattel mortgage of the tenant's goods, executed after the making of the first lease, but before the making of the second lease, the lien of the landlord upon such goods for rent accruing under the second lease, for the period covered by the first lease, is not postponed to that of the chattel mortgage, if the landlord had no knowledge of it at the time of making the second lease.[6]

593. A landlord cannot distrain for rent after the term has expired, and the tenant has surrendered the possession.[7]

---

[1] Garther v. Stockbridge (Md.), 9 Atl. Rep. 632.

[2] Gilbert v. Greenbaum, 56 Iowa, 211.

[3] Beall v. White, 94 U.S. 382, 389, per Clifford, J.; Cahill v. Lee, 55 Md. 319; Bain v. Clark, 10 Johns. (N. Y.) 424.

[4] Martin v. Stearns, 52 Iowa, 345.

[5] Peters v. Newkirk, 6 Cow. (N. Y.) 103.

[6] Rollins v. Proctor, 56 Iowa, 326.

[7] Terboss v. Williams, 5 Cow. (N. Y.) 407; S. C. 2 Wend. 148; Greider's App. 5 Pa. St. 422.

A statutory right to distrain goods removed from the premises within thirty days, or other certain period, exists only during the continuance of the lease and the tenant's possession of the premises,[1] unless otherwise specially provided.

A landlord cannot distrain after the determination of his own estate by surrender to the owner of the paramount estate, though rent be in arrear and due from his former tenant, and the goods of the latter remain on the premises.[2]

594. A landlord's lien is not impaired by his tenant's sub-letting the premises. The sub-lessee's property may be thereby subjected to a double lien, — that of the landlord and that of his immediate lessor; but the lien of the landlord is paramount. The lessee can pass no better estate and no better right to the use of the land than he himself possessed.[3]

A lessee who has parted with his whole term cannot distrain on his sub-lessee.[4]

595. A landlord's lien or privilege upon the goods of his tenant is lost by their destruction by fire, and does not attach to the insurance money.[5]

VI. *The Remedy of Distress and the Enforcement of Liens.*

596. In a proceeding by distress for rent, notice to the tenant was unnecessary at common law. In a case in the Exchequer Chamber,[6] Parke, Baron, delivering the judgment of the court, said: " We think that the common law casts no such obligation on the distrainor. It has been expressly laid down that, if the lord distrains for rent or services, he has no occasion to give notice to the tenant for what thing he distrains, for the tenant, by intendment, knows what things are in arrear for his lands ;[7] and the authority for this is Year Book, Pasch. 45 Edw. III.,[8] where the Lord Chief Justice Fyncheden, in answer to the argument that the lord, on the taking of a distress,

---

[1] Burr *v.* Van Buskirk, 3 Cow. (N. Y.) 263 ; Terboss *v.* Williams, 5 Cow. (N. Y.) 407.

[2] Walbridge *v.* Pruden, 102 Pa. St. 1.

[3] Montague *v.* Mial, 89 N. C. 137; Ledbetter *v.* Quick, 90 N. C. 276.

[4] Ragsdale *v.* Estis, 8 Rich. (S. C.) 429.

[5] *In re* Reis, 3 Woods, 18.

[6] Tancred *v.* Leyland, 16 Q. B. 669; Trent *v.* Hunt, 9 Exch. 14; Keller *v.* Weber, 27 Md. 660, 666.

[7] 1 Roll. Abr. 674 (*a*), tit. Distress (8), pl. 1.

[8] Fol. 9, A. pl. 13.

ought to give notice to the tenant of the cause of the takin;
says it is not so, for the tenant is always held, by common inten
ment, to know what things are in arrear from his land, as rei
and service, etc."

597. Under statutes which substantially adopt the con
mon law remedy of distress, no notice to the tenant is ne
essary, or demand upon him,[1] before seizure. The statute ;
such case becomes a part of the contract of leasing, and reg
lates and limits the rights of the parties. Virtually, the lan
lord, in pursuing this remedy, takes possession of the property ;
pursuance of the contract of leasing, which usually embraces
consent that the possession may be so taken in default of pa
ment. The service of the warrant is a sufficient notice. Tl
warrant is a process of law with reference to this contract. .
is substantially a proceeding *in rem,* under which a seizure
the property in the possession of the owner for the enforcemei
of a lien upon it, is held to be a sufficient notice to the owner,
no other notice is required by the statute.[2]

This remedy, by which the property liable to seizure is levie
upon without personal notice to the tenant, is not in conflict wit
the constitutional provisions which secure the right of trial b
jury, and declare that no person shall be deprived of propert
without due process of law.[3] Especially is this the case und
statutes which provide that the tenant may replevy the propert
taken on distress within a limited time, and that the tenar
thereupon may have the matters in dispute tried by a jury.[4]

598. Who may distrain. — At common law only the less
could distrain for rent.[5] By statute this remedy may of cours
be given to the landlord's personal representative for rent b
coming due before his death, or to his grantee or assignee. Rer
accruing after the death of the landlord belongs to the heirs[6]
devisees.[7] Under statutes conferring a lien for rent, this may b
enforced by the landlord himself, or by any one standing legall

---

[1] Blanchard *v.* Raines, 20 Fla. 467;
Keller *v.* Weber, 27 Md. 660, 666;
Buffington *v.* Hilley, 55 Ga. 655.

[2] Blanchard *v.* Raines, *supra.*

[3] Blanchard *v.* Raines, *supra.*

[4] Blanchard *v.* Raines, *supra.*

[5] Co. Lit. 162 *a ;* Bagwell *v.* Jami-
son, Cheves (S. C.), 249 ; 32 Hen
VIII. ch. 37.

[6] Sherman *v.* Dutch, 16 Ill. 283
Wright *v.* Williams, 5 Cow. (N. Y
501.

[7] Lewis's App. 66 Pa. St. 312.

in his place, as by his grantor, assignee, heir, or personal representative. In either case the relation of landlord and tenant must exist either by direct contract or indirectly by operation of law.[1]

The right of distress is inseparable from the reversion.[2] Therefore a tenant who has sublet a portion of the demised premises, for the entire period of the term, cannot distrain for rent.[3] Otherwise if he has sublet for a part only of his term.[4] Tenants in common may distrain severally,[5] each for his own share of the rent; or one may distrain in the name of all if not forbidden by the others to do so.[6] One tenant in common who has leased his interest to his co-tenant may distrain for rent.[7]

If the lessors be joint tenants, all must join in the distress, unless one distrains in the name of all.[8] But one of two executors may distrain when the contract of rent was made with him alone.[9]

599. Whether a purchaser at a foreclosure sale can distrain for the rent of the premises depends upon his relation to the tenant. Where the property was already subject to a lease for a term of years at the time of making the mortgage, the mortgagee may be considered as the assignee of the reversion, and entitled, after condition broken, to all the remedies for the collection of accruing rent. But if a lease be made of premises already subject to a mortgage, upon the foreclosure of the mortgage the leasehold estate is extinguished with the equity of redemption. A purchaser at a foreclosure sale of such a mortgage cannot distrain for accruing rent unless the tenant attorns to him; and a mere notice by the purchaser to the tenant, to pay the rent to him when the tenant does not consent, does not make the tenant liable to him for the rent. The relation of landlord and tenant does not exist in such case.[10]

---

[1] McGillick v. McAllister, 10 Bradw. (Ill.) 40 ; M'Kircher v. Hawley, 16 Johns. (N. Y.) 289 ; Wright v. Link, 34 Miss. 266.

[2] Cornell v. Lamb, 2 Cow. (N. Y.) 652 ; Schuyler v. Leggett, Ib. 660.

[3] Prescott v. De Forest, 16 Johns. (N. Y.) 159.

[4] Ege v. Ege, 5 Watts (Pa.), 134.

[5] De Coursey v. Guarantee Trust & Safe Deposit Co. 81 Pa. St. 217.

[6] Dutcher v. Culver, 24 Minn. 584 ; Waring v. Slingluff, 63 Md. 53 ; Jones v. Gundrim, 3 W. & S. (Pa.) 531.

[7] Luther v. Arnold, 8 Rich. (S. C.) 24.

[8] Waring v. Slingluff, *supra*.

[9] Carter v. Walters, 63 Ga. 164.

[10] Reed v. Bartlett, 9 Bradw. (Ill.) 267; and see M'Kircher v. Hawley, *supra*. See, also, Drakford v. Turk, 75 Ala. 339.

600. Against whom distraint may be had. — At common law the remedy by distress for rent was confined to the lessor and his representatives, against the tenant for life, or in tail, and his representatives, but did not exist against the personal representatives of tenants for years. Goods in their hands are *in custodia legis*.[1] By statute and adjudication, in several states, the proceeding by distress upon the death of any tenant survives, and may be prosecuted against his personal representative.[2]

A landlord, by accepting administration of his tenant's estate, waives his right to distrain.[3]

Upon the death of the tenant the landlord may distrain, before administration is granted, for rent due and in arrear, for no notice is necessary before distress.[4]

601. The landlord may have an injunction against the tenant or his assignee to restrain the sale or removal of the property subject to the lien from the demised premises, in the absence of a special statutory provision for the purpose.[5] But if the landlord can enforce his lien by attachment, as provided by statute, an injunction will not be issued.[6]

VII. *Statutory Provisions, and Adjudications under the same, in the several States.*

602. Alabama.[7] — Landlords of storehouses, dwelling-houses, and other buildings have a lien for rent upon the goods, furniture, and effects of tenants, and this lien is superior to all other liens on such property except that for taxes. This lien may be enforced by attachment whenever the tenant has fraudulently disposed of the goods, or is about to do so, or has made an assignment for the benefit of his creditors, or has made a transfer of all his goods without the consent of his landlord, or has failed to pay any instalment of the rent when due.

[1] So, also, by Stat. 32 Henry VIII. ch. 37 ; Smith *v.* Bobb, 12 S. & M. (Miss.) 322 ; Salvo *v.* Schmidt, 2 Speers (S. C.), 512.

[2] McLaughlin *v.* Riggs, 1 Cranch C. C. 410. **Illinois:** Rauh *v.* Ritchie, 1 Bradw. 188. **Mississippi :** Smith *v.* Bobb, *supra.* **New York :** Morrill *v.* Jenkins, 2 N. Y. Leg. Obs. 214. **Indiana :** Merkle *v.* O'Neal, 5 Blackf. 289.

[3] Hovey *v.* Smith, 1 Barb. (N. Y.) 372.

[4] Keller *v.* Weber, 27 Md. 660 ; Longwell *v.* Ridinger, 1 Gill (Md.), 57. See, however, Hughes *v.* Sébre, 2 A. K. Marsh. (Ky.) 227.

[5] Garner *v.* Cutting, 32 Iowa, 547.

[6] Rotzler *v.* Rotzler, 46 Iowa, 189.

[7] Acts 1883, p. 175, No. 102. The common law remedy of distress was abolished in 1812. Frazier *v.* Thomas, 6 Ala. 169.

This lien may be enforced by the transferee of the landlord's claim for rent.

603. Alabama[1] *(continued)*. **Landlords' liens upon crops.** — A landlord has a lien[2] on the crop grown on rented land[3] for rent for the current year,[4] and for advances,[5] made in money or other

[1] Acts 1878–79, p. 72, No. 67; Code 1875, §§ 3467–3478.

[2] This lien attaches only where the relation of landlord and tenant exists, and not where there is an implied liability for use and occupation, or where one of several tenants in common occupies and cultivates the entire premises. Kennon *v.* Wright, 70 Ala. 434 ; Tucker *v.* Adams, 52 Ala. 254 ; Hadden *v.* Powell, 17 Ala. 314. It arises under a contract whereby the landlord rents land to another to be cultivated for a stipulated part of the crops to be grown thereon ; for such a contract creates the relation of landlord and tenant. Wilson *v.* Stewart, 69 Ala. 302.

Prior to this statute a contract between the lessee of land and his laborers for the cultivation of the land on shares, did not create the relation of landlord and tenant between them, or give the lessee a lien on the crops for advances made to his laborers during the year. Shields *v.* Kimbrough, 64 Ala. 504. The statute contemplates only the conventional relation of landlord and tenant, subsisting because of the contract between the parties. A mortgagee under a mortgage executed prior to the entry of the tenant is not, on giving notice to his mortgagor's tenant, entitled to the statutory lien on the crops grown on the rented premises for the payment of the rent, and he cannot enforce this by attachment. Drakford *v.* Turk, 75 Ala. 339.

[3] The lien attaches to the crop whether this be raised by the tenant or by some one under the tenant. Givens *v.* Easley, 17 Ala. 385. But it seems that the attachment must issue against the tenant, and not against the under-tenant, unless the contract with the latter has been assigned to the landlord. Simmons *v.* Fielder, 46 Ala. 304.

[4] As to the landlord's rights against an under-tenant, and the equities of creditors of the under-tenant, see Robinson *v.* Lehman, 72 Ala. 401.

The landlord's writ of attachment is usually in the form of a mandate to attach so much of the crops grown on the rented premises as may be sufficient to satisfy his demand with costs. This authorizes an attachment not only of the crops belonging to his tenant, but also the crops raised on the premises by an under-tenant. Agee *v.* Mayer, 71 Ala. 88. The statute, § 3476, requires in express terms that the crop of the tenant in chief shall be exhausted before a levy is made on the crop of the under-tenant, unless the tenant in chief has not made a crop, or it is insufficient to satisfy the lien ; and a levy made in violation of this provision "shall be vacated on motion, at the first term thereafter." But the under-tenant may intervene at the return term of the writ and move a vacation of the levy on his crop. Lehman *v.* Howze, 73 Ala. 302.

[5] The lien for advances is of equal dignity with the lien for rent; Wilson *v.* Stewart, 69 Ala. 302 ; Thompson *v.* Powell, 77 Ala. 391 ; unless there be some fact or agreement which operates as a waiver, as in Coleman *v.* Siler, 74 Ala. 435. See, also, Foster *v.* Napier, 74 Ala. 393.

The landlord's lien for advances is

thing of value,[1] whether made directly by him, or at his instance
and request, by another person, or for which he has assumed the
legal responsibility,[2] at or before the time at which such advances
were made, for the sustenance or well-being of the tenant or his
family, for preparing the ground for cultivation, or for cultivating, gathering, saving, handling, or preparing the crop for market ; and he shall have a lien also upon each and every article advanced, and upon all property purchased with money advanced,
or obtained by barter in exchange for any articles advanced, for
the aggregate price or value of all such property or articles
so advanced ; and such liens for rent and advances shall be
paramount, and have preference of all other liens.[3]

much more comprehensive than the lien given to any other person making advances, and embraces everything useful for the purposes enumerated, or tending to the substantial comfort and well-being of the tenant, his family, or persons employed about the service ; and this lien laps over from year to year for any balance due, so long as the tenancy continues. Cockburn v. Watkins, 76 Ala. 486 ; Thompson v. Powell, 77 Ala. 391.

[1] As regards the landlord's advances, the words of the statute are very comprehensive, and it would be difficult to define what articles of commerce are beyond its terms. Lake v. Gaines, 75 Ala. 143.

If the advances are not paid for in the current year, the residue becomes a lien on the next crop, if the tenancy continues. Code, § 3469 ; Lake v. Gaines, supra.

[2] This provision was not intended to confer upon the landlord the power to appoint another to make advances to his tenant, and thereby clothe such person with the lien ; but merely to afford him indemnity against any liability he might assume for his tenant. Therefore, if advances are made by a third person with the understanding that he is to look to the tenant, and not to the landlord, for payment, al-though made at the instance of the

landlord and on his request, if there is no liability resting on the landlord the lien does not exist. Bell v. Hurst 75 Ala. 44.

[3] A landlord's lien for advances is superior to the lien of another person for advances made after the renting, though before any advances were made by the landlord. Wells v. Thompson, 50 Ala. 83.

But he may by his acts estop himself from denying the liability of the property to another in preference to his lien. Brown v. Hamil, 76 Ala. 506.

But the landlord may maintain a special action against one who, with notice of the lien, destroys, removes, or converts the crop, or so changes its character that the landlord cannot enforce his lien. Hussey v. Peebles, 53 Ala. 432 ; Lake v. Gaines, supra ; Hurst v. Bell, 72 Ala. 336 ; Kennon v. Wright, 70 Ala. 434 ; Thompson v. Powell, supra.

Notice to a purchaser from the tenant that the crop was raised on rented land and that the rent is unpaid, does not operate as notice that the landlord had made advances to the tenant and that he has a lien therefor. Wilson v. Stewart, 69 Ala. 302 ; Wilkinson v. Ketler, 69 Ala. 435.

Actual knowledge is not necessary to charge a purchaser with notice of

The landlord may assign his claim, and the assignee takes his rights and remedies.[1]

The lien is enforced by attachment either when the claim is due or before it is due, in case the tenant is about to remove or dispose of the crop, or has removed it without consent, or the the landlord has good cause to believe the tenant is about to dispose of the articles advanced or purchased.

604. Alabama[2] (*continued*). Persons who farm on shares, or who raise crops by joint contributions in such manner as

the lien, but anything that should put him upon inquiry is sufficient. Lomax *v.* Le Grand, 60 Ala. 537.

A purchaser in good faith from the tenant, after the latter has removed the crop from the rented premises, is protected as a purchaser without notice. Scaife *v.* Stovall, 67 Ala. 237.

The affidavit need not specify the particular articles advanced, or set forth an itemized account. It is sufficient if it shows that the relation of landlord and tenant existed, that advances for the purposes specified were made, that a specified balance remains unpaid, and that a statutory ground for attachment exists. Cockburn *v.* Watkins, 76 Ala. 486 ; Bell *v.* Allen, 76 Ala. 450. If the claim for advances is past due, the affidavit should aver specially that a demand for payment was made before the action was brought. Bell *v.* Allen, *supra.*

The affidavit is to be construed liberally, and is sufficient if it sets forth with substantial accuracy the general facts, either expressly, or by necessary implication. Gunter *v.* Du Bosc, 77 Ala. 326 ; Fitzsimmons *v.* Howard, 69 Ala. 590.

[1] Simmons *v.* Fielder, 46 Ala. 304. Otherwise before so provided. Foster *v.* Westmoreland, 52 Ala. 223; Hussey *v.* Peebles, 52 Ala. 432 ; Lavender *v.* Hall, 60 Ala. 214 ; Lomax *v.* Le Grand, *supra ;* Hudson *v.* Vaughan, 57 Ala. 609 ; Barnett *v.* Warren Ala.), 2 So. Rep. 457.

The remedy of the landlord against a purchaser of the crop with notice of the lien, who has received and converted it to his own use, is by special action on the case. He cannot maintain a bill in equity unless he shows thath is remedy at law is inadequate. Kennon *v.* Wright, 70 Ala. 434. Otherwise where the statutory remedy cannot be pursued. Abraham *v.* Hall, 59 Ala. 386.

Until he has sued out a valid attachment, and had it levied on the crop, he cannot recover in a statutory suit against a third person to try the right of property. Jackson *v.* Bain, 74 Ala. 328.

The landlord cannot maintain trover for the conversion of the crop by a wrong-doer. His lien has no element of property. He has neither a *jus in re* nor a *jus ad rem.* Corbitt *v.* Reynolds, 68 Ala. 378 ; Folmar *v.* Copeland, 57 Ala. 588. He has merely a statutory right to charge the crop with the payment of the rent and advances in priority to all other rights or liens. The property and the right of property remain in the tenant. The later may therefore make a *bonâ fide* sale to a purchaser, which would prevail over the landlord's lien. Wilson *v.* Stewart, 69 Ala. 302 ; Stern *v.* Simpson, 62 Ala. 194 ; Blum *v.* Jones, 51 Ala. 149 ; Thompson *v.* Spinks, 12 Ala. 155.

[2] Code 1876, §§ 3479, 3480.

to make them tenants in common in such crops, or their assignees, have a lien upon the interest of the other in such crops for any balance due for provisions, supplies, teams, materials, labor, services, and money, or either, furnished to aid in the cultivating and gathering such crops under contract, or furnished when the interests of such crops require it, in case of a failure of either to contribute the amount and means as agreed upon by the parties.

This lien may be enforced in the same manner as a landlord's lien is enforced; but it may also be enforced in any other appropriate mode.

605. Arizona Territory.[1] — Any person who shall rent land for agricultural purposes shall, on filing the lease of such land for record in the office of the county recorder of the county where the lands lie, have a lien on all the crops raised on such lands during the continuance of the lease for the amount of rent therein specified; but such liens shall cease and determine on the first day of September next following the filing of the lease for record, unless before that time the lessor or his assignee shall have commenced an action in some court of competent jurisdiction to recover his rent.

If the rent reserved be payable in grain, or other products of the land rented, and it be not paid or delivered as stipulated, the lessor, if he has acquired a lien, may recover of the lessee in cash the highest market value of such rent at the place where the same was to be delivered, at any time between the day of delivery specified and the day of trial, provided the action has been commenced before the expiration of the lien.

This lien does not affect the rights of any mortgagee whose mortgage has been recorded, or the rights of any lien-holder whose lien has attached, at the time of filing the lease for record.

606. Arkansas.[2] — Every landlord shall have a lien upon the crop grown upon the demised premises in any year for rent that shall accrue for such year, and such lien shall continue for six months after such rent shall become due and payable.[3]

---

[1] Laws 1881, p. 84, No. 46, § 1.

[2] Dig. Stats. 1884, ch. 96, §§ 4453–4455, 4462; Acts of July 23, 1868, and Jan. 8, 1875.

[3] If the rent contract includes other indebtedness in the amount expressed as rent, the landlord's lien is limited to the amount due for rent only; and

Whenever any landlord shall indorse upon any written agreement made by and between his tenant and the employees of such tenant his written consent to the terms of such agreement, then, and in that case only, shall the lien of such employees have precedence over that of the landlord, and that only for the compensation specified in such agreement, the services therein specified having been rendered toward the production of the crop against which the landlord's lien attaches.

Any person sub-renting lands or tenements shall only be held responsible for the rent of such as are cultivated or occupied by him.

Any landlord who has a lien on the crop for rent shall be entitled to bring suit before a justice of the peace, or in the Circuit Court, as the case may be, and have a writ of attachment for the recovery of the same, whether the rent be due or not, in the following cases: First. When the tenant is about to remove the crop from the premises without paying the rent. Second. When he has removed it, or any portion thereof, without the consent of the landlord.[1]

in a contest between the landlord and another incumbrancer, the latter may show the true amount due for rent. Roth v. Williams, 45 Ark. 447; Varner v. Rice, 39 Ark. 344; Hammond v. Harper, 39 Ark. 248.

But a creditor who has no lien on the property cannot complain that the landlord has applied a part of the crop to the satisfaction of a debt for which the landlord has no lien. Hammond v. Harper, *supra.*

The landlord's lien does not pass to an assignee of the rent debt. Varner v. Rice, *supra;* Nolen v. Royston, 36 Ark. 561; Bernays v. Feild, 29 Ark. 218; Roberts v. Jacks, 31 Ark. 597.

But if the debt is reassigned to the landlord, the lien revives. Varner v. Rice, *supra.* And though the note for rent be executed by the tenant to a creditor of the landlord with his consent, and it is afterwards redelivered by the creditor to the landlord, the lien, which before was dormant, revives and unites in the landlord the debt and the right to enforce satis-

faction out of the crop. The original payee of the note may properly be made a party to the suit for the protection of the tenant. Varner v. Rice, *supra.*

Although the assignment of the rent note does not carry the landlord's lien, yet, if the tenant delivers the crop to one holding the rent note as collateral security for a debt due from the landlord, the payment will be upheld as against a mortgagee of the crop. Watson v. Johnson, 33 Ark. 737. Though the landlord's lien cannot be transferred, it can be released. Buckner v. McIlroy, 31 Ark. 631.

[1] A landlord's lien gives him no right of possession of the crop, and he cannot therefore maintain replevin. He must proceed by attachment. Bell v. Matheny, 36 Ark. 572.

While a landlord must refrain from an active injury to a junior incumbrancer, he is under no obligation to collect his debt, or to husband the crop so as to make it cover both debts. If the tenant wrongfully disposes of a

Before such writ of attachment is issued, the landlord must make and file an affidavit that the amount claimed is due for rent, stating the time when the same became or will become due, and that he has a lien on the crop for the rent.[1]

The writ may be levied on the crop in the possession of the tenant, or of any one holding it in his right, or in the possession of a purchaser from him with notice of the lien of the landlord.[2]

607. Arkansas[3] **(*continued*). Lien for supplies advanced.** — In addition to the lien now given by law to landlords, if any landlord, to enable his tenant or employee to make and gather the crop, shall advance such tenant or employee any necessary supplies, either of money, provisions, clothing, stock, or other necessary articles, such landlord shall have a lien upon the crop raised upon the premises for the value of such advances, which lien shall have preference over any mortgage or other conveyance of such crop made by such tenant or employee. Such lien may be enforced by an action of attachment before any court or justice of the peace having jurisdiction, and the lien for advances and for rent may be joined and enforced in the same action.

The purchaser or assignee of the receipt of any ginner, warehouse holder, or cotton factor, or other bailee, for any cotton, corn, or other farm products in store or custody of such ginner, warehouseman, cotton factor, or other bailee, shall not be held to be an innocent purchaser of any such produce against the lien of any landlord or laborer.

608. Delaware.[4] — A distress lies for any rent in arrear

part of the crop subject to his lien, he may enforce his lien against the residue of the crop. Lemay *v.* Johnson, 35 Ark. 225, 233; Hammond *v.* Harper, 39 Ark. 248.

[1] The affidavit may be amended. Nolen *v.* Royston, 36 Ark. 561. It is not impaired by including in the demand a claim for which he has no lien. Kurtz *v.* Dunn, 36 Ark. 648.

[2] As against a purchaser of the crop with notice of the lien, the landlord's remedy is by specific attach-

ment, while the crop is in the purchaser's hands, or by bill in equity, if he has sold it, to have the proceeds applied to the payment of the rent. Reavis *v.* Barnes, 36 Ark. 575.

An action by the landlord against one taking the crop, with a knowledge of the existence of the lien, will be barred in six months after the maturity of the rent. King *v.* Blount, 37 Ark. 115; Valentine *v.* Hamlett, 35 Ark. 538.

[3] Acts 1885, ch. 134, §§ 1–3.

[4] R. Code 1874, ch. 120, §§ 19–66.

either of money, or a quantity or share of grain or other produce, or of anything certain or that can be reduced to certainty, and whether the same be a rent accruing upon a demise for life, or a term of one or more years, or a less time, or at will, or a rent-charge, rent-seck, quit-rent, or otherwise, issuing out of, or charged upon, any lands, tenements, or hereditaments.

The person entitled to such rent, whether the original lessor, or an assignee, heir, executor, or administrator, may distrain for the same, either personally or by his bailiff.

A distress may be made either during the demise or afterward, while the tenant, or any person coming into possession by or under him, shall continue to hold the demised premises, and the title to said premises shall remain in the person to whom the rent accrued, or his heirs, devisees, executors, or administrators, or be in his immediate reversioner or remainder-man.

A distress may be as well of the grain, grass, and other produce found upon the premises out of which the rent issues, or upon which it is charged, whether growing or severed, in sheaves, stacks, or otherwise, as the horses, cattle, and other goods and chattels being upon said premises ; except goods and chattels not the property of the tenant, but being in his possession in the way of his trade, or upon the said premises in the regular course of any occupation or business there carried on,[1] which exception shall extend to horses and carriages at a livery-stable, to property of boarders in a boarding-house, and to the beasts of a drover depastured while passing through the county, as well as to the more obvious cases of exemption at common law ; also except stoves not the property of, but hired by, the tenant, and beasts not the property of the tenant, escaping into the said premises through defect of fences, which the tenant, or his landlord, was bound to repair.

If the tenant, either during his term or estate, or after the end thereof, remove his goods and chattels, or any of them, from the said premises without payment of the rent due, or growing due, for the said premises, and without license from the landlord or his agent in writing under his hand, the goods and chattels so removed, unlesss old fairly for a valuable consideration

---

[1] The goods of a sub-tenant, removed from the demised premises after the expiration of the term, are not liable to distress, on a warrant at the suit of the landlord against the original tenant, for rent in arrears. New v. Pyle, 2 Houst. 9.

and delivered to the buyer, shall be liable, wherever found, to be distrained for said rent for forty days after the removal, or, if the rent be not in arrear at the time of the removal, for forty days after the rent shall become in arrear.

The person on whose demand a distress is made has a special property in the things distrained until replevin or sale thereof, so that he may take the same wherever found, and recover damages for carrying away or injuring them.

If the property distrained be not replevied within five days after written notice to the tenant of the property distrained, and the cause of the distress, it must be appraised at its true value.

After the expiration of six days from the day of appraising the property, it may be sold at public vendue to the highest bidder, first giving at least six days' notice of the sale.

If the goods and chattels of a tenant be seized upon execution or attachment, they are liable for one year's rent of the premises, in arrear, or growing due, at the time of the seizure, in preference to such process. A prior distress of such goods for rent in arrear does not preclude the landlord from such preference.[1]

609. District of Columbia.[2] — The landlord has a tacit lien upon such of the tenant's personal chattels on the premises as are subject to execution for debt, to commence with the tenancy and continue for three months after the rent is due,[3] and until

---

[1] After execution has been levied on the tenant's goods, the landlord cannot distrain on a portion of them, and take the proceeds of a sale of them on a claim of a balance due him for the preceding year, and then claim an entire year's rent out of the sale of the residue on the execution, for the current year. Hopkins v. Simpson, 3 Houst. 90. See, also, State v. Vandever, 2 Harr. 397; Biddle v. Biddle, 3 Harr. 539.

If, at an execution sale of the tenant's goods, the landlord buys in the unexpired term, he is not entitled to a year's rent growing due at the time of sale, to be paid out of the proceeds of it, in preference to the execution creditor, but he is entitled to the rent growing due up to the time of the purchase of the term. Gause v. Richardson, 4 Houst. 222.

[2] R. S. 1874, §§ 678, 679. The first section of the statute abolishes the common law right of the landlord to distrain for rent The statute is a substitute for the right abolished. Wallach v. Chesley, 2 Mack. 209. See, also, on this statute, Fowler v. Rapley, 15 Wall. 328; Webb v. Sharp, 13 Wall. 14; Beall v. White, 94 U. S. 382.

[3] Where the tenant's chattels have been sold by virtue of an assignment for the benefit of his creditors, the landlord's claim upon the fund, to the extent of three months' rent, has priority over the claims of simple contract creditors. Fox v. Davidson, 1 Mack. 102.

the termination of any action for such rent brought within the said three months.

This lien may be enforced, — *First*. By attachment, to be issued upon affidavit that the rent is due and unpaid, or, if not due, that the defendant is about to remove or sell all or some part of said chattels ;[1] or, *Second*. By judgment against the tenant and execution, to be levied on said chattels or any of them, in whosesoever hands they may be found ;[2] or, *Third*. By action against any purchaser of any of said chattels, with notice of the lien, in which action the plaintiff may have judgment for the value of the chattels purchased by the defendant, but not exceeding the rent, arrear, and damages.[3]

610. Florida.[4] — All claims for rent shall be a lien on agri-

The lien is for the periodical rent accruing when the levy is made, but not for succeeding periods, during which the officer keeps the goods upon the premises. Harris *v.* Dammann, 3 Mack. 90.

[1] If the rent is payable monthly, the landlord may issue his attachment for rent which will be due and payable for the month during a part of which the tenant occupied the premises. Joyce *v.* Wilkenning, 1 MacArt. 567.

[2] The landlord has no right to an attachment against the tenant's chattels which have been removed from the premises before the rent is due. His remedy is by judgment against the tenant and execution, to be levied upon such chattels or any of them, in whosesoever hands they may be found. Wallach *v.* Chesley, 2 Mack. 209. The statute provides for several conditions of things : " First, when the rent is due; and, next, when the rent is not yet matured. When the rent is due, the lien may be enforced by an attachment issued upon an affidavit that the rent is due and unpaid. There is no trouble about that. But it will occur to anybody, that the tenant may, just before the maturity of his rent, and in order to avoid com-

pulsory payment of it, remove his chattels, or change the property in them. To meet that contingency, it is further provided that, even before the rent is due, if the landlord will make affidavit that the tenant is about to remove or sell all or some part of his chattels, the attachment may issue. And those are the only two cases provided for in the statute, in which an attachment is the remedy intended." Per Cox, C. J.

[3] If the goods subject to a landlord's lien be seized and sold upon execution by another creditor, the landlord may move the court out of which the execution issued for an order for the payment of the rent out of the proceeds of the sale. This motion may be made at any time before the money is paid over, the officer being bound, on notice from the landlord, to retain the money. Gibson *v.* Gautier, 1 Mack. (D. C.) 35.

[4] Dig. of Laws 1881, ch. 137, §§ 1, 12; being parts of Acts of 1879, ch. 3131, and 1881, ch. 3247. The former act repealed the Act of 1866, ch. 1498.

Under the last named statute, which simply provided that on the tenant's failure to pay rent the landlord might obtain a warrant of distress, there was

413

cultural products raised on the land rented, and shall be superior to all other liens and claims, though of older date, and also a superior lien on all other property of the lessee or his sub-lessee, or assigns, usually kept on the premises, over any lien acquired subsequent to such property having been brought on the premises leased.

Landlords shall have a lien on the crop grown on rented land for rent for the current year, and for advances made in money, or other things of value, whether made directly by them or at their instance and request by another person, or for which they have assumed the legal responsibility, at or before the time at which such advances were made, for the sustenance or well-being of the tenant or his family, for preparing the ground for culti- vation, or for cultivating, gathering, saving, handling, or pre- paring the crop for market; and they shall have a lien also upon each and every article advanced, and upon all property purchased with money advanced, or obtained by barter in exchange for any articles advanced, for the aggregate price or value of all such property or articles so advanced; and such liens for rent and advances shall be paramount and have preference of all other liens.

The lien is enforced [1] by a distress warrant [2] directed to the sheriff or constables of the county in which the rented land lies. This is issued upon an affidavit stating the amount or quality and value of the rent due, and whether it is payable in money, cotton, or other agricultural product or thing. If the prop- erty levied upon be not replevied within ten days, it is sold, and the proceeds applied to the payment of the lien claim and costs.[3]

---

no lien for rent until a warrant of dis- tress was issued. Patterson v. Taylor, 15 Fla. 336.

[1] Dig. of Laws 1881, ch. 137, §§ 2–11.

[2] The landlord's lien for rent, and also his lien for advances, may be en- forced by a single distress warrant covering both claims; the claim for advances being a lien upon the crop only, while the lien for rent may be satisfied out of the crop and other property kept on the premises. Blan- chard v. Raines, 20 Fla. 467.   A seizure of the property in the tenant's possession is a sufficient notice of the proceeding. Ib.

[3] If the tenant claims that certain property is exempt from levy and sale, the question should be settled in law. The landlord cannot invoke the aid of a court of equity to enforce his lien. Haynes v. McGeehee, 17 Fla. 159.

611. **Georgia.**[1] — Landlords have a special lien for rent on crops made on land rented from them, superior to all other liens except liens for taxes,[2] to which they shall be inferior, and shall also have a general lien on the property of the debtor liable to levy and sale, and such general lien shall date from the time of the levy of a distress warrant to enforce the same.[3] Such general lien of landlords shall be inferior to liens for taxes and the general and special lien of laborers, but shall rank with other liens, and with each other, according to date, the date being from the time of levying a distress warrant as aforesaid. The special liens of landlords for rent shall date from the maturity of the crops on the lands rented, unless otherwise agreed on, but shall not be enforced by distress warrants until said rent is due, unless the tenant is removing his property, when the landlord may, as provided elsewhere in this code, enforce said liens, both general and special.[4]

[1] Code 1882, §§ 1977, 1978; Act of 1873. Prior to this statute the landlord had no lien except by contract on the crop until the levy of a distress warrant.

[2] Saulsbury *v.* McKellar, 59 Ga. 301. This lien is superior to an agreement between the tenant and one who cultivated the premises with him on shares, whereby the latter was to have all the cotton to be raised thereon. Alston *v.* Wilson, 64 Ga. 482.

The tenant is not entitled to any exemption out of the crop till the rent of the land upon which the crop was raised is paid. Davis *v.* Meyers, 41 Ga. 95.

This special lien can be enforced only by distress warrant. The title to the crop is not in the landlord, and therefore he cannot sue for it in trover or for its value in assumpsit. Worrill *v.* Barnes, 57 Ga. 404.

Before the landlord can assert his lien on a crop, he must prove that it was raised on the rented land. The burden of this proof is upon him. Saulsbury *v.* McKellar, 55 Ga. 322.

[3] When the hire of animals or other personalty upon a farm is included in the rent for the whole, the entire sum is rent, and may be collected by distress. Lathrop *v.* Clewis, 63 Ga. 282.

An affidavit to enforce the special lien should allege a demand and refusal to pay the rent. Hill *v.* Reeves, 57 Ga. 31; Lathrop *v.* Clewis, *supra.* This is not necessary in case of a general lien. Buffington *v.* Hilley, 55 Ga. 655.

The affidavit to foreclose the landlord's lien for supplies is sufficient if it sets out fully the relation of landlord and tenant, states that the landlord furnished the tenant with supplies to make a crop for a particular year, states the amount claimed, and a demand and refusal to pay after the debt became due. It is not necessary to set out the property on which the lien is claimed. Ware *v.* Blalock, 72 Ga. 804; Scruggs *v.* Gibson, 40 Ga. 511.

[4] An ordinary distress for rent implies that the plaintiff is the landlord. An assignee can succeed to a landlord's lien only by an assignment of the same in writing. Code, § 1996; Driver *v.* Maxwell, 56 Ga. 11. With-

Landlords[1] furnishing supplies, money, farming utensils, or other articles of necessity to make crops, and also all persons furnishing clothing and medicines, supplies or provisions for the support of families, or medical services, tuition, or school-books, have the right to secure themselves from the crops of the year in which such things are done or furnished, upon such terms as may be agreed upon by the parties with the following conditions : [2] —

1. The liens shall arise by operation of law from the relation of landlord and tenant, as well as by special contract in writing, whenever the landlord shall furnish the articles enumerated in said section, or any one of them, to the tenant, for the purposes therein named.

2. Whenever said liens may be created by special contract in writing as now provided by law, the same shall be assignable by the landlord, and may be enforced by the assignees in the manner provided for the enforcement of such liens by landlords.

3. They shall only exist as liens on the crop of the year in which they are made, and may be foreclosed before the debt is

out such assignment, the right to enforce the lien remains in the landlord. If the proceeding be by an assignee, both the contract and the assignment must be set out or described in the affidavit. Lathrop v. Clewis, 63 Ga. 282. Inasmuch as the landlord's special lien dates from the maturity of the crop, and his general lien from the levy of a distress warrant, a mere transfer of a note given for rent, which transfer is made in writing before either of these events happens, is not an assignment of any lien. Lathrop v. Clewis, *supra.*

If the tenant is removing his property the landlord may distrain before the rent is due. Rosenstein v. Forester, 57 Ga. 94.

[1] If a landlord having a lien for his rent and a lien for supplies assigns the latter lien for the purpose of enabling the tenant to procure supplies of the assignee, and the supplies are furnished by the assignee on the faith of this lien, the landlord is estopped from

attacking the validity of the lien in the hands of the assignee. Zachry v. Stewart, 67 Ga. 218.

In order to have a lien for supplies the landlord must himself furnish them. He has no lien by reason of having become his tenant's surety for the price of the articles, when these are furnished by some other person directly to the tenant. The landlord may furnish them directly from his own stores, or may order them from others on his credit. He has a lien if he is the real purchaser for the tenant, and it does not matter that the tenant has joined him in a joint and several note for the price. If, however, the tenant is the real purchaser in the first instance, there is no lien. Scott v. Pound, 61 Ga. 579.

[2] The lien may be enforced as provided in § 1991, which is a general provision for the enforcement of liens upon personal property. See Chap. XXII., *infra.*

due, if the tenant is removing, or seeking to remove, his crop from the premises.

4. Every person giving a lien under this section, having previously given a lien or liens under it, or any other lien, shall, when giving a new lien under this section, on the same property, to another person, inform such person, if interrogated as to the facts, of the amount of such lien or liens, and to whom given.[1]

612. Georgia (*continued*). Distress for rent.[2] — The landlord shall have power to distrain for rent as soon as the same is due, or before due if the tenant is seeking to remove his goods from the premises.

The landlord's lien for his rent shall attach from the time of levying his distress warrant, but it shall take precedence of no lien of older date except as to the crop raised on the premises.

Any person who may have rent due may, by himself, his agent or attorney, make application to any justice of the peace within the county where his debtor may reside, or where his property may be found, and obtain from such justice a distress warrant for the sum claimed to be due, on the oath of the principal, his agent or attorney, in writing, for the said rent, which may be levied by any constable, duly qualified, on any property belonging to said debtor, whether found on the premises or elsewhere, who shall advertise and sell the same, as in case of levy and sale under execution : provided, if the sum claimed to be due exceeds one hundred dollars and said warrant shall be levied by a constable, it shall be his duty to deliver the warrant, with a return of the property levied upon, to the sheriff of said county,

---

[1] Such person giving false information as to the facts aforesaid shall be deemed a common cheat and swindler, and, on conviction thereof, shall be punished as prescribed in § 4310 of the Code. These liens are hereby declared to be superior in rank to other liens, except liens for taxes, the general and special liens of laborers, and the special liens of landlords, to which they shall be inferior, and shall, as between themselves and other liens not herein excepted, rank according to date. Code 1882, § 1978, pl. 5, 6.

[2] Code 1882, §§ 2285, 2286, 4082–4084. To justify a distress warrant, the relation of landlord and tenant must exist. Cohen *v.* Broughton, 54 Ga. 296; Payne *v.* Holt, 61 Ga. 355; Ferguson *v.* Hardy, 59 Ga. 758. A tenant who sublets to another stands in the relation of landlord to him, and may distrain. Harrison *v.* Guill, 46 Ga. 427.

or his deputy, who shall advertise and sell as now provided by law for sheriffs' sales.

The party distrained may in all cases replevy the property so distrained by making oath that the sum, or some part thereof, distrained for is not due, and give security for the eventual condemnation money; and in such case the levying officer shall return the same to the court having cognizance thereof, which shall be tried by a jury as provided for in the trial of claims.

When property distrained may be claimed by a third person, the same shall be claimed on oath, and bond given as required in cases of other claims, which shall be returned and tried as provided by law for the trial of the right of property levied upon by execution.

613. Illinois.[1] — In all cases of distress for rent, the landlord, by himself, his agent or attorney, may seize for rent any personal property of his tenant that may be found in the county where such tenant shall reside;[2] and in no case shall the property of any other person, although the same may be found on the premises, be liable to seizure for rent due from such tenant.[3]

The person making the distress must immediately file with a justice of the peace, or clerk of a court of record of competent jurisdiction, a copy of the distress warrant, with an inventory of the property.[4]

Upon the filing of such copy the justice of the peace or clerk issues a summons to the party against whom the distress warrant is issued, returnable as any other summons.

---

[1] Annotated Stats. 1885, ch. 80, §§ 16–30; R. S. 1845, p. 334. The statutes of this state in regard to the landlord's right of distress do not create the right, but recognize and regulate the right which existed by common law. Penny v. Little, 3 Scam. 301; Johnson v. Prussing, 4 Bradw. 575.

It is not necessary that the lease should reserve the right. Penny v. Little, *supra*.

[2] Under this statute the landlord has no lien upon the personal property of the tenant prior to the actual levy of the distress warrant. Leopold v. Godfrey, 11 Biss. 158.

[3] The landlord cannot distrain the goods of a stranger or a sub-tenant, the latter being liable only to his immediate lessor. Gray v. Rawson, 11 Ill. 527; Emmert v. Reinhardt, 67 Ill. 481. The distress can be levied only upon the property of the tenant found in the county. Uhl v. Dighton, 25 Ill. 154.

[4] As to requisites of allegation, proof, and practice, see Bartlett v. Sullivan, 87 Ill. 219; Rauh v. Ritchie, 1 Bradw. 188; Alwood v. Mansfield, 33 Ill. 452; Cox v. Jordan, 86 Ill. 560, 561.

The suit thereupon proceeds as in case of an attachment.

The defendant may avail himself of any set-off or other defence which would have been proper if the suit had been for rent.[1]

The judgment has the same effect as in suits commenced by summons,[2] and execution may issue thereon, not only against the property distrained, but also against the other property of the defendant. But the property distrained, if the same has not been replevied or released from seizure, shall be first sold.

If the property distrained is of a perishable nature and in danger of immediate waste or decay, and it has not been replevied or bonded, the landlord or his agent may, upon giving notice to the defendant or his attorney, if either can be found in the county, or if neither can be found, apply to a judge or master in chancery of the court in which, or justice of the peace before whom, the suit is pending, for an order of sale, upon such time and such notice, terms, and conditions as the judge, master, or justice of the peace shall think to be for the best interests of all the parties concerned. The money arising from such sale must be deposited with the clerk of the court in which, or justice of the peace before whom, the suit is pending, there to abide the event of the suit.

The right of the landlord to distrain the personal goods of the tenant shall continue for the period of six months after the expiration of the term for which the premises were demised or the tenancy is terminated.[3]

When the rent is payable wholly or in part in specific articles of property, or products of the premises, or labor, the landlord may distrain for the value of such articles, products, or labor.[4]

The same articles of personal property which are by law exempt from execution, except the crops grown or growing upon

---

[1] See Cox v. Jordan, 86 Ill. 560; Lindley v. Miller, 67 Ill. 244; Alwood v. Mansfield, 33 Ill. 452. In an action of trespass by a tenant against his landlord for an illegal distress, the latter, it seems, may recoup to the extent of the rent unpaid, although this may not be due. Cunnea v. Williams, 11 Bradw. 72.

[2] See Clevenger v. Dunaway, 84 Ill. 367.

[3] A warrant issued afterwards is illegal and void, and affords no protection to the officer levying it. Werner v. Ropiequet, 44 Ill. 522.

[4] A warrant under this section is not vitiated by the use of the term "damages" instead of "rent." Craig v. Merime, 16 Bradw. 214.

the demised premises, shall also be exempt from distress for rent.

614. Illinois'[1] (*continued*).   Lien upon crops. — Every landlord shall have a lien upon the crops grown or growing upon the demised premises for the rent thereof, whether the same is payable wholly or in part in money, or specific articles of property, or products of the premises, or labor, and also for the faithful performance of the terms of the lease.   Such lien shall continue for the period of six months after the expiration of the term for which the premises were demised.

In all cases where the demised premises shall be sublet, or the lease is assigned, the landlord shall have the same right to enforce his lien against the sub-lessee or assignee that he has against the tenant to whom the premises were demised.

If the tenant abandons the premises, the landlord may seize any grain or crops growing upon the premises, whether the rent be due or not.   He may harvest or gather the crops and sell the

---

[1] Annotated Stats. 1885, ch. 80, §§ 31, 32, 35.

This statute makes a distinction between agricultural products and the general personal property of the tenant.

A lien is given upon the crops grown in any year for the rent that shall accrue during such year, but no specific lien is given as to any other property of the tenant. The giving of a lien upon crops by implication excludes the idea of a lien on any other property of the tenant. Hadden *v.* Knickerbocker, 70 Ill. 677; Herron *v.* Gill, 112 Ill. 247. The distinction was doubtless owing to the fact that agriculture is the chief industry of the state. It may have been thought that it could work no serious injury to trade if one kind of property alone were subject to a statutory lien, but that to extend this lien to all the personal property owned by a tenant in the county would interfere with it very materially. Morgan *v.* Campbell, 22 Wall. 381, 390, per Davis, J.

The levy of a distress warrant is not

essential to the landlord's right of possession of the property upon which he has a lien for rent. Such warrant is not his exclusive remedy for the assertion and protection of his lien. The statute gives him a lien upon the crop. The lien does not grow out of the levy of the distress warrant. The landlord may take possession of the crop, and he may hold it as against a purchaser from the tenant or an attaching creditor to the extent of the rent due him. Hunter *v.* Whitfield, 89 Ill. 229 ; Wetsel *v.* Mayers, 91 Ill. 497 ; Thompson *v.* Mead, 67 Ill. 395; Mead *v.* Thompson, 78 Ill. 62; Miles *v.* James, 36 Ill. 399; Prettyman *v.* Unland, 77 Ill. 206.

The landlord is not entitled to possession as against the tenant until the rent is due. Watt *v.* Scofield, 76 Ill. 261. The lien can only be lost by waiver, or by failing to enforce it within the proper time. The abandonment of proceedings by distress is not a waiver of the lien. Wetsel *v.* Mayers, *supra.*

same, and apply the proceeds to the payment of his expenses and the rent. The tenant may redeem at any time before sale by tendering the rent due, and the expenses of cultivation and harvesting.[1]

If any tenant shall, without the consent of his landlord, sell and remove, or permit to be removed, or be about to sell and remove, or permit to be removed, from the demised premises, such part or portion of the crops raised thereon as shall endanger the lien of the landlord upon such crops for the rent agreed to be paid, it shall and may be lawful for the landlord to institute proceedings by distress before the rent is due, as is now provided by law, in case of the removal of the tenant from the demised premises ; and thereafter the proceedings shall be conducted in the same manner as is now provided by law in ordinary cases of distress where the rent is due and unpaid.

615. Indiana.[2] — In all cases where a tenant agrees to pay, as rent, a part of the crop raised on the leased premises, or rent in kind, or a cash rent, the landlord shall have a lien on the crop raised under such contract for the payment of such rent ; which lien, if the tenant refuse or neglect to pay or deliver to the landlord such rent when due, may be enforced by sale of such crop, in the same manner as the lien of a chattel mortgage containing a power to sell : provided that nothing herein contained shall prohibit the tenant, after notice in writing to the landlord or his agent, from removing from such leased premises his own part of said growing crop, and no more than such part, and from also disposing of the same whenever the rent is to be paid in part of the crop raised ; but in other cases he may remove not more than one half of the crop growing or matured.

616. Iowa.[3] — A landlord shall have a lien for his rent upon all crops grown upon the demised premises,[4] and upon any other

---

[1] The landlord's rights are not affected by notice from the tenant of his intention to leave. Hare *v.* Stegall, 60 Ill. 380. See Hammond *v.* Will, 60 Ill. 404.

[2] R. S. 1881, § 5224 ; Act of May 20, 1852, § 17, amended March 11, 1875 ; Kennard *v.* Harvey, 80 Ind. 37.

[3] R. Code 1880, § 2017 ; Rev. 1860, § 2302 ; Code 1851, § 1270.

[4] The lien attaches to crops grown upon the demised premises by a sublessee of the tenant. Houghton *v.* Bauer (Iowa), 30 N. W. Rep. 577. The lien is not divested by a sale of the crops by the tenant, but the landlord may follow them into the hands

personal property of the tenant which has been used[1] on the premises during the term, and not exempt from execution, for the period of one year after a year's rent, or the rent of a shorter period claimed, falls due; but such lien shall not in any case continue more than six months after the expiration of the term.

The lien may be effected by the commencement of an action, within the period above prescribed, for the rent alone, in which action the landlord will be entitled to a writ of attachment, upon filing with the proper clerk or the justice an affidavit that the

---

of the purchaser; and if he has consumed them, he is liable to the landlord in damages. Holden v. Cox, 60 Iowa, 449.

[1] A different rule applies to sales of other personal property. Thus, if a tenant keeps a stock of goods upon the demised premises merely for sale, he may make sales in the ordinary course of business, and the landlord cannot follow the goods sold. Grant v. Whitwell, 9 Iowa, 152. In like manner it is held that the landlord's lien does not follow a tenant's cow which the tenant has sold, for it is presumed that the cow is not kept solely for use, but partly for sale. Nesbitt v. Bartlett, 14 Iowa, 485. The reason for this distinction is said to be that, in the case of the stock of goods, the lien rested upon the stock as a mass. When goods are sold in the ordinary course of trade, they are sold with the view to replenishment. The stock as a mass is preserved, and the lien-holder suffers no detriment. The same thing may be said, with some slight propriety at least, of the mass of live-stock with which a farmer stocks his farm. Sales may be made, but the proper conduct of the farm requires the continuity of the mass. With annual crops it is different. Each year's sales and consumption may properly enough exhaust the mass. Per Adams, J., in Holden v. Cox, supra.

The property must be actually used

on the premises to entitle the landlord to a lien thereon for rent. Grant v. Whitwell, supra. Horses and wagons used in connection with a grocery business carried on upon the leased premises, but kept in another place, are not subject to the landlord's lien. Van Patten v. Leonard, 55 Iowa, 520.

No lien is given by the statute upon notes and accounts due the tenant and kept on the premises. Van Patten v. Leonard, supra.

The word "used" is not employed in the limited sense in which it is applied to agricultural implements. Grant v. Whitwell, supra. The landlord has a lien on property kept upon the premises for the purpose of sale, although not used for any other purpose. The lien is given only upon the property of the tenant. The landlord has no lien upon the property of third persons, although it be used by the tenant upon the demised premises during the term of the lease. Thus, a lessor of a hotel has no lien on the property of the lessee's wife used in furnishing the hotel; and if the lessee sells his lease and the wife also sells her furniture to the same purchaser, subject to a recorded mortgage upon it which she had given, and the purchaser takes possession, the lessor has no lien upon such property as against the holder of the mortgage. Perry v. Waggoner, 68 Iowa, 403.

action is commenced to recover rent accrued within one year previous thereto upon premises described in the affidavit.[1]

617. Kansas.[2]— Any rent due for farming land shall be a lien on the crop growing or made on the premises. Such lien may be enforced by action and attachment therein.[3]

When any such rent is payable in a share or certain proportion of the crop, the lessor shall be deemed the owner of such share or proportion; and may, if the tenant refuse to deliver him such share or proportion, enter upon the land and take possession of the same, or obtain possession thereof by action of replevin.

The person entitled to the rent may recover from the purchaser of the crop, or any part thereof, with notice of the lien, the value of the crop purchased, to the extent of the rent due and damages.[4]

When any person who shall be liable to pay rent (whether the

---

[1] § **2018.** The word "effected," as used by the statute, must be regarded the same as "enforced," for it does not require an action to effectuate the lien. It exists for and during the statutory period, although no action is brought to enforce it. If, however, it is desired to enforce the lien, then an action is required. A tenant sold certain wheat on which his landlord had a lien. The landlord sued his tenant *before* the expiration of the six months prescribed, and recovered judgment, and, after the expiration of that time, sued the purchaser of the wheat for the amount of the prior judgment. It was held that the lien was not effected by the action against the tenant, and that the action against the purchaser was barred. Mickelson *v.* Negley (Iowa), 32 N. W. Rep. 487. This remedy is purely statutory, and must be strictly construed. Merrit *v.* Fisher, 19 Iowa, 354.

An action for rent, commenced by ordinary attachment before rent is due, cannot be deemed an action to effect a landlord's lien, and the plaintiff takes thereby only such a lien as an ordinary attachment gives. Clark *v.* Haynes, 57 Iowa, 96. The action under the statute to effect the lien cannot be commenced before the rent is due, and if the landlord needs to aid his lien by preventing a disposition of the property, he must do so by an application in equity for an injunction. Garner *v.* Cutting, 32 Iowa, 547, 552.

An attachment may be issued against the crop of a sub-lessee grown upon the lands demised to the tenant, in an action by the landlord on a promissory note given by the tenant to secure the rent. Houghton *v.* Bauer, 30 N. W. Rep. 577.

A mortgagee of chattels, after being garnished by a creditor of the mortgagor, may pay over to the landlord, out of the surplus in his hands, after satisfying the mortgage debt, the rent accrued upon the building in which the goods were kept, and which was in arrear when the mortgagee took possession. Doane *v.* Garretson, 24 Iowa, 351, 354.

[2] Comp. Laws 1885, ch. 55, §§ 24–28.

[3] Neifert *v.* Ames, 26 Kans. 515.

[4] See Neifert *v.* Ames, *supra*.

423

same be due or not, if it be due within one year thereafter, and whether the same be payable in money or other thing) intends to remove, or is removing, or has within thirty days removed, his property, or the crops, or any part· thereof, from the leased premises, the person to whom the rent is owing may commence an action in the court having jurisdiction ; and upon making an affidavit stating the amount of rent for which such person is liable, and one or more of the above facts, and executing an undertaking as in other cases, an attachment shall issue in the same manner, and with the like effect, as is provided by law in other actions.[1]

In an action to enforce a lien on crops for rent of farming lands, the affidavit for an attachment shall state that there is due from the defendant to the plaintiff a certain sum, naming it, for rent of farming lands, describing the same, and that the plaintiff claims a lien on the crop made on such land. Upon making and filing such affidavit and executing an undertaking as prescribed in the preceding section, an order of attachment shall issue as in other cases, and shall be levied on such crop, or so much thereof as may be necessary ; and other proceedings in such attachment shall be the same as in other actions.

618. Kentucky.[2] — Rent may be recovered by distress or attachment, but no landlord shall issue his own distress warrant. When rent is reserved in money,[3] he may, before a justice of the peace, police judge, or a judge of a county court, make oath to the amount of rent due him and in arrear, and thereupon such officer issues a distress warrant directed to the sheriff, marshal, or

---

[1] Land was rented to be cultivated in wheat, the rent being a share of the crop. When the wheat was ripe the tenant harvested and removed the entire crop from the premises against the protest of the landlord, who afterwards commenced an action against the tenant for the value of his share of the wheat, and at the same time procured an order of attachment to be issued and levied upon the entire crop. It was held that the action with the order of attachment was rightly brought and could be maintained. The landlord had a lien upon the whole crop for the payment of his share ; and was not confined to the remedy of replevin under § 25 of the act, but could proceed by attachment under § 27. Tarpy v. Persing, 27 Kans. 745. And see Neifert v. Ames, 26 Kans. 515.

[2] G. S. 1873, ch. 66, art. 2. As to constitutionality of the act, see Burket v. Boude, 3 Dana, 209.

[3] Distress is available only when rent is payable in money. Myers v. Mayfield, 7 Bush, 212, 213 ; Poer v. Peebles, 1 B. Mon. 1, 3.

constable, authorizing such officer to distrain the personal estate of the tenant for the amount due, with interest and costs.   The personal estate of a sub-tenant or assignee found on the premises is also liable to distress.   If the tenant has removed his property to another county, the distress may be directed to such county.

A distress warrant may issue although the lease be not ended, but only for rent then due, and not after the lapse of six months from the time it was due.

All valid liens upon the personal property of a lessee, assignee, or under-tenant, created before the property was carried upon the leased premises, prevail against a distress warrant, or attachment for rent.   If liens be afterwards created on property upon which the landlord has a superior lien, then, to the extent of one year's rent, whether the same accrued before or after the creation of the lien, a distress or attachment has preference, provided the same is sued out in ninety days from the time the rent was due.[1]

619. Kentucky (*continued*). **Lien for rent.** — A landlord shall have a superior [2] lien on the produce of the farm or premises rented, on the fixtures, on the household furniture, and other personal property of the tenant, or under-tenant, owned by him, after possession is taken under the lease ; but such lien shall not be for more than one year's rent due or to become due, nor for any rent which has been due for more than one hundred and twenty days.[3]   But if any such property be removed openly from

---

[1] A creditor who levies execution upon property subject to a landlord's lien must, upon notice, tender the rent in arrear not exceeding one year. Craddock *v.* Riddlesbarger, 2 Dana, 209 ; Burket *v.* Boude, 3 Ib. 209 ; Williams *v.* Wood, 2 Metc. 41. To render the lien effectual against an attaching creditor, if the rent is not due at the time of such attachment, the landlord should sue out an attachment or a distress warrant and have it levied on the attached property on which he has a lien.   Williams *v.* Wood, *supra*.

[2] The lien is superior as against the tenant's creditors, but not as against *bonâ fide* purchasers who take the

property off the premises.   Stone *v.* Bohm, 79 Ky. 141.   The landlord, however, has priority over the tenant's mortgagees whose liens have been acquired after the property has been taken to the leased premises, to the extent of one year's rent, if the remedy has been pursued within the time allowed by law.   English *v.* Duncan, 14 Bush, 377 ; Fisher *v.* Kollerts, 16 B. Mon. 398, 408 ; Williams *v.* Wood, *supra*.

[3] Under § 12 of this statute the landlord, in order to prevail against other liens, must assert his rent claim in ninety days ; and under § 13, to prevail against all other rights and equities of third persons, he must as-

the leased premises, and without fraudulent intent, and not returned, the lien of the landlord shall be lost as to it, unless the same be asserted by proper procedure within fifteen days from removal.[1]

Property distrained for rent, or so much as is sufficient to make satisfaction, is sold by the officer, unless within ten days from the day of levy the demand be replevied, or by other legal procedure a sale is prevented.

A distress for rent, at any time before sale, may be replevied for three months by the defendant's giving a bond with surety.

620. Louisiana.[2] — The lessor has, for the payment of his rent and other obligations of the lease, a right of pledge on the movable effects of the lessee which are found on the property leased.[3]

sert it in one hundred and twenty days. A distress warrant not issued within the latter time cannot prevail against the tenant's assignee under an assignment for the benefit of his creditors. Petry v. Randolph (Ky.), 3 So. West Rep. 420.

[1] This provision is a material change from the statutes of 8 Anne, ch. 14, and 2 George II. ch. 19, under which, in order to preserve the lien after removal of the property, it was necessary to show that the removal was fraudulent. Under the statute of Kentucky it is immaterial whether the removal be with a fraudulent intent or not. Stone v. Bohm, 79 Ky. 141, 144.

[2] R. Civ. Code 1870, arts. 2705–2709, 3218.

[3] The lease need not be recorded. Johnson v. Tacneau, 23 La. Ann. 453, 454.

Furniture lodged by the lessee upon the leased premises is pledged for the rent. A seizure by the landlord, and a release of the seizure by the lessee's giving bond, does not destroy or impair the privilege. Harrison v. Jenks, 23 La. Ann. 707. The landlord's privilege springs from the nature of the debt. A seizure does not give the privilege, and a release of the

seizure does not take it away. The bond is only an additional security. The privilege still exists against the property. Ib. See Conrad v. Patzelt, 29 La. Ann. 465.

The landlord's privilege, for rent due and for rent not due, prevails against a seizure by a judgment creditor of the lessee. Harmon v. Juge, 6 La. Ann. 768; Robinson v. Staples, 5 La. Ann. 712; Gleason v. The Sheriff, 20 La. Ann. 266. The sheriff may be ordered to retain in his hands the proceeds of the property sold, and such order continues the landlord's privilege in force. New Orleans v. Vaught, 12 La. Ann. 339. As to the landlord's remedies in such case, see Robb v. Wagner, 5 La. Ann. 111.

The lessor is not bound to enforce his privilege before pursuing the lessee's sureties. Ledoux v. Jones, 20 La. Ann. 539.

Agreements in the lease whereby the lessee is to repair, are secured by the privilege. Warfield v. Oliver, 23 La. Ann. 612.

But on the other hand the covenant of a landlord to pay for improvements erected by a tenant does not constitute a lien on the premises. Confiscation Cases, 1 Woods, 221.

In case of predial estates, this right embraces everything that serves for the labors of the farm,[1] the furniture of the lessee's house, and the fruits produced during the lease of the land, and in case of houses and other edifices, it includes the furniture of the lessee,[2] and the merchandise contained in the house or apartment, if it be a store or shop.

But the lessee shall be entitled to retain, out of the property subjected by law to the lessor's privilege, his clothes and linens, and those of his wife and family, his bed, bedding, and bedsteads, and those of his wife and family; his arms, military accoutrements, and tools and instruments necessary for the exercise of the trade or profession by which he gains his living and that of his family.[3]

This right of pledge includes, not only the effects of the principal lessee or tenant, but those of the under-tenant,[4] so far as the latter is indebted to the principal lessee at the time when the proprietor chooses to exercise his right.[5]

A payment made in anticipation, by the under-tenant to his principal, does not release him from the owner's claim.

This right of pledge affects, not only the movables of the lessee and under-lessee, but also those belonging to third persons, when their goods are contained in the house or store by their own consent, express or implied.[6]

The lessor has no privilege on a debt due the lessee. Edwards *v.* Fairbanks, Louque's Dig. 583.

But a banker's movable effects, subject to the privilege, embrace notes, certificates of stock, and the like, on the premises. Matthews *v.* Creditors, 10 La. Ann. 718.

[1] The lessor's privilege extends to horses and carts kept by the lessee on the premises. Bazin *v.* Segura, 5 La. Ann. 718.

[2] Lalaurie *v.* Woods, 8 La. Ann. 366.

[3] The lessor cannot seize a piano, organ, or other musical instrument hired for use, and not the property of the inmates or sub-lessee. Act 1874, No. 63, p. 112.

[4] *Under - tenant* is the same as under-lessee. University Publishing Co. *v.* Piffet, 34 La. Ann. 602.

[5] Goods of a sub-lessee are only liable to seizure for rent that is past due. Sanarens *v.* True, 22 La. Ann. 181.

If the sub-lessee does not disclose the title under which he occupies the premises, the lessor's privilege will cover the goods for the whole amount of rent due. Simon *v.* Goldenberg, 15 La. Ann. 229.

If the sub-lessee owes no rent to the lessee, the landlord cannot seize his goods. Kittridge *v.* Ribas, 18 La. Ann. 718; Simon *v.* Goldenberg, *supra ;* Powers *v.* Florance, 7 La. Ann. 524; Wallace *v.* Smith, 8 Ib. 374. One who pays storage on his goods in a warehouse is a sub-lessee. Vairin *v.* Hunt, 18 La. 498.

[6] Therefore, if goods of a third person be consigned by their owner to the lessee, to be sold by the latter at a price fixed by the owner, with the

Movables are not subject to this right when they are only transiently or accidentally in the house, store, or shop, such as the baggage of a traveller in an inn, merchandise sent to a workman to be made up or repaired, and effects lodged in the store of an auctioneer to be sold.[1]

In the exercise of this right, the lessor may seize the objects which are subject to it, before the lessee takes them away, or within fifteen days after they are taken away, if they continue to be the property of the lessee and can be identified.[2]

agreement that the lessee shall keep, as his compensation, all that he should obtain above such price, and that no rent should be charged, the goods are affected by the privilege. Goodrich v. Bodley, 35 La. Ann. 525.

The goods of a third person who is allowed to occupy a portion of the leased premises without rent, the lessor's motive being an expected benefit to his own business from having such person in his house, are subject to the landlord's privilege. University Publishing Co. v. Piffet, 34 La. Ann. 602.

As to the consent which makes the goods of a third person liable, see, also, Twitty v. Clarke, 14 La. Ann. 503.

When the lessor's privilege has attached before a sale by the lessee, the purchaser cannot defeat a seizure by the lessor. Davis v. Thomas, 23 La. Ann. 340. Otherwise if sale take place before any default. Smith v. Blois, 8 La. Ann. 10.

Goods on the leased premises belonging to a partnership are subject to the lessor's privilege where the lessee is a member of the partnership. Hynson v. Cordukes, 21 La. Ann. 553.

Property of a wife carrying on a separate trade in a building leased to husband is liable for the rent. Deslix v. Jonc, 6 Rob. 292.

Under the rule that privileges are *stricti juris*, the court is precluded from assuming that the effects of a third person are affected by the lessor's privilege after their removal from his house or store. The privilege must be restricted as against third persons to the conditions imposed by this article. Merrick v. La Hache, 27 La. Ann. 87; Silliman v. Short, 26 Ib. 512 ; Bailey v. Quick, 28 Ib. 432.

The effects of a third person removed from the premises cannot be seized by the lessor, even within fifteen days of their removal. Merrick v. La Hache, *supra*. If a lessee not in default for his rent transfers goods back to a vendor, and obtains credit for the price, and the vendor sells to another, the lessor's privilege is defeated, though the lessee was in an embarrassed condition at the time. Smith v. Blois, *supra*.

[1] Sugar and molasses manufactured for third persons from cane belonging to them, and grown on another plantation, are not liable to the landlord's privilege. Lesseps v. Ritcher, 18 La. Ann. 653; Coleman v. Fairbanks, 28 La. Ann. 93. Nor on goods of a third person transiently stored. Rea v. Burt, 8 La. 509, 511.

[2] A lessor who makes a seizure before the rent is due is not liable in damages although the lessee had no fraudulent intent, provided the lessor acts without malice and in the honest belief or fear that the lessee will remove his property from the leased premises. Dillon v. Porier, 34 La. Ann. 1100.

The attempt of a lessee or of his

The right which the lessor has over the products of the estate, and on the movables which are found on the place leased, for his rent, is of a higher nature than a mere privilege.[1] The latter is only enforced on the price arising from the sale of movables to which it applies. It does not enable the creditor to take or keep the effects themselves specially. The lessor, on the contrary, may take the effects themselves and retain them until he is paid.[2]

Privileges on crops are ranked in the order of preference: [3] —

1. Privilege of the laborer.[4]

2. Privilege of the lessor.[5]

3. Privilege of the overseer.

4. Pledges for advances.

5. Privilege of furnishers of supplies and of money, and of the physician.

When a lessor sues for rent, whether the same be due or not due, he may obtain the provisional seizure of such furniture or property as may be found in the house, or attached to the land leased by him; [6] and in all cases it shall be sufficient, to entitle a lessor to said writ, to swear to the amount which he claims, whether due or not due, and that he has good reasons to believe

---

vendee to forcibly remove from the leased premises property subject to the lessor's privilege is a trespass, sounding in damages. Cooper v. Cappel, 29 La. Ann. 213.

The privilege cannot be asserted against goods removed except within the time limited. Langsdorf v. Le Gardeur, 27 La. Ann. 363 ; Haralson v. Boyle, 22 La. Ann. 210 ; Farnet v. Creditors, 8 La. Ann. 372.

[1] R. Civ. Code 1870, art. 3218 ; Garretson v. Creditors, 1 Rob. 445 ; Hoey v. Hews, 3 La. Ann. 704.

[2] As against others having a legal right to the property, the lessor cannot detain the lessee's property continuously ; he cannot prevent a sale of the property on the pretence that it would not bring the amount of his debt. No right of his is violated by a sale made in the exercise of a legal right of another against the property. If his right is preserved and his debt

is paid in whole or in part by the appropriation of the entire proceeds of the property, he has no just ground of complaint. Case v. Kloppenburg, 27 La. Ann. 482. And see Cooper v. Cappel, supra.

The lessors have the first privilege on movables seized upon a plantation, except on the crops, upon which the laborers have a preference. Duplantier v. Wilkins, 19 La. Ann. 112.

[3] Act No. 89 of 1886.

[4] Under Act No. 66 of 1874.

[5] The privilege of a vendor who has delivered personal property is inferior to that of a lessor. Gale's Succession, 21 La. Ann. 487; Harrison v. Jenks, 23 Ib. 707.

[6] Code of Practice, 1882, arts. 287, 288. As to seizure, when demand for rent be made within the jurisdiction of a justice of the peace, see art. 1125.

that such lessee will remove the furniture or property on which he has a lien or privilege out of the premises, and that he may be thereby deprived of his lien : provided that, in case the rent be paid when it falls due, the costs of seizure shall be paid by the lessor, unless he prove that the lessee did actually remove, or attempt or intend to remove, the property out of the premises : provided that, in all cases of provisional seizure of furniture or other property at the instance of lessors, the lessee shall be permitted to have the seizure released upon executing a forthcoming bond or obligation with a good, solvent security for the value of the property to be left in his possession, or for the amount of the claim with interest and costs : provided further, that the value of the property shall be fixed by the sheriff, or one of his deputies, with the assistance of two appraisers selected by the parties, twenty-four hours' notice being previously given to the lessor or his counsel to select an appraiser.

The lessor may seize, even in the hands of a third person, such furniture as was in the house leased,[1] if the same has been removed by the lessee, provided he declare on oath that the same has been removed without his consent, within fifteen days previous to his suit being brought.

621. **Maine.**[2] — When a lease of land, with a rent payable, is made for the purpose of erecting a mill or other buildings thereon, such buildings and all the interest of the lessee are subject to a lien and liable to be attached for the rent due. Such attachment, made within six months after the rent becomes due, is effectual against any transfer of the property by the lessee.

In all cases where land rent accrues and remains unpaid, whether under a lease or otherwise, all buildings upon the premises while the rent accrues are subject to a lien and to attachment for the rent due, as provided in the preceding section, although other persons than the lessee may own the whole or part thereof, and whether or not the land was leased for the purpose of erecting such buildings : provided, however, that if any person except the lessee is interested in said buildings, the proceedings shall be substantially in the forms directed for enforcing liens against vessels, with such additional notice to supposed

---

[1] Factors and agents of the lessee are not third persons in the sense of this provision. Tupery *v.* Edmondson, 32 La. Ann. 1146.

[2] R. S. 1883, ch. 91, §§ 36, 37.

or unknown owners as any justice of the Supreme Judicial Court orders, or the attachment and levy of execution shall not be valid except against the lessee.

622. **Maryland.**[1] **Distress for rent.** — A landlord or his agent,[2] before levying a distress, must make oath before a justice of the peace that the tenant is justly indebted in the sum named, or is entitled to a certain quantity or proportion of the produce raised by the tenant, for rent in arrear and already due, and that no part of it has been received except the credits given.[3]

When the distress is for grain or produce the bailiff shall summon two appraisers to estimate the money value of the same, and thereupon the distress is levied as in ordinary cases, taking the estimated value to be the money rent. At any time before such grain or produce is sold, the tenant may deliver the grain or other produce, with the expenses of the distress, whereupon the proceedings shall cease.[4]

[1] R. Code 1878, art. 67, vii., §§ 8–23. Certain property, specifically named, is exempt from distress. Laws 1884, ch. 310.

The property of a boarder or sojourner in a boarding-house is exempt by the statute. But it must be such property as is in the personal use of the boarder or his family, and not such as is in general use by the household. Leitch v. Owings, 34 Md. 262. And see Trieber v. Knabe, 12 Md. 491.

[2] What agency sufficient : Giles v. Ebsworth, 10 Md. 333; Jean v. Spurrier, 35 Md. 110.

A distress for rent is a remedy by the act of the party, and a landlord may constitute any person as his bailiff to make it. Myers v. Smith, 27 Md. 91. It is customary, however, to have the warrant directed to a sheriff, who may execute it by his deputy. Myers v. Smith, supra.

[3] If by mistake a larger sum is alleged to be due than is actually due, the whole distress is not rendered void, but the landlord may recover what is actually due. Jean v. Spurrier, supra.

The object of the provision was to protect the tenant from onerous and oppressive proceedings and from an excessive distress, and the statute is to receive a reasonable construction. Cross v. Tome, 14 Md. 247. It is not necessary to state the terms of the renting, or the items of the charges and credits. But the account must state when the rent became due, so that the tenant may be protected against being called on a second time for the same debt, and so that it may be known that the rent is in arrear and may be collected by distress. Cross v. Tome, supra; Butler v. Gannon, 53 Md. 333, 346. No action lies for distraining for more rent than is due and in arrear. Hamilton v. Windolf, 36 Md. 301.

[4] No notice or demand preliminary to the levy of the distress is necessary; Offutt v. Trail, 4 Har. & J. 20; but there must be notice preliminary to the sale. Keller v. Weber, 27 Md. 660.

Before sale the goods must be appraised by two sworn appraisers. These must be reasonably competent,

Whenever property shall be removed from premises which have been rented, within sixty days prior or subsequent to the time when the rent has or will become due, and whether such removal be by night or day, it shall be lawful for the landlord to follow, seize, and sell such property, under distress for the rent due, at any time within sixty days after the time when the rent becomes due: provided, that such property shall not have been sold to a *bonâ fide* purchaser without notice, or taken in execution.[1]

The rents of real estate of minors, or of leasehold estates that may not be due at the death of such minor, shall, for the year in which such minor may die, be paid to the guardian, who may maintain distress or suit to recover such rent.

If such guardian dies before the recovery of said rent, the executor or administrator of such guardian may recover the same by distress or suit.

Whenever any landlord shall give notice of rent due, to the sheriff or constable who may be about to sell the goods and chattels of his tenant under execution, there shall be appended to said notice an affidavit of the amount of his rent claimed to be due.

623. Maryland (*continued*). **Lien on crops.** — In all cases of renting lands wherein a share of the growing crops is reserved as rent, the rent reserved is a lien on such crops, which cannot be divested by any sale made by the tenant, or by his assignment in bankruptcy or insolvency, or by the process of law issued against the tenant.

In all cases wherein advances by the landlord have been made upon the faith of the crops to be grown, the rent reserved, and such advances made, are a lien on such crops, which shall not be divested by any sale made by the tenant, or by any administrator of a deceased tenant, or by the assignment of the tenant in insolvency, or by the process of law issued against the tenant: provided, that at the time of the said renting the con-

but need not be professional appraisers. Cahill *v.* Lee, 55 Md. 319.

[1] R. Code 1878, ch. 7, §§ 20–23; Neale *v.* Clautice, 7 H. & J. 373.

Where a receiver has taken possession of the tenant's goods and sold them, the landlord is not entitled to a lien on the proceeds of such sale for rent becoming due after the sale and removal of the goods by the purchaser, notwithstanding this provision. Gaither *v.* Stockbridge (Md.), 9 Atl. Rep. 632.

tract, under and by which the said advances are to be made, shall be reduced to writing, duly attested, and executed by the said landlord and tenant.[1]

624. Minnesota.[2] — The landlord's common law right of dis tress for rent in arrear, as modified by the statute 2 William & Mary, ch. 3, allowing the property to be sold, existed in this state until the remedy was abolished by statute in 1877.[2] The common law of a state or territory which had no political existence before the Revolution, is the common law as modified and amended by English statutes passed prior to our Revolution.[3]

625. Mississippi.[4] — Every lessor of land shall have a lien on all the agricultural products of the leased premises,[5] however and by whomsoever produced, to secure the payment of the rent, and the fair market value of all advances made by him to his tenant, for supplies for tenant and others for whom he may con tract, and for his business carried on upon the leased premises; and this lien shall be paramount to all other liens, claims, or demands of any kind upon such products;[6] and the claim of the lessor for supplies furnished may be enforced in the same man-

---

[1] These provisions apply only to the counties of St. Mary's, Prince George's, Charles, and Calvert.

[2] Laws 1877, ch. 140; G. S. 1878, ch. 75, § 39; Dutcher v. Culver, 24 Minn. 584.

[3] Coburn v. Harvey, 18 Wis. 147.

[4] R. Code 1880, §§ 1301, 1302. Section 1301 is an addition to the law of landlord and tenant, as it ex isted before the Code of 1880. Under the Codes of 1871 and 1857, the land lord's common law remedy for rent was assumed to exist, and was regu lated and modified by those codes. Fitzgerald v. Fowlkes, 60 Miss. 270. The common law process of distress was abolished by the statute, which provides for a summary method of attaching the tenant's property, and selling the same to pay the rent due by him. Marye v. Dyche, 42 Miss. 347.

[5] The right of the landlord to en force this lien is not prejudiced or in any manner diminished by the termi nation of the lease and removal of the tenant from the demised premises, nor by the removal of the products from the premises. The lien in either event continues until it is extinguished by lapse of the period prescribed by statute for its enforcement, just as if there had been no removal of the ten ant or of the products. Fitzgerald v. Fowlkes, supra.

[6] A third person can assert his lien only as subject to the landlord's lien, but the tenant can defeat a recovery of possession by such third person by setting up the landlord's lien. McGill v. Howard, 61 Miss. 411. This statute (1873) took away the power of the tenant to incumber the crop so as to impair the lien of the landlord. Ar buckle v. Nelms, 50 Miss. 556; Storm v. Green, 51 Miss. 103. See, also, Strauss v. Baley, 58 Miss. 131.

ner, and under the same circumstances, as his claim for rent may be ; and all the provisions of law, as to attachment for rent and proceedings under it, shall be applicable to a claim for supplies furnished, and such attachment may be levied on any goods and chattels [1] liable for rent, as well as on the agricultural products aforesaid.

The remedy is by attachment in the nature of a distraint, and sale of the property after at least ten days' notice.[2]

Attachment may be made upon apprehension that the tenant will remove his effects from the leased premises. Attachment may also be made after such removal within thirty days after the rent becomes due.[3]

If a tenant removes his chattels from the premises leaving any part of the rent unpaid, the landlord may, within thirty days afterwards, cause them to be seized wherever they may be found, as a distress for the arrears of rent ; but no goods so carried off

---

[1] There is a distinction between the agricultural products of the leased premises and other goods and chattels of the tenant. The statute creates a lien on the former, and gives the attachment to enforce it, while only a right to seize the latter is conferred. Goods and chattels of the tenant, other than agricultural products of the leased premises, are not subject to a lien for rent or advances for supplies, and they can be seized only on the premises, or off of them within the time prescribed by statute; but this limitation of time or place is not applicable to the agricultural products of the leased premises, on which the landlord has a lien, with the right to enforce it by seizure under attachment wherever and whenever found. Henry *v.* Davis, 60 Miss. 212, per Campbell, C. J.; Fitzgerald *v.* Fowlkes, 60 Miss. 270.

See, further, as to the nature of the lien, Westmoreland *v.* Wooten, 51 Miss. 825.

[2] R. C. 1880, §§ 1302, 1303. A distress for rent is not the commencement of a suit, but a seizure of the tenant's goods for the satisfaction of the rent, just as if a judgment had been rendered therefor. Towns *v.*

Boarman, 23 Miss. 186; Canterberry *v.* Jordan, 27 Miss. 96. And under the statute an attachment is not a *mesne process* returnable into a court, but is in the nature of a final process. Maxey *v.* White, 53 Miss. 80, 83. No lien for rent, either by common law or by statute, existed in this state prior to the Agricultural Lien Act of 1873. Arbuckle *v.* Nelms, 50 Miss. 556. The right of distress by attachment, under the statutes of this state modifying the common law of distress, exists not because of any lien, but because of rent in arrear, or because of a contemplated removal. Stamps *v.* Gilman, 43 Miss. 456; Marye *v.* Dyche, 42 Miss. 347.

[3] R. C. §§ 1304, 1305. To authorize a distress on account of apprehension that the tenant will remove his property before the rent is due, the landlord must have some ground for this apprehension, and must show this by evidence, else the distress will be wrongful. Briscoe *v.* McElween, 43 Miss. 556. The removal, moreover, must be such as would endanger or defeat a distress for rent. Stamps *v.* Gilman, *supra.*

and sold in good faith, before such seizure, shall be seized for rent.[1]

Distress may be made after the termination of the lease, provided it be made within six months afterwards, and during the continuance of the landlord's title, and during the possession of the tenant.[2]

The distress must be reasonable, and must not be removed from the county.[3]

No goods or chattels found on the demised premises, and not belonging to the tenant, or to some person liable for the rent, shall be distrained for rent ; but a limited interest in such goods may be distrained. No person claiming title to such property shall avail himself of this provision, unless by making and filing an affidavit that the goods distrained are his property, and not the property of the tenant, nor held in trust for the tenant, and giving bond and security in the manner directed for the tenant.[4]

626. Missouri.[5] — Every landlord shall have a lien upon the crops grown on the demised premises in any year, for the rent that shall accrue for such year, and such lien shall continue for eight months after such rent shall become due and payable, and no longer. When the demised premises, or any portion thereof,

[1] R. C. § 1306. To authorize a seizure of goods and chattels of the tenant away from the leased premises, within thirty days after their removal, it is not necessary that the affidavit for attachment shall state that the goods and chattels have been removed from the premises. Henry v. Davis, 60 Miss. 212.

[2] R. C. § 1308.

[3] Ibid. § 1309.

[4] Ibid. § 1317. A person claiming the goods distrained is precluded from maintaining an action for them if he has failed to interpose a claim in pursuance of this provision. Paine v. Hall's Safe and Lock Co. (Miss.) 1 So. Rep. 56.

[5] 1 R. S. 1879, § 3083. The right of distress for rent has never existed in this state. Crocker v. Mann, 3 Mo. 331, 333.

The lien given by statute can only be enforced by process of law. The landlord cannot himself seize the crops. Knox v. Hunt, 18 Mo. 243.

By express stipulation in the lease the landlord may be authorized to take possession of the crop and sell it. Sheble v. Curdt, 56 Mo. 437.

The crop during the continuance of the lien is not subject to process of law at the suit of any other creditor of the tenant. Knox v. Hunt, supra.

If the tenant abandons the crop, and the landlord harvests it, it is not subject to seizure by a creditor of the tenant. Sanders v. Ohlhausen, 51 Mo. 163.

If there is no indebtedness for rent, though the tenant may be otherwise indebted to the landlord, the tenant may dispose of the crop. Brown v. Turner, 60 Mo. 21.

are used for the purposes of growing nursery stock, a lien shall exist and continue on such stock until the same shall have been removed from the premises and sold, and such lien may be enforced by attachment in the manner hereinafter provided.

Whether the rent is due or not, if it will be due within one year, and the person liable to pay it intends to remove, or has within thirty days' removed, his property from the leased premises, or attempts to dispose of it so as to endanger or delay the collection of the rent, or when the rent is due and unpaid, the landlord may, upon affidavit of the fact, obtain an attachment of such property, including the crops grown on the premises.[1]

627. New Jersey.[2] Distress for rent. — All distresses shall be reasonable and not too great. No person shall take any distress wrongfully,[3] or cause any distress to be driven or conveyed out of the county. No person shall be distrained for any cause whatsoever by his beasts of the plough, or sheep, or by the implements of his trade, while other distress or chattels whereof the debt or demand may be levied, or sufficient for the same, may be found.

---

[1] R. S. § 3091. The landlord has a lien under this statute on the whole crop. The tenant is not prohibited from removing any portion of it, provided he does not endanger the landlord's collection of his rent. This is a question for the jury, to be determined with reference to the property remaining on the premises. Haseltine v. Ausherman, 87 Mo. 410; Meier v. Thomas, 5 Mo. App. 584.

A lien under § 3083 for *rent due and unpaid* may be enforced under § 3091 by attachment, accompanied by the affidavit required. Chamberlain v. Heard, 22 Mo. App. 416.

The growing crop of a tenant may be attached by the landlord for rent due. Crawford v. Coil, 69 Mo. 588.

Though the provision for attachment in favor of the landlord was not enacted for the purpose of enforcing the lien upon the crop grown upon the premises, yet it may be properly used for that purpose. Hubbard v. Moss, 65 Mo. 647. This remedy is not exclusive. The landlord may proceed under the general attachment law. Sanders v. Ohlhausen, 51 Mo. 163; Price v. Roetzell, 56 Mo. 500.

The proceeding may be maintained by the landlord, not only against his immediate lessee, but also against a sub-lessee, provided the rent accrued during the term of such lessee. Therefore, where an under-tenant had removed a wheat crop from the land within thirty days next before the commencement of the suit for an attachment, and while the rent was still owing by the lessee to the landlord, it was held that the landlord was entitled to an attachment against the under-tenant's wheat for the rent due by the lessee to the landlord. Garroutte v. White, 4 So. West. Rep. 681.

[2] R. S. 1877, p. 308, §§ 1–14.

[3] A landlord cannot distrain for rent, unless he can maintain an action for it. Oliver v. Phelps, Spen. 180.

Where any goods or chattels shall be distrained for any rent reserved and due, and the tenant or owner of the goods so distrained shall not within ten days next after such distress, and notice thereof, with the cause of such taking, left at the chief mansion-house or other most notorious place on the premises charged with the rent distrained for, replevy the same, with sufficient security to be given to the sheriff, according to law, then in such case, after such distress and notice and expiration of the said ten days, the person distraining may, on two days' notice to the tenant, with the sheriff or under-sheriff of the county, or with the constable of the township, precinct, or place where such distress shall be taken, cause the goods and chattels so distrained to be inventoried and appraised by three sworn appraisers, and after such inventory and appraisement may lawfully sell at public vendue the goods and chattels so distrained (giving five days' public notice by advertising the articles to be sold, and the time and place of sale, in at least three of the most public places in the township where such distress shall be made), for the best price that can be gotten for the same, towards satisfaction of the rent for which the said goods and chattels shall be distrained, and of the charges of such distress, appraisement, and sale, leaving the overplus, if any, in the hands of such sheriff, under-sheriff, or constable, for the owner's use.

The landlord may seize in distraint sheaves, cocks, or stacks of grain or corn, or grain or corn loose or in the straw, or flax, hemp, or hay in any barn, stack, or rick, and may lock up the same in the place where the same may be found.

The landlord may seize as a distress for arrears of rent any of the goods and chattels of his tenant, and not of any other person,[1] although in possession of such tenant, which may be found on the demised premises, except such goods and chattels as are by law privileged from distress ; and also any hogs, horses, cattle,

---

[1] The right of distress is limited to the goods of the tenant. Woodside v. Adams, 40 N. J. L. 417.

The goods of one of several joint lessees may be distrained. Hoskins v. Paul, 4 Halst. 110.

Goods of which the tenant is a joint owner with a stranger may be distrained; but only his interest can be distrained and sold. Allen v. Agnew, 24 N. J. L. 443.

Goods of a tenant on the premises may be distrained although the tenant has made an assignment of them under the insolvent act. Hoskins v. Paul, *supra.*

There is no lien on the goods of the tenant except from the time of actual seizure under the distress warrant. Woodside v. Adams, *supra.*

or stock of his tenant, and not of any other person, although in possession of such tenant, feeding on the demised premises, or upon
any common appendant or appurtenant, or anyways belonging to
the premises demised;[1] and also to take or seize any grain or produce whatsoever growing or being on the premises, as a distress
for arrears of rent,[2] and the same to cut, dig, pull, gather, make,
cure, carry, and lay up in some proper and convenient place on
the premises, and for want thereof in some other place to be procured by such lessor or landlord (due notice of such place being
given to such tenant or lessee, or left at his or her place of
abode), and to appraise, sell, and dispose of the same in the time
and manner hereinbefore directed : provided always, that it shall
not be lawful for any lessor or landlord, at any one time, to distrain for more than one year's rent in arrear, and that such distress must be made within six months after the same shall become
due, or, where the rent is payable in instalments, then within
six months after the year's rent shall have become due.

If any tenant or lessee for life or lives, term of years, at will,
sufferance, or otherwise of any lands, shall convey away or carry
off or from such premises his goods or chattels, leaving the rent
or any part thereof unpaid, the landlord or lessor, within the
space of thirty days next after such conveying away or carrying
off such goods or chattels, may take and seize such goods and
chattels wherever the same shall be found, as a distress for the
said arrears of rent, and the same to sell or otherwise dispose of,
in such manner as if the said goods and chattels had actually
been distrained in and upon such premises : provided always,
that no landlord or lessor, or other person entitled to such arrears
of rent, shall take or seize any such goods or chattels as a distress for the same, which shall be sold *bonâ fide*, or for a valuable
consideration, before such seizure made, to any person not privy
to such fraud. This section shall extend to all cases where rent
shall have accrued and shall be unpaid upon any demise or con-

---

[1] By the ancient rule of law, the
cattle of the tenant, being on a common appendant or appurtenant to the
demised premises, were not subject to
the landlord's levy. This clause extends his remedy to such property.
Guest v. Opdyke, 31 N. J. L. 552,
555.

[2] The power of distress as to produce "growing or being on the premises " is not limited to such as belongs
exclusively to the tenant. Guest v.
Opdyke, *supra*. It follows that the
lessor's right to distrain growing crops
is not affected by the sale of such
crops by the tenant. Bird v. Anderson, 41 N. J. L. 392.

tract hereafter made, although by the terms thereof the rent shall not be payable.[1]

628. New Jersey [2] **(*continued*.) Liens for rent. When tenant's goods seized on execution.** — No goods or chattels upon any land or tenements leased for term of life or years, at will or otherwise, shall be liable to be taken by virtue of any execution, attachment, or other process, unless the party at whose suit the said execution or other process is sued out shall, before the removal of such goods from the premises, pay to the landlord all rent due for the premises at the time of the taking such goods, or which shall have accrued up to the day of the removal of the goods from the premises, whether by the terms of lease the day of payment shall have come or not, making a rebate of interest on the sum, the time of payment of which, by the terms of the lease, shall not have come : provided, the said arrears of rent do not amount to more than one year's rent ; and in case the said arrears shall exceed one year's rent, then the said party at whose suit such process is sued out, paying the landlord one year's rent, may proceed to execute his process ; and the sheriff

[1] This provision construed : Weiss *v.* Jahn, 37 N. J. L. 93.

[2] Revision 1877, p. 570, §§ 4–6. The landlord must give notice to the officer of the rent due him, before the removal of the goods. Ayres *v.* Johnson, 2 Halst. 119. If the sheriff wrongfully proceeds to sell and remove the goods after such notice, he is liable for the tort, but the plaintiff in execution is not. Princeton Bank *v.* Gibson, Spen. 138.

As to distress of goods which have already been seized upon execution, see Newell *v.* Clark, 46 N. J. L. 363.

A levy and sale of the goods amount to a removal, whether the goods are actually taken from the premises or not, for a sale effects the very evil which the statute was designed to remedy. Ryerson *v.* Quackenbush, 26 N. J. L. 236.

It is proper practice for a landlord, who is entitled to have his arrears of rent paid before the removal or sale of goods levied on, to apply to the court for a rule that the proceeds of the sale under execution be applied to the payment of his rent. Fischel *v.* Keer, 45 N. J. L. 507. This was done as early as 1718, under the Act 8 Anne, ch. 14, passed in 1710 ; Waring *v.* Dewberry, 1 Str. 97 ; and the practice has continued down to the present time. Henchett *v.* Kimpson, 2 Wils. 140; Central Bank *v.* Peterson, 24 N. J. L. 668. If the rent be not due, the landlord has no right to demand payment before removal, except by force of the statute. Schenck *v.* Vannest, 1 South. 329.

To authorize a payment out of the proceeds of an execution sale of rent to the landlord, it must appear that rent was due to him upon such a lease or contract as would give him the right to distrain. Kirkpatrick *v.* Cason, 30 N. J. L. 331. The fact that the rent is reserved to be applied to a special purpose does not affect its character as rent. Ryerson *v.* Quackenbush, *supra.*

439

or other officer is empowered and required to levy and pay to the plaintiff as well the money so paid for rent as the money to be made by virtue of such process.

If the goods have been removed from the leased premises by virtue of such process, the same shall not be sold until ten days after such removal, and then not unless the plaintiff shall, before the sale, pay to the landlord all rent due as above provided : provided the landlord shall, before the expiration of the said ten days from the time of such removal, give notice to the officer holding the execution or other process of the amount of the rent in arrear, and claim the same.[1]

No such goods shall be removed from the premises except openly and in the daytime, and then not unless the officer shall at the time of such removal give notice thereof to the defendant, or, in his absence, to some person of his family residing on the premises.

629. New York.[2] — Distress for rent under the common law rules as modified by statute prevailed in this state down to 1845, when it was abolished by statute.

630. New Mexico.[3] — Landlords shall have a lien on the property of their tenants which remain in the house rented, for the rent due, and said property may not be removed from said house without the consent of the landlord until the rent is paid or secured.

No person is entitled to a lien who has taken collateral security for the debt.

To enforce the lien a written notice may be served on the debtor, setting forth the amount of the indebtedness and the nature of it, and if the same is not paid within ten days after the service of such notice, the property may be advertised by posting for twenty days and then sold at auction. The lien claimant may bid for or purchase the property at such sale.

The lien may also be enforced by suit in the ordinary form,

---

[1] Before this provision (Act March 4, 1835), the landlord could not follow the goods beyond the demised premises, when removed by an officer by virtue of an execution. Peacock v. Hammitt, 3 Green, 165.

[2] Williams v. Potter, 2 Barb. 316; Gould v. Rogers, 8 Ib. 502 ; Van Rensselaer v. Snyder, 13 N. Y. 299.

[3] Comp. Laws 1884, §§ 1537–1546.

and sale of the property upon which the lien has attached upon execution, as in other cases. If such property does not satisfy the execution, other property of the defendant may be levied upon.

631. North Carolina.[1] — When lands shall be rented or leased by agreement, written or oral, for agricultural purposes, or shall be cultivated by a cropper, unless otherwise agreed between the parties to the lease or agreement, any and all crops raised on said lands shall be deemed and held to be vested in possession of the lessor or his assigns at all times, until the rents for said lands shall be paid,[2] and until all the stipulations contained in the lease or agreement shall be performed, or damages in lieu thereof shall be paid to the lessor or his assigns, and until said party or his assigns shall be paid for all advancements made and expenses incurred in making and saving said crops.[3] This lien

[1] Code 1883, vol. i. §§ 1754, 1759. Distress for rent is unknown in this state. Dalgleish v. Grandy, Cam. & N. 22; Deaver v. Rice, 4 Dev. & B. L. 431. Under this statute the landlord has a first lien upon the crop to secure his rent and advances, with the right of possession. Ledbetter v. Quick, 90 N. C. 276.

[2] The landlord has such a property in his tenant's crop by virtue of his lien and right of possesion that he can maintain an action for the recovery of the same. Montague v. Mial, 89 N. C. 137; Levingston v. Farish, Ib. 140; Ledbetter v. Quick, supra; Rawlings v. Hunt, 90 N. C. 270.

The landlord's title is not impaired by the tenant's conveying the crop to a third person, who purchases without notice of the landlord's claim. Belcher v. Grimsley, 88 N. C. 88. A tenant who retains actual possession of the crop cannot be indicted for larceny for secretly taking away part of the crop. State v. Copeland, 86 N. C. 691.

Otherwise if the tenant's actual possession has terminated by a delivery to the landlord. State v. Webb, 87 N. C. 558.

[3] The advances, whether made in money or merchandise, must be such as go directly or indirectly to make or save the crop, and the tenant must be the judge of what best serves his purpose. Womble v. Leach, 83 N. C. 84.

Supplies necessary to make and save a crop are such articles as are in good faith furnished to and received by the tenant for that purpose. It may be properly left to the jury to find whether upon the evidence a mule and wagon were treated as advancements. Ledbetter v. Quick, supra. The debt for advances must be created in good faith. It must not be made collusively. The landlord cannot be allowed to supply such things as advancements as are manifestly not such, and which he has good reason to believe are not so intended. Ledbetter v. Quick, supra.

Advances by the landlord to a sub-lessee, made without the knowledge and privity of the lessee, are not entitled to priority over advances procured by the lessee for the sub-lessee from a third person. Moore v. Faison (N. C.), 2 So. East Rep. (169.)

shall be preferred to all other liens, and the lessor or his assigns shall be entitled, against the lessee or cropper, or the assigns of either, who shall remove the crop or any part thereof from the lands without the consent of the lessor or his assigns, or against any other person who may get possession of said crop or any part thereof, to the remedies given in an action upon a claim for the delivery of personal property.

In case there is any controversy between the parties, this may be determined in court forthwith ; but in case of a continuance or appeal, the lessee must give an undertaking to pay whatever the adverse party may recover in the action. If the lessee fails to give the undertaking, the officer delivers the property to the lessor, on his giving an undertaking to return it in case judgment be against him. In case neither party gives such undertaking, the clerk of court issues an order to the officer, directing him to take into his possession the property, or so much as is necessary to satisfy the claimant's demand and costs, and to sell the same in the manner prescribed for the sale of personal property under execution, and to hold the proceeds subject to the decision of the court.[1]

Any lessee or cropper, or the assigns of either, or any other person, who shall remove said crop, or any part thereof, from such land, without the consent of the lessor or his assigns, and without giving him or his agent five days' notice of such intended removal, and before satisfying all the liens held by the lessor or his assigns on said crop, shall be guilty of a misdemeanor; and if any landlord shall unlawfully, wilfully, knowingly, and without process of law, and unjustly, seize the crop of his tenant when there is nothing due him, he shall be guilty of a misdemeanor.[2]

632. Pennsylvania.[3] — Any person having any rent in arrear [4]

---

[1] Code 1883, §§ 1756-1758. The lien includes costs as well as rents. Slaughter v. Winfrey, 85 N. C. 159.

[2] As to indictments under this provision, see State v. Pendor, 83 N. C. 651; State v. Rose, 90 N. C. 712; Varner v. Spencer, 72 N. C. 381.

[3] 2 Brightly's Purdon's Digest, 1883, p. 1011, §§ 1, 4, 5, 7, 10, 14, 15.

[4] A landlord issuing a distress is required to credit on the rent all actual payments of rent, and such sums as the parties have agreed to treat as payment on account of rent. But he is under no obligation to deduct any claim for unliquidated damages which the tenant may have against him. Therefore the fact that he fails, in issuing the warrant of distress, to credit on the rent such claim for unliquidated damages, does not entitle the tenant to recover damages for distraining for more rent than was in

or due upon any lease for life or lives, or for one or more years, or at will, ended or determined, may distrain for such arrears, after the determination of the said respective leases, in the same manner as he might have done if such lease had not been ended : provided, that such distress be made during the continuance of such lessor's title or interest.[1]

The landlord may take and seize as a distress for arrears of rent any cattle or stock of his tenant, feeding or depasturing upon all or any part of the premises demised or holden ; and also all sorts of corn and grass, hops, roots, fruit, pulse, or other product whatsoever, which shall be growing on any part of the estate so demised, in the same manner as other goods and chattels may be seized, distrained, and disposed of.[2] And the purchaser of any such product shall have free egress and regress to and from the same where growing, to repair the fences from time to time, and, when ripe, to cut, gather, make, cure, and lay up and thresh, and after to carry the same away, in the same manner as the tenant might legally have done had such distress never been made.

Property to the value of three hundred dollars, exclusive of all wearing apparel of the defendant and his family, and all bibles and school-books in use in the family (which shall remain exempted as heretofore), and no more, owned by or in possession

arrear. Spencer v. Clinefelter, 101 Pa. St. 219.

As to the recovery of damages for an excessive distress, see Fernwood Masonic Hall Asso. v. Jones, 102 Pa. St. 307; Richards v. McGrath, 100 Ib. 389 ; McElroy v. Dice, 17 Ib. 163 ; M'Kinney v. Reader, 6 Watts, 34.

A distress cannot be made on Sunday; Mayfield v. White, 1 Browne, 241 ; nor by breaking open an outer door. Ib.

[1] The right continues after the termination of the term, without limitation as to time. The statute gives the landlord this right whenever the rent is in arrear, and he retains the title. Moss's App. 35 Pa. St. 162 ; Clifford v. Beems, 3 Watts, 246 ; Lewis's App. 66 Pa. St. 312 ; Whiting v. Lake, 91 Pa. St. 349.

A lessee for years who transfers all his interest to a third person, with a reservation of rent, cannot distrain unless the instrument of transfer reserves an express power of distress. Manuel v. Reath, 5 Phila. 11.

After the determination of the landlord's estate by surrender to the owner of the paramount estate, the landlord has no right to distrain, for rent in arrear, on the goods of his former tenant, remaining on the premises. An officer acting under such a warrant is a trespasser. Walbridge v. Pruden, 102 Pa. St. 1.

[2] Property of a stranger on the demised premises is generally liable to distress for rent. Kleber v. Ward, 88 Pa. St. 93.

of any debtor, shall be exempt from levy and sale on execution, or by distress for rent.[1]

In case any lessee shall fraudulently or clandestinely convey or carry off or from such demised premises [2] his goods and chattels, with intent to prevent the landlord or lessor from distraining the same for arrears of such rent so reserved as aforesaid, it shall and may be lawful to and for such lessor, within the space of thirty days next ensuing such conveying away or carrying off such goods or chattels as aforesaid, to take and seize such goods and chattels,[3] wherever the same may be found, as a distress for the said arrears of such rent, and the same to sell or otherwise dispose of, in such manner as if the said goods and chattels had actually been distrained by such lessor or landlord in and upon such demised premises, for such arrears of rent.

When any goods or chattels shall be distrained for any rent reserved and due, and the tenant or owner shall not, within five

---

[1] Joint owners of chattels levied on, under distress for rent due upon their joint lease, are not entitled to the benefit of the exemption law. Bonsall v. Comly, 44 Pa. St. 442.

A sub-tenant, or assignee of the tenant, who has not been recognized as such by the landlord, cannot claim the benefit of the exemption law, as against a distress for rent, when the goods are levied on as those of the original lessee. Neither the relation of landlord and tenant, nor that of debtor and creditor, exists between the landlord and such sub-tenant or assignee. Rosenberger v. Hallowell, 35 Pa. St. 369.

A privilege from distress may be waived. M'Kinney v. Reader, 6 Watts, 34 ; Winchester v. Costello, 2 Pars. (Pa.) 279, 283; Bowman v. Smiley, 31 Pa. St. 225.

[2] A removal in the daytime, though without the knowlege of the landlord, is not fraudulent. Grant's App. 44 Pa. St. 477; Grace v. Shively, 12 S. & R. 217 ; Hoops v. Crowley, Ib. 219, n.; Purfel v. Sands, 1 Ash. 120 ; Morris v. Parker, Ib. 187.

[3] The goods of a stranger cannot be

followed and distrained under this clause. Sleeper v. Parrish, 7 Phila. 247; Adams v. La Comb, 1 Dall. 440. But goods of an assignee after term may be followed. Jones v. Gundrim, 3 W. & S. 531. Nor can goods fairly sold to an innocent purchaser be distrained. Clifford v. Beems, 3 Watts, 246.

Such goods cannot be distrained for rent not due at the time of removal. Conway v. Lowry, 7 W. N. C. 64 ; Grace v. Shively, supra.

As to the law applicable to Philadelphia, see 2 Brightly's Purdon's Dig. p. 1013, § 9. The same applied to Pittsburgh and Allegheny. Act 29 March, 1876.

In Pennsylvania, outside of Philadelphia, Pittsburgh, and Allegheny, a landlord has no right to distrain upon goods fraudulently removed from the demised premises with intent to defraud the landlord of his distress, for rent that is not yet due, nor has a court of equity jurisdiction to detain the goods upon the premises until the landlord is in a condition to distrain. Jackson's Appeal (Pa.), 9 Atl. Rep. 306.

days after such distress and notice thereof,[1] with the cause of such taking left on the premises, replevy the same,[2] then the person distraining may cause the goods to be appraised by two reputable freeholders under oath, and after such appraisement may, after six days' public notice, sell the goods distrained for the satisfaction of the rent and charges.[3]

633. Pennsylvania[4] (*continued*). Tenant's goods seized on execution. — The goods and chattels upon any lands or tenements which are demised for life or years, or otherwise, taken by virtue of an execution, and liable to the distress of the landlord, are liable for the payment of any sums of money due for rent at the time of taking such goods in execution :[5] provided, that such rent shall not exceed one year's rent.[6]

[1] The day of making the distress is to be excluded in computing the time, and if the last day fall on Sunday, the landlord has until the next day to remove the goods. M'Kinney *v.* Reader, 6 Watts, 34, 37; Brisben *v.* Wilson, 60 Pa. St. 452.

[2] Replevin is the only remedy for an unlawful distress where notice has been given and the goods appraised. Sassman *v.* Brisbane, 7 Phila. 159.

[3] The landlord ought not to sell the goods after a tender of the rent and costs made at any time before the sale. Richards *v.* McGrath, 100 Pa. St. 389; and see Johnson *v.* Upham, 2 El. & El. 250.

Even after the sale has commenced, if the tenant tenders the difference between the amount realized by the sale and the full amount of the rent claimed, with costs, and the landlord refuses the tender and proceeds with the sale, he is liable in an action of trespass for the value of the goods afterwards sold. Richards *v.* Mc-Grath, *supra.*

[4] Brightly's Purdon's Dig. 1883, p. 752, §§ 58, 59 ; p. 1015, §§ 14, 15.

[5] This right is confined to goods which were upon the demised premises at the time of the levy, and which were liable to distress. When the tenant's goods were removed from the premises and the removal was neither clandestine nor fraudulent, and the landlord distrained a part of them at the place of removal, he cannot, as against an execution creditor whose execution was levied the day after, claim any portion of the proceeds for rent due. He should have returned the goods to the demised premises, so that if the sheriff levied upon them they would have been liable for the rent within the terms of the statute. Grant's App. 44 Pa. St. 477.

[6] The landlord's preference for one year's rent is not confined to the rent for the year immediately preceding the execution. Richie *v.* McCauley, 4 Pa. St. 471.

But the landlord is entitled only to the rent due at the time of the levy, out of the proceeds of the property. Case *v.* Davis, 15 Pa. St. 80.

Only the immediate landlord of the defendant, either by a direct lease or by a legal assignment of the lease, is entitled to receive one year's rent out of the proceeds of the sheriff's sale. Bromley *v.* Hopewell, 2 Miles, 414.

The landlord's right to be paid out of the proceeds of a sheriff's sale, depends on his power to distrain the

After sale by the officer of such goods, he must first pay out of the proceeds the rent so due.[1]

634. South Carolina.[2] — No goods or chattels, lands or tenements, which are or shall be leased for life or lives, term of years, at will, or otherwise, shall be liable to be taken by virtue of any execution or any pretence whatsoever, unless the party at whose suit the said execution is sued out shall, before the removal of such goods from off the said premises, by virtue of such execution or extent, pay to the landlord of the said premises or his bailiff all such sum or sums of money as are or shall be due for rent for the said premises at the time of the taking such goods or chattels by virtue of such execution : provided, the said arrears of rent do not amount to more than one year's rent.

In case any lessee shall, fraudulently or clandestinely, convey

goods sold. Lewis's App. 66 Pa. St. 312.

After a levy of an execution upon goods liable to distress, the plaintiff cannot stay proceedings without the consent of the landlord first had in writing. The rent is a prior charge by law, and the sale under execution is for the benefit of the landlord. Barnes's App. 76 Pa. St. 50.

This right continues after the determination of the term. Moss's App. 35 Pa. St. 162.

The landlord is entitled to claim rent payable in advance out of the proceeds of a sheriff's sale of the tenants' goods upon the demised premises. Collins's App. 35 Pa. St. 83.

The tenant's waiver of the benefit of the exemption law in favor of the execution creditor, gives the latter no preference over the claim of the landlord, in whose favor there is no such waiver. Collins's App. *supra.*

[1] Of course the landlord must give notice of his claim for rent before the return of the execution. Mitchell *v.* Stewart, 13 S. & R. 295.

The landlord may distrain upon goods on the demised premises which have been previously taken in execu-

tion and released. Gilliam *v.* Tobias, 11 Phila. 313.

In case the landlord had previously to the levy and sale distrained the property and the tenant had replevied it, the landlord would be entitled to have out of the proceeds of the sale only the amount of rent that had accrued subsequently to the distress. Gray *v.* Wilson, 4 Watts, 39.

[2] G. S. 1882, §§ 1824–1828. Distress for rent was abolished in 1868. 14 Stat. 106. But in 1878 the law as it formerly existed was restored, with the single exception that no property could be taken except such as belonged to the tenant in his own right. 16 Stat. 511; Mobley *v.* Dent, 10 S. C. 471, 472; Sullivan *v.* Ellison, 20 S. C. 481. After an execution has been levied upon the tenant's personal property subject to distress, the landlord may, before removal of the property, give notice of his claim for rent, and have judgment against the officer for the proceeds of the sale, or for so much of the proceeds as may be necessary to pay his claim for rent for that year before satisfying the execution. Sullivan *v.* Ellison, *supra.*

or carry off or from such demised premises his goods or chattels, with intent to prevent the landlord or lessor from distraining the same for arrears of such rent so reserved as aforesaid, it shall and may be lawful to and for such lessor or landlord, within the space of five days next ensuing such conveying away or carrying off such goods or chattels as aforesaid, to take and seize such goods and chattels, wherever the same shall be found, as a distress for the said arrears of such rent; and the same to sell or otherwise dispose of, in such manner as if the said goods and chattels had actually been distrained by such lessor or landlord, in and upon such demised premises, for such arrears of rent; any law, usage, or custom to the contrary in anywise notwithstanding.

Nothing herein contained shall extend, or be construed to extend, to empower such lessor or landlord to take or seize any goods or chattels, as a distress for arrears of rent, which shall be sold *bonâ fide* and for a valuable consideration before such seizure made; and no property shall be seized under a distress warrant for such, except such as belongs to the tenant in his own right.[1]

When tenants *pur autre vie*, and lessees for years or at will, hold over the tenements to them devised after the determination of such leases, it shall and may be lawful for any person or persons, to whom any rent is in arrear or due, to distrain for such arrears, after the determination of the said respective leases, in the same manner as they might have done if such lease or leases had not been ended or determined: provided, that such distress be made within the space of six calendar months after the determination of such lease, and during the continuance of such landlord's title or interest, and during the possession of the tenant from whom such arrears became due.

635. South Carolina[2] (*continued*). Lien for rent and advances for agricultural purposes. — Each landlord leasing lands for agricultural purposes[3] shall have a prior and preferred

---

[1] This provision includes goods on the premises as well as those removed therefrom; but property mortgaged *bonâ fide* by the tenant before seizure under the distress warrant, though still on the premises, does not, within the meaning of the statute, *belong* to the tenant, and is therefore not liable to be distrained for rent due. Knobeloch v. Smith (S. C.), 2 So. East Rep. 612.

[2] G. S. 1882, § 2399; Acts 1885, p. 146, No. 77. As to enforcement before trial justices, see Acts 1884, p. 749.

[3] The lien arises from the contract

lien for rent to the extent of all crops raised on the lands leased by him, whether the same be raised by the tenant or other persons, and enforcible in the same manner as liens for advances, which said lien shall be valid without recording or filing: provided, that, subject to such lien and enforcible in the same way, the landlord shall have a lien on all the crops raised by the tenant for all advances made by the landlord during the year: provided, further, every lien for advances and for rent, when the agreement is for more than one third of the crop,[1] shall be indexed in the office of the register of mesne conveyances of the county in which the lienor resides within thirty days from the date of the lien (and the indexing of the said lien shall constitute notice thereof to all third persons, and entitle the same to the benefit of this chapter): said index shall show the names of the lienor and lienee, the date and amount of lien, and a brief description of the place so cultivated; and said indexing shall be a sufficient record of the same, and the property covered by said lien so indexed as aforesaid, if found in the hands of subsequent purchasers or creditors, shall be deemed liable to said lien.

The landlord shall have a lien upon the crops of his tenant for his rent in preference to all other liens. Laborers who assist in making any crop shall have a lien thereon to the extent of the amount due them for such labor next in priority to the landlord, and as between such laborers there shall be no preference. All other liens for agricultural supplies shall be paid next after the

of renting without an express agreement that there shall be a lien. Carter v. Du Pre, 18 S. C. 179; Kennedy v. Reames, 15 S. C. 548.

A landlord having a first lien for rent is not estopped from asserting it as against a second lien for supplies by reason of paying, or allowing to be paid, a first lien for supplies in preference to the lien for rent. Carter v. Du Pre, supra.

[1] A landlord, to secure a lien for advances made to his tenant, or for rent exceeding one third of the crop, must comply with the statute relating to agricultural advances. This statute was not intended to do more than to secure the rent proper to the landlord,

and then leave him to make agricultural advances to his tenants upon the same terms and conditions, as to recording and the like, as are imposed upon all others. Therefore, where a landlord leased land to a tenant for a stipulated rent, and also agreed to make advances, which were to be repaid out of the crop, but the contract was not recorded nor filed, it was held that the landlord could not recover for such advances the crop made by the tenant, which had been seized under a warrant issued upon a merchant's recorded lien of later date. Whaley v. Jacobson, 21 S. C. 51. See, also, Kennedy v. Reames, supra.

satisfaction of the liens of the landlord and laborers, and shall rank in other respects as they do now under existing laws.

No writing or recording shall be necessary to create the liens of the landlord, but such lien shall exist from the date of the contract, whether the same be in writing or verbal.

636. Tennessee.[1] — Any debt by note, account, or otherwise, created for the rent of land, is a lien on the crop growing or made on the premises, in preference to all other debts, from the date of the contract.[2]

The lien continues for three months after the debt becomes due, and until the termination of any suit commenced within that time for such rent.

This lien may be enforced:[3] 1. By original attachment issued on affidavit that the rent is due and unpaid, or, before due, on affidavit that the defendant is about to remove or sell the crop;[4] 2. Or by judgment at law against the tenant and execution to be delivered on the crop in whosesoever hands it may be.

The person entitled to the rent may recover from the purchaser of the crop, or of any part of it, the value of the property not exceeding the amount of the rent and damages.[5]

---

[1] Code 1884, §§ 4280–4285.

[2] The lien exists when the farming is on shares, as well as when the rent is payable in money. Sharp v. Fields, 1 Heisk. 571.

The lien attaches to the crop whether raised by the lessee or a sub-lessee; and it attaches as against a sub-lessee, although he may have paid the tenant the rent due from him. Rutlege v. Walton, 4 Yerg. 458. The lien is superior to the laws exempting property from execution. Hill v. George, 1 Head, 394.

[3] A court of equity also has jurisdiction of an attachment to enforce a landlord's lien for rent. Sharp v. Fields, supra.

Damages for the tenant's failure to comply with an implied contract for good husbandry, where the renting is for a part of the crop, cannot be enforced under those provisions giving attachment for rent. He must seek these by an action on the case. Patterson v. Hawkins, 3 Lea, 483.

[4] The lien begins from the date of the contract.

The landlord may make his inchoate lien specific, before the rent has become due, by attaching the crop upon the premises. The lien thus fixed relates back to the date of the contract, and overreaches any title acquired by a purchaser of the crop from the tenant, though without notice of the lien. Phillips v. Maxwell, 1 Bax. 25.

[5] The landlord may maintain a suit against a purchaser of the crop from the tenant, before he has recovered any judgment against the tenant for the rent due. Richardson v. Blakemore, 11 Lea, 290.

A factor who sells cotton for a tenant, and appropriates the proceeds to a debt due him with the tenant's consent, is not liable to the landlord. The

The landlord, in addition to liens already given him by law, shall have a further lien on the growing crop for necessary supplies of food and clothing furnished by the landlord or his agent to the tenant, for himself or those dependent on him, to enable the tenant to make the crop :[1] provided an account of such necessary supplies is kept as the articles are furnished, and is sworn to before some justice of the peace before the enforcement of the lien. This lien shall be secondary to that of the landlord for his rent, and may be enforced in the same manner.[2]

637. Tennessee (*continued*). **Furnishers' liens.**[3] — Any debt by note, account, or otherwise, contracted for supplies, implements of industry, or work stock furnished by the owners of the land to lessees, or by lessees to sub-tenants,[4] and used in the cultivation of the crop, shall be and constitute a lien upon the crop growing or made during the year upon the premises, in as full and perfect a manner as provided with regard to rents :[5] provided the said lien is expressly contracted for on the face of the note or writing between the owner of the land or lessees, or between the lessees and sub-tenants.[6] The agreement or con-

factor is not a purchaser, but a seller; and the fact that the tenant paid him the proceeds does not make him a purchaser within the meaning of this provision. Armstrong *v.* Walker, 9 Lea, 156.

[1] This lien, unlike the lien for general supplies, may be created without any contract in writing. Lewis *v.* Mahon, 9 Bax. 374.

[2] The landlord may join in one suit demands for rent and for supplies which are a lien on the same crop, but he must give the amount of each demand constituting the aggregate sum. Dougherty *v.* Kellum, 3 Lea, 643.

The affidavit need not state the form of the demand, as, whether it is a note or account; but it must state that an account of the supplies was kept as the articles were furnished, and the account must be sworn to at or before the time of suing out the attachment. An account meets the requirements of the act, though it be a mere memorandum upon a loose

sheet of paper. Dougherty *v.* Kellum, *supra.*

[3] Code 1882, § 4284.

[4] This section was intended to give the owner a security for supplies furnished, and also at the same time to give security to a tenant as against his sub-tenant, subordinate, however, to the lien of the landlord for rent. This lien is given only to the landlord and to lessees. It has all the incidents of a landlord's lien, and is enforced in the same way. It is not a right of property in the crop, but a right to enforce a charge created by contract. Whitmore *v.* Poindexter, 7 Bax. 248. A landlord has no lien for supplies furnished upon a parol contract. Hughes *v.* Whitaker, 4 Heisk. 399.

[5] See §§ 4280, 4283 of Code.

[6] An agreement in writing to "bind and trust his half of the crop to the said [creditor] for any debt he may owe or contract to him," creates no lien for advances. Dunlap *v.* Aycock, 10 Heisk. 561.

tract so entered into shall not have priority of the lien of the owner of the land for the rent.

638. Texas.[1] — All persons renting or leasing lands or tenements, at will or for a term, shall have a preference lien [2] upon the property of the tenant, hereinafter indicated, upon such premises,[3] for any rent that may become due, and for all money and the value of all animals, tools, provisions, and supplies furnished by the landlord to the tenant to enable the tenant to make a crop on such premises, and to gather, secure, house, and put the same in condition for market, the money, animals, tools, provisions, and supplies so furnished being necessary for that purpose, whether the same is to be paid in money, agricultural products, or other property; and this lien shall apply only to animals, tools, and other property furnished by the landlord to the tenant, and to the crop raised on such rented premises.

All persons leasing or renting any residence or storehouse or other building shall have a preference lien upon all the property of the tenant in said residence or storehouse or other building [4] for the payment of the rents due and that may become due, and such lien shall continue and be in force as long as the tenant shall occupy the rented premises, and for one month thereafter.[5]

[1] R. S. 1879, arts. 3107 – 3118, 3122 a.

[2] A claim for rent due by an insolvent lessee is a lien superior to attachments of the property subject to the lien, and is entitled to be first satisfied out of the moneys arising from a sale of the attached property. Sullivan v. Cleveland, 62 Tex. 677.

[3] The landlord's lien attaches upon whatever property the lessee has on the rented premises when the warrant issues and is levied, without reference to the time when the debt for the rent accrued. One who has purchased the property from the lessee not in the ordinary course of business stands in this respect in the same position as the lessee. Block v. Latham, 63 Tex. 414.

A landlord's lien under art. 3107, and the remedy by distress warrant prescribed by the statute, are inconsistent with the relationship of tenant in common, and none of the consequences resulting from such relationship can be inferred in such a case. Texas & Pacific Ry. Co. v. Bayliss, 62 Tex. 570.

[4] Where a married woman is the lessee of a hotel, her furniture in the hotel, whether it be her separate property or community property, is subject to the lien. Biesenbach v. Key, 63 Tex. 79.

[5] This article, 3122 a, of the Revised Statutes, is a legislative addition to title LVIII., which regulates rural or farm renting. It is apparent, taking all the provisions together, that the legislature intended to limit the operation of the landlord's lien to a yearly renting. The provision of the statute, that the lien shall continue in

451

It shall not be lawful for the tenant, while the rent and such advances remain unpaid, to remove or permit to be removed from the premises so leased or rented any of the agricultural products produced thereon, or any of the animals, tools, or property furnished as aforesaid, without the consent of the landlord. Such preference lien shall continue as to such agricultural products, and as to the animals, tools, and other property furnished to the tenant as aforesaid, so long as they remain on such rented or leased premises, and for one month thereafter; and such lien, as to agricultural products, and as to animals and tools furnished as aforesaid, shall be superior to all laws exempting such property from forced sales.

Such lien shall not attach to the goods, wares, and merchandise of a merchant, trader, or mechanic, sold and delivered in good faith in the regular course of business to the tenant.

The removal of the agricultural products, with the consent of the landlord, for the purpose of being prepared for market, shall not be considered a waiver of such lien, but such lien shall continue and attach to the products so removed the same as if they had remained on such rented or leased premises.

When any rent or advances shall become due, or the tenant shall be about to remove from such leased or rented premises, or to remove his property from such premises, it shall be lawful for the person to whom the rents or advances are payable, his agent, attorney, assigns, heirs, or legal representatives, to apply to a

force so long as the tenant shall occupy the rented premises, prescribes the rule only when the lien has attached by reason of rents due or such as are accruing, and will certainly become due, under the particular tenancy. It does not impose a charge in advance upon the property of the tenant for any rents that might by possibility become due for another term or tenancy, whether such term be created by contract or by the tenant's holding over.

Therefore, when a tenant from month to month mortgages the personal property on the mortgaged premises to another, and the rent for the month in which the mortgage is executed has been paid, and the property remains upon the premises by permission of the mortgagee from month to month, the lien of the landlord is subordinate to that of the mortgage. At the time the mortgage is made in such case, the tenant holds the property free from any charge and unincumbered by any lien. He could then remove it from the rented premises, dispose of it by sale, or incumber it at will. The mortgagee occupies the same position with respect to the landlord's lien as if the mortgage had been executed before the property had been brought upon the rented premises. Hempstead Assoc. v. Cochran, 60 Tex. 620.

justice of the peace of the precinct where the premises are situated for a warrant to seize the property of such tenant.[1]

The plaintiff, his agent or attorney, shall make oath that the amount sued for is for rent or advances, or shall produce a writing signed by such tenant to that effect, and shall further swear that such warrant is not sued out for the purpose of vexing and harassing the defendant;[2] and the person applying for such warrant shall execute a bond, with two or more good and suffi-

---

[1] The lien, being given by statute, exists independently of a distress warrant, which is only a means of securing the property and making the lien effective. Templeman v. Gresham, 61 Tex. 50. The lien is therefore superior to an assignment to secure creditors. Rosenberg v. Shaper, 51 Tex. 134.

The lien is not lost by the failure of the landlord to sue out a distress warrant for rent, nor acquired by his resort to that remedy; but the lien may be preserved by suit to foreclose, which will prevent its loss by the expiration of the time limited in the statute for its continuance. Bourcier v. Edmondson, 58 Tex. 675; Rosenberg v. Shaper, supra.

The landlord is not restricted to the use of the summary remedy by distress provided by the statute. It allows him this remedy in case he is willing to subject himself to the burden prescribed by it. But he may also use the remedies appropriate for the enforcement of liens upon personal property. He may foreclose the lien by suit, though by so doing he takes the chances of finding the property forthcoming to answer his judgment. Bourcier v. Edmondson, supra.

If a tenant's goods are attached upon the rented premises, and there remain until they are sold under the process, he is liable for rent during the entire period of such occupancy; and though the goods are not subject to seizure for rent under a distress warrant while they are in the custody of the law, yet, immediately upon a sale being made under the attachment, the landlord's lien can be enforced by seizure of the goods while they are still upon the premises for all the rent due up to the time of seizure. Meyer v. Oliver, 61 Tex. 584. The remedy by distraint under the statute is not dependent upon the ownership of the premises at the time the writ is issued, nor is it in any way affected by the fact that the relation of landlord and tenant has then ceased. If rent is due and the lien subsists, a distress warrant may issue to enforce the lien. Meyer v. Oliver, supra.

In a proceeding to enforce the lien by foreclosure, if the landlord does not have access to the premises so as to enable him to inventory the articles which he wishes to subject to his lien, it is sufficient that he describes them in a general way, as by referring to the property as a quantity of household furniture and other personal property owned by the tenant, and now in his possession on the rented premises. A general description, with the exact locality of the house containing it, the name of person in possession and of the owner, is sufficient. Bourcier v. Edmondson, supra.

[2] Affidavit that the warrant was not sued out for " injuring or harassing " is sufficient. Biesenbach v. Key, 63 Tex. 79.

The amount must be stated definitely, not " about " a given sum. Jones v. Walker, 44 Tex. 200.

cient sureties, to be approved by the justice of the peace, payable to the defendant, conditioned that the plaintiff will pay the defendant such damages as he may sustain in case such warrant has been illegally and unjustly sued out, which bond shall be filed among the papers of the cause; and in case the suit shall be finally decided in favor of the defendant, he may bring suit against the plaintiff and his sureties on such bond, and shall recover such damages as may be awarded to him by the proper tribunal.

Upon the filing of such oath and bond, it shall be the duty of such justice of the peace to issue his warrant to the sheriff or any constable of the county, commanding him to seize the property of the defendant, or so much thereof as will satisfy the demand.

It shall be the duty of the officer to whom such warrant is directed to seize the property of such tenant, or so much thereof as shall be of value sufficient to satisfy such debt and costs, and the same in his possession safely keep, unless the same is replevied as herein provided, and make due return thereof to the court to which said warrant is returnable, at the next term thereof.

The defendant shall have the right at any time within ten days from the date of said levy to replevy the property so seized.

If the property is of a perishable or wasting kind, and the defendant fails to replevy as herein provided, the officer making the levy, or the plaintiff or the defendant, may apply to the court or judge thereof to which the warrant is returnable, either in term time or vacation, for an order to sell such property.

639. **Virginia**[1] **and West Virginia.**[2] — Rent of every kind may be recovered by distress or action. He to whom rent or compensation is due, whether he have the reversion or not, his personal representative or assignee, may recover it, whatever be the estate of the person owing it, or though his estate or interest in the land be ended.

Rent may be distrained for within five[3] years from the time it becomes due, and not afterwards, whether the lease be ended or

---

[1] Code 1873, ch. 134, §§ 7–15. As to exemptions, see ch. 49, §§ 32–38.

[2] 2 R. S. ch. 113, §§ 7–15. See

As Acts 1882, ch. 65. As to exemptions, see Acts 1881, §§ 18–29.

[3] In **West Virginia**, one year.

not. The distress shall be made by a constable, sheriff, or other officer of the county or corporation wherein the premises yielding the rent, or some part thereof, may be, or the goods liable to distress may be found, under warrant from a justice, founded upon an affidavit of the person claiming the rent, or his agent, that the amount of money or other thing to be distrained for (to be specified in the affidavit), as he verily believes, is justly due to the claimant, for rent reserved upon contract, from the person of whom it is claimed.

The distress may be levied on any goods of the lessee, or his assignee or under-tenant, found on the premises, or which may have been removed therefrom not more than thirty days. If the goods of such lessee, assignee, or under-tenant, when carried on the premises, are subject to a lien which is valid against his creditors, his interest only in such goods shall be liable to such distress. If any lien be created thereon while they are upon the leased premises, they shall be liable to distress, but for not more than one year's rent, whether it shall have accrued before or after the creation of the lien. No other goods shall be liable to distress than such as are declared to be so liable in this section. If, after the commencement of any tenancy,[1] a lien be obtained

---

[1] If, after the commencement of a tenancy for a year, the tenant mortgages his furniture on the leased premises, and the rent for that year is paid, but the tenant holds over under a new lease, the lien of the mortgage is valid against the lien of the landlord for rent, the former being a lien when the latter lease commenced. Richmond v. Duesberry, 27 Gratt. 210.

Real estate was leased to a firm for the term of three years, to commence on the 1st of January. 1876. On the 19th day of June, 1876, before the rent of that year became due, one of the lessees executed a deed of trust on the furniture. The rent for the year 1876 was paid. The rent for 1877 was assigned to a third party, who levied a distress warrant upon the furniture on the leased premises for that year's rent, which was in arrear; the holder of the note claiming, among other things, that the trust deed constituted a prior lien on the property to the rent for the year 1877, and praying an injunction to stop the sale of the property levied on until the rights of the parties could be determined, and for the appointment of a receiver. It was held: 1. That the deed of trust was created "after the commencement of the tenancy" under which the distress was made, — that the tenancy of the two years (1876 and 1877) was the same; 2. That the payment of the rent for the year 1876 was no discharge of the prior right of the lessors or their assignee to "one year's rent," within the meaning of the statute; 3. That goods carried on the leased premises and incumbered "after the commencement of the tenancy," are charged with a definite portion of the rent arising under the tenancy during the term, and not with the specific

or created by deed of trust, mortgage, or otherwise, upon the interest or property in goods on premises leased or rented, of any person liable for the rent, the party having such lien may remove said goods from the premises on the following terms, and not otherwise : that is to say, on the terms of paying to the person entitled to the rent so much as is in arrear, and securing to him so much as is to become due, what is so paid or secured not being more altogether than a year's rent in any case. If the goods be taken under legal process, the officer executing it shall, out of the proceeds of the goods, make such payment of what is in arrear ; and as to what is to become due, he shall sell a sufficient portion of the goods on a credit till then, taking from the purchasers bonds with good security, payable to the person so entitled, and delivering such bonds to him. If the goods be not taken under legal process, such payment and security shall be made and given before their removal.[1]

Where goods are distrained or attached for rent reserved in a share of the crop, or in anything other than money, the claimant of the rent, having given the tenant ten days' notice, or, if he be out of the county, having set up the notice in some con-

rent of any particular year or period of time. "One year's rent" and "a year's rent" are used in the statute to denote the *amount* of rent to be distrained for in the one case, and to be paid or secured in the other. And it matters not for what year it accrued, or whether it was before or after the creation of the lien, or whether or not other rents may have accrued after the lien was created and been paid by the tenants. As long as any rent arising under the tenancy remains unpaid by the persons liable therefor, as soon as it becomes due the person entitled to it may distrain the goods for an amount not exceeding the rent for a year. Wades *v.* Figgatt, 75 Va. 575.

As to marshalling proceeds of sale as between successive mortgages of property subject to distress, see Jones *v.* Phelan, 20 Gratt. 229.

A tenant under a lease for a term of years, which contained no covenant or stipulation for a renewal, executed a deed of trust which conveyed the machinery and other personalty on the premises. Thereafter, but before registration of the deed of trust, an agreement for renewal of the lease was entered into. It was held that possession under the agreement for renewal was to be treated as a new tenancy, and that the lien of the trust deed took priority over the landlord's lien for rent accruing after the expiration of the original term. Upper Appomattox Co. *v.* Hamilton (Va.), 2 So. East. Rep. 195.

[1] This statute creates a lien in favor of the landlord, and a lien of a high and peculiar character. The lien it creates must be respected and enforced. The landlord's lien under that statute is given by the statute independently of proceedings by distress-warrant or attachment, which remedies, in case of a bankrupt, are superseded by the effect and operation of the bankrupt act. *In re* Wynne, Chase's Dec. 227.

spicuous place on the premises, may apply to the court to which the attachment is returnable, or the court of the county or corporation in which the distress is made.   The court having ascertained the value, either by its own judgment, or, if either party require it, by the verdict of a jury impanelled without the formality of pleading, shall order the goods distrained or attached to be sold to pay the amount so ascertained.

640. Wisconsin.[1] — The common law right of distress, as it existed in England prior to the American Revolution, existed in this state [1] down to 1866, when it was abolished by statute.[2]

[1] Coburn v. Harvey, 18 Wis. 147.   [2] Laws 1866, ch. 74.

457

CHAPTER XIII.

LIENS OF LIVERY-STABLE KEEPERS AND AGISTORS.

I. *Statutory Provisions and their Construction.*

641. Liens of livery-stable keepers and agistors. — Agistors of cattle and livery-stable keepers have no lien at common law for the keeping of cattle or horses. Such a lien can arise only by virtue of a statute, or of a special agreement in the nature of a pledge.[1] " By the general law," said Baron Parke,[2] " in the absence of any specific agreement, whenever a party has expended labor and skill in the improvement of a chattel bailed to him, he has a lien upon it. Now the case of an agistment does not fall within that principle, inasmuch as the agistor does not confer an additional value on the article, either by the exertion of any skill of his own, or indirectly, by means of any instrument in his possession, as was the case with the stallion in Scarfe *v.* Morgan ;[3] he simply takes the animal to feed it."

The livery-stable keeper does not come within the reason of

[1] 3 Kent's Com. 365; Chapman *v.* Allen, Cro. Car. 271; Bevan *v.* Waters, 3 C. & P. 520; Wallace *v.* Woodgate, 1 C. & P. 575; Jackson *v.* Cummins, 5 M. & W. 342; Yorke *v.* Grenaugh, 2 Ld. Raym. 866; Judson *v.* Etheridge, 1 C. & M. 743 ; Richards *v.* Symons, 15 L. J. (N. S.) Q. B. 35.

Iowa : Munson *v.* Porter, 63 Iowa, 453; McDonald *v.* Bennett, 45 Iowa, 456.

Massachusetts : Goodrich *v.* Willard, 7 Gray, 183; Vinal *v.* Spofford, 139 Mass. 129 ; Goell *v.* Morse, 126 Mass. 480.

New York : Jackson *v.* Kasseall, 30 Hun, 231; Fox *v.* McGregor, 11

Barb. 41; Grinnell *v.* Cook, 3 Hill, 485, 491; Bissell *v.* Pearce, 28 N. Y. 252.

Vermont : Wills *v.* Barrister, 36 Vt. 220; for keeping sheep, Cummings *v.* Harris, 3 Vt. 244.

Other States : Miller *v.* Marston, 35 Me. 153, 155 ; Kelsey *v.* Layne, 28 Kans. 218; Lewis *v.* Tyler, 23 Cal. 364; Hickman *v.* Thomas, 16 Ala. 666 ; Mauney *v.* Ingram, 78 N. C. 96; Jackson *v.* Holland, 31 Ga. 339; Millikin *v.* Jones, 77 Ill. 372; Saint *v.* Smith, 1 Coldw. (Tenn.) 51.

[2] Jackson *v.* Cummins, *supra.*

[3] 4 M. & W. 270.

the rule of law which gives a lien to an innkeeper, namely, that the innkeeper is bound to entertain and provide for any one who presents himself in the character of a guest ; for the keeper of a livery-stable is under no obligation to take and feed the horse of a customer.[1]

642. Nor can such a lien be created by the force of any usage prevailing in a particular town or city ; but to acquire the force of law, such usage or custom must have been established, and have become general, so that a presumption of knowledge by the parties can be said to arise.[2]

The lien may be created by force of a special agreement, and in such case, if the owner of a horse remove it for the purpose of defrauding the keeper of his lien, the latter may retake the horse, and his lien will revive with the restored possession.[3]

643. In a Pennsylvania case the doctrine of the cases which deny the agistor of cattle a lien is called in question.[4] In this case Chief Justice Gibson dissents from the view that liens are confined to bailments for skilled labor ; that the lien results from the labor and care of any bailee, whether skilled

[1] Munson v. Porter, 63 Iowa, 453, per Adams, J.

[2] Saint v. Smith, 1 Coldw. (Tenn.) 51.

[3] Wallace v. Woodgate, Ry. & M. 193.

[4] Steinman v. Wilkins, 7 W. & S. (Pa.) 466. This case is cited, and the views of Chief Justice Gibson approved, in Hoover v. Epler, 52 Pa. St. 522, per Thompson, J., and in Kelsey v. Layne, 28 Kans. 218, 224. In the latter case Brewer, J., said : "The theory of the common law was, that if the labor and skill of the bailee increased the value of the article bailed, he had a lien. In other words, it was the profit of the bailor, and not the loss of the bailee, which determined the lien. Now it would seem far more just that, when the bailee parted with anything, either property or labor, at the instance of the bailor, he should be protected irrespective of the question whether such property or labor increased the value of the thing bailed, or simply preserved it in existence. Oftentimes, indeed, as suggested by Chief Justice Gibson in the quotation just made, the feeding and care of the agistor actually increase the intrinsic value. Further, it may be remarked that the general tendency of all legislation and adjudication is to afford protection to him who parts with labor or material for the benefit of another. Witness the various mechanics' lien laws for the protection of those who bestow labor or furnish material for the improvement of real estate, the law requiring railroads to give a bond to secure the payment of all laborers, and the statutes like the one now in consideration before us. These statutes, which rest upon obvious considerations of justice, are to be reasonably construed in order to accomplish the ends intended."

or not, and not from the improved condition of the thing bailed. "It is," he says, "difficult to find an argument for the position that a man who fits an ox for the shambles, by fattening it with his provender, does not increase its intrinsic value by means exclusively within his control." The learned Chief Justice refers to the argument of Baron Parke in Jackson v. Cummins,[1] that the lien extends only to cases in which the bailee has directly conferred additional value by labor or skill, or indirectly by the instrumentality of an agent under his control, as in the case of Scarfe v. Morgan,[2] where the owner of a stallion was allowed to have a lien for a single service, which resulted in the mare's being with foal. In the latter case the lien, of course, could have no other foundation than the improved condition and increased value of the mare, independently of the consideration of skill. "In Jackson v. Cummins," said Gibson, C. J., in conclusion, "we see the expiring embers of the primitive notion that the basis of the lien is intrinsic improvement of the thing by mechanical means ; but if we get away from it at all, what matters it how the additional value has been imparted, or whether it has been attended with an alteration in the condition of the thing? It may be said that the condition of a fat ox is not a permanent one, but neither is the increased value of a mare in foal permanent, yet in Scarfe v. Morgan the owner of a stallion was allowed to have a lien for the price of the leap. The truth is, the modern decisions evince a struggle of the judicial mind to escape from the narrow confines of the earlier precedents, but without having as yet established principles adapted to the current transactions and convenience of the world."

644. But a livery-stable keeper has a lien at common law on a horse which he keeps for the purpose of exercising and training to run at races,[3] although the races be for bets and wagers which are made illegal by statute, and the stable-keeper knew that the horse was so used while in his possession.[4] Even though the parties were *in pari delicto, potior est conditio possi-*

---

[1] 5 M. & W. 342, above cited.
[2] 4 M. & W. 270, above cited.
[3] Bevan v. Waters, 3 C. & P. 520; S. C. Moo. & M. 235; Scarfe v. Morgan, 4 M. & W. 270, 283; Forth v. Simpson, 13 Q. B. 680; Jacobs v. La-

tour, 5 Bing. 130; S. C. 2 Moo. & P. 20; Harris v. Woodruff, 124 Mass. 205; Shields v. Dodge, 14 Lea (Tenn.), 356; Towle v. Raymond, 58 N. H. 64.
[4] Harris v. Woodruff, *supra.*

dentis, and the law will not assist the owner of the horse to obtain possession without paying the keeper and trainer.[1]

It may happen that a trainer, while having a lien at common law for his labor bestowed upon a horse, may have a statutory lien for boarding the horse. Whether both liens, in such case, can be enforced together, depends upon the law of the state under which the liens arise.[2]

One who takes a horse to be kept and cared for has a lien for the service,[3] but the lien arises from the special service in caring for the horse, if he needs medical treatment. A stable-keeper has no lien for incidental treatment of a horse rendered in the usual course of keeping it without a special contract for a lien.[4]

645. The owner of a stallion has a lien upon a mare for the charge for serving the mare.[5] The lien is specific, and the mare cannot be retained for a general balance of account. This lien is given upon the general principle that, where a bailee has expended his labor and skill in the improvement of a chattel delivered to him, he has a lien for his charge in that respect.

In this country a similar lien has in several states been conferred by statute.[6] The lien is sometimes extended so as to

[1] Harris *v.* Woodruff, 124 Mass. 205.

[2] Towle *v.* Raymond, 58 N. H. 64.

[3] Lord *v.* Jones, 24 Me. 439.

[4] Miller *v.* Marston, 35 Me. 153.

[5] Scarfe *v.* Morgan, 4 M. & W. 270, 283. Parke, B., said: "The object is that the mare may be made more valuable by proving in foal. She is delivered to the defendant that she may by his skill and labor, and the use of his stallion for that object, be made so; and we think, therefore, that it is a case which falls within the principle of those cited in argument."

[6] **Alabama:** Owners of stallions, jacks, bulls, rams, ram-goats, and boars, who keep them for profit, have a lien on the mare or jenny, cow, ewe, or sow, and also upon the colt, calf, lambs, or pigs, for the stipulated price of the service, which lien may be enforced by attachment. Acts 1882–83, p. 157, No. 85.

Arkansas: The owner or keeper of any jack, stallion, bull, ram, or boar has a lien upon the mares, jennets, cows, ewes, and sows served, for the care and labor of such owner or keeper, for the price of such service. The lien is enforced like a laborer's lien. Acts 1885, p. 53.

Colorado: Keepers of stallions, jacks, bulls, rams, and boars have liens upon the get of such, for one year from the birth of the same, for the payment of the service. *Bonâ fide* purchasers without notice are not affected by the lien. G. S. 1883, § 3193.

Dakota Territory: The owner or person having in charge a stallion or bull has a lien for the service of the same upon the mare or cow and upon the offspring of the same. Notice must be filed in the registry of deeds within ninety days afterwards. Laws 1883, ch. 85; Laws 1885, ch. 112.

Georgia: Owners of stallions, jacks,

attach also to the offspring, and sometimes it is made to attach to the offspring alone. The lien is also generally enlarged so that it does not depend upon possession, but without possession may be asserted within a limited time by attachment.

646. The statutes of the several states giving liens to agistors, stable-keepers, and others, differ much in terms. Generally the lien attaches only to the animals taken care of; and it does not attach to wagons, carriages, harnesses, and other articles left with the horses and cattle which are to be kept.[1] But in a few states it is provided that the lien shall attach to such articles.[2] In some states the lien is given only to livery-

and bulls have a lien for the service of the same upon the young begotten. Laws 1882–83, p. 132, No. 352.

Kentucky: Owners of stud horses, jacks, stallions, and bulls have a lien upon the get for one year after birth of same. G. S. 1883, p. 982.

Maine : A lien is given on colts for the use of the stallion in begetting the same, until they are five months old. Acts 1887, ch. 52. For enforcement, see Chap. XXII., **Maine.**

Mississippi : The owner of a stallion, jackass, or bull shall have a lien on each foal or calf begotten by it for the price agreed to be paid therefor, and may enforce such lien in the manner provided for enforcing the lien of employers and employees, subject to the provisions of the act on that subject. R. Code 1880, § 1394.

Nebraska : The owners of stallions, jacks, and bulls have a lien upon the get for six months after the birth of the same. Comp. Laws 1885, ch. 4, art. 1, § 40.

North Carolina : The owner of a stud horse, jack, or bull has a lien on the colt or calf for one year after the birth of the same, for the price charged for use of the same for the season. Code 1883, §§ 1797, 1798; Laws 1885, ch. 72.

Ohio : The keeper or owner of a stallion has a lien upon the get for

the period of one year after the birth of the same. An affidavit of the amount due must be filed with county recorder within ten months after the rendition of the service. Laws 1885, p. 207; Laws 1884, p. 43.

Tennessee : Any person keeping a stallion, jack, bull, or boar for public use, has a lien on the offspring for the season, provided the lien is enforced in ten months from the birth. The lien is enforced in the same manner as a landlord's lien. Code 1884, §§ 2758, 2759. As to superiority of lien to subsequent mortgage, see Sims v. Bradford, 12 Lea, 434.

South Carolina : The owner of any stock horse, jack, bull, boar, or ram, having a claim by contract for service, has a prior lien on the issue for the amount of such claim, provided an action shall be instituted to enforce such claim within twelve months from the time such claim shall have accrued. G. S. 1882, § 2349.

[1] Thus a lien given by statute upon a horse for his keeping does not extend to any other property intrusted to the stable-keeper, such as carriages and harness. Hartshorne v. Seeds, 1 Chester Co. (Pa.) Rep. 460.

[2] As in **Delaware, § 653; Missouri, § 666; New Jersey, § 671; Virginia, § 680;** and **Wisconsin, § 682.**

462

stable keepers; in others it is also given to agistors, ranchmen, and farmers. In some the statutes apply in favor of those whose business it is to board horses, or to pasture or feed cattle; while others seem to be broad enough to cover isolated cases of boarding horses or keeping cattle.

The statutes of several states expressly provide that the lien shall not attach to property which has been stolen, or which does not belong to the person who intrusts it to a stable-keeper or agistor.[1] The reason for an innkeeper's lien attaching to such property does not hold in case of stable-keepers and agistors, and therefore the lien does not attach to such property unless it is expressly made to attach. If the statute is silent on the subject, it does not apply to stolen animals or such as belong to other persons.[2]

647. **Alabama.**[3] — Keepers, owners, or proprietors of livery-stables have a lien on all stock kept and fed by them, and have power to retain such stock, or so much thereof as may be necessary to secure the keepers, owners, or proprietors in the payment of charges due for keeping and feeding such stock.

If the charges when due are not paid within ten days from demand thereof, the keepers, owners, or proprietors are authorized, after giving thirty days' notice, once a week for three successive weeks, in a newspaper published in the county in which such stables are located, or, if there be no such paper, by posting the notice for thirty days in three conspicuous places in the county, to sell the stock, and out of the proceeds of such sale pay the charges and expenses incident thereto; and the balance, if any, to be paid to the owner of such stock.

648. **Arkansas.**[4] — Keepers of livery, sale, or feed stables, or wagon yards, have a lien for their reasonable charges and costs on all horses, mules, or other stock or property left in their charge to be kept, sheltered, fed, sold, or otherwise cared for. Such keepers are authorized to keep possession of such property until such charges are paid or tendered to them by the owner thereof.

---

[1] **Dakota Territory,** § 652; **Montana Territory,** § 667; **Wyoming Territory,** § 681.

[2] Gump *v.* Showalter, 43 Pa. St. 507.

[3] Code 1876, §§ 3494, 3495.

[4] Dig. of Stats. 1884, §§ 4463–4466.

In case any such property is left with such keeper and not called for by the owner, and the charges and costs thereon paid before they shall amount to the value thereof, and the cost of selling the same, it shall be lawful for such keeper to cause the same to be sold.

Such sale shall be at public outcry, after first giving the owner thirty days' actual notice or constructive notice, to be published in a newspaper authorized to publish legal notices, specifying the day, hour, and place of such sale, and out of the proceeds of such sale shall be paid : 1st. The costs and expenses of sale ; 2d. The amount due such keeper for his charges; and the balance, if any, shall be held by such keeper for the use, and subject to the order, of the owner of the property so sold.

649. California.[1] — Livery or boarding or feed stable proprietors, and persons pasturing horses or stock, have a lien, dependent on possession, for their compensation in caring for, boarding, feeding, or pasturing such horses or stock.

650. Colorado.[2] — Any ranchman, farmer, agistor, or herder of cattle, tavern-keeper, or livery-stable keeper, to whom any horses, mules, asses, cattle, or sheep shall be intrusted, for the purpose of feeding, herding, pasturing, or ranching, shall have a lien upon such horses, mules, asses, cattle, or sheep until the said amount is paid.

651. Connecticut.[3] — When a special agreement shall have been made between the owner of any cattle, horses, sheep, or swine, and any person who shall keep and feed them, regarding the price of such keeping, such cattle, horses, sheep, and swine shall be subject to a lien for the price of such keeping in favor of the person keeping the same ; and such person so keeping said cattle, horses, sheep, or swine may detain the same until such debt shall be paid ; and if it be not paid within twenty-one days after it is due, he may sell such cattle, horses, sheep, or swine, or so many thereof as shall be necessary, at public auction, upon

---

[1] Codes and Stats. 1885, § 3051 of Civ. Code. As to former statute of 1870, and the Code before it was amended in 1878, see Johnson v. Perry, 53 Cal. 351.

[2] G. S. 1883, § 2118. For mode of enforcing, see general provision, Chap. XXII., *infra.*

[3] Acts 1875, ch. 77, p. 45.

giving written notice to the owner of the time and place of said sale at least six days before said sale, and apply the proceeds to the payment of such debts, returning the surplus, if any, to said owner.

652. Dakota Territory.[1] — Any farmer, ranchman, or herder of cattle, tavern-keeper, or livery-stable keeper, to whom any horses, mules, cattle, or sheep shall be intrusted for the purpose of feeding, herding, pasturing, or ranching, shall have a lien upon said horses, mules, cattle, or sheep for the amount that may be due for such feeding, herding, pasturing, or ranching, and shall be authorized to retain possession of such horses, mules, cattle, or sheep until the said amount is paid: provided, that these provisions shall not be construed to apply to stolen stock.

These provisions shall not be construed to give any farmer, ranchman, or herder of cattle, tavern-keeper, or livery-stable keeper any lien upon horses, mules, cattle, or sheep put into their keeping for the purposes mentioned in the previous section, when said property was not owned by the person intrusting the same at the time of delivering them into the possession of said farmer, ranchman, herder, tavern-keeper, or livery-stable keeper.

653. Delaware.[2] — Any hotel-keeper, innkeeper, or other person who keeps a livery or boarding-stable, and for price or reward at such stable furnishes food or care for any horse, or has the custody or care of any carriage, cart, wagon, sleigh, or other vehicle, or any harness, robes, or other equipments for the same, shall have a lien upon such horse, carriage, cart, wagon, sleigh, vehicle, harness, robes, or equipments, and the right to detain the same to secure the payment of such price or reward, and may, after the expiration of fifteen days from the time the same, or any part thereof, became due and payable, the same remaining unpaid in whole or in part, sell the property upon which he has such lien at public sale, at such livery or boarding-stable, to the highest and best bidder or bidders therefor, first giving at least ten days' notice of such sale.

If the keeper of the stable has parted with the custody of the property subject to such lien, he may at any time within ten days

---

[1] Code of Civil Procedure, 1883, §§ 672, 673. For mode of enforcing liens, see Chap. XXII., *infra*.

[2] Laws 1885, vol. 17, pt. 2, p. 920.

from the parting of such custody make an affidavit describing the property and stating the amount due, and thereupon a warrant may issue for the seizure of the property and the delivery thereof to the keeper of the stable.

654. Florida.[1] — All keepers of livery, sale, and feed stables shall have a lien upon any horse or other animal put in their charge for feeding or taking care of said animal, and the owners shall not have a right to recover the possession of any such animals as against the person so having the same in charge, until all amounts due for feeding or taking care of such animals shall be paid.

655. Georgia.[2] — Innkeepers and livery-stable keepers have a lien for their dues on the stock placed in their care for keeping, which shall be superior to other liens, except liens for taxes, special liens of landlords for rent, liens of laborers, and all general liens of which they had actual notice before the property claimed to be subject to lien came into their control, to which excepted liens they shall be inferior.

The keeper of a livery-stable is a depositary for hire, and is bound to the same diligence and entitled to the same lien as an innkeeper.

656. Illinois.[3] — Stable - keepers and other persons have a lien upon the horses, carriages, and harness kept by them, for the proper charges due for the keeping thereof and expenses bestowed thereon at the request of the owner, or the person having the possession thereof.

Agistors and other persons keeping, yarding, feeding, or pasturing domestic animals, have a lien upon the animals agistored, kept, yarded, or fed, for the proper charges due for the agisting, keeping, yarding, or feeding thereof.

657. Indiana.[4] — The keepers of livery-stables and all others

---

[1] Laws 1885, No. 63, p. 60.

[2] Code 1882, §§ 1986, 2124. For mode of enforcing the lien, see general provisions, Chap. XXII., **Georgia.** As to priority, see Colquitt v. Kirkman, 47 Ga. 555.

[3] Annotated Stats. 1885, ch. 82,

§§ 49, 50. For mode of enforcing liens, see Chap. XXII., **Illinois.**

[4] R. S. 1881, § 5292. The statute does not apply to isolated cases of feeding cattle. Conklin v. Carver, 19 Ind. 226.

engaged in feeding horses, cattle, hogs, and other live-stock, shall have a lien upon such property for the feed and care bestowed by them upon the same, and shall have the same rights and remedies as are provided for tradesmen, mechanics, and others.[1]

658. Iowa.[2] — Keepers of livery and feed stables, herders and feeders and keepers of stock for hire, have a lien on all stock and property coming into their hands as such, for their proper charges, and for the expense of keeping when the same have been received from the owner or from any person : provided, however, this lien shall be subject to all prior liens of record.

The owner or claimant of the property may release the lien and shall be entitled to the possession of the property on tendering to the person claiming the lien a good and sufficient bond, signed by two sureties, residents of the county, who shall justify, the penalty in the bond being at least three times the amount of the lien claimed, and conditioned to pay any judgment the person claiming the lien shall obtain, for which the property was liable under the lien.

659. Kansas.[3] — The keepers of livery-stables, and all others engaged in feeding horses, cattle, hogs, or other live-stock, shall have a lien upon such property for the feed and care bestowed by them upon the same ; and if reasonable or stipulated charges for such feed and care be not paid within sixty days after the same becomes due, the property, or so much thereof as may be necessary to pay such charges and the expense of publication and sale, may be sold.[4]

660. Kentucky.[5] — All owners and keepers of livery-stables in this state have a lien upon the horses, cattle, or other stock placed in such stable by the owner or owners thereof, for their reasonable charges for keeping and caring for the same ; and this lien shall attach whether the horses, cattle, or other stock

---

[1] See § **758.**

[2] R. Code 1880, p. 585, §§ 1, 2. Prior to the enactment of this statute, March 10, 1880, a livery-stable keeper in this state had no lien. McDonald v. Bennett, 45 Iowa, 456 ; Munson v. Porter, 63 Iowa, 453. The statute giving a lien upon personal property stored or left with a warehouseman or *other depositary* did not give such a lien. McDonald v. Bennett, *supra.*

[3] Comp. Laws 1885, § 3259.

[4] For mode of enforcing this lien see § **349.**

[5] G. S. 1883, ch. 70, §§ 1–3.

are merely temporarily lodged, fed, and cared for, or are placed at such stables for regular board; but it shall be subject to the limitations and restrictions as provided in case of a landlord's lien for rent.

When such lien exists in favor of any person, he may, before a justice of the peace, or a judge of the county court, or a police judge of any town or city, where such livery-stable is situated, by himself or agent, make affidavit to the amount due him and in arrear for keeping and caring for such stock, and describing, as near as may be, the horses, cattle, or other stock so kept by him; and thereupon such officer shall issue a warrant, directed to the sheriff or any constable or town or city marshal of said county, authorizing him to levy upon and seize the said horses, cattle, or other stock, for the amount due, with interest and costs: but if the said horses, cattle, or other stock have been removed from the custody of the livery-stable keeper with his consent, the lien herein provided for shall not continue longer than ten days from and after such removal; nor shall such lien, in any case of such removal, be valid against any *bond fide* purchaser without notice at any time within ten days after such removal. A warrant, as herein provided, may be issued to another county than that in which the livery-stable keeper resides.

Such warrant shall be made returnable, and the proceedings thereunder and the right of replevy shall be in all respects the same as is provided in cases of distress warrants for rent.

661. Louisiana. — Under the provision of the Code [1] which entitles a party to the expenses incurred in the preservation of property and to the right to retain it, it is held that the feeding of horses may be classed among the expenses incurred in their preservation, and that a privilege exists therefor.[2]

But a keeper of public stables has no privilege on horses placed with him on livery for money loaned to their owner.[3]

---

[1] Civ. Code, arts. 3191–3193.

[2] Andrews v. Crandell, 16 La. Ann. 208.

In Powers v. Hubbell, 12 La. Ann. 413, it was held that the keeper of a livery stable has no privilege by law upon carriages kept in his stable. Whether he has a privilege for preserving the horses by feeding them, the court deemed it unnecessary to decide.

[3] Whiting v. Coons, 2 La. Ann. 961.

662. **Maine.**[1]— Whoever pastures, feeds, or shelters animals by virtue of a contract with or by consent of the owner, has a lien thereon for the amount due for such pasturing, feeding, or sheltering, to secure payment thereof with costs, to be enforced in the same manner as liens on goods in possession and choses in action.[2]

663. **Massachusetts.**[3]— Persons having proper charges due them for pasturing, boarding, or keeping horses or other domestic animals brought to their premises or placed in their care by or with the consent of the owners thereof, have a lien on such horses or other domestic animals for such charges.

At the expiration of ten days after a demand in writing, petition may be made for the sale of the property, and notice thereon may be served seven days before the hearing.[4]

664. **Michigan.**[5]— Whenever any person shall deliver to any person any horse, mule, neat cattle, sheep, or swine to be kept or cared for, such person shall have a lien thereon for the keeping and care of such animals, and may retain possession of the same until such charges are paid.

The person having such lien may commence a suit for the recovery of such charges, by summons in the usual form, before any justice of the peace of the city or township in which he

[1] R. S. 1883, ch. 91, § 41; Acts 1887, ch. 1.

[2] See § 531.

After a sale under execution issued upon a petition to enforce the lien, a second petition to enforce a lien for keeping the animals during the time intervening between the dates of the two petitions cannot be maintained, though commenced while the animals still remain in the possession of the lienholder, and there is a surplus arising from the proceeds of the sale. After the sale there is nothing upon which the lien can attach. It cannot attach to the surplus. Lord v. Collins, 76 Me. 443, 446, per Foster, J.: "There is nothing in the statute we are considering which, by express words or by necessary implication, contemplates the enforcement of a lien upon any-

thing other than the animals which have been furnished food or shelter. The petitioner claims to sustain this petition as against said animals in addition to the judgment of lien in his behalf before granted, and to have his claim satisfied 'out of said property or the proceeds thereof.' The statute does not go to that extent, where, by the petitioner's own motion, the property has been sold to satisfy a lien in favor of the same party and originating from one and the same bailment."

[3] Pub. Stats. 1882, ch. 192, §§ 32, 33.

[4] In other respects the lien is enforced under the general provisions stated in Chap. XXII., **Massachusetts.**

[5] Annot. Stats. 1882, §§ 8399, 8402–8405, 8407.

resides, or in any court, as the case may require, against the person liable for the payment thereof. If such summons be returned personally served upon the defendant, the same proceedings shall thereupon be had, in all respects, as in other suits commenced by summons, in which there is a personal service of process, and judgment shall be rendered in such suit in like manner. If the officer return upon such summons that the defendant cannot be found within his county, the same proceedings shall be thereupon had, in all respects as near as may be, as in suits commenced by attachment, in which there is not a personal service of a copy of the attachment upon the defendant, and judgment shall be rendered in such suit in like manner. If the plaintiff recover judgment in such suit, execution shall issue thereon in the same manner and with the like effect as upon judgment rendered in suits commenced by attachment; and the property upon which the plaintiff holds such lien, or so much thereof as shall be sufficient to satisfy such execution, may be sold thereon in the same manner as if it had been seized and held upon an attachment in such suit.

If the property upon which any such lien shall be enforced consist of horses, cattle, sheep, swine, or other beasts, and any expenses shall have been incurred by the person having such lien after the same accrued, in keeping and taking care of such property, the amount of such expenses shall be an additional lien upon the property, and shall be computed and ascertained upon the trial or assessment of damages, and included in the judgment.

665. **Minnesota.**[1] — Any keeper of a livery or boarding-stable, and any person pasturing or keeping any horses, mules, cattle, or stock, at the request of the owner or lawful possessor thereof, shall have a lien for all his charges for keeping, supporting, and caring for such property, and a right to hold and retain the possession thereof, and a power of sale for the satisfaction of his reasonable charges and expenses. If such charges are not paid within three months, a person having such lien may sell the property at public auction on giving notice by advertise-

---

[1] Laws 1885, ch. 81; G. S. 1878, ch. 90, §§ 16, 17.

The lien takes precedence of a chattel mortgage executed before such keeping. Smith v. Stevens, 31 N. W. Rep. 55.

ment for three weeks in the manner prescribed for enforcing liens of mechanics and carriers.[1]

666. Missouri.[2] — Every person who shall keep, board, or train any horse, mule, or other animal shall, for the amount due therefor, have a lien on such animal and on any vehicle, harness, or equipment coming into his possession therewith ; and no owner or claimant shall have the right to take any such property out of the custody of the person having such lien, except with his consent or on the payment of such debt ; and such lien shall be valid against said property in the possession of any person receiving or purchasing it with notice of such claim.

The lien provided for in the preceding paragraph shall be enforced as follows : The person claiming the lien shall file with a justice of the peace of the ward, district, or township in which he resides a statement, duly verified by himself, his agent, or attorney, setting forth his account and a description of the property on which the lien is claimed ; and thereupon the justice shall issue a summons as in ordinary civil actions, returnable forthwith, and, upon the return of the summons duly served, shall set the cause for hearing at any time after the lapse of one day. If summons be returned "defendant not found," and if it be proven to the satisfaction of the justice that the defendant is not a resident of the county, the justice shall order a notice of the proceedings to be published for three successive days in a daily newspaper, if one be published in the county, and if there be none, then once in a weekly, if such be published in the county; and if no paper be published in the county, then by six handbills put up in six public places in the county, notifying the defendant of the filing and the particulars of the account, the description of the property on which the lien is claimed, its whereabouts, and the day and place set for the hearing of the cause, which shall be at least ten days from the day of the last publication of the notice ; and the proof of such publication shall be filed in the justice's office on or before the day of trial. When the defendant shall have been summoned or notified as aforesaid the cause shall, on the day fixed for trial, be tried as any ordinary case in a justice's court. If the judgment be for the plaintiff, the justice shall order the property, upon which the lien shall have been found to exist, to be sold to satisfy the same. If the

---

[1] See § 354.   [2] 1 R. S. 1879, §§ 3196, 3197.

lien be not established, and the defendant shall not have been summoned or shall not have voluntarily appeared to the action, the cause shall be dismissed at the cost of the plaintiff; if the defendant shall have been summoned or shall have appeared to the action, and the plaintiff shall have established an indebtedness on the account sued on, but shall have failed to establish the lien claimed, the judgment shall be for the plaintiff for such indebtedness, but the costs of suit, or any part thereof, may be taxed against him.

667. **Montana Territory.**[1] — Any ranchman, farmer, agistor, or herder of cattle, tavern-keeper, or livery-stable keeper, to whom any horses, mules, asses, cattle, or sheep shall be intrusted, and a contract for their keeping be entered into between the parties for the purpose of feeding, herding, pasturing, or ranching, shall have a lien upon said horses, mules, asses, cattle, or sheep, for the amount that may be due for such feeding, herding, pasturing, or ranching, and shall be authorized to retain possession of such horses, mules, asses, cattle, or sheep until the said amount is paid: provided, that the provisions of this section shall not be construed to apply to stolen stock.

668. **Nebraska.**[2] — When any person shall procure, contract with, or hire any other person to feed and take care of any kind of live-stock, it shall be unlawful for him to gain possession of the same by writ of replevin, or other legal process, until he has paid or tendered the contract price, or a reasonable compensation, for taking care of the same.

669. **Nevada.**[3] — Any ranchman, or other person or persons,

---

[1] G. L. 1879, § 848.

[2] Comp. Stats. 1885, art. 1, ch. 4, § 28; art. 3, ch. 2, § 2.

This statute was enacted, February 18, 1867, and is probably the earliest statute passed by any Western state or territory for the protection of feeders and herders of cattle. State Bank v. Lowe, 33 N. W. Rep. 482. Cobb, J., in this case, said : " Our legislature seems to have proceeded with great caution ; and instead of adopting the language of the statutes of New Hampshire and other Eastern states, which give in express terms to the agistors of cattle, they only created an estoppel against the person contracting, hiring, or procuring the feeding and caring for of live-stock to gain possession of such stock, by replevin or other legal means, until he should make payment or tender therefor." It was accordingly held, that the statute did not create a lien superior to that of a chattel mortgage previously executed, delivered, and recorded.

[3] 1 Comp. Laws 1873, ch. 20, § 144.

keeping corrals, livery or feed stables, or furnishing hay, grain, pasture, or otherwise boarding any horse or horses, mule or mules, ox or oxen, or other animal or animals, shall have a lien upon and retain possession of the same, or a sufficient number thereof, until all reasonable charges are paid, or suit can be brought and judgment obtained for the amount of such charges, and execution issued and levied on said property: provided, nothing in this act shall be so construed as to include any debt other than for the boarding, keeping, or pasture of such animal or animals, together with costs of suit and sale. Sales of such animal or animals shall be made as other sales of personal property under execution. The officer making such sale shall be entitled to such fees for his services as are allowed by law in cases of other sales of personal property.

670. **New Hampshire.**[1] — Any person to whom any horses, cattle, sheep, or other domestic animals shall be intrusted to be pastured or boarded, shall have a lien thereon for all proper charges due for such pasturing or board, until the same shall be paid or tendered.

671. **New Jersey.**[2] — All livery-stable, boarding, and exchange stable-keepers shall have a lien on all horses and other animals left with them in livery for board, or sale, or exchange; and also upon all carriages, wagons, sleighs, and harness left with them for storage, sale, or exchange, for the amount of the bill due to the proprietor of any such stable for the board and keep of any such horse or other animal, and also for such storage;

[1] G. L. 1878, ch. 139, § 2. For mode of enforcing see general provision, Chap. XXII., **New Hampshire.**

Under this statute a person pasturing a milch cow for the season, in the usual manner, under an agreement with the owner, is so far intrusted with the animal as to have a lien upon it for the charge of pasturing, as against the owner, and third persons having no title or right of possession. Smith *v.* Marden, 60 N. H. 509, 512, per Doe, C. J.: "The statute does not expressly exclude a lien when the contract is to pasture or board an animal a month, a week, a day, or parts of successive days, or where the owner is to have the use and possession of it a part of every day, and there is not satisfactory evidence of an intent to leave the creditor, in such cases as this, without equitable security." It is also declared that the right of the owner to take the cow from the pasture daily to milk is as consistent with a lien, as the right of a boarder to carry various articles of his luggage from his boarding-house without affecting the boarding-house keeper's lien.

[2] Revision 1877, p. 496, §§ 72, 73.

and shall have the right, without the process of law, to retain the same until the amount of such said indebtedness is discharged.

All property held by any such livery-stable, boarding, and exchange stable-keeper shall, after the expiration of thirty days from the date of such detention, be sold at public auction, upon a notice of said sale being first published, for the space of two weeks, in some newspaper circulating in the city or township in which said livery, or boarding and exchange stable is situate, and also after five days' notice of said sale set up in five of the most public places in said city or township; and the proceeds of said sale shall be applied to the payment of such lien and the expenses of such sale, and the balance, if any remaining, shall be paid over to the owner of such property or his representatives; and if the said balance is not claimed by such owner within sixty days after such sale, then the said balance to be paid over to the overseer of the poor of said city or township for the support of the poor.

672. New Mexico.[1] — Livery-stable keepers, and those who furnish feed or shelter for the stock of others, have a lien on the stock while the same is in their possession, and until the same is paid for. After ten days' notice in writing stating the amount of the indebtedness, and then after giving twenty days' notice by posting, the lien may be enforced by sale at auction.

673. New York.[2] — Persons keeping any animals at livery or pasture, or boarding the same for hire, under any agreement with the owner thereof, may detain such animals until all charges under such agreement for the care, keep, pasture, or board of such animals shall have been paid:[3] provided, however, that notice in writing shall first be given to such owner in person, or at his last known place of residence, of the amount of such charges, and the intention to detain such animal or animals until such charges shall be paid;[4] and such persons may at any time main-

---

[1] Comp. Laws 1884, §§ 1542–1544.

[2] 2 R. S. 7th ed. p. 1284; Laws 1872, ch. 498; Laws 1880, ch. 145.

[3] The statute gives no lien upon any wagons, harnesses, or robes that may be kept with a horse, but only upon the horse itself. Jackson v. Kasseall, 30 Hun, 231.

[4] Under this statute, when the owner of a horse demands it from a livery-stable keeper without offering to pay him his charges for keeping it,

tain an action in any of the courts of this state to enforce such lien and procure a sale of the said animals for the payment of said keeping, pasture, and board, and the costs of such action, whenever such sum shall exceed fifty dollars. From the time of giving such notice, and while such horse or horses are so detained, and no longer, such livery-stable keeper or other person shall have a lien upon such horse or horses for the purpose of satisfying any execution which may be issued upon a judgment obtained for such charges.

674. Ohio.[1] — A person who feeds or furnishes food and care for any horse, mare, foal, filly, gelding, mule, or ass, by virtue of any contract or agreement with the owner thereof, shall have a lien therefor to secure the payment of the same upon such animal.

A person feeding or furnishing food and care for any horse, mare, foal, filly, gelding, mule, or ass shall retain such animal

the livery-stable keeper is entitled to a reasonable time in which to make up the account of what is due and serve it, with notice of the lien, in the manner required by the statute. "Otherwise it would be in the power of an unscrupulous debtor, by suddenly making such a demand, to cut off the livery-stable keeper altogether from his lien, unless he were prepared at the moment to hand the debtor the bill of charges, and the notice in writing, which the statute requires. Such a construction would operate rather to defeat the statute than to aid the enforcement of the remedy, which is the construction required in remedial statutes. Where an account is running on from day to day, or from week to week, for the keeping of a horse, the livery-stable keeper would have to be continually serving written notices of his lien and his charges under such a construction as the justice has given; and it is a much more reasonable one that, when the owner of a horse demands the animal without offering to pay what is due for keeping it, the livery-stable keeper should have there-

after a reasonable length of time to make up the account, and serve it with the notice in the formal manner which the statute requires for his protection; and, as in this case, an account running over a period of eight months has to be made up of charges, credits, and offsets, four or five hours was not an unreasonable length of time to enable the defendant to do so." Eckhard v. Donohue, 9 Daly (N. Y.), 214, 216, cited with approval in Lessells v. Farnsworth, 3 How. (N. Y.) Pr. N. S. 364. If a stable-keeper boards a horse which is already subject to a mortgage, the mortgagee has a superior lien.

One who desires to assert his right to the possession of a horse by virtue of his lien, must ascertain the real owner and serve notice on him. A notice directed to and served upon the husband, when in fact the horse belonged to his wife, is a nullity. Armitage v. Mace, 16 J. & S. (N. Y.) 107; S. C. on another point, 96 N. Y. 538.

[1] R. S. 1880, §§ 3212, 3213.

for the period of ten days, at the expiration of which time, if the owner does not satisfy such lien, he may sell such animal at public auction, after giving the owner ten days' notice in a newspaper of general circulation in the county where the services were rendered; and after satisfying the lien and costs that may accrue, any residue remaining shall be paid to the owner.

675. Oregon.[1] — Any person who shall depasture or feed any horses, cattle, hogs, sheep, or other live-stock, or bestow any labor, care, or attention upon the same, at the request of the owner or lawful possessor thereof, shall have a lien upon such property for his just and reasonable charges for the labor, care, and attention he has bestowed and the food he has furnished, and he may retain possession of such property until such charges be paid.   Lien is enforced by sale after notice.[2]

676. Pennsylvania.[3] — All livery-stable keepers and innkeepers have a lien upon any and every horse delivered to them to be kept in their stables, for the expense of the keeping; and in case the owner of the said horse or horses, or the person who delivered them for keeping to the keeper of the livery-stable or innkeepers, shall not pay and discharge the said expense, provided it amount to thirty dollars, within fifteen days after demand made of him personally, or in case of his removal from the place where such livery-stable or inn is kept, within ten days after notice of the amount due, and demand of payment in writing left at his last place of abode, the livery-stable keeper or innkeeper may cause the horse or horses aforesaid to be sold at public sale, according to law; and, after deducting from the amount of sales the costs of sale and the expense of keeping, shall deliver the residue upon demand to the person who delivered the horse or horses for keeping..

---

[1] Laws 1878, p. 102, § 2.

[2] For general provision for enforcement of this and other liens, see Chap. XXII., **Oregon.**

[3] 1 Brightly's Purdon's Dig. 1883, p. 890, § 16. This lien is joint and several on all the horses kept. Young v. Kimball, 23 Pa. St. 193.

The lien is restricted to the board of the horses, and does not cover the board of their drivers. McManigle v. Crouse, 34 Leg. Int. 384. Or the care of wagons and the like. Hartshorne v. Seeds, 1 Chest. Co. Rep. 460.

The lien does not attach to stolen horses. Gump v. Showalter, 43 Pa. St. 507; Hoopes v. Worrall, 1 Del. Co. (Pa.) Rep. 111.

677. **Tennessee.**[1] — Whenever any horse or other animal is received to pasture for a consideration, the farmer shall have a lien upon the animal for his proper charges, the same as the innkeeper's lien at common law.

This lien shall include the charges for the service of any stallion, jack, bull, or boar, when the charge for the service of such animal shall have been stipulated and agreed upon between the parties.

Livery-stable keepers are entitled to the same lien on all stock received by them for board and feed, until all reasonable charges are paid.

· 678. **Texas.**[2] — Proprietors of livery or public stables have a special lien upon all animals placed with them for feed, care, and attention, as also upon such carriages, buggies, or other vehicles as may have been placed in their care, for the amount of the charges against the same.

679. **Vermont.**[3] — Persons having charges due them for pasturing, boarding, or keeping horses or other domestic animals, brought to their premises, or placed, with the consent of the owners thereof, in the care of such persons, may, if the charges become due while such animals remain in their possession, retain the possession of such animals until such charges are paid.

680. **Virginia.**[4] — When an agreement, expressed or implied, shall have been made between the keeper of any ordinary, house of private entertainment, or livery-stable, and any person keeping horses or other animals, vehicles, or harness at such livery-stable, regarding the price of stabling and provender or pasturage for such horses or other animals, all the animals, vehicles, or harness so kept by such person at such ordinary, house of private entertainment, or livery-stable shall be subject to a lien in favor of the keeper of such ordinary, house of private entertainment, or livery-stable for all such sums as shall be at any time due from such person for keeping and providing for such horses or other animals; and the keeper of any such ordinary, house of private entertainment, or livery-stable may retain such horses or

---

[1] Code 1882, §§ 2756, 2757, 2760.
[2] R. S. 1879, art. 3183. For manner of enforcing the lien, see general provision, Chap. XXII., **Texas.**
[3] Laws 1884, No. 91.
[4] Acts 1879, ch. 84, § 2.

other animals, vehicles, and harness, until such debt shall be paid; and if not paid within thirty days after it is due, he may, after due notice, sell said property, or so much thereof as may be necessary, at public auction, and apply the proceeds to the payment of such debt.

681. **Wyoming Territory.**[1] — Any ranchman, farmer, agistor, or herder of cattle, tavern-keeper, or livery-stable keeper, to whom any horses, mules, asses, cattle, or sheep shall be intrusted, for the purpose of feeding, herding, pasturing, or ranching, shall have a lien upon said horses, mules, asses, cattle, or sheep for the amount that may be due for such feeding, herding, pasturing, or ranching, and shall be authorized to retain possession of such horses, mules, asses, cattle, or sheep until the said amount is paid: provided, that the provisions of this section shall not be construed to apply to stolen stock.

682. **Wisconsin.**[2] — Every keeper of a livery or boarding-stable, and every person pasturing or keeping any horses, carriage, harness, mules, cattle, or stock, shall have a lien upon and may retain the possession of any such horses, carriage, harness, mules, cattle, or stock for the amount which may be due him for the keeping, supporting, and care thereof, until such amount is paid.

683. **A statute creating the lien attaches from its enactment.** The fact that the keeping of a horse began before the enactment of the statute giving a lien does not deprive the keeper of a lien for the keeping subsequent to such enactment, especially if the keeping of the horse subsequent to the enactment was not in pursuance of a contract made prior thereto. In such case the lien does not attach for that part of the account which accrued prior to the taking effect of the statute; but it does attach for that part of the account accruing subsequently.[3]

---

[1] Comp. Laws 1876, p. 462; Act Dec. 13, 1873, § 1.

[2] R. S. 1878, § 3344.

An action of contract for the care and keeping of horses cannot be changed into one to enforce a specific lien upon such horses. A complaint for legal relief cannot be changed by amendment into one for equitable relief. Brothers v. Williams, 65 Wis. 401.

[3] Munson v. Porter, 63 Iowa, 453.

684. Though the horses, cattle, or other stock upon which the statute gives a lien be exempt from execution and from distress for rent, the property is subject to the lien in the same manner as other property not so exempt.[1] The lien attaches to such property, although the lien can be enforced only by execution.[2]

685. Inasmuch as the lien of a stable-keeper is purely statutory, it is for him to comply with all the conditions precedent which the statute requires. Thus, if a statute requires the giving of notice to the owner of an intention to claim a lien and of the amount of the charges, the person claiming the lien must ascertain the real owner of the property, and serve notice of his lien upon that person. If the notice be directed to and served upon a person who is not the owner, it is a nullity as against the person who is.[3]

686. A statutory lien for the keeping of several horses is a joint and several lien upon all the horses, and one horse may be detained for the keeping of all of them.[4]

687. A statute giving a lien to a livery-stable keeper, and to those engaged in feeding horses and cattle, does not include isolated cases of feeding, but only those whose business it is to feed horses and cattle.

But where it appears that for three or four years a farmer has been keeping, feeding, and caring for stock belonging to a neighbor, such farmer will be entitled to a lien upon the stock for his feed and care, notwithstanding it may appear that he fed and pastured no other stock for third parties, and that the number of cattle belonging to such neighbor so kept and cared for at no time exceeded twelve in number.[5] Brewer, Justice, delivering the opinion of the court, said : "This is not a case where a farmer has only for a single season pastured a single head of stock for a neighbor, but where year after year the party has pastured and fed several head of stock. It is true that he only did this

[1] See § 510 ; Fitch v. Steagall, 14 Bush (Ky.), 230; Munson v. Porter, 63 Iowa, 453.

[2] Munson v. Porter, supra.

[3] Armitage v. Mace, 16 J. & S. (N. Y.) 107, 113.

[4] Young v. Kimball, 23 Pa. St. 193.

[5] Conklin v. Carver, 19 Ind. 226; Kelsey v. Layne, 28 Kans. 218, 225. See Alt v. Weidenberg, 6 Bosw. (N. Y.) 176.

for one person, but still he did it to such an extent and for such a length of time that it seems to us he comes fairly within the protection of the statute. He was engaged in feeding his stock. That, *pro hac vice*, may be considered his business. No one would for a moment seriously contend that a party must engage in it as an exclusive business before becoming entitled to the protection of the statute. Suppose, as in the case of Brown *v.* Holmes,[1] that ninety-two cattle were wintered for a single person : could it be said for a moment that the agistor was not engaged in the business of feeding and taking care of cattle, simply because he had only the cattle of one person ? So in this case, while the number of cattle is not so great, yet the length of time is much greater."

688. No lien arises under a statute for keeping a horse under a special agreement whereby the stable-keeper is to use the horse for the joint benefit of himself and the owner ; as where he was to take the horse around the country and enter it for races, the owner to pay all expenses, and to divide the earnings with the stable-keeper. For expenses which the stable-keeper has paid for the care and board of the horse at other stables the statute gives him no lien, though the expenses are for board which would give other persons a lien.[2]

689. A servant hired as a groom to a horse has no lien upon the horse for his services, but he has a lien for feed furnished by him which the owner ought to have furnished. If the horse is in the groom's custody at his own stable, he is a bailee, and entitled to the lien of a bailee. A contract to feed and keep the horse is not necessary in order to create a lien ; but the case stands as if the horse had been left for keep and care without more being said, in which case it is clear that the owner could not have demanded the horse without paying the charges.[3]

690. Where a statute gives a lien provided notice in writing shall first be given to the owner of the amount of the charges and the intention to claim a lien,[4] an inchoate lien attaches when a horse is placed in a stable; and it becomes com-

[1] 13 Kans. 482.
[2] Armitage *v.* Mace, 96 N. Y. 538, affirming *S. C.* 14 J. & S. 550.
[3] Hoover *v.* Epler, 52 Pa. St. 522 ; *S. C.* 1 Pearson, 255.
[4] As in New York, § 673.

plete from the time of giving such notice. It then relates back, and covers all charges due for the care and board of the horse from the beginning. Such a statute is a remedial one, giving a lien where none existed before, and should be liberally construed to advance the remedy. The lien is not cut off by a sale of the horse before the notice is given.[1]

II. *Priority as regards Chattel Mortgages and other Liens and Sales.*

691. A chattel mortgage upon a horse is superior to a subsequent lien of a stable-keeper, where the horse is placed in the stable by the mortgagor, after the making of the mortgage, without the knowledge or consent of the mortgagee.[2] It is not to be supposed that a statute giving a lien for the keeping of animals was intended to violate fundamental rights of property by enabling the possessor to create a lien without the consent of the mortgagee, when the person in possession could confer no rights as against the mortgagee by a sale of the animals. The keeper of animals intrusted to him by the mortgagor undoubtedly acquires a lien as against the mortgagor, but it is a lien only upon such interest in them as the mortgagor had at the time, and not a lien as against the mortgagee, between whom and the keeper of the animals there is no privity of contract. The mortgagor, though in possession, is in no sense the mortgagee's agent, nor does he sustain to the mortgagee any relations which authorize

---

[1] Lessells *v.* Farnsworth, 3 How. (N. Y.) Pr. N. S. 73; *S. C.* Ib. 364; Eckhard *v.* Donohue, 9 Daly (N. Y.), 214. There are some statements inconsistent with the foregoing in Jackson *v.* Kasseall, 30 Hun (N. Y.), 231. It is there said that if the notice operates retrospectively, it would be immaterial, for the purposes of the lien, at what stage of the period of keeping the notice is given; one given on the last day would be as effectual as one given on the first day. Such a construction would defeat the very object of requiring a notice to be given, which evidently is to advise the owner and all others interested that a lien is claimed, and to enable them to take such action as they may deem neces-

sary in view of such claim. Per Smith, J. It is, however, expressly declared by the court that it was not intended to deal with the question whether a lien could be created as against the *owner* for past charges; and the court only decided that no such lien could be created as against a mortgagee holding a mortgage duly filed. This case is referred to and explained in Lessells *v.* Farnsworth, 3 How. (N. Y.) Pr. N. S. 364, 367.

[2] Jackson *v.* Kasseall, 30 Hun (N. Y), 231; Bissell *v.* Pearce, 28 N. Y. 252; Charles *v.* Neigelson, 15 Bradw. (Ill.) 17; Sargent *v.* Usher, 55 N. H. 287; State Bank *v.* Lowe (Neb.), 33 N. W. Rep. 482.

him to contract any liability on his behalf. The statute cannot be construed to authorize the mortgagor to subject the mortgagee's interest to a lien without his knowledge or consent, as security for a liability of the mortgagor, unless such a construction clearly appears from the language of the statute to be unavoidable.

692. On the other hand, some authorities hold that the lien of an agistor or livery-stable keeper is paramount to a previous mortgage of the animals.[1] While it is conceded that no contract lien could be placed upon the property to take precedence of the prior chattel mortgage, a statutory lien which arises from the mere fact of the keeping of the cattle has such precedence. " The possession of the agistor was rightful, and, the possession being rightful, the keeping gave rise to the lien ; and such keeping was as much for the interest of the mortgagee as the mortgagor. The cattle were kept alive thereby ; and the principle seems to be, that where the mortgagee does not take the possession, but leaves it with the mortgagor, he thereby assents to the creation of a statutory lien for any expenditure reasonably necessary for the preservation or ordinary repair of the thing mortgaged. Such indebtedness really inures to his benefit. The entire value of his mortgage may rest upon the creation of such indebtedness and lien, as in the case at bar, where the thing mortgaged is live-stock, and the lien for food. And while it seems essential that this should be the rule, to protect the mechanic or other person given by statute a lien upon chattels for labor or material, the rule, on the other hand, will seldom work any substantial wrong to the mortgagee. The amount due under such liens is generally small, a mere trifle compared with the value of the thing upon which the lien is claimed. The work or material enhances or continues the value of that upon which the work is done, or to which the material is furnished ; and the mortgagee can always protect himself against such liens, or, at least, any accumulation of debt thereon, by taking possession of the chattel mortgaged." [2]

---

[1] Case v. Allen, 21 Kans. 217, 220; Smith v. Stevens (Minn.), 31 N. W. Rep. 54. In this case Berry, J., said: " A mortgagee, when he takes a mortgage, takes it, in legal contemplation, with full knowledge and subject to the right of a person keeping it, at the request of the mortgagor or other lawful possessor, to the statutory lien, as he would do to a common law lien." See Colquitt v. Kirkman, 47 Ga. 555.

[2] Case v. Allen, supra, per Brewer, J.

693. A lien given by statute to the keeper of a stallion on the offspring is held to be superior to the right of a subsequent mortgagee to whom the mare is conveyed while in foal, though the mortgage is registered before the foal is dropped. The statute is regarded as giving the lien from the time of the performance of the service, to be enforced at any time after the birth of the colt.[1] As in the case of the analogous liens of landlords for rent and mechanics for work and materials, all persons must take notice of the lien at their peril.

694. The possession of animals by a stable-keeper or agistor entitled to a lien for keeping them, is constructive notice to a purchaser of the right to the lien.[2] He is not estopped from claiming a lien because he has not given notice of it previous to the purchase, or previous to payment by the purchaser, unless the stable-keeper or agistor has done something to mislead the purchaser into making the purchase, or has done something to lead the purchaser to suppose that no lien is claimed.

695. A subsequent mortgage made by the owner while in temporary possession has priority. Where a livery-stable keeper received a span of horses to feed and care for, but the owner was allowed to retain possession of the horses and use them daily, and while in possession he mortgaged them to secure a debt, it was held that the claim of the mortgagee was superior to that of the livery-stable keeper.[3] Continuance of possession is indispensable to the existence of a lien at common law, and the abandonment of the custody of the property, over which the right extends, divests the lien. The lien-holder in such case is deemed to surrender the security he has upon the property, and to rely on the personal responsibility of the owner. If, however, a sale of the property be made by the owner while it is in the possession of the person holding it under the lien, the lien will not divest it. The purchaser in that case takes it subject to the incumbrance.[4]

---

[1] Sims v. Bradford, 12 Lea (Tenn.), 434 ; Burr v. Graves, 4 Ib. 552, 557.

[2] Lessells v. Farnsworth, 3 How. (N. Y.) Pr. N. S. 73 ; S. C. Ib. 364.

[3] Marseilles Manufacturing Co. v. Morgan, 12 Neb. 66.

[4] Marseilles Manufacturing Co. v. Morgan, supra, per Maxwell, C. J.

696. A lien for the keeping of a horse, created by agreement, will not hold against a mortgage subsequently executed and recorded, if the owner is afterwards permitted to use the horse at his pleasure. By the mortgage a good title to the property is given subject to the lien of the livery-stable keeper. If afterwards, the horse is repeatedly, with the consent of the livery-stable keeper, suffered to be taken by the mortgagor into his possession, to be used by him at his pleasure in carrying on the particular business in which he is engaged, this, as against the mortgagee, is such a relinquishment of possession as extinguishes and discharges the previously existing lien. The mortgage then becomes prior in right, and the incumbrance created by it continues without interruption, disturbance, or discharge from and after the time when this lien was lost; and the mortgagee thereby acquires a paramount right and title to the property.[1]

697. If the owner of a horse upon which there is a lien for board be allowed to use it in his business, and while it is away from the stable sells it without the knowledge of the stable-keeper, the lien is lost, and the stable-keeper cannot regain it by taking the horse from the possession of the purchaser.[2] The lien is created by statute. "But it gives no intimation that it uses the word ' lien ' in any different sense from that which is known to the common law. On the contrary, it in terms supposes that the animals in question have been placed in the care, that is to say, in the possession, of the party to whom the lien is given. The provisions for sale would seem to imply the same thing. To admit that it was intended to create a tacit hypothecation like that enforced from necessity, but within narrow limits, in the admiralty, would be to go in the face of the whole policy of our statutes, which always strive to secure public registration when possession is not given and retained, and which expressly provide for such registration when they in terms create a lien not depending on possession. It follows from what we have said, that, even if the defendant had had a lien for the keeping of the horse after the sale, or whatever might be the rule when the animal was voluntarily restored to his possession, he lost it

[1] Perkins *v.* Boardman, 14 Gray (Mass.), 481, 483.

[2] Vinal *v.* Spofford, 139 Mass. 126, 130.

by allowing the plaintiff to take possession, and could not revive his right by seizing the horse." [1]

III. *Waiver of the Lien.*

698. A livery-stable keeper does not necessarily lose his lien by delivering a horse to the owner for use by him. Thus, if horses belonging to a mail contractor are used by him regularly in his business, the stable-keeper does not lose his right to a lien for previous charges every time he allows the horses to be taken away from his stable. It is a necessary part of the contract in such a case that the horses should be delivered to the owner as they are needed, and this course of business is consistent with the right of lien that belongs to the stable-keeper, and does not impair that lien.[2]

A livery-stable keeper does not lose his lien upon a horse for board by permitting the owner to ride the horse occasionally; and his lien is superior to the lien of an execution levied upon the horse while temporarily in the owner's possession.[3]

699. The lien is waived or lost by allowing the owner to take and keep possession longer than for a temporary daily use. The owner of a horse had been in the habit of taking it from the stable where it was boarded, and using it each day in his business, and returning it to the stable at night. On one occasion he did not return the horse as usual, and the stable-keeper some three weeks afterwards, finding it in the owner's possession, took possession of it under a claim of lien, and left it in charge of an agent at a stable where the owner kept it. The agent on the following day left the horse, and went with the owner to see the stable-keeper who claimed the lien. The owner then made an offer of settlement, which was refused, and then promised to return the horse next day, but did not. It was held that there had been a waiver of the lien.[4]

---

[1] Vinal *v.* Spofford, 139 Mass. 126, per Holmes, J.

[2] Young *v.* Kimball, 23 Pa. St. 193.

[3] Caldwell *v.* Tutt, 10 Lea (Tenn.), 258, 260. Per Freeman, J.: "Neither party thought of terminating the contract, or of the one taking and the other yielding possession, so as to give an individual credit alone for the board, and release thereby the lien of the livery man."

[4] Papineau *v.* Wentworth, 136 Mass. 543. And see Estey *v.* Cooke, 12 Nev. 276; Cardinal *v.* Edwards, 5 Nev. 36.

700. Acts of ownership by lien-holder. — The owner of a mare placed her in the possession of a stable-keeper under an agreement that the latter should train her for the track, and should run her from time to time, and should divide the track-money and premiums with the owner. The mare was placed upon the track, but the owner received no share of the gains, if any were obtained. Subsequently the owner borrowed a sum of money of a third person, and gave a bill of sale of the mare as security. On the owner's failure to pay the loan it was paid by the stable-keeper, and the bill of sale was transferred to him. Afterwards the stable-keeper, continuing in possession of the mare, caused her to be gotten with foal, and later again placed her upon the track. The owner then went to the stable and took the mare away. The stable-keeper brought an action of replevin to recover the mare on the ground that he had a lien upon her for her keeping. It was held that he was entitled to recover, inasmuch as he had such a lien, as well as a lien for the money advanced upon the assignment of the bill of sale.[1] The action of the stable-keeper in apparently assuming absolute ownership of the mare, by keeping all the premiums and causing the mare to be gotten with foal, was held not to destroy any lien which he had for her keeping.

701. If one having a lien includes a claim to which the lien does not attach, he waives his lien. Thus, where a stable-keeper, who had boarded a horse which had been mortgaged, gave notice to the mortgagee of his claim of a lien upon the horse, and afterwards rendered a bill for the board of the horse both before and after the notice, and demanded payment of this as a condition of surrendering possession of the horse, it was held that he rendered himself liable for a conversion of the horse, and that the mortgagee could maintain a suit for the conversion without a tender of the amount due for keeping the horse after notice for which a valid lien might have existed.[2] "Had the stable-keeper claimed distinct liens for distinct debts for what accrued before and what accrued after the notice to the mortgagee, it may be that he would not thereby have waived a valid lien for one of the debts only, without the refusal of a tender of that alone; but the demand for the whole as one debt, and the refusal to de-

---

[1] Hartman *v.* Keown, 101 Pa. St. 338.   [2] Hamilton *v.* McLaughlin, 12 N. East. Rep. 424.

liver the property unless the whole was paid, was a refusal to deliver the property upon the payment of the amount which had accrued after the notice, or to accept a tender of that, and rendered a tender of it unnecessary." [1]

[1] Hamilton *v.* McLaughlin, 12 N. East. Rep. 424, per W. Allen, J.

CHAPTER XIV.

I. Statutory provisions, 702–719. | II. Interpretation and construction, 720–730.

I. *Statutory Provisions.*

702. At common law, laborers engaged in cutting, hauling, and driving timber had no lien thereon.[1] It is indispensable to the continuance of such a lien that it should be accompanied by possession. The moment that possession is voluntarily surrendered, the lien is gone. A laborer cutting, hauling, and driving logs could retain possession only by placing them upon his own land, or upon the land of another under agreement that such other should hold possession for him. Practically the laborer cannot retain possession. If he parts with the possession he can have a lien only by statute or by special contract. If it be agreed between the parties that the laborer or contractor shall cut timber and deliver it upon the owner's premises, and it be further stipulated that the laborer or contractor shall have a lien upon the logs until he is paid, he may resume possession and assert his lien. The owner, having made such an agreement and having failed to make payment, is not allowed to come into court and say that the claimant has parted with possession and thereby relinquished his lien.[2]

Moreover, a laborer who does work for a contractor can have no lien at common law, even if the contractor has such a lien; for if any one has possession it is the contractor. The possession of the laborer is the possession of the contractor, with whom alone the owner deals, and to whom alone he gives possession of the property.[3] A lien cannot be acquired through a possession unlawfully obtained; and therefore a contractor cannot give his

---

[1] Oakes *v.* Moore, 24 Me. 214; Oliver *v.* Woodman, 66 Me. 54, 56, per Virgin, J.; Arians *v.* Brickley, 65 Wis. 26, per Orton, J.

[2] Oakes *v.* Moore, *supra.*

[3] Wright *v.* Terry (Fla.), 2 So. Rep. 6.

laborers a lien through possession, for he alone is entitled to possession as against the owner.[1]

703. Lien at common law where possession is retained. — One who has cut and hauled to his mill a quantity of timber from the land of another, under a contract with him, has a lien at common law for his labor upon the lumber in his possession remaining manufactured from the timber, and also upon the logs unsawed.[2] In like manner one who saws the logs of another into lumber and shingles has a common law lien thereon for the value of such work.[3]

704. In states in which lumbering is an important industry, liens are generally given by statute to those engaged in the work. In some states the laborers alone are protected, and in others contractors as well as laborers are within the protection of the statute. The most characteristic feature of these statutes is that they generally make this lien paramount to all other liens or claims against the property, on the ground, doubtless, that the labor of the lumberman in cutting, hauling, or driving logs greatly increases their value for the benefit of áll persons who may have an interest in the property, whether such persons be claimants under other liens or under mortgages executed and recorded before the lumberman's lien attaches.

705. Arizona Territory.[4] — All persons who shall perform work or labor upon any tract or tracts of land by cutting and cording the timber or wood growing or being thereon, pursuant to a contract therefor with the person or persons owning such tracts of land, or in possession of the same under a *bonâ fide* claim or title thereto, shall have and may each respectively claim and hold a lien upon the wood or timber so cut and corded, for the amount in value of the work or labor so performed, by retaining possession of the same until the whole amount due for such work or labor shall have been paid : provided, that any lien claimed and held as aforesaid shall be deemed to be waived unless an action be brought in some court of competent jurisdiction, for the recovery of the amount for which such lien is

---

[1] Wright *v.* Terry (Fla.), 2 So. Rep. 6, per Raney, J.

[2] Palmer *v.* Tucker, 45 Me. 316.

[3] Arians *v.* Brickley, 65 Wis. 26.

[4] Laws 1885, No. 93, § 20.

claimed as security, within thirty days after such wood or timber shall have been taken in possession by the claimant; and the fact that such lien is claimed shall be set out in the complaint, together with the description of and the number of cords of wood or timber retained in possession of the claimant. If the judgment be for the plaintiff in such action, the execution shall direct the same, with costs, to be satisfied out of the wood or timber so retained, if the same shall be sufficient; if not, then the balance to be satisfied out of any other property of the defendant not exempt from execution in the manner provided by law. Justices of the peace have jurisdiction of all actions under these provisions, when the amount claimed does not exceed three hundred dollars.

706. California.[1] — A person who labors at cutting, hauling, rafting, or driving logs or lumber, or who performs any labor in or about a logging camp necessary for the getting out or transportation of logs or lumber, shall have a lien thereon for the amount due for his personal services, which shall take precedence of all other claims, to continue for thirty days after the logs or lumber arrive at the place of destination, for sale or manufacture, except as hereinafter provided.

The lien hereby created shall cease and determine unless the claimant thereof shall, within twenty days from the time such labor shall have been completed, file and record in the office of the county recorder of the county where such labor was performed a verified claim, containing a statement, — 1. Of his demand, after deducting all just credits and offsets; 2. The time within which such labor was done; 3. The name of the person or persons for whom the same was done; 4. The place where the logs or timber upon which such lien is claimed are believed to be situated, and the marks upon the same; 5. The reputed owner thereof; and, 6. The reputed owner of the land from which the same were cut and hauled.

All liens hereby provided for shall cease and determine unless suit to foreclose the same shall be commenced in the proper court within twenty-five days from the time the same are filed.[2]

---

[1] 2 Codes and Stats. 1885; § 1183 of Code Civ. Proced. amended in Stats. 1887, ch. 42, by providing for the consolidation of separate actions.

This statute does not apply to contracts entered into before its passage. Shuffleton v. Hill, 62 Cal. 483.

[2] The complaint must allege that

The plaintiff in any such suit, at the time of issuing the summons, or at any time afterward, may have the logs or timber upon which such lien subsists attached, as further security for payment of any judgment he may recover, unless defendant give him good and sufficient security to pay such judgment, in which event such logs shall be forthwith discharged by the sheriff from such attachment, and from the lien hereby created.

The clerk of the court must issue the writ of attachment upon receiving an affidavit by or on behalf of the plaintiff, showing: 1. That the defendant is indebted to the plaintiff upon a demand for labor, for which his claim has been duly filed in accordance with section two of this act; 2. That the sum for which the attachment is asked is an actual *bonâ fide* existing debt, due and owing from the defendant to the plaintiff, and that the attachment is not sought, and the action is not prosecuted, to hinder, delay, or defraud any creditor or creditors of the defendant.

The writ must be directed to the sheriff of the county, and must require him to attach and safely keep the logs and timber specified in such lien, or so much thereof as may be sufficient to satisfy plaintiff's demand, unless the defendant give good and sufficient security, as provided in this act, in which case to take such security and discharge any attachment he may have made, and to deliver up such logs to the defendant, who shall receive the same free from the lien upon which such suit is brought.

707. Florida.[1] — Laborers and contractors, contracting and engaging to cut, raft, or sell logs or timber of any kind, or to perform any labor in connection with the sale and delivery of any such logs or timber, shall have a first lien on such logs or timber, or any lumber, boards, staves, laths, or shingles manufactured therefrom, until the compensation for services shall be fully paid and satisfied to the amount agreed upon by the contracting parties, unless a contrary stipulation be entered into at the time the contract is made or work done, which lien shall be enforced in like manner as the lien provided for builders, mechanics, material-men, and laborers.[2]

something was due from the defendants to the original contractor when the lien of the plaintiff was filed, or that the defendant was notified or had knowledge of the claim of the plaintiff prior to the payment in full of the amount due to the original contractor under the contract. Wilson v. Barnard, 67 Cal. 422.

[1] Dig. of Laws 1881, ch. 143, § 39.

[2] Only laborers with whom the owner contracts can have the benefit

708. Georgia.[1] — All persons furnishing sawmills with timber, logs, provisions, or any other thing necessary to carry on the work of sawmills, shall have liens on said mills and their products, which shall, as between themselves, rank according to date.

709. Idaho Territory.[2] — When any person or persons make an express contract in writing with the owner or owners of any tract or tracts of land, or with the person or persons who were at the time of such contract in the actual *bonâ fide* possession of such tract or tracts of land, by himself or themselves, or tenant or tenants, to cut and cord the timber growing or being thereon, or any portion thereof, or for the purchase of said timber, or any portion thereof, to be paid for when the same shall be cut and corded, and shall go on and complete such contract, he or they shall have a lien on such wood so. cut and corded for the amount contracted to be paid, and may hold, take, and retain possession of such wood until such contract price shall be paid; and if not paid within one month after the contract shall be completed, or work done, or purchase made, as aforesaid, then all the provisions respecting the mode of securing and enforcing mechanics' liens shall apply thereto; and any person or persons cutting cordwood, saw-logs, or other timber upon any of the public lands for another, may have a lien upon such cordwood, saw-logs, or other timber so cut for the amount due for cutting the same, and may retain possession thereof until the amount due shall be paid, and, if not paid within a month, may file and enforce their lien in accordance with the aforesaid provisions; and any person hauling or handling any such cordwood, saw-logs, or timber may likewise hold the same, and file and enforce a lien thereon in accordance with such provisions.

of this lien. Wright *v.* Terry (Fla.), 2 So. Rep. 6.

¹ Code 1882, § 1985.

Under this statute, one furnishing money for carrying on the business has no lien. The lien is derogatory to common rights, and gives an immediate and harsh remedy, and therefore should be strictly construed. While money is necessary to carry on the work of a sawmill, by buying the things necessary for that work, still it is not primarily the thing necessary.

It buys from others what is used to carry it on. Those who actually furnish the timber, or provisions, or other things necessary, have the lien; the money-lender does not. Dart *v.* Mayhew, 60 Ga. 104; and see Saulsbury *v.* Eason, 47 Ga. 617.

A sale made on the foreclosure of a lien for logs furnished a sawmill, where there was a prior mortgage, conveyed only the equity of redemption subject to the mortgage. Townsend Savings Bank *v.* Epping, 3 Woods, 390.

² R. L. 1875, p. 615, § 11.

710. Maine.[1] — Whoever labors at cutting, hauling, rafting, or driving logs or lumber, or at cooking for persons engaged in such labor, has a lien thereon for the amount due for his personal services, and for the services performed by his team,[2] which takes precedence of all other claims except liens reserved to the state;[3] continues for sixty days after the logs or lumber arrive at the place of destination for sale or manufacture,[4] and may be enforced by attachment.[5] In such actions the court has the same power to allow and apportion costs as in equity.

The officer making such attachment may pay the boomage thereon, not exceeding the rate per thousand on the quantity actually attached by him, and return the amount paid on the writ, which shall be included in the damages recovered. The action or lien is not defeated by taking a note, unless it is taken in discharge of the amount due and of the lien. Such notice of the suit as the court orders, shall be given to the owner of the logs or lumber, and he may be admitted to defend it.[6]

---

[1] R. S. 1883, ch. 91, §§ 38, 39.

[2] A lien given by a former statute for " personal services " was held not to include services rendered by the laborer's team. Coburn v. Kerswell, 35 Me. 126. Under the present statute, giving a lien not only for his " personal services," but for " the services performed by his team," it is held that the laborer is entitled to the earnings of a team rightfully in his possession and control, though he may not own it. Kelley v. Kelley, 77 Me. 135.

[3] This lien takes precedence of a prior mortgage. Oliver v. Woodman, 66 Me. 54. The rule is the same under analogous statutes, — statutes, for instance, giving liens upon vessels. Deering v. Lord, 45 Me. 293; Perkins v. Pike, 42 Me. 141; Donnell v. The Starlight, 103 Mass. 227; The Granite State, 1 Sprague, 277, 278.

[4] The sixty days within which attachment must be made do not commence to run, as to any of the logs upon which the lien exists, until all the logs subject to the same lien have arrived at their destination, within the boom: provided the logs have been driven together, and the driving has not been suspended after a portion of them has reached the boom, but has been continuously kept up until all the logs have been driven in. Sheridan v. Ireland, 66 Me. 65.

[5] For provisions for enforcement of liens by attachment, see Chap. XXII., Maine.

[6] Such notice of the suit is imperative and cannot be disregarded. It cannot be dispensed with, though there be an appearance upon the docket of parties claiming to own the logs or lumber; for the court cannot judicially know whether such claimants are the owners, without giving a notice that shall be binding upon the owner, whoever he may be. The notice ordered should be a public notice by posting or publication, as well as a specific notice to the supposed owners. Sheridan v. Ireland, 61 Me. 486; Parks v. Crockett, 61 Me. 489. These cases differ from Bean v. Soper, 56 Me. 297, inasmuch as it appears in that

It is also provided[1] that whoever labors at cutting, peeling, or yarding hemlock bark, or cutting cordwood, or at cooking for persons engaged in such labor, has a lien thereon for his personal services, and the services performed by his team, which takes precedence of all other claims, continues for thirty days after the contract is completed, and may be enforced by attachment: provided, such lien shall not continue after the bark or wood has arrived at a market.

711. Maine (*continued*). **Enforcement of the lien.**[2] — Under this statute, one who contracts with the owner of the logs has a claim against him *in personam*, and a claim *in rem* against the logs. The proceeding by attachment operates in both ways so far as the contractor is concerned. But a sub-contractor, or a laborer employed by the contractor, has no claim against the owner *in personam*, but only a claim against the property, and his proceedings must be strictly *in rem*. No other property of the owner is liable except that upon which the lien attaches. Therefore a sub-contractor or laborer must obtain a valid judgment *in rem* against the identical logs with reference to which the labor was done.[3] The identity of claim and of property must coexist, and must be traceable till the fruits of the judgment have been obtained by satisfaction of the execution. The

case that the notice required by statute was given. See, also, Redington v. Frye, 43 Me. 578, 587, per Cutting, J. As to the form of proceeding and practice relative thereto, see Parks v. Crockett, 61 Me. 489.

The action, as it comes through a contract, though not a part of it, should be against the employer, whether he be the owner of the logs or not. It should not be against the owner where there is no contract with him. Oliver v. Woodman, 66 Me. 54.

The action does not inure to a trespasser. Spofford v. True, 33 Me. 283; Doe v. Monson, 33 Me. 430 : Hamilton v. Buck, 36 Me. 536.

It is not necessary to allege in the writ the ownership of the logs, or that the owner is unknown. Parker v. Williams, 77 Me. 418.

Where several owners separately

employ the same person to drive their logs, the laborer's lien is not upon the whole mass collectively, but is to be apportioned, *pro rata*, to each. Oliver v. Woodman, *supra;* Hamilton v. Buck, *supra;* Doyle v. True, 36 Me. 542.

But where different owners severally employ sufficient laborers to drive their respective logs, the lien of each laborer is confined to the logs he is employed to drive, although all the logs become intermingled in driving, and are collectively driven by all the laborers. Doe v. Monson, *supra*.

[1] R. S. 1883, ch. 91, § 29; Acts 1885, ch. 280; Acts 1887, ch. 21.

[2] For provisions for enforcing liens, see Chap. XXII., **Maine.**

[3] Bicknell v. Trickey, 34 Me. 273; Reddington v. Frye, *supra*.

identity of the property must be established, else the lien cannot attach; and the labor must be shown to have been done upon the specific property seized. The attachment must be of the thing upon which the lien is claimed, and the lien must be established by a valid judgment.[1] The record of the judgment must show that the logs upon which the labor was expended are the same which the writ commands to be attached, and which were attached. The officer's return of an attachment of logs having similar marks with those described in the plaintiff's writ and declaration, does not sufficiently establish the identity;[2] but such identity is sufficiently established if, in addition, it appears that all the parties interested were summoned and appeared, and admitted the truth of the facts set forth in the declaration, and that the logs described therein were attached.[3] Moreover, a laborer's claim of lien, when the person with whom he contracted is other than the owner, must not be joined in the same suit with a claim for which he has no lien. If a judgment embracing both claims be rendered, the lien claim is regarded as waived or merged. The lien claim and the personal claim should in such case be enforced by separate suits, in each of which the plaintiff may recover costs.[4]

712. Michigan.[5] — Any person who performs any labor or services in cutting, skidding, falling, hauling, scaling, banking, driving, running, rafting, or booming [6] any logs, timber, cedar posts, telegraph poles, railroad ties, tan bark, shingle bolts, or staves in this state, has a lien thereon for the amount due for such labor or services, and the same shall take precedence of all other claims or liens thereon.[7] The word "person" shall be inter-

---

[1] Annis v. Gilmore, 47 Me. 152.

[2] Thompson v. Gilmore, 50 Me. 428.

[3] Bean v. Soper, 56 Me. 297.

[4] Bicknell v. Trickey, 34 Me. 273.

[5] Annot. Stats. 1882, § 8412.

[6] A boom company's lien is acquired if the work is done by its agent, though the agent is paid a gross sum for the job. Hall v. Tittabawassee, 51 Mich. 377.

[7] A boom company has a lien for its services in breaking jams and driving logs whose owners have not put on a sufficient force of laborers to do the work. Hall v. Tittabawassee, *supra.* Where the logs of an individual owner have become intermingled with those in charge of a boom company without his consent, but without the fault of the company, the latter acquires a lien for its services in driving them, which it does not waive by refusing to deliver them to the owner, unless he shall tender not only a reasonable compensation in driving them, but also for separating his logs from the others. Hall v. Tittabawassee, *supra.*

preted to include cooks, blacksmiths, artisans, and all others actually employed in performing such labor and services.

A statement in writing under oath must be filed in the office of the clerk of the county, setting forth the amount due and a description of the property, within thirty days from the completion of the labor or services. The lien is enforced by attachment.[1]

713. **Minnesota.**[2] — Any person who may do or perform any manual labor in cutting, banking, driving, rafting, cribbing, or stowing any logs, railroad cross-ties,[3] or timber, shall have a lien thereon as against the owner thereof, and all other persons except the state, for the amount due for such services, and the same shall take precedence of all other claims thereon ; and any verbal or written agreement, expressed or implied, made by or between any person or persons or chartered company or companies, designed to act as a waiver of any right under this act, or any portion thereof, shall be wholly void. The lien herein created shall not attach as against the claim of the owner or legal occupant of the land upon which logs or timber were cut, in cases of trespass, or when the logs and timber were cut and carried away without the consent of such owner or legal occupant.

A statement under oath by the claimant[4] must be filed in the office of the surveyor-general of the district, setting forth the

---

[1] Annotated Stats. 1882, §§ 8413–8426. The proceedings to enforce the lien must conform strictly to the statute. The affidavit for the attachment is jurisdictional, and if it omits material averments the writ affords no protection to the officer executing it. Woodruff v. Ives, 34 Mich. 320.

The lien is lost if the conditions in regard to the filing of a statement of the lien, and commencing suit to enforce it, within limited periods, are complied with. Haifley v. Haynes, 37 Mich. 535.

See Clark v. Adams, 33 Mich. 159, as to service of notice, and general interpretation of the lien law of 1873.

Under the provision that a proceeding to enforce a lien on logs shall be commenced in the county where the property or any part of it is situated,

the petition is defective if it does not allege that the logs, or some of them, are within the county where the suit is begun. The court cannot take judicial notice that the boom is within the county so as to cure the omission of this averment. The appearance and plea of a claimant is no waiver of the defect, for, the judgment sought being one against the logs, the court must have actual jurisdiction. Pine Saw-Logs v. Sias, 43 Mich. 356.

[2] Stats. 1878, ch. 32, §§ 63–65.

[3] Laws 1885, ch. 86.

[4] If the statement be not made by the claimant, it must be made by some one with authority from him to make it, and the oath should state such authority. Griffin v. Chadbourne, 32 Minn. 126.

date of the commencement and termination of such labor, the amount or balance due, and a description of the logs on which the lien is claimed.

For labor performed between first day of October and first day of April the statement must be filed before the first day of May next thereafter; and for labor performed in any other part of the year the statement must be filed within thirty days after completion of same.

The lien is enforced by an attachment against such logs or lumber. Before the attachment is issued, the claimant must make affidavit that the defendant is indebted in a certain sum (to be stated as near as may be), and that such indebtedness is for labor or services on logs or lumber, and that the claimant has filed a lien thereon.[1]

It is further provided,[2] that this act is intended only for the protection of laborers for hire, and shall not inure to the benefit of any person interested in contracting, cutting, hauling, banking, or driving logs by the thousand.[3]

714. Nevada.[4] — All persons who shall perform work or labor upon any tract or tracts of lands, by cutting or cording the wood or timber growing or being thereon, shall have, and may each respectively claim and hold, a lien upon the wood or timber so cut or corded, for the amount in value of the work or labor so performed, by retaining possession of the same until the whole amount due for such work or labor shall have been paid: provided, that any lien claimed and held, as aforesaid, shall be deemed to be waived, unless an action be brought in some court of competent jurisdiction for the recovery of the amount for which such lien is claimed as security, within sixty days after such wood or timber shall have been taken into possession by the claimant.

Possession of wood or timber within the meaning of this section shall be deemed to be in the person or persons cutting or cording wood or timber, for the purposes of this act, from the

---

[1] The lien can only be enforced by attachment as provided. Griffin *v.* Chadbourne, 32 Minn. 126.

[2] Ch. 32, § 76.

[3] It is held that this provision is intended to distinguish the contractor who employs others to do the work from a laborer who does the work himself, and should be interpreted as if it read that it "shall not inure to the benefit of any person interested in contracting for cutting, hauling," etc. King *v.* Kelly, 25 Minn. 522.

[4] Stats. 1879, ch. 45.

times of cutting or cording the same; and shall not be deemed to have been released or yielded by the person or persons performing the work or labor as herein provided, except such person or persons, by word or act, clearly and distinctly declare or evidence his or their intention to so release or yield possession.

715. New Hampshire.[1] — Any person who, by himself or others, or by teams, shall perform labor or furnish supplies to the amount of fifteen dollars or more toward rafting, driving, cutting, hauling, or drawing wood, bark, lumber, or logs, or at cooking or hauling supplies in aid of such labor, shall have a lien thereon for such labor or supplies, which lien shall take precedence of all prior claims except liens on account of public taxes, to continue ninety days after the services are performed or supplies furnished, and may be secured by attachment.

The officer making such attachment may pay the boomage thereon not exceeding the rate per thousand on the quantity actually attached by him, and return the amount paid on the writ, which shall be included in the damages recovered.

Any person who labors at cutting, hauling, or drawing wood, bark, logs, or lumber, by himself or others, under a contract with an agent, contractor, or sub-contractor of the owner thereof, by giving notice in writing to said owner, or the person having charge of said property, that he shall claim a lien for labor to be performed, shall have the same lien as above provided, to be secured in the same manner.[2]

716. Oregon.[3] — Any laborer in a timber or in any logging camp shall have a lien upon any timber or logs cut or manufactured by him, or in such camp, for the amount due him for labor on or about the same.

Such laborer shall file a copy of his demand, verified by his oath, in the county clerk's office, within thirty days of his ceasing work on such timber or in such camp, or, in lieu of such filing, such laborer or laborers may take and hold possession of such timber or logs, subject to the payment of their demand: provided, however, that if such timber or logs should be sold at

---

[1] G. L. 1878, ch. 139, §§ 13, 14, 16, as amended in Session Laws 1879, p. 370, § 25.

[2] This last section was added after the decision in Jacobs v. Knapp, 50 N. H. 71.

[3] Laws 1882, p. 53, §§ 1, 2.

any time while such laborers are still at work, they may take possession of such logs and hold the same as aforesaid at any time before said logs are delivered at the mill where they are to be manufactured into lumber.

717. Vermont.[1] — A person cutting or drawing logs shall have a lien thereon for his wages, which shall take precedence of other claims except public taxes, and shall continue sixty days after the services are performed. But such lien shall not attach until the person claiming it files in the town clerk's office of the town where he performed the services, or, if the town is not organized, in the county clerk's office, a brief statement of the contract under which he claims a lien, and his purpose to enforce it against the property for the amount due for such service.

Such lien shall have no validity against a subsequent purchaser unless a suit is brought and the logs attached thereon within thirty days from the time the plaintiff's right of action accrues against the person for whom he performed the service, and shall be vacated as to all persons unless a suit is brought and the logs attached thereon within sixty days from such time.

Such attachment shall be made by leaving a copy of the process in the town clerk's office of the town where the services were performed and also where the logs are, and, if either town is unorganized, in the county clerk's office.

718. Washington Territory.[2] — Every person performing labor upon or assisting in obtaining or securing saw-logs, spars, piles, and other lumber, shall have a lien upon the same for the work or labor done upon or in obtaining or securing the same, whether such work or labor be done at the instance of the owner of the same or his agent. The cook in a logging camp shall be regarded as a person who assists in obtaining or securing the timber herein mentioned.

Every person performing labor upon or assisting in manufacturing saw-logs into lumber shall have a lien upon such lumber, while the same remains at the mill where manufactured, whether such work or labor be done at the instance of the owner of such logs or his agent.

Any person who shall permit another to go upon his timber

---

[1] R. L. 1880, §§ 1988–1990.
[2] Code 1881, §§ 1941–1956.

land and cut thereon saw-logs spars, piles, and other timber, shall have a lien upon such logs, spars, piles, and timber for the price agreed to be paid for such privilege, or for the price such privilege would be reasonably worth in case there was no express agreement fixing the price.

These liens are preferred liens, and are prior to any other liens, and no sale or transfer of any saw-logs, spars, piles, and other timber, or manufactured lumber, shall divest the lien thereon as herein provided.

The person rendering the service or doing the work or labor named is only entitled to the liens as provided herein for services, work, or labor for the period of eight calendar months, or any part thereof, next preceding the filing of the claim.

The person granting the privilege to another to cut logs upon his land is only entitled to the lien as provided therein for saw-logs, spars, piles, and other timber cut during the eight months next preceding the filing of the claim.

Every person, within thirty days after the close of the rendition of the services, or after the close of the work or labor mentioned in sections three and four of this act, claiming the benefit hereof, must file for record with the county auditor of the county in which such saw-logs, spars, piles, and other timber was cut, or in which such lumber was manufactured, a claim containing a statement of his demand, and the amount thereof, after deducting as near as possible all just credits and offsets, with the name of the person by whom he was employed, with a statement of the terms and conditions of his contract, if any, and in case there is no express contract the claim shall state what such service, work, or labor is reasonably worth; and it shall also contain a description of the property to be charged with the lien, sufficient for identification with reasonable certainty, which claim must be verified by the oath of himself or some other person to the effect that affiant believes the same to be true.[1]

Every person claiming the benefit of the lien for the purchase price of timber must file for record, with the county auditor of the county in which such saw-logs, spars, piles, and other timber was cut, a claim in substance the same as provided in the preceding section, and verified as therein provided.

No lien above provided for binds any saw-logs, spars, piles, or other timber, or any lumber for a longer period than twelve cal-

[1] The form of the claim is given in the statute.

endar months after the claim has been filed, unless a civil action be commenced in a proper court within that time to enforce the same.

The lien is enforced by a civil action. Any number of persons claiming liens may join in the same action.

719. Wisconsin.[1] — Any person who shall do or perform any labor or services in cutting, felling, hauling, running, driving, rafting, booming, cribbing, towing, sawing, or manufacturing into lumber any logs or timber in any of the counties in this state, shall have a lien upon such logs, timber, or lumber for the amount due, or to become due, for such labor or services, which shall take precedence of all other claims or liens thereon.[2]

In certain counties there is a lien for supplies in cutting, felling, and driving logs.[3]

II. *Interpretation and Construction.*

720. Whether this lien be merely for the personal services or manual labor of the claimant, as is the case under

[1] Laws 1885, c. 469, § 1. The statute, though limited to certain counties, is a *general law* within the meaning of the constitution. Collins *v.* Cowan, 52 Wis. 634. As to the effect of forming a new county out of one to which the statute extended, see Shevlin *v.* Whelen, 41 Wis. 88.

As to the mode of enforcing such lien, see Laws 1885, ch. 449, § 2–6. As to the description of the property in the judgment, see Paulsen *v.* Ingersoll, 62 Wis. 312.

A lien is also given for labor in cutting, peeling, or hauling bark. R. S. 1878, § 3341.

As to time within which petition must be filed, see Cuer *v.* Ross, 49 Wis. 652.

[2] A prior statute gave a lien on logs and timber, but not upon lumber. "While the property remains in the form of logs or timber, it can be traced, described, and identified by reference to location and marks; but after it is cut and sawed into lumber, it becomes more portable, more liable to be scat-tered, and more difficult to describe or identify. It also then becomes more peculiarly an article of commerce, and more liable to pass into the hands of innocent purchasers." Babka *v.* Eldred, 47 Wis. 189. See, also, Arians *v.* Brickley, 65 Wis. 26. The word "timber," however, includes railroad ties. These are usually made from the stems of small trees. They are as much timber as squared sticks of timber. Kollock *v.* Parcher, 52 Wis. 393.

[3] Under a statute giving a lien to one furnishing any supplies in such business, one who cooks food for the men at work on the logs directly is entitled to a lien thereon for his wages. Young *v.* French, 35 Wis. 111; Winslow *v.* Urquhart, 39 Wis. 260.

The word "supplies" also includes the board of the men, even when furnished at a hotel in a city several miles from the place where they are at work, if the charges for such board are reasonable for men so engaged. Kollock *v.* Parcher, *supra.*

the statutes of Maine [1] and Vermont,[2] or includes services performed by his servants and teams, as is the case under the statutes of New Hampshire [3] and of Wisconsin,[4] depends much upon the terms of the statutes, though statutes substantially in the same terms have received diverse interpretations in different states. In the latter state the Supreme Court has declared that the words " labor and services " in a statute giving a lien should be construed as broadly as their common use will allow; and without other restrictive words this language would include labor and services performed by servants and agents, as well as personally, just as in the common count in assumpsit, for work and labor done, recovery may be had for work and labor not personally and manually performed by the plaintiff.[5]

721. In some states it is held that a laborer has a· lien upon the logs and lumber benefited by his work, whether such work was performed under a contract with the owner or not; and that, where the labor in such case is not employed by the general owner of the logs, the latter is not required to be made a party to the action to enforce the lien. In Wisconsin it was declared that the owner in such a case is not deprived of his day in court, but that he may bring an action against the officer who has seized the logs at the suit of the lien claimant, and is entitled to show in such action that there was collusion between such lien claimant and his employer, or that the amount adjudged to be due the former, in his action against his employer, was not in fact due him.[6] This view was adhered to in a later decision which affirmed the constitutionality of the statutes declaring such lien.[7]

On the other hand, the authorities generally hold that the lien is limited to the party who contracts with the owner of the property upon which the labor of the contractor and all his sub-contractors or servants is expended, unless the statute expressly or impliedly includes the latter.[8] At common law the

[1] See § 710. The present statute includes the amount due for services performed by the laborer's team.

[2] See § 717.

[3] See § 715, expressly so provided.

[4] Hogan v. Cushing, 49 Wis. 169.

[5] Hogan v. Cushing, *supra.* Per Orton, J.

[6] Munger v. Lenroot, 32 Wis. 541, Dixon, C. J., dissenting, and approving of Jacobs v. Knapp, 50 N. H. 71.

[7] Winslow v. Urquhart, 39 Wis. 260. So in **Michigan** : Reilly v. Stephenson, 29 N. W. Rep. 99.

[8] Jacobs v. Knapp, 50 N. H. 71; Gross v. Eiden, 53 Wis. 543; § 737.

lien belongs to the person with whom the owner contracts for the work or service, and not to the servants or others employed by him. A statute should not be regarded as changing this principle of the common law, unless its terms are such that the intention of the legislature to make such a change seems too apparent to be mistaken; for such a change would be likely to work much confusion by giving to various persons, having no connection with each other and none with the owner of the property, liens upon the whole property for labor expended upon different parts of it under different contracts. To give all the various workmen and servants each an independent lien, without preference, upon the same property, would be inconvenient and practically unjust to the owner. Liens are sometimes given to sub-contractors, but when this is done some special provision is made for avoiding the embarrassment that would arise from giving a right of lien upon the same property to several persons at the same time; and this is usually done by providing that, when the work is done under a contract with the owner, no person shall have the benefit of a lien unless, within a prescribed time, he shall give notice to the owner that he is so employed and will claim the benefit of the lien.[1]

Only laborers with whom the owner of logs or lumber contracts, and not employees of a person contracting with the owner who are not employees of the owner, can claim the benefit of this lien.[2]

722. **The contractor is not in general an agent of the owner to employ men, and bind the owner or his property.** Where one contracted with the owner of logs to drive them to a certain place at a stipulated price, and the owner was to supply provisions and money to a limited amount to pay off men who might be discharged, "all other men to be paid by the owner at the end of the drive," it was held that the contract did not

[1] After the decision in Jacobs v. Knapp, 50 N. H. 71, a section was added to the statute of New Hampshire, giving the lien to persons who perform labor under a contract with an agent or contractor of the owner. Laws 1871, ch. 1; G. L. 1878, ch. 169, § 16.

[2] Wright v. Terry (Fla.), 2 So. Rep. 6. "The lien is given to the laborers or contractors with whom the owner of the logs contracts. If he hires laborers, his laborers have a lien; if his agreement for rafting is with a contractor who is to raft the logs and employ his own help, the contracting parties are the owner and the contractor. The hired help, or employees of the contractor, are not contracting parties with the owner; they are not his laborers." Per Raney, J.

constitute the contractor the owner's agent to employ men, and
that the men employed by the contractor were his own and not
the owner's employees, and that the contract did not give the
employees a lien on the logs for their wages.[1]   The purpose and
legal effect of the provision for the payment of the men " at the
end of the drive " was to authorize the owner to pay them and
charge the amount to the contractor, and thereby protect himself, if he so desired, from any annoyance that might arise from
the contractor's not paying them, but it did not render the owner
liable to such men for their pay.

723. Whether a statute which allows a lien in favor of
one not in privity of contract with the owner of the property
is unconstitutional is a question upon which the cases are not
in entire harmony.   A statute providing for the enforcement of
a laborer's lien, by an action against the person or property of
a party between whom and the plaintiff no privity of contract
ever existed, without making the owner a party, is unconstitutional.[2]   No person can be deprived of his property except by
due process of law, or by the law of the land.   The law of the
land was defined by Mr. Webster, in his argument in the Dartmouth College case, as the law " which hears before it condemns,
which proceeds upon inquiry, and renders judgment only after
trial."   The person whose property is to be affected by a judgment of court must have notice of the proceeding and an opportunity to defend.   A statute which provides for enforcing a lien
against property without giving the owner an opportunity to
come into court and be heard is unconstitutional.[3]

724. The term "personal services" in these statutes has
been judicially considered in several cases.   Under a former
statute in Maine, it was held that the lien given for " personal
services " did not include the services rendered by the laborer's
team, though the present statute expressly includes the services
of his team.[4]   But in New Hampshire, under the present statute,
it is held that the term " personal services " includes not only

---

[1] Wright v. Terry (Fla.), 2 So. Rep.
6, citing Jacobs v. Knapp, 50 N. H.
71; Landry v. Blanchard, 16 La. Ann.
173, a case relating to an artisan's lien;
and Harlan v. Rand, 27 Pa. St. 511,
a case relating to a mechanic's lien.

[2] Jacobs v. Knapp, *supra.*

[3] Quimby v. Hazen, 54 Vt. 132;
Redington v. Frye, 43 Me. 578, 587.
See *contra*, § 721.

[4] Coburn v. Kerswell, 35 Me. 126;
McCrillis v. Wilson, 34 Me. 286.

services accomplished by the laborer's own hands, but those aided by the use of such appliances of his own as are indispensable to the performance of his labor. " We have, therefore," say the court in a recent case,[1] " little hesitation in holding that the personal services of the lumberman include the use and the earnings of his own oxen, chain, cant-hook, and the use of his own team and sled, if these are actually used by him and are essential to the service rendered. We do not, in this case, go so far as to hold, that if the claimant did not labor himself, or if, acting as a common laborer, he loaned the use of his team on the same work, he could successfully claim the benefit of the lien on account of his team."[2]

Under the present statute of Maine, which expressly includes services performed by the laborer's team, it is held that the latter are included, although he may not own the team, provided it is in his rightful possession and control.[3]

725. Under a statute giving a lumberman a lien for " personal services " in cutting and hauling lumber, a contractor has no lien for labor performed by his servants.[4] The object of the statute was to protect the man whose subsistence

[1] Hale v. Brown, 59 N. H. 551, 558, per Foster, J.

[2] The court suggest that possibly this was the real question decided in the two cases cited from Maine.

[3] Kelley v. Kelley, 77 Me. 135, 137. " To hold otherwise would be doing violence to the spirit, if not to the letter, of a statute remedial in its objects, and calculated to make certain the payment for the labor which has actually gone to increase the value of the timber." Per Foster, J.

[4] Hale v. Brown, supra; S. C. 47 Am. Rep. 224, per Foster, J. " Whether a person in the plaintiff's position, a contractor, one who assumes the responsibility of performing a certain piece of work, and employs and superintends others in the performance of it, 'labors,' within the meaning of the statute granting one a lien for his 'personal services,' might be a question of no little difficulty in the absence of any judicial construc-

tion of this or similar statutes. The stock-broker, the clergyman, the student, the farmer, and the wood-chopper, all labor, but in different ways, requiring the exercise of different mental and physical powers. From the original and comprehensive meaning of the word itself, no reason, perhaps, could be suggested why a person who accomplishes a certain amount of work by the exercise of his mental powers, in connection with the physical exertion of others, could not be said to labor. The two classes or kinds of labor are dependent, the one on the other, and without both nothing would be accomplished. But when we study the legislative intention in the enactment of a law granting those who work chiefly through physical means certain privileges, it is possible to see that the term 'labor' is used in a restricted sense, and not in its broad and comprehensive meaning." See, also, Wentroth's App. 82 Pa. St. 649.

depends on the wages earned by his own manual labor, and not the contractor, who does no manual labor himself, but draws his compensation from the profits derived from the employment of others. "Most of the authorities that we have examined," say the court, "support this view of the law, except in cases where, from the wording of the statutes, a different intention clearly appeared. And we are not disposed to question the wisdom of those cases."[1]

Under a similar statute in Vermont which gives a lien to "any person who labors at cutting or drawing logs," it was held that the lien must be enforced by the person who actually cuts and hauls the logs; and that it cannot be enforced by a contractor who employs others to perform the labor. The statute is primarily designed to protect employees against employers.[2]

726. What are logs or lumber. — Under a statute giving a lien on logs or lumber for cutting and hauling, the sawing of logs into sticks four feet long for shingle rift does not destroy the lien.[3] Railroad ties have been considered "logs and timber" under such a statute.[4] A lien upon logs and timber does not include the lumber into which timber is manufactured.[5] Such a lien does not include laths,[6] or shingles.[7]

727. A lumberman's lien has priority of a lien by contract and of a prior mortgage, though previously executed and recorded.[8] It is declared to be the intention of the statute conferring such lien to give to the laborers mentioned an absolute lien, where they are employed to do the work by any one having competent authority, as against everybody, upon the principle

[1] Hale v. Brown, 59 N. H. 551, citing Weymouth v. Sanborn, 43 N. H. 171; Balch v. N. Y. & O. M. R. R. 46 N. Y. 521; Parker v. Bell, 7 Gray, 429; Stryker v. Cassidy, 10 Hun (N. Y.), 18; Wentroth's Appeal, 82 Pa. St. 469; Jones v. Shawham, 4 W. & S. (Pa.) 257; Ericsson v. Brown, 38 Barb. 390; Aikin v. Wasson, 24 N. Y. 482; Sullivan's Appeal, 77 Pa. St. 107; Winder v. Caldwell, 14 How. 434; Hoatz v. Patterson, 5 W. & S. (Pa.) 537, 538.

[2] Quimby v. Hazen, 54 Vt. 132.

[3] Sands v. Sands, 74 Me. 239.

[4] Kolloch v. Parcher, 52 Wis. 393; S. C. 26 Alb. L. J. 402.

[5] Gross v. Eiden, 53 Wis. 543.

[6] Babka v. Eldred, 47 Wis. 189.

[7] Gross v. Eiden, supra. "It is an absurdity to say that the laborer shall have a lien upon logs and timber for work done upon them in manufacturing them into lumber." Per Cole, C. J.

[8] The statutes generally give this lien precedence over all other liens or claims. Oliver v. Woodman, 66 Me. 54.

that their labor enhances the value of the property of every one who has any interest in it. " It was designed to make it like the sailor's lien for wages. The labor of workmen in running and rafting logs is of a very similar nature, and the design of the statute was to give them a like lien. And whosoever makes such contract as the plaintiff made in this case, which contemplates the performance of this kind of labor for the benefit of both the contracting parties, must be held to intend that the lien of the laborers shall attach according to the law, and that his own shall be subject to it, precisely as one taking a bottomry bond or mortgage upon a vessel must be held to contemplate that such vessel will continue subject to the lien for sailors' wages thereafter performed, which will take precedence of his own." [1]

An attachment upon logs or lumber under a general attachment act, though prior in time, is subordinate to an attachment for the enforcement of this lien.[2]

728. **As a general rule, the property upon which the lien is claimed must be identified as the property upon which the labor was done.** To entitle one to claim a lien, it must appear that his services, or those of his team, have been performed upon the logs upon which he seeks to enforce his lien.[3] But these statutes should be liberally construed in the interests of labor. A strict construction as regards the identity of the property would in many instances defeat the lien. Accordingly, the lien of a teamster who has worked with several others in hauling and banking logs which are mixed together, is not limited to the identical logs which he himself hauled and banked, but may be enforced against any portion of the lot of logs upon which he and the others worked.[4]

If the owner has intermingled the logs upon which there is a lien with other logs of the same mark, so that the former cannot be distinguished, an attachment of the whole lot may be made to enforce the lien.[5]

729. **If several owners of logs employ several laborers to**

[1] Paine v. Woodworth, 15 Wis. 298, 304, per Paine, J. And see Paine v. Gill, 13 Wis. 561 ; Kline v. Comstock, 67 Wis. 473 ; Reilly v. Stephenson (Mich.), 29 N. W. Rep. 99.

[2] Halpin v. Hall, 42 Wis. 176.

[3] Kelley v. Kelley, 77 Me. 135 ; Annis v. Gilmore, 47 Me. 152. See, also, § 711.

[4] Jacubeck v. Hewitt, 61 Wis. 96. See, also, Kline v. Comstock, supra.

[5] Parker v. Williams, 77 Me. 418.

drive their logs, the lien of each of the laborers is solely upon the logs he was employed to drive, although the logs of the several owners become intermixed in driving, and are driven collectively by all the laborers employed by all the owners.[1] In like manner, if several owners contract with one person who employs the same drivers, and in the drive all the logs become intermixed, their respective liens are not collectively upon the whole mass of logs, but are distributed upon the logs of each owner according to the amount of the labor bestowed thereon.[2] If, however, logs belonging to the same owner, though cut under different contracts, are, with his consent, mingled together, the liens of the laborers attach to all the logs thus mingled together.[3]

730. **A person who performs services on the same logs for different persons** may enforce the entire lien by one action. The action bears some analogy to a libel *in rem*, and proceedings thereon in admiralty. It is the performance of the labor, and not the contract of employment, or other relation that the employer bears to the logs, that creates the lien. It saves a multiplicity of suits to treat the lien as an entirety capable of being enforced in one action. It gives each employer who may have the same interest in the logs an opportunity of contesting the amount and right of lien, not only under his employment, but also as to the others. It further saves the common property from being consumed by costs in several suits, which seem unnecessary for the protection of any right.[4]

---

[1] Doe *v.* Monson, 33 Me. 430; Marsh *v.* Flint, 27 Me. 475, 478.

[2] Hamilton *v.* Buck, 36 Me. 536;

Oliver *v.* Woodman, 66 Me. 54; Doyle *v.* True, 36 Me. 542.

[3] Spofford *v.* True, 33 Me. 283.

[4] Collins *v.* Cowan, 52 Wis. 634.

508

CHAPTER XV.

I. *At Common Law.*

731. By the common law, a workman who by his skill
and labor has enhanced the value of a chattel has a lien
on it for his reasonable charges, provided the employment be
with the consent, either express or implied, of the owner.[1] And
it is immaterial whether there be an agreement to pay a stipulated price for such skill and labor, or there be only an implied
agreement to pay a reasonable price.[2]

Except as declared by modern statutes, this lien rests upon
immemorial recognition, or, in other words, upon the common
law. It exists in favor of every bailee for hire who takes property in the way of his trade and occupation, and by his labor
and skill imparts additional value to it.[3] A tailor who has made

[1] Cowper *v.* Andrews, Hobart, 39,
41 ; Green *v.* Farmer, 4 Burr. 2214;
Close *v.* Waterhouse, 6 East, 523 ;
Scarfe *v.* Morgan, 4 M. & W. 270,
per Baron Parke.

　Indiana : Hanna *v.* Phelps, 7 Ind.
21 ; East *v.* Ferguson, 59 Ind. 169.

　New York : Morgan *v.* Congdon,
4 N. Y. 552, 553, per Jewett, J.; Mc-
Farland *v.* Wheeler, 26 Wend. 467;
Grinnell *v.* Cook, 3 Hill, 485, 491;
White *v.* Hoyt, 7 Daly, 232 ; Hazard
v. Manning, 8 Hun, 613 ; Myers *v.*
Uptegrove, 3 How. Pr. N. S. 316.

　Pennsylvania : Hensel *v.* Noble,
95 Pa. St. 345 ; Mathias *v.* Sellers, 86
Pa. St. 486 ; M'Intyre *v.* Carver, 2
W. & S. 392 ; Pierce *v.* Sweet, 33
Pa. St. 151.

　Vermont : Cummings *v.* Harris, 3
Vt. 244 ; Burdict *v.* Murray, 3 Vt.
302.

　Wisconsin : Chappell *v.* Cady, 10
Wis. 111 ; Arians *v.* Brickley, 65
Wis. 26.

　Other States : Pinney *v.* Wells, 10
Conn. 104, 105 ; Wilson *v.* Martin, 40
N. H. 88 ; Nevan *v.* Roup, 8 Iowa,
207 ; Oakes *v.* Moore, 24 Me. 214 ;
White *v.* Smith, 44 N. J. L. 105.

[2] Morgan *v.* Congdon, 4 N. Y. 551;
Hanna *v.* Phelps, *supra;* Steinman *v.*
Wilkins, 7 W. & S. (Pa.) 466.

[3] Green *v.* Farmer, 4 Burr. 2214,
2221 ; Bevan *v.* Waters, Moody & M.
235 ; Scarfe *v.* Morgan, 4 M. & W.
270, 283 ; Trust *v.* Pirsson, 1 Hilt.
(N. Y). 292 ; Grinnell *v.* Cook, 3 Hill

a coat out of cloth delivered to him by the owner, is not bound to deliver the coat until he is paid for his labor.[1] Neither is a shoemaker bound to restore a shoe which he has mended ; nor a jeweller a gem which he has set ; nor a wheelwright a wagon which he has repaired ; nor a ship carpenter a ship which he has made seaworthy, until his services are paid for.[2]

732. The lien which the common law gives to every one who bestows labor and expense upon a chattel in the way of his trade or occupation is a particular or specific lien ; or, in other words, it secures the payment of his services in respect to property upon which a lien is claimed.[3] It does not secure a general balance of account, or any debt other than that created by labor upon the specific property detained. In particular trades there may perhaps be general usages which entitle them to claim a general balance for work done in the course of their trades ;[4] or

(N. Y.), 485, 491; Crommelin v. Harlem R. R. Co. 4 Keyes (N. Y.), 90, per Hunt, C. J. ; White v. Smith, 44 N. J. L. 105; Mathias v. Sellers, 86 Pa. St. 486; Oakes v. Moore, 24 Me. 214.

A specific lien for work done arises in favor of a dyer who dyes clothes : Green v. Farmer, 4 Burr. 2214; in favor of a carriage-maker who repairs carriages : Rushforth v. Hadfield, 7 East, 224 ; Pinnock v. Harrison, 3 M. & W. 532; in favor of a wagon-maker who makes a wagon out of materials furnished by another : Gregory v. Stryker, 2 Den. (N. Y.) 628 ; in favor of a carpenter who makes doors out of lumber furnished by another: Curtis v. Jones, How. App. Cas. (N. Y.) 137 ; M'Intyre v. Carver, 2 W. & S. (Pa.) 392 ; in favor of one to whom logs are delivered to be converted into boards or into shingles : Pierce v. Sweet, 33 Pa. St. 151; Comstock v. McCracken, 53 Mich. 123 ; Morgan v. Congdon, 4 N. Y. 552 ; Arians v. Brickley, 65 Wis. 26 ; in favor of a manfacturer of starch: Ruggles v. Walker, 34 Vt. 468 ; in favor of one who manufactures brick in a brick-yard furnished by another: Moore v. Hitchcock, 4 Wend.

(N. Y.) 292; King v. Indian Orchard Canal Co. 11 Cush. (Mass.) 231 ; in favor of a person engaged in rendering lard and barrelling the same: Hanna v. Phelps, 7 Ind. 21 ; in favor of a raftsman on lumber rafted: Farrington v. Meek, 30 Mo. 578 ; in favor of a harness-maker for oiling a harness: Wilson v. Martin, 40 N. H. 88 ; in favor of a farrier for shoeing horses: Lane v. Cotton, 1 Salk. 18; Cummings v. Harris, 3 Vt. 245 ; Lord v. Jones, 24 Me. 439 ; in favor of one who threshes grain : Nevan v. Roup, 8 Iowa, 207; in favor of one who kills and packs hogs : East v. Ferguson, 59 Ind. 169 ; in favor of one who effects an exchange of stocks for bonds: Chappell v. Cady, 10 Wis. 111.

[1] Cowper v. Andrews, Hob. 39, 42; Blake v. Nicholson, 3 M. & S. 167, per Lord Ellenborough, C. J.

[2] Story's Bailments, § 440.

[3] Green v. Farmer, supra; Rushforth v. Hadfield, 6 East, 519, 522 ; Mathias v. Sellers, 86 Pa. St. 486; Moulton v. Greene, 10 R. I. 330 ; Nevan v. Roup, supra.

[4] Rose v. Hart, 8 Taunt. 499; Rushforth v. Hadfield, supra.

tradesmen in particular places may, by resolution or agreement among themselves, acquire a general lien, if such resolution or agreement be brought to the notice of their customers and assented to by them.[1]

But it would seem to be essential, except in the case of a general usage well known, that knowledge of the resolution or agreement for a general lien should be brought home to the customer in such way that there is practically an assent on his part that a general lien may be claimed and asserted against him.

733. To entitle one to a lien for work done upon a chattel, the work must be done at the owner's request, or with his consent. The fact that one has purchased a chattel in good faith from a person claiming to be the owner, gives him no lien upon it for expenditures made in repairs before discovering that the property belonged to another.[2]

The employment must be by the owner whose property is affected by the lien, or by his consent, express or implied. Thus a coachmaker to whom a carriage had been delivered for repairs by the owner's servant, was denied a lien because the carriage had been broken by the negligence of the servant, without the knowledge of the master, and had been taken by the servant to the coachmaker for repairs without the master's orders.[3] And so where one having purchased a machine in an unfinished state contracted with the seller to finish it for a stipulated price, and the latter, without the purchaser's knowledge, employed a mechanic to do the work, it was held that the latter acquired no lien in his own right for the labor done on the machine, as against the owner, although, while the work was in progress, the owner knew that the mechanic was performing the work.[4]

734. But the consent of the owner to a bailment of a chattel for repairs may be implied. Such consent need not be given with such formalities or in such manner as would create a personal liability on the part of the owner to pay the charges. If the property is improved and enhanced in value by the work-

---

[1] Kirkman c. Shawcross, 6 T. R. 14; Weldon v. Gould, 3 Esp. 268.

[2] Clark v. Hale, 34 Conn. 398 ; White v. Smith, 44 N. J. L. 105, per Depue, J.

[3] Hiscox v. Greenwood, 4 Esp. 174.

[4] Hollingsworth v. Dow, 19 Pick. (Mass.) 228. See M'Intyre v. Carver, 2 W. & S. (Pa.) 392, which is hardly consistent.

man's labor, the authority of the owner to have it done on the footing of a workman's lien may be implied from the relation of the parties, or from the circumstances of the case.[1]   Accordingly, where a wagon owned by a wife was put in the husband's charge for use in a business which was carried on for the support of the family, and he took it to a wheelwright to be repaired, it was held that the latter had a lien upon it for his reasonable charges for the repairs, though the wheelwright, thinking that it belonged to the husband, had charged the bill for repairs to him.[2] " It was in the contemplation of all the parties," said Mr. Justice Depue, delivering the judgment of the court, " that the wagon could be made useful for the purpose for which it was designed to be used only by being kept in repair. The repairs were beneficial to the interests of both parties, — to the husband in fitting the wagon for use ; to the wife in enhancing the value of the property by the repairs put upon it. I think it clear that the husband had authority from the wife — implied from the manner in which she permitted the wagon to be used — to have the repairs done ; and if so, the property became by law subject to a lien for the workman's charges."

735. **Such consent may be inferred when the owner of property by his neglect gives some one else the right to incur labor and expense upon his property.**   A canal-boat loaded with stone was accidentally sunk in the harbor of Buffalo, and then deserted by her master and crew, who made no effort to raise the boat, and the wreck formed a serious obstruction and hindrance to commerce and navigation.   The common council of the city, in pursuance of the powers conferred by the charter, ordered the boat and cargo to be removed without delay, and decided that, if the owner did not do this in three days, the harbor master should remove the same at the expense of the boat and cargo.   In accordance with such order the harbor master caused the boat to be raised and the cargo saved, at a large expense.   It was held that the city acquired a lien at common law upon the boat and cargo for the amount of such expense, and that this lien could be enforced in equity.[3]   The very act of the

---

[1] White v. Smith, 44 N. J. L. 105, 110, per Depue, J.

[2] White v. Smith, *supra.*

[3] City of Buffalo v. Yattan, Shel-

don (N. Y.), 483, 487, per Smith, J. " The common law right of lien, in respect to personal property, in many cases, rests upon the duty of the party

owner in reclaiming the property in its improved condition was regarded as a recognition of the city's right to indemnity, and consequently to a lien for its expenses in saving the property.

736. A city or town or its agents may acquire a lien at common law for expenses incurred upon property under statutory authority in the removal of nuisances, or in the preservation of the public health. Thus, under a regulation of the board of health of the city of Boston, made in pursuance of

upon whom it is conferred to render services or incur expenses. Thus, the legal obligation to exercise one's trade when requested, as in the case of an innkeeper to receive a guest, has vested in him a lien upon the goods intrusted to him, or those which the guest carries with him, for the particular service rendered or entertainment and necessaries supplied. Says Justice Bronson, in Grinnell *v.* Cook, 3 Hill, 491, 'The right of lien has always been admitted where the party was bound by law to receive the goods.' So where goods have been taken under a legal right, and expenses have been necessarily incurred in their preservation, as in the case of the lord of a manor who had seized a horse as an estray. Henry *v.* Walsh, 2 Salk. 686. The right of lien has always been favored by courts, as consonant with every principle of equity and justice. Within a recent period, indeed, they have recognized and allowed, without restriction, the right of every bailee, whether voluntary or involuntary, to a lien on the goods bailed to hire, when he has conferred an additional value on the chattel, either directly by the exercise of personal labor or skill, or indirectly by the performance of any duty or the use of any means within his control. Upon these principles, I think it safe and just to establish and enforce the lien claimed by the plaintiff in this case. In the discharge of a duty which it could neither evade nor ne-

glect, it has become the involuntary bailee of the boat, and has thus incurred large expenses. The plaintiff performed this duty, as it was bound to, in such manner as to preserve, protect, and save the boat, rather than to suffer it to be destroyed or injured. It is now of more than sufficient value to yield indemnity for these expenses. The plaintiff waited ample time for the owner of the boat to remove and save his property, before taking any action for that purpose. He does not even now claim the boat, or set up any right to have her restored to him. He rests simply upon a denial of the plaintiff's claim. If he has, indeed, abandoned the property, and intends never to reclaim it, no injury can result to him by the adjudication which equity will give the plaintiff. If, on the other hand, he asserts a right to have the property returned to him, he ought to pay the necessary expenses incurred in saving and protecting his property. The very act of reclaiming the property, which he once abandoned for, at least, so long as to require the plaintiff to act, and receiving it in its improved and more valuable condition, would be an implied recognition of the plaintiff's right to indemnity. If this be not so, then the defendants have not only the right to recover the property, but to demand of the plaintiff damages for its detention. The law will permit no such injustice."

513

statutory authority, ordering rags imported into the city to be disinfected at the expense of the owner, it was in a recent case held that a lien arises for such expense ; and that the work of disinfection may be delegated by the board of health to a third person, who is entitled to claim and enforce a lien upon the rags for his reasonable charges for the work done.[1] Mr. Justice Devens, delivering the judgment of the Supreme Court of Massachusetts in this case, said : " It cannot be important that, in this commonwealth, the creditor has a right of attachment on mesne process.   Such a remedy is very imperfect, as compared with that afforded by a lien, which is a usual and efficient remedy where work is done upon a chattel by a bailee, to whom it is confided under any agreement, either express or implied, with the owner thereof.   Nor is it important that, while expenditures may be made upon real estate under the orders of the board of health, a lien can only exist upon personal property, and thus that this remedy is partial.   There is no reason why a well-recognized remedy as to personal property should not be enforced, because there may be cases coming within the statute affecting real estate to which it would not be applicable.   Even if a lien might exist in favor of the city, if it had done the work through its officers, agents, or servants, and the plaintiffs contend that this was the only mode in which it was authorized to do it, they further argue that no lien can exist in the case at bar ; that there can be none in favor of the city, as it has done no work ; and none in favor of the defendant, as it was an independent contractor with the city, and there was no debt due to such contractor from the plaintiffs as the owners of the goods.   The board of health might certainly delegate the work to an independent contractor ; it was not necessarily to be done by it or its immediate servants, and under its personal supervision ; it was sufficient if it prescribed the method, and this was complied with. The board, in the language of the statute, was to ' cause ' the goods to be purified.   It had a right to make a reasonable contract for the disinfection of the goods ; the duty of paying for the expenses thus incurred was by the statute cast upon the plaintiffs, and their promise to pay therefor is one implied by law. Where a party is subjected to such a duty, this obligation is to be performed, and the law will, of its own force, imply a promise, even against his protestation and express declaration.

---

[1] Train v. Boston Disinfecting Co. 144 Mass. 523, 532.

Such a contract necessarily implies a lien in favor of the contractor into whose hands the goods are taken for disinfection, to secure him for the expenses properly incurred in his work."

737. The lien belongs strictly to the person who has contracted with the owner to do the work. A servant or journeyman or sub-contractor of such person has no lien.[1]

Where a physician rendered services to one member of a firm in consideration of the firm's agreement to repair his sleigh and charge the expense to that partner, the firm's assignee in insolvency has no possessory lien on the sleigh for the work done on it by the firm before the assignment, nor for that done by himself afterwards without the physician's knowledge. There is no privity of contract between the assignee and the physician.[2]

738. A lien is acquired by virtue of the work done, and it is immaterial whether the work be done by the claimant or by his agents. Thus the statutory lien of a boom company for driving logs is acquired by virtue of the work done under the contract of the parties; and it is immaterial that the work is done by the company's agent who is paid a gross sum for the work. It is as competent for the company to employ an agent to do the whole labor for a specified sum, as it is to do it through laborers employed by the day or the month.[3]

An artisan has a lien for work done in the way of his trade by another than himself outside his shop. Thus, when a chronometer was left with a watchmaker in Nova Scotia to be repaired, and the watchmaker, finding that he could not make the repairs, sent it to Boston to be repaired, it was held that the watchmaker had a lien for the charges paid by him for the repairs done in Boston.[4]

739. The lien extends to every portion of the goods delivered under one contract, and attaches to every part for the whole service. Where a quantity of logs were delivered on different days to the owner of a sawmill to be sawed into boards,

---

[1] White v. Smith, 44 N. J. L. 105, per Depue, J.; Quillian v. Central R. R. & Banking Co. 52 Ga. 374.

[2] Morrill v. Merrill, 6 Atl. Rep. 602. See § 721.

[3] Hall v. Tittabawassee Boom Co. 51 Mich. 377. See §§ 724, 725.

[4] Webber v. Cogswell, 2 Canada S. C. 15.

and he sawed a part of them and delivered them to the bailor without receiving payment for the sawing, it was held that the mill-owner had a lien upon the logs remaining in his possession for his account. The sawing was an entire work, and the lien extended to every portion of the logs.[1]

A delivery of a part of the articles received under one contract, does not defeat the lien upon the remainder for the entire contract price.[2]

740. Where an entire contract is made for making or repairing several articles for a gross sum, the mechanic or tradesman has a lien on any one or more of the articles in his possession, not only for their proportionate part of the sum agreed upon for making or repairing the whole, but for such amount as he may be entitled to for labor bestowed upon all the articles embraced in the contract.[3] Thus a tailor employed to make a suit of clothes has a lien for the whole and upon any part of the suit in his possession.[4] Thus also, under a special contract between the owner of a wagon and a blacksmith that the latter should re-tire two wheels for three dollars, the former left one wheel, and after the tire was set, came and demanded that wheel upon a tender of half that sum, saying that he would not have the other wheel repaired. The blacksmith, however, had cut, bent, and welded the iron for the other wheel, and therefore refused to deliver the wheel that had been repaired. It was held that he had a right to retain that wheel for the work done upon both wheels under the contract.[5]

741. The fact that the chattels are delivered to a workman in different parcels, and at different times, does not interfere with his right to detain any part of them for the payment of the amount due upon all of them, provided all the work be done under one bargain.[6] Where a lien was claimed on carriages repaired, not only for the work done on those carriages but also upon other carriages, it was held that the carriages

[1] Morgan v. Congdon, 4 N. Y. 551.
[2] See § 320. Steinman v. Wilkins, 7 W. & S. (Pa.) 466; Myers v. Uptegrove, 3 How. (N. Y.) Pr. N. S. 316.
[3] Partridge v. Dartmouth College,

5 N. H. 286; McFarland v. Wheeler, 26 Wend. (N. Y.) 467.
[4] Blake v. Nicholson, 3 M. & S. 167, per Lord Ellenborough, C. J.
[5] Hensel v. Noble, 95 Pa. St. 345.
[6] Chase v. Westmore, 5 M. & S. 180; Myers v. Uptegrove, *supra*.

might be reclaimed upon payment of the charges for the repairs done upon the specific carriages, in the absence of any proof that the other carriages were a part of an entire lot delivered at the same time, or at different times under one arrangement.[1]

If wheat be sent to a miller at different times to be ground, but it is all sent under one contract, he may detain the whole until he has received the price for grinding it.[2]

742. It is an essential element of an artisan's lien at common law, that he has conferred additional value upon the chattel, either directly by his own labor or skill, or indirectly by the use of some instrument or means within his control.[3] If additional value has not been conferred upon the chattel there is no lien, though labor and skill may have been expended upon it. An agistor, or one who takes charge of horses or cattle, has no lien for keeping and feeding them, because he does not confer any additional value on the animal by taking charge of it and feeding it.[4] But on the other hand one has a lien on a mare covered by his stallion, because the mare is made more valuable by being in foal.[5]

743. A printer has no lien upon type set up by him and used for printing, for no additional value is imparted to the type by the use of it. On the contrary the inference might well be that, by setting the type and printing from it, its value would be diminished.[6] Neither has a printer any lien upon stereotype plates which have been furnished him to print from.[7] But the printer has a lien upon a book printed from the type or plate, for the book is the thing produced by his labor and skill. In the case of the book, the paper and other materials used in its

---

[1] Moulton v. Greene, 10 R. I. 330.

[2] Chase v. Westmore, 5 M. & S. 180.

[3] Chapman v. Allen, Cro. Car. 271; Wallace v. Woodgate, 1 C. & P. 575; White v. Smith, 44 N. J. L. 105, per Depue, J.

[4] Jackson v. Cummins, 5 M. & W. 342. See § 641.

[5] Scarfe v. Morgan, 4 M. & W. 270.

[6] De Vinne v. Rianhard, 9 Daly (N. Y.), 406; S. C. 11 Weekly Dig. 268.

[7] Bleaden v. Hancock, Mood. & M. 465; S. C. 4 Car. & P. 152. In **Florida** by statute, § **755.**

A publisher may, it is said, under an agreement with an author to receive a share of the profits on a book to be published, have a lien on the copyright for his disbursements. Brook v. Wentworth, 3 Anst. 881. But how can the publisher have a lien upon a copyright unless it has been taken in his name or assigned to him?

manufacture are enhanced in value by the printer's labor and skill.[1] An engraver has a lien on the plates, impressions, and prints in his possession for the work done upon them.[2]

744. Whether this lien takes precedence of a chattel mortgage previously recorded or filed, depends upon the circumstances attending the creation of the lien. It is certain that the mortgagor cannot by contract create any lien which shall have priority over such mortgage.[3] But the mortgagee's authority for the creation of such a lien may be implied, and the implication arises from the mortgagor's being allowed to remain in possession of the chattel, and to use it for profit.[4] Thus, where the subject of a mortgage was a hack let for hire, and it was described as " now in use " at certain stables, and it was stipulated that the mortgagor might retain the possession and use of it, it was regarded as the manifest intention of the parties that the hack should continue to be driven for hire, and should be kept in a proper state of repair for that purpose, not merely for the benefit of the mortgagor, but for that of the mortgagee also, by preserving the value of the security and affording a means of earning wherewithal to pay off the mortgage debt.[5]

But the authority of the mortgagor to create a lien was held not to be implied where one manufacturing engines for certain boats under a contract mortgaged them when they were only partly built, and afterwards proceeded with their construction under a verbal agreement with the mortgagee that he might go on with the work and finish the engines. This agreement did

---

[1] Blake v. Nicholson, 3 M. & S. 167; De Vinne v. Rianhard, 9 Daly (N. Y.), 406, per Daly, J.

[2] Marks v. Lahee, 3 Bing. N. C. 408.

[3] Jones on Chattel Mortgages, § 472; Bissell v. Pearce, 28 N. Y. 252.

[4] Hammond v. Danielson, 126 Mass. 294; Loss v. Fry, 1 City Ct. (N. Y.) 7.

[5] Hammond v. Danielson, supra. " The case is analogous," says Gray, C. J., " to those in which courts of common law, as well as of admiralty, have held, upon general principles, independently of any provision of statute, that liens for repairs made by mechanics upon vessels in their pos-

session take precedence of prior mortgages." Williams v. Allsup, 10 C. B. (N. S.) 417; The Scio, L. R. 1 Adm. & Eccl. 353, 355; The Granite State, 1 Sprague, 277; Donnell v. The Starlight, 103 Mass. 227, 233 ; The St. Joseph, 1 Brown Adm. 202.

It may be stated as a rule that a mortgagor of a vessel who is allowed to remain in possession has an implied authority to create liens for repairs which will take priority of the mortgage. Jones Chattel Mortgages, § 535 ; Beall v. White, 94 U. S. 382; Scott v. Delahunt, 5 Lans. 372; S. C. affirmed, 65 N. Y. 128.

not give the mortgagor himself a lien against the mortgagee for
the work afterwards done upon the engines, nor did it authorize
him to employ any one else to work upon them in such a manner as to create a lien for such work.[1]

745. Possession is essential to the existence of this lien.
If the mechanic delivers the chattel on which he has worked to
the owner his lien is gone, and he has only a right of action
against him for the value of the work done.[2] A blacksmith
ironed a sled and claimed a lien for his services, whereupon the
owner agreed with him that the sled should be his till the charge
should be paid. The owner took and kept possession of the
sled, always recognizing the blacksmith's ownership. A creditor
of the owner afterwards attached the sled and sold it upon
execution. It was held that the blacksmith lost his lien by his
agreement with the owner for a conditional sale, and by delivering the sled to him, and that the sale was invalid as against the
creditors of the latter.[3] If, after having parted with the possession of the chattel, he again come into possession of it without
the consent or agreement of the owner, his lien is not reinstated.[4]
He cannot recover his lien by stopping the goods *in transitu*,
after he has shipped them to the owner at the owner's risk and
on his account.[5]

A tailor does not lose his lien by allowing his customer to try
on the clothes made for him if this be done in the tailor's presence.[6]

746. The possession of an officer of a corporation acting
in its behalf is the possession of the corporation, and he cannot by means of such possession acquire a lien as against the
corporation. Thus, where the secretary of a railroad corporation bought a set of books with his own money and entered in

[1] Globe Works *v.* Wright, 106 Mass. 207.
[2] Stickney *v.* Allen, 10 Gray (Mass.), 352; King *v.* Indian Orchard Canal Co. 11 Cush. (Mass.) 231; Morse *v.* Androscoggin R. R. Co. 39 Me. 285; Nevan *v.* Roup, 8 Iowa, 207; Bailey *v.* Quint, 22 Vt. 474; McDougall *v.* Crapon, 95 N. C. 292; Tucker *v.* Taylor, 53 Ind. 93.
[3] Kitteridge *v.* Freeman, 48 Vt. 62.
[4] Hartley *v.* Hitchcock, 1 Stark. 408; Howes *v.* Ball, 7 B. & C. 481; S. C. 1 Man. & R. 288; Nevan *v.* Roup, *supra*.
[5] Sweet *v.* Pym, 1 East, 4, per Lord Kenyon.
[6] Hughes *v.* Lenny, 5 M. & W. 183, 187, per Parke, B.

them the minutes of the proceedings of the corporation, it was held, that upon going out of office he had no lien on the books either for the purchase money, or for his services as secretary, for his possession of the books was the possession of the company as soon as he began to enter in them the minutes and accounts of the company. By entering the records and accounts of the company in these books, he so mixed his own property with the property of the company that they could not be separated, and, according to the well established principle of law, the whole property thereby became the property of the company.[1]

747. One who is by contract bound to deliver property upon which he has expended labor, before the stipulated time of payment, has no lien. One who contracts to haul and deliver lumber on board cars, at an agreed price to be paid when the lumber is sold in the market and the proceeds are received by the owner, has no lien thereon for his labor. The obligation to deliver the lumber before payment negatives the right to detain until payment.[2] He has waived the lien by his contract, and cannot set it up in violation of his contract. A tanner who contracts to tan hides furnished him by the owner, and to return the leather made from them in a reasonable time, at a price agreed upon for tanning and transportation, payable after delivery, has no right to detain the leather after it is finished and ready for delivery.[3]

A mechanic repaired a wagon under an agreement that he should receive payment in the use of the wagon and the owner's horse for a journey. When the wagon was repaired, the mechanic, not being ready for his journey, allowed the owner to take it away. After some three weeks he was ready for his journey and the owner delivered to him the wagon and a horse, which directly kicked the dash-board off the wagon and broke the shafts. The mechanic gave up his journey and asserted a lien on the wagon. It was held that he had no lien. If any lien ever existed, he lost it by parting with the possession; and, moreover, the agreement of the parties seems to have contemplated payment at a future day, so that the lien was waived from the beginning. Detention of the wagon by the mechanic until he

[1] State v. Goll, 32 N. J. L. 285.   [3] Lee v. Gould, 47 Pa. St. 398.
[2] Stillings v. Gibson, 63 N. H. 1.

should find it convenient to take his journey would seem to have been inconsistent with the understanding of the parties.[1]

748. The mode of payment agreed upon may be inconsistent with a lien, as where a carriage-maker agrees to repair a physician's carriages, and to take payment in medical services.[2]

II. *By Statute.*

749. In most of the states there are statutes giving to mechanics, artisans, and others who bestow labor on personal property, a lien therefor. The purpose of these statutes is in general to extend the common law lien in respect of the persons who can acquire such lien, and to give an effectual remedy for its enforcement, either by sale after notice, or by attachment and sale under execution. In a few states the lien is extended so that it may be availed of within a limited time after the property has been delivered to the owner.[3] But generally these statutes in most respects are merely declaratory of the common law, and must be interpreted in accordance with its principles. Especially is this so as regards the necessity of retaining possession of the property in order to retain a lien upon it.[4] "The lien under the statute is of the same nature that it formerly was, and the same circumstances must combine to create it. There must be a possession of the thing; otherwise there cannot, without a special agreement to that effect, be any lien. The term *lien* as used in the statute means the same it ever did, — the right to hold the thing until the payment of the reasonable charges for making, altering, repairing, or bestowing labor upon it. Possession of the article is essential."[5]

750. Alabama.[6] — Blacksmiths, wood-workmen, and all other mechanics, who contribute their labor and material, or labor or material only, to the production or repairs of any article, implement, machine, or article of any kind, have a lien thereon in the hands of the party for whom such vehicle or implement, ma-

---

[1] Tucker *v.* Taylor, 53 Ind. 93.

[2] Morrell *v.* Merrill (N. H.), 6 Atl. Rep. 602.

[3] As in **Alabama,** § **750** ; **Louisiana,** § **760.**

[4] McDearmid *v.* Foster, 14 Oregon,

417 ; McDougall *v.* Crapon, 95 N. C. 292.

[5] McDearmid *v.* Foster, *supra*, per Thayer, J.

[6] Acts 1884–85, p. 92, No. 26.

chine or article, was made, sold, or repaired, and in the hands
of a purchaser, with notice of such lien, for the value of the
labor and material, or the labor or material, contributed to the
production, manufacture, or repair of the same.

Parties shall be entitled to process of attachment to enforce
their rights, to be issued by the same officers and under the same
conditions as reqired by law in other cases of attachments; and
the affidavit shall set forth all the facts necessary to the creation
of such lien under the section above quoted, and, in addition
thereto, one or the other of the following causes: 1. That the
party for whom such article was made, sold, or repaired is the
owner thereof, and that the price of the article, or for the repair
thereof, or some part of either, is due and unpaid; 2. That the
party for whom such article was made, sold, or repaired has
transferred the article to a purchaser, with notice of such lien,
and that the price of the article, or for the repair thereof, or
some part of either, is due and unpaid.   Such lien shall be enforced only within six months from the time when the account
or claim becomes due.

751. Arizona Territory.[1] — Any artisan or mechanic who
shall make, alter, or repair any article of personal property, at
the request of the owner or legal possessor of such property, shall
have a lien on such property so made, altered, or repaired, for
his just and reasonable charges for his work done and materials
furnished, and may hold and retain possession of the same until
such just and reasonable charges shall be paid; and if not paid
within the space of two months after the work shall be done,
such mechanic, artisan, or laborer may proceed to sell such
property by him so made, altered, or repaired, at public auction,
giving twenty days' public notice of such sale by advertisement
in some newspaper published in the county in which the work
was done, or, if there is no such newspaper, then by posting up
notices of such sale in three of the most public places in the
town or township where such work was done, and the proceeds
of such sale shall be applied first to the discharge of such lien
and the costs and expenses of keeping and selling such property,
and the remainder, if any, shall be paid out to the owner
thereof.

[1] Laws 1885, p. 240, No. 93, § 19.

752. California [1] and Dakota Territory.[2] — Every person who, while lawfully in possession of an article of personal property, renders any service to the owner thereof, by labor or skill, employed for the protection, improvement, safe keeping, or carriage thereof, has a special lien thereon, dependent on possession, for the compensation, if any, which is due to him from the owner for such service.

A person who makes, alters, or repairs any article of personal property, at the request of the owner or legal possessor of the property, has a lien on the same for his reasonable charges for work done and materials furnished, and may retain possession of the same until the charges are paid. If not paid within two months after the work is done, the person may proceed to sell the property at public auction, by giving ten days' public notice of the sale by advertising in some newspaper published in the county in which the work was done; or, if there be no newspaper published in the county, then by posting up notices of the sale in three of the most public places in the town where the work was done, for ten days previous to the sale. The proceeds of the sale must be applied to the discharge of the lien and the cost of keeping and selling the property; the remainder, if any, must be paid over to the owner thereof.

753. Colorado.[3] — Any mechanic or other person who shall make, alter, repair, or bestow labor upon any article of personal property, for the improvement thereof, at the request of the owner of such personal property, or of the materials from which the same is made, shall, in like manner, have a lien upon such articles of personal property for his reasonable charges for the labor performed and materials furnished and used in such making, alteration, repair, or improvement.

754. District of Columbia.[4] — Any mechanic or artisan who shall make, alter, or repair any article of personal property, at the request of the owner, shall have a lien thereon for his just and reasonable charges for his work done and materials furnished, and he may retain the same in his possession until such charges shall be paid; and if not paid at the end of six months

[1] 2 Codes and Stats. 1885, §§ 3051, 3052, of Civ. Code.

[2] 2 Dak. Codes 1883, §§ 1806, 1814, of Civ. Code.

[3] G. S. 1883, § 2120.

[4] Stats. U. S. 1884, ch. 143, § 13.

after the work is done, he may proceed to sell the property at public auction, by giving notice once a week for three consecutive weeks in some daily newspaper published in the District of Columbia; and the proceeds of such sale shall be applied first in the discharge of such lien and the expense of selling such property, and the remainder, if any, shall be paid over to the owner thereof.

755 Florida.[1] — Any person who shall manufacture, alter, or repair any article of value, shall have a lien upon the same for a period of ninety days after the delivery of the same to the purchaser or person having such article or articles altered or repaired, if the same be delivered on credit, with written stipulations for a lien; and such article so delivered shall at any time within said ninety days be subject to attachment to satisfy all claims of the person so delivering the same, upon an affidavit of the facts before a justice of the peace; and after judgment is obtained, the same may be sold according to law to satisfy such judgment.

All persons, of whatsoever trade or craft, performing any labor whatsoever upon and with any machinery, apparatus, fixtures, or any other thing, shall have a lien on such machinery, apparatus, fixtures, or thing for a period of ninety days from the date of failure or refusal of the owners thereof to pay for such labor performed upon and with such machinery, apparatus, fixtures, or thing; and at any time within said ninety days such machinery, apparatus, fixtures, or thing shall be subject to attachment to satisfy the lien hereby created. This section shall be so construed as to give printers and other employees of printing offices and other similar establishments, stores, etc., a lien upon the presses, types, stock, fixtures, etc., of such establishment.

756. Georgia.[2] — All mechanics of every sort, for work done and material furnished in manufacturing personal property, or for repairing personal property, shall have a special lien on the same, which must be asserted by retention of such property, and not otherwise. Said liens shall be lost by the surrender of such personal property to the debtor, and shall be superior to all liens

---

[1] Laws 1885, p. 53, ch. 3611, §§ 4, 5.

For enforcement, see Chap. XXII., Georgia.

[2] Code 1882, §§ 1981, 2100, 2101.

but liens for taxes, and such other liens as the mechanic may have had actual notice of before the work was done or material furnished.

The bailee, for hire of labor and service, is entitled to the possession of the thing bailed, pending the bailment. He has, also, a special lien upon the same for his labor and services, until he parts with possession; and if he delivers up a part, the lien attaches to the remainder in his possession for the entire claim under the same contract.

If the thing bailed for labor and services be destroyed, without fault on the part of the bailee, the loss falls upon the bailor, and the bailee may demand compensation for the labor expended and materials used upon it.

757. Idaho Territory.[1] — Any artisan or mechanic who shall make, alter, or repair any article of personal property, at the request of the owner or legal possessor of such property, shall have a lien on such property, so made, altered, and repaired, for his just and reasonable charges for his work done and material furnished, and may hold and retain possession of the same until such reasonable and just charges be paid; and if not paid within two months after the work shall be done, such mechanic or artisan may proceed to sell the property by him so made, altered, or repaired, at public auction, by giving three weeks' notice of such sale by advertisement in some newspaper published in the county in which the work may be done, or, if there is no such newspaper, then by posting up notices of such sale in three of the most public places in the town where such work was done; and the proceeds of said sale shall be applied, first, to the discharge of such lien and the costs and expenses of keeping and selling such property, and the remainder, if any, shall be paid over to the owner thereof.

758. Indiana.[2] — Whenever any person shall intrust to any

[1] R. L. 1875, p. 616, § 15.

[2] R. S. 1881, § 5304–5309. Under a statute whereby an execution operates as a lien from the time it comes to the officer's hands on the property of the judgment debtor liable to be seized on it, which can only be divested in favor of some other writ in the hands of another officer which shall be first levied upon the property, it is held that, if a wagon which is subject to the lien of an execution on a judgment against the owner be left by the execution debtor with a mechanic for repairs, the latter takes the same subject to such lien and to the right of the officer to levy

mechanic or tradesman materials to construct, alter, or repair
any article of value, such mechanic or tradesman, if the same be
completed and not taken away, and his fair and reasonable
charges not paid, may, after six months from the time such
charges became due, sell the same; or, if the same be susceptible
of division without injury, he may sell so much thereof as is
necessary to pay such charges; and such sale shall be at public
auction, for cash, or on reasonable credit, taking sufficient sureties in case of a sale on time.

Notice of the time and place of sale must be given by posting,
or advertisements set up for ten days in three public places in
the city or township where he resides, one of which shall be in
some conspicuous part of his shop, or place of business; or, if
the value of the article be ten dollars or more, by publishing the
same three weeks successively in a newspaper in the county, if
any.[1]

The proceeds of such sale, after payment of charges for construction or repair, and for publication and notice aforesaid, shall,
if the owner be absent, be deposited with the treasurer of the
proper county by the person making such sale, he taking the
treasurer's receipt therefor, and shall be subject to the order of
the person legally entitled thereto.

These provisions shall apply to all cases of personal property
on which the bailee or keeper has by law a lien for any feed or
care by him bestowed on such property : provided that, in cases
where the person liable shall die before the expiration of six
months from the time such charges had accrued, such sale shall
not be made until the expiration of six months from the time of
his decease.

In cases embraced in the last preceding section, if the property
bailed or kept be horses, cattle, hogs, or other live-stock, and in
all cases embraced in this act where the property is of a perishable nature and will be greatly injured by delay, the person to
whom such charges may be due may, after the expiration of thirty
days from the time when such charges shall have become due,

thereon, though he made the repairs
without knowledge of the execution.
McCrisaken *v.* Osweiler, 70 Ind. 131.

[1] Notice of the sale of property by
a livery-stable keeper to satisfy his
lien, if the value is ten dollars or
more, is sufficient if given by publishing the same three weeks successively
in a newspaper in the county. Shap-
pendocia *v.* Spencer, 73 Ind. 128.

A notice of a sale to be made " on
the —— day of ——, 1877," is not a
notice of the time and place of sale.
Ibid.

proceed to dispose of so much of such property as may be necessary, as hereinbefore provided.

Additional compensation for expenses in keeping and taking care of such property, necessarily incurred, may be taken from the proceeds of sale, as part of the charges.

759. Kansas.[1] — Whenever any person shall intrust to any mechanic, artisan, or tradesman materials to construct, alter, or repair any article of value, or any article of value to be altered or repaired, such mechanic, artisan, or tradesman shall have a lien on such article, and, if the same be completed and not taken away, and his fair and reasonable or stipulated charges be not paid, may, after three months from the time such charges become due, sell the same; or, if the same be susceptible of division without injury, he may sell so much thereof as is necessary to pay such charges, and the expenses of publication and sale.[2]

760. Louisiana.[3] — The debts of a workman or artisan for the price of his labor are privileges on the movables which he has repaired or made, if the thing still continues in his possession, or the possession of the person for whom they were repaired.

761. Maine.[4] — Whoever digs, hauls, or furnishes rock for the manufacture of lime, has a lien thereon for his personal services, and on the rock so furnished, for thirty days after such rock is manufactured into lime, or until such lime is sold or shipped on board a vessel; whoever labors in quarrying or cutting and dressing granite in any quarry, has a lien for his wages on all the granite quarried or cut and dressed in the quarry by him or his co-laborers for thirty days after such granite is cut or dressed, or until such granite is sold, or shipped on board a vessel; and

---

[1] Comp. Laws 1885, § 3258.

[2] See § 349.

[3] Rev. Laws, 1884, § 2873, amending art. 3217 of the Civil Code by the addition of the last line.

This privilege exists only in favor of him who has contracted to do the work, and not to journeymen and other mechanics whom he has employed to work under him. Landry v. Blanchard, 16 La. Ann. 173. Privileges are *stricti juris*, and the party claiming a privilege must point to the express law which gives him such right of preference on account of the nature of the debt. Landry v. Blanchard, *supra*.

[4] R. S. 1883, ch. 91, § 27.

whoever labors in mining, quarrying, or manufacturing slate in any quarry,[1] has a lien for the wages of his labor on all slate mined, quarried, or manufactured in the quarry by him or his co-laborers for thirty days after the slate arrives at the port of shipment: such liens have precedence of all other claims, and may be enforced by attachment within the time aforesaid.[2]

Whoever performs labor, or furnishes labor or wood, for manufacturing and burning bricks, has a lien on such bricks for such labor and wood, taking precedence of all other claims, and continuing in force for thirty days after the same are burned suitable for use, provided that said bricks remain in the yard where burnt, such lien to be enforced by attachment within that time, which attachment shall have precedence of all attachments and incumbrances not made to secure a similar lien; and such suit may be maintained although the employer or debtor is dead and his estate has been rendered insolvent, and in that case his executor or administrator may be summoned to answer thereto : and judgment shall be rendered as in other cases against executors and administrators, and execution issued and enforced to satisfy such lien.[3]

Whoever furnishes corn or other grain or fruit, for canning or preservation otherwise, has a lien on such preserved article, and all with which it may have been mingled, for its value when delivered, including the cans and other vessels containing the same, and the cases, for thirty days after the same has been delivered, and until it has been shipped on board a vessel or laden in a car, which lien may be enforced by attachment within that time.[4]

762. **Massachusetts.**[5] — Whoever has a lien for money due to him on account of work and labor, care and diligence, or money expended on or about personal property, by reason of any contract, express or implied, if such money is not paid within

---

[1] The statute giving a lien for wages on slate quarried and manufactured "in the quarry" does not give a lien to one who labors in manufacturing slate at a place other than "in the quarry." Union Slate Co. v. Tilton, 73 Me. 207.

[2] This statute is construed to mean that, if the lien is enforced within the time named, it will have precedence of sales within that time; and that after that time the lien may be enforced so long as the granite remains unsold and not shipped on board a vessel. Collins Granite Co. v. Devereux, 72 Me. 422.

[3] R. S. 1883, ch. 91, § 28.

[4] R. S. 1883, ch. 91, § 40.

[5] Pub. Stat. 1882, ch. 192, §§ 24.

sixty days after a demand in writing delivered to the debtor, or left at his usual place of abode, if within this commonwealth, or made by letter addressed to him at his usual place of abode without the commonwealth, and deposited in the post-office to be sent to him, may apply by petition to a police, district, or municipal court, or to a trial justice in the county where the petitioner resides, for an order for the sale of the property in satisfaction of the debt.

763. Michigan.[1] — Whenever any person shall deliver to any mechanic, artisan, or tradesman any materials or articles for the purpose of constructing in whole or in part, or completing, any furniture, jewelry, implement, utensil, clothing, or other article of value, or shall deliver to any person any horse, mule, neat cattle, sheep, or swine, to be kept or cared for, such mechanic, artisan, tradesman, or other shall have a lien thereon for the just value of the labor and skill applied thereto by him, and for any materials which he may have furnished in the construction or completion thereof, and for the keeping and care of such animals, and may retain possession of the same until such charges are paid.

When any person shall deliver to any mechanic, artisan, or tradesman any watch, clock, article of furniture or jewelry, implement, clothing, or other article of value, to be altered, fitted, or repaired, such mechanic, artisan, or tradesman shall have a lien thereon for the just value of the labor and skill applied thereto by him, and may retain possession of the same until such charges are paid.[2]

764. Minnesota.[3] — Whoever makes, alters, repairs, or bestows labor on any article of personal property, at the request of the owner or legal possessor thereof, shall have a lien on such property so made, repaired, altered, or upon which labor has been bestowed, for his just and reasonable charges for the labor he has performed, and the materials he has furnished, and such person may hold and retain possession of the same until such just and reasonable charges are paid; and if they are not paid within

[1] Annot. Stats. 1882, §§ 8399, 8400, 8402.

[2] This lien is enforced by summons and sale of the property upon judgment in the manner presented in the statute given under the title Livery-Stable Keepers, § 664.

[3] Stats. 1878, p. 875, ch. 90, § 16.

three months after the labor is performed or the materials are furnished, the person having such lien may proceed to sell the property by him so made, altered, or repaired, or upon which labor has been bestowed, at public auction, by giving public notice of such sale, by advertisement for three weeks in some newspaper printed and published in the county, or, if there is none, then by posting up notice of such sale in three of the most public places in the county three weeks before the time of sale; and the proceeds of such sale shall be applied first to the discharge of such lien, and the costs and expenses of keeping and selling such property, and the remainder, if any, shall be paid over to the owner thereof.

765. Mississippi.[1] — All carriages, buggies, wagons, ploughs, or any other article constructed or repaired, shall be liable for the price of the labor and material employed in constructing or repairing the same; and the mechanic to whom the price of said labor and material may be due shall have the right to retain possession of such things so constructed or repaired, until the same shall be paid for; and if the same shall not be paid within thirty days, shall commence his suit in any court of competent jurisdiction; and upon proof of the value of the labor and materials employed in such repairs or construction, shall be entitled to judgment against the party for whom such labor or materials were furnished, with costs, as in other cases, and to a special order for the sale of the property upon which the lien exists for the payment thereof, with costs, and to an execution, as in other cases, for the residue of what remains unpaid after sale of the property.

766. New Jersey.[2] — The lien which any person may have upon any chattel in his possession for labor or materials bestowed or employed in the repair or construction thereof, shall be in no wise waived, merged, or impaired by the recovery of any judgment for the moneys due for such labor or materials; and such lien may be enforced by levy and sale under execution upon such judgment.

767. New Mexico.[3] — All artisans and mechanics shall have

---

[1] R. Code, 1880, § 1383.
[2] Laws 1885, ch. 15.
[3] Comp. Laws 1884, § 1536.

a lien on things made or repaired by them, for the amount due for their work, and may retain possession thereof until said amount is paid; and a voluntary parting with the possession of the thing shall be deemed a waiver of the lien.

768. North Carolina.[1] — Any mechanic or artisan who shall make, alter, or repair any article of personal property at the request of the owner or legal possessor of such property, shall have a lien on such property so made, altered, or repaired for his just and reasonable charge for his work done and material furnished, and may hold and retain possession of the same until such just and reasonable charge shall be paid; and if not paid for within the space of thirty days — provided it does not exceed fifty dollars, if over fifty dollars, ninety days — after the work shall have been done, such mechanic or artisan may proceed to sell the property so made, altered, or repaired at public auction, by giving two weeks' public notice of such sale by advertising in some newspaper in the county in which the work may have been done, or, if there be no such newspaper, then by posting up notice of such sale in three of the most public places in the county, town, or city in which the work may have been done, and the proceeds of the said sale shall be applied first to the discharge of the said lien, and the expenses and costs of keeping and selling such property, and the remainder, if any, shall be paid over to the owner thereof.

769. Oregon.[2] — Any person who shall make, alter, repair, or bestow labor on any article of personal property, at the request of the owner or lawful possessor thereof, shall have a lien on such property so made, altered, or repaired, or upon which labor

---

[1] Code 1883, § 1783.

This is a self-executing enactment, conferring upon the mechanic or artisan the means of making his claim out of the property by his own act, by sale without any judicial proceeding. But possession is essential to give him the right to enforce his claim by sale. If he has never had possession and cannot get possession, he has no lien. If he repairs a wagon and surrenders it to the owner, he loses his lien. McDougall *v.* Crapon, 95 N. C. 292.

[2] Laws 1878, p. 102, § 1.

Possession of the thing claimed is essential to support a lien under this statute. This possession must be actual and exclusive. It must be such a possession as would support a lien at common law. A laborer cannot have a lien on a crop of wheat for harvesting and stacking it on the farmer's land. McDearmid *v.* Foster, 14 Oregon, 417; *S. C.* 12 Pac. Rep. 813.

has been bestowed, for his just and reasonable charges for the labor he has performed and the material he has furnished, and such person may hold and retain possession of the same until such just and reasonable charges shall be paid.

Lien is enforced by sale or after notice.[1]

770. South Carolina.[2] — It shall be lawful for any mechanic in this state, when property may be left at his shop for repair, to sell the same, at public outcry, to the highest bidder, after the expiration of one year from the time such property shall have been repaired, and the same shall be sold by any trial justice of the county in which the work was done : provided that the said trial justice shall, before selling such property, advertise the same, for at least ten days, by posting a notice in three of the most conspicuous places in his township. And he shall, after deducting all proper costs and commissions, pay to the claimant the money due to him, taking the receipt for the same ; after which he shall deposit the said receipt, as well as the items of costs and commissions, with the remainder of money or proceeds of the sale, in the office of the clerk of the court, subject to the order of the owner thereof, or his legal representatives.

771. Tennessee.[3] — Silversmiths, lock and gunsmiths, blacksmiths, and artisans generally, who do work for the public, are hereby empowered, at the expiration of one year from the time of the contract and leaving the material with them, or the article to be repaired, if not claimed or called for by the owner or owners, to sell the same at public outcry, after giving thirty days' notice, to be conspicuously posted in three public places in the county wherein the sale is to be made, one notice to be posted at the court-house door.

772. Texas.[4] — Whenever any article, implement, utensil, or vehicle shall be repaired with labor and material, or with labor and without furnishing material, by any carpenter, mechanic, artisan, or other workman in this state, such carpenter, mechanic, artisan, or other workman is authorized to retain possession of said article, implement, utensil, or vehicle until the amount due

---

[1] See general provisions for enforcement of liens, Chap. XXII., *infra.*
[2] G. S. 1882, § 1667.
[3] Code 1882, § 2763.
[4] R. S. 1879, arts. 3184–3190.

on the same for repairing by contract shall be fully paid off and discharged.

In case no amount is agreed upon by contract, then said carpenter, mechanic, artisan, or other workman shall retain possession of such article, implement, utensil, or vehicle until all reasonable, customary, and usual compensation shall be paid in full.

When possession of any of the property has continued for sixty days after the charges accrued, and the charges so due have not been paid, it shall be the duty of the persons so holding said property to notify the owner, if in the state and his residence be known, to come forward and pay the charges due ; and on his failure within ten days after such notice has been given him to pay said charges, the persons so holding said property, after twenty days' notice, are authorized to sell said property at public sale, and apply the proceeds to the payment of said charges, and shall pay over the balance to the person entitled to the same.

If the owner's residence is beyond the state or is unknown, the person holding said property shall not be required to give the ten days' notice before proceeding to sell.

If the person who is legally entitled to receive the balance is not known, or has removed from the state or from the county in which such repairing was done or such property was so held, it shall be the duty of the person so holding said property to pay the balance to the county treasurer of the county in which said property is held, and take his receipt therefor.

Whenever any balance shall remain in the possession of the county treasurer for the period of two years unclaimed by the party legally entitled to the same, such balance shall become a part of the county fund of the county in which the property was so sold, and shall be applied as any other county fund or money of such county is applied or used.

Nothing in this title shall be construed or considered as in any manner impairing or affecting the right of parties to create liens by special contract or agreement, nor shall it in any manner affect or impair other liens arising at common law, or in equity, or by any statute of this state, or any other lien not treated under this title.

773. Virginia.[1] — Where an agreement shall have been made

[1] Acts 1880, ch. 191.

between any mechanic and any other person whatsoever, regarding the price for the repairs of any gun, pistol, plough, wagon, or any other article whatsoever, the said gun, pistol, plough, wagon, or other article, as the case may be, shall be subject to a lien in favor of said mechanic for any amount that may be due said mechanic for repairs as aforesaid, and the said mechanic may retain the said gun, pistol, plough, wagon, or other article, as the case may be, until said amount due for said repairs be paid ; and if it be not paid within thirty days after it is due, the said mechanic shall have the same remedies for the enforcement of his lien as are given by existing law to a landlord having a lien on personal property for rent.

774. Wisconsin.[1] — Every mechanic who shall make, alter, or repair any article of personal property, at the request of the owner or legal possessor of such property, shall have a lien thereon for his just and reasonable charges therefor, and may retain possession of such property until such charges are paid.

775. Wyoming Territory.[2] — Any mechanic, or other person who shall make, alter, repair, or bestow labor upon any article of personal property, at the request of the owner of such property, or of the materials from which the same is made, shall have a lien upon all such articles for his reasonable charges for the labor performed and materials furnished and used in such making, alteration, repair, or improvement.

If any such charges for which a lien is given by the preceding section be not paid after the same become due and payable, the mechanic or other person to whom such lien is given may apply to any justice of the peace of the county wherein he resides to appoint appraisers to appraise the several articles of personal property when such lien is claimed. Such justice shall thereupon appoint by warrant, under his hand and seal, the appraisers, being responsible householders of the county, not interested in the matter, to appraise such personal property.

No mortgage on personal property shall be valid as against the rights and interest of any person entitled to a lien under the provisions of this law.

No lien upon personal property shall be valid as against an

[1] R. S. 1878, § 3343. As to enforcement, see § 373.

[2] Comp. Laws 1876, p. 462; Act Dec. 13, 1873, §§ 3, 4, 13, 16.

innocent and *bonâ fide* purchaser, unless the person having the right of such lien shall notify said purchaser, before he makes payment for such property, of the existence of such lien, in which case the purchaser shall be responsible to the person having such lien claim against said property for the full amount of his claim, and all legitimate costs and expenses, and payment made on such lien claim shall apply on payment for such personal property.

III. *Agricultural Laborers.*

776. Laborers upon a farm have no lien for their wages upon the crops produced unless given by statute,[1] or by special contract. They have no possession of the crops so long as they are growing; and even after they are harvested they have no possession if they are gathered and stored on the farmer's land. Thus, a laborer employed to cut and stack wheat on the premises has no such possession of it as entitles him to a lien upon it at common law.[2] The laborer has only a qualified possession of the crops while he is laboring in gathering them. While they remain upon the farmer's premises, and are subject to his control, as they must necessarily be, unless he has by contract surrendered the control, he is in actual possession, and no one can have a lien at common law upon them. These acts providing as they generally do for a remedy summary in its character and contrary to the course of the common law, must receive a strict construction. Claimants under them must bring themselves strictly within the terms of the acts.[3]

777. Alabama.[4] — A lien is created in favor of agricultural laborers and superintendents of plantations upon the crops grown during the current year, in and about which they are employed, for the hire and wages due them for labor and services rendered by them in and about the cultivation of the crops under any contract for such labor and services during the current year ; which

[1] Hunt *v.* Wing, 10 Heisk. (Tenn.) 139.

[2] McDearmid *v.* Foster, 14 Oregon, 417; *S. C.* 12 Pac. Rep. 813. Thayer, J., delivering judgment, said : "There could, to my mind, be no greater absurdity than to hold that an employee of a farmer, to perform labor upon the farm, would be entitled to a lien for the work bestowed in cultivating the land or harvesting the crop, in the absence of a special contract creating it, to be followed by an actual and physical change of possession in the nature of a pledge."

[3] Flournoy *v.* Shelton, 43 Ark. 168.

[4] Code 1876, §§ 3482–3485.

lien is subordinate to the landlord's lien for rent, and to the lien for supplies furnished to make the crops, as now provided by law.[1]

The lien is held to be waived and abandoned at the expiration of six months after the work shall have been completed, unless proceedings are within that time commenced to enforce the lien. The lien is enforced by attachment. No greater portion of the crop than is sufficient to satisfy the claim, with costs of the suit, shall be attached.

778. Arkansas.[2] — Laborers who perform work and labor for any person under a written or verbal contract, if unpaid for the same, have an absolute lien on the production of their labor for such work.[3]

---

[1] This lien prevails against any purchaser with notice, actual or constructive. In the case of a superintendent, if a purchaser has knowledge of his employment or relation to the owner, and of the fact that the crops were raised under his supervision during the year, he is chargeable with constructive notice of the lien. Townsend v. Brooks, 76 Ala. 308; Lomax v. Le Grand, 60 Ala. 537.

[2] Dig. 1884, ch. 96, §§ 4425–4427, 4436, 4439.

It is provided by Acts 1885, p. 73, No. 57, that the owner of any land, houses, boats, or vessel, shall have the right to withhold one third of the amount due any contractor, to be held in trust for any mechanic, laborer, or other person to whom such contractor may be indebted.

[3] This statute has reference solely to movable property, and the labor performed thereon. " Thus, ordinary farm hands, employed in the cultivation of a crop, would have a lien on the crop produced by their labor. But it may well be doubted whether the laborer, who built fires whilst a man of genius wrote a poem, would have a lien either upon the rhythm or the manuscript, although he may have contributed to the comfort and convenience of the poet. This word ' all,' as it is used in this act, is not to be construed literally as giving to every laborer a lien for his labor. The clerk of a merchant or banker, in one sense of the word, is a laborer, and so are ordinary house servants ; but they do not come within the purview of this act, because they produce nothing to which a lien could attach." Dano v. M. O. & R. R. Railroad Co. 27 Ark. 564, 567.

A farm overseer is not a laborer within the meaning of this act. Flournoy v. Shelton, 43 Ark. 168 ; Isbell v. Dunlap, 17 S. C. 581, 583; Whitaker v. Smith, 81 N. C. 340.

For penalty for removing property subject to such lien, see § 1695 of Dig. 1884.

One who raises a crop upon the land of another for an agreed share is a laborer and not a tenant, and is entitled to a lien. Burgie v. Davis, 34 Ark. 179.

The laborer's lien given by this act is personal and not assignable ; it must arise out of contract ; and the laborer must bring himself strictly within the statute. The first nine sections apply only to movable property. The remedy is summary, and should be strictly construed. Dano v. M. O. & R. R.

Every person who has such lien, and wishes to avail himself of the same, shall make a sworn statement of the amount due after all just credits are given, to the best of his knowledge and belief, and the kind of service, and for whom rendered, and materials furnished. The statement shall also contain a list of land, property, crops, or other productions of his labor charged. The truth of the sworn statement may be put in issue, as in cases of attachment.

A lien under this act is in full force and effect from the time the labor is performed.

Proceedings to enforce this lien must be commenced within eight months after the work is done.[1] The employer, however, may bring the laborer to settlement before a proper officer any time after the labor is performed, by giving the laborer or his agent ten days' notice.

779. Arkansas[2] (continued). Specific liens in favor of employers. — Specific liens are reserved upon so much of the produce raised, and articles constructed or manufactured, by laborers during their contract, as will secure all moneys and the value of all supplies furnished them by the employers, and all wages or shares due the laborer.

When no written contract is made, the employer shall have a lien upon the portion of the crop going to the employee for any debt, incident to making and gathering the crop, owing to such employer by such employee, without any necessity for recording any contract of writing giving such lien; and no mortgage or conveyance of any part of the crop made by the person cultivating the land of another shall have a validity, unless made with the consent of the employer or owner of the land or crop,

Railroad Co. 27 Ark. 564; Taylor v. Hathaway, 29 Ark. 597.

Hay is the production of the laborer who cuts and rakes the grass, and he has a lien on it for the price or value of his labor. Emerson v. Hedrick, 42 Ark. 263.

A laborer who cultivates land, or clears and prepares the same for cultivation, is not entitled to a lien thereon for his wages. The statute only gives a lien upon the production

of his labor. Taylor v. Hathaway, 29 Ark. 597.

[1] For provisions to enforce the lien, see §§ 4428–4440 of Dig. 1884.

[2] Dig. 1884, §§ 4441, 4452. Contracts for a longer period than one month must be signed, witnessed by two witnesses, or acknowledged. The contract does not affect third persons unless a copy of it is filed in the recorder's office.

which consent must be indorsed upon such mortgage or conveyance.

780. Florida.[1] — A lien is created in favor of agricultural laborers on the respective crops cultivated by them to the extent of the value of such labor, whether it be rendered in consideration of money wages, or for a share in the crops; and such lien shall have equal and undivided application with the landlord's lien, and be prior to all other liens.

A writ of attachment may issue upon application of a laborer when any portion of the crops are removed, or attempted to be removed, from the premises without full payment of all wages due him.

781. Georgia.[2] — Laborers shall have a general lien upon the property of their employers, liable to levy and sale, for their labor, which is hereby declared to be superior to all other liens, except liens for taxes, the special liens of landlords on yearly crops, and such other liens as are declared by law to be superior to them.

Laborers shall also have a special lien on the products of their labor, superior to all other liens except liens for taxes, and special liens of landlords on yearly crops, to which they shall be inferior.[3]

[1] Dig. Laws 1881, ch. 143, §§ 30, 31.

[2] Code 1882, §§ 1974–1976.

The word *laborer* as used in the statute means one engaged in manual labor, and not one whose employment is associated with mental labor and skill, as a clerk, for instance. Hinton *v.* Goode, 73 Ga. 233 ; Ricks *v.* Redwine, 73 Ga. 273 ; Richardson *v.* Langston, 68 Ga. 658.

A laborer, though a mechanic, who performs actual manual labor for his employer, is entitled to a laborer's lien on the property of the latter.

But though a contractor may be a mechanic, if he does not perform manual labor, he is not entitled to a laborer's lien under this statute. Adams *v.* Goodrich, 55 Ga. 233 ; Sa-

vannah & Charleston R. R. Co. *v.* Callahan, 49 Ga. 506.

[3] A laborer has a special lien on particular property, and also a general lien on all the property of his employer, for work done, and, if properly asserted, it will date from the completion of the work. But in order to receive the advantage of this lien, it must be foreclosed as provided by law, and, as to realty, recorded.

Where a laborer neither recorded nor foreclosed his lien as such, but brought complaint on an open account for the amount due him, and recovered judgment, his claim was postponed to judgments junior to the performance of the work, but senior to the date of his judgment. That a laborer desires to claim a general lien on all the prop-

Liens of laborers shall arise upon the completion of their contract of labor, but shall not exist against *bonâ fide* purchasers without notice, until the same are reduced to execution and levied by an officer; and such liens in conflict with each other shall rank according to date, dating each from the completion of the contract of labor.[1]

782. Louisiana.[2]—The following debts to agricultural laborers are privileged:—

The appointments or salaries of the overseer for the current year, on the crops of the year and the proceeds thereof; the wages of laborers employed in working the same, on the crops of the year, and on everything which serves to the working of the farm.[3]

erty of his employer, and is unable to describe such property specifically, does not relieve him from asserting his lien and enforcing it as such. It does not matter that he might be compelled to enforce his lien on the personalty of his employer in one action and on the realty in another. Love *v.* Cox, 68 Ga. 269.

The lien must be established by judgment, and process must issue upon the judgment, before he can claim money arising from the sale of property under an execution in favor of another party. Cumming *v.* Wright, 72 Ga. 767.

[1] While these liens by the terms of the statute yield to *bonâ fide* purchasers without notice, yet it is held that they take precedence of mortgages, though the holders took them in good faith and without notice. Langston *v.* Anderson, 69 Ga. 65.

A distress warrant, levied before the work for which the lien was claimed is completed, takes precedence. Hight *v.* Fleming, 74 Ga. 592.

Upon a summary process to enforce a laborer's lien for wages, the defendant cannot set up by way of set-off a negotiable note of the laborer, bought up by the employer after the contract

of hiring, in the absence of any request or encouragement on the part of the laborer to make the purchase, or of any promise to allow the note as payment or as set-off. Where the claim in set-off arises out of transactions wholly disconnected with the labor or the wages, it is thought to be a defence not contemplated by the provisions of the code relating to the enforcement of liens. Fuller *v.* Kitchens, 57 Ga. 265.

If a laborer be employed by his creditor, the amount due him for his wages will be applied in payment of his debt, in the absence of any express agreement that they shall not be so applied. If after the hiring the employer makes advances in money or property to the laborer, in the absence of a stipulation to the contrary, such advances are applied to the payment of the claim for wages. Fuller *v.* Kitchens, *supra*, per Bleckley, J.

[2] R. Civ. Code, art. 3217; Rev. Laws 1884, §§ 2873–2875; Acts 1886, No. 89.

[3] The privilege "on everything which serves to the working of the farm" is construed to apply only to such things as serve to the working of the farm but do not constitute a part of the farm itself; that is, to mova-

The privileges granted to the overseer, the laborers, the furnishers of supplies, and the party advancing money necessary to carry on any farm or plantation, are concurrent, and shall not be divested by any prior mortgage, whether conventional, legal, or judicial, or by any seizure or sale of the land while the crop is on it. The privileges granted on crops shall be ranked in the following order of preference, viz.:[1]—

First. Privilege of the laborer.

Second. Privilege of the lessor.

Third. Privilege of the overseer.

783. Mississippi.[2]— Every employer shall have a lien on the share or interest of his employee in any crop made under such employment, for all advances of money, and for the fair market value of all other things advanced to him, or any one at his request, for supplies for himself and his family and business, during the existence of such employment, which lien such employer may offset, recoup, or otherwise assert and maintain, according to the exigency; and every employee, laborer, cropper, part owner,

bles by nature and destination,— movables serving to the working of the farm, but not belonging to the owner. Rogers v. Walker, 24 Fed. Rep. 344.

[1] In the distribution of the proceeds of a plantation sold to satisfy a mortgage, upon the intervention of laborers claiming a lien, there may be two funds, a crop fund and a plantation fund. On the crop fund there is, first, the laborer's lien; and, second, the factor's lien. On the plantation fund, to the extent of the mules, etc., the maxim, *qui prior est tempore, potior est jure*, is applicable. Rogers v. Walker, *supra*.

[2] R. Code 1880, §§ 1360–1363. These statutes are intended only to give liens upon the crops, and to provide means for the enforcement of the same between the classes enumerated, namely, the employer and employee, the landlord and his tenant, or the cropper on shares and the supply-man and the party supplied. An overseer is not within either of these classes,

and is not entitled to a lien. Hester v. Allen, 52 Miss. 162.

As regards the nature of the indebtedness for which the lien may be created, it is clear that there can be no lien for a debt which has no relation to agriculture, or to supplies for the family. But where a farmer has in good faith taken up the goods on the faith of the lien, and it is questioned whether this article or that falls within the law, there ought to be evidence that the things were not needed for farm purposes, or that they are of such nature of themselves as to be unfit for that use, in order to defeat the lien. Where a planter pays his laborers for wages in goods obtained from a merchant, the latter would have a lien for them, whether they were of the class embraced in the provisions of the statute or not; for it would be the same as advancing money to pay the wages of the laborers, and the statute gives a lien for this. Herman v. Perkins, 52 Miss. 813.

or other person, who may aid by his labor to make, gather, or prepare for sale or market any crop, shall have a lien on the interest of the person who contracts with him for such labor, for his wages, or share or interest in such crop, whatever may be the kind of wages or the nature of such interest; and such liens shall be paramount to all liens or encumbrances or rights of any kind created by or against the person so contracting for such assistance, except the lien of the lessor of the land on which the crop is made for rent, and supplies furnished, as provided in the act in relation to landlord and tenant.[1]

Said liens shall exist by virtue of the relation of the parties as employer and employee, and without any writing or recording.

784. North Carolina.[2] — Personal property is subject to a lien for the payment of all debts contracted for work done on the same. The lien for work on crops or farms is preferred to every other lien or incumbrance which attached upon the property subsequent to the time at which the work was commenced.[3]

---

[1] Such lien is superior to a mortgage of the crop executed after the passage of this act. The mortgagor in such case has the right to employ laborers, and thereby, by operation of law, to create the lien in their behalf, although such employment be subsequent to the execution of the mortgage. Buck v. Paine, 50 Miss. 648.

The lien is also paramount to a mortgage of the crop made for supplies furnished to enable a farmer to make the crop, though the mortgage was made before the laborer was employed and was duly recorded, and the contract with the laborer was verbal only. The lien is implied by law. It requires no writing and rests upon no record to uphold it. Buck v. Payne, 52 Miss. 271 ; Leak v. Cooke, 52 Miss. 799 ; Herman v. Perkins, 52 Miss. 813.

The laborer may waive his implied lien in favor of the mortgagee, and thus make the mortgage paramount to the lien. Whether he has done so verbally or by his act, is a question for the jury. After such waiver, a sale by the laborer of his interest in the crop passes only such interest as the laborer had after his waiver, and his vendee cannot protect himself from the waiver on the ground that he did not know of it. The purchaser is bound to inform himself of the facts, and can claim no better right than the laborer himself. Buck v. Payne, *supra*.

A mortgage of the crop made before the passage of the act creating liens in favor of laborers, is a vested right, by contract, which is paramount to any liens under such statute. Leak v. Cook, *supra*.

[2] Code 1883, §§ 1781, 1782, 1796.

[3] See Warren v. Woodard, 70 N. C. 382.

An overseer is not entitled to a laborer's lien for his wages upon the crop or land of his employer over which he has superintendence. Whitaker v. Smith, 81 N. C. 340.

Whenever servants and laborers in agriculture shall by their contracts, orally or in writing, be entitled for wages to a part of the crops cultivated by them, such part shall not be subject to sale under executions against their employers, or the owners of the land cultivated.

785. South Carolina.[1] — Whenever laborers are working on shares of a crop, or for wages in money, or other valuable consideration, they shall have a prior lien upon said crop, in whosesoever hands it may be. Such portion of the crop to them belonging, or such amount of money or other valuable consideration due, shall be recoverable by an action in any court of competent jurisdiction.

786. Tennessee.[2] — Whenever any person shall perform any labor, or render service to another in accordance with a contract, written or verbal, for cultivating soil, and shall produce a crop, he shall have a lien upon the crop produced, which shall be the result of his labor, for the payment of such wages as were agreed upon in the contract.[3]

This lien shall exist three months from the fifteenth day of November of the year in which the labor is performed, and shall be enforced by execution or attachment, as landlord's liens are enforced.

---

[1] G. S. 1882, §§ 2083, 2403.

An overseer is not an agricultural laborer. Isbell v. Dunlap, 17 S. C. 581.

[2] Code 1882, §§ 2771, 2772.

[3] Laborers upon a farm, who stipulate for a share of the crop in lieu of wages, cannot, as against third persons who have a fixed lien, as by mortgage, upon a portion of the crop, subject such portion to the payment of their claims against the entire crop. They must show that the portion attempted to be subjected is the product of their labor, and then can only subject their stipulated part of such portion to their lien. Hunt v. Wing, 10 Heisk. (Tenn.) 139.

CHAPTER XVI.

PARTNERSHIP LIENS.

787. Each member of a partnership has an equitable lien on the partnership property for the balance of account between himself and his copartners, which he may enforce as against them, and all persons claiming under them, in their individual capacity.[1] The partnership property belongs to the partnership, and not to the individuals of whom the partnership is composed. It is the right of each individual member of the partnership to require that the partnership property shall be applied to the payment of the partnership debts. The share of each member is his share of the surplus remaining after the settlement of all the firm's debts and accounts. The lien covers a partner's account as made up in the partnership dealings; but it does not cover an individual debt due from one partner to the other.[2]

[1] Garbett v. Veale, 5 Q. B. 408; Pitzpatrick v. Flannagan, 106 U. S. 648; Case v. Beauregard, 99 U. S. 119, per Strong, J.; Kirby v. Schoonmaker, 3 Barb. (N. Y.) Ch. 46; Saunders v. Reilly, 6 N. Y. St. Rep. 452; Evans v. Bryan, 95 N. C. 174; Freeman v. Stewart, 41 Miss. 138; Pierce v. Jackson, 6 Mass. 242; Gibson v. Stevens, 7 N. H. 352; Christian v. Ellis, 1 Gratt. (Va.) 396; Miller v. Price, 20 Wis. 117; Roop v. Herron, 15 Neb. 73; S. C. 17 N. W. Rep. 353; Matlock v. Matlock, 5 Ind. 403; Dunham v. Hanna, 18 Ind. 270; Pilcher's Succession (La.), 1 So. Rep. 929; Duryea v. Burt, 28 Cal. 569; Hodges v. Holeman, 1 Dana (Ky.), 50.

California and Dakota Territory: Each member of a partnership may require its property to be applied to the discharge of its debts, and has a lien upon the shares of the other partners for this purpose, and for the payment of the general balance, if any, due to him.

Property, whether real or personal, acquired with partnership funds, is presumed to be partnership property. Cal. §§ 2405, 2406, of Civ. Code; Dak. T. §§ 1411, 1412, of Civ. Code.

Each member of a mining partnership has a lien on the partnership property for the debts due the creditors thereof, and for money advanced by him for its use. This lien exists notwithstanding there is an agreement among the partners that it must not. Cal. § 2514 of Civ. Code.

This lien may exist in favor of one partner, although the partnership property is in the actual possession of the other. Morganstern v. Thrift, 66 Cal. 577.

[2] Evans v. Bryan, 95 N. C. 174.

788. A creditor of a partnership has no equitable lien upon its effects in the first instance to compel their application to the payment of partnership debts. Each member of a partnership has a right to require the application of the joint property to the payment of the joint debts, before any portion can be diverted to the individual debts of the separate partners.[1] But a partnership creditor has no specific lien, legal or equitable, upon the joint funds, any more than any individual creditor has upon the private estate of his debtor. This has been the settled doctrine on this subject since Lord Eldon's decision in 1801 of the case of *Ex parte* Ruffin.[2] A creditor of a partnership has, as a general rule, no direct lien upon the partnership property until he acquires it by legal process, that is, by the levy of an attachment or of an execution. His indirect, or *quasi* lien is derived from the lien or equity of the individual partners. It is practically a subrogation to the lien of the individual partners. If the partners are not themselves in a condition to enforce an equitable lien upon the partnership property, the creditors of the partnership cannot enforce a lien derived from them, or from one of them.[3] The equity of the partnership creditor continues so long as the equity of the individual partner continues, and no longer.

789. It is only through the operation of administering the equities between the partners themselves that the joint creditors have the benefit of a quasi lien upon the partnership property.[4] These equities can be asserted only through the ac-

[1] *Ex parte* Ruffin, 6 Ves. 119; Taylor *v.* Fields, 4 Ves. 396; *Ex parte* King, 17 Ib. 115 ; Campbell *v.* Mullett, 2 Swanst. 551; Fitzpatrick *v.* Flannagan, 106 U. S. 648, per Matthews, J.

New York : Saunders *v.* Reilly, 6 N. Y. St. Rep. 452; *S. C.* 25 Cent. L. J. 201; Nicoll *v.* Mumford, 4 Johns. (N. Y.) Ch. 522.

Ohio : Gwin *v.* Selby, 5 Ohio St. 96; Sigler *v.* Knox Co. Bank, 8 Ohio St. 511; Wilcox *v.* Kellogg, 11 Ohio, 394 ; Phillips *v.* Trezevant, 67 N. C. 370 ; Allen *v.* Center Valley Co. 21 Conn. 130; M'Donald *v.* Beach, 2 Blackf. (Ind.) 55; Freeman *v.* Stewart, 41 Miss. 138.

[2] 6 Ves. 119.

[3] Fitzpatrick *v.* Flannagan, *supra;* Case *v.* Beauregard, 99 U. S. 119; Bank of Kentucky *v.* Herndon, 1 Bush (Ky.), 359.

[4] Story Part. § 360; Case *v.* Beauregard, 99 U. S. 119; *S. C.* 101 U. S. 688; Fitzpatrick *v.* Flannagan, *supra;* *In re* Lloyd, 22 Fed. Rep. 90; Woodmansie *v.* Holcomb, 34 Kans. 35; Allen *v.* Grissom, 90 N. C. 90; Philips *v.* Trezevant, *supra;* Burns *v.* Harris, 67 N. C. 140; Gallagher's Appeal (Pa.), 7 Atl. Rep. 237; Coo-

tion of the partners, or of one of them, or through the insolvency of the firm, which puts the property into the custody of the law, or through the death of one partner, which devolves the settlement of the partnership affairs upon the survivor. Simple contract creditors of the partnership have no lien upon its property until it is acquired by process of law, or the property has passed *in custodia legis.* The partnership creditors have what is termed a *quasi* lien upon the partnership property, but this does not exist independently of the partners. " The partners have the lien, and especially the solvent ones, and have a right to insist that the joint funds shall pay the joint debts, and in this way, and by enforcing the equities or lien of the partners, the creditors of the partnership come to their rights, whatever they are, and thus these rights are ' worked out,' as the authorities say." [1]

A simple contract creditor of a partnership can enforce his equity only when the partnership property is within the control of the court, and, in the course of administration, brought there by proceedings in bankruptcy or insolvency, or by an assignment for the benefit of creditors, or by the creation of a trust in some other way. Neither the partners nor the creditors of the partnership have any specific lien, nor is there any trust that can be enforced until the property has passed in *custodiam legis.*[2]

790. If there be no joint property there can be no equity in favor of joint creditors.[3] Thus, where two persons entered into partnership under an agreement that one should have the exclusive ownership of the property until the other should contribute a certain sum of money, and before he did this a separate

ver's Appeal, 29 Pa. St. 9; York Co. Bank's Appeal, 32 Pa. St. 446 ; Baker's Appeal, 21 Ib. 76 ; McNutt v. Strayhorn, 39 Pa. St. 269; Rice v. Barnard, 20 Vt. 479; Wilcox v. Kellogg, 11 Ohio, 394: Day v. Wetherby, 29 Wis. 363; Schmidlapp v. Currie, 55 Miss. 597; White v. Parish, 20 Tex. 688 ; Hawk Eye Woolen Mills v. Conklin, 26 Iowa, 422; Poole v. Seney, 66 Iowa, 502 ; Jones v. Lusk, 2 Met. (Ky.) 356; Whitehead v. Chadwell, 2 Duv.(Ky.) 432; Bank of Kentucky v. Herndon, 1 Bush (Ky.), 359; Freeman v. Stewart, 41 Miss. 139. See, however, Menagh v. Whitwell, 52 N. Y. 146.

[1] Allen v. Center Valley Co. 21 Conn. 130, 135, per Church, C. J.

[2] Fitzpatrick v. Flannagan, 106 U. S. 648; Case v. Beauregard, 99 U. S. 119, per Strong, J.; Saunders v. Reilly, 6 N. Y. St. Rep. 452; Austin v. Seligman, 18 Fed. Rep. 519.

[3] Case v. Beauregard, *supra,* Scull's Appeal (Pa.), 7 Atl. Rep. 588.

creditor of the other partner levied an execution upon the property, and afterwards a joint creditor levied upon the same goods, it was held that the separate execution creditor was entitled to the preference acquired by priority of seizure. The property was individual property. The partner who had not become entitled to an interest in the property had no lien upon it, and the joint creditors could work out no equity through him.[1]

If the contract of partnership be of such a nature that the partners cannot, as between themselves, enforce a lien upon the partnership funds for the payment of partnership liabilities, as where there is a community of goods between them, and they and their families are supported from the joint property without any account being kept by one as against the other, the partnership creditors cannot enforce any such preference.[2]

And so, if property which has once been property of the partnership has been in good faith transferred by the partnership to an individual member of the firm or to a third person, the equities of the partners are extinguished, and consequently the equities of the creditors of the partnership are at the same time extinguished.[3]

791. One of two partners may extinguish all partnership equities by transferring his interest to the other, provided the property has not previously passed *in custodia legis*, and provided the transfer be made in good faith.[4] This has been the recognized rule ever since it was declared by Lord Eldon at the beginning of this century.[5]

Where one partner transfers all his interest in the partnership property to the other, and is content with his personal undertaking to pay the partnership debts, the retiring partner has no longer any lien in equity upon the effects of the partnership, but the continuing partner may dispose of them as he chooses, and may transfer them in trust for the payment of his own

---

[1] York Co. Bank's Appeal, 32 Pa. St. 446; Baker's Appeal, 21 Pa. St. 76.

[2] Rice v. Barnard, 20 Vt. 479, and see York Co. Bank's Appeal, *supra;* Case v. Beauregard, 99 U. S. 119.

[3] M'Donald v. Beach, 2 Blackf. (Ind.) 55.

[4] Fitzpatrick v. Flannagan, 106 U. S. 648; Case v. Beauregard, *supra; S. C.* 101 U. S. 688; Hapgood v. Cornwell, 48 Ill. 64 ; Robb v. Mudge, 14 Gray (Mass.), 534 ; Kimball v. Thompson, 13 Met. (Mass.) 283. See cases collected by Mr. Corliss, 34 Alb. L. J. 346.

[5] *Ex parte* Ruffin, 6 Ves. 119.

debts; and the partnership creditors cannot follow these effects, to subject them to the payment of the partnership debts.[1]

, Of a firm consisting of five members two withdrew, assigning their interests to the remaining three, who agreed to pay the debts of the firm. Some time afterwards one of the remaining three sold his interest to the remaining two partners. The latter, after contracting debts, made an assignment of their partnership property to pay the debts of the last partnership. It was held that the creditors of the first and second partnerships had no right to claim any portion of the property assigned for the benefit of the creditors of the last partnership.[2]

792. One member of a partnership may, with the concurrence of his copartner, transfer in good faith his interest in the firm to any individual creditor, and a simple contract creditor of the firm cannot maintain a bill to subject the property to the payment of his debt, although both the firm and the individual members of it were insolvent at the time of such transfer.[3] The transfer converts the partnership property into property held in severalty, or at least operates to terminate the equity of any partner to require the application of the partnership property to the payment of the joint debts. The partnership creditor can sustain such bill only upon proof that the transfer was fraudu-

[1] Rankin v. Jones, 2 Jones' (N. C.) Eq. 169; Potts v. Blackwell, 4 Ib. 58; White v. Griffin, 2 Jones' (N. C.), L. 3; Allen v. Grissom, 90 N. C. 90; Flack v. Charon, 29 Md. 311; Griffith v. Buck, 13 Md. 102; Jones v. Fletcher, 42 Ark. 422, 451; Goembel v. Arnett, 100 Ill. 34; Andrews v. Mann, 31 Miss. 322; White v. Parish, 20 Tex. 688.

In a few cases, however, it has been held that if one partner buys out his copartners, agreeing to pay the debts of the firm, the partnership property remains bound for the firm debts; and the lien of the firm creditors upon such property is preferred to the lien of an individual creditor of such remaining partner, though the lien of the latter first attached. Conroy v. Woods, 13 Cal. 626; Sedam v. Williams, 4 McLean, 51; Bowman v. Spalding (Ky.), 2 S. W. Rep. 911.

[2] Baker's Appeal, 21 Pa. St. 76.

[3] Case v. Beauregard, 99 U. S. 119; S. C. 101 U. S. 688; Fitzpatrick v. Flannagan, 106 U. S. 648; Woodmansie v. Holcomb, 34 Kan. 35; Schmidlapp v. Currie, 55 Miss. 597.

Some authorities hold, however, that if the firm is insolvent at the time of such payment or transfer, it is fraudulent and void as to existing creditors of the firm, and will be set aside under insolvency proceedings, or at the suit of a creditor who has obtained a judgment against the firm. Goodbar v. Cary, 16 Fed. Rep. 316; Wilson v. Robertson, 21 N. Y. 587, 589; Menagh v. Whitwell, 52 N. Y. 146; Ransom v. Van Deventer, 41 Barb. (N. Y.) 307. See Saunders v. Reilly, 6 N. Y. St. Rep. 452; Patterson v. Seaton (Iowa), 28 N. W. Rep. 598; Keith v. Fink, 47 Ill. 272.

lent. He has no specific claim upon the property, and there is no trust in his behalf which a court of equity can enforce.

But a sale and transfer by one partner, without the assent and concurrence of his copartner, of all his interest in the partnership property to a trustee, to pay all his individual and partnership debts, does not divest or defeat the implied lien of the other partner upon the partnership property ; but such implied lien continues till the partnership debts have been paid, and upon the insolvency of the partnership may be enforced by the partnership creditors.[1]

793. The partnership may pay the debts of individual members although it has not in fact sufficient assets to pay its liabilities in full, provided it remains in the exclusive possession and control of its assets, and acts in good faith. The mere inability of a partnership to pay its debts does not deprive the partners of their legal control of their property, and their right to sell and dispose of it as may seem just and proper.[2] If proceedings in bankruptcy or insolvency are afterwards instituted by or against the firm, the validity of the appropriation must be tested by statutes and rules regulating such proceedings.[3]

If, upon a dissolution of a partnership by mutual agreement, the members, honestly believing that the outstanding accounts and notes due the firm are sufficient to pay all its debts, divide the merchandise between them, the title to this vests in the individual members, and one partner cannot afterwards rescind such division, and compel a restoration of the goods, or the proceeds thereof, from another partner or from his assignee in insolvency, except for fraud.[4]

794. Upon the dissolution of a partnership by the death of one of its members, the survivor may pay his individual debts out of the assets, unless the intervention of the court is sought to wind up its affairs. If no bill is filed by the representatives of the deceased partner, or by the firm creditors, asking a court of equity to wind up the business, marshal its assets and

[1] Bank of Kentucky v. Herndon, 1 Bush (Ky.), 359.

[2] Case v. Beauregard, 99 U. S. 119 ; Sigler v. Knox Co. Bank, 8 Ohio St. 511 ; and see Wilcox v. Kellogg, 11 Ohio, 394.

[3] National Bank of Metropolis v. Sprague, 20 N. J. Eq. 13 ; Schæffer v. Fithian, 17 Ind. 463 ; Jones v. Lusk, 2 Met. (Ky.) 356.

[4] Whitworth v. Benbow, 56 Ind. 194.

apply them to the firm debts, the surviving partner may, in the absence of an actual intent to defraud, pay his individual indebtedness with such assets.[1] If, in good faith, with the acquiescence of the personal representatives of the deceased partner, he uses the firm property to continue the business on his own account and in his name, he does it without other liability than to be held accountable to the estate of the deceased partner for a share of the profits.[2]

If the surviving partner continues the business under a new firm, no lien attaches upon the property of the new firm in favor of the creditors of the old firm, although the representatives of the deceased partner do not sanction the continuance of the business. The creditors of the new firm have priority of payment out of the property of the new firm, if the equities are administered in court. To prevent the attaching of such new equities, the representatives of the deceased partner or the creditors of the old firm must stop the carrying on of the business, and obtain a winding up of the old firm.[3]

795. If the creditor of an individual partner levies an execution upon the partnership property, he acquires no interest thereby in the property itself as against the partnership, but only a lien upon the interest of the judgment debtor in the surplus remaining after all partnership debts and liens should be paid.[4] The *corpus* of the partnership property cannot be taken and held upon a levy of such execution. And so upon a sale by one member of a firm, to a person not a member, of his interest in the firm property, the purchaser takes no part of the *corpus* of the firm property, but only such interest as remains after the equities between the partners have been adjusted and the firm debts paid.[5] Even if all the members of a firm severally convey to different persons each his interest in the firm property, the purchasers do not take any of the *corpus* of the firm property, but only the interest of each partner after the firm debts are paid, and the equities between the partners adjusted.[6]

[1] Fitzpatrick *v.* Flannagan, 106 U. S. 648; Schmidlapp *v.* Currie, 55 Miss. 597 ; Locke *v.* Lewis, 124 Mass. 1.

[2] Fitzpatrick *v.* Flannagan, *supra.*

[3] Payne *v.* Hornby, 25 Beav. 280 ; *S. C.* 4 Jur. (N. S.) 446 ; Hoyt *v.* Sprague, 103 U. S. 613.

[4] Donellan *v.* Hardy, 57 Ind. 393;

Conroy *v.* Woods, 13 Cal. 626; Chase *v.* Steel, 9 Cal. 64; Jones *v.* Parsons, 25 Cal. 100; Coover's Appeal, 29 Pa. St. 9.

[5] Saunders *v.* Reilly, 6 N. Y. St. Rep. 452 ; *S. C.* 25 Cent. L. J. 201.

[6] Menagh *v.* Whitwell, 52 N. Y. 146.

796. When real property is conveyed to partners for the benefit of the firm, the legal title, which at common law would vest in the grantees as joint tenants, under the statutes in this country relative to joint tenancies, vests in them as tenants in common. A purchaser or mortgagee who obtains the legal title to an undivided portion of partnership lands, without notice of the equitable rights of other partners in the property as a part of the funds of the partnership, is entitled to protection in courts of equity as well as in courts of law. But as between the partners themselves, such real estate is to be treated as the property of the firm, and subject to the equitable rights of the partners. It is chargeable with the debts of the partnership, and with any balance that may be due from one copartner to another upon the winding up of the affairs of the firm.[1]

It is immaterial whether the title to real property be taken in the name of one partner or in the names of all the partners; if the property be purchased with partnership funds for partnership uses, it is in equity treated as partnership property, so far as it is necessary for the payment of the debts of partnership and the adjustment of the equities of the partners.[2]

797. But a purchaser or mortgagee dealing with an individual partner may be affected with notice of the partnership equities, so that any title he acquires to such property will be subject to such equities.[3] He has such notice if he is apprised of facts sufficient to put him on inquiry, and to lead him by such inquiry to a discovery of the truth. Thus, if, while a mining partnership is engaged in working its mining grounds, one partner sells his interest in the mine, the purchaser will be deemed to buy with notice of any lien resulting from the relation of the partners to each other, and to the creditors of the partnership.[4]

798. The character of partnership property may be impressed upon real estate which has not been purchased with partnership funds, but which has been purchased and paid for

See examination of this case by Mr. Corliss, 34 Alb. L. J. 364.

[1] Shanks v. Klein, 104 U. S. 18; Dyer v. Clark, 5 Met. (Mass.) 562; Buchan v. Sumner, 2 Barb. (N. Y.) Ch. 165; Duryea v. Burt, 28 Cal. 569; Smith v. Evans, 37 Ind. 526.

[2] Shanks v. Klein, supra; Smith v. Jones (Neb.), 25 N.W. Rep. 624.

[3] Duryea v. Burt, supra; Whitmore v. Shiverick, 3 Nev. 288.

[4] Duryea v. Burt, supra.

by individual members of the partnership; as where such property has been purchased with a view to the formation of the partnership, and has been, by agreement of the partners or by their acts, brought into the firm and used for its purposes.[1]

Land transferred to two attorneys at law who are partners, to secure a debt due to the firm for professional services, is partnership property, and cannot be subjected to the claims of the individual creditors of one of the firm until the partnership debts are paid.[2] It was urged that the land could not be used in or appropriated to the firm business, and hence could not be treated as partnership property. The authorities are conflicting as to what is requisite to convert real estate into personalty for the purposes of a partnership. It is really a question of intention to be gathered from all the attending circumstances; but unless a contrary intention appears, it is presumed that partnership real estate is to be treated as partnership assets. " It is unnecessary to review the numerous cases. To do so we would have to begin with the opinions of Lord Thurlow upon one side and those of Lord Eldon upon the other; and we shall content ourselves with saying that we think the true principle, deducible from all of them, is, that if real property has been purchased with the firm means, and is held in the joint names of the partners as partnership property, then, in the absence of any agreement between them to the contrary, it should be regarded at law as held and owned by them as tenants in common; but that in equity it should be treated as held by them in trust for the firm, subject to the rules applicable to partnership personal property, and liable to the debts of the firm, and the claims of each partner upon the others; and after these claims are satisfied, the residue of it, if any be left, will belong, both at law and in equity, to the partners as tenants in common, unless they have by an agreement, either express or implied, impressed upon it the character of personal property for all purposes." [3]

799. Upon the dissolution of a firm by the death of one partner, the survivor can sell the partnership real estate; and, though he cannot transfer the legal title which passed to the heirs or devisees of the deceased partner, the sale vests the equi-

---

[1] Roberts v. McCarty, 9 Ind. 16; Duryea v. Burt, 28 Cal. 569.

[2] Flanagan v. Shuck, 82 Ky. 617.

[3] Flanagan v. Shuck, supra, per Holt, J.

table ownership in the purchaser, who can in a court of equity compel the holders of the legal title to convey it to himself.[1] The surviving partner has something more than an equitable lien, such as belongs to the representatives of the deceased partner, to require the application of such real estate to the payment of the debts of the firm and the settlement of the partnership accounts. " It is," in the language of Mr. Justice Miller,[2] " an equitable *right* accompanied by *an equitable title.* It is an *interest in the property* which courts of chancery will recognize and support. What is that right? Not only that the court will, when necessary, see that the real estate so situated is appropriated to the satisfaction of the partnership debts, but that for that purpose, and to that extent, it shall be treated as personal property of the partnership, and, like other personal property, pass under the control of the surviving partner. This control extends to the right to sell it, or so much of it as may be necessary to pay the partnership debts, or to satisfy the just claims of the surviving partner."

[1] Shanks *v.* Klein, 104 U. S. 18, 22 ; Dyer *v.* Clark, 5 Met. (Mass.) 562; Delmonico *v.* Guillaume, 2 Sandf. N. Y. Ch. 366; Dupuy *v.* Leavenworth, 17 Cal. 262; Andrews *v.* Brown, 21 Ala. 437.

[2] Shanks *v.* Klein, *supra.*

CHAPTER XVII.

I. *Nature and Extent of the Lien.*

800. A seller of goods has a lien upon them for the price, so long as they remain in his possession and the purchaser neglects to pay the price according to the terms of sale.[1]

[1] Parks *v.* Hall, 2 Pick. (Mass.) 206; Clark *v.* Draper, 19 N. H. 419; Milliken *v.* Warren, 57 Me. 46; White *v.* Welsh, 38 Pa. St. 396; Wanamaker *v.* Yerkes, 70 Pa. St. 443; Barr *v.* Logan, 5 Harr. (Del.) 52; Carlisle *v.* Kinney, 66 Barb. (N. Y.) 363; Cornwall *v.* Haight, 8 Ib. 327; Morse *v.* Sherman, 106 Mass. 430, per Colt, J.; Haskins *v.* Warren, 115 Mass. 514, per Wells, J.; Ware River R. R. Co. *v.* Vibbard, 114 Mass. 447; Southwestern Freight & Cotton Press Co. *v.* Stanard, 44 Mo. 71; Bradley *v.* Michael, 1 Ind. 551; Owens *v.* Weedman, 82 Ill. 409; Welsh *v.* Bell, 32 Pa. St. 12.

In a few states there are statutes declaring the seller's lien. Thus, in **California** and **Dakota Territory**, it is provided by code that one who sells personal property has a special lien thereon, dependent on possession, for its price, if it is in his possession when the price becomes payable, and may enforce his lien in like manner as if the property was pledged to him for the price. 1 Codes and Stats. Cal.

1885, § 3049 of Civ. Code ; R. Codes Dak. 1883, § 1804 of Civ. Code.

In **Louisiana**, the seller of movables has a preference over the other creditors of the purchaser, whether the sale was made on credit or without, if the property still remains in the possession of the purchaser. The seller of agricultural products of the United States in New Orleans has a lien for five days only after the day of delivery, and may seize the same in whatsoever hands or place they may be found. This lien may be waived by a written order for delivery without the vendor's privilege. R. Civ. Code, §§ 3227–3231. See Gumbel *v.* Beer, 36 La. Ann. 484; Scannell *v.* Beauvais, 38 La. Ann. 217.

Under this statute the lien of a vendor of cotton, when enforced in five days, is superior to that of the holder for value of a bill of lading of the cotton. Harris *v.* Nicolopulo, 38 La. Ann. 12; Allen *v.* Jones, 24 Fed. Rep. 11.

Tennessee. When merchants, factors, or cotton-brokers sell cotton, a

"A lien for the price is incident to the contract of sale, when there is no stipulation therein to the contrary ; because a man is not required to part with his goods until he is paid for them."[1] In a leading case before the King's Bench, Bayley, J., upon this point said :[2] " Where goods are sold and nothing is said as to the time of the delivery, or the time of payment, . . . and everything the seller has to do with them is complete, the property vests in the buyer, so as to subject him to the risk of any accident which may happen to the goods, and the seller is liable to deliver them whenever they are demanded upon payment of the price ; but the buyer has no right to have possession of the goods till he pays the price. . . . If the seller has dispatched the goods to the buyer, and insolvency occurs, he has a right, in virtue of his original ownership, to stop them *in transitu.* Why ? Because the property is vested in the buyer, so as to be subject to the risk of any accident ; but he has not an indefeasible right to the possession, and his insolvency, without payment of the price, defeats that right. And if this be the case after he has dispatched the goods, and whilst they are *in transitu, à fortiori,* is it when he has never parted with the goods, and when no transitus has begun ? The buyer, or those who stand in his place, may still obtain the right of possession if they will pay or tender the price, or they may still act upon their right of property if anything unwarrantable is done to that right."

801. Part payment of the purchase-money for goods sold for cash, or on credit, does not divest the seller of his lien so long as he retains possession.[3] But payment in full for a severed portion of the goods divests the seller of his lien in respect of that portion of the goods which has been actually paid for. The sale may be apportionable, although in one sense the contract is an entire contract. Thus, if a certain quantity

special lien in behalf of the vendors for the purchase-money exists for five days from and after the day of sale or delivery thereof, unless the purchase-money be sooner paid. Code 1884, § 2761.

[1] Arnold *v.* Delano, 4 Cush. (Mass.) 33, 39, per Shaw, C. J.; Southwestern Freight & Cotton Press Co. *v.* Stanard, 44 Mo. 71.

[2] Bloxam *v.* Sanders, 4 B. & C.

941. To like effect, see Leonard *v.* Davis, 1 Black, 476.

[3] Hodgson *v.* Loy, 7 T. R. 440 ; Craven *v.* Ryder, 6 Taunt. 433; Bunney *v.* Poyntz, 4 B. & Ad. 568; Feise *v.* Wray, 3 East, 93; Welsh *v.* Bell, 32 Pa. St. 12; Buckley *v.* Furniss, 17 Wend. (N. Y.) 504; Williams *v.* Moore, 5 N. H. 235; Hamburger *v.* Rodman, 9 Daly, N. Y. 93.

of steel rails be sold at an entire price to be delivered at intervals, and each portion to be settled for separately, and the contract is carried out in substance though not at the exact times, nor in the exact amounts, which had been arranged, but payment is made for a portion of the goods substantially as agreed, the vendor can have no lien on that portion of the goods which has been fully paid for.[1]

802. This right has sometimes been said to be not a mere lien, but a special interest in the goods sold growing out of the vendor's original ownership. Thus, in a case before the Court of the King's Bench in 1825, Bayley, J., said:[2] "The vendor's right in respect of the price is not a mere lien which he will forfeit if he parts with the possession, but grows out of his original ownership and dominion; and payment or a tender of the price is a condition precedent on the buyer's part, and until he makes such payment or tender he has no right of possession." And again, in 1840, in a case before the Queen's Bench, where goods were sold and removed to a warehouse used by the purchaser, but belonging to a third person, the course of dealing was that the goods should remain there till paid for, and it was held that, although there was a sufficient delivery and acceptance to enable the seller to maintain an action for goods sold and delivered, "consistently with this, however, the vendor had, not what is commonly called a lien, determinable on the loss of possession, but a special interest, sometimes, but improperly, called a lien, growing out of his original ownership, independent of the actual possession, and consistent with the property being in the purchaser. This he retained in respect of the term agreed on, that the goods should not be removed to their ultimate place of destination before payment. But this lien is consistent with the possession having passed to the buyer, so that there may have been a delivery to and actual receipt by him."[3]

803. Even where goods have been sold to be paid for in the notes of a third person, and he becomes insolvent before the time fixed for delivery, the seller is not bound to deliver

---

[1] Merchants' Banking Co. v. Phœnix Bessemer Steel Co. 5 Ch. D. 205.

[2] Bloxam v. Sanders, 4 B. & C.

941; and see Audenreid v. Randall, 3 Cliff. 99, 106, per Clifford, J.

[3] Dodsley v. Varley, 12 Ad. & E. 632, 634.

upon a tender of such notes, though they be not entirely worth-less.[1]

804. A seller's lien is only for the price, and for any charges or expenses incurred in keeping the goods.[2] In a case before the House of Lords, upon the question whether a person who has a lien upon a chattel can make a claim against the owner for keeping it, Lord Wensleydale said:[3] "No authority can be found affirming such a proposition, and I am clearly of opinion that no person has, by law, a right to add to his lien upon a chattel a charge for keeping it till the debt is paid; that is, in truth, a charge for keeping it for his own benefit, not for the benefit of the person whose chattel is in his possession."

805. The effect of the seller's exercising his right of lien is not to rescind the contract of sale;[4] and therefore the seller continues to hold possession by virtue of his lien until that is foreclosed, or the purchaser waives the contract of sale.

But if a seller of merchandise, in order to maintain his lien for its price, refuses to permit the purchaser to take possession of it, he may thereby prevent an acceptance of it by the purchaser within the statute of frauds; and if there be no memoran-

---

[1] Benedict v. Field, 16 N. Y. 595; Roget v. Merritt, 2 Caines (N. Y.), 117; Southwestern Freight & Cotton Press Co. v. Stanard, 44 Mo. 71, per Wagner, J.

In Roget v. Merritt, supra, Judge Spencer said : "In this case I hold there was a valid contract, executory in its nature; but before the period of its execution arrived, the consideration agreed to be given by the plaintiff (the buyer) wholly failed, in the insolvency of Lyon (the maker of the note which was to be given in payment). The offer of the plaintiff to pay in the note of a bankrupt was not an offer of payment." In Benedict v. Field, supra, the court, approving the foregoing decision and the language of Judge Spencer, said : "The agreement was executory, as we have said, in respect to the title : it certainly was in respect to the de-

livery; and before the time of performance arrived, the essential consideration on which it was based had failed. It is true that the sale, looking only to the precise letter of the contract, was not defeasible in the event which occurred. But when the parties contracted, the firm (whose note was to be received in payment) was in good credit, and was supposed to be solvent. Their notes were to be accepted as payment, but the ability of that firm to give good notes was assumed, and was really the consideration of the defendant's engagement to sell and deliver the goods." Per Comstock, J.

[2] British Empire Shipping Co. v. Somes, E., B. & E. 353; S. C. Ib. 367.

[3] Somes v. British Empire Shipping Co. 8 H. L. Cas. 338, 445.

[4] Martindale v. Smith, 1 Q. B. 389.

dum in writing of the contract, and no part payment to bind the bargain, the seller cannot maintain an action for the price of the goods. If, in such case, the goods are destroyed by fire, the loss will fall upon the seller.[1]

II. *Possession Essential to its Existence.*

806. It is a well-settled rule that the seller's right of lien depends upon his possession.[2] He can never maintain it without having the actual or constructive possession of the goods. He can never maintain it after the goods have come into the possession of the purchaser. It is generally immaterial whether the delivery be actual or constructive. It is true that it has sometimes been doubted whether a constructive delivery is sufficient to take away the seller's right of lien ; and while it would perhaps be going too far to say that in every possible case a constructive delivery would have this operation, the general rule is that such a delivery, as well as an actual delivery, defeats the lien.[3] Thus, if the goods be stored in the seller's warehouse, his delivery of the key of the warehouse to the purchaser, with the view of giving him possession, amounts to a constructive delivery of the goods, and defeats the seller's lien.[4]

Upon a sale of lumber to be delivered by the seller at a railroad station, and to be paid for by the buyer as shipped by him from the station, there is a complete delivery, which will defeat the seller's lien, when he has delivered the lumber to the buyer at the station, and the latter has with the knowledge of the seller measured and piled it, marked it with his initials, and left it in charge of the station master with directions to ship it. The lien having been lost, it cannot be reëstablished in such case by proof that the vendee, upon being requested to pay for the lumber lying at the station, said to the vendor, "You are all right any way. You have the lumber there at Bronte Station."[5]

807. There may be a constructive delivery of the goods

---

[1] Safford *v.* McDonough, 120 Mass. 290.

[2] Parks *v.* Hall, 2 Pick. (Mass.) 206 ; Pickett *v.* Bullock, 52 N. H. 354; Welsh *v.* Bell, 32 Pa. St. 12 ; Bowen *v.* Burk, 13 Pa. St. 146 ; Boyd *v.* Mosely, 2 Swan (Tenn.), 661 ; Obermier *v.* Core, 25 Ark. 562; Gay *v.* Hardeman, 31 Tex. 245; McNail *v.* Ziegler, 68 Ill. 224; Thompson *v.* Wedge, 50 Wis. 642.

[3] Parks *v.* Hall, *supra*, per Wilde, J.

[4] Ellis *v.* Hunt, 3 T. R. 464, 468, per Lord Kenyon.

[5] Mason *v.* Hatton, 41 U. C. Q. B. 610, 612.

sold which will pass the title but which will not destroy the seller's lien.[1] If goods be sold and counted out and set apart for the purchaser, there is such a constructive delivery that the title will vest in the purchaser and the property will be at his risk, and yet the seller has the indisputable right to refuse to deliver without payment.[2] Thus, two persons agreed with the managers of a lottery to take a large number of tickets, and to give approved security on the delivery of the tickets. Part of the tickets were delivered and paid for, and the remainder were selected, and the package marked by the managers with the name of the purchasers. The drawing of the lottery thereupon began, and on the second day one of the tickets in this package drew a large prize, and the managers, upon a subsequent tender of the price of this package of tickets, refused to deliver them. It was held that the property in the tickets, subject to a lien for the purchase-money, had passed to the purchasers.[3]

808. **Marking and setting aside the goods sold do not amount to a delivery** sufficient to divest the vendor of his lien;[4] though they may be sufficient to pass the title to the

[1] Lickbarrow v. Mason, 5 T. R. 367 ; S. C. 1 Smith's Lead. Cas. 8th Eng. ed. 789 ; Owens v. Weedman, 82 Ill. 409 ; Sigerson v. Kahmann, 39 Mo. 206 ; Southwestern Freight & Cotton Express Co. v. Stanard, 44 Mo. 71.

[2] Southwestern Freight & Cotton Express Co. v. Plant, 45 Mo. 517 ; Owens v. Weedman, *supra*.

[3] Thompson v. Gray, 1 Wheat. 75, 83. Chief Justice Marshall said the purchasers were absolutely bound to take the designated tickets. "A refusal to do so would have been a breach of contract, for which they would have been responsible in damages. When the parties proceed one step further ; when the vendee, in execution of the contract, selects the number of tickets he has agreed to purchase, and the vendor assents to that selection ; when they are separated from the mass of tickets, and those not actually delivered are set apart and marked as the property of the vendee, — what, then, is the state of the contract? It certainly stands as if the selection had been previously made and inserted in the contract itself. An article purchased in general terms from many of the same description, if afterwards selected and set apart with the assent of the parties as the thing purchased, is as completely identified, and as completely sold, as if it had been selected previous to the sale, and specified in the contract. . . .

"The stipulation respecting security could not in such a case be considered as a condition precedent, on the performance of which the sale depended. Certainly the managers could have required and have insisted on this security ; but they might waive it without dissolving the contract." And see United States v. Lutz, 3 Blatch. 383.

[4] Dixon v. Yates, 5 B. & Ad. 313 ; Goodall v. Skelton, 2 H. Bl. 316 ; Proctor v. Jones, 2 C. & P. 532, per Best, C. J.

vendee. "There is manifestly a marked distinction between those acts which, as between vendor and vendee, upon a contract of sale, go to make a constructive delivery and to vest the property in the vendee, and that actual delivery by the vendor to the vendee which puts an end to the right of the vendor to hold goods as security for the price." [1] Marking, measuring, weighing, and setting aside goods which are the subject of sale, serve only to identify the goods; for if they are capable of being identified without these acts, the title passes by the contract of sale. Thus, if the whole of a quantity of iron lying in a pile be sold and pointed out to the purchaser, there is no need of any further act of delivery to pass the property. But so long as the iron remains upon the premises of the vendor, and thus in his possession, he has the right to detain it until the price is paid.[2]

809. There may even be a qualified delivery of goods to the buyer, which will not destroy the seller's lien for the price. Thus, if it be shown that by the intention of the parties the delivery was for the purpose of allowing the buyer an opportunity to examine the goods, and not for the purpose of giving absolute possession to the buyer, the lien is not lost; and a usage of trade in conformity with such intention may be shown.[3] But if it appear that the goods were delivered for the purpose of completing the sale, evidence of a usage that the sale is not completed is inadmissible, and a usage that no title passes upon an ordinary sale and delivery without payment is unreasonable and invalid.[4]

A delivery of goods to the buyer to hold as bailee of the

---

[1] Arnold v. Delano, 4 Cush. (Mass.) 33, 38.

[2] Thompson v. Baltimore & Ohio R. R. Co. 28 Md. 396, 407, per Miller, J. "So long as the vendor does not surrender actual possession, his lien remains, although he may have performed acts which amount to a constructive delivery, so as to pass the title or avoid the statute. In all cases of symbolical delivery, which is the only species of constructive delivery sufficient to give a final possession to the vendee, it is only because of the manifest intention of the vendor utterly to abandon all claim and right of possession, taken in connection with the difficulty or impossibility of making an actual and manual transfer, that such a delivery is considered as sufficient to annul the lien of the vendor."

[3] Haskins v. Warren, 115 Mass. 514.

[4] Haskins v. Warren, supra.

vendor, does not divest the latter of his lien. But if the buyer, after the completion of the contract of sale, delivers the property to the seller to hold as his bailee, the latter cannot by virtue of such possession have a lien for the price,[1] unless the express terms of the sale be for ready money, or such as to imply that the property is not to be taken away until it is paid for.[2]

810. A seller has the right to insist upon his lien for the price until he has made actual and absolute delivery to the buyer. In all cases of inchoate delivery, until the delivery is complete, he may suspend it and insist upon his lien. Thus, if the seller has given to the buyer an order on a warehouseman for the goods, and, before the buyer has presented the order to the warehouseman and taken the goods, or had them transferred by the warehouseman to the name of the buyer, or of some other person, the buyer becomes insolvent, the seller may reclaim the goods under his lien; and he may do this although the buyer has indorsed and delivered the order for value to another who did not know that the buyer had not paid for the goods.[3]

811. But a seller of personal property has no lien upon it after a fair and absolute delivery of it to the purchaser.[4] The rule in relation to real estate, that a vendor has a lien for the purchase-money, although he has conveyed the land to the purchaser absolutely and has delivered possession to him, has no application to personal property. Even as regards the rule as to real property, it is one that does not exist at common law; but it is a doctrine of equity, and was transplanted into equity from the civil law.[5]

There is no lien for the purchase-money after the goods are delivered, although the purchaser was insolvent at the time, and he knew that he was unable to pay for them. The seller may

---

[1] Marvin v. Wallis, 6 E. & B. 726.

[2] Tempest v. Fitzgerald, 3 B. & Ald. 680.

[3] Keeler v. Goodwin, 111 Mass. 490.

[4] Lupin v. Marie, 6 Wend. (N. Y.) 77; Blackshear v. Burke, 74 Ala. 239; Beam v. Blanton, 3 Ired. (N. C.) Eq. 59; James v. Bird, 8 Leigh (Va.),

510; Baker v. Dewey, 15 Grant Ch. (U. C.) 668.

[5] By the Roman law the vendor of personal property could resort to the property in the hands of the purchaser for the payment of the price. The sale, though positive in terms, was regarded as made upon the condition that the price be paid.

have a right in equity for that reason to rescind the sale ; but he has no right of lien which he can enforce for this reason.[1]

In Louisiana, however, the vendor's privilege on movables continues so long as the vendee's possession continues, but is lost by a sale and delivery of them by the vendee to a third person. But a sale without delivery does not defeat the vendor's lien ; and a delivery, in order to defeat it, must be actual and undoubted, and the change of possession must be continued.[2]

A vendor is, however, estopped by taking security for the purchase-money from claiming his lien, especially as against a subsequent *bonâ fide* purchaser or pledgee.[3]

812. Whenever the ownership of property is transferred, as shown from the whole transaction, and the seller only reserves a security for the price, it matters not what designation the parties may give to the transaction, the contract is ineffectual to create a valid lien in favor of the seller, unless it be a chattel mortgage, and the formalities required to make such a mortgage valid are observed. Thus, where printing materials were delivered by the owner to another under a contract whereby the latter in terms borrowed the property, but it was to become his on payment of the price, and he promised absolutely to pay the price, and it was provided that, if the borrower failed to pay the price, the lender might take them and dispose of them, rendering to the borrower all surplus, if any, after paying the price agreed upon, it was held that the ownership of the property was transferred, and that the contract was invalid as against a mortgagee of the purchaser.[4] "Where it is clear from the whole transaction," say the court, "that for all practical purposes the ownership of property was intended to be transferred, and that the seller only intended to reserve a security for the price, any characterization of the transaction by the parties, or any mere denial of its legal effect, will not be regarded. The question, it is true, is one of intention ; but the intention must be collected from the whole transaction, and not from any particular feature of it. In the present case it seems to us that the intention must be taken

---

[1] Johnson *v.* Farnum, 56 Ga. 144 ; Echols *v.* Head, 68 Ga. 152.

[2] Civ. Code, § 3227 ; Flint *v.* Rawlings, 20 La. Ann. 557 ; Musson *v.* Elliott, 30 Ib. 147 ; Fetter *v.* Field, 1

Ib. 80 ; Elkin *v.* Harvy, 20 Ib. 545. See § 800.

[3] Musson *v.* Elliott, *supra.*

[4] Palmer *v.* Howard (Cal.), 13 Pac. Rep. 858.

to have been to transfer the ownership of the property, reserving a security for the price and nothing more. The possession was delivered. The promise to pay was absolute."

813. Upon a sale of goods already in the possession of the purchaser as agent of the seller, no delivery is necessary, beyond the completion of the contract of sale, to destroy the seller's lien.[1]

If goods stored in a warehouse in the name of the owner's broker be sold by the owner to such broker, the seller's lien for the purchase-money is lost without any further delivery of the goods.[2] But if in such case the owner does not sell the goods to such broker in whose name the goods are stored, but to a third person who gives notice of his purchase to the broker, but not to the warehouseman, the possession is not changed, and the lien of the seller will revive on the insolvency of the purchaser.[3]

814. A condition of sale, that notes or bills shall be given for the price of the goods, is waived by an absolute delivery without demanding the notes.[4] Such delivery, when not procured by fraud, vests the absolute property in the purchaser. The rule does not differ from that which applies where goods are sold to be paid for in cash, and delivery is made without demanding the money; the title vests in the purchaser. But a delivery of part of the goods is no waiver of the condition as regards the part not delivered. Because the seller has dispensed with the condition of being paid in the manner provided in delivering part of the goods, it cannot be said that the property in the whole of the goods vested in the purchaser, so that the seller is bound to deliver the remainder. The waiver is only *pro tanto*, and the seller is entitled at any time to stand on his rights as established by the contract.[5]

815. But not every delivery of goods without insisting upon the performance of such condition is absolute. Un-

---

[1] Edan v. Dudfield, 1 Q. B. 302; *In re* Batchelder, 2 Lowell, 245; Warden v. Marshall, 99 Mass. 305; Martin v. Adams, 104 Mass. 262; Linton v. Butz, 7 Pa. St. 89.

[2] *In re* Batchelder, *supra.*

[3] *In re* Batchelder, *supra.*

[4] Lupin v. Marie, 6 Wend. (N. Y.) 77; Furniss v. Hone, 8 Ib. 247; Smith v. Dennie, 6 Pick. (Mass.) 262; Freeman v. Nichols, 116 Mass. 309. And see McCraw v. Gilmer, 83 N. C. 162.

[5] Payne v. Shadbolt, 1 Camp. 427.

doubtedly a delivery without any demand of performance of the condition is presumptive evidence of a waiver of the condition of present payment, and of a lien upon the property. This presumption may, however, be rebutted by the acts and declarations of the parties, or by the circumstances of the case. The intention of the parties in this respect is a question of fact for the jury. If the jury find that the delivery was not absolute, but that the condition of payment in money or by note attached to it, the seller may reclaim the goods upon the vendee's refusal to comply with the condition.[1]

816. The seller may by special contract retain a lien upon goods sold, which, as between the parties, will not be dependent upon his continued possession. When the common law itself raises a lien, its continuance depends upon the vendor's possession. But the lien may be created and continued by contract irrespective of possession. The contract may stipulate the mode in which the lien may be retained; and if it provides that the vendor shall retain a lien upon the property in the hands of the vendee until the purchase-money shall be paid, there is no rule of law to defeat the stipulation.[2]

817. But a lien by contract is in general good only between the parties themselves, after delivery of the goods, and is ineffectual as against those who had acquired any interest under the vendor. But such a lien would usually be regarded as a mortgage.[3] Thus, where it was agreed between the vendor and vendee of a large number of cattle, that the former should retain a lien upon them until the purchase-money should be paid, and that for the purpose of preserving the lien an agent of the vendor should accompany the cattle, and accordingly an agent did accompany them, and, the purchase-money not being paid at maturity, took forcible possession of the cattle, it was held that the lien, which depended upon a contract and not upon possession, might be enforced as between the parties, no rights of third parties having intervened, according to the

[1] Osborn v. Gantz, 60 N. Y. 540, affirming S. C. 6 J. & S. 148; Smith v. Lynes, 5 N. Y. 41. And see Hammett v. Linneman, 48 N. Y. 399; Leven v. Smith, 1 Denio (N. Y.)

571; Marston v. Baldwin, 17 Mass. 606.
[2] Sawyer v. Fisher, 32 Me. 28.
[3] Dunning v. Stearns, 9 Barb. (N. Y.) 630.

terms of the contract. But the court spoke of the charge upon the property as being in the nature of a mortgage.[1]

If standing timber be sold, the seller reserving a lien upon "said timber and saw-logs cut therefrom" until the conditions of sale shall be performed, and the buyer cuts the logs, removes them from the seller's land, and sells them to an innocent purchaser, who has no knowledge of the lien reserved, the lien cannot be enforced against such purchaser.[2]

818. No lien or charge upon goods valid as against purchasers and creditors can be created in favor of a seller not in possession, except by mortgage.[3] When the seller delivers the goods, the right of property becomes absolute in the buyer, and the seller can have no claim upon them except by force of an instrument which can operate as a mortgage, and be made effectual by recording it as such.[4]

If a lien be expressly reserved in the contract of sale, while it may continue to exist as against the vendee after a delivery of the property to him,[5] it does not exist as against one who has purchased from him for value and without notice after such delivery, unless the lien be in the form of a chattel mortgage, and this be duly recorded.[6]

819. An agreement that the purchaser of chattels shall give a mortgage upon them for the purchase-money constitutes an equitable lien as between the parties, which is not defeated by the omission of the seller to demand the mortgage at the time of the delivery of the property, or to make the delivery conditional upon the execution of the mortgage ; but the agreement creating the equitable lien is one which can be specifically enforced in equity as against the purchaser and all persons claiming under him, except *bonâ fide* purchasers having no notice of the lien.[7] If, in pursuance of such agreement, a mortgage be executed which is not in itself sufficient to create a legal lien, as, for instance, if the purchasers be a mercantile firm, and the mortgage be executed by one member of the firm in his own

[1] Gregory *v.* Morris, 96 U. S. 619.
[2] Bunn *v.* Valley Lumber Co. 51 Wis. 376.
[3] Obermier *v.* Core, 25 Ark. 562.
[4] Gay *v.* Hardeman, 31 Tex. 245.
[5] Barnett *v.* Mason, 7 Ark, 253; Bradeen *v.* Brooks, 22 Me. 463.
[6] Barnett *v.* Mason, *supra.*
[7] Husted *v.* Ingraham, 75 N. Y. 251.

name, yet if it appears, from the recitals in the mortgage or otherwise, that this was given with the intention of performing the agreement, the equitable lien will not be lost, but will be protected in equity. If a receiver of the partnership property be afterwards appointed for the purpose of winding up its affairs, the seller may apply to the court to restrain a sale of the property by him ; or may apply to have the property made expressly subject to the lien ; or may apply to have the proceeds of any sale of it made by the receiver first applied to the payment of the lien. But no relief could be obtained in such case by a suit at law.[1]

820. Under a conditional sale, or an executory contract of sale, the property does not pass though possession be delivered. The seller in such case has no lien, but instead the title to the property.[2] The seller can have a lien only when the

[1] Husted *v.* Ingraham, 75 N. Y. 251; Hale *v.* Omaha Nat. Bank, 64 N. Y. 555; *S. C.* 49 Ib. 626.

[2] Harkness *v.* Russell, 7 Sup. Ct. Rep. 51; Frick *v.* Hilliard, 95 N. C. 117.

Conditional sales, in the absence of fraud, are generally valid as well against third persons as between the parties to the transaction.

England: Barrow *v.* Coles, 3 Camp. 92; Swain *v.* Shepherd, 1 Moody & R. 223; Brandt *v.* Bowlby, 2 Barn & Ad. 932; Berhap *v.* Stillito, 2 Barn & Ald. 329, note *a; Ex parte* Crawcour, 9 Ch. D. 419; Crawcour *v.* Salter, 18 Ib. 30. Otherwise under the ●English bankrupt laws. Horn *v.* Baker, 9 East, 215; Holroyd *v.* Gwynne, 2 Taunt. 176.

United States: Copland *v.* Bosquet, 4 Wash. 588; Harkness *v.* Russell, *supra.*

Alabama : Fairbanks *v.* Eureka, 67 Ala. 109; Sumner *v.* Woods, Ib. 139.

Connecticut: Forbes *v.* Marsh, 15 Conn. 384; Hart *v.* Carpenter, 24 Conn. 427.

Georgia. Must be recorded as chattel mortgages.   Code 1882, § 1955 *a.*

Indiana : Hodson *v.* Warner, 60 Ind. 214; McGirr *v.* Sell, Ib. 249; Bradshaw *v.* Warner, 54 Ind. 58; Dunbar *v.* Rawles, 28 Ind. 225; Shireman *v.* Jackson, 14 Ind. 459.

Iowa. Must be recorded as chattel mortgages.   R. C. 1880, § 1922.

Maine: George *v.* Stubbs, 26 Me. 243 ; Boynton *v.* Libby, 62 Me. 253 ; Rogers *v.* Whitehouse, 71 Me. 222. Now not valid unless made and signed in a note, or recorded. Acts 1874, ch. 181 ; R. S. 1883, ch. 111, § 5.

Massachusetts: Hussey *v.* Thornton, 4 Mass. 405; Marston *v.* Baldwin, 17 Mass. 606; Barrett *v.* Pritchard, 2 Pick. 512; Coggill *v.* Hartford & N. H. R. R. Co. 3 Gray, 545; Deshon *v.* Bigelow, 8 Gray, 159; Hirschorn *v.* Canney, 98 Mass. 149; Chase *v.* Ingalls, 122 Mass. 381; Acts 1884, ch. 313.   Now conditional sales of furniture or household effects must be in writing, and copy furnished vendee, on which all payments must be indorsed.

Michigan: Whitney *v.* McConnell, 29 Mich. 12 ; Smith *v.* Lozo, 42 Mich. 6; *S. C.* 3 N. W. Rep. 227; Marquette Manuf'g Co. *v.* Jeffery, 49 Mich. 283; *S. C.* 13 N. W. Rep. 592.

title passes to the purchaser. If the title does not pass, the person to whom the possession is delivered can confer no valid

Minnesota. Must be filed in town where vendee resides. Record ceases to be notice after one year. G. S. 1878, ch. ˙39, §§ 15, 16; Laws 1883, ch. 38; Laws 1885, ch. 76.

Missouri : Ridgeway v. Kennedy, 52 Mo. 24; Wangler v. Franklin, 70 Mo. 659; Sumner v. Cottey, 71 Mo. 121. Now must be recorded in same manner as chattel mortgages. R. S. 1879, § 2505.

Nebraska. Must be filed in county where vendee resides. Ceases to be valid after five years, unless filing renewed. Comp. Stat. 1885, ch. 32, § 26.

New Hampshire: Sargent v. Gile, 8 N. H. 325; McFarland v. Farmer, 42 N. H. 386; King v. Bates, 57 N. H. 446. Now not valid unless vendor takes a written memorandum, signed by the purchaser, witnessing the sum due, and causes it to be recorded in the town clerk's office where the purchaser resides, if in the state, otherwise where the vendor resides, within ten days after delivery. An affidavit of good faith, signed by both parties, must be appended and recorded. Laws 1885, ch. 30, §§ 1, 2.

New Jersey: Cole v. Berry, 42 N. J. L. 308.

New York: Haggerty v. Palmer, 6 Johns. Ch. 437; Strong v. Taylor, 2 Hill, 326; Herring v. Hoppock, 15 N. Y. 400; Ballard v. Burgett, 40 N. Y. 314; and see Dows v. Kidder, 84 N. Y. 121 ; Parker v. Baxter, 86 N. Y. 586; Bean v. Edge, 84 N. Y. 510. Void unless contract or a copy be filed in the town where purchaser resides, if in the state, otherwise in town where property is. Record ceases to be notice after one year, unless re-filed within thirty days. Laws 1884, ch. 315.

North Carolina: Vasser v. Buxton, 86 N. C. 335; *S. C.* 14 Rep. 121.

Ohio : Call v. Seymour, 40 Ohio St. 670 ; Sanders v. Keber, 28 Ohio St. 630. Contract void unless made under oath and signed by purchaser, and filed in city where he resides, or where property is. Acts 1885, p. 238.

South Carolina. Must be recorded in same manner as chattel mortgages. Acts 1882, No. 20.

Texas. Must be recorded as chattel mortgages. Laws 1885, ch. 78.

Vermont : Hefflin v. Bell, 30 Vt. 134 ; Fales v. Roberts, 38 Vt. 503 ; Duncans v. Stone, 45 Vt. 118, 123. Not valid unless memorandum signed by both parties be recorded in town clerk's office where purchaser resides, if in the state, otherwise where seller resides, within thirty days. R. S. 1880, §§ 1992–1994 ; Acts 1884, No. 93. One who purchases such property after the lien is recorded, acquires no title, for the seller has none to give. Church v. McLeod, 58 Vt. 541.

West Virginia. Condition or reservation must be recorded in county where property is. R. S. 1878, ch. 96, § 3.

Wisconsin. Not valid unless filed in town where vendee resides, or where property is. R. S. 1878, § 2317.

In a few states conditional sales, or secret liens which treat the vendor of personal property, who has delivered possession of it to the purchaser, as owner until payment of the purchase-money, cannot be maintained; being regarded as constructively fraudulent.

Colorado. Must be recorded as chattel mortgages. G. S. 1883, § 169; George v. Tufts, 5 Colo. 162.

Illinois: Murch v. Wright, 46 Ill. 488; McCormick v. Hadden, 37 Ill. 370 ; Ketchum v. Watson, 24 Ill. 591; Van Duzor v. Allen, 90 Ill. 499; Hervey v. R. I. Locomotive Works, 93 U. S. 664.

Kentucky : Hart v. Barney &

claim to the property to another, even a *bonâ fide* purchaser for value.[1] If the title does pass, and a lien is in some form reserved, though this may be a valid contract between the parties, it does not protect the property from seizure by creditors of the purchaser, or from passing by a sale made by him.[2]

If the contract of sale provides that the seller may at his option resume possession of the property, he should give notice of his option before taking the property by replevin, especially if considerable time has elapsed since default.[3]

III. *What Change of Possession Destroys It.*

821. There is often difficulty in determining what constitutes such a change of possession from the seller to the buyer as will put an end to the seller's lien. If the goods are delivered to the buyer's own servant, agent, or carrier, they are in legal effect delivered to the buyer himself.[4] But a common carrier is not the servant of the buyer, and therefore, although the goods have left the actual possession of the seller, he retains his lien while they are in the hands of the carrier, until they have reached their destination, or the actual custody of the seller, and may be stopped by him *in transitu*.[5] Even after the goods have reached their destination, the seller has the right to stop them, so long as they have not passed into the actual custody of the buyer, and he has exercised no act of ownership over them. But so far as the seller's right of lien is concerned, this right is at an end and the delivery is complete when the seller has placed the goods in possession of a carrier to be transported to the buyer. The seller's only right in respect to the goods after such delivery is his right of stoppage *in transitu*, — which is an equitable right in the nature of a lien, but well distinguished from it, — to repossess himself of the goods while in the carrier's hands and before they have come into the actual possession of the buyer, upon the buyer's insolvency.[6]

Smith Manuf'g Co. 7 Fed. Rep. 543; Vaughn *v.* Hopson, 10 Bush, 337; Greer *v.* Church, 13 Bush, 430.

[1] Kohler *v.* Hayes, 41 Cal. 455; Hegler *v.* Eddy, 53 Cal. 597, 598; Palmer *v.* Howard (Cal.), 13 Pac. Rep. 858.

[2] Heryford *v.* Davis, 102 U. S. 235.

[3] Wheeler & Wilson Manufacturing Co. *v.* Teetzlaff, 53 Wis. 211.

[4] Arnold *v.* Delano, 4 Cush. (Mass.) 33, 39, per Shaw, C. J.; Muskegon Booming Co. *v.* Underhill, 43 Mich. 629.

[5] Arnold *v.* Delano, *supra.*

[6] Bullock *v.* Stcherge (U. S. C. C. D. Iowa, 1882), 14 Rep. 39; Boyd *v.* Mosely, 2 Swan (Tenn.), 661.

822. A seller is deemed to have parted with the possession of chattels sold where the buyer has changed the character of the property by expending labor or money upon it, in pursuance of the contract of sale. Thus, if the owner of land sells wood standing upon it, giving authority to the purchaser to cut it within a certain time, the seller has no lien on the wood for the price, in case of the purchaser's insolvency after the wood is cut, and before it is removed. The purchaser having expended labor and money in felling the trees and preparing the wood for the market, he must be regarded as having taken it into his actual possession. His acts have wrought such a change of possession as to defeat any right of lien in the seller.[1]

823. A delivery order upon a warehouseman does not, without some positive act done under it, operate as a constructive delivery, nor deprive the seller of his right of lien for the price, even as against a third person who has in good faith purchased the goods of the buyer holding such order.[2] The indorsee of a bill of lading may have a better title to the goods which it represents than the indorser had; but the indorsee of a delivery order has no better title through the indorsement than the indorser had.[3] Even the fact that the sub-vendee was induced by the original vendee to purchase and pay for the goods, by receiving the delivery orders given by the original vendor, does not estop the latter from setting up his right, as an unpaid

---

[1] Douglas v. Shumway, 13 Gray (Mass.), 498.

[2] M'Ewan v. Smith, 2 H. L. Cas. 309; Townley v. Crump, 5 Nev. & M. 606; S. C. 4 Ad. & El. 58; Imperial Bank v. London Docks Co. 5 Ch. D. 195, 200; Griffiths v. Perry, 1 E. & E. 680; Winks v. Hassall, 9 B. & C. 372.

[3] Lord Chancellor Cottenham, delivering judgment in M'Ewan v. Smith, supra, said: "It is said that, though the delivery note does not pass the property as a bill of lading would have passed it, by being indorsed over from one party to another, still it operates as an estoppel upon the party giving it, so far, at all events, as a

third party is concerned; and it is argued that it is a kind of fraud for a person to give a delivery note which the person receiving it may use so as to impose upon a third person, and then to deprive that third person of its benefit. But that argument is merely putting the argument as to the effect of a delivery note in another form, and it assumes that such a document has all the effect of a bill of lading. But, as the nature and effects of these two documents are quite different from each other, it seems to me that such an argument has no foundation at all, and cannot be adopted without converting a delivery note into a bill of lading."

vendor, to withhold the goods.[1] In a case before the Common Pleas Division, where a sub-vendee claimed that the vendor was estopped from setting up his right, all the judges said the order obviously contained no representation of any fact, and the sub-vendee had no right to rely upon it as a representation, and consequently he did not bring himself within the conditions of an estoppel.

824. A delivery order differs materially in its effects from a bill of lading;[2] for, while a delivery order does not divest the seller of possession until the order is accepted or actual possession is taken under it, the transfer of a bill of lading immediately divests the seller of possession, and consequently of his right of lien. But in England, by the recent Factors' Act, the transfer of a delivery order by a vendor to his vendee seems to have the same effect as the transfer of a bill of lading in defeating any vendor's lien, or right of stoppage *in transitu*.[3]

A bill of lading is an instrument of title representing the property, and the delivery of it by the vendor to the vendee passes the title and the right of possession. It of course implies that the actual possession of the goods represented has passed from the vendor to the carrier who has issued the bill of lading. Moreover, the delivery of the instrument of title is a complete legal delivery of the goods themselves. The vendor is consequently divested of his lien by the delivery of the bill of lading; but, as will hereafter be noticed, the vendor may, until the goods have come to the actual possession of the vendee, or he has transferred the bill of lading to a third person for value, intercept the goods in case the buyer becomes insolvent before paying the price.

825. A warehouse receipt or dock-warrant also differs

[1] Farmeloe *v.* Bain, 1 C. P. D. 445. The delivery order in this case was as follows: "We hereby undertake to deliver to your order, indorsed hereon, twenty-five tons merchantable sheet zinc off your contract of this date." Lindley, J., said: "The document amounts to no more than this: 'You have a contract with me for the sale of certain zinc; and I am willing to deliver twenty-five' tons off that contract, on the terms of that contract.' That clearly does not amount to a representation that the vendee was at liberty to transfer to his vendee a property in the zinc which he himself did not possess."

[2] Keeler *v.* Goodwin, 111 Mass. 490.

[3] Factors' Act 1877, 40 & 41 Vict. ch. 39, § 4; Benjamin on Sales, 4th ed. § 1207.

materially from a delivery order. It is so far a document of title that the indorsement or transfer of it for value amounts to a delivery of the goods represented, and divests the vendor of his lien.[1] In the case of Spear *v.* Travers,[2] decided in 1815, the gentlemen of the special jury observed, that in practice the indorsed dock-warrants and certificates are handed from seller to buyer as a complete transfer of the goods.

A warehouseman who has issued his own receipt to a purchaser is himself estopped from denying his liability for the goods to the holder of the receipt; and he is estopped although the goods have not been separated from others of the same kind.[3]

826. A wharfinger's certificate, that certain goods are at the vendor's works ready for shipment, is not a document of title, and therefore the delivery of it does not pass the goods and divest the vendor of his right of lien as against either the vendee or a purchaser from him.[4] In a case before the Court of Appeal in Chancery, it appeared that an iron manufacturer had contracted to sell a large quantity of iron rails for shipment to Russia, and that in pursuance of the contract he delivered to the purchaser wharfinger's certificates to the effect that a certain number of tons of such rails were lying at the works of the manufacturer ready for shipment under the contract. The purchaser obtained advances on the security of such certificates, and became insolvent before his acceptances for the price became due. The person who advanced the money claimed the rails, on the ground that the wharfinger's certificates were equivalent to warrants or documents of title, and passed both the right of property and the right of possession. But this claim was repudiated by the court. "A document of title," said Mellish, L. J., "is something which represents the goods, and from which, either immediately or at some future time, the possession of the goods may be obtained. In this way a bill of lading represents the goods while they are at sea, and by which, when the goods arrive at the port of destination, the possession of the goods may be ob-

---

[1] Whether an indorsement of the warrants of the West India Docks Co. would pass the property in the goods therein mentioned, was left an undecided question in Lucas *v.* Dorrien, 7 Taunt. 278; though Dallas, J., said that he felt no doubt on the question.

[2] 4 Camp. 251.

[3] Adams *v.* Gorham, 6 Cal. 68; Goodwin *v.* Scannell, Ib. 541.

[4] Gunn *v.* Bolckow, L. R. 10 Ch. 491.

tained. So, also, a delivery order is an order for a delivery of the goods either immediately or at some future time ; generally, immediately on the presentation of the delivery order, the party is entitled to the goods. Therefore it represents the goods. . . . Then it is said that there is a custom of the trade to treat these certificates as warrants. Now, in the first place, there is no evidence of such a custom. That these certificates are often pledged, and that, as between the party who pledges them and the party who advances money, they would be evidence of an equitable charge, is, I think, very probable. The iron trade, we know, is a very speculative trade. I dare say those who are engaged in it raise money in that way. But if the custom were proved, I cannot understand how any practice of raising money in that way can affect the vendor's rights. The vendor, having agreed by this contract that he would give the wharfinger's certificate in order that the purchaser may have evidence that the goods have been actually made, and now are actually ready to be shipped, cannot help giving the certificate ; and how the fact of his giving that certificate, which does not profess to be negotiable, and does not profess to require the delivery of the goods to order or to bearer, or anything of the kind, can affect his lien as vendor, merely because the purchaser chooses to borrow money on the faith of it, I am at a loss to conceive."

827. But, by usage of a particular trade, a delivery warrant, without anything more, may be sufficient to estop the vendor from setting up his lien as against an assignee for value of such warrant. Thus, where it was proved to be the custom of the iron trade in England to treat such a warrant as giving to the holder thereof title to the iron described, free from any claim by the vendor who gave the warrant for the purchase-money, it was held that the vendor could not set up his lien as against a pledgee of such warrant.[1]

[1] Merchant Banking Co. *v.* Phœnix Bessemer Steel Co. 5 Ch. D. 205. The warrant in this case was as follows :—

"The under-mentioned iron will not be delivered to any party but the holder of this warrant. Stacked at the works, etc. Warrant for (specified) steel rails. Iron deliverable (f. o. b.) to (purchasers), or to their assigns, by indorsement hereon."

The vendor had already given to the purchaser an invoice of the goods with a similar warrant attached. Jessell, M. R., referring to the terms of the warrant and to the fact that an invoice and warrant had already been delivered, said : "The very form of

828. There is an actual change of possession under a delivery order where the warehouseman has entered the goods in the name of the purchaser, though the goods themselves are not moved from their place. When a delivery order has been lodged with the warehouse-keeper in whose warehouse the goods lie, whether this be the vendor's warehouse or belongs to another, and the warehouseman has transferred the goods in his books into the name of the purchaser, the vendor's lien is gone. From that moment the warehouseman becomes the bailee of the purchaser, and the delivery is as complete as if the goods had been delivered into his own hands.[1] And so, if the warehouseman, on receiving an order from the vendor to hold the goods on account of the purchaser, gives a written acknowledgment that he so holds them, he cannot set up, as a defence for not delivering them to the purchaser, that by the usage of that particular trade the property in them is not transferred till it is remeasured, and that, before they were remeasured, the purchaser became insolvent. By the acknowledgment the warehouseman attorned to the purchaser.[2]

Even the verbal assent of the warehouseman to the order, upon the purchaser's communicating it to him, will effect a change of possession without an actual transfer of the goods in his books to the name of the purchaser.[3]

829. But a mere notice of a sale given to a warehouse-man, or other bailee in possession of the goods, does not

the warrant shows the purpose. In my opinion, considering that they had already given a document of title which was quite clear and independent and satisfactory to the purchaser, this was something they were issuing for a different purpose. . . . On these two grounds I am in the plaintiffs' favor : first, on account of the general custom of the trade ; and, secondly, because I think you must impute to the defendant company special notice and special knowledge that the warrant was intended to be used for some such purpose, and, having that knowledge, they issued the document in this particular form, for it is inconceivable for what purpose it could have been used except that for which it was actu-ally used, of course, including the selling as well as pledging the goods. I have in this case the distinction, that the company purposely issued a second document of title with a view of its being used for a special purpose. On those grounds I think the company are not entitled to set up in this case the vendors' lien at all against the plaintiffs."

[1] Harman v. Anderson, 2 Camp. 242; Arnold v. Delano, 4 Cush. (Mass.) 33, 39, per Shaw, C. J.; Parker v. Byrnes, 1 Lowell, 539.

[2] Stonard v. Dunkin, 2 Camp. 344; Hawes v. Watson, 2 B. & C. 540; Gosling v. Birnie, 7 Bing. 339; Holl v. Griffin, 10 Bing. 246.

[3] Lucas v. Dorrien, 7 Taunt. 278.

generally deprive the seller of his lien; but the bailee must enter into some obligation with the vendee, or recognize him in some way, so that he shall become his bailee instead of the vendor's bailee.[1] " Notice may be enough to put him on his guard, and to render him liable to an action if he does anything inconsistent with the notice ; and a notice silently received may be evidence of acquiescence, and it may even be conclusive evidence thereof, by way of estoppel, if third persons have been misled ; but, as between the vendor and vendee, I understand that the possession is not changed until the warehouseman has in some way acknowledged the change, and has become the agent of the vendee. In the analogous law of stoppage *in transitu*, the carrier who receives goods very often has notice that the consignee has bought them, and is in fact their owner, and he is notified and directed to deliver to the vendee ; but until he has either delivered them, or changed his relation in some way so as to become the exclusive agent of the vendee, they may be stopped, if the occasion arises. In short, such an order is revocable in the case of the failure of the vendee, unless it has been acted on." [2]

830. **Possession under a delivery order obtained by artifice or mistake does not divest the seller of his lien.** Thus a seller of certain casks of oil directed the wharfinger to transfer them to the purchaser's name, and he accordingly did so, and gave to the seller a transfer order addressed to the purchaser, acknowledging that he held the goods for him. The seller thereupon, through his clerk, offered the transfer order to the buyer, and demanded payment, which he was entitled to upon delivery. The buyer refused to make payment, but retained the transfer order. The seller immediately gave notice to the wharfinger not to deliver the oil, but the latter, in defiance of the order, afterwards delivered it to the buyer. In trover by the seller for the oil, it was held that neither the property nor the right of possession passed to the buyer.[3] " There is no doubt upon the authorities," said Williams, J., " that, if that transfer order had been delivered to the buyer, and he had carried it to the wharfinger, and the latter had consented to hold the oil therein specified for him, or if, after the order had been left with the wharf-

---

[1] *In re* Batchelder, 2 Lowell, 245, 247.

[2] *In re* Batchelder, *supra*, per Lowell, J.

[3] Godts *v.* Rose, 17 C. B. 229.

inger by the seller's clerk, the wharfinger had communicated it
to the buyer, and the latter had assented to it either tacitly or
explicitly, that would have constituted a complete transfer, inasmuch as the transaction would amount to an arrangement between
the three — the vendor, the wharfinger, and the vendee — that
the oil should remain in the wharfinger's hands as the agent of
·the vendee. It is impossible to say that the facts here show that
any arrangement of that kind was come to. The person who
took the order from the wharfinger to the vendee was induced to
part with it by a species of force. I am clearly of opinion that
the property in the oil, notwithstanding what took place, remains
in the plaintiff."

831. Of course a delivery order upon a warehouseman,
given, not by the owner in whose name the goods are stored,
but by his vendee, does not make a constructive delivery as between such vendee and a sub-vendee, so as to put an end to the
first vendee's lien for the price.[1]

832. A charge of warehouse rent by the seller upon the
goods left in his possession, and stored in his own warehouse, does not affect his right of lien for the unpaid purchase-
money ;[2] though a payment of such rent by a sub-vendee for the
whole of the goods, and acceptance of the same by the seller,
would rightly be regarded as a delivery of the whole.[3] But if
the warehouse rent is not actually paid, but only charged, such
charge amounts to a notification by the seller to the purchaser
that he is not to have the goods until he has paid, not only the
price of the goods, but also the rent.[4] And so, if a sub-vendee
pays the warehouse rent upon part of the goods upon receiving
such part, upon an order from the original vendee, the vendor's
lien upon the remainder of the goods is not affected. His control and lien remain entire over the whole until the delivery of
the part. It is, however, divisible, and, when part is taken away,

[1] Lackington v. Atherton, 7 M. &
G. 360.

[2] Miles v. Gorton, 2 Cr. & M. 504;
Bloxam v. Sanders, 4 B. & C. 941;
Grice v. Richardson, 3 App. Cas. 319;
Winks v. Hassall, 9 B. & C. 372;

Hammond v. Anderson, 1 B. & P. N.
R. 69.

[3] Hurry v. Mangles, 1 Camp. 452.

[4] Miles v. Gorton, 2 Cr. & M.
504, 513, per Bayley, B.

the lien remains on the goods which were not delivered, and for which the warehouse rent has never been paid.[1]

833. **A seller loses his lien by giving an acknowledgment that he holds the goods as bailee for the purchaser.** In a case where a negotiable note was taken for the price of goods sold, the seller at the same time gave the buyer a certificate that he held them for the seller upon storage. Afterwards the buyer verbally offered to cancel the sale if the seller would surrender the note. He agreed to this, but, the note having been discounted at a bank, he did not tender the note till several days afterwards. In the mean time the buyer had assigned the goods to certain of his creditors, informing them, however, of the conversation in regard to cancelling the sale. These assignees brought an action of trover against the seller for the goods, whereupon it was held that the property vested in the buyer, and that the seller had no lien for the price of the goods.[2] The contract to cancel the sale was conditional ; and, as a resale of the goods, it was void by the statute of frauds, the value of the goods being more than fifty dollars.

834. **A delivery of a part of the goods sold does not operate as a delivery of the whole,** so as to destroy the vendor's lien, or right of stoppage *in transitu*, unless there be something to show that the parties intended that such delivery of a part should be equivalent to a delivery of the whole.[3] Upon this point Willes, J., has well stated the modern doctrine: " There have been different expressions of opinion at various times as to whether the delivery of a portion of the goods, the subject of an entire contract, operates as a constructive delivery of the whole, so as to put an end to the right of stopping *in transitu*. It was supposed to have been thrown out by Taunton, J., that a delivery of part operated as a constructive delivery of the whole, but that doctrine has since been called in question and dissented from ; and it is now held that the delivery of part operates as a constructive delivery of the whole only where the delivery of

[1] Miles *v.* Gorton, 2 Cr. & M. 504, 513, per Bayley, B.

[2] Chapman *v.* Searle, 3 Pick. (Mass.) 38.

[3] *Ex parte* Cooper, 11 Ch. D. 68 ;

Bunney *v.* Poyntz, 4 B. & Ad. 568; Payne *v.* Shadbolt, 1 Camp. 427; Hamburger *v.* Rodman, 9 Daly (N. Y.), 93.

part takes place in the course of the delivery of the whole, and the taking possession by the buyers of that part is the acceptance of constructive possession of the whole."[1]

835. When part of a quantity of goods is sold, there can be no delivery until the part sold is separated or set apart for the purchaser. Thus, if a thousand bushels of corn, part of a larger quantity lying in bulk, be sold, no title passes until separation of this part is made in some form.[2]   But if in such case the grain be stored in an elevator, and the seller delivers to the buyer an order on the proprietor of the elevator or upon the warehouseman, and the buyer presents the order to the proprietor or warehouseman, and the latter agrees thenceforward to hold that quantity for the buyer, a valid title with constructive possession is acquired by the buyer, and the seller's lien is defeated.[3]

Trees lying on the land of a third person were sold, the purchaser having the privilege of removing them when he pleased. He marked the trees, ascertained their cubical contents, and removed some of them.   It was held, that the transfer of the whole was complete, and that, upon the bankruptcy of the purchaser, the vendor could not enforce any lien upon the portion not removed.[4]

836. The rule has sometimes been stated to be that the delivery of part of the goods sold on an entire contract is a virtual delivery of the whole, and vests in the purchaser the entire property:[5] so stated, subject, however, to qualifications, de-

[1] Bolton v. Lancashire & Yorkshire Ry. Co. L. R. 1 C. P. 431, 440.

[2] Keeler v. Goodwin, 111 Mass. 490.

[3] Keeler v. Goodwin, supra, per Wells, J.; Cushing v. Breed, 14 Allen (Mass.), 376.

[4] Tansley v. Turner, 2 Bing. N. C. 151; and see Ex parte Gwynne, 12 Ves, 379 ; Cooper v. Bill, 3 H. & C. 722.

[5] Slubey v. Heyward, 2 H. Bl. 504; Hammond v. Anderson, 1 B. & P. N. R. 69. Pollock, C. B., referring to these two cases in Tanner v. Scovell, 14 M. & W. 28, 37, says they are the only ones, so far as he has observed, which bear the semblance of an authority that a mere part delivery is sufficient to put an end to the vendor's lien, or his right to stoppage in transitu.

In Ex parte Cooper, 11 Ch. D. 68, Brett, L. J., said, with reference to these two cases : " It seems to me that in the former case the ground of decision was that the captain of the ship had altered his position from that of a mere carrier, and had undertaken, with the consent of the assignees of the bill of lading, to hold the whole of the cargo for them ; and, in the latter case, the wharfinger, who for a time had held for the persons who had put

pending upon the terms of the particular contracts and the intention of the parties. "As, for instance," says Judge Wilde,[1] "if
goods are sold by weight or measure, and a part is weighed or measured and delivered, and a part not, the property in the goods not
weighed or measured still remains in the vendor;[2] or if anything remains to be done by the vendor before delivery as to the
part not delivered;[3] or if a part is retained by the vendor until
the price shall be paid ; or if the goods are to be paid for on delivery, and a part only is paid for and delivered. In all these
cases the property not delivered will not vest in the vendee."

The vendor's right of lien in such cases depends, of course
upon the rule that governs as to delivery.

837. **The rule as above stated applies only where there
was no intention to separate the particular part** delivered
from the remainder. In that case the incipient or inchoate delivery will amount to a determination of the vendor's lien.
Chief Baron Pollock, reviewing the early cases upon this point,
says of the leading case of Slubey v. Heyward,[4] that the part
delivery of the cargo there was in truth a delivery of the whole
cargo, for each part was taken away with the intention to take
possession of the whole, and not to separate the part that was
delivered from the remainder. In Jones v. Jones,[5] also, the ven-

the goods into his hands, had altered
his position, and, with the consent of
the person to whom the goods were
transferred, had agreed to hold them
no longer for the person who had put
them into his hands, but for the vendee. In both cases there was an attornment by the person who held the
goods, and, unless something equivalent to an attornment is shown on the
part of the carrier, so that he has altered his position from that of carrier,
and holds them in another capacity,
it seems to me the *transitus* cannot be
at an end." Parks v. Hall, 2 Pick.
(Mass.) 206 ; *Ex parte* Gwynne, 12
Ves. 379.

[1] Parks v. Hall, *supra.*

[2] Citing Hanson v. Meyer, 6 East,
614.

[3] Citing Dixon v. Yates, 5 B. & Ad.
313 ; Simmons v. Swift, 5 B. & C.

857 ; Young v. Austin, 6 Pick.
(Mass.) 280 ; Merrill v. Hunnewell,
13 Ib. 213; Riddler v. Varnum, 20 Ib.
280.

[4] 2 H. Bl. 504. Lord Tenterden,
referring to this case in Bunney v.
Poyntz, 4 B. & Ad. 568, 571, says that
that was "the delivery of part of the
cargo, made in the progress of, and
with a view to the delivery of the
whole."

[5] 8 M. & W. 431.

In *Ex parte*, Cooper, 11 Ch. D.
68, 77, Lord Justice Cotton, referring
to this case, said : "It looks at first
a little more like one which supports
the general proposition which is put
forward. But when it is examined it
amounts only to this, that the court
came to the conclusion as a matter of
fact that there was an intention to
take the whole when part only was

dee, who was an assignee under a trust deed, took possession of part of a cargo, with the intention of obtaining possession of the whole, for the purposes of the trust, and therefore such taking possession of a part put an end to the transaction.

In illustration of this rule may be mentioned a case which turned upon the legal effect of a partial delivery of a cargo of wheat. Bills of lading of the wheat were transmitted by the seller to the purchaser, whose assignee, upon the arrival of the ship, received delivery of part of the cargo, when the vendor ordered the master not to deliver the residue. The court held that the vendor had no authority to countermand his order of delivery, for a delivery of a part was the delivery of the whole, there appearing to be no intention, either previous to or at the time of the delivery, to separate part of the cargo from the rest.[1]

838. Wherever an intention appears to separate a part of the goods from the residue, delivery of a part only will not divest the seller's lien upon such residue.[2] If, for instance, goods be sold to be paid for on delivery, and the seller, as a favor, allows the purchaser to carry away part of them without payment, there is no waiver of the condition, but the seller is entitled at any time to assert his rights, and detain the remainder of the goods until payment is made according to the terms actually taken; and, that being so, it is only an authority that where a purchaser taking part shows an intention, acquiesced in by the carrier, to receive and take possession of the whole, that is a constructive possession of the whole by the acquiescence of both parties. It does not in any way support the proposition that the mere delivery of a part of the cargo, as in the present case, can be looked upon as a constructive delivery of the whole, or as putting the consignee in constructive possession of the whole so as to defeat the vendor's right to stop in transitu, or the right of the consignee, if he so desires under the circumstances, to put an end to the contract."

[1] Slubey v. Heyward, 2 H. Bl. 504. In Betts v. Gibbons, 2 Ad. & E. 57, 73, Taunton, J., in reply to counsel, who asserted that a delivery of a part amounted to a delivery of the whole only when the circumstances showed that it was meant as such, said: "No; on the contrary, a partial delivery is a delivery of the whole, unless circumstances show that it is not so meant." This dictum is questioned by Pollock, C. B., in Tanner v. Scovell, 14 M. & W. 28, 37.

[2] Valpy v. Oakeley, 16 Q. B. 941; Griffiths v. Perry, 1 E. & E. 680; Miles v. Gorton, 2 Cr. & M. 504; Leonard v. Sheard, 1 E. & E. 667, per Crompton, J.; Hanson v. Meyer, 6 East, 614; Bunney v. Poyntz, 4 B. & Ad. 568, 571; Williams v. Moore, 5 N. H. 235; Haskell v. Rice, 11 Gray (Mass.), 240; Wanamaker v. Yerkes, 70 Pa. St. 443.

of the sale. Such a delivery of a part is a separation of that part from the whole bulk, and not an inchoate delivery of the whole.[1]

A vendee taking possession of a part of the goods sold, not meaning thereby to take possession of the whole, but to separate that part, and to take possession of that part only, puts an end to the vendor's lien only with respect to that part and no more; and the right of lien and the right of stoppage *in transitu* on the remainder still continue.[2]

839. If during the delivery of goods sold, and before it is completed, the purchaser sells or pledges them to a third person, without the knowledge of the original vendor, the lien of the latter is not affected. Thus, where a raft of lumber upon the Hudson River was sold to be paid for on delivery upon the dock of a lumber dealer at Albany, after nearly all the lumber had been taken from the water and piled upon the dock, the seller, having learned that the buyer had absconded, forbade the piling of any more of it upon the dock. When part of the lumber had been piled upon the dock, the buyer obtained an advance upon it from the owner of the dock, and the latter claimed title to the lumber. But it was held that the vendor was entitled to the lumber by virtue of his lien. The court said, that the sale was of the whole raft to be delivered upon the dock, that the vendor had no right to demand payment of any part until the whole was delivered, and that, being present to demand payment as soon as the whole should be placed upon the dock, he had not lost his lien.[3]

840. The vendor may retain the goods still in his hands, not only for the price of such goods, but also for the price of any part of the goods already delivered.[4] The insolvency of the purchaser does not put an end to the contract of sale, but, if the insolvent has any beneficial interest under it, it is the right of his assignee, in behalf of his creditors, to complete the contract by paying the remainder of the unpaid purchase-money. The

---

[1] Dixon *v.* Yates, 5 B. & Ad. 313, per Parke, J.; Townley *v.* Crump, 5 Nev. & M. 606.

[2] Tanner *v.* Scovell, 14 M. & W. 28, 38, per Pollock, C. B.

[3] Palmer *v.* Hand, 13 Johns. (N. Y.) 434.

[4] *Ex parte* Chalmers, L. R. 8 Ch. 289.

assignee cannot, however, claim damages for the non-delivery of an instalment of the goods sold, without tendering payment not only of the price of that, but also of the unpaid price of a prior instalment already delivered.

IV. When Seller Estopped by a Resale.

841. A purchaser who has not obtained possession cannot defeat the seller's lien by making a sale to another person.[1] The purchaser without possession can confer no better title than he has himself. An invoice of the goods without actual possession, or a delivery order which shows his right of possession, does not enable the purchaser to confer a title upon another as against the seller's lien.[2]

A resale of the goods to a third person by the first purchaser does not affect the rights of the unpaid vendor, unless he has in some way estopped himself from asserting them, as against the sub-purchaser.[3]

A bill of lading in the hands of the purchaser enables him to sell and confer a title upon a purchaser from him. But a vendor may preserve his lien by consigning goods to an agent or bailee instead of the purchaser, and taking a bill of lading to the vendor's own order. Then, upon the arrival of the goods at their destination, the bailee may take possession of them and hold them until payment is made. If, in such case, the vendor draws against the goods and obtains a discount of his draft upon a pledge of the bill of lading, and, the purchaser having become insolvent, the pledgee attaches the goods, upon their arrival at their destination, as the purchaser's goods, such attachment will have no effect upon the lien of the vendor, but he may pay the draft, and by virtue of his lien replevy the goods from the attaching officer.[4]

842. The unpaid seller may by his acts or declarations estop himself from claiming his lien as against a sub-pur-

---

[1] Dixon v. Yates, 5 B. & Ad. 313.

[2] Dixon v. Yates, supra; Ware River R. R. Co. v. Vibbard, 114 Mass. 447; Hamburger v. Rodman, 9 Daly (N. Y.), 93.

[3] Craven v. Ryder, 6 Taunt. 433; Miles v. Gorton, 2 Cr. & M. 504;

Farmeloe v. Bain, 1 C. P. D. 445; Townley v. Crump, 4 Ad. & El. 58; Haskell v. Rice, 11 Gray (Mass.), 240; Hamburger v. Rodman, supra.

[4] Seymour v. Newton, 105 Mass. 272.

chaser.[1] Thus, timber lying at the owner's wharf was sold and marked with the initials of the buyer, who gave his acceptances on time for the price. Before the acceptances became due, the buyer sold all the timber except a small part which had been delivered to him. The last purchaser notified the original vendor of his purchase, who answered, " Very well ; " and the purchaser went with him to the wharf, and there marked the timber with his own initials, and directed the vendor to send no more of the timber to the original vendee. Upon the insolvency of the latter, it was held that the vendor could not retain the lumber as against the last purchaser.[2] Lord Ellenborough, referring to the assent of the vendor to the last purchase in saying " Very well," and in making no objection to the marking of the timber in the name of the last purchaser, said : " If that be not an executed delivery, I know not what is so." The other judges also declared that there was an express assent to such transfer of the lumber, and that the seller could not retain it.

843. Same (*continued*). A purchaser of barley, which was in the seller's warehouse, resold a part of it, and gave to the purchaser a delivery order addressed to the station-master. The second purchaser sent this order to the station-master, saying, " Please confirm this transfer." The station-master showed the delivery order to the seller, who still had possession of the barley, and he said, " All right. When you get the forwarding note I will put the barley on the line." The first purchaser became bankrupt, and the seller refused to deliver the grain. The Court of Queen's Bench held that the seller was estopped by his statement to the station-master from denying that the property had passed to the second purchaser ; for, by making such statement, he induced the plaintiff to rest satisfied under the belief that the property had passed, and so to alter his position by abstaining from demanding back the money which he had paid to his vendor.[3]

A case not distinguishable from the foregoing was decided upon the same grounds by the Court of Appeals of New York.

---

[1] Stoveld *v.* Hughes, 14 East, 308; Parker *v.* Crittenden, 37 Conn. 148.

[2] Stoveld *v.* Hughes, *supra.* For a similar case, see Chapman *v* Shepard, 39 Conn. 413.

[3] Knights *v.* Wiffen, L. R. 5 Q. B. 660. For similar cases see Woodley *v.* Coventry, 2 H. & C. 164 ; Pooley *v.* Great Eastern Ry. Co. 34 L. T. N. S. 537.

A purchaser of a quantity of cotton in store pledged the invoice, and gave to the pledgee an order upon the warehouseman. The pledgee presented the order to the warehouseman, who, with the consent of the vendor, gave to the pledgee the ordinary warehouse receipt for the cotton. Three days afterwards the purchaser of the cotton failed, without having paid for it. It was held that the seller was estopped from claiming the cotton as against the pledgee, because the latter had a right to rely upon the warehouse receipt. Had the pledgee not obtained the warehouse receipt, he might have resorted to some process to recover the loan, or to secure some indemnity against loss.[1]

844. A seller is estopped from setting up his lien, as against a purchaser from his vendee, by recognizing such purchaser's delivery order, and delivering several parcels to him without objection. Thus, sugar lying in the seller's warehouse was sold, and the buyer's acceptances taken in payment. The buyer resold the sugar, and gave a delivery order to the purchaser, who handed it to the original vendor, and received from him a part of the sugar. Afterwards this purchaser, on several occasions, gave his own delivery orders on the vendor for portions of the goods. Before the acceptances became due, the first purchaser became insolvent, and the vendor refused to deliver the remainder of the goods to the last purchaser. It was held that he could not detain the goods; that, by accepting his buyer's delivery order without making claim to any lien upon the goods, he had recognized the second purchaser as having the right of property and of possession of the goods, and that he could not set up any lien upon the goods as against such purchaser.[2] Lord Campbell, C. J., said: "The title of the purchaser being once acknowledged by the warehouseman, the purchaser has a right to treat the warehouseman as his agent; and the latter cannot afterwards set up a right in respect of a third party. The right claimed by the vendor is analogous to a right of stoppage *in transitu;* and, as to that, there are many cases in which it has been decided that, after the first vendee has parted with the possession of the goods to the second vendee, and ac-

---

[1] Voorhis *v.* Olmstead, 66 N. Y. 113, citing and approving Wiffen, L. R. 5 Q. B. 660.

[2] Pearson *v.* Dawson, E., B. & E. 448. Knights *v.*

knowledged his title, he cannot afterwards stop them *in transitu* on account of any claim against the first vendee."

845. In such cases the result is the same, whether the sub-vendee has paid his purchase-money before or after the acts or representations of the vendor which estop him, as against such sub-vendee, from setting up his lien. If at the time of such acts or representations the sub-vendee has not paid the price of the goods, but in consequence of such acts or representations he alters his position by paying the price either wholly or in part, the vendor is held to be bound by his acts or declarations.[1] If at the time of such acts or declarations the sub-vendee has already paid the price of the goods, nevertheless his position may be altered thereby; for he may be induced to rest satisfied that the property had passed to him, and would take no steps to demand back the money he had paid to the first purchaser before he became bankrupt. If once the fact is established that the sub-vendee's position is altered by relying upon the acts or declarations of the vendor, and taking no further steps, the latter is estopped, just as he is in the case first stated.[2]

846. If the owner of goods in any way allows them to be so situated that a stranger has a right to assume that the title is in another, and on the faith of such indicia of ownership deals with the apparent owner, the true owner is estopped from asserting his title.[3] But in such case it is an essential part of the estoppel that the third party dealt with the apparent owner on the faith of the indicia of ownership with which the owner has invested him. The owner is not estopped if he has not invested another with any indicia of ownership, and no third party has in consequence parted with his money or assumed any liability. Thus, where one sold wheat to be paid for on delivery on a car at a railroad station, and the buyer, before any wheat had been placed on board the car, by false representations obtained from the railroad company a bill of lading of the wheat, and afterwards the seller of the wheat, without any knowledge

[1] Woodley *v.* Coventry, 2 H. & C. 164.

[2] Knights *v.* Wiffen, L. R. 5 Q. B. 660. See Stonard *v.* Dunkin, 2 Camp.

344; Hawes *v.* Watson, 2 B. & C. 540.

[3] Marsh *v.* Titus, 6 T. & C. (N. Y.) 29.

of the fraudulent act of the buyer, put the wheat into the car, it was held that he had not delivered the wheat, but that he had the right to move it if the price were not paid, both as against the railroad company and as against the buyer.[1]

If a seller remaining in possession of the goods shows them to a third person as the goods of the vendee without claiming any lien upon them, and such third person thereupon buys the goods of the vendee and pays for them, the seller may be estopped as against him from asserting his lien upon the subsequent insolvency of the vendee.[2]

847. But the seller retains his lien as against a sub-purchaser if he has in no way assented to or induced the resale. Logs were sold on credit, with an agreement that they should remain in the seller's yard for a certain time, free of storage, the purchaser being free to send for them whenever he pleased. At the request of the purchaser, and to enable him to resell, an invoice containing an enumeration of the measurement of the logs was delivered to him by the seller. Subsequently the purchaser resold the logs to one who paid him the price in cash, without having seen the bill given by the original vendor, or having communicated with the latter in any way respecting the ownership of the logs; although before such resale he was seen by one of the original vendors in the yard, engaged in an examination of the logs, in company with the original purchaser. Part of the logs were delivered on a verbal order of the original purchaser, who shortly afterwards failed. It was held that the lien of the vendor attached to the logs remaining in his possession; and as the resale did not appear to have been made with his knowledge or approval, nor in any way induced by him, the case did not come within the application of the rule that, where one of two innocent persons must suffer by the act of a third, he who has enabled such third person to occasion the loss must himself bear it.[3]

848. A vendor's lien is waived when the parties make any agreement inconsistent with the existence of such lien, or from which a waiver may be fairly inferred.[4] There may be

---

[1] Toledo, Wabash & Western Ry. Co. v. Gilvin, 81 Ill. 511.

[2] Hunn v. Bowne, 2 Caines (N. Y.), 38.

[3] Hamburger v. Rodman, 9 Daly (N. Y.), 93; S. C. 9 Rep. 417.

[4] Pickett v. Bullock, 52 N. H. 354.

an actual waiver of the lien, and yet the court may not be justified in finding a waiver as a matter of law. In ordinary cases,
where the contract of sale and the agreement of the parties
made in connection with it are merely verbal, the question should
be submitted to the jury whether the lien was intended and understood by the parties to be waived or not. And so, if any
agreement not in writing is made after the sale affecting the
lien, the jury should find, from this and all the attendant circumstances, what the understanding of the parties was concerning it.[1]

849. A seller of goods waives his lien by attaching them
as the property of the purchaser, in a suit against him. The
attachment is an affirmance of the sale and delivery under it.[2]
But a suit by the seller against the purchaser for the price of
the goods, where these have remained in the seller's possession,
is no waiver of the lien.[3] An admission or averment in the
petition that the goods had been delivered is not conclusive
against the seller when in fact he had retained possession, but
was ready to deliver possession upon payment of the price.[4]

V. *When Lien Waived by Giving Credit.*

850. The giving of credit by the seller generally defeats
his right of lien; for, on a promise to pay at a future time, the
buyer, in the absence of any special agreement to the contrary,
is entitled to the immediate possession of the goods, and he may
enforce this right by action.[5] Accordingly, the taking of a
promissory note or bill of exchange payable at a future day, for
the price of the goods sold, operates as a bar to the vendor's
right of lien. The giving of a credit of any kind for the price of
the goods sold, implies the right of the buyer to take them away
into his own actual possession; and when he exercises this right,

---

[1] Pickett *v.* Bullock, 52 N. H. 354,
per Sargent, C. J.

[2] Heller *v.* Elliott, 45 N. J. L. 564;
Leavy *v.* Kinsella, 39 Conn. 50.

[3] Rhodes *v.* Mooney, 43 Ohio St.
421.

[4] Rhodes *v.* Mooney, *supra.*

[5] Spartali *v.* Benecke, 10 C. B. 212;
Chase *v.* Westmore, 5 M. & S. 180;
Crawshay *v.* Hornfray, 4 B. & Ald.
50; Houlditch *v.* Desanges, 2 Stark.

337; Feise *v.* Wray, 3 East, 93;
Edwards *v.* Brewer, 2 M. & W. 375;
Cowell *v.* Simpson, 16 Ves. 275; Jones
v. Thurloe, 8 Mod. 172; Hewison *v.*
Guthrie, 2 Bing. N. C. 755, 759; Demp-
sey *v.* Carson, 11 U. C. C. P. 462; Leon-
ard *v.* Davis, 1 Black, 476; Arnold *v.*
Delano, 4 Cush. (Mass.) 33, 39, per
Shaw, C. J.; Baker *v.* Dewey, 15
Grant Ch. (U. C.) 668.

the vendor's right of lien is gone, this being a right incident to the possession. "If goods are sold upon credit, and nothing is agreed upon as to the time of delivering the goods, the vendee is immediately entitled to the possession, and the right of possession and the right of property vest at once in him : but his right of possession is not absolute; it is liable to be defeated if he becomes insolvent before he obtains possession." [1]

851. Whether evidence is admissible of a usage in a particular trade, that the seller is not bound to deliver goods without payment, in case a term of credit is given by a written contract of sale not ambiguous in its language, is a question upon which there has been some diversity of opinion. Thus, where thirty bales of goats' wool were sold, " to be paid for by cash in one month, less five per cent. discount," it was held that the vendee was entitled to have the goods delivered to him immediately, or within a reasonable time, but was not bound to pay for them until the end of the month, and that evidence of a usage to the contrary was inadmissible.[2] "The objection to the admissibility of the evidence is, that the incident sought to be annexed by such evidence is inconsistent with, and contradictory to, the express terms of the contract, and is by those terms, if not expressly, certainly by implication, excluded." [3]

But this decision was overruled by the Exchequer Chamber, in Field v. Lelean.[4] There a sale was made by one broker to another of shares in a mine, " payment half in two months, and half in four months." It was held that evidence was admissible of a custom among brokers in mining shares, that, in contracts relating to the sale and purchase of such shares, the delivery

[1] Bloxam v. Sanders, 4 B. & C. 941, per Bayley, J.

[2] Spartali v. Benecke, 10 C. B. 212. See, also, Ford v. Yates, 2 M. & G. 549.

[3] Spartali v. Benecke, supra, per Wilde, C. J.

[4] 6 H. & N. 617. Wightman, J., delivering the judgment of the court, said : " The judgment of the Court of Common Pleas in the case of Spartali v. Benecke, supra, in which the circumstances were hardly distinguishable from the present, is no doubt directly against the admissibility of evidence of usage in this case; but that decision proceeds on what appears to me to be the mistaken ground that the effect of the introduction of a custom as to the time of delivery of the thing sold, would be to alter or vary the time fixed for payment by the written contract; whereas the time for payment would not be altered, and the custom would only affect the time for delivery, with respect to which the written contract is silent."

takes place at the time appointed for payment. The usage was regarded as not varying the time of payment as fixed by the contract of sale, but as determining the time of delivery.

852. But if the buyer allows the goods to remain in the seller's possession until the period of credit has elapsed and then fails to make payment, the seller's lien revives and may be asserted in the same manner as it might have been had no credit been given, and he may hold the goods as security for the price. Though the vendor waives his lien for the price by giving credit for it, this waiver is upon the implied condition that the vendee does not become bankrupt or insolvent.[1] Thus, if the owner of a large quantity of wood, lying in a pile upon his own land, sell it on a credit of six months, with an agreement that the purchaser may remove it within a year, and before the purchaser removes the wood he becomes insolvent, the vendor may retain the wood against the assignee in insolvency of the purchaser.[2]

Where a sale was made of a number of bales of drillings, which were to be delivered to the purchaser as fast as he needed them, for manufacturing into bags, and it was agreed that the purchaser should store the manufactured bags and deliver the warehouse receipts to the seller in pledge, it was held that, upon the delivery of the goods to the purchaser, the title vested in him, and that the seller had no lien thereon, and no lien on the manufactured bags, until the warehouse receipts were delivered to him. The agreement showed that the seller was willing to trust the purchaser for a portion of the goods, and that, upon his pledging the bags manufactured from that portion, he was willing to trust him for another portion. If the seller delivered a second portion to the purchaser without requiring a delivery in pledge of the manufactured bags, this was a waiver of the condition, and the title to both vested absolutely in the purchaser.[3]

[1] Grice v. Richardson, 3 App. Cas. 319; Gunn v. Bolckow, L. R. 10 Ch. 491; M'Ewan v. Smith, 2 H. L. 309; Martindale v. Smith, 1 Q. B. 389, 395; Dixon v. Yates, 5 B. & Ad. 313; Castle v. Sworder, 5 H. & N. 281; Miles v. Gorton, 2 Cr. & M. 504; Ex parte Chalmers, L. R. 8 Ch. 289; Griffiths v. Perry, 1 E. & E. 680; Valpy v. Oakeley, 16 Q. B. 941; Arnold v. Delano, 4 Cush. (Mass.) 33, per Shaw, C. J.; Milliken v. Warren, 57 Me. 46; Hamburger v. Rodman, 9 Daly (N. Y.), 93.

[2] Arnold v. Delano, supra; Miles v. Gorton, supra.

[3] Hewlet v. Flint, 7 Cal. 264.

853. The fact that the vendor has taken a negotiable note or bill of exchange for the purchase-money does not defeat his lien upon the subsequent insolvency of the purchaser before he has taken actual possession of the goods.[1] "When the bill is dishonored, there is no longer payment, or anything which can be considered as equivalent to payment; and it seems to me that the assignee of the bankrupt cannot, after what has taken place, insist on delivery without actual payment."[2] A bill of exchange, taken for the price of goods sold, is not absolute payment therefor, but conditional on its being honored at maturity. "No doubt, if the buyer does not become insolvent, that is to say, if he does not openly proclaim his insolvency, then credit is given by taking the bill; and during the time that the bill is current there is no vendor's lien, and the vendor is bound to deliver. But if the bill is dishonored before delivery has been made, then the vendor's lien revives; or if the purchaser becomes openly insolvent before the delivery actually takes place, then the law does not compel the vendor to deliver to an insolvent purchaser."[3]

The fact that the vendor has negotiated acceptances of the vendee for the price of the goods does not defeat the vendor's lien upon the goods, upon the subsequent insolvency of the vendee before meeting his acceptances.[4] This is certainly the rule if the bills are not secured in any way, and do not bear the name of any third person.

854. The taking of a negotiable note payable on demand for the price of goods does not divest the seller of his lien.[5]

855. If property sold at auction be delivered to the purchaser on his promise to pay for it in a few days, without any reservation of the title by the vendor, and the delivery is not obtained by fraud, the lien is waived just as it is in any case

---

[1] Gunn v. Bolckow, L. R. 10 Ch. 491; Miles v. Gorton, 2 Cr. & M. 504; Arnold v. Delano, 4 Cush. (Mass.) 33, 44; Thurston v. Blanchard, 22 Pick. (Mass.) 18; Millikin v. Warren, 57 Me. 46.

[2] Miles v. Gorton, supra, per Bayley, J.

[3] Gunn v. Bolckow, L. R. 10 Ch. 491, 501, per Mellish, J.

[4] Gunn v. Bolckow, supra. In Bunney v. Poyntz, 4 B. & Ad. 568, the fact that the vendor had taken the vendee's promissory note for the price of goods sold, and had negotiated it, and it was still outstanding, was regarded as substantially a payment, and it was consequently held that the vendor had no lien.

[5] Clark v. Draper, 19 N. H. 419.

of a sale and delivery of property on credit. Such sale and delivery pass the title, and it is not divested merely because the purchaser fails to pay for the property.[1]

856. If goods be ordered by letter without mentioning the time of payment, parol evidence is admissible to show that the goods were supplied on credit, the letter not being a valid contract within the statute of frauds.[2]

[1] Thompson *v.* Wedge, 50 Wis. 642; Singer Manuf. Co. *v.* Sammons, 49 Wis. 316.

[2] Lockett *v.* Nicklin, 2 Ex. 93.

589

CHAPTER XVIII.

I. *Its Nature and Effect.*

857. This right is an equitable extension of the vendor's right of lien at common law for the unpaid purchase-money.[1] These rights are not distinct and independent, but are, under different names, the same right at different stages of the execution of the contract of sale. The vendor's right of lien is his right to detain goods which he has sold until the price is paid, and it exists while the goods remain in his own possession or control. His right of stoppage *in transitu* is his right to retake the goods after they have passed out of his own possession and control, and exists so long as the goods are in the hands of a carrier for delivery to the purchaser. In one respect, however, the latter right differs from the former; for, while a vendor may retain the goods still in his possession for the payment of the price,

[1] Lord Romilly, M. R., in Fraser *v.* Witt, L. R. 7 Eq. 64; D'Aquila *v.* Lambert, 2 Eden, 75, 77, note; Ellis *v.* Hunt, 3 T. R. 464, 469; Rowley *v.* Bigelow, 12 Pick. (Mass.) 307, 313; Grout *v.* Hill, 4 Gray (Mass.), 361; White *v.* Welsh, 38 Pa. St. 396, 420, per Lowrie, C. J.; Benedict *v.* Schaettle, 12 Ohio St. 515; Babcock *v.* Bonnell, 80 N. Y. 244, 251; Blossom *v.* Champion, 28 Barb. (N. Y.) 217, 223, per Sutherland, J.; Loeb *v.* Peters, 63 Ala. 243, 249; Atkins *v.* Colby, 20 N. H. 154, 155, per Gilchrist, C. J.; Bucker *v.* Donovan, 13 Kans. 251, per Brewer, J.; Morris *v.* Shryock, 50 Miss. 590, 598.

In **California** and **Dakota Territory** it is declared by statute that a seller or consignor of property, whose claim for its price or proceeds has not been extinguished, may, upon the insolvency of the buyer or consignee becoming known to him after parting with the property, stop it while on its transit to the buyer or consignee, and resume possession thereof. Cal. § 3076 of Civ. Code; Dak. § 1815 of Civ. Code.

whether the purchaser be insolvent or not, he can retake the goods while they are in the possession of a third person, in transit to the purchaser, only upon the insolvency of the latter. The vendor's possession is the essential condition of his right of lien, and possession by a third person is the essential condition of his right of stoppage *in transitu*. " The sale is not executed before delivery; and, in the simplicity of former times, a delivery into the actual possession of the vendee or his servant was always supposed. In the variety and extent of dealing which the increase of commerce has introduced, the delivery may be presumed from circumstances, so as to vest a property in the vendee. A destination of the goods by the vendor to the use of the vendee, marking them, or making them up to be delivered, or removing them for the purpose of being delivered, may all entitle the vendee to act as owner, to assign, and to maintain an action against a third person into whose hands they have come. But the title of the vendor is never entirely divested till the goods have come into the possession of the vendee. He has therefore a complete right, for just cause, to retract the intended delivery, and to stop the goods *in transitu*." [1]

The right of stoppage *in transitu*, being based on an equitable principle, is highly favored.

858. The right of stoppage in transitu was first asserted as an equitable right,[2] though it has now become a legal pos-

[1] Mason *v.* Lickbarrow, 1 H. Bl. 357, 364, per Lord Loughborough.

[2] D'Aquila *v.* Lambert, 2 Eden, 75, 77, note; *S. C.* Amb. 399; *S. C.* 1 Smith's Lead. Cas. 8th ed. 797.

In Lickbarrow *v.* Mason, 6 East, 21, 27, note, Mr. Justice Buller upon this point said: " The right of stopping *in transitu* is founded wholly on equitable principles, which have been adopted in courts of law; and, as far as they have been adopted, I agree they will bind at law as well as in equity. So late as the year 1690, this right, or privilege, or whatever it may be called, was unknown to the law."

The ground on which the adoption of this equitable right by courts of law is justified are stated by the same eminent judge as follows : —

" I have always thought it highly injurious to the public that different rules should prevail in the different courts on the same mercantile case. My opinion has been uniform on that subject. It sometimes happens that in questions of real property, courts of law find themselves fettered with rules from which they cannot depart, because they are fixed and established rules, though equity may interpose, not to contradict, but to correct, the strict and rigid rules of the law. But in mercantile questions no distinction ought to prevail. The mercantile law of this country is founded on principles of equity; and when once a rule is established in that court as a rule of property, it ought to be adopted in a court of law. For this reason

sessory right, and is recognized and favored by courts of law. The earliest case in which this right is recognized is said to be Wiseman v. Vandeputt,[1] in the year 1690. Two Italians had consigned cases of silk to merchants in London ; but before the ship set sail from Leghorn news came that the merchants had failed, and thereupon the Italians changed the consignment to another person, against whom the assignees in bankruptcy of the merchants brought their bill for discovery and relief. " The court declared the plaintiffs ought not to have had so much as a discovery, much less any relief in this court, in regard that the silks were the proper goods of the two Florentines, and not of the Bonnells (the bankrupts), nor the produce of their effects ; and therefore, they having paid no money for the goods, if the Italians could by any means get their goods again into their hands, or prevent their coming into the hands of the bankrupts, it was but lawful for them so to do, and very allowable in equity."

Lord Kenyon said :[2] " The doctrine of stopping goods in transitu is bottomed on the case of Snee v. Prescot ;[3] . . . on this all the other cases are founded." In that case Lord Hardwicke, stating the case hypothetically, said : " Suppose such goods are actually delivered to a carrier to be delivered to A., and while the carrier is upon the road, and before actual delivery to A. by the carrier, the consignor hears A., his consignee, is likely to become bankrupt, or is actually one, and countermands the delivery, and gets them back into his own possession again, I am of opinion that no action of trover would lie for the assignees of A. because the goods, while they were in transitu, might be so countermanded. . . . Though goods are even delivered to the principal, I could never see any substantial reason why the origi-

courts of law of late years have said that, even where the action is founded on a tort, they would discover some mode of defeating the plaintiff, unless his action were also founded in equity ; and that, though the property might on legal grounds be with the plaintiff, if there were any claim or charge by the defendant, they would not consider the retaining of the goods as a conversion." Tooke v. Hollingworth, 5 T. R. 229.

But the fact that stoppage in transitu is only a remedial proceeding,

doubtless had much to do with its early adoption by the courts of law.

See, further, Gibson v. Carruthers, 8 M. & W. 321, per Lord Abinger.

[1] 2 Vern. 203. The next case was Snee v. Prescot, 1 Atk. 245, which occurred in 1743; and the next case was Ex parte Wilkinson (1755), cited in D'Aquila v. Lambert, supra (1761).

Adopted into common law courts by Lord Mansfield, Burghall v. Howard, 1 H. Bl. 366 n.

[2] Ellis v. Hunt, 3 T. R. 464.

[3] 1 Atk. 246, 248 (1743).

nal proprietor, who never received a farthing, should be obliged to quit all claim to them, and come in as a creditor only for a shilling, perhaps, in the pound, unless the law goes upon the general credit the bankrupt has gained by having them in his custody. But, while goods remain in the hands of the original proprietor, I see no reason why he should not be said to have a lien upon them till he is paid and reimbursed what he so advanced ; and therefore I am of opinion the defendant had a right to retain them for himself and company."

859. The civil law did not recognize the right of stoppage in transitu.[1] It was a rule of the ancient Roman law, as old as the Twelve Tables, that things sold and delivered were not acquired by the buyer until he had paid or secured the price. The unpaid vendor might pursue and retake the goods even in the hands of a third person who had in good faith bought and paid for them. If the sale was upon credit, the vendor by action might establish a claim to goods so long as they remained in the hands of the purchaser, though not against a *bonâ fide* purchaser from him for value.[2] These rules were adopted by most of the nations of continental Europe, and continued in force till about the beginning of the present century, when the necessities of commerce demanded greater security in the transfer of property, and gradually brought about a change in the law of sales and the adoption of a right of stoppage *in transitu*, substantially the same as that which had existed in England for a century or more.[3]

In Louisiana the code gives the seller a preference over other

---

[1] Domat, bk. 3, tit. 1, § 5, art. 4.

[2] This right of the unpaid vendor was called, in the civil law, revindication. *In re* Westzynthius, 2 Nev. & M. 650 *n.*

[3] In France the old rule of *revindication* was rejected, and the principle of stoppage *in transitu* adopted in the Code de Commerce in 1807. The right was shown to exist in Holland in a case tried by Lord Loughborough in 1789; Mason *v.* Lickbarrow, 1 H. Bl. 357, 364 ; and it was formally introduced into that country with the Code Napoleon in 1811.

The doctrine exists in Russia as a part of the Code of Mercantile Navigation Laws (1781), as is shown in the case of Bothlingk *v.* Inglis, 3 East, 381, 386.

In Scotland, down to 1790, it seems to have been presumed that if the buyer became bankrupt within three days after delivery to him of goods sold, he had fraudulently concealed his bankruptcy, and the vendor might retake the goods. But in that year the English doctrine of stoppage *in transitu* was adopted. Jaffrey *v.* Allan, 3 Paton, 191.

creditors of the purchaser for the price, whether the sale be on credit or not, so long as the property remains in the possession of the purchaser. If the sale be made without credit, the restitution must be made within eight days of the delivery. This privilege is not conditional, or dependent upon the solvency or insolvency of the buyer. It is positive without condition so long as the property remains in the possession of the purchaser.[1] Stoppage *in transitu* is a right which does not exist in Louisiana; but the courts of Louisiana will recognize and enforce a right of stoppage *in transitu* arising from a sale in another state to an insolvent residing in Louisiana.[2]

860. **This right, though originating in equity, has become altogether a legal right,** so that a court of equity will not ordinarily enforce it. Indeed, Lord Eldon has said :[3] " There is no instance, that I recollect, of stopping *in transitu* by a bill in equity. There have been many cases where questions have arisen respecting the property in the ship itself, in which the court has interfered ; but I do not remember one of stoppage *in transitu.*" In the case then before the court it was held that a bill would not lie to restrain by injunction the sailing of a vessel containing goods which a vendor wished to resume possession of on account of the insolvency of the consignee, though the reason given was that this might be highly inconvenient to the other shippers.

861. **The effect of the vendor's exercising this right is to restore the goods to his possession** so that he can hold them by virtue of his lien.[4] In an early case Lord Kenyon remarked,[5] that " the right of the vendor to stop goods *in transitu*, in case of the insolvency of the vendee, was a kind of equitable lien adopted by the law for the purposes of substantial justice, and that it did not proceed, as the plaintiff's counsel supposed, on the

[1] Converse *v.* Hill, 14 La Ann. 89.

[2] Blum *v.* Marks, 21 La. Ann. 268.

[3] Goodhart *v.* Lowe, 2 Jac. & W. 349.

[4] Wentworth *v.* Outhwaite, 10 M. & W. 436. Since the case of Goodhart *v.* Lowe, *supra*, decided in 1819, the courts have more clearly shown a disposition to hold that stoppage *in* *transitu* does not rescind the contract, but only gives or restores to the vendor a lien for the price. Schotsmans *v.* Lancashire & Yorkshire Ry. Co. L. R. 2 Ch. 332, 340, per Cairns, L. J.

[5] Hodgson *v.* Loy, 7 T. R. 440, 445.

ground of rescinding the contract." Notwithstanding this declaration, and other statements to like effect by other judges,[1] Lord Tenterden remarked in 1829 that there did not appear to be any case in which it had been expressly decided whether the effect of the stoppage was to rescind the contract or not. Even so late as 1842 Baron Parke said : " What the effect of stoppage *in transitu* is, whether entirely to rescind the contract, or only to replace the vendor in the same position as if he had not parted with the possession, and entitle him to hold the goods until the price be paid down, is a point not fully decided, and there are difficulties attending each construction."

Since that time, however, the principle has become well established that the effect of the stoppage is not to revest the title in the vendor, but to reinstate him in his lien for the price. He is revested in his rights as an unpaid vendor.[2]

862. The vendor, after gaining possession of the goods, holds them by virtue of his lien. The right of stoppage *in*

[1] *Ex parte* Gwynne, 12 Ves. 379, per Erskine, L. C.; Feise *v.* Wray, 3 East, 93.

[2] Martindale *v.* Smith, 1 Q. B. 389; Tarling *v.* Baxter, 6 B. & C. 360; Valpy *v.* Oakeley 16 Q. B. 941; Griffiths *v.* Perry, 1 E. & E. 680; Kemp *v.* Falk, L. R. 7 App. Cas. 573, 581, per Lord Blackburn : "It is pretty well settled now that it would not have rescinded the contract." And see Schotsmans *v.* Lancashire & Yorkshire Ry. Co. 2 Ch. 332, where Lord Cairns pointed out that, if the contract were regarded as rescinded, a court of equity would have no jurisdiction to enforce the right of stoppage *in transitu.* Newhall *v.* Vargas, 15 Me. 314; *S. C.* 13 Me. 93; Stanton *v.* Eager, 16 Pick. (Mass.) 467, 475, per Shaw, C. J.; Rowley *v.* Bigelow, 12 Ib. 307, 313, per Shaw, C. J.; Arnold *v.* Delano, 4 Cush. (Mass.) 33, 39; Rogers *v.* Thomas, 20 Conn. 53; Inslee *v.* Lane, 57 N. H. 454, 458, per Foster, C. J.; Patten's Appeal, 45 Pa. St. 151; Cox *v.* Burns, 1 Iowa, 64; Rucker *v.* Donovan, 13 Kans. 251;

Chandler *v.* Fulton, 10 Tex. 2; Morris *v.* Shryock, 50 Miss. 590; White *v.* Solomonsky, 30 Md. 585; Jordan *v.* James, 5 Ohio, 88, 98; Benedict *v.* Schættle, 12 Ohio St. 515; Cross *v.* O'Donnell, 44 N. Y. 661, 665, per Earl, C. ; Harris *v.* Pratt, 17 N. Y. 263. In Babcock *v.* Bonnell, 80 N. Y. 244, 251, Chief Justice Church said that the question had never been definitely decided in that state. " As an original question," he said, " the doctrine of rescission commends itself to my judgment as being more simple, and in most cases more just to both parties, than the notion that the act of stoppage is the exercise of a right of lien; but, in deference to the prevailing current of authority, I should hesitate in attempting to oppose it by any opinion of my own."

In **California** and **Dakota Territory** it is provided by code that stoppage in transit does not of itself rescind a sale, but it is a means of enforcing the lien of the seller. Cal. § 3080 of Civ. Code; Dak. § 1819 of Civ. Code.

transitu being an enlargement of the common law right of lien, it follows that the vendor, after exercising this right, must hold the property in the same manner that he would be required to hold it in case he had a lien upon it for the price. If the property was sold upon credit, he must hold it until the expiration of the credit, so as to be able to deliver it upon the payment of the price. But if the purchaser does not pay the price at the time stipulated, the vendor may, as in case of a lien, sell the property upon giving notice.[1] In the mean time the purchaser or his assignee may enforce his claim to the goods upon payment of the purchase-money, according to the terms of the original contract, provided he acts without unreasonable delay.[2] The vendor, by the exercise of his right of stoppage *in transitu*, can only recover the goods in the condition they are at the time he exercises the right. He cannot recover insurance upon them for loss or damage suffered in the transit.[3]

The vendor may also, notwithstanding his exercise of the right of stoppage, maintain an action against the vendee for the price of the goods bargained and sold, provided he be ready and willing to surrender the goods according to the terms of the contract.[4]

863. The vendor, after reasonable notice to the vendee, may sell the goods, and the contract of sale is then so far determined by the default of the vendee, and the action of the vendor thereupon, that the vendor may, after applying the proceeds of the sale to the payment of the price of the goods, maintain an action for the balance remaining unpaid.[5]

[1] Babcock *v.* Bonnell, 80 N. Y. 244, 249, per Church, C. J. "The general rule upon the theory of a lien must be that the vendor, having exercised the right of stoppage *in transitu*, is restored to his position before he parted with the possession of the property. The property is vested in the vendee, and the vendor holds possession as security for the payment of the purchase-price."

[2] Patten's Appeal, 45 Pa. St. 151, per Strong, J.

[3] Berndston *v.* Strang, L. R. 3 Ch. 588.

[4] Lickbarrow *v.* Mason, 6 East, 21 *n*, 27; *S. C.* 1 Smith's Lead. Cas. 8th Eng. ed. 789; Kymer *v.* Suwercropp, 1 Camp. 109; Rhodes *v.* Mooney, 43 Ohio St. 421; Newhall *v.* Vargas, 15 Me. 314, 326. "The absence of decided cases (on this point) may partly be accounted for by supposing that the vendor, usually obtaining all the goods sold, finds he is fully paid; or if not, that the object of pursuing the insolvent vendee is not worth the trouble and expense."

[5] Kymer *v.* Suwercropp, *supra;* Newhall *v.* Vargas, *supra.*

864. The vendor may also make proof of his claim against the insolvent estate of the vendee ; but whether he make proof of his entire claim for the price of the goods, or whether he must deduct from his whole claim the value of the goods in his hands, or the amount he has received from a sale of the goods, depends upon the statute or rule adopted with reference to the proof of claim for which the creditor holds security, or holds goods or money which is applicable to the claim against the insolvent's estate. In several states the vendor may in such case prove his whole claim due at the date of the assignment, though he has subsequently sold a portion or the whole of the goods stopped *in transitu*, and applied the proceeds to the payment of the debt for the price of the goods.[1]

865. There may be a resale or rescission of the contract, by the act of the vendee, which in its effect amounts to very much the same thing as a stoppage *in transitu*, and is sometimes spoken of as such.[2] Thus, if the vendee, before he receives the goods from the carrier, finds that he is insolvent, and he leaves the goods in the hands of the carrier or of a third person, for the use of the vendor, whom he notifies of his act, and the latter

[1] Patten's Appeal, 45 Pa. St. 151, following the rule adopted in Keim's Appeal, 27 Pa. St. 42 ; and in Miller's Appeal, 35 Pa. St. 481.

[2] Atkin *v.* Barwick, 1 Stra. 165; Salte *v.* Field, 5 T. R. 211; Smith *v.* Field, Ib. 402; Neate *v.* Ball, 2 East, 117; Bartram *v.* Farebrother, 4 Bing. 579 ; Nicholson *v.* Bower, 1 E. & E. 172; Lane *v.* Jackson, 5 Mass. 157; Scholfield *v.* Bell, 14 Mass. 40; Naylor *v.* Dennie, 8 Pick. (Mass.) 198 ; Grout *v.* Hill, 4 Gray (Mass.), 361; Lewis *v.* Mason, 36 U. C. Q. B. 590, 604; Mason *v.* Redpath, 39 Ib. 157.

In the leading case of Atkin *v.* Barwick, *supra*, the goods sold and sent by the vendors actually reached the hands of the vendees; but the latter, being satisfied they could not pay, delivered them to one Penhallow, to be redelivered to the vendors. Shortly after the delivery to Penhallow, the vendees wrote to their vendors, stating their inability, and expressing an unwillingness that the goods should go to pay their creditors. This letter was sent two days after they had become bankrupts, though the goods had been received and delivered to Penhallow some time before. The latter may have been a mere stranger to the vendors and not their agent. At any rate the vendors got no notice of the delivery to him till after the vendee's bankruptcy. They then assented.

All the judges held that the property in the goods revested in the vendors, from the time when they were delivered to Penhallow, subject to the dissent of the vendors ; and that the precedent debt was a sufficient consideration. Although this case has been frequently questioned, it has never been overruled; on the contrary, it has been many times approved.

expressly or tacitly assents to it, there is a good resale or stoppage *in transitu.*   And so, if the vendee, upon ascertaining that he is insolvent, before the arrival of the goods executes a bill of sale to the vendor, and delivers this to a third person for him, his act amounts to a resale or stoppage *in transitu*, and his assignee in insolvency cannot recover the goods or their value from the vendor, or from the third person to whom the bill of sale was made.[1]   An insolvency messenger, before the appointment of an assignee, cannot cut off the seller's right by accepting the goods and paying the freight after the insolvent purchaser has refused to receive them, in order that the seller might reclaim them.   A messenger is a mere custodian who has no authority to accept or reject, or to affirm or disaffirm, the act of the insolvent purchaser.[2]

The assent of the purchaser to a resumption of possession by the unpaid vendor, does not make his possession illegal under the bankrupt law, because the vendor could exercise this right without the assent of the purchaser, and thereby gain the same preference over other creditors which he acquires with the voluntary assent of the purchaser.   " It is not giving a preference to a creditor, when a debtor, peaceably and for convenience, assents to the doing by the creditor of what the creditor, if objection and collision arose, could lawfully do in spite of objection." [3]
Therefore the vendor may retain the goods voluntarily surrendered by the purchaser under such circumstances, and may prove his claim against the estate of the purchaser in bankruptcy for any balance of account not satisfied by such surrender.[4]

866. Perhaps in some cases of this nature it should be said that there is a resale or rescission of the contract rather than a stoppage *in transitu*, for the latter act is in its nature adverse to the vendee.[5]   Whether the transaction be called a re-

---

[1] Grout *v.* Hill, 4 Gray (Mass.), 361.

[2] Tufts *v.* Sylvester (Me.), 9 Atl. Rep. 357.

[3] *In re* Foot, 11 Blatchf. 530, 533, per Woodruff, J.

[4] *In re* Foot, *supra.*

[5] Siffken *v.* Wray, 6 East, 371, per Lord Ellenborough, C. J.; Ash *v.* Put-

nam, 1 Hill (N. Y.), 302; Cox *v.* Burns, 1 Iowa, 64.

But in saying that stoppage *in transitu* is an adverse proceeding, and must be exercised adversely to the vendee, the courts mean " no more than that the right of stopping *in transitu* cannot be exercised under a title derived from the consignee; not that

particular purpose, and the consignee becomes insolvent, payment of the money may be stopped.[1]

Property sold in violation of a statute, as, for instance, intoxicating liquors, may be stopped *in transitu* by notice to the carrier, or demand upon him. But, under a statute which provides that no action shall be maintained for the recovery or possession of intoxicating liquors, a right of stoppage *in transitu* of such property cannot be enforced by an action of replevin.[2]

II. *Who may Exercise the Right.*

869. Not only a vendor, but any person substantially in the position of a vendor, may exercise this right.[3] Thus a commission merchant, or factor, or consignor, or other agent who has bought goods on his own credit, though by order and on account of another, may exercise a vendor's right of stoppage. But the agent must pay for the goods, or render himself liable for them, in order to be entitled to stop them *in transitu* as a vendor.[4]

The vendor may exercise this right even when he has consigned goods to the joint account of himself and the consignee, and a bill of lading has been sent to the latter making the goods deliverable to him or his assigns;[5] unless the vendor has indorsed the bill of lading in trust to secure drafts drawn against the consignment.[6]

870. The right can be exercised only by one who holds the relation of vendor to the consignee. If one buys goods and directs his vendor to consign them to a customer of his own with whom the vendor has no privity, and the vendor accordingly ships the goods to such third person, he cannot stop them *in transitu* to him upon the insolvency of his immediate purchaser. Thus, a merchant at Dardanelle, in Arkansas, ordered goods of merchants at St. Louis. They sent the order to merchants at

New Orleans, with directions to ship the goods to the purch[aser] at Dardanelle, which they did, and sent the bill and bill of [lad]ing to the St. Louis merchants, and charged the goods to t[hem.] During the transit from New Orleans to Dardanelle th[e St.] Louis merchants failed, and the New Orleans merchants, c[laim]ing a right of stoppage *in transitu*, demanded the goods o[f the] carrier and obtained possession of them. In a suit by the [con]signee against the carrier, it was held that the New Orl[eans] merchants were not the vendors of the consignee; that t[here] was no right of privity between him and them; and that [they] had no right to stop the goods, and consequently the carrier [was] liable to the consignee for their value.[1]

871. A principal may stop goods in transitu consigne[d to] his factor upon the insolvency of the latter, though he has [ac]cepted bills upon the faith of the consignment, and paid a [por]tion of the freight. A factor has no lien on goods for a gen[eral] balance until they come into his possession, when he holds t[hem] in pledge, or has a lien upon them, neither of which can be [en]forced except through possession.[2]

872. A pledgee of the bill of lading may exercise [the] **right.**[3] To the extent of his interest in the property he [is a] quasi vendor, and is entitled to use all lawful means to pro[tect] his interest.

873. But one who has only a lien upon goods cannot s[top] them *in transitu* after he has shipped them to the general ow[ner] at the expense of the latter.[4] Lord Kenyon said, upon t[his] point:[5] "The right of lien has never been carried further th[an] while the goods continue in the possession of the party claim[ing] it. Here the goods were shipped by the order and on account [of] the bankrupt, and he was to pay the expense of the carriage [of] them; the custody, therefore, was changed by the delivery [to] the captain."

[1] Smith *v.* Bowles, 2 Esp. 578; Muller *v.* Pondir, 55 N. Y. 325; *S C.* 6 Lans. 472.

[2] Howe *v.* Stewart, 40 Vt. 145.

[3] Feise *v.* Wray, 3 East, 93; Ireland *v.* Livingston, L. R. 5 H. L. 395; Snee *v.* Baxter, 1 Aik. 285; *Ex parte* Banner, 2 Ch. D. 278; Ogle *v.* Atkinson, 5 Taunt. 759; Patten *v.* Thompson, 5 M. & S. 350; Tucker *v.* Humphrey, 4 Bing. 516; Turner *v.* Liverpool Dock Co. 6 Ex. 543; Ellershaw *v.* Magniac, Ib. 570; Newhall *v.* Vargas, 13 Me. 93; Gossler *v.* Schepeler, 5 Daly (N. Y.), 476.

[4] Oakford *v.* Drake, 2 F. & F. 493.

[5] Newsom *v.* Thornton, 6 East, 17.

[6] Haille *v.* Smith, 1 B. & P. 563.

[1] Memphis & L. R. R. R. Co. *v.* Freed, 38 Ark. 614. And see, also, Stubbs *v.* Lund, 7 Mass. 453; Eaton *v.* Cook, 32 Vt. 58.

[2] Kinloch *v.* Craig, 3 T. R. 119; *S. C.* Ib. 783; *S. C.* affirmed, 4 Brown C. P. 47.

[3] Gossler *v.* Schepeler, 5 Daly (N. Y.), 476.

[4] Sweet *v.* Pym, 1 East, 4; Gw[ynn] *v.* Richmond & Danville R. R. C[o.,] 85 N. C. 429; *S. C.* 13 Rep. 473.

[5] Sweet *v.* Pym, *supra.*

874. A surety for the price of goods has no right to stop them in transitu, upon the failure of the consignee, without authority from the vendor;[1] unless the circumstances of the case are such that the title to the goods, with the lien of the vendor, has passed to the surety, who is then not merely a surety, but occupies the position of the vendor himself.[2]

875. A general agent may exercise this right in behalf of his principal. The authority of an agent of the vendor to stop the goods *in transitu* need not be specified, that is, having reference to that particular measure, or to that particular transaction.[3] The authority of an agent acting within the general scope of his principal's business is sufficient to enable him to exercise the right of stoppage *in transitu*. A merchant to whom goods are sent to be forwarded to the purchaser, may stop them *in transitu* for the benefit of the vendor, provided the latter affirms the act.

A vendor's agent who is vested with the legal title to the property, by transfer of the bill of lading, may stop it *in transitu* in his own name;[4] and may, moreover, in his own name, upon refusal of the person in possession to surrender it, sue for and recover it.[5]

Of course the vendor may give notice to stop delivery by an authorized agent.[6] He may also avail himself of the act of another in giving the notice in his behalf by ratifying and adopting such act, so that the notice will have the same effect as if it had been specially authorized.[7] But a ratification after the goods have reached the possession of the vendee is too late to give validity to an unauthorized demand.[8]

876. The act of one who stops goods in transitu, without any previous general or special authority, may be ratified by

[1] Siffken *v.* Wray, 6 East, 371.
[2] Imperial Bank *v.* London & St. Katharine Docks Co. 5 Ch. D. 195.
[3] Hutchings *v.* Nunes, 1 Moo. P. C. N. S. 243; Reynolds *v.* Boston & Me. R. R. Co. 43 N. H. 580; Bell *v.* Moss, 5 Whart. (Pa.) 189; Chandler *v.* Fulton, 10 Tex. 2.
[4] Morison *v.* Gray, 2 Bing. 260; S. C. 9 Moore, 484; Jenkyns *v.* Us-

borne, 7 M. & G. 678. But see Waring *v.* Cox, 1 Camp. 369.
[5] Morison *v.* Gray, *supra.*
[6] Holst *v.* Pownal, 1 Esp. 240.
[7] Wood *v.* Jones, 7 Dow. & Ry. 126; Hutchings *v.* Nunes, *supra*; Bailey *v.* Culverwell, 8 B. & C. 448; Bartram *v.* Farebrother, 4 Bing. 579.
[8] Bird *v.* Brown, 4 Ex. 786.

sale or a rescission, the effect is the same; though if the transaction be a resale, it follows that the property vested in the vendee and was revested by his act in the vendor; while, if it be a rescission or refusal to accept, the vendor was never divested of the property.[1] If, on the other hand, the refusal of the vendee to receive the goods on account of his insolvency, taken in connection with the vendor's assent to such refusal and his subsequent taking back the goods, be regarded as a species of stoppage *in transitu*, it must follow that the vendor, upon receiving them, has only a lien upon them for his purchase-money, and not an absolute title.

867. A rescission may take place after the right of stoppage has ceased to exist. But after the vendee has actually received the goods, intending to make them his own, he cannot rescind the contract so as to defeat the claim of the general body of his creditors.[2] After the right of stoppage has once ended through a delivery to the vendee, it cannot be revived by a subsequent refusal of the consignee to accept a portion of the goods, by reason of their not being merchantable or salable, under the terms of the contract of purchase.

868. Upon what property the right may be exercised. — This right is usually exercised upon merchandise or personal chattels, because these are more frequently the subject-matter of sales and shipments by carriers. But there is no reason why the right should not exist as well under like circumstances in respect to such property as specie, bank bills, or negotiable paper. Thus, if a person remits money on a particular account, or for a

it should be exercised in hostility to him." Per Parker, C. J., in Naylor *v.* Dennie, 8 Pick. (Mass.) 198, 204; quoted and approved in Cox *v.* Burns, 1 Iowa, 64, 68.
[1] Ash *v.* Putnam, 1 Hill (N. Y.), 302, per Cowen, J.; Cox *v.* Burns, 1 Iowa, 64.

A rescission or resale is complete before the assent of the vendor is actually given or expressed, provided he does subsequently assent; or, in other words, his subsequent assent relates back to the time of the vendee's

act; and therefore an attachment of the goods made by a creditor of the vendee after the vendee's act of rescission, and before the vendor's assent to it, is ineffectual. Sturtevant *v.* Orser, 24 N. Y. 538.
[2] Barnes *v.* Freeland, 6 T. R. 80; Neate *v.* Ball, 2 East, 117; Smith *v.* Field, 5 T. R. 402; Heinekey *v.* Earle, 8 E. & B. 410. See, in connection with the foregoing, Dixon *v.* Baldwin, 5 East, 175; Byrnes *v.* Fuller, 1 Brev. (S. C.) 316; Wilds *v.* Smith, 2 Ont. App. 8.

the vendor, but it is said that the act of ratification must take place at a time, and under circumstances, when the ratifying party might himself have lawfully done the act which he ratifies. A merchant in New York sold and shipped goods to a merchant in Liverpool, who became bankrupt before the arrival of the goods at Liverpool. Another merchant at Liverpool, who was not the general agent of the seller, though he had purchased some of the bills drawn upon the purchaser for the goods, claimed to stop the goods *in transitu* in behalf of the seller upon their arrival at Liverpool and before the transitus was at an end. Soon afterwards, on the 11th day of May, the assignees in bankruptcy of the buyer made formal demand for the goods of the master of the vessel and tendered the freight; but the master refused to deliver them, and delivered them to the merchant, claiming to act in behalf of the seller. The latter, having heard of the insolvency of the buyer, on the 29th day of the previous April, executed a power of attorney to another person in Liverpool authorizing him to stop the goods *in transitu*. This agent received the power on the 13th day of May, and on the same day confirmed the previous stoppage by the merchant who had assumed to act for the seller. Subsequently the seller adopted and ratified all that had been done in his behalf by both these agents. In trover for the goods by the assignees of the bankrupt, against the merchant holding them, it was held that the ratification of the stoppage by the seller had not the effect of altering retrospectively the ownership of the goods, which had already vested in the assignees.[1]

III. *Conditions under which the Right Exists.*

877. There is no right of stoppage in case the goods have been paid for in full. Neither is there any such right in case the goods have been shipped to pay a precedent debt.[2]

---

[1] Bird *v.* Brown, 4 Ex. 786, 800. "In the present case, the stoppage could only be made during the transitus. During that period the defendants, without authority from the vendor, made the stoppage. After the transitus was ended, but not before, the vendor ratified what the defendants had done. From that time the stoppage was the act of the vendor, but it was then too late for him to stop. The goods had already become the property of the plaintiffs, free from all right of stoppage." Per Rolfe, B. This case referred to and distinguished from Hutchings *v.* Nunes, 1 Moo. P. C. N. S. 243 ; also in Durgy Cement & Umber Co. *v.* O'Brien, 123 Mass. 12.

[2] Wood *v.* Roach, 1 Yeates (Pa.), 177.

If the state of accounts between the vendor and vendee is such that the former is indebted to the latter in a sum equal to or greater than the value of the goods consigned, there is no right of stoppage *in transitu*, for the goods are in fact paid for.[1] If payment has been made to the vendor's agent, though he has never paid over the money to the vendor, the right does not exist.[2]

878. The fact that the vendee has given his note or acceptance for the price of the goods does not defeat the vendor's right of stoppage *in transitu;*[3] and the vendor need not tender back the purchaser's note or acceptance before exercising this right.[4]

The vendor's right of stoppage *in transitu* is not taken away by the purchaser's acceptance of bills for the price of the goods, without tendering back the bills,[5] for, though the bills may be proved against the estate of the purchaser in bankruptcy, and part payment obtained by this means, this is no objection ; for a part payment does not destroy the vendor's right of stopping *in transitu*, but only reduces the amount of his lien upon them after he has got them into his possession.

879. If, however, the goods be paid for by the note, order, or accepted bill of a third person, without the indorsement or guaranty of the purchaser, the vendor has no right of stoppage *in transitu*.[6]

880. The fact that the vendor is indebted to the vendee upon an unadjusted account does not defeat his right of stoppage *in transitu*. He is not bound to wait for the settlement of the mutual accounts to ascertain the fact or extent of his indebtedness to the vendee, but he may act at once upon the

[1] Vertue v. Jewell, 4 Camp. 31.

[2] Bunney v. Poyntz, 4 B. & Ad. 568.

[3] Inglis v. Usherwood, 1 East, 515; Bothlingk v. Inglis, 3 East, 381; Feise v. Wray, 3 East, 93; Edwards v. Brewer, 2 M. & W. 375; Miles v. Gorton, 2 Cr. & M. 504; S. C. 4 Tyr. 295, 299; Lewis v. Mason, 36 U. C. Q. B. 590; Clapp v. Peck, 55 Iowa, 270; Clapp v. Sohmer, Ib. 273; Buckley v. Furniss, 15 Wend. (N. Y.) 137; Atkins v. Colby, 20 N. H. 154.

[4] Hays v. Mouille, 14 Pa. St. 48.

[5] Feise v. Wray, *supra;* Edwards v. Brewer, *supra;* Patten v. Thompson, 5 M. & S. 350. But in Cowasjee v. Thompson, 5 Moore P. C. 165, where the vendor had the option of taking payment by bill or in cash, and he elected the former mode of payment, it was held that he had waived the right of stoppage.

[6] Eaton v. Cook, 32 Vt. 58.

insolvency of the vendee, and by the exercise of his right of stoppage make himself secure against loss.[1] But the right may often depend on the state of accounts between the parties.[2] If the consignor is indebted to the consignee to the full amount of the value of the goods consigned, and they are expressly consigned on account of such indebtedness, the right of stoppage *in transitu* does not apply, for there can be no risk of loss to the consignor.[3]

The circumstance that the shipment is made at the risk of the consignor does not in such case impair the consignee's claim to it.[4]

The fact that the consignment has been made by the debtor to his creditor at the request of the latter, or at least was made with notice to him, is material.[5]

881. Part payment of the purchase-money does not affect the vendor's right of stoppage in transitu.[6] It has already been noticed that such payment does not affect his right of lien.[7] In an early case respecting the effect of such payment, Lord Kenyon [8] said " he did not think that this took the case out of the general rule, and that he should be sorry to let in such an exception, because it would destroy the rule itself: since every payment, however small, even the payment of a farthing by way of earnest, would, if such an exception were introduced, prevent the operation of the general rule of stopping *in transitu*." On this point, however, a second argument was ordered at the request of the other judges; but judgment was entered without further argument, because the judges finally had no doubt on the subject. Lord Kenyon then said: " When the distinction was first taken at the bar, I thought it not well founded; and, on looking into the cases that were referred to in support of it, we are clearly of opinion that the circumstance of the vendee

[1] Wood *v.* Jones, 7 Dow. & Ry. 126; and see Masters *v.* Barreda, 18 How. 489.

[2] Vertue *v.* Jewell, 4 Camp. 31.

[3] Clark *v.* Mauran, 3 Paige (N. Y.), 373; Summeril *v.* Elder, 1 Binn. (Pa.) 106; Wood *v.* Roach, 1 Yeates (Pa.), 177.

[4] Haille *v.* Smith, 1 B. & P. 563, 571; Clark *v.* Mauran, *supra.*

[5] Walter *v.* Ross, 2 Wash. 283 ; Clark *v.* Mauran, *supra.*

[6] M'Ewan *v.* Smith, 2 H. L. Cas. 309; Gibson *v.* Carruthers, 8 M. & W. 321.

[7] § 801.

[8] Hodgson *v.* Loy, 7 T. R. 440, 445; recognized in Feise *v.* Wray, 3 East, 93.

having partly paid for the goods does not defeat the vendor's right to stop them *in transitu*, the vendee having become bankrupt; and the vendor has a right to retake them unless the whole price has been paid."

But a composition by the vendor with his vendee for the price of undelivered goods operates as an abandonment of the right of stoppage, and the vendor is bound to deliver the goods on receiving payment agreed upon in the composition.[1]

882. **The bankruptcy of the buyer does not of itself rescind the contract of sale,** and therefore, unless the goods are stopped by the seller, the buyer or his assignee may take possession of the goods, and put an end to the transit and to the vendor's right of stoppage.[2] This rule does not apply, however, to a consignment to a factor. As Lord Kenyon said:[3] " If goods be sent to a factor to be disposed of, who afterwards becomes a bankrupt, and the goods remain distinguishable from the general mass of his property, the principal may recover the goods in specie, and is not driven to the necessity of proving his debt under the commission of bankrupt; nay, if the goods be sold and reduced to money, provided that money be in separate bags and distinguishable from the factor's other property, the law is the same."

And so if goods are ordered by a merchant who is at the time insolvent, and they are sent to him by the vendor without knowledge of this fact, and afterwards the purchaser dies, his administrator is entitled to receive the goods upon their arrival, and the vendor not having exercised his right of stoppage *in transitu*,

---

[1] Nichols *v.* Hart, 5 C. & P. 179.
[2] Ellis *v.* Hunt, 3 T. R. 464, 467.

In Snee *v.* Prescot, 1 Atk. 245, 249, Lord Hardwicke said: " Though goods are even delivered to the principal, I could never see any substantial reason why the original proprietor, who never received a farthing, should be obliged to quit all claim to them and come in, as a creditor only, for a shilling, perhaps, in the pound, unless the law goes upon the general credit the bankrupt has gained by having them in his custody." And see Scott *v.* Pettit, 3

B. & P. 469. But this suggestion has never been followed; and when an argument of this sort, supported by this quotation, was addressed to Judge Story, he said : " Nothing is better settled — if an uninterrupted series of authorities can settle the law — than the doctrine that the vendor, in cases of insolvency, can stop the property only while it is in its transit." Conyers *v.* Ennis, 2 Mason, 236, 238.

[3] Tooke *v.* Hollingworth, 5 T. R. 215, 226.

sale or a rescission, the effect is the same ; though if the transaction be a resale, it follows that the property vested in the vendee and was revested by his act in the vendor ; while, if it be a rescission or refusal to accept, the vendor was never divested of the property.[1] If, on the other hand, the refusal of the vendee to receive the goods on account of his insolvency, taken in connection with the vendor's assent to such refusal and his subsequent taking back the goods, be regarded as a species of stoppage *in transitu*, it must follow that the vendor, upon receiving them, has only a lien upon them for his purchase-money, and not an absolute title.

867. A rescission may take place after the right of stoppage has ceased to exist. But after the vendee has actually received the goods, intending to make them his own, he cannot rescind the contract so as to defeat the claim of the general body of his creditors.[2] After the right of stoppage has once ended through a delivery to the vendee, it cannot be revived by a subsequent refusal of the consignee to accept a portion of the goods, by reason of their not being merchantable or salable, under the terms of the contract of purchase.

868. Upon what property the right may be exercised. — This right is usually exercised upon merchandise or personal chattels, because these are more frequently the subject-matter of sales and shipments by carriers. But there is no reason why the right should not exist as well under like circumstances in respect to such property as specie, bank bills, or negotiable paper. Thus, if a person remits money on a particular account, or for a

---

it should be exercised in hostility to him." Per Parker, C. J., in Naylor *v.* Dennie, 8 Pick. (Mass.) 198, 204 ; quoted and approved in Cox *v.* Burns, 1 Iowa, 64, 68.

[1] Ash *v.* Putnam, 1 Hill (N. Y.), 302, per Cowen, J.; Cox *v.* Burns, 1 Iowa, 64.

A rescission or resale is complete before the assent of the vendor is actually given or expressed, provided he does subsequently assent; or, in other words, his subsequent assent relates back to the time of the vendee's

act ; and therefore an attachment of the goods made by a creditor of the vendee after the vendee's act of rescission, and before the vendor's assent to it, is ineffectual. Sturtevant *v.* Orser, 24 N. Y. 538.

[2] Barnes *v.* Freeland, 6 T. R. 80; Neate *v.* Ball, 2 East, 117; Smith *v.* Field, 5 T. R. 402; Heinekey *v.* Earle, 8 E. & B. 410. See, in connection with the foregoing, Dixon *v.* Baldwin, 5 East, 175; Byrnes *v.* Fuller, 1 Brev. (S. C.) 316; Wilds *v.* Smith, 2 Ont. App. 8.

particular purpose, and the consignee becomes insolvent, payment of the money may be stopped.[1]

Property sold in violation of a statute, as, for instance, intoxicating liquors, may be stopped *in transitu* by notice to the carrier, or demand upon him. But, under a statute which provides that no action shall be maintained for the recovery or possession of intoxicating liquors, a right of stoppage *in transitu* of such property cannot be enforced by an action of replevin.[2]

II. *Who may Exercise the Right.*

869. Not only a vendor, but any person substantially in the position of a vendor, may exercise this right.[3] Thus a commission merchant, or factor, or consignor, or other agent who has bought goods on his own credit, though by order and on account of another, may exercise a vendor's right of stoppage. But the agent must pay for the goods, or render himself liable for them, in order to be entitled to stop them *in transitu* as a vendor.[4]

The vendor may exercise this right even when he has consigned goods to the joint account of himself and the consignee, and a bill of lading has been sent to the latter making the goods deliverable to him or his assigns;[5] unless the vendor has indorsed the bill of lading in trust to secure drafts drawn against the consignment.[6]

870. The right can be exercised only by one who holds the relation of vendor to the consignee. If one buys goods and directs his vendor to consign them to a customer of his own with whom the vendor has no privity, and the vendor accordingly ships the goods to such third person, he cannot stop them *in transitu* to him upon the insolvency of his immediate purchaser. Thus, a merchant at Dardanelle, in Arkansas, ordered goods of merchants at St. Louis. They sent the order to merchants at

[1] Smith *v.* Bowles, 2 Esp. 578 ; Muller *v.* Pondir, 55 N. Y. 325; *S C.* 6 Lans. 472.

[2] Howe *v.* Stewart, 40 Vt. 145.

[3] Feise *v.* Wray, 3 East, 93 ; Ireland *v.* Livingston, L. R. 5 H. L. 395; Snee *v.* Baxter, 1 Aik. 285; *Ex parte* Banner, 2 Ch. D. 278; Ogle *v.* Atkinson, 5 Taunt. 759 ; Patten *v.* Thompson, 5 M. & S. 350; Tucker *v.* Humphrey, 4 Bing. 516; Turner *v.* Liverpool Dock Co. 6 Ex. 543; Ellershaw *v.* Magniac, Ib. 570 ; Newhall *v.* Vargas, 13 Me. 93; Gossler *v.* Schepeler, 5 Daly (N. Y.), 476.

[4] Oakford *v.* Drake, 2 F. & F. 493.

[5] Newsom *v.* Thornton, 6 East, 17.

[6] Haille *v.* Smith, 1 B. & P. 563.

New Orleans, with directions to ship the goods to the purchaser at Dardanelle, which they did, and sent the bill and bill of lading to the St. Louis merchants, and charged the goods to them. During the transit from New Orleans to Dardanelle the St. Louis merchants failed, and the New Orleans merchants, claiming a right of stoppage *in transitu*, demanded the goods of the carrier and obtained possession of them. In a suit by the consignee against the carrier, it was held that the New Orleans merchants were not the vendors of the consignee; that there was no right of privity between him and them; and that they had no right to stop the goods, and consequently the carrier was liable to the consignee for their value.[1]

871. A principal may stop goods in transitu consigned to his factor upon the insolvency of the latter, though he has accepted bills upon the faith of the consignment, and paid a portion of the freight. A factor has no lien on goods for a general balance until they come into his possession, when he holds them in pledge, or has a lien upon them, neither of which can be enforced except through possession.[2]

872. A pledgee of the bill of lading may exercise this right.[3] To the extent of his interest in the property he is a quasi vendor, and is entitled to use all lawful means to protect his interest.

873. But one who has only a lien upon goods cannot stop them *in transitu* after he has shipped them to the general owner at the expense of the latter.[4] Lord Kenyon said, upon this point:[5] "The right of lien has never been carried further than while the goods continue in the possession of the party claiming it. Here the goods were shipped by the order and on account of the bankrupt, and he was to pay the expense of the carriage of them; the custody, therefore, was changed by the delivery to the captain."

[1] Memphis & L. R. R. R. Co. v. Freed, 38 Ark. 614. And see, also, Stubbs v. Lund, 7 Mass. 453 ; Eaton v. Cook, 32 Vt. 58.

[2] Kinloch v. Craig, 3 T. R. 119; S. C. Ib. 783; S. C. affirmed, 4 Brown C. P. 47.

[3] Gossler v. Schepeler, 5 Daly (N. Y.), 476.

[4] Sweet v. Pym, 1 East, 4 ; Gwyn v. Richmond & Danville R. R. Co. 85 N. C. 429 ; S. C. 13 Rep. 473.

[5] Sweet v. Pym, *supra*.

874. A surety for the price of goods has no right to stop them in transitu, upon the failure of the consignee, without authority from the vendor;[1] unless the circumstances of the case are such that the title to the goods, with the lien of the vendor, has passed to the surety, who is then not merely a surety, but occupies the position of the vendor himself.[2]

875. A general agent may exercise this right in behalf of his principal. The authority of an agent of the vendor to stop the goods *in transitu* need not be specified, that is, having reference to that particular measure, or to that particular transaction.[3] The authority of an agent acting within the general scope of his principal's business is sufficient to enable him to exercise the right of stoppage *in transitu*. A merchant to whom goods are sent to be forwarded to the purchaser, may stop them *in transitu* for the benefit of the vendor, provided the latter affirms the act.

A vendor's agent who is vested with the legal title to the property, by transfer of the bill of lading, may stop it *in transitu* in his own name;[4] and may, moreover, in his own name, upon refusal of the person in possession to surrender it, sue for and recover it.[5]

Of course the vendor may give notice to stop delivery by an authorized agent.[6] He may also avail himself of the act of another in giving the notice in his behalf by ratifying and adopting such act, so that the notice will have the same effect as if it had been specially authorized.[7] But a ratification after the goods have reached the possession of the vendee is too late to give validity to an unauthorized demand.[8]

876. The act of one who stops goods in transitu, without any previous general or special authority, may be ratified by

[1] Siffken *v.* Wray, 6 East, 371.
[2] Imperial Bank *v.* London & St. Katharine Docks Co. 5 Ch. D. 195.
[3] Hutchings *v.* Nunes, 1 Moo. P. C. N. S. 243 ; Reynolds *v.* Boston & Me. R. R. Co. 43 N. H. 580 ; Bell *v.* Moss, 5 Whart. (Pa.) 189 ; Chandler *v.* Fulton, 10 Tex. 2.
[4] Morison *v.* Gray, 2 Bing. 260; *S. C.* 9 Moore, 484 ; Jenkyns *v.* Usborne, 7 M. & G. 678. But see Waring *v.* Cox, 1 Camp. 369.
[5] Morison *v.* Gray, *supra*.
[6] Holst *v.* Pownal, 1 Esp. 240.
[7] Wood *v.* Jones, 7 Dow. & Ry. 126; Hutchings *v.* Nunes, *supra ;* Bailey *v.* Culverwell, 8 B. & C. 448; Bartram *v.* Farebrother, 4 Bing. 579.
[8] Bird *v.* Brown, 4 Ex. 786.

the vendor, but it is said that the act of ratification must take place at a time, and under circumstances, when the ratifying party might himself have lawfully done the act which he ratifies. A merchant in New York sold and shipped goods to a merchant in Liverpool, who became bankrupt before the arrival of the goods at Liverpool. Another merchant at Liverpool, who was not the general agent of the seller, though he had purchased some of the bills drawn upon the purchaser for the goods, claimed to stop the goods *in transitu* in behalf of the seller upon their arrival at Liverpool and before the transitus was at an end. Soon afterwards, on the 11th day of May, the assignees in bankruptcy of the buyer made formal demand for the goods of the master of the vessel and tendered the freight; but the master refused to deliver them, and delivered them to the merchant, claiming to act in behalf of the seller. The latter, having heard of the insolvency of the buyer, on the 29th day of the previous April, executed a power of attorney to another person in Liverpool authorizing him to stop the goods *in transitu*. This agent received the power on the 13th day of May, and on the same day confirmed the previous stoppage by the merchant who had assumed to act for the seller. Subsequently the seller adopted and ratified all that had been done in his behalf by both these agents. In trover for the goods by the assignees of the bankrupt, against the merchant holding them, it was held that the ratification of the stoppage by the seller had not the effect of altering retrospectively the ownership of the goods, which had already vested in the assignees.[1]

III. *Conditions under which the Right Exists.*

877. There is no right of stoppage in case the goods have been paid for in full. Neither is there any such right in case the goods have been shipped to pay a precedent debt.[2]

---

[1] Bird *v.* Brown, 4 Ex. 786, 800. "In the present case, the stoppage could only be made during the transitus. During that period the defendants, without authority from the vendor, made the stoppage. After the transitus was ended, but not before, the vendor ratified what the defendants had done. From that time the stoppage was the act of the vendor, but it was then too late for him to stop." The goods had already become the property of the plaintiffs, free from all right of stoppage." Per Rolfe, B. This case referred to and distinguished from Hutchings *v.* Nunes, 1 Moo. P. C. N. S. 243 ; also in Durgy Cement & Umber Co. *v.* O'Brien, 123 Mass. 12.

[2] Wood *v.* Roach, 1 Yeates (Pa.), 177.

If the state of accounts between the vendor and vendee is such that the former is indebted to the latter in a sum equal to or greater than the value of the goods consigned, there is no right of stoppage *in transitu*, for the goods are in fact paid for.[1] If payment has been made to the vendor's agent, though he has never paid over the money to the vendor, the right does not exist.[2]

878. The fact that the vendee has given his note or acceptance for the price of the goods does not defeat the vendor's right of stoppage *in transitu*;[3] and the vendor need not tender back the purchaser's note or acceptance before exercising this right.[4]

The vendor's right of stoppage *in transitu* is not taken away by the purchaser's acceptance of bills for the price of the goods, without tendering back the bills,[5] for, though the bills may be proved against the estate of the purchaser in bankruptcy, and part payment obtained by this means, this is no objection ; for a part payment does not destroy the vendor's right of stopping *in transitu*, but only reduces the amount of his lien upon them after he has got them into his possession.

879. If, however, the goods be paid for by the note, order, or accepted bill of a third person, without the indorsement or guaranty of the purchaser, the vendor has no right of stoppage *in transitu*.[6]

880. The fact that the vendor is indebted to the vendee upon an unadjusted account does not defeat his right of stoppage *in transitu*. He is not bound to wait for the settlement of the mutual accounts to ascertain the fact or extent of his indebtedness to the vendee, but he may act at once upon the

---

[1] Vertue *v.* Jewell, 4 Camp. 31.

[2] Bunney *v.* Poyntz, 4 B. & Ad. 568.

[3] Inglis *v.* Usherwood, 1 East, 515; Bothlingk *v.* Inglis, 3 East, 381; Feise *v.* Wray, 3 East, 93; Edwards *v.* Brewer, 2 M. & W. 375; Miles *v.* Gorton, 2 Cr. & M. 504; *S. C.* 4 Tyr. 295, 299; Lewis *v.* Mason, 36 U. C. Q. B. 590; Clapp *v.* Peck, 55 Iowa, 270; Clapp *v.* Sohmer, Ib. 273; Buckley *v.* Furniss, 15 Wend. (N. Y.) 137; Atkins *v.* Colby, 20 N. H. 154.

[4] Hays *v.* Mouille, 14 Pa. St. 48.

[5] Feise *v.* Wray, *supra;* Edwards *v.* Brewer, *supra;* Patten *v.* Thompson, 5 M. & S. 350. But in Cowasjee *v.* Thompson, 5 Moore P. C. 165, where the vendor had the option of taking payment by bill or in cash, and he elected the former mode of payment, it was held that he had waived the right of stoppage.

[6] Eaton *v.* Cook, 32 Vt. 58.

insolvency of the vendee, and by the exercise of his right of stoppage make himself secure against loss.[1] But the right may often depend on the state of accounts between the parties.[2] If the consignor is indebted to the consignee to the full amount of the value of the goods consigned, and they are expressly consigned on account of such indebtedness, the right of stoppage *in transitu* does not apply, for there can be no risk of loss to the consignor.[3]

The circumstance that the shipment is made at the risk of the consignor does not in such case impair the consignee's claim to it.[4]

The fact that the consignment has been made by the debtor to his creditor at the request of the latter, or at least was made with notice to him, is material.[5]

881. Part payment of the purchase-money does not affect the vendor's right of stoppage in transitu.[6] It has already been noticed that such payment does not affect his right of lien.[7] In an early case respecting the effect of such payment, Lord Kenyon [8] said " he did not think that this took the case out of the general rule, and that he should be sorry to let in such an exception, because it would destroy the rule itself : since every payment, however small, even the payment of a farthing by way of earnest, would, if such an exception were introduced, prevent the operation of the general rule of stopping *in transitu*." On this point, however, a second argument was ordered at the request of the other judges ; but judgment was entered without further argument, because the judges finally had no doubt on the subject. Lord Kenyon then said : " When the distinction was first taken at the bar, I thought it not well founded ; and, on looking into the cases that were referred to in support of it, we are clearly of opinion that the circumstance of the vendee

[1] Wood *v.* Jones, 7 Dow. & Ry. 126; and see Masters *v.* Barreda, 18 How. 489.

[2] Vertue *v.* Jewell, 4 Camp. 31.

[3] Clark *v.* Mauran, 3 Paige (N. Y.), 373; Summeril *v.* Elder, 1 Binn. (Pa.) 106; Wood *v.* Roach, 1 Yeates (Pa.), 177.

[4] Haille *v.* Smith, 1 B. & P. 563, 571; Clark *v.* Mauran, *supra*.

[5] Walter *v.* Ross, 2 Wash. 283 ; Clark *v.* Mauran, *supra*.

[6] M'Ewan *v.* Smith, 2 H. L. Cas. 309; Gibson *v.* Carruthers, 8 M. & W. 321.

[7] § 801.

[8] Hodgson *v.* Loy, 7 T. R. 440, 445; recognized in Feise *v.* Wray, 3 East, 93.

having partly paid for the goods does not defeat the vendor's right to stop them *in transitu*, the vendee having become bankrupt; and the vendor has a right to retake them unless the whole price has been paid."

But a composition by the vendor with his vendee for the price of undelivered goods operates as an abandonment of the right of stoppage, and the vendor is bound to deliver the goods on receiving payment agreed upon in the composition.[1]

882. The bankruptcy of the buyer does not of itself rescind the contract of sale, and therefore, unless the goods are stopped by the seller, the buyer or his assignee may take possession of the goods, and put an end to the transit and to the vendor's right of stoppage.[2] This rule does not apply, however, to a consignment to a factor. As Lord Kenyon said:[3] " If goods be sent to a factor to be disposed of, who afterwards becomes a bankrupt, and the goods remain distinguishable from the general mass of his property, the principal may recover the goods in specie, and is not driven to the necessity of proving his debt under the commission of bankrupt; nay, if the goods be sold and reduced to money, provided that money be in separate bags and distinguishable from the factor's other property, the law is the same."

And so if goods are ordered by a merchant who is at the time insolvent, and they are sent to him by the vendor without knowledge of this fact, and afterwards the purchaser dies, his administrator is entitled to receive the goods upon their arrival, and the vendor not having exercised his right of stoppage *in transitu*,

---

[1] Nichols *v.* Hart, 5 C. & P. 179.

[2] Ellis *v.* Hunt, 3 T. R. 464, 467.

In Snee *v.* Prescot, 1 Atk. 245, 249, Lord Hardwicke said: " Though goods are even delivered to the principal, I could never see any substantial reason why the original proprietor, who never received a farthing, should be obliged to quit all claim to them and come in, as a creditor only, for a shilling, perhaps, in the pound, unless the law goes upon the general credit the bankrupt has gained by having them in his custody." And see Scott *v.* Pettit, 3 B. & P. 469. But this suggestion has never been followed; and when an argument of this sort, supported by this quotation, was addressed to Judge Story, he said : " Nothing is better settled — if an uninterrupted series of authorities can settle the law — than the doctrine that the vendor, in cases of insolvency, can stop the property only while it is in its transit." Conyers *v.* Ennis, 2 Mason, 236, 238.

[3] Tooke *v.* Hollingworth, 5 T. R. 215, 226.

cannot reclaim them upon the ground of the purchaser's insolvency.[1]

883. But if the goods pass into the hands of the bankrupt vendee or of his assignee after a valid notice to stop them has been given to the carrier, as where the carrier after receiving such notice delivers the goods to such vendee by mistake, the vendor may recover the goods, or maintain trover therefor. In such case, inasmuch as the goods have not come into the possession of the bankrupt or of his assignee with the consent of the owner, they are not a part of the bankrupt's estate.[2] The right of possession is revested in the vendor by his notice to the carrier, and the assignee has no other or greater right to the goods than the vendee himself would have.

884. The right of stoppage in transitu can be exercised only in case the buyer becomes insolvent.[3] But it is not necessary that proceedings by or against him should have been commenced before the seller can stop the goods *in transitu*, and much less that he should have been adjudicated a bankrupt or insolvent debtor;[4] but only that the buyer should have shown in some way a general inability to pay his debts in the usual course of business.[5] It is enough that the affairs of the vendee

[1] Conyers v. Ennis, 2 Mason, 236; and see Scott v. Pettit, 3 B. & P. 469; Bothlingk v. Inglis, 3 East, 381.

[2] Litt v. Cowley, 7 Taunt. 169.

[3] The Constantia, 6 Rob. Adm. 321; Wilmshurst v. Bowker, 7 M. & G. 882; Walley v. Montgomery, 3 East, 585; O'Brien v. Norris, 16 Md. 122; *In re* the St. Joze Indians, 1 Wheat. 208.

In **California** and **Dakota Territory** it is provided by code that a seller or consignor of property, whose claim for its price or proceeds has not been extinguished, may, upon the insolvency of the buyer or consignee becoming known to him after parting with the property, stop it while on its transit to the buyer or consignee, and resume possession thereof. A person is insolvent when he ceases to pay his debts in the manner usual with persons of his business, or when he declares his inability or unwillingness to do so. Codes and Stats. Cal. 1876, §§ 8076, 8077; R. Codes Dak. 1877, §§ 1815, 1816.

[4] Ogle v. Atkinson, 1 Marsh. 323, 327; Durgy Cement & Umber Co. v. O'Brien, 123 Mass. 12, per Morton, J.; and see Parker v. Gossage, 2 Cr., M. & R. 617; Queen v. Saddlers' Co. 10 H. L. Cas. 404; Thompson v. Thompson, 4 Cush. (Mass.) 127.

[5] O'Brien v. Norris, *supra*; Secomb v. Nutt, 14 B. Mon. (Ky.) 324; James v. Griffin, 2 M. & W. 623; Edwards v. Brewer, Ib. 375; Bloomingdale v. Memphis & Charleston R. R. Co. 6 Lea (Tenn.), 616; Inslee v. Lane, 57 N. H. 454, 458, per Foster, C. J.; Benedict v. Schættle, 12 Ohio St. 515.

are so involved that he is unable to pay for the goods; and it does not matter that his insolvency is not known or declared at the time of the stoppage, provided he becomes actually insolvent before he obtains possession of the goods.[1]   The vendor has the right to judge for himself of the danger of the vendee's insolvency, and to take measures to guard against it.[2]   He, of course, acts at his peril, but he has the right so to act, subject to risk of being required to restore the goods to the consignee, or to respond in damages if the latter proves to be solvent at the time the goods should have been delivered to him and paid for.

885. The question of the buyer's insolvency is one of fact to be determined by the jury, and any evidence bearing upon this fact is competent.[3]   The fact that the buyer has stopped payment is of course sufficient evidence of his insolvency to warrant a stoppage *in transitu ;*[4] and his failure to pay a single undisputed debt in the usual course of mercantile business may be sufficient for this purpose.[5]

If the vendee has, before the stoppage *in transitu,* afforded the ordinary apparent evidences of insolvency, he ought not to complain of the precautionary act of the vendor in exercising this right, though it should afterwards turn out that the vendee was ultimately able to pay ; and, on the other hand, he ought not to complain in case the vendor exercised this right when no evidences of the vendee's insolvency had become manifest, if the

---

[1] Gardner *v.* Tudor, 8 Pick. (Mass.) 205.

[2] Stanton *v.* Eager, 16 Pick. (Mass.) 467, 474, per Shaw, C. J. ; Patten *v.* Thompson, 5 M. & S. 350, 368, per Holroyd, J.

[3] Hays *v.* Mouille, 14 Pa. St. 48 ; Reynolds *v.* Boston & Me. R. R. Co. 43 N. H. 580.

[4] Vertue *v.* Jewell, 4 Camp. 31 ; Dixon *v.* Yates, 5 B. & Ad. 313 ; Bird *v.* Brown, 4 Ex. 786 ; Dodson *v.* Wentworth, 4 M. & G. 1080 ; Jackson *v.* Nichol, 5 Bing. N. C. 508.

[5] Benedict *v.* Schættle, 12 Ohio St. 515, 519, per Gholson, J. ; O'Brien *v.* Norris, 16 Md. 122.

In **Connecticut** an exceptional rule on this point prevails. It is de-

clared that an essential requisite to the exercise of this right is the insolvency of the vendee, consisting not merely of a general inability to pay his debts, but in his having taken the benefit of an insolvent law, or in his having stopped payment, or in his having failed in business. His insolvency should consist of some visible change in his pecuniary situation, — some open, notorious act on his part, calculated to affect his credit, — some change in his apparent circumstances which would operate as a surprise on the vendor. Rogers *v.* Thomas, 20 Conn. 53. This case is now only cited to be criticised and disapproved. See Benedict *v.* Schættle, 12 Ohio St. 515, 521, and many other cases.

fact of insolvency existed at the time the goods reached their destination.[1]

A confession of judgment by the vendee, and a levy of execution upon his property, has been held to be sufficient evidence of his insolvency.[2]   An admission by the vendee of the fact of his insolvency is sufficient evidence of it.[3]

886. The vendor is bound to deliver the goods if the vendee is solvent when they arrive at their destination; and he is also liable in damages to the vendee for any delay, loss, or expense occasioned by the unwarranted stoppage. If the vendor has acted upon an apprehension of the consignee's insolvency which proves to be without foundation, his stoppage of the goods is unlawful, and the property belongs to the consignee, and he is entitled to restitution, which may be specifically enforced in a court of admiralty.[4]

Where a merchant in Bahia ordered goods from a merchant in Pittsburgh, with instructions to send them by sailing vessel direct or *via* Pernambuco, and the goods were shipped by the vendor to a forwarding agent in New York with instructions to ship them to Bahia, saying nothing of a shipment *via* Pernambuco, and the agent finding no vessel to Bahia, the vendor after some months ordered a sale of the goods in New York, without alleging the insolvency of the consignee or other equivalent cause, it was held, in a suit by the latter against the vendor, that the sale was illegal, and that the measure of damages was the price of the goods at Bahia when they should have arrived there, less the invoice price, expenses, costs, and charges of transportation.[5]

887. That the insolvency existed at the time of the sale is immaterial if the vendor was ignorant of the fact.[6]   The object in allowing the privilege of stoppage *in transitu* to the

---

[1] Benedict *v.* Schættle, 12 Ohio St. 515, 519.

[2] Loeb *v.* Peters, 63 Ala. 243.

[3] Secomb *v.* Nutt, 14 B. Mon. (Ky.) 324.

[4] The Constantia, 6 Rob. Adm. R. 321 ; The Tigress, 32 L. J. Adm. 97.

[5] Schmertz *v.* Dwyer, 53 Pa. St.

335; and see Eby *v.* Schumacker, 29 Pa. St. 40.

[6] Bohtlingk *v.* Inglis, 3 East, 381; Litt *v.* Cowley, 1 Holt N. P. Cas. 338 ; Inslee *v.* Lane, 57 N. H. 454 ; Reynolds *v.* Boston & Me. R. R. Co. 43 N. H. 580; Buckley *v.* Furniss, 15 Wend. (N. Y.) 137 ; Loeb *v.* Peters, *supra;* O'Brien *v.* Norris, 16 Md. 122.

vendor being to protect him against the insolvency of the vendee, this privilege, unless waived by the vendor, should apply
as well to cases of insolvency existing at the time of sale as to
cases of insolvency occurring afterwards at any time before the
actual delivery of the goods; the only exception being in case
the insolvency was known to the vendor at the time of the sale,
and the contract was made in view of this fact.[1]

IV. *Mode of Exercising the Right.*

888. To exercise this right it is only necessary for the
vendor or his agent to give notice of his claim to the carrier or other person. It is not necessary that he should demand
a delivery of the goods to himself.[2] Much less is it necessary
that he should make an actual seizure of the goods. A demand
for the goods of the person in possession, or a notice to him to
stop the goods, or a claim of possession under his right of stoppage *in transitu*, and an endeavor to get possession, is sufficient.[3]
No particular form of notice or demand is required. If the carrier is clearly informed that it is the intention and desire of the
vendor to exercise his right of stoppage, the notice is sufficient.[4]

It is not necessary that the vendor should take possession of
the goods to complete the stoppage and revest the right of possession. "It was formerly held," said Chief Justice Gibbs,[5]
" that, unless the vendor recovered back actual possession of the
goods by a corporeal seizure of them, he could not exercise his
right of stoppage *in transitu*. Latterly it has been held that
notice to the carrier is sufficient, and that, if he deliver the goods

---

[1] Reynolds *v.* Boston & Me. R. R.
Co. 43 N. H. 580 ; Benedict *v.* Schættle, 12 Ohio St. 515; Hayes *v.* Mouille, 14 Pa. St. 48; Blum *v.* Marks,
21 La. Ann. 268 ; Buckley *v.* Furniss, 15 Wend. 137 ; Schwabacher *v.*
Kane, 13 Mo. App. 126. The case of
Rogers *v.* Thomas, 20 Conn. 53, to
the contrary, is criticised and repudiated in Benedict *v.* Schættle, 12
Ohio St. 515, 521 ; Reynolds *v.* Boston & Me. R. R. Co. *supra;* Loeb
v. Peters, 63 Ala. 243, 248 ; Reynolds
v. Boston & Me. R. R. Co. 43 N.
H. 580, 588 ; Schwabacher *v.* Kane,
supra.

[2] Northey *v.* Field, 2 Esp. 613 ;

Reynolds *v.* Boston & Me. R. R. Co.
supra; Bell *v.* Moss, 5 Whart. 189,
207.

In **California** and **Dakota** Territory, it is provided by code that stoppage in transit can be effected only by
notice to the carrier or depositary of
the property, or by taking actual possession thereof. Codes and Stats. Cal.
1876, § 3079 ; R. Codes Dak. 1877,
§ 1818.

[3] Rucker *v.* Donovan, 13 Kans. 251.
[4] Jones *v.* Earl, 37 Cal. 630 ;
Bloomingdale *v.* Memphis & Charleston R. R. Co. 6 Lea ('Tenn.), 616.
[5] Litt *v.* Cowley, 7 Taunt. 169 ; *S.
C.* 2 Marsh. 457.

after such notice, he is liable. That doctrine cannot be controverted, and it is supported by all modern decisions."

889. A demand by the vendor of the bills of lading which are in possession of the ship-owner, having never been delivered to the consignee to whose order they are made out, because he had not paid the freight, is an effectual stoppage *in transitu.* Goods were shipped from England to Shanghai for the account of a merchant in London. Soon after the vessel sailed, the merchant committed an act of bankruptcy, and was adjudicated a bankrupt. Both the vendor and the bankrupt's trustee claimed the bills of lading, which were still in the hands of the ship-owners in London ; and it was finally arranged that the goods should be sold by the agent of the ship-owners at Shanghai, and the proceeds paid to the person who should be entitled to them. It was held that the vendor's demand of the bills of lading was an effectual stoppage *in transitu.*[1] James, L. J., delivering the judgment, said : " It so happens, luckily for the vendor, that the documents of title have never left the ship-owners' possession. . . . The vendor comes to the ship-owners and says, ' Deliver the goods to me,' and the ship-owners have undertaken to sell the goods and hand over the proceeds of sale to the real owner. I am of opinion that the goods have been effectually stopped *in transitu,* because the ship-owners are to sell them and deal with the proceeds according to the legal and equitable rights of the parties."

890. The vendor may claim the goods in the hands of any person who may have charge of them before the transit ends.[2] Thus he may claim them not only while they are in the hands of the carrier, but also while they are in the hands of a depositary or warehouseman not acting for the vendee, or while in the possession of the collector of customs awaiting the payment of duties before the vendee has taken actual possession.[3]

891. Notice to the carrier's agent, who has the actual custody of the goods in the regular course of his agency, is

[1] *Ex parte* Watson, 5 Ch. D. 35, 43. And see Inglis *v.* Usherwood, 1 East, 515.

[2] Northey *v.* Field, 2 Esp. 613.

[3] Newhall *v.* Vargas, 13 Me. 93, 109; *S. C.* 15 Me. 314.

notice to the carrier.[1] A letter from the vendor, delivered to the carrier's agent in possession of the goods, stating that the purchaser's property had been attached, that the vendor desired to save the goods, of which he gave a bill of particulars, and directing the agent to deliver the goods to no one but to the vendor's own agent, was held to be a sufficient demand.[2]

A station agent who has control of goods received by railroad at that station is an agent upon whom notice of stoppage *in transitu* may be made.[3]

892. If a railroad company has deposited goods in a customs warehouse belonging to the company, to await the payment of duties as well as the payment of the freight due the carrier, notice by the consignor to stop the goods given to the company is sufficient, though in such a case it may be advisable to give notice also to customs officers.[4] Where imported goods are entered in bond by the importer, and are sold by him and sent in bond by railroad to a purchaser at an interior city, the railroad company is regarded as being in possession of the goods while they are in transit over the road, and notice to stop them should be given to the railroad company. Thus, where the goods go into a bonded warehouse belonging to the railroad company at their place of destination, it would seem that the goods are still in charge of the railroad company.

[1] Bierce v. Red Bluff Hotel Co. 31 Cal. 160; Jones v. Earl, 37 Cal. 630; Bloomingdale v. Memphis & Charleston R. R. Co. 6 Lea (Tenn.), 616; Poole v. Railroad Co. 58 Tex. 134, 139.

[2] Jones v. Earl, *supra.*

[3] Poole v. Railroad Co. *supra.* "The rule is elementary, that where the principal holds out an agent in such manner as to induce the public to believe that the agent is authorized to transact business of any particular kind, the principal will be bound for the acts of the agent in that particular. Here the station agent was, to all appearances, held out to the public as the representative of the company at that point, in regard to freights either shipped to or from that station. And it would seem to follow that a notice to him of a stoppage *in transitu* of goods in transit to that point, upon the soundest principles of law and justice ought to be considered as notice to the company." Per Watts, J.

[4] Ascher v. Grand Trunk Ry. Co. 36 U. C. Q. B. 609, 614. Chief Justice Richards, delivering the judgment of the court, said: " We think it is not unreasonable to hold that notice may be given to the railway company, when the goods which have been sent forward by them are in their own warehouse, and under their own charge, subject to the directions of the government as to being held for duties thereon.''

893. Notice of a stoppage in transitu given to a ship-owner doubtless imposes a duty on him to communicate it with reasonable diligence to the master of the ship, though the notice, if so communicated, will not be effectual until it reaches the master.   In the recent case of *Ex parte* Falk,[1] Bramwell, L. J., remarked that he did not think that the giving of such notice to the ship-owner imposed any duty upon him to stop the goods. But when this case came before the House of Lords,[2] Lord Blackburn expressed a different view, saying : " I had always myself understood that the law was that when you became aware that a man to whom you had sold goods which had been shipped had become insolvent, your best way, or at least a very good way, of stopping them *in transitu* was to give notice to the ship-owner in order that he might send it on.   He knew where his master was likely to be, and he might send it on ; and I have always been under the belief that although such a notice, if sent, cast upon the ship-owner who received it an obligation to send it on with reasonable diligence, yet if, though he used reasonable diligence, somehow or other the goods were delivered before it reached the master, the ship-owner would not be responsible.   I have always thought that a stoppage, if effected thus, was a sufficient stoppage *in transitu ;* I have always thought that when the ship-owner, having received such a notice, used reasonable diligence and sent the notice on, and it arrived before the goods were delivered, that was a perfect stoppage *in transitu.*"

But if the notice be given to the principal when the goods are in the custody of his agent or servant, the notice will not be effectual unless it be given at such a time and under such circumstances that the principal, by the exercise of reasonable diligence, may communicate it to his servant in time to prevent the delivery to the consignee.   Baron Parke uses forcible language on this point, saying : [3] " To hold that a notice to a principal at a distance is sufficient to revest the property in the unpaid vendor, and render the principal liable in trover for a subsequent delivery by his servants to the vendee, when it was impossible, from the distance and want of means of communication, to prevent that delivery, would be the height of injustice.   The only duty that can be imposed on the absent principal is to use reasonable diligence to prevent the delivery."

[1] 14 Ch. D. 446, 455.

[2] Kemp *v.* Falk, 7 App. Cas. 573, 585.

[3] Whitehead *v.* Anderson, 9 M. & W. 518.

If the goods are on board a ship, the vendor may demand them of the master,[1] or give notice to him.

894. The vendor does not ordinarily demand the goods of the vendee; for, if the latter is in actual possession, the vendor's right of stoppage *in transitu* is at an end, and he can only make demand of the person in actual possession at the time.[2] But, if the vendee is not already in possession of the goods, a demand upon him may be effectual. Thus, in a Pennsylvania case, Chief Justice Gibson, discussing this point, said:[3] " A demand of the carrier is a countermand of the previous order to deliver; and, where he is not accessible at the time, there is no reason why an equivalent for it should not be found in a countermand of the consignee's authority to receive. If there were a specific object to be accomplished by a demand on the carrier, it would be to make him liable; but his responsibility is seldom looked to, the object being to prevent the consignee's ownership from becoming absolute; for which purpose any act that warns him of an enforcement of the lien ought to be taken for a sufficient protest against his possession." In the case under consideration, the vendor's agent wrote to the assignees of the insolvent purchaser, before the arrival of the vessel carrying the goods, proposing that the goods should either be delivered to this agent, or that the assignees should receive them and keep a separate account of sales; and in the latter alternative he demanded the proceeds as the property of the vendor. In consequence of this, the parties agreed that the goods should remain without being sold till the question of title should be determined by a competent tribunal, and that the rights of the parties should not be varied by the agreement. It was held that there was a sufficient exercise of the right of stoppage *in transitu*, and that a demand of, or notice to, the carrier was not necessary.

895. In demanding goods of the carrier, it is not requisite

---

[1] Bohtlingk *v.* Inglis, 3 East, 381, 397.

[2] Rucker *v.* Donovan, 13 Kans. 251.

[3] Bell *v.* Moss, 5 Whart. (Pa.) 189, 206. The learned chief justice also remarked that " the countermand of the original order to deliver to the consignee, which is the usual act of stoppage, is so invariably communicated to the master, or other person in possession, that I have seen but one case in which it was communicated to any one else."

that the vendor should prove that the conditions exist which give him the right of stoppage. Thus, he need not prove that the vendee has not negotiated the bill of lading delivered or indorsed to him. As Dr. Lushington has said:[1] " Were it otherwise, were the vendor obliged formally to prove his title to exercise the right of stoppage *in transitu*, that right would be worthless; for the validity of a stoppage *in transitu* depends upon several conditions. First, the vendor must be unpaid; secondly, the vendee must be insolvent; thirdly, the vendee must not have indorsed over for value. But the proof that these conditions have been fulfilled would always be difficult for the vendor, — often impossible: for instance, whether the vendor is or is not unpaid, may depend upon the balance of a current account; whether the vendee is insolvent may not transpire till afterwards, when the bill of exchange for the goods becomes due; for it is, as I conceive, clear law, that the right to stop does not require the vendee to have been found insolvent. And, lastly, whether the vendee has or has not indorsed the bill of lading over, is a matter not within the cognizance of the vendor. He exercises his right of stoppage *in transitu* at his own peril, and it is incumbent upon the master to give effect to a claim as soon as he is satisfied it is made by the vendor, unless he is aware of a legal defeasance of the vendor's claim. Such, according to my opinion, is the law as laid down by Lord Campbell in Gurney v. Behrend.[2] Lord Campbell uses these words : ' *Primâ facie* the defendants had a right to stop the wheat, for it was still *in transitu*, and they were unpaid vendors. The onus is on the plaintiffs to prove that they had become the owners, and that the right to stop *in transitu* was gone.' "

It would seem, however, that the carrier, in a suit against him by the vendor for delivering the goods to the purchaser after receiving notice from the vendor to stop them, might show the fact that the purchaser was solvent after the delivery, and that by due diligence the debt might have been collected, and therefore the vendor was not injured by the wrongful delivery of the goods.[3]

In Georgia the Code declares that the carrier cannot dispute

---

[1] The Tigress, 32 L. J. Adm. 97, 101.

[2] 3 E. & B. 622.

[3] Bloomingdale v. Memphis & Charleston R. R. Co. 6 Lea (Tenn.), 616, per Freeman, J.; and see Rosenfield v. Express Co. 1 Woods, 131.

the title of the person delivering the goods to him by setting up
adverse title in himself, or a title in third persons, which is not
being enforced against him.[1]   It is further declared that a stoppage *in transitu* by the vendor relieves the carrier from his obligation to deliver, and he is not thenceforward responsible for
more than ordinary diligence in the care of the goods.[2]

896. A carrier, when in doubt as to the authority of an
agent to act for the vendor in stopping the goods, is entitled to
reasonable time to make inquiry into the facts, and the agent is
also entitled to reasonable time to produce his authority and to
furnish indemnity.   The carrier, having received notice from an
agent, is bound to ascertain his authority, and he acts at his peril
in delivering the goods after such notice.[3]

897. A carrier who, without good reason, refuses to deliver
the goods to the vendor when he rightly exercises his right of
stoppage *in transitu*, is guilty of a conversion of the goods, and
is liable for their value.[4]

A vendor is not estopped from maintaining a suit against a
carrier for a wrongful delivery to the purchaser after notice to
stop the goods, by bringing suit upon the debt and recovering
judgment against the purchaser.   On the contrary, the carrier,
under some circumstances, might well set up the defence that
the vendor could have recovered his debt by suit against the
purchaser, and had failed in diligently prosecuting such legal
remedy.[5]

---

[1] Code 1882, § 2076. In Macon &
Western R. R. *v.* Meador, 65 Ga. 705,
it was said to be very questionable
whether, under this provision, the
carrier can buy the vendee's title, as
against the vendor's right of stoppage
in transitu.

[2] Code 1882, § 2074.

[3] Reynolds *v.* Boston & Me. R. R.
Co. 43 N. H. 580.

[4] Thompson *v.* Trail, 2 C. & P. 334;
S. C. 6 B. & C. 36; 9 D. & R. 31;
Bloomingdale *v.* Memphis & Charleston R. R. Co. 6 Lea (Tenn.), 616.
In Childs *v.* Northern Ry. Co. 25 U. C.
Q B. 165, it was held that a railroad
company which has received a valid
and sufficient notice of stoppage *in
transitu*, but has nevertheless delivered the goods to the insolvent consignee, is not liable to the vendor in
trover, because, by the sale and delivery to the carrier, the property
passed to the purchaser, and the stoppage did not give the vendor the right
of property and possession necessary
to sustain such action.

[5] Bloomingdale   *v.*   Memphis   &
Charleston R. R. Co. *supra.*

898. It is the duty of the carrier to determine which of two different claimants of goods has the better right. Thus, if bills of lading are presented to a ship-master by two different holders, and he delivers the goods to the one not entitled to them, the other who is entitled to them may hold the master accountable for the value of the goods.[1]

If bills of lading are presented to the master or other carrier by two different holders, it is incumbent upon him to deliver to the rightful claimant, or to bring an action of interpleader. But he is entitled to deliver to the person first producing a bill of lading, no matter which part it is, so long as he has no notice or knowledge of any dealing with the other parts.[2] "Where the master has notice, or probably even knowledge, of the other indorsement, I think he must deliver at his peril to the rightful owner, or interplead."

If the bill of lading has been assigned for value to a *bonâ fide* assignee, and the vendor seizes the goods in an action of replevin, claiming a right to stop them *in transitu*, it is the duty of the carrier to intervene in the suit, and either interplead or contest the claim of the vendor; otherwise he will render himself liable to the indorsee of the bill of lading for the value of the goods.[3]

899. Liability for delivery after notice. — Both the carrier and the consignee, or his assignee, are liable in trover to the vendor if the carrier by mistake delivers the goods to the consignee after receiving a valid notice to stop them.[4] Chief Justice Gibbs declared[5] it would be monstrous to say, after such notice, that a transfer made by the carrier's mistake should be such as to bind the vendor, and to vest a complete title in the bankrupt purchaser or his representative. The bankrupt has no title to the goods except what he derived from the dry act of delivery, and that, being founded on a mistake, conveyed no property at

[1] The Tigress, 32 L. J. Adm. 97.

[2] Glyn v. East and West India Dock Co. 7 App. Cas. 591, affirming S. C. 6 Q. B. D. 475, reversing S. C. 5 Q. B. D. 129.

[3] The Schooner Mary Ann Guest, 1 Olc. Adm. 498; affirmed 1 Blatchf. 358.

[4] Litt v. Cowley, 7 Taunt. 168; S. C. 12 Marsh. 457; Poole v. Railroad Co. 58 Tex. 134.

[5] Litt v. Cowley, *supra*. As the modern doctrine is that the effect of a stoppage is not to rescind the contract, but only to put the vendor in possession so that he can enforce his lien, the assertion of the learned judge that *the property is revested* in the vendor is not correct, but rather it should be said that the *possession is revested* in the vendor.

all. " As soon as notice was given, the property returned to
the vendor, and he was entitled to maintain trover, not only
against the carrier, but against the assignees of the bankrupt
or any other person.   Until notice, the vendor cannot sue the
carrier, but the purchaser may ; after notice, the case is reversed,
because the property is divested out of the purchaser and revested in the vendor.   I cannot conceive a stronger case in which
the property is in the vendor and not in the vendee."

In a recent case in Texas it appeared that after the carrier, a
railroad company, had received a valid notice to stop *in transitu*
a shipment of goods, and before the goods arrived at their destination, the purchaser assigned the bill of lading without consideration to his attorney, who intercepted the goods at an intermediate station, effaced the marks upon them, remarked them
with a fictitious name, and reshipped them to their original destination, where the agent of the railroad company, though suspecting that the goods were those of which notice of stoppage
had been given, delivered them to the original purchaser.   In a
suit by the vendor against the railroad company and the attorney,
it was held that the attorney, having assumed the apparent ownership of the goods with the intention of committing a fraud
upon the creditor, could not be heard to deny his liability for
the loss; and that, as to the railroad company, the question of
the good faith of its agents should be submitted to the jury with
appropriate instructions.[1]

900. The vendor, upon demanding possession of the carrier or seizing the goods by legal process, should pay the
carrier's charges, for the latter has a lien upon the goods for
such charges, and may insist upon retaining possession until such
charges are paid.   But the vendor, or other person acting in his
behalf, upon paying these charges, is substituted to the carrier's
right of lien and possession respecting the goods.[2]

The vendor's right of stoppage *in transitu* is subject to the
carrier's lien for the freight.   If the goods be consigned to one
person under one contract, the carrier has a lien upon the whole
for the freight and charges on every part; and a delivery of a
part of the goods does not discharge his lien upon the rest without proof of an intention so to do, even as against the right of

[1] Poole *v.* Railroad Co. 58 Tex.   [2] Rucker *v.* Donovan, 13 Kans.
134.   251.

the consignor to stop *in transitu* the goods not delivered; but the carrier may charge against those goods the freight on the whole consignment.[1]

901. **The vendor's right of stoppage in transitu prevails as against a carrier's lien for a general balance of account due from the consignee.** A usage for carriers to retain goods for such a lien cannot affect the vendor's right; and it would seem that such a lien could not be established even by agreement between the carrier and the vendee.[2] The law gives the consignee a specific lien upon the goods, and he should not be allowed to engraft a new lien upon his own laches, especially as against the vendor. I think, said Heath, J., in the leading case,[3] that the right of stopping *in transitu* is a common law right, arising out of the ancient power and dominion of the consignor over his property, which at the time of delivering his goods to the carrier he reserves to himself; and this is paramount as to any sort of agreement between the carrier and consignee.

But the owners of a ship are not entitled to freight, as against the vendor who has stopped the goods *in transitu*, in case the goods were shipped on a vessel belonging to the vendee, and the master, with full authority so to do, issued bills of lading to the vendor, "freight for the said goods free on owners' account;" and it does not matter in such case that the ship had been sold and transferred before the shipment, no notice of the transfer having reached the master or the vendor. The new owners of the ship were bound by the contract of the master entered into pursuant to his original instructions.[4]

V. *During what Time Goods are in Transitu.*

902. **In general the right of stoppage *in transitu* may be exercised at any time after the goods have been delivered to the carrier until they have come into the actual possession of the buyer.**[5] During this time the title is in the buyer. He may also

[1] Potts *v.* N. Y. & N. E. R. R. Co. 131 Mass. 455.

[2] Oppenheim *v.* Russell, 3 B. & P. 42; Jackson *v.* Nichol, 5 Bing. N. C. 508, 518; *S. C.* 7 Scott, 577, 591; Butler *v.* Woolcott, 2 B. & P (N. R.) 64; Leuckhart *v.* Cooper, 3 Bing. N.

C. 99; Potts *v.* N. Y. & N. E. R. R. Co. *supra;* Macon & Western R. R. *v.* Meador, 65 Ga. 705.

[3] Oppenheim *v.* Russell, *supra*.

[4] Mercantile and Exchange Bank *v.* Gladstone, L. R. 3 Ex. 233.

[5] *Ex parte* Rosevear China Clay Co.

have the right of possession, and even constructive possession.
The vendor has parted with the title, the right of possession, and
actual possession; but until the vendee has gained actual possession, upon his insolvency the vendor may stop the goods and
resume the actual possession. This right exists till the goods
have got home into the hands of the purchaser, or of some one
who receives them in the character of his servant or agent, and
not merely as carrier. A carrier, unless he be the purchaser
himself, is a mere intermediary between the seller and the buyer.
The possession of this intermediary is only the constructive possession of the buyer. The actual possession is in the third person, and such possession is a necessary condition to the exercise
of this right. Lord Cranworth (then Baron Rolfe) expressed
this view : [1] " I consider it to be of the very essence of that doctrine, that during the transitus the goods should be in the custody of some third person intermediate between the seller who
has parted with, and the buyer who has not yet acquired, actual
possession."

In Georgia [2] the Code declares that the right of stoppage *in
transitu* exists wherever the vendor in a sale on credit seeks to
resume the possession of goods while they are in the hands of a
carrier or middle-man, in their transit to the vendee or consignee,
on his becoming insolvent. It continues until the vendee obtains
actual possession of the goods.

If the goods are delivered before the price is paid, the seller
cannot retake because of failure to pay; but, until actual receipt
by the purchaser, the seller may at any time arrest them on the
way and retain them until the price is paid. If credit has been
agreed to be given, but the insolvency of the purchaser is made

---

[1] Ch. D. 560; James *v.* Griffin, 2 M.
& W. 623; *S. C.* 1 Ib. 20; White *v.*
Welsh, 38 Pa. St. 396; Atkins *v.*
Colby, 20 N. H. 154; Stubbs *v.* Lund,
7 Mass. 453; Calahan *v.* Babcock, 21
Ohio St. 281; Aguirre *v.* Parmelee,
22 Conn. 473; Lane *v.* Robinson, 18
B. Mon. (Ky.) 623, Halff *v.* Allyn,
60 Tex. 278.

[1] Gibson *v.* Carruthers, 8 M. & W.
321, 328. His language has been
adopted by Lord Cairns and Vice-
Chancellor Wood, in Berndtson *v.*

Strang, L. R. 4 Eq. 481; *S. C.* L. R. 3
Ch. 588, 590 ; by Lord Justice James,
in *Ex parte* Rosevear China Clay Co.
11 Ch. D. 560; and by Burton, J.,
in Wiley *v.* Smith, 1 Ont. App. 179,
188.

[2] Code 1882, §§ 2075, 2649; Macon
& Western R. R. *v.* Meador, 65 Ga.
705. In this case Jackson, C. J., said:
" We think that our Code contemplates actual delivery and possession
as distinguished from constructive possession."

known to the seller, he may still exercise the right of stoppage *in transitu*.

In California[1] and Dakota Territory[2] it is provided by code that the transit of property is at an end when it comes into the possession of the consignee, or into that of his agent, unless such agent is employed merely to forward the property to the consignee.

903. Goods shipped to seller's own order. — Inasmuch as the right of stoppage *in transitu* presupposes the actual custody of the goods by a third person intermediate between the seller and the buyer, it is as important to the existence of the right that the vendor should have parted with the actual possession as it is that the vendor should not have acquired it.   Therefore the right does not exist in case the vendor has shipped goods to his own order, or to the order of his own exclusive agent, and the bill of lading has not been assigned to the purchaser or to any third person.[3]

904. There are many kinds of actual delivery; or, in other words, actual delivery to the vendee may be made in various ways and under different circumstances.   Baron Parke enumerates four kinds of delivery, in the following passage:[4]   "The actual delivery to the vendee or his agent, which puts an end to the transitus, or state of passage, may be at the vendee's own warehouse, or at a place which he uses as his own, though belonging to another, for the deposit of goods;[5] or at a place where he means the goods to remain until a fresh destination is communicated to them by orders from himself;[6] or it may be by the vendee's taking possession by himself or agent at some point short of the original intended place of destination."

Judge Woodruff states, as the result of the cases on this point: "That a merely constructive delivery, though sufficient to entitle the vendor to demand the price of the goods, and to place the goods at the vendee's risk, does not alone defeat the right of stoppage.   That while the goods are in transportation to the

---

[1] Codes and Stats. 1876, § 8078.

[2] R. Codes Dak. 1877, § 1817.

[3] *In re* St. Joze Indiano, 1 Wheat. 208, 210 ; Ilsley *v.* Stubbs, 9 Mass. 65 ; *In re* San Joze Indiano, 2 Gall. 268.

[4] James *v.* Griffin, 2 M. & W. 623, 633.

[5] Scott *v.* Pettit, 3 B. & P. 469 ; Rowe *v.* Pickford, 8 Taunt. 83.

[6] Dixon *v.* Baldwen, 5 East, 175.

place of destination, or are in the hands of an intermediate agent or warehouseman for the purpose of being forwarded, they are not subject to this right. That after their arrival at the place of destination, and while in the hands of the carrier, or a wharfinger, or a warehouseman, for the mere purpose of delivery to the vendee, the vendor may resume the possession. That delivery to the vendee's special agent on board the vendee's own conveyance, or a conveyance chartered by him, if the purpose of the delivery is transportation to the vendee, does not defeat the right. But that the right is lost if the vendee received actual possession; or if after their arrival at the place of destination he exercise acts of ownership over the goods; or if his agents, having authority and power of disposal, exercise like acts."[1]

There is, of course, no right of stoppage when the seller has put the buyer in possession of the goods before the transit has commenced.[2]

905. Where the transit has not commenced, and the vendor is still in control of the goods, he may refuse to allow the transit to commence under the same circumstances that would justify him in stopping the goods after the transit had commenced.[3] The question is then more often one of a vendor's lien; yet the question of stoppage may arise, especially where the goods are at the time of sale in the possession of a warehouseman or other agent, and the vendor transfers possession by a delivery order, which in itself does not amount to a constructive delivery, but requires acceptance by the warehouseman in order to confer such possession upon the holder.[4] The transfer

---

[1] Harris v. Hart, 6 Duer (N. Y.), 606, 607 ; affirmed 17 N. Y. 249.

[2] Loeb v. Blum, 25 La. Ann. 232 ; Lupin v. Marie, 2 Paige (N. Y.), 169.

[3] White v. Welsh, 38 Pa. St. 396, 420. "Judges do not ordinarily distinguish between the retainder of goods by a vendor, and their stoppage *in transitu* on account of the insolvency of the vendee ; because these terms refer to the same right, only at different stages of perfection and execution of the contract of sale. If a vendor has a right to stop *in transitu, à fortiori*

he has a right of retainer before any transit has commenced." Per Lowrie, C. J.

[4] Farina v. Home, 16 M. & W. 119, 123. "This warrant is no more than an engagement by the wharfinger to deliver to the consignee, or any one he may appoint ; and the wharfinger holds the goods as the agent of the consignor, and his possession is that of the consignor, until an assignment has taken place, and the wharfinger has attorned, so to speak, to the assignee, and agreed with him to hold

of a delivery order operates differently in this respect from the transfer of a bill of lading or a warehouse receipt. The warehouseman upon whom a delivery order is given remains the agent of the vendor until the order is presented to him, and he becomes the agent of the purchaser, by a transfer of the goods to the name of the purchaser or by some other equivalent act. In the mean time, upon the happening of the purchaser's insolvency, the vendor may stop the goods in hands of the warehouseman, just as he might in the hands of a carrier ; but after the order has been presented to the warehouseman, and he has transferred the goods to the name of the purchaser, the delivery to him is complete and the right of stoppage is gone.[1]

906. The procuring of a warehouse certificate for goods as the property of the vendee preliminary to their transit, and not at the termination of it, does not deprive the vendor of his right to stop them *in transitu*. Thus, whiskey in a government bonded warehouse in Indiana was sold to a purchaser in Boston. The storekeeper gave his certificate for the whiskey as the property of the purchaser, and the seller sent it to him. It was part of the terms of sale, that the seller should from time to time, as the buyer should request, ship the whiskey to Boston, and pay the storage charges, taxes, and insurance, and draw on the buyer for the amounts. The whiskey could not be taken from the warehouse until the taxes were paid. The whiskey was shipped by railroad in accordance with these terms, but while in the hands of the railroad company the buyer became insolvent and the seller stopped the goods. It was held that his right of stoppage *in transitu* was not lost. The transitus in such case would not be at an end until the goods reached Boston, and were taken into custody by the purchaser. It would be no answer to say that there was a constructive delivery of the whiskey to the buyer by virtue of the delivery of the warehouse receipt to him, and that he had the right to take possession of it and withdraw it from the

for him. Then, and not till then, the wharfinger is the agent or bailee of the assignee, and his possession that of the assignee, and then only is there a constructive delivery to him. In the mean time, the warrant, and the indorsement of the warrant, is nothing more than an offer to hold the goods as the warehouseman of the assignee." Per Parke, B.

See Benjamin, §§ 1244 *et seq.*

[1] Wood *v.* Tassell, 6 Q. B. 234 ; Lackington *v.* Atherton, 7 M. & Gr. 360 ; Tanner *v.* Scovell, 14 M. & W. 28 ; Swanwick *v.* Sothern, 9 A. & E. 895.

warehouse; for the purchaser did not take possession of it at the warehouse, but left it in charge of the seller, and to be shipped by him. The seller therefore had the right to exercise his right of stoppage *in transitu* until the goods reached the purchaser at the place contemplated by the parties as the place of their destination.[1]

907. Ordinarily a delivery of goods to a carrier is not a constructive delivery to the purchaser to whom the carrier is to take them, so far as the right of stoppage *in transitu* is concerned; for the carrier is not the special agent of the purchaser, but a general agent for the carriage of the goods; and this is the case even although the carrier may have been specially designated or appointed by the purchaser.[2] But the terms of the contract and the circumstances of the case may show that the parties intended the delivery to the carrier to be a complete delivery to the vendee, so that the vendor will not retain his right to stop the goods in their passage. Bills of lading or carriers' receipts sent to the consignee, making the goods deliverable to him, may be evidence of an intention on the part of the vendor to vest the property and the possession in the consignee. In such a case, Parke, B., giving judgment, observed:[3] "If the intention of the parties to pass the property, whether absolute or special, in certain ascertained chattels, is established, and they are placed in hands of a depositary, no matter whether such depositary be a common carrier or ship-master employed by the consignor, or a third person, and the chattels are so placed on account of the person who is to have that property, and the depositary assents, it is enough, and it matters not by what documents this is effected."

908. It is immaterial that the carrier has been designated by the purchaser or hired by him; for even in such case a delivery to the carrier is only a constructive delivery to the purchaser, and not an actual delivery to him. "The delivery, by the vendor of goods sold, to a carrier of any description, either expressly or by implication named by the vendee, and who is to

[1] Mohr *v.* Boston & Albany R. R. Co. 106 Mass. 67.

[2] *In re* Frances, 8 Cranch, 418.

[3] Bryans *v.* Nix, 4 M. & W. 775,

791. And see Evans *v.* Nichol, 4 Scott N. R. 43; Cowasjee *v.* Thompson, 5 Moore P. C. C. 165; Meletopulo *v.* Ranking, 6 Jur. 1095.

carry on his account, is a constructive delivery to the vendee ; but the vendor has a right, if unpaid, and the vendee be insolvent, to retake the goods before they are actually delivered to the vendee, or some one whom he means to be his agent, to take possession of and keep the goods for him, and thereby to replace the vendor in the same situation as if he had not parted with the actual possession." [1]

909. **When goods have been delivered to one who is only a carrier, though named by the purchaser,** but not his agent for any other purpose, such delivery is only a constructive delivery to the purchaser.[2] If goods are placed on board a ship chartered by the purchaser, ordinarily the transit is not over until the carriage is over.

The distinction between a constructive delivery to a purchaser by delivery on board a vessel chartered by him, and an actual delivery to him, is well illustrated in the recent English case of the Rosevear China Clay Company. A contract was entered into for the sale of some china clay to be delivered free on board at a specified port. The purchaser chartered a ship, and the clay was delivered on board at the port agreed upon. The destination of the clay was not communicated to the vendors. Before the ship left the harbor, the vendors heard of the insolvency of the purchaser, and gave notice to the master to stop the clay *in transitu*. It was held by the Court of Appeal in Chancery that, the clay being in the possession of the master of the ship only as carrier, the transit was not at an end and the notice to stop was given in time.[3] Lord Justice James said : " The principle is this, — that, when the vendor knows that he is delivering the goods to some one as carrier, who is receiving them in that character, he delivers them with the implied right, which has been established by the law, of stopping them so long as they remain in the possession of the carrier as carrier. I am of opinion that in the present case, although the vendors' liability was at an end when they had delivered the clay on board the ship,

---

[1] James *v.* Griffin, 2 M. & W. 623, 632, per Parke, B.

[2] Lickbarrow *v.* Mason, 1 Smith's Lead. Cas. 7th ed. 818 ; Berndtson *v.* Strang, L. R. 4 Eq. 481 ; *S. C. L. R.* 3 Ch. 588 ; *Ex parte* Rosevear China Clay Co. 11 Ch. D. 560 ; Ruck *v.* Hatfield, 5 B. & Ald. 632 ; Lane *v.* Bartlett, 18 B. Mon. (Ky.) 623.

[3] *Ex parte* Rosevear China Clay Co. *supra.*

which indeed is the case in most instances of stoppage *in transitu*, that did not deprive them of the right to stop *in transitu*, so long as the clay was in possession of the master of the ship as carrier." In the same case, Brett, L. J., said : " The clay was placed on board the ship for the purpose of being carried to Glasgow ; it was in the actual possession of the ship-owner, and only in the constructive possession of the purchaser. Therefore the right of stoppage *in transitu* existed. If the purchaser had been the owner of the ship, the vendors would have had no such right, unless they had reserved it by express stipulation. But, in the actual state of things, I think that, both on principle and on the authorities, the transit was not over and the right to stop *in transitu* remained." Colton, L. J. : " I am of the same opinion. . . . The contract with a carrier to carry goods does not make the carrier the agent or servant of the person who contracts with him, whether he be the vendor or the purchaser of the goods. Here the verbal agreement which the purchaser entered into to charter the ship did not make the captain the agent or servant of the purchaser ; he was only a carrier."

910. A delivery to a carrier is under some circumstances a delivery to the vendee, and then there can be no stoppage *in transitu* of the goods in the hands of the carrier.[1] Thus, if the goods are delivered on board of a vessel appointed by the vendee to receive them, not for the purpose of transportation to him, or to a place appointed by him for his use, but to be shipped in his name from his own place of business to a third person at another port, there is a delivery to the vendee when the goods are put on board such vessel, and the vendor has no right afterwards to stop the goods to obtain payment of the price.[2] But whether a delivery on board the purchaser's own ship, or upon his own cart, is a delivery to him, is a question of fact, and de-

---

[1] Fowler *v.* M'Taggart, cited in 1 East, 522; *S. C.* 3 East, 388; Noble *v.* Adams, 2 Marsh. 366.

[2] Memphis & L. R. R. R. Co. *v.* Freed, 38 Ark. 614; Treadwell *v.* Aydlett, 9 Heisk. (Tenn.) 388 ; Eaton *v.* Cook, 32 Vt. 58; Rowley *v.* Bigelow, 12 Pick. (Mass.) 307 ; Stubbs *v.* Lund, 7 Mass. 453. In the latter case, Parsons, C. J., said that the dis-tinction in such case depends upon the terms of shipment as shown by the bill of lading ; the right of stoppage ceases on the shipment if no transit is contemplated ; but that the right exists if the delivery to him is to be made after the termination of the voyage. This distinction is criticised in Bolin *v.* Huffnagle, 1 Rawle (Pa.), 9, a leading case.

pends upon the circumstances of the delivery, and particularly upon such circumstances as show the intention of the parties in making such delivery. It is well said by Jessell, M. R.,[1] that "it neither follows, as a proposition of law, that because a purchaser sends his cart for goods, and they are given to him in the cart, the transit is at an end, nor does it follow it is not: it is to be considered as a question of what in law is called a question for the jury, that is, a question of inference from known facts as to what the real intention of the parties was."

911. A delivery on board the purchaser's own ship is ordinarily a delivery to him so as to preclude a stoppage *in transitu* by the vendor before the delivery of the goods at the port of consignment.[2] In the words of Baron Parke,[3] "delivery on the vendee's own ship is a final delivery at the place of destination." In such case an essential condition to the exercise of the right of stoppage *in transitu* is wanting, namely, the custody of the goods by a third person intermediate between the seller and the buyer after the former has parted with actual possession, and before the latter has acquired it.[4] But when goods are delivered absolutely and unconditionally on board the buyer's own ship, and the master signs bills of lading making the goods deliverable to the buyer or his assigns, without any reservation to the seller of control over them, there is no intermediate third person in custody of the goods; for the master being the servant or agent of the buyer, the delivery to the master is a delivery to the buyer.[b]

In this respect there is no well-founded distinction between the case of a ship of the vendee sent out expressly to receive

[1] Merchants' Banking Co. *v.* Phœnix Bessemer Steel Co. 5 Ch. D. 205, 219.

[2] Van Casteel *v.* Booker, 2 Ex. 691; Turner *v.* Liverpool Docks Co. 6 Ex. 543; Ogle *v.* Atkinson, 5 Taunt. 759; Inglis *v.* Usherwood, 1 East, 515; Blakey *v.* Dinsdale, 2 Cowp. 661, 664; Fowler *v.* M'Taggart, cited 1 East, 522, and 7 T. R. 442 ; Bolin *v.* Huffnagle, 1 Rawle (Pa.), 9; Thompson *v.* Stewart, 7 Phila. (Pa.) 187; Pequeno *v.* Taylor, 38 Barb. (N. Y.) 375.

[3] Van Casteel *v.* Booker, 2 Ex. 691, 708.

[4] Gibson *v.* Carruthers, 8 M. & W. 328, per Rolfe, B.

[5] Schotsmans *v.* Lancashire & Yorkshire Ry. Co. L. R. 2 Ch. 332, 336. Per Lord Chelmsford, L. C. : "If the vendor desires to protect himself under these circumstances, he may restrain the effect of such delivery, and preserve his right of stoppage *in transitu*, by taking bills of lading, making the goods deliverable to his order or assigns."

the goods, and the case of a general ship belonging to him taking the goods without any previous arrangement for the purpose.[1]

912. But the right of stoppage may exist even when goods are shipped upon the buyer's own vessel, consigned to him at his place of residence.[2]   A vendor, after putting a cargo on board the vendee's ship, and taking bills of lading making the goods deliverable to the vendee, before the sailing of the ship heard of the vendee's insolvency, and thereupon prevailed upon the master to give up the bills of lading already signed, and to sign other bills of lading deliverable to the vendor's own agent.   The vendee had in the mean time executed a bill of sale of the cargo.   In an action of replevin for the goods brought by the assignee, it was held that the vendor so far had control of goods after the goods had been put on board, that he might rightfully alter their destination, or might stop them *in transitu*.[3]

It seems also that a delivery on board the vendee's own ship should have the effect of a delivery to the vendee himself, only when the vendor has full knowledge that the vendee is the owner; for it would be scarcely just that a vendor who has delivered goods to be carried to his vendee, under the belief that he could exercise the ordinary right of an unpaid vendor over them, should be deprived of that right because he had ignorantly placed the goods on board the vendee's own ship, and must therefore be taken to have made an absolute delivery of them.[4]

913. If the vendor takes a bill of lading making the goods deliverable to his own order, this goes to show that no property passes to the vendee, and that the vendor, though shipping the goods by the vendee's own vessel, intends to retain control

---

[1] Schotsmans *v.* Lancashire & Yorkshire Ry. Co. L. R. 2 Ch. 332, 336, per Lord Chelmsford, L. C.   The case of Mitchel *v.* Ede, 11 Ad. & E. 888, sometimes relied upon as creating such a distinction, was not a case of stoppage *in transitu*, or of vendor and purchaser.

[2] Ilsley *v.* Stubbs, 9 Mass. 65; Cross *v.* O'Donnell, 44 N. Y. 661, 666. See, however, Bolin *v.* Huffnagle, 1 Rawle (Pa.), 9.

[3] Ilsley *v.* Stubbs, *supra*. And see *Ex parte* Rosevear China Clay Co. 11 Ch. D. 560.

[4] Schotsmans *v.* Lancashire & Yorkshire Ry. Co. *supra*.

of the goods till he should do some further act, such as indorsing the bill of lading to the vendee.[1] Merchants at Liverpool sent orders to merchants at Charleston to ship a quantity of cotton for the homeward voyage of a ship of theirs then at that port. The Charleston merchants accordingly purchased cotton and shipped it on board this vessel. The master signed for the consignors a bill of lading making the cotton deliverable at Liverpool " to order or to our assigns, paying for freight of the cotton nothing, being owners' property ; " and the consignors indorsed the bill of lading to order of their own agents at Liverpool, and drew upon the consignees for the consignment, and pledged the bill of lading for advances upon the draft. The consignees having become bankrupt before the arrival of the vessel at Liverpool, the consignors by their agent stopped the cargo *in transitu.* The assignees in bankruptcy of the consignees claimed the cotton ; but it was held that the property did not vest absolutely in the consignees, notwithstanding the delivery on board their ship ; for, by the terms of the bill of lading, the consignors reserved to themselves a *jus disponendi* of the goods, which the master acknowledged by signing the bill of lading making the cotton deliverable to their order, although by so doing the master might have exceeded his authority.[2]

914. Receipt that goods are shipped on seller's account. — If a vendor, upon delivering goods on board a vessel named by the vendee, takes a receipt from the person in charge, stating that the goods are shipped on the seller's account, he preserves his right of stoppage until he exchanges his receipt for a bill of lading ; and he does not lose his right though the ship-master inadvertently gives the bill of lading to the purchaser or his assigns.[3] " I take it," said Gibbs, C. J.,[4] " that the regular practice is, that the person who is in possession of the receipt is alone entitled to the bill of lading ; and the captain, therefore, ought

---

[1] Seymour *v.* Newton, 105 Mass. 272.

[2] Turner *v.* Liverpool Docks, 6 Ex. 543. See, also, Ellershaw *v.* Magniac, 6 Ex. 570, n. ; Wait *v.* Baker, 2 Ex. 1. In Ogle *v.* Atkinson, 5 Taunt. 759, the general circumstances bore a close resemblance to the above case ; but the case is distinguishable, because a fraud was practised upon the master of the vessel to induce him to sign a bill of lading with the name of the consignee in blank.

[3] Craven *v.* Ryder, 2 Marsh. 127; *S. C.* 6 Taunt. 433.

Cowasjee *v.* Thompson, 5 Moore P. C. 165, is to be distinguished.

[4] Craven *v.* Ryder, *supra.*

not to give the bill of lading except to the person who can give the receipt in exchange; consequently the person holding the receipt has a control over the goods till he has exchanged the receipt for a bill of lading."

915. Though the vendor takes a bill of lading by which the goods are to be delivered to the purchaser, this is not conclusive that the delivery on board the purchaser's own ship is a delivery to him. Thus, where a planter residing in Jamaica was indebted to a London merchant, and shipped sugars on board a vessel belonging to the latter, and received from the master a bill of lading by which the goods were to be delivered to the London merchant, he paying freight, the planter made an indorsement on the bill of lading that the goods were to be delivered to the merchant only upon his giving security for certain payments, and otherwise to the planter's agent. The planter then indorsed and delivered the bill to a third person, to whom he was indebted in more than the value of the goods. It was held that the planter had a right to change the destination of the goods before the delivery of them or of the bill of lading to the merchant, and that the property had not passed to the latter, although the planter was indebted to him in a greater sum than the value of the sugars.[1]

916. Notwithstanding the form of the bill of lading, the vendor may have acted as agent for the vendee in taking it. If, therefore, the bill of lading be made "freight free," and the invoice shows that the goods were shipped for and on account of the vendee, and it appears that both the bill of lading and invoice are immediately assigned to the vendee, it is a question for the jury whether the goods were not really delivered on board the vendee's ship, to be carried for and on his account, and, if so, the right of stoppage would end with the delivery of the goods on board the vendee's ship.[2]

---

[1] Mitchel v. Ede, 11 A. & E. 888; and see Moakes v. Nicolson, 19 C. B. N. S. 290; Inglis v. Usherwood, 1 East, 515.

[2] Van Casteel v. Booker, 2 Ex. 691. Also see Wait v. Baker, 2 Ex. 1; Turner v. Liverpool Docks Co. 6 Ex. 543; Ellershaw v. Magniac, Ib. 570; Brown v. North, 8 Ex. 1; Jenkyns v. Brown, 14 Q. B. 496; Browne v. Hare, 3 H. & N. 484; Ruck v. Hatfield, 5 B. & Ald. 632; Joyce v. Swann, 17 C. B. N. S. 84.

917. As a general rule, the transit continues until the goods have arrived at the original destination contemplated by the purchaser and named to the vendor.[1] Such destination is the place to which the goods are to be conveyed by the carrier, and where they will remain unless fresh orders be given for their subsequent disposition.[2]

When the goods have arrived by vessel at their place of destination, and the purchaser has indorsed the bills of lading, and delivered them to a railroad company, in order that the goods may be forwarded to the purchaser at another place, they cannot be stopped by the vendor while in possession of the latter carrier, for the transitus prescribed by the vendor is at an end, and the railroad company is the agent of the purchaser.[3]

918. Where a port of call is named at which the vessel must touch for orders to proceed to the place of its final destination, the arrival of the vessel at the port of call does not ordinarily end the transitus. A merchant at Bahia shipped a cargo of sugar to a sugar-refining company at Glasgow by a ship chartered by the vendor. The charter-party provided that the ship should proceed " either direct or *via* Falmouth, Cowes, or Queenstown, for orders, to a port in the United Kingdom, or to a port on the continent (between certain limits)." The bill of lading, which was indorsed to the consignee, and the invoice, specified the destination of the cargo in similar terms. The ship arrived at Falmouth, and the master, in pursuance of written instructions from the vendor, announced its arrival to his agents in London, and asked them for orders. The agents applied to the consignee for instructions as to the destination of the ship; but, before any instructions were given, the latter became insolvent, and thereupon the vendor's agents stopped the cargo. It was held that the cargo had not been constructively delivered to the vendee, that the transitus was not over, and that the stoppage was valid.[4] Lord Romilly, M. R., delivering judgment,

[1] Whitehead *v.* Anderson, 9 M. & W. 518, 534; Coates *v.* Railton, 6 B. & C. 422; Dixon *v.* Baldwen, 5 East, 185; Leeds *v.* Wright, 3 B. & P. 320; Rowe *v.* Pickford, 8 Taunt. 83; Coventry *v.* Gladstone, L. R. 6 Eq. 44, per Wood, V. C.; Rodger *v.* The Comptoir d'Escompte de Paris, L. R. 2 P. C. 393; Stokes *v.* La Riviere, cited 3 T. R.

466, and 3 East, 397; Parker *v.* M'Iver, 1 Des. (S. C.) 274.

[2] Wentworth *v.* Outhwaite, 10 M. & W. 436, 450, per Parke, B.; Blackman *v.* Pierce, 23 Cal. 508; Halff *v.* Allyn, 60 Tex. 278.

[3] *Ex parte* Gibbes, 1 Ch. D. 101.

[4] Fraser *v.* Witt, L. R. 7 Eq. 64, 71.

said: [1] " The question is, whether there was delivery at a place
where the vendee meant the goods to remain until a fresh destination was communicated to them by orders from himself. If
the ship had, under the direction of the company, proceeded to
the Clyde, still the transitus would not have been over ; but if,
on its arrival, the company had determined to send the cargo to
another port, not within the original charter-party, and had for
that purpose chartered the vessel afresh, and thereby made the
master their own agent, then the constructive delivery pointed out
by Lord Wensleydale would have occurred, and it would have
been the same thing in substance as if the cargo had been taken
from the vessel and put on board another vessel under the direction and control of the company. The purchaser must not only
be the owner of the goods, but he must be the owner for the
time being of the receptacle in which the goods are placed. This
was not so in the present case : the company could not have sent
the sugar to any port in the Mediterranean, or, indeed, to any
port, except one within the limits specified in the charter-party,
effected by the vendor; and even if directions had been given
by the company to proceed to one of the ports specified in the
charter-party, still there would have been no delivery to the
company until after the arrival of the cargo in that port, and
some act done by which the possession and absolute control over
the sugar had been vested in the company. But, in truth, not
even this was done; for the agents did not desire the company
to give the master directions whither he was to go, or put him
under their control, but they wrote to the company and said :
' Give us instructions as to the port to which we are to send the
vessel ; ' and even then instructions never came until after the
delivery of the goods had been stopped by the agents of the
vendor."

919. It is generally conceded that the vendee may anti-
cipate the delivery at the place of consignment, and take possession at any place on the route where he may direct the carrier
to deliver the goods, though he thereby shortens the transit and
puts an end to the vendor's right of stoppage.[2] Baron Parke, in

[1] Fraser v. Witt, L. R. 7 Eq. 64,
71.
[2] Wright v. Lawes, 4 Esp. 82;
Wood v. Yeatman, 15 B. Mon. (Ky.)

270; Muskegon Booming Co. v. Underhill, 43 Mich. 629; Stevens v. Wheeler,
27 Barb. (N. Y.) 656, 660. In this
case goods consigned to the buyer

a case which did not directly involve this point, expressed this view strongly, saying:[1] "The law is clearly settled, that the unpaid vendor has a right to retake the goods before they have arrived at the destination originally contemplated by the purchaser, unless in the mean time they have come to the actual or constructive possession of the vendee. If the vendee take them out of the possession of the carrier into his own before their arrival, with or without the consent of the carrier, there seems to be no doubt that the transit would be at an end; though in the case of the carrier's consent it may be a wrong to him, for which he would have a right of action."

920. But a mere demand by the consignee without a delivery of the goods to him is not sufficient to intercept them on their passage, and determine the vendor's right of stoppage. Upon this point Chief Justice Tindal observed that, "although it might be conceded to be the better opinion, that if the vendee actually receives the possession of his goods on their passage to him, and before the voyage has completely terminated, that the delivery is complete, and the right of stoppage gone, yet no

in Brooklyn were taken possession of by him in New York. There are *dicta* and implications to this effect in several cases. Whitehead *v.* Anderson, 9 M. & W. 518; Jackson *v.* Nichol, 5 Bing. N. C. 508; James *v.* Griffin, 2 M. & W. 623; Mills *v.* Ball, 2 B. & P. 457; Foster *v.* Frampton, 6 B. & C. 107; Dixon *v.* Baldwen, 5 East, 175; Kendall *v.* Marshall, 48 L. T. R. N. S. 951; *S. C.* 16 Rep. 511; Secomb *v.* Nutt, 14 B. Mon. (Ky.) 324; Chandler *v.* Fulton, 10 Tex. 2.

In Mohr *v.* Boston & Albany R. R. Co. 106 Mass. 67, 72, Morton, J., remarked: "In all cases of delivery of goods to a common carrier for the purpose of transit, the vendee, acting in good faith, has the right to intercept the goods before they reach their destination, and, by taking actual possession of them, to defeat the vendor's lien."

In a modern case, which did not, however, involve the question of the vendor's right of stoppage *in transitu*, it was held that the carrier was not bound to deliver the goods at the place of consignment, but might deliver them at any place at which the consignee should order their delivery; and Bramwell, B., said: "It would probably create a smile anywhere but in a court of law, if it were said that a carrier could not deliver to the consignee at any place except that specified by the consignor. The goods are intended to reach the consignee, and, provided he receives them, it is immaterial at what place they are delivered. The contract is to deliver the goods to the consignee at the place named by the consignor, unless the consignee directs them to be delivered at a different place." London & N. W. Ry. Co. *v.* Bartlett, 7 H. & N. 400, 407.

[1] Whitehead *v.* Anderson, *supra.* See, also, Oppenheim *v.* Russell, 3 B. & P. 42, per Chambre, J.

authority has been cited for the position, and the principle seems the other way, that a mere demand by the vendee, without any delivery, before the voyage has completely terminated, deprives the consignor of his right of stoppage."[1]

921. Whether an intermediate delivery before the goods have reached their ultimate destination terminates the transitus or not, depends upon the authority of the person to whom the intermediate delivery is made. If he be merely an agent to forward the goods in accordance with the original directions, the vendor's right continues;[2] but if he has authority to receive the goods for the consignee, and to give them a new destination not originally intended, the transitus ends with the delivery to him. If the goods upon their intermediate delivery have so far reached the end of their journey that they await new orders from the purchaser to put them in motion again, and give them another substantive destination, and if without such new orders they must remain stationary, then the delivery is complete and the lien of the vendor has expired.[3]   If the person into whose hands

[1] Jackson *v.* Nichol, 5 Bing. N. C. 508.

[2] Smith *v.* Goss, 1 Camp. 282; Coates *v.* Railton, 6 B. & C. 422; Jackson *v.* Nichol, *supra; Ex parte* Watson, 5 Ch. D. 35 ; Nicholls *v.* Le Feuvre, 2 Bing. N. C. 81 ; Rodger *v.* Comptoir d'Escompte de Paris, L. R. 2 P. C. 393 ; Markwald *v.* Creditors, 7 Cal. 213 ; Blackman *v.* Pierce, 23 Cal. 508 ; Atkins *v.* Colby, 20 N. H. 154 ; Lane *v.* Robinson, 18 B. Mon. (Ky.) 623 ; Secomb *v.* Nutt, 14 Ib. 324 ; Wood *v.* Yeatman, 15 Ib. 270 ; Halff *v.* Allyn, 60 Tex. 278; Cabeen *v.* Campbell, 30 Pa. St. 254; Hays *v.* Mouille, 14 Pa. St. 48 ; Buckley *v.* Furniss, 15 Wend. (N. Y.) 137; Harris *v.* Pratt, 17 N. Y. 249, affirming Harris *v.* Hart, 6 Duer, 606; Covell *v.* Hitchcock, 23 Wend. (N. Y.) 611, 613. In this case Walworth, Chancellor, said : "The law appears to be well settled that the right of stoppage *in transitu* exists so long as the goods remain in the hands of a middle-man on the way to the place of their destination, and that the right terminates whenever the goods are or have been, either actually or constructively, delivered to the vendee ; a delivery to the general agent of the vendee being of course tantamount to a delivery to himself. The time during which the right exists, therefore, is during the whole period of the transit from the vendor to the purchaser, or the place of ultimate destination as designated to the vendor by the buyer ; and this transit continues so long as the goods remain in the possession of the middle-man, whether he be the carrier either by land or water, or the keeper of a warehouse or place of deposit connected with the transmission and delivery of the goods."

[3] This is the doctrine of the leading case of Dixon *v.* Baldwen, 5 East, 175 ; and of Leeds *v.* Wright, 3 B. & P. 320; Scott *v.* Pettit, Ib. 469 ; Valpy *v.* Gibson, 4 C. B. 837; Wentworth *v.* Outhwaite, 10 M. & W. 436; Dodson *v.* Wentworth, 4 M. & G.

the goods come does not receive them for the purpose of expediting their further transportation, but simply as the agent of the purchaser for his use for general purposes unconnected with transportation, it is virtually the possession of the purchaser himself, and the transitus is at an end.[1]

922. **The transitus continues while the goods are in the hands of an agent appointed by the purchaser for the purpose of forwarding the goods.** Though the agent may be the agent of the purchaser, designated, paid, and employed by him, yet, if the purpose of his employment is to expedite the property towards its destination, or to aid those engaged in forwarding it, the seller's right to stay the final delivery continues.[2] "When the seller attempts to claim the goods, the question is whether they have arrived at the end of their transit, and this usually depends upon the further question whether the party in whose hands they are found is acting in the character of an agent for transportation, or as the agent of the purchaser, holding them simply for his use unconnected with the business of forwarding them. It sometimes happens that the seller delivers goods sold on credit immediately to an agent of the purchaser, or that, as in the present case, he sends them a part of the way to their final destination, and they are delivered to such agent of the buyer. When they have been so delivered according to the vendee's direction, either immediately upon the sale, or after being carried a part of the distance, the question arises whether the seller retains a right to stop them on account of the failure of the purchaser. Under certain circumstances the de-

1080 ; James *v.* Griffin, 2 M. & W. 623, 631, per Parke, B. ; Smith *v.* Hudson, 6 B. & S. 431, per Cockburn, C. J.; Rowe *v.* Pickford, 8 Taunt. 83 ; Cooper *v.* Bill, 3 H. & C. 722 ; Harman *v.* Anderson, 2 Camp. 243 ; Lucas *v.* Dorrien, 7 Taunt. 279 ; Kendall *v.* Marshall, 48 L. T. R. N. S. 951 ; *S. C.* 16 Rep. 511 ; Guilford *v.* Smith, 30 Vt. 49, where the cases are reviewed at length ; Biggs *v.* Barry, 2 Curtis, 259 ; Pottinger *v.* Hecksher, 2 Grant (Pa.), 309 ; Hays *v.* Mouille, 14 Pa. St. 48.

[1] Harris *v.* Pratt, 17 N. Y. 249 ; Covell *v.* Hitchcock, 23 Wend. (N.

Y.) 611 ; Becker *v.* Hallgarten, 86 N. Y. 167 ; Hoover *v.* Tibbits, 13 Wis. 79; Atkins *v.* Colby, 20 N. H. 154 ; Inslee *v.* Lane, 57 N. H. 454, 459, per Foster, C. J.

[2] Stokes *v.* La Riviere, reported in Bohtlingk *v.* Inglis, 3 East, 381 ; Coates *v.* Railton, 6 B. & C. 422 ; Nicholls *v.* Le Feuvre, 2 Bing. N. C. 81; Jackson *v.* Nichol, 5 Ib. 508 ; Tucker *v.* Humphrey, 4 Bing. 516 ; Harris *v.* Pratt, 17 N. Y. 249, per Denio, J., who reviews at length the earlier cases ; Hays *v.* Mouille, *supra.*

positary in these cases is considered as the general agent of the purchaser, and the goods when in his hands are adjudged to be virtually in the possession of such purchaser and not *in transitu;* while, under a state of facts somewhat different, the person into whose custody they thus came is regarded as an agent for expediting them, and the right of stoppage continues until they come to the purchaser's hands at his place of business, or at some other place where he has directed them to be sent."[1]

Wool was purchased in New York by a manufacturing company located at Enfield, through their agent, to be paid for by the paper of this company when delivered at Enfield. The wool was delivered to the agent upon an order of the vendor to the storekeeper to deliver it to the company named or bearer. The agent of this company was also the agent of another manufacturing company located at Simsbury, and it was his usual course of business to divide between these two companies any large lots of wool purchased for either, each company giving its own notes for its respective share of the wool when received. The agent accordingly divided the wool purchased in this case, and forwarded a portion of it to the corporation located at Simsbury without the knowledge of the vendor. Before the wool was received both corporations became insolvent, and the portion of the wool forwarded to the Simsbury company was attached as its property while in the hands of the carrier. It was held that the transitus of the wool was not terminated by the delivery to the agent, nor by his act in sending a portion of it to the Simsbury company; and that the vendor might exercise his right of stoppage.[2]

923.   If the vendee repudiates the purchase, and declines to receive the goods after they have arrived at their destination, the transitus is not at an end, and the unpaid vendor has the right to stop them.[3] " The property in these goods passed by the contract to the vendee. Unless the property passed, there would be no need of the right of stopping *in transitu.* The only effect of the property passing is, that from that time the

---

[1] Harris *v.* Pratt, 17 N. Y. 249, per Denio, J.

[2] Aguirre *v.* Parmelee, 22 Conn. 473.

[3] Bolton *v.* Lancashire & York-shire Ry. Co. L. R. 1 C. P. 431, 439 ; Nicholls *v.* Le Feuvre, 2 Bing. N. C. 81 ; Mason *v.* Wilson, 43 Ark. 172 ; Greve *v.* Dunham, 60 Iowa, 108.

goods are at the risk of the buyer. But it by no means follows that the buyer is to have possession unless he is prepared to pay for the goods. As long as the goods remain in the warehouse of the vendor, or in the hands of one who holds as his agent, his lien upon them for the unpaid price remains. But, when once they have got into the posssession of an agent for the buyer, the vendor parts with his lien. The right to stop *in transitu* upon the bankruptcy of the buyer remains, even when the credit has not expired, until the goods have reached the hands of the vendee, or of one who is his agent, as a warehouseman, or a packer, or a shipping-agent, to give them a new destination. Until one of these events has happened, the vendor has a right to stop the goods *in transitu*. It must be observed that there is, besides the propositions I have stated, and which are quite familiar, one other proposition which follows as deducible from these, viz., that the arrival which is to divest the vendor's right of stoppage *in transitu* must be such as that the buyer has taken actual or constructive possession of the goods; and that cannot be so long as he repudiates them. This is the alphabet of the doctrine of stoppage *in transitu*." [1]

If after such refusal of the buyer to receive the goods, finding himself insolvent, they are attached by one of his creditors, the sheriff paying the freight, the seller may still assert his right of stoppage *in transitu*, though, upon taking the goods from the sheriff by replevin suit, he may be required to repay to the attaching creditor the amount advanced by him for payment of the freight.[2]

A purchaser of goods which had been shipped to him, and were stored in the freight-house of the railroad company, finding on the day of their arrival that he was insolvent, re-marked the goods, and ordered the agent of the railroad company to return them to the seller. While for that purpose they were being transferred from the freight-house to the cars, a sheriff took possession of the goods, under insolvency proceedings, as the property of the purchaser. The seller, upon hearing of the insolvency, wrote a letter for the return of the goods, which, however, was never received. It was held that there had been no effectual exercise of the right of stoppage *in transitu*.[3]

---

[1] Bolton *v.* Lancashire & Yorkshire Ry. Co. L. R. 1 C. P. 431, 439.
[2] Greve *v.* Dunham, 60 Iowa, 108.

[3] Millard *v.* Webster (Conn.), 8 Atl. Rep. 470, Granger, J., dissenting.

924. The refusal of the buyer after his insolvency to take the goods upon their arrival may determine the question whether there has been a delivery or not, for it may show the intention with which the buyer has directed that they should be landed or stored.[1]   Goods were consigned to a London merchant, and by the bill of lading were made deliverable to him in the river Thames.   On the arrival of the vessel in the river, the master of the ship pressed the consignee to have them landed immediately, and the latter accordingly sent his son to the master with directions to land them at a wharf where he was accustomed to have goods landed; but being then insolvent, he at the same time told his son not to meddle with the goods, that he did not intend to take them, and that the vendor ought to have them. The goods were accordingly landed at the wharf, and were then stopped *in transitu* by the vendor.   In an action for the goods by the consignee's assignee in bankruptcy, it was held that the declarations so made by the consignee to his son were admissible in evidence, although they were not communicated to the vendor or to the wharfinger; and that they showed that the consignee had not taken possession of the goods as owner, and therefore that the transitus was not determined.[2]   Baron Parke, delivering the judgment of the court, said: " If the order was given to land at the wharf, with intent to make it the place of deposit for the goods as the bankrupt's own property, at which place he meant to deal with them as his own, to sell to his customers, or to give them from thence a fresh destination, doubtless the transitus was at an end.   The wharf became the warehouse of the vendee, and the landing there was a taking possession. . . . On the other hand, if his intention in landing the goods had been to make the wharfinger an instrument of further conveyance to his own warehouse, then the transitus still continued; or, if the goods were placed there with the intention of preventing any liability on his part to the captain for demurrage, and that they might remain *in medio*, or that they might remain for the benefit of the owners, the transitus had not ended; they had not arrived at the end of their journey; they were not actually delivered to the

---

[1] James *v.* Griffin, 2 M. & W. 623; S. C. 1 Ib. 20, 29 ; Bartram *v.* Farebrother, 4 Bing. 579 ; Cox *v.* Burns, 1 Iowa, 64 ; Mason *v.* Redpath, 39 U. C. Q. B. 157. And see Heinekey *v.*

Earle, 8 E. & Bl. 410 ; Mills *v.* Ball, 2 B. & P. 457.

[2] James *v.* Griffin, *supra*, Lord Abinger, C. B., dissenting ; S. C. 1 M. & W. 20.

vendee, or one who was an agent of his for the purpose of keeping possession on his account.   The whole question then is, with
what intent was the order to land given ?   Of that there is on
the evidence no doubt, — the bankrupt did not mean to take
possession as owner."

925. In another similar case it appeared that goods were
sent by railway to the buyer, who gave notice to the seller before they arrived, that he would not receive them on account of
their alleged bad quality ; and after their arrival he gave the
railway company orders to take the goods back to the seller.
The latter refused to receive them, and ordered them back to
the buyer.   The goods, being thus rejected by both the buyer
and the seller, remained in the hands of the railway ; and while
they so remained the buyer became bankrupt, and the vendor
stopped the goods.   In an action against the railway company
by the assignees of the buyer, it was held that the transit was not
at an end, and the vendor could exercise his right of stoppage.[1]
Erle, J., said: "It was urged that, being repudiated by both
parties to the contract, the goods remained in the hands of the
railway company as warehousemen for the real owner, that is,
for the buyer.   There is no doubt but that the carrier may, and
often does, become a warehouseman for the consignee ; but that
must be by virtue of some contract or course of dealing between
them, that when arrived at their destination the character of
carrier shall cease, and that of warehouseman supervene."   And
Willes, J., said : " The right to stop *in transitu* upon the bankruptcy of the buyer remains, even when the credit has not expired, until the goods have reached the hands of the vendee or
of one who is his agent, as a warehouseman, or a packer, or a
shipping agent, to give them a new destination.   Until one of
these events has happened, the vendor has a right to stop the
goods *in transitu*.   It must be observed that there is, besides the
propositions I have stated, and which are quite familiar, one
other proposition which follows as deducible from these, namely,
that the arrival which is to divest the vendor's right of stoppage
in transitu must be such that the buyer has taken actual or constructive possession of the goods, and that cannot be as long as
he repudiates them."

[1] Bolton *v.* Lancashire & Yorkshire Ry. Co. L. R. 1 C. P. 431.

926. The right of stoppage in transitu remains so long as the carrier holds the goods as carrier, and not as the purchaser's agent by virtue of an agreement with him, though he has delivered a part. Of course the same principle will apply under like circumstances when the goods are in the hands of a warehouseman or wharfinger. A cargo of one hundred and fourteen tons of iron castings was consigned to the purchaser, he paying the freight, on board a ship chartered by the vendor. After thirty tons of the cargo had been delivered to the purchaser, the vendor gave notice to stop the delivery. At this time, only part of the freight had been paid. The purchaser having become insolvent and a receiver having been appointed, he paid the balance of the freight, and claimed the remainder of the iron. It was held, that, inasmuch as it could not be supposed that the master of the ship intended to abandon his lien for the unpaid freight, the delivery of the thirty tons did not operate as a constructive delivery of the whole cargo, and that, consequently, the transitus was not at an end as to the remainder of the cargo, and the vendor's notice to stop *in transitu* was given in time.[1] Lord Justice James, delivering judgment, said : " It seems to me quite clear there was nothing like a constructive delivery of the whole by the captain, or a constructive acceptance of the whole by the vendee. How it might have been if the whole freight had been paid, so that the captain had no lien that he could exercise on behalf of the owners of the ship, and the delivery had begun, what difference that would have made it is not necessary now to say. It appears to me quite clear that, as there was not an actual delivery of the whole, there could not be a constructive delivery of the whole, because it must be assumed that the captain would not have delivered the whole until he had received the whole of the freight ; and if the captain had not constructively delivered the whole, it would be impossible to say that the vendee had constructively accepted a delivery which was never made." Goods remain *in transitu* while the carrier holds them in actual possession, and has not wrongfully refused to deliver them.[2]

---

[1] *Ex parte* Cooper, 11 Ch. D. 68, 72.

[2] Crawshay *v.* Eades, 1 B. & C. 181; Holst *v.* Pownal, 1 Esp. 240; Tucker *v.* Humphrey, 4 Bing. 516; Lackington *v.* Atherton, 8 Scott N. S. 38.

vendee, or one who was an agent of his for the purpose of keeping possession on his account. The whole question then is, with what intent was the order to land given? Of that there is on the evidence no doubt, — the bankrupt did not mean to take possession as owner."

925. In another similar case it appeared that goods were sent by railway to the buyer, who gave notice to the seller before they arrived, that he would not receive them on account of their alleged bad quality; and after their arrival he gave the railway company orders to take the goods back to the seller. The latter refused to receive them, and ordered them back to the buyer. The goods, being thus rejected by both the buyer and the seller, remained in the hands of the railway; and while they so remained the buyer became bankrupt, and the vendor stopped the goods. In an action against the railway company by the assignees of the buyer, it was held that the transit was not at an end, and the vendor could exercise his right of stoppage.[1] Erle, J., said: "It was urged that, being repudiated by both parties to the contract, the goods remained in the hands of the railway company as warehousemen for the real owner, that is, for the buyer. There is no doubt but that the carrier may, and often does, become a warehouseman for the consignee; but that must be by virtue of some contract or course of dealing between them, that when arrived at their destination the character of carrier shall cease, and that of warehouseman supervene." And Willes, J., said: "The right to stop *in transitu* upon the bankruptcy of the buyer remains, even when the credit has not expired, until the goods have reached the hands of the vendee or of one who is his agent, as a warehouseman, or a packer, or a shipping agent, to give them a new destination. Until one of these events has happened, the vendor has a right to stop the goods *in transitu*. It must be observed that there is, besides the propositions I have stated, and which are quite familiar, one other proposition which follows as deducible from these, namely, that the arrival which is to divest the vendor's right of stoppage *in transitu* must be such that the buyer has taken actual or constructive possession of the goods, and that cannot be as long as he repudiates them."

[1] Bolton *v.* Lancashire & Yorkshire Ry. Co. L. R. 1 C. P. 431.

926. The right of stoppage in transitu remains so long
as the carrier holds the goods as carrier, and not as the purchaser's agent by virtue of an agreement with him, though he
has delivered a part. Of course the same principle will apply
under like circumstances when the goods are in the hands of
a warehouseman or wharfinger. A cargo of one hundred and
fourteen tons of iron castings was consigned to the purchaser,
he paying the freight, on board a ship chartered by the vendor.
After thirty tons of the cargo had been delivered to the purchaser, the vendor gave notice to stop the delivery. At this
time, only part of the freight had been paid. The purchaser having become insolvent and a receiver having been appointed, he
paid the balance of the freight, and claimed the remainder of the
iron. It was held, that, inasmuch as it could not be supposed
that the master of the ship intended to abandon his lien for the
unpaid freight, the delivery of the thirty tons did not operate
as a constructive delivery of the whole cargo, and that, consequently, the transitus was not at an end as to the remainder of
the cargo, and the vendor's notice to stop *in transitu* was given
in time.[1] Lord Justice James, delivering judgment, said : " It
seems to me quite clear there was nothing like a constructive
delivery of the whole by the captain, or a constructive acceptance of the whole by the vendee. How it might have been if
the whole freight had been paid, so that the captain had no lien
that he could exercise on behalf of the owners of the ship, and
the delivery had begun, what difference that would have made
it is not necessary now to say. It appears to me quite clear that,
as there was not an actual delivery of the whole, there could not
be a constructive delivery of the whole, because it must be assumed that the captain would not have delivered the whole until
he had received the whole of the freight ; and if the captain had
not constructively delivered the whole, it would be impossible to
say that the vendee had constructively accepted a delivery which
was never made." Goods remain *in transitu* while the carrier
holds them in actual possession, and has not wrongfully refused
to deliver them.[2]

---

[1] *Ex parte* Cooper, 11 Ch. D. 68,
72.
[2] Crawshay *v.* Eades, 1 B. & C.
181; Holst *v.* Pownal, 1 Esp. 240;
Tucker *v.* Humphrey, 4 Bing. 516;
Lackington *v.* Atherton, 8 Scott N.
S. 38.

927. The transitus is not at an end until the carrier parts with the possession of the goods.[1] He has the right to retain possession until the freight due him is tendered or paid. Of course he may assent to the consignee's having possession of the goods without paying the freight; but such assent will not be presumed. Iron was sold and shipped by water to the purchaser. The carrier, upon reaching the purchaser's wharf, landed a part of the iron, but, finding that the purchaser had stopped payment, reloaded it on board his barge, and took the entire shipment to his own premises. The freight had not been paid or tendered, and, there being nothing to show that the carrier intended to part with possession without the payment of his freight, it was held that he still had possession of the iron, and that the consignor had a right to stop it *in transitu*.[2] "When part of the iron was landed upon the wharf," said Bayley, J., "it might more properly be considered as in a course of delivery than as actually delivered. By placing it upon the wharf, the carrier did not mean to assent to the vendee's taking it away without paying the freight. Besides, a carrier has a lien on the entire cargo for his whole freight; and, until the amount is either tendered or paid, the special property which he has in his character of carrier does not pass out of him to the vendee, unless, indeed, he does some act to show that he assents to the vendee's taking possession of the property before the freight is paid. . . . In order to divest the consignor's right to stop *in transitu*, there ought to be such a delivery to the consignee as to divest the carrier's lien upon the whole cargo."

928. But the transitus is at an end when the consignee has claimed the goods, and the carrier has wrongfully refused to deliver them, and has thus rendered himself liable for them in trover.[3] In Bird *v.* Brown, it appeared that, upon the arrival of the goods by vessel at their port of destination, the consignee formally demanded them of the master, and tendered the freight, but he delivered them to one who claimed to act for

[1] McFetridge *v.* Piper, 40 Iowa, 627; Alsberg *v.* Latta, 30 Iowa, 442; Greve *v.* Dunham (Iowa, 1882), 15 Rep. 232; Blum *v.* Marks, 21 La. Ann. 268.

[2] Crawshay *v.* Eades, 1 B. & C. 181; *S. C.* 2 D. & R. 288.

[3] Bird *v.* Brown, 4 Exch. 786; Walley *v.* Montgomery, 3 East, 585; Davis *v.* McWhirter, 40 U. C. Q. B. 598; Reynolds *v.* B. & M. R. R. Co. 43 N. H. 580.

the vendor. The Court of Exchequer held that the master could not, by wrongfully detaining the goods, prolong the transitus, and so extend the period during which stoppage might be made. " The transitus," said Rolfe B.,[1] " was at an end when the goods had reached the port of destination, and when the consignees, having demanded the goods and tendered the amount of the freight, would have taken them into their possession but for a wrongful delivery of them to other parties."

929. Goods are still in transitu after they have arrived at the place of their destination, but are in the hands of a local carrier for local delivery.[2] " The real and indeed the only question in all these cases is, whether the transitus is over ; in other words, whether the goods have been delivered to the buyer : if they have, then the right to stop is gone, and the only remedy of the seller is by action at law, or by proof against the estate of the buyer."[3] The vendor's right is terminated only by the passage of the goods into the actual or constructive possession of the vendee.[4]

930. Goods are in transitu, and may be stopped by the vendor, although the ship has arrived at the port of destination, but has been ordered out for quarantine, and it does not matter that the assignee of the bankrupt purchaser has taken possession of the goods on board the ship while she was in port.[5] In the case cited it was argued that the consignee had a right to go out to sea to meet the ship ; but Lord Kenyon declared that this argument could not be supported, as it might go the length of saying that the consignee might meet the vessel coming out of the port from whence she had been consigned, and divest the consignor of the property and vest it in himself, — a position which could not be supported, as there would then be no possibility of any stoppage *in transitu* at all.[6] In the case before

---

[1] 4 Exch. 786, 797.

[2] White v. Mitchell, 38 Mich. 390; Jackson v. Nichol, 5 Bing. N. C. 508; Chicago, Burling. & Quincy R. R. Co. v. Painter, 15 Neb. 394; Mason v. Wilson, 43 Ark. 172; O'Neil v. Garrett, 6 Iowa, 480; Calahan v. Babcock, 21 Ohio St. 281; Reynolds v. B. & M. R. R. Co. 43 N. H. 580.

[3] Fraser v. Witt, L. R. 7 Eq. 64, 69, per Lord Romilly, M. R.

[4] McFetridge v. Piper, 40 Iowa, 627; Greve v. Dunham, 60 Iowa, 108; Halff v. Allyn, 60 Tex. 278; Chandler v. Fulton, 10 Tex. 2, 13.

[5] Holst v. Pownal, 1 Esp. 240.

[6] See, however, *dictum* of Lord A - vanley, C. J., in Mills v. Ball, 2 B. & P. 457, 461.

the court it was held that the vendor stopped the goods in time because the voyage was not completed until the vessel had performed quarantine.

931. Goods are in transitu after they have been placed by the carrier in the custom-house, or government storehouse, to await the payment of duties.[1] In such case it does not matter that the assignee of the purchaser has demanded possession of the goods before the vendor has interposed to exercise his right of stoppage *in transitu*,[2] if the assignee has only made demand and has not taken actual possession ; nor does it matter that the vendee has paid the freight and given his note for the price of the goods, which, in consequence of the loss of the invoice, are stored in the custom-house, and there remain until the dishonor of the note, for until the duties are paid the goods remain *in custodia legis*.[3] The goods are still *in transitu* after the vessel has arrived at the place of destination, but has been ordered out and placed in quarantine.

932. Even the entry of the goods by the consignee at the custom-house without the payment of duties does not terminate the right. In such case the goods are in the legal possession of the government or its officers, and have not come to the possession of the vendee so as to deprive the vendor of his right.[4]

---

[1] Northey *v.* Field, 2 Esp. 613; Nix *v.* Oliver, cited in Abbott on Shipping, 393; Burnham *v.* Winsor, 5 Law Rep. 507; Parker *v.* Byrnes, 1 Lowell, 539; Burr *v.* Wilson, 13 U. C. Q. B. 478 ; Lewis *v.* Mason, 36 Ib. 590; Ascher *v.* Grand Trunk Ry. Co. Ib. 609 ; Mottram *v.* Heyer, 5 Denio (N. Y.), 629, per Walworth, C. ; Holbrook *v.* Vose, 6 Bosw. (N. Y.) 76, 104, per Woodruff, J. ; *In re* Bearns, 18 N. Bank. Reg. 500, per Choate, J.; Hoover *v.* Tibbits, 13 Wis. 79; Newhall *v.* Vargas, 13 Me. 93; *S. C.* 15 Me. 314; Donath *v.* Broomhead, 7 Pa. St. 301.

[2] Northey *v.* Field, *supra;* Holst *v.* Pownal, 1 Esp. 240.

[3] Donath *v.* Broomhead, *supra.*

[4] Harris *v.* Pratt, 17 N. Y. 249, 262; Mottram *v.* Heyer, *supra;* Holbrook *v.* Vose, *supra;* Burnham *v.* Winsor, *supra;* Nix *v.* Oliver, *supra.*

Otherwise after the consignee has made a warehouse entry at the custom-house, and taken a warehouse receipt and transferred this in pledge. Cartwright *v.* Wilmerding, 24 N. Y. 521; Harris *v.* Pratt, *supra;* Fraschieris *v.* Henriques, 6 Abb. (N. Y.) Pr. N. S. 251.

In the latter case, Judge Barrett, after reviewing the cases, deduced from them the following rules : " 1. Where the goods are removed under general orders, in default of an entry, the right of stoppage *in transitu* is not terminated.

And so, if imported goods are entered at a custom-house by the vendee at the port of entry for transportation to an interior city under bond to be delivered to the collector of customs at the latter place, the legal custody of the goods during the transit is in the government, but the actual possession is in the carriers, and neither the vendee nor his agent has such possession as will defeat the vendor's right of stoppage *in transitu.* "We apprehend," said Woodruff, J.,[1] "that the true principle upon which it must be held that the entry of the goods and their being held by the government to secure the payment of duties, does not defeat the vendor's right to stop, is, that so long as the goods are in the custody of the government, there is not, and cannot be, any reduction of the goods by the vendee to his own possession. They are kept, for the time being, from reaching such possession. By this, of course, we do not mean that enough was not done by the vendors to perfect the contract of sale, nor that the possession of the carriers was not for many purposes to be deemed the possession of the actual owners (the vendees), but the possession of the carriers was a possession for the purpose of transportation to the vendees, and was subject to the right of the vendors to stop the goods, if those events which create that right should happen while the goods were in course of such transportation. The goods had not come to the actual possession of any agent of the vendees, for the purpose of disposal. Nor did the carriers hold them subject to the directions of the vendees for disposal, nor as a deposit in a warehouse, subject to the order of the vendees for disposal. The only substantial change in the conditions of the goods was, that they were placed in a course of transmission to the vendees, and were in the actual possession of a middleman for that purpose; and it may be stated, as a general proposition, that a delivery of goods to a carrier or other agent of the buyer, for the purpose of being carried forward to the buyer, does not terminate the transit."

933. For stronger reasons the right continues when they have been stored in a government warehouse in the name of

---

"2. Where a formal entry is made, but is not followed up by proper bonding, the right continues.

"3. But where there is a perfect entry, and the goods are thereupon regularly bonded and warehoused, the right ceases."

[1] Holbrook *v.* Vose, 6 Bosw. (N. Y.) 76.

the seller, so that it is impossible for the consignee to get them without the written consent of the former.[1]

The mere fact that goods imported from abroad upon the order of a buyer have come into the hands of the officers of the customs, and have been by them put into a warehouse, does not determine the transit though the buyer has paid freight and given his note for the price of the goods.[2]

It has been held, however, that a vendee has constructive possession of goods entered by him at a custom-house at the place of their destination to await the payment of duties.[3] Whatever possession the government may have, is said to be under the owner, and to be at most but a qualified or special possession, for the purpose of securing a lien by way of pledge. The goods are at all times subject to the order of the owner upon payment of duties and expenses, and upon the payment of these he is entitled to actual possession. He can sell them subject to the duties and expenses. Although he has not paid the duties he has constructive possession.

934. After the consignee has paid the duties or given a bond for their payment, the customs officer cannot be considered a middleman, so that the consignor could, by notice to him, stop the goods *in transitu*.[4] " From the moment the col-

[1] *In re* Bearns, 18 N. Bank. Reg. 500, 502, Judge Choate, delivering the judgment, said: "The right of stoppage *in transitu* depends upon the fact that the goods have not come to the actual or constructive possession of the vendee, and it is not necessary that the obstacle which has prevented this should be one that was purposely interposed by the vendor for this purpose, nor that it was one created by him directly or indirectly. If the existing regulation of the Treasury Department has prevented that possession being consummated, the nature of that regulation is of no more consequence on this question than the nature of any other fact or accident that may have led to the same result."

[2] Donath v. Broomhead, 7 Pa. St. 301; Parker v. Byrnes, 1 Lowell, 539,

per Lowell, J.; Mottram v. Heyer, 1 Den. (N. Y.) 483; S. C. 5 Ibid. 629; Barrett v. Goddard, 3 Mason, 107, doubted.

[3] Guilford v. Smith, 30 Vt. 49, reviewing Mottram v. Heyer, *supra*.

In Guilford v. Smith, *supra*, Bennet, J., remarks that, in Northey v. Field, 2 Esp. 613, the possession of the carrier was still continued; and that neither in this case nor in Donath v. Broomhead, *supra*, had the consignees themselves exercised any ownership over the property by entering the goods at the custom-house. But in Mottram v. Heyer, *supra*, Walworth, C., remarks that the entry of the goods by the vendee without payment of the duties is not a termination of the transitus.

[4] Wiley v. Smith, 1 Ont. App. 179, 191, overruling Graham v. Smith, 27

lector of customs receives the bond of the vendee, there is as complete a delivery as if the goods had been delivered into his own hands. The collector has a lien on the goods, and would be justified in detaining them until it is satisfied ; but as between vendor and vendee the goods are at home, and constructively in the possession of the purchaser ; the customs authorities (subject to the payment of the duties) having by the acceptance of the bond undertaken to hold them for the use of the purchaser, and subject to such sales or dispositions as he might choose to make." [1]

935. Goods placed by the carrier in a warehouse at the place of their destination, to await the consignee's sending for them and paying the freight, are still *in transitu* while in the warehouse, and may be stopped by the vendor.[2] And so goods placed by the carrier in the hands of any other depositary, if not designated by the purchaser as his agent, nor his agent in fact to receive and hold the goods for him, are still *in transitu.*[3] And even if the depositary be designated by the vendee, he may still be the agent of the carrier to hold the goods for the purpose of collecting freight and charges, and in that case the goods cannot be considered as in the hands of the vendee so as to defeat the right of the vendor to stop them. If in any case there is evidence to show that the warehouseman received the goods as agent of the carrier, and held them as such at the time the vendor asserted his right to stop them, it is erroneous to instruct the jury that, if the vendee directed that the goods should be sent to that warehouseman, and they were so sent in pursuance of that direction, they had come into the possession of the vendee so as to deprive the vendor of the right of stoppage. The jury should be left free to determine, upon all the evidence, whether the warehouseman received the goods as the agent of the carrier, or as the agent of the vendee.[4]

936. A wharfinger to whom a carrier has delivered goods

U. C. C. P. 1 ; and Howell *v.* Alport, 12 U. C. C. P. 375.

Wiley *v.* Smith, 1 Ont. App. 179, 191, is followed in Wilds *v.* Smith, 2 Ont. App. 8 ; *S. C.* 41 Q. B. 136, 142.

[1] Wiley *v.* Smith, *supra,* per Burton, J.

[2] Edwards *v.* Brewer, 2 M. & W.

375 ; Covell *v.* Hitchcock, 23 Wend. (N. Y.) 611 ; Calahan *v.* Babcock, 21 Ohio St. 281 ; Clapp *v.* Peck, 55 Iowa, 270 ; Greve *v.* Dunham (Iowa, 1882), 15 Rep. 232.

[3] Hoover *v.* Tibbits, 13 Wis. 79.

[4] Hoover *v.* Tibbits, *supra.*

to be forwarded to the consignee at another place is a middleman, in whose hands the goods may be stopped by the vendor.[1] A trader living in the country, about twenty-five miles from Exeter, ordered goods from London to be sent by ship *via* Exeter. On their arrival at Exeter a wharfinger received them on the trader's account, and paid the freight and charges; and, while they remained in the wharfinger's possession, the trader wrote to the vendor informing him of his insolvency, and that he should not take the goods. The vendor thereupon demanded the goods of the wharfinger; and it was held that he had a right to stop them in the wharfinger's hands.[2] Lord Alvanley, C. J., remarked that the only question was, whether the goods are to be considered as having been in the hands of a middleman, or as having been taken in the possession of the person for whom they were ultimately intended; and he was of opinion that the wharfinger, not having been particularly employed by the vendee, was to be considered as a middleman. The other judges concurred; Brooke, J., saying that the consignee did nothing to take possession of the goods while they remained with the wharfinger before the vendor made his claim; and Chambre saying, upon the question whether the goods were *in transitu*, that they were directed to be sent to the town where the purchaser lived, and, having been carried as far as they could go by water, they were delivered to a wharfinger to be forwarded to the purchaser. While they were with the wharfinger the demand was made, no act having been done to shorten the journey. We cannot, therefore, say the goods were not *in transitu*.

937. Goods carried by railroad are in transitu while in a car at their place of destination awaiting delivery to the consignee. Thus, a car containing the goods consigned was set out upon a side-track, where, according to custom, the goods were to be taken from the car immediately by the consignee, or, if not so taken, were liable to be charged a certain sum daily for demurrage. There was no agreement or understanding between the carrier and the consignee that the goods should be held by the former as warehouseman, or as agent of the consignee. A truckman, who had a standing order from the consignee to take

---

[1] Mills v. Ball, 2 B. & P. 457; *Ex parte* Barrow, 6 Ch. D. 783; Holst v. Pownal, 1 Esp. 240; Smith v. Goss, 1 Camp. 282; Hunt v. Ward, cited 3 T. R. 467.

[2] Mills v. Ball, *supra*.

any goods he might find at the railroad station and fetch them to the consignee's store, was notified of the arrival of the goods by an agent of the carrier; but he did not remove them, the consignee having absconded. The goods, while so situated, were attached by a creditor of the consignee; but it was held that the consignor's right of stoppage was not then terminated, and that he might maintain trover against the attaching officer for the goods.[1]

Goods carried by railroad were, upon arrival at their destination, set aside by the railroad company in its depot, under an agreement made by it with the consignee that the goods should be sold, and the proceeds used to pay past-due freights, the balance, if any, to go to the consignee. The consignee did not receive the goods and turn them over to the railroad company, nor did he assign to it the bill of lading, nor pay the freight. While the goods were so situated, the consignor sought to stop them *in transitu*. It was held that no delivery had taken place so as to prevent a stoppage *in transitu*.[2]

938. After the vendee has once taken possession of the goods and exercised dominion over them, the transit is at an end, though for a special purpose they come again into the hands of the vendor. Thus, goods bought for exportation were sent to the purchaser's agent to be forwarded, and were by him shipped on board a vessel, but were afterwards relanded and sent back to the vendor to be repacked. While the goods were in the vendor's possession for this purpose the purchaser became bankrupt. It was held that the transit had been determined, and that the vendor acquired no new right by the redelivery to him.[3] In delivering judgment, Wilde, C. J., said: "The goods being sold on credit, and the complete property and possession having vested in the vendee, they become his absolutely, without any lien or right of the vendor's attaching to them any more than on any other property of the vendee; and their delivery to the vendor to be repacked could not have the effect of creating a lien for the price without an agreement to that effect."

A delivery of the goods by the carrier to a third person upon the order of the vendee is equivalent to a delivery to him, and terminates the right of the vendor to stop them.[4]

---

[1] Inslee *v.* Lane, 57 N. H. 454.

[2] Macon & Western R. R. *v.* Meador, 65 Ga. 705.

[3] Valpy *v.* Gibson, 4 C. B. 837, 865.

[4] Stevens *v.* Wheeler, 27 Barb. (N. Y.) 658.

939. What constitutes such an actual or constructive possession by the vendee as will put an end to the transitus, and with it to the vendor's right to stop the goods, has frequently been a matter of discussion in the courts. Lord Kenyon, in an early case, said :[1] " There have, indeed, been cases where nice distinctions have been taken on the fact whether the goods had or had not got into the possession of the vendee; but they all profess to go on the ground of the goods being *in transitu* when they were stopped. As to the necessity of the goods coming to the ' corporal touch' of the bankrupt, that is merely a figurative expression, and has never been literally adhered to. For there may be an actual delivery of the goods without the bankrupt's seeing them; as a delivery of the key of the vendor's warehouse to the purchaser." In the case under consideration, goods were sent by wagon from Sheffield to the buyer in London. Part of the goods were brought to an inn in London, and were there attached by a creditor of the buyer, who had become a bankrupt. The assignee in bankruptcy went to the inn where the goods remained under attachment, and put his mark upon them, but did not take them away. It was held that when they were so marked they were delivered to the buyer so far as the circumstances of the case would permit, and that the vendor could not afterwards stop them.

This decision is, however, called in question by Baron Parke,[2] who said it appeared very doubtful whether an act of marking, without any removal from the possession of the carrier, would amount to a constructive possession. In the case before the court, it appeared that a cargo of timber having arrived at its port of destination, the agent of the assignees of the purchaser, who had become bankrupt, went on board the vessel and told the captain he had come to take possession of the cargo. He

[1] Ellis v. Hunt, 3 T. R. 464, 467. In Hunter v. Beale, cited in the above case at p. 466, Lord Mansfield is said to have used the expression, "they must have come to the *corporal touch* of the vendee, otherwise they may be stopped *in transitu*."

Lord Ellenborough, in Dixon v. Baldwen, 5 East, 184, also disapproved of the ruling attributed to Lord Mansfield.

And see Wright v. Lawes, 4 Esp.

82, 85, where Lord Kenyon said : " I once said that to confer a property on the consignee, a corporal touch was necessary. I wish the expression had never been used, as it says too much ; . . . but all that is necessary is, that the consignee exercise some act of ownership on the property consigned to him."

[2] Whitehead v. Anderson, 9 M. & W. 518, 535.

went into the cabin, into which the ends of timber projected, and saw and touched the timber. He then went ashore, and the vendor shortly afterwards served a notice to stop the cargo *in transitu.* It was held that no actual possession was taken by the assignees, and that, as the master did not undertake to hold possession for them, they had not taken constructive possession. Although the master told the agent he would deliver the cargo when he was satisfied about the freight, this was no more than a promise to fulfil the original contract and deliver in due course to the consignee. His relation to the consignee was not changed.

940. The vendee may obtain constructive possession of the goods while they still remain in the hands of the carrier.[1] But to effect such a possession the carrier must, by some agreement with the vendee, express or implied, change his relation from that of carrier to that of agent for the vendee ; he must expressly or impliedly enter into a new agreement with the vendee, distinct from the original contract for carriage, to hold the goods in a new character as his agent, and subject to his order.[2] " A case of constructive possession," said Baron Parke,[3] " is where the carrier enters expressly, or by implication, into a new agreement, distinct from the original contract for carriage, to hold the goods for the consignee as his agent, not for the purpose of expediting them to the place of original destination, pursuant to that contract, but in a new character, for the purpose of custody on his account, and subject to some new or further order to be given to him." The carrier cannot become the buyer's agent without the buyer's consent. His intention to take possession, and to make the carrier his agent to hold the goods, is a material fact.[4]

There is an exception to the rule that the transitus continues until there is an actual delivery to the consignee, in case the carrier by agreement with him becomes his agent to keep the goods

---

[1] *Ex parte* Cooper, 11 Ch. D. 68; Reynolds *v.* B. & M. R. R. Co. 43 N. H. 580.

[2] James *v.* Griffin, 2 M. & W. 623; Jackson *v.* Nichol, 5 Bing. N. C. 508; Bolton *v.* Lancashire & Yorkshire Ry. Co. L. R. 1 C. P. 431; Donath *v.* Broomhead, 7 Pa. St. 301; McFetridge *v.* Piper, 40 Iowa, 627; Alsberg *v.* Latta, 30 Iowa, 442; O'Neil *v.* Garrett, 6 Iowa, 480; *In re* Foot, 11 Blatchf. 530.

[3] Whitehead *v.* Anderson, 9 M. & W. 518, 535; Langstaff *v.* Stix (Miss.), 1 So. Rep. 97.

[4] James *v.* Griffin, *supra;* Whitehead *v.* Anderson, 9 M. & W. 518, 529, per Parke, B.

on storage for him;[1] and such an agreement may be inferred where the consignee has been in the habit of using the warehouse of the carrier or wharfinger as his own.[2]

After a consignee has paid the freight on goods carried by railroad, has receipted for them, and left them at the depot to be called for, the right of stoppage *in transitu* is at an end, and the agent of the railroad company has no right to detain them upon afterwards discovering, upon opening his mail, that he had instructions not to deliver them. The railroad company, in holding the goods till they should be sent for, became the agent of the purchaser.[3]

941. The transitus is at an end when the goods have arrived at their destination and the consignee has made the carrier his own agent to hold them upon storage, or to forward them to a new place of destination.[4] Thus, where a purchaser of several hogsheads of sugar, upon notice from the carrier of their arrival, took samples from them, and directed the carrier to let them remain in his warehouse until he should receive further instructions, it was held that the transitus was at an end. The purchaser made the carrier his agent, and used his warehouse as his own. The carrier ceased to be a carrier, and, at least by implication, entered into a new relation distinct from the contract for the carriage.[5] Baron Parke, referring to this, said there were circumstances which indicated an agreement on the part of the carrier to hold the goods for the consignee as his agent. He remarked, however:[6] " It appears to us to be very doubtful whether an act of marking or taking samples, or the like, without any removal from the possession of the carrier, though done with the intention to take possession, would amount to a constructive possession, unless accompanied with such cir-

[1] Richardson *v.* Goss, 3 B. & P. 119, 127; Scott *v.* Pettit, 3 B. & P. 469; Rowe *v.* Pickford, 1 Moore, 526; Molley *v.* Hay, 3 M. & R. 396; Allan *v.* Gripper, 2 C. & J. 218; Reynolds *v.* B. & M. R. R. Co. 43 N. H. 580.

[2] Tucker *v.* Humphrey, 4 Bing. 516, 521; Foster *v.* Frampton, 6 B. & C. 107, 109.

[3] Langstaff *v.* Stix (Miss.), 1 So. Rep. 97.

[4] Foster *v.* Frampton, *supra;* Richardson *v.* Goss, *supra;* Scott *v.* Pettit, *supra;* Whitehead *v.* Anderson, 9 M. & W. 518, 534; Tucker *v.* Humphrey, *supra;* Rowe *v.* Pickford, 1 Moore, 526.

[5] Foster *v.* Frampton, *supra.* It appeared, also, that the purchaser was in the habit of leaving goods in the warehouse of the carrier.

[6] Whitehead *v.* Anderson, *supra.*

cumstances as to denote that the carrier was intended to keep, and assented to keep, the goods in the nature of an agent for custody."

942. The carrier may by agreement become the buyer's agent to keep the goods, although at the same time he claims a lien upon them for freight and charges. Thus, where goods were conveyed by a carrier by water, and deposited in the carrier's warehouse for the convenience of the buyer, to be delivered out as he should want them, it was held that the transitus was at an end, and the vendor's right to stop the goods gone, although it appeared that the carrier claimed a lien on them.[1] Under such circumstances it is immaterial whether the carrier has a lien or not. "The payment or the non-payment of the charges and duties may have some bearing upon the character of the possession which a third person may have, but when it is found that such third person has the custody of the goods to keep for the vendee, and await a further order from him, the non-payment of freight or duties becomes of no importance. The vendee has then a constructive possession, subject to all liens."[2] In other words, although the fact that the carrier claims a lien upon the goods for unpaid freight raises a presumption that he continues to hold the goods as carrier, yet this presumption may be rebutted; but, to overcome this presumption, proof should be adduced of an arrangement, express or implied, between the buyer and the carrier, whereby the latter becomes the buyer's agent to keep the goods for him.

In a case where the purchaser had absconded before the arrival of the goods at their destination, and the carrier stored them until they were stopped by the vendor, it was held that the transit was not ended, and that the carrier did not hold the goods as agent of the purchaser, because, from the circumstances of the case, he could never have consented to such an arrangement.[3]

943. On the other hand the carrier cannot, without his own consent, be made the buyer's agent to hold the goods

---

[1] Allan *v.* Gripper, 2 Cr. & J. 218; *S. C.* 2 Tyrw. 217; and see Foster *v.* Frampton, 6 B. & C. 107; Oppenheim *v.* Russell, 3 B. & P. 42.

[2] Guilford *v.* Smith, 30 Vt. 49, 72, per Bennett, J.

[3] *Ex parte* Barrow, 6 Ch. D. 783. And see, also, a similar case, Crawshay *v.* Eades, 1 B. & C. 181.

after their arrival. Thus, upon the arrival of a cargo of timber at the port of destination, the assignee of the vendee, who had become bankrupt, went on board the vessel and told the captain he had come to take possession of the cargo. The captain told him he would deliver it when he was satisfied about his freight. Shortly afterwards the vendor stopped the goods *in transitu.* It was held that, as there was no contract by the master to hold the goods as the agent of the purchaser's assignees, the latter had not obtained constructive possession of them, and the transitus was not at an end when the vendor exercised his right of stoppage.[1]

944. When goods are placed in the warehouse of a third person which the purchaser uses as his own, the transit is ordinarily at an end. This is the case although the warehouseman does not charge any rent, if he has previously been in the habit of receiving goods for the purchaser and holding them as his agent until he should take them away, or give further orders for their disposition.[2] The fact that the goods have reached their destination, and have been placed in a warehouse with which the carriers have no connection, but is substantially the purchaser's warehouse, is conclusive that a delivery has been made to him. But, while the fact that the warehouse does not belong to the carrier makes it more certain that the carrier does not any longer hold them as carrier, yet, if it appear by an agreement, express or implied, that the consignee has made the carrier's warehouse his own, the transit is equally at an end.[3]

If the goods by the direction of the purchaser are forwarded to a particular warehouseman, who acts as the agent of the purchaser in receiving them, the transitus is at an end.[4]

If goods are sold, and by agreement with the vendor are stored in his warehouse, rent free, the warehouse of the vendor becomes for the occasion the purchaser's warehouse, and, the delivery being complete, the transit is ended, and the vendor has no right of lien or stoppage.[5]

---

[1] Whitehead *v.* Anderson, 9 M. & W. 518.

[2] Dodson *v.* Wentworth, 4 M. & G. 1080; Richardson *v.* Goss, 3 B. & P. 119; Scott *v.* Pettit, Ib. 469; Leeds *v.* Wright, Ib. 320; Wiley *v.* Smith, 1 Ont. App. 179, 195, per Moss, J.;

Hoover *v.* Tibbits, 13 Wis. 79; Frazer *v.* Hilliard, 2 Strobh. (S. C.) 309.

[3] Smith *v.* Hudson, 6 B. & S. 431.

[4] Hoover *v.* Tibbits, *supra*, per Cole, J.

[5] Barrett *v.* Goddard, 3 Mason, 107;

945. Goods landed at a wharf belonging to a third person, at which the vendee usually receives goods without charge for wharfage, the carrier having no lien on them for freight or charges, are not subject to stoppage *in transitu*. In such case the possession of the carrier has ceased; the wharfinger has nothing to do with the goods, and, unless they are to be considered as being in the possession of the vendor, no person has any possession of them.[1]

VI. *How the Right is Waived or Defeated.*

946. The assignment of the bill of lading or other document of title by the vendee to a third person for value, defeats or impairs the vendor's right of stoppage *in transitu*.[2] But if the assignee of the bill of lading takes it with notice of the vendee's insolvency, the vendor has the same right of stoppage

Frazer *v.* Hilliard, 2 Strobh. (S. C.) 309.

[1] Sawyer *v.* Joslin, 20 Vt. 172, 180. Hall, J., said: "When the goods were landed on the wharf, the result of the original impulse, impressed upon them by the vendor in transmitting them to the vendee, was accomplished. They would go no farther under that impulse. They were not in the hands of a middleman, to be forwarded by other carriers. The wharfinger had no charge of them, and could not therefore be a middleman; and there was no other person standing in that character. The wharf, in the language of the books, became the warehouse of the vendee for the reception of the goods, and must consequently be considered the place contemplated by the consignor as that of their ultimate destination. The vendee could not have remained in his store with his arms folded, expecting the goods to be driven up to his door. He must have looked for them at the wharf, which, for the purposes of their reception, he had made his own; and when they arrived there, their transitus, so far as regarded the right of the vendor to stop them, must, I think, be considered as ended."

[2] Lickbarrow *v.* Mason, 2 T. R. 63; *S. C.* 1 H. Bl. 357, 5 T. R. 683, 1 Smith's Lead. Cas. 8th ed. 753, Gurney *v.* Behrend, 3 E. & B. 622, 637; Castanola *v.* Missouri Pac. Ry. Co. 24 Fed. Rep. 267. The Schooner Mary Ann Guest, 1 Olc. Adm. 498; affirmed, 1 Blatchf. 358; Lee *v.* Kimball, 45 Me. 172; Walter *v.* Ross, 2 Wash. 283; Ryberg *v.* Snell, 2 Wash. 294; Dows *v.* Greene, 24 N. Y. 638; *S. C.* 32 Barb. 490; Dows *v.* Perrin, 16 N. Y. 325; Rawls *v.* Deshler, 4 Abb. (N. Y.) App. Dec. 12, affirming *S. C.* 28 How. Pr. 66; Blossom *v.* Champion, 28 Barb. (N. Y.) 217; Jordan *v.* James, 5 Ohio, 89; Curry *v.* Roulstone, 2 Overt. (Tenn.) 110; Conard *v.* Atlantic Ins. Co. 1 Pet. 386; Audenreid *v.* Randall, 3 Cliff. 99; Becker *v.* Hallgarten, 86 N. Y. 167; Halliday *v.* Hamilton, 11 Wall. 560; First Nat. Bank *v.* Pettit, 9 Heisk. (Tenn.) 447.

In Georgia it is provided that a *bonâ fide* assignee of the bill of lading of goods for a valuable consideration, and without notice that the same were unpaid for, and the purchaser insolvent, will be protected in his title against the seller's right of stoppage *in transitu*. Ga. Code 1882, § 2650.

in transitu against the assignee that he had against the vendee himself.[1] Such knowledge on the part of the vendee tends to show that he did not purchase in good faith. Mere knowledge by the indorsee that the goods have not been paid for does not defeat his rights, for one may have a perfect right to buy goods of one who has not paid for them. He is only defeated by knowledge of circumstances such as render the bill of lading not fairly and honestly assignable.[2]

A transfer of the " duplicate " bill of lading, the original not being accounted for, does not carry with it necessarily the title to the goods ; and if the purchaser had notice which should have put him upon inquiry for the original, the transfer does not defeat the right of the seller to stop the goods *in transitu*.[3] But mere notice to the indorsee that the consignee has not paid for the goods does not prevent his holding them under the bill of lading as against the consignor, unless the indorsee also knows that by the terms of the sale the vendor is entitled to receive payment from the consignee before he disposes of the goods or assigns the bill of lading.[4] If, for instance, the goods have been sold on credit, and the consignee has given his note or acceptance for the price, and this is not due at the time he assigns the bill of lading for value, his knowledge of this fact does not make it unfair for him to accept an assignment of the bill of lading. In such a case, Lord Ellenborough, C. J., said :[5] " If a bill of lading should be held by us not assignable under these circumstances, the consequence would be that no bill of lading could be deemed safely assignable before the goods arrived, unless the assignee of the bill of lading was perfectly assured that the goods were paid for in money, or paid for in account between the parties, which is the same thing ; a position which would

---

[1] Vertue *v.* Jewell, 4 Camp. 31; Loeb *v.* Peters, 63 Ala. 243.

[2] Cuming *v.* Brown, 9 East, 506; Salomons *v.* Nissen, 2 T. R. 674, 681.

[3] Castanola *v.* Missouri Pac. Ry. Co. 24 Fed. Rep. 267.

[4] Cuming *v.* Brown, *supra.* This qualification of the rule has been criticised on the ground that " where there has been no delivery of the goods, and the transferee acts upon the faith of the bill of lading, he necessarily knows that the goods are in transit,

and that if not paid for they are subject to the vendor's right to stop them if the vendee becomes insolvent. It would not therefore be inequitable to hold that, with such knowledge, and knowledge also that the goods have not been paid for, he makes his advances subject to the vendor's right, and does so voluntarily with knowledge of all the facts." Holbrook *v.* Vose, 6 Bosw. (N. Y.) 76, 109, per Woodruff, J.

[5] Cuming *v.* Brown, *supra.*

tend to overturn the general practice and course of dealing of the commercial world on this subject, and which is warranted, as we conceive, by no decided case on the subject."

947. It does not matter that the instrument is not strictly a bill of lading, if it be substantially such.[1] But if the instrument signed by the carrier be a mere receipt acknowledging possession of the goods, but not making them deliverable to any one, it being made in this form because the goods were being transported in bond from the seaboard to the collector of customs at an interior city, the transfer of such receipt by the consignee does not have the effect to defeat the vendor's right of stoppage during such transit.[2]

Advances made on a promise to procure and deliver bills of lading are not made on the faith of such bills, and the lender is not protected as against the vendor.[3]

948. Assignee for creditors not a purchaser for value. — If the bill of lading be assigned in trust for the creditors of the insolvent vendee, such assignee is not a purchaser for value, and consequently takes subject to the exercise of any right of stoppage in transitu which might exist against the vendee himself.[4]

949. A pre-existing debt is a valuable consideration for a transfer of a bill of lading, and will protect the transferee from a subsequent stoppage in transitu.[5] There is no distinction in principle between cases relating to the consideration for a transfer of a bill of lading and cases relating to the consideration for a transfer of negotiable paper.

But by some courts it is held that a transfer in security or in payment of an existing indebtedness, without anything advanced, given up, or lost, on the part of the transferee, does not

---

[1] Rawls v. Deshler, 4 Abb. (N. Y.) App. Dec. 12, affirming S. C. 28 How. Pr. 66.

[2] Holbrook v. Vose, 6 Bosw. (N. Y.) 76, 109.

[3] Holbrook v. Vose, 6 Bosw. (N. Y.) 76, 104, 111; Barnard v. Campbell, 65 Barb. (N. Y.) 286, 292.

[4] Harris v. Pratt, 17 N. Y. 249;

Stanton v. Eager, 16 Pick. (Mass.) 467, 476.

[5] Leask v. Scott, 2 Q. B. D. 376 (dissenting from Rodger v. Comptoir d'Escompte de Paris, L. R. 2 P. C. 393); Clementson v. Grand Trunk Ry. Co. 42 U. C. Q. B. 263; Lee v. Kimball, 45 Me. 172.

constitute such an assignment as will preclude the vendor from exercising the right of stoppage *in transitu*.[1]

950. Whether a transfer of the bill of lading by the vendee, after a stoppage in transitu, has the same effect as such a transfer made before such stoppage, is a question which was for the first time decided in a recent case by the Supreme Court of California. In that case the bill of lading which the vendor sent to the buyer was indorsed by the latter for advances made upon it in good faith, after the seller had given notice to the carrier to stop the goods *in transitu;* and it was held that the indorser of the bill of lading was entitled to the goods as against the seller. Mr. Justice Crockett, delivering the judgment of the court, stated very clearly the grounds of the decision, saying:[2] "The vendor has voluntarily placed in the hands of the vendee a muniment of title, clothing him with the apparent ownership of the goods; and a person dealing with him in the usual course of business, who takes an assignment for a valuable consideration, without notice of such circumstances as render the bill of lading not fairly and honestly assignable, has a superior equity to that of the vendor asserting a recent lien, known perhaps only to himself and the vendee.[3] These being the conditions which determine and control the relative rights of the vendor and assignee, where the assignment is made before the notice of stoppage is given, precisely the same principles, in my opinion, are applicable when the assignment is made after the carrier is notified by the vendor. Notwithstanding the notice to the carrier, the vendor's lien continues to be only a secret trust as to a person who, in the language of Mr. Benjamin in his work on Sales, takes an assignment of a bill of lading 'without notice of such circumstances as render the bill of lading not fairly and honestly assignable.' The law provides no method by which third persons are to be affected with constructive notice of acts transpiring between the vendor and carrier; and, in dealing with the vendee, whom the vendor has

---

[1] Lesassier *v.* The Southwestern, 2 Woods, 35; Loeb *v.* Peters, 63 Ala. 243.

[2] Newhall *v.* Cent. Pac. R. R. Co. 51 Cal. 345, 350.

This would seem to hold good only in states where bills of lading are made negotiable, for, ordinarily, an indorser can give no better title than he himself has.

[3] Brewster *v.* Sime, 42 Cal. 139.

invested with the legal title and apparent ownership of the goods, a stranger, advancing his money on the faith of this apparently good title, is not bound at his peril to ascertain whether possibly the vendor may not have notified a carrier — it may be on some remote portion of the route — that the goods are stopped *in transitu*. If a person taking an assignment of a bill of lading is to encounter these risks, and can take the assignment with safety only after he has inquired of the vendor, and of every carrier through whose hands the goods are to come, whether a notice of stoppage in transition has been given, it is quite certain that prudent persons will cease to advance money on such securities, and a very important class of commercial transactions will be practically abrogated."

951. **Pledge by a factor or agent.** — By the common law, a consignee who was a mere factor or agent of the consignor could only defeat the latter's rights by a sale, and not by a pledge, of the bill of lading.[1]   But now, under the factors' acts, a factor or agent may make a valid pledge of a bill of lading or other document of title, which operates as an assignment of the contract, and defeats the consignor's rights.[2]

952. **An apparent sale of the bill of lading, fraudulently made,** without consideration, for the purpose of defeating the right of stoppage, will not have that effect.[3]   The fraudulent assignee, if he effectually aids the original vendee in obtaining possession of the goods, may make himself personally liable for the loss sustained by the vendor.[4]

And so, if the bill of lading has been obtained from the consignor by fraud, his right of stoppage *in transitu* is not defeated, either as against his immediate indorsee, or as against a subsequent indorser for value, for the latter can obtain no better title to the goods than his indorser had.[5]

953. **The transfer of a bill of lading as security does not absolutely defeat the vendor's right of stoppage in transitu,**

[1] Lickbarrow *v.* Mason, 1 Sm. Lead. Cas. 8th ed. 753; Walter *v.* Ross, 2 Wash. 283.

[2] Thompson *v.* Dominy, 14 M. & W. 403 ; Howard *v.* Shepherd, 9 C. B. 297.

[3] Rosenthal *v.* Dessau, 11 Hun (N. Y.), 49; Poole *v.* H. & T. C. Railroad Co. 58 Tex. 134.

[4] Poole *v.* Railroad Co. *supra.*

[5] Gurney *v.* Behrend, 3 E. & B. 622; Dows *v.* Perrin, 16 N. Y. 325.

but he may resume possession of the goods upon satisfying the pledgee's claim.[1] When the vendor has done this, he stands exactly in the same position as to everybody else, both the original purchaser and those claiming under him, as if there had never been any pledge of the bill of lading. His right of stoppage *in transitu* covers every interest in the goods which has not passed by the pledging of the bill of lading. The vendor, moreover, has in such case the equitable right of having the assets marshalled; that is, the pledgee may be called upon to exhaust any other securities he has for the same debt before proceeding against the goods claimed by the unpaid pledgor.[2]

954. After the purchaser has transferred the bill of lading in pledge, he can make no sale that will discharge the vendor's right of stoppage *in transitu;* for he can transfer no greater or better title than he has; and the right which he has is a right subject to the vendor's right of stoppage *in transitu*, for the indorsement of the bill of lading transfers the title to the pledgee, and not to any other person.[3] A sub-purchaser in such case is like any sub-purchaser without a document of title; he has no greater rights than the original purchaser. It has been suggested that in such case the sub-purchaser, having an equitable interest in the goods subject to the rights of the pledgee and of the vendor, might come in and satisfy the claim of the vendor who has stopped the goods *in transitu*, after paying off the claim of the pledgee.[4]

955. The fact that the vendee has indorsed the bill of lading to his factor does not impair the vendor's right to stop the goods *in transitu* upon the insolvency of the vendee, provided the indorsement was not in pledge, though the vendee is indebted to the factor on general account.[5]

[1] Kemp *v.* Falk, 7 App. Cas. 573, affirming *S. C.* 14 Ch. D. 446; *In re* Westzinthus, 5 B. & Ad. 817; Berndtson *v.* Strang, L. R. 4 Eq. 481; *S. C.* 3 L. R. Ch. 588; Spalding *v.* Ruding, 6 Beav. 376; Turner *v.* Liverpool Docks, 6 Ex. 543; Chandler *v.* Fulton, 10 Tex. 2 ; and see *Ex parte* Golding, 13 Ch. D. 628.

[2] Aldrich *v.* Cooper, 2 White & Tudor's Lead. C. in Eq. 6th Eng. ed. (1886) 82.

[3] Kemp *v.* Falk, *supra.*

[4] Kemp *v.* Falk, *supra,* per Lord Selborne, L. C.

[5] Patten *v.* Thompson, 5 M. & S. 350. See Vertue *v.* Jewell, 4 Camp. 31, where it is asserted that the right of stoppage *in transitu* does not exist in case the shipment is made in payment of a balance of account.

956. After a consignee has made advances to the consignor upon the bill of lading, the latter has no right to stop them *in transitu*.[1]

957. The indorsement of the bill of lading by the vendor to the vendee does not affect the right of the former to stop the goods *in transitu*.[2] This does not amount to a negotiation of the bill of lading, such as is ordinarily meant by the use of that term in this connection. The negotiation which puts an end to the right of stoppage *in transitu* is a negotiation by the vendee to a third person for a valuable consideration.

958. A delivery order given by the vendor to his vendee, and transferred by the latter to a purchaser from him, does not defeat the vendor's right of stoppage.[3]

The delivery of a shipping note, with an order on a warehouseman to deliver the goods to a third person, does not pass the property in the goods so as to prevent a stoppage *in transitu*.[4] And so a delivery of the original bill of parcels, in which the vendor acknowledges he has received the price in the vendee's notes, secured by mortgage, together with an order for the delivery of the goods, does not protect the sub-purchaser in his title against the vendor, unless the sub-purchaser has obtained possession of the goods.[5]

959. But a warehouse receipt differs in its legal effect from a delivery order, for the latter is not binding upon the warehouseman until he has accepted it, while the former is in itself a document of title. Of late years the factors' acts have generally placed such receipts upon the same footing as bills of lading, as being documents of title, conferring upon the holder who has received them from the true owner, for the purpose of

---

[1] Burritt *v.* Rench, 4 McLean, 325.

[2] The Tigress, 32 L. J. Adm. 97, per Dr. Lushington.

[3] Jenkyns *v.* Usborne, 7 M. & G. 678, 680; M'Ewan *v.* Smith, 2 H. L. Cas. 309; Akerman *v.* Humphrey, 1 C. & P. 53; Ives *v.* Polak, 14 How. (N. Y.) Pr. 411.

[4] Akerman *v.* Humphrey, *supra*.

[5] Holbrook *v.* Vose, 6 Bosw. (N. Y.) 76, 106.

If the vendor has given a bill of parcels of the goods sold, together with an order on a warehouseman for their delivery, and the vendee, on the strength of these, sells the goods, and the purchaser from him fairly obtains possession, the right of stoppage *in transitu* is gone. Hollingsworth *v.* Napier, 3 Caines (N. Y.), 182.

enabling him to dispose of the property, full power to sell or pledge the property by transferring such documents of title.[1] A factor making a warehouse entry at a custom-house, and taking a warehouse-keeper's receipt, which enables him to withdraw the goods at his pleasure upon discharging the lien for government duties, is regarded as in possession, and so enabled to effectually pledge them.[2]

960. **A mere sale of goods in transitu, without indorsement of the bill of lading, does not determine the transitus.**[3] It has even been said that a transfer of the bill of lading to the sub-purchaser, or the making of a bill of lading in his name, does not of itself destroy the right of the vendor to stop the goods *in transitu*. It is only when the sub-purchaser has taken possession of the goods, or changed their destination, or paid value for them, that the right of stoppage *in transitu* is affected by the sub-sale. If the vendor has given notice to stop *in transitu* before his vendee has received the purchase-money from the sub-purchaser, the vendor is entitled to have his purchase-money satisfied out of the unpaid purchase-money of the sub-purchaser.[4]

[1] Cartwright v. Wilmerding, 24 N. Y. 521.

[2] Cartwright v. Wilmerding, *supra.* This he might do irrespective of the factors' act.

[3] Kemp v. Falk, 7 App. Cas. 573.

[4] *Ex parte* Golding, 13 Ch. D. 628, 638.

Cotton, L. J., in giving his opinion, said : " Except so far as it is necessary to give effect to interests which other persons have acquired for value, the vendor can exercise his right to stop *in transitu*. It has been decided that he can do so when the original purchaser has dealt with the goods by way of pledge. Here we have rather the converse of that case. There has been an absolute sale of the goods by the original purchaser, but the purchase-money has not been paid. Can the vendor make effectual his right of stoppage *in transitu* without defeating in any way the interest of the sub-purchaser? In my opinion he can. He can say, ' I claim a right to retain my vendor's lien. I will not defeat the right of the sub-purchaser, but what I claim is to defeat the right of the purchaser from me, that is, to intercept the purchase-money which he will get, so far as is necessary to pay me.' That, in my opinion, he is entitled to do, not in any way thereby interfering with the rights of the sub-purchaser, but only, as against his own vendee, asserting his right to resume his vendor's lien and to obtain payment by means of an exercise of that right, interfering only with what would have been a benefit to the vendee, who would otherwise have got his purchase-money without paying for the goods, but in no way interfering with any right acquired by the sub-purchaser of the goods."

See, also, Craven v. Ryder, 6 Taunt. 433; Dixon v. Yates, 5 B. & Ad. 313; Davis v. Reynolds, 4 Camp. 267; Seymour v. Newton, 105 Mass. 272, 275; Secomb v. Nutt, 14 B. Mon. (Ky.) 324; Macon & Western R. R. v.

But the proposition, that a right of stoppage *in transitu* can be exercised as against the purchase-money payable by a sub-purchaser to his vendor, was called in question by Lord Selborne in the House of Lords.[1] " I am bound to say that it is not consistent with my idea of the right of stoppage *in transitu* that it should apply to anything except to the goods which are *in transitu*. But when the right exists as against the goods which are *in transitu*, it is manifest that all other persons who have, subject to that right, any equitable interest in those goods by way of contract with the original purchaser, or otherwise, may come in, and, if they satisfy the claim of the seller who has stopped the goods *in transitu*, they can of course have effect given to their rights : and I apprehend that a court of justice, in administering the rights which arise in actions of this description, would very often find that the rights of all parties were properly given effect to, if so much of the purchase-money payable by the sub-purchasers were paid to the original vendor as might be sufficient to discharge his claim ; and, subject of course to that, the other contracts would take effect in their order and in their priorities."

961. But if the original vendor has notice of the resale of the goods by his vendee, and consigns them to the second vendee, his right of stoppage *in transitu* is gone.[2] There is in such case a final and irrevocable delivery from the time of the commencement of the carriage of the goods to the second purchaser.

There is no right of stoppage *in transitu* of goods shipped in the name of the buyer to a third person as consignee. The seller, by shipping the goods in this way and taking a bill of lading in the buyer's name as consignor, recognizes his right to control the goods as owner, and to vest the title of the goods in the consignee.[3]

962. The delivery of a part of a cargo does not determine the right of stoppage in transitu of the whole cargo, unless the circumstances show that a delivery of part was intended to have that effect.[4] Lord Blackburn well expressed the law upon

---

Meador, 65 Ga. 705; Clapp *v.* Sohmer, 55 Iowa, 273; Pattison *v.* Culton, 33 Ind. 240; Holbrook *v.* Vose, 6 Bosw. (N. Y.) 76, 106.

[1] Kemp *v.* Falk, 7 App. Cas. 573, 587.

[2] Eaton *v.* Cook, 32 Vt. 58.

[3] Treadwell *v.* Aydlett, 9 Heisk. (Tenn.) 388.

[4] Turner *v.* Scovell, 14 M. & W. 28; Slubey *v.* Heywood, 2 H. Bl. 504; Hammond *v.* Anderson, 4 B. & P. 69; Betts *v.* Gibbins, 2 Ad. & E. 57, 73;

this point in a recent case before the House of Lords:[1] "It is said that the delivery of a part is a delivery of the whole. It may be a delivery of the whole. In agreeing for the delivery of goods with a person, you are not bound to take an actual corporeal delivery of the whole in order to constitute such a delivery, and it may very well be that the delivery of a part of the goods is sufficient to afford strong evidence that it is intended as a delivery of the whole. If both parties intend it as a delivery of the whole, then it is a delivery of the whole; but if either of the parties does not intend it as a delivery of the whole, if either of them dissents, then it is not a delivery of the whole. I had always understood the law upon that point to have been an agreed law, which nobody ever doubted since an elaborate judgment in Dixon v. Yates,[2] by Lord Wensleydale, who was then Parke, J. The rule I had always understood, from that time down to the present, to be that the delivery of a part may be a delivery of the whole if it is so intended, but that it is not such a delivery unless it is so intended, and I rather think that the onus is upon those who say that it was so intended."

The same rule applies in case of a stoppage *in transitu* of a portion of the goods after the delivery of another portion. The vendor's lien on the part so stopped *in transitu* is restored, and it covers not only the price of such part of the goods, but also the price of the portion already delivered.[3]

963. In case the goods are resold and a part delivered when the notice to stop in transitu is given by the vendor, though the vendor loses by the resale the right to stop the goods *in transitu*, he is entitled, if he gives that which would have been a valid notice of stoppage *in transitu* had there been no resale, to intercept, to the extent of his own unpaid purchase-money, so much of the sub-purchaser's purchase-money as remains unpaid by him.[4]

Miles v. Gorton, 2 Cr. & M. 504; *Ex parte* Gibbs, 1 Ch. D. 101; Jones v. Jones, 8 M. & W. 431; Crawshay v. Eades, 1 B. & C. 181; Buckley v. Furniss, 17 Wend. (N. Y.) 504; Secomb v. Nutt, 14 B. Mon. (Ky.) 324; Hamburger v. Rodman, 9 Daly (N. Y.), 93; *In re* Bearns, 18 N. Bank. Reg. 500.

[1] Kemp v. Falk, 7 App. Cas. 573, 586, affirming *Ex parte* Falk, 14 Ch. D. 446.

[2] 5 B. & Ad. 313, 339.

[3] Wentworth v. Outhwaite, 10 M. & W. 436, 452, per Parke, B.

[4] *Ex parte* Falk, *supra*, following *Ex parte* Golding, 13 Ch. D. 628.

964. After a vendee has resold the goods and delivered the bill of lading to his vendee, the right of stoppage *in transitu* by the original vendor is gone, because the last purchaser is entitled to rely upon the title and possession of his vendor as evidenced by his holding and indorsing the bill of lading.[1] And in like manner one purchasing from a vendee who has acquired actual possession from the carrier, may properly rely upon such possession, if the sale be made in good faith and without knowledge of any claim to their possession on the part of the original vendor. Thus, if goods at a railroad station at the place of their destination are received by the purchaser, who pays the freight and thereupon sells and delivers them to another while they are still at the station, the right of stoppage *in transitu* is gone.[2]

965. An attachment or seizure upon execution of the goods while in the hands of the carrier by another creditor of the purchaser as his property does not defeat the seller's right of stoppage *in transitu*.[3] Even an attachment by the holder of the draft drawn by the seller upon the buyer does not affect the seller's right to stop the goods *in transitu* upon the insolvency of the buyer.[4] But an attachment of the goods by the vendor as the property of the vendee, while they are in the course of transportation, destroys the vendor's right to stop them *in transitu*.[5]

[1] Newsom v. Thornton, 6 East, 17, 43; Loeb v. Peters, 63 Ala. 243.

[2] United States Engine Co. v. Oliver, 16 Neb. 612.

[3] Smith v. Goss, 1 Camp. N. P. 282; Morley v. Hay, 3 M. & Ry. 396; Oppenheim v. Russell, 3 B. & P. 42; Jackson v. Nichol, 5 Bing. N. C. 508, 518, per Tindal, C. J.; Naylor v. Dennie, 8 Pick. (Mass.) 198; Seymour v. Newton, 105 Mass. 272; Durgy Cement & Umber Co. v. O'Brien, 123 Mass. 12; Covell v. Hitchcock, 23 Wend. (N. Y.) 611; Aguirre v. Parmelee, 22 Conn. 473; Chicago, Burlington & Quincy R. R. Co. v. Painter, 15 Neb. 394; Inslee v. Lane, 57 N. H. 454; Rucker v. Donovan, 13 Kans. 251; Morris v. Shryock, 50 Miss. 590; Schwabacher v. Kane, 13 Mo. App. 126; Chandler v. Fulton, 10 Tex. 2; Mississippi Mills v. Union & Planters' Bank, 9 Lea (Tenn.), 314; Hays v. Mouille, 14 Pa. St. 48; Pottinger v. Hecksher, 2 Grant (Pa.), 309; Calahan v. Babcock, 21 Ohio St. 281; Benedict v. Schættle, 12 Ohio St. 515; O'Brien v. Norris, 16 Md. 122; Greve v. Dunham (Iowa), 14 N. W. Rep. 130; O'Neil v. Garrett, 6 Iowa, 480; Cox v. Burns, 1 Iowa, 64; Blackman v. Pierce, 23 Cal. 508; Hause v. Judson, 4 Dana (Ky.), 9, 11; Wood v. Yeatman, 15 B. Mon. (Ky.) 270; Blum v. Marks, 21 La. Ann. 268; Sherman v. Rugee, 55 Wis. 346; S. C. 14 Rep. 640; Buckley v. Furniss, 15 Wend. (N. Y.) 137. *Contra*, Boyd v. Mosely, 2 Swan (Tenn.), 661.

[4] Seymour v. Newton, *supra*.

[5] Woodruff v. Noyes, 15 Conn. 335;

The goods are subject to attachment at the suit of the consignor's creditors if the consignee sustains the relation of agent or factor of the consignor, so that the latter is the owner of the goods, and may dispose of them at his will.[1]

Fox *v.* Willis, 60 Tex. 373; Ferguson *v.* Herring, 49 Tex. 126, 129.

[1] Dickman *v.* Williams, 50 Miss. 500; Sproule *v.* McNulty, 7 Mo. 62.

CHAPTER XIX.

WAREHOUSEMEN AND WHARFINGERS' LIENS.

I. *Of Warehousemen.*

967. A warehouseman's lien is a common law lien. The duties of a warehouseman are similar to those of a carrier. The latter receives goods to be delivered at a different place; the former receives them to deliver at a different time. Neither the carrier nor the warehouseman adds anything to the intrinsic value of the property; but the relative value to the owner is increased by the services rendered, either by the one or the other, else the owner would not have undertaken to pay for them.[1]

A warehouseman's lien is a specific lien for the charges due upon the particular goods that have been stored.[2] A warehouseman has no lien upon the goods in his possession for any indebtedness to him from the owner, disconnected with the charges for storage. He has no lien for a balance of accounts relating to different transactions of storage. His lien is specific upon the goods stored for the particular charges for such storage.[3]

A warehouseman's lien may, however, be made a general one by express agreement, and possibly by an agreement implied from a well-established custom, or from the circumstances of a particular case.[4]

968. In some states a person not a warehouseman, and

---

[1] Steinman *v.* Wilkins, 7 W. & S. (Pa.) 466, per Gibson, C. J.

[2] Steinman *v.* Wilkins, *supra.*

[3] Scott *v.* Jester, 13 Ark. 437, 446. "Warehousemen certainly have not a general lien, authorizing a detention of goods not only for demands accruing out of the article retained, but for a balance of accounts relating to dealings of a like nature." Per Scott, J.

[4] Holderness *v.* Collinson, 1 Man. & R. 55; *S. C.* 7 B. & C. 212.

not in the business of storing goods, has no lien on goods for his compensation for storing them, unless there be an express agreement for a lien, or it is the legal duty of one to receive and hold the goods.[1] A mere volunteer, under no such obligation, who accepts the temporary custody of goods, without any agreement for a lien, can claim none for his compensation.[2]

The statutes declaring this lien generally confer it upon any person who stores goods at the request of the owner.

969. As already stated, a carrier may store goods which the consignee neglects or refuses to receive, and create a lien upon the goods for such storage, or he may himself hold them as warehouseman and claim a lien for his services in that capacity. If the consignee does not receive the goods after notice of their arrival, the carrier may subject them to a warehouseman's lien without notifying either the consignor or consignee that he has stored the goods. "We are not aware," says Devens, J., in a recent case,[3] "that it has ever been held to be the duty of the carrier to notify the owner or consignor of goods of a refusal to accept them before he can terminate his own liability as carrier, and thereafter hold them himself, or transfer them to another to hold as a warehouseman. It is for the owner or consignor of goods to have some one at the place of delivery, when their transit is completed, to accept them. If he does not, the rule which imposes a duty upon the carrier to hold them himself as warehouseman, or to store them in some convenient place, sufficiently protects the goods he has shipped. It would be unreasonable that the carrier should not be allowed to terminate his contract of carriage until after notice to the consignor, and subsequent assent by him to the storage of the goods. The assent of the owner or consignor of goods that a lien thereon for storage shall, under certain circumstances, be created, is one to be inferred from the contract of shipment he has made. If his consignee cannot be found, or, being found, refuses to accept, he must be held to authorize the storage of the goods. If the car-

---

[1] **New York** : *In re* Kelly, 18 Fed. Rep. 528; Trust *v.* Pirsson, 1 Hilt. 292; Alt *v.* Weidenberg, 6 Bosw. 176; Rivara *v.* Ghio, 3 E. D. Smith, 264. So declared by statute.

[2] Rivara *v.* Ghio, *supra*, per Woodruff, J.

[3] Barker *v.* Brown, 138 Mass. 340, 343.

rier is authorized to store them, it does not require argument to
show that he may subject them to a lien for the necessary storage
charges, and that the owner cannot thereafter sell or transfer
them so as to divest the lien."

970. A warehouseman may claim a lien for freight charges
he has paid to a carrier upon goods which the carrier has placed
in his warehouse upon the neglect or refusal of the consignee to
receive the goods upon their arrival at their destination.[1]   In
such case the warehouseman really acts as the agent of the carrier, both in holding possession of the goods and in collecting the
freight charges.   But a warehouseman can maintain no lien for
freight charges advanced by him when the carrier by his negligence has failed to fulfil his contract.[2]   If the goods have been
injured by the carrier, and the warehouseman received them in
apparent good order without knowledge of the injury, the consignee must look to the carrier for his damages, and cannot offset
them in an action by the warehouseman for carrier's charges paid
by him.[3]

971. A mortgagor of chattels has no authority, implied
from his being allowed to remain in possession, to charge
them with a lien for storage as against a mortgagee whose
mortgage is recorded.[4]   The warehouseman has notice of the
mortgage from the record, and therefore he is not at liberty to
assume that the mortgagor has an absolute *jus disponendi* from
his possession alone; and, if storage is necessary, he is chargeable with notice that the mortgagee has a right to judge for
himself where it should be, if his interest is to be charged with
the cost.[5]   If the mortgagee is afterwards informed of the storage
of the mortgaged goods, but is not informed that any attempt
would be made to charge him or the goods with the storage expenses, the fact that he expresses no disapproval does not render
him liable for the charges for storage.

972. A person who has a lien upon a chattel cannot add
to the amount a charge for keeping the chattel till the debt

---

[1] Alden *v.* Carver, 13 Iowa, 253;
Bass *v.* Upton, 1 Minn. 408; Sage *v.*
Gittner, 11 Barb. (N. Y.) 120.
[2] Bass *v.* Upton, *supra.*

[3] Sage *v.* Gittner, *supra.*
[4] Storms *v.* Smith, 137 Mass. 201.
[5] Storms *v.* Smith, *supra,* per
Holmes, J.

is paid; that is, in truth, a charge for keeping it for his own benefit, not for the benefit of the owner of the chattel.[1]

An artificer has no lien upon a chattel for taking care of it after he has completed his work upon it, and while he detains it to enforce his lien. "The owner of the chattel can hardly be supposed to have promised to pay for the keeping of it while, against his will, he is deprived of the use of it; and there seems to be no consideration for such a promise. Then the chattel can hardly be supposed to be wrongfully left in the possession of the artificer, when the owner has been prevented by the artificer from taking possession of it himself. If such a claim can be supported it must constitute a debt from the owner to the artificer, for which an action might be maintained."[2] The right of detaining goods on which there is a lien is a remedy which is to be enforced by the act of the party who claims the lien, and, having such remedy, he is not generally at common law allowed the costs of enforcing it.

Accordingly it was held by Lord Ellenborough that a coachmaker, after having repaired a coach, could not claim any lien for storage, unless there was an express contract to that effect, or unless the owner left the property on the premises beyond a reasonable time, and after notice had been given him to remove it.[3] And so where a shipwright repaired a ship in his own dock, and after the repairs were completed the owner was not prepared to pay for them, and the shipwright gave him notice that he should detain the ship and claim a certain sum per day for the use of the dock during the detention, it was held by the Exchequer Chamber, affirming the judgment of the Queen's Bench, that the shipwright had no lien for the use of the dock during the detention.[4]

One claiming possession of goods adversely to the owner cannot have a lien upon the goods for money paid by him for their storage. The owner can recover in an action of trover without tendering the rent paid for their storage.[5]

But where the purchaser of swine returned them to the seller,

---

[1] Somes *v.* British Empire Shipping Co. 8 H. L. Cases, 338, 345.

[2] British Empire Shipping Co. *v.* Somes, E., B. & E. 353, 365, per Lord Campbell, C. J.; *S. C.* Ib. 367; affirmed in House of Lords, 8 H. L. Cas. 338.

[3] Hartley *v.* Hitchcock, 1 Stark. 408.

[4] British Empire Shipping Co. *v.* Somes, *supra.*

[5] Allen *v.* Ogden, 1 Wash. 174.

claiming to rescind the contract, and the seller afterwards obtained a judgment for the price, it was held that he had a lien for the expense of keeping the swine, because he had been made a bailee by compulsion, though he had lost his lien as vendor by obtaining judgment for the price.[1]

973. A warehouseman waives his lien by claiming to hold the goods, when demanded of him, upon a different ground, as that they are his own property, without making mention of his lien.[2]

He waives his lien by stating to an officer, who is about to seize the goods upon legal process, that he has no charge against them.[3]

He waives his lien by accepting a note for the amount due him for storage and delivering the goods; and he cannot revive the lien by again taking possession of the goods.[4]   And so, if by the course of trade the wharfage due upon goods is not due until Christmas following the importation, whether the goods are removed in the mean time or not, the course of business, which amounts to an agreement between the parties, prevents the wharfinger from maintaining his lien.[5]

A warehouseman does not lose his lien for grain actually stored by fraudulently issuing receipts for other grain not in store.[6]

A warehouseman does not waive his lien for storage by giving a receipt which is expressly made subject to such lien and charge for storage; but he waives it by permitting the purchaser or holder of such receipt to remove the goods without paying the

---

[1] Leavy v. Kinsella, 39 Conn. 50.

[2] Boardman v. Sill, 1 Camp. 410, n.

[3] Blackman v. Pierce, 23 Cal. 508.

[4] Hale v. Barrett, 26 Ill. 195.

[5] Crawshay v. Homfray, 4 B. & Ald. 50. See in this connection, as to the effect of a course of trade, Fisher v. Smith, 39 L. T. R. 430; Dunham v. Pettee, 1 Daly (N. Y.), 112.

In Crawshay v. Homfray, *supra*, Holroyd, J., said : " The principle laid down in Chase v. Westmore, Selw. N. P. 1322, where all the cases came under the consideration of the court, was this, that a special agree-

ment did not of itself destroy the right to retain, but that it did so only where it contained some term inconsistent with that right. Now, if by such agreement the party is entitled to have the goods immediately, and the payment in respect of them is to take place at a future time, that is inconsistent with the right to retain the goods till payment. That was the case here : the wharfage was not payable till Christmas, and by the sale the plaintiffs had a right to an immediate delivery of the goods."

[6] Low v. Martin, 18 Ill. 286.

charges for storage. He does not, however, forfeit his right to demand the amount of the storage charges as a personal debt of the holder of the receipt.[1]

974. A warehouseman may deliver a part of the goods and retain the residue for the price chargeable on all the goods received by him under the same bailment, provided the ownership of the whole is in the same person. The lien attaches to the whole and every part of the goods for the storage of the whole, if the goods were received together under one transaction.[2]

975. A warehouseman or wharfinger does not lose his lien because the goods have a fraudulent trade-mark. A wine merchant brought an action against another wine merchant to restrain an infringement of a trade-mark on the corks of champagne bottles. Some of the bottles with the pirated trade-mark were in the possession of wharfingers acting for a consignee, and the wharfingers were made defendants in the action. In their statement of defence they disclaimed all interest in the matter, and submitted to act as the court should direct upon the payment of their costs. They contended at the trial that the plaintiff, if he should establish his right, ought not to touch the bottles, for the purpose of removing the branded corks, without first paying their warehouse charges. It was held that the wharfingers had a prior lien upon the bottles for their charges, and that if the plaintiff had any lien for his costs, this must be postponed to the wharfingers' lien. There was nothing to deprive them of their lien as wharfingers because the corks in the champagne bottles had fraudulent marks which they knew nothing about.[3] "The lien of the wharfinger is, I assume," said Lord Justice Cotton, "only as against the bottles and wine when the fraudulent corks have been removed; but I cannot see any possible ground, when these have been removed, for saying that their lien for warehouse expenses loses any priority

---

[1] Cole v. Tyng, 24 Ill. 99.

[2] Schmidt v. Blood 9 Wend. (N. Y.) 268; Steinman v. Wilkins, 7 W. & S. (Pa.) 466. And see Blake v. Nicholson, 3 M. & S. 167; Morgan v. Congdon, 4 N. Y. 551.

[3] Moet v. Pickering, 8 Ch. D. 372, reversing S. C. 6 Ch. D. 770, where Mr. Justice Fry held that the plaintiff had a lien for the costs of his action in priority to the lien of the wharfinger for his charges.

that it before had, and which was a first charge against these goods."

976. **Enforcement.** — A warehouseman's lien, like other common law liens, confers no right to sell the property to which the lien attaches, but only a right to hold it till his charges are paid.[1] In most of the states, however, a remedy by sale is provided by statute. Only in a few states are there any statutes expressly enacted for the purpose of providing a remedy for the enforcement of warehousemen's liens;[2] but in quite a number of states there are statutes applicable to the enforcement of all common law liens; and in other states the statutes which provide for the sale of unclaimed goods are expressly made applicable to goods in the hands of warehousemen.[3]

II. *Of Wharfingers.*

977. There is an important distinction between the lien of a warehouseman and that of a wharfinger. The former is a common law lien; the latter is a commercial or customary lien. The lien of a warehouseman is specific, not general. A wharfinger's lien, on the other hand, is general.[4] " There is a well known distinction," says Chief Justice Gibson,[5] " between

---

[1] See § 335.

[2] In **Alabama** it is provided that warehousemen, to whom goods are delivered by a common carrier, may advertise and sell for the same purposes and in the same manner as common carriers are authorized to do. Code 1876, § 2143. See § 339.

In **Indiana**, any forwarding and commission merchant, having a lien upon goods which may have remained in store for one year or more, may proceed to advertise and sell, at public auction, so much thereof as may be necessary to pay the amount of the lien and expenses. R. S. 1881, § 531.

As to **Montana Territory**, see § 981.

In **Wisconsin**, a warehouseman having a lien for charges which have remained unpaid for three months,

may sell the property at auction if its value does not exceed one hundred dollars, and apply the proceeds to the payment of the amount due him. R. S. 1878, § 3347. See § 373, last paragraph. As to **Utah Territory**, see § 981.

[3] As in **Colorado**, see § 342; **Connecticut**, § 343; **Delaware**, § 345; **Iowa**, § 348; **Kansas**, § 349; **Maine**, § 350; **Michigan**, § 353; **Minnesota**, § 354; **Missouri**, § 356; **Nebraska**, § 357; **Nevada**, § 358; **Ohio**, § 362; **Oregon**, § 363; **Pennsylvania**, § 364; **Vermont**, § 370; **Washington Territory**, § 372; **Wisconsin**, § 373.

[4] Rex v. Humphrey, 1 M'Clel. & Y. 173.

[5] Steinman v. Wilkins, 7 W. & S. (Pa.) 466. The learned chief justice criticises the position taken by Baron

a commercial lien, which is the creature of usage, and a common law lien, which is the creature of policy. The first gives a right to retain for a balance of accounts; the second, for services performed in relation to the particular property. Commercial or general liens, which have not been fastened on the law merchant by inveterate usage, are discountenanced by the courts as encroachments on the common law."

Considered as a new question and upon general principles, there seems to be no reasonable foundation for this distinction between the lien of a warehouseman and that of a wharfinger. Upon general principles it would seem that in both cases the lien should be a specific lien on the goods for the storage or wharfage. The lien, perhaps, should not be based upon the ground that the property had been given an additional value, though there is very much the same reason for saying that the property has been given an additional value, by keeping it in a warehouse, as there is in the case of a carrier for saying that the goods have been improved by carriage to a different place; but the lien may perhaps be placed upon the broader ground that care and labor have been expended upon goods at the request of the owner.

A wharfinger's lien is likened to that of a factor, and a warehouseman's lien to that of a carrier. The likeness in the former case may have arisen from the custom of wharfingers in earlier times to make advances upon the goods.

978. That a wharfinger's lien is a general lien seems to have been an established rule since the cases at *nisi prius* in Espinasse's Reports. In the first of these, tried before Lord Kenyon in 1794,[1] it appeared that a person having twenty-five hogsheads of sugar stored with a wharfinger sold the sugar, but the wharfinger refused to deliver it to the purchaser, claiming to hold it for a balance of account due him from the seller on account of wharfage and advances not relating to this particular sugar. Lord Kenyon said: " A lien from usage was matter of

Graham in Rex *v.* Humphrey, 1 McClel. & Y. 194, that a warehouseman has a general lien.

[1] Naylor *v.* Mangles, 1 Esp. 109. Spears *v.* Hartly, 3 Esp. 81, tried at *nisi prius* before Lord Eldon, was a similar case. The distinguished judge

said: " This point has been ruled by Lord Kenyon, and considered as a point completely at rest. I shall therefore hold it as the settled law on the subject, that he has such a lien as claimed in the present case."

evidence; the usage in the present case has been proved so
often, it should be considered as a settled point that wharfingers
had the lien contended for." In a later case before the Court
of Exchequer,[1] the cases in Espinasse's Reports are referred to
as clearly establishing this lien. The court regarded the wharfinger's lien for a general balance of account as equally clear and
decided as in the case of a factor who has by custom the same
lien. Baron Graham, delivering the judgment, said: "After
these cases, it seems to me to be infinitely too much to be
argued in a court of law, that this right of wharfingers is not
perfectly clear and universally admitted."

979. If it appears that a wharfinger's right to a general
lien is a matter in dispute at the port where it is claimed,
the right cannot be inferred. "The onus of making out a right
of general lien lies upon the wharfinger. There may be an
usage in one place varying from that which prevails in another.
Where the usage is general, and prevails to such an extent that a
party contracting with a wharfinger must be supposed conusant
of it, then he will be bound by the terms of that usage. But
then it should be generally known to prevail at that place. If
there be any question as to the usage, the wharfinger should protect himself by imposing special terms, and he should give notice
to his employer of the extent to which he claims a lien. If he
neglects to do so, he cannot insist upon a right of general lien
for anything beyond the mere wharfage."[2]

In this case the court, while sustaining the wharfinger's claim
of a general lien for his wharfage, refused to allow the lien for
labor, such as landing, weighing, and delivering, and for warehouse rent, because the custom proved was not sufficiently certain and uniform to found such a general lien upon for these mat-

---

[1] Rex v. Humphrey, 1 McClel. & Y.
173, 194. Graham, B., said he had always considered the case of a wharfinger and of a warehouseman as standing on the same ground. The other
judges intimated a doubt on this point,
which was afterwards held to be immaterial to the case. It is said to be
to this intimation of a doubt by a majority of the barons in this case that

we owe the impression of a difference
between the lien of a warehouseman
and that of a wharfinger. 23 Am.
Law Reg. 465, 469. But this view assumes that there was no difference in
the origin of these liens.

[2] Holderness v. Collinson, 7 B. & C.
212, per Bayley, J.; S. C. 1 Man. &
R. 55.

ters. As to such charges his lien is specific, attaching only to the goods with respect to which the services were rendered.[1]

980. The wharfinger's general lien may be reduced to a specific lien if the property does not vest in the consignee against whom the wharfinger claims a general balance. If the contract of sale to the consignee be rescinded before the arrival of the goods, the wharfinger, though he receives and stores the goods without having been informed of the determination of the contract, acquires no general lien upon the goods. Thus, where a merchant shipped goods to a customer who, before their arrival, wrote to say that he was in failing circumstances and would not apply for the goods on their arrival, and the merchant, as soon as possible, applied to the wharfinger, at whose wharf the goods had meanwhile arrived, and tendered the freight and charges upon the goods, but the wharfinger refused to deliver them except upon payment of a general balance due him from the consignee, it was held that, the contract of sale having been rescinded previously to the arrival of the goods, the wharfinger had no right to detain them as the property of the consignee subject to a general lien.[2]

The result is the same if the consignee sells the goods before their arrival. The wharfinger, though not informed of the sale before the arrival of the goods, cannot hold them under a claim of lien for a general balance due him from the consignee.[3]

The lien does not attach until the goods are actually landed at the wharf.[4]

981. In several states the lien of a warehouseman is declared by statute. These statutes are generally merely declaratory of the common law. In New York the privilege is confined to persons exclusively engaged in the business of storing goods.

In Colorado[5] and Wyoming Territory,[6] any warehouseman or other person who shall safely keep or store any personal property at the request of the owner, or person lawfully in possession thereof, shall have a lien upon all such personal property for his

[1] Holderness v. Collinson, 7 B. & C. 212, per Bayley, J.

[2] Richardson v. Goss, 3 B. & P. 119.

[3] Crawshay v. Homfray, 4 B. & Ald. 50.

[4] Stephen v. Coster, 1 W. Bl. 413, 423; S. C. 3 Burr. 1408; Syeds v. Hay, 4 T. R. 260.

[5] Gen. Stats. 1883, § 2119.

[6] Comp. Laws 1876, p. 462, § 2.

reasonable charges for the storage or keeping thereof, and for all reasonable and proper advances made thereon by him, in accordance with the usage and custom of warehousemen.

In Iowa[1] personal property transported by, or stored or left with, any warehouseman, forwarding and commission merchant, or other depositary, express company, or carrier, shall be subject to a lien for the just and lawful charges on the same, and for the transportation, advances, and storage thereof.[2]

In Louisiana[3] he who, having in his possession the property of another, whether on deposit or on loan or otherwise, has been obliged to incur any expense for its preservation, acquires against the owner and his creditors a right in the nature of a pledge, by virtue of which he may retain the thing until the expenses which he has incurred are paid.

In Minnesota[4] and Oregon[5] any person who safely keeps or stores any personal property, at the request of the owner or lawful possessor thereof, shall have the same lien for his charges, and the same right to hold and retain the possession thereof, and the same power of sale for the satisfaction of his reasonable charges and expenses, as are provided in case of a mechanic or artisan having a lien upon personal property.

In Missouri the same lien is given to warehousemen that is given to carriers.[6]

In Montana Territory[7] any storage or commission merchant who has received any goods for storage, after keeping them in store for ninety days, may, in default of the payment of the storage or freight on such goods, advertise and sell the same at public auction, first giving notice by publication for at least thirty days before the sale.

In New York[8] a warehouseman, or person lawfully engaged exclusively in the business of storing goods, wares, and merchandise for hire, shall have a lien for his storage charges, for moneys

---

[1] R. Code 1880, p. 582, § 2177.

[2] For proceedings for sale of such goods see Ib. §§ 2178–2180.

[3] R. Civ. Code 1870, arts. 3224–3226. Under this provision there is a privilege for storage. Where a carrier stores goods in a warehouse at the port of destination, the charges of the warehouse-keeper for storage forms a privilege superior in rank to that of the carrier for freight. Powers v. Sixty Tons of Marble, 21 La. Ann. 402.

[4] Laws 1885, ch. 81.

[5] Laws 1878, p. 102, § 2.

[6] 2. R. S. 1879, § 6277. See § 356, supra.

[7] R. S. 1879, §§ 1179–1181.

[8] Laws 1885, ch. 526.

advanced by him for cartage, labor, weighing, and coopering, paid on goods deposited and stored with him, and such lien shall extend to and include all legal demands for storage, and said above-described expenses paid, which he may have against the owner of said goods ; and it shall be lawful for him to detain said goods until such lien is paid.

In Tennessee [1] the owners and proprietors of wharves and landings, where wharfage is allowed by law, have a lien on all boats, rafts, and other water craft, and their loading, for the payment of their wharfage fees, and the same may be enforced by attachment within three months after the lien accrued.

In Utah Territory,[2] whenever a special agreement has been made between the owner of a storage warehouse and parties storing any description of property therein regarding the price of such storage, such property shall be subject to a lien for the charges for freight, storage, and insurance, and, in case of nonpayment for the period of six months, such storage warehouse owner shall have the right to sell the property, or so much of it as may be necessary to pay such charges.

The sale is made in accordance with the provisions for sales by innkeepers.[3]

[1] Code 1882, § 2753.
[2] Laws 1884, ch. 18.

[3] Compiled Laws 1876, § 1195. See § 538, *supra.*

CHAPTER XX.

ASSIGNMENTS OF LIENS.

I. *Of Common Law Liens.*

982. A common law lien is not a proper subject of sale or assignment, for it is neither property nor is it a debt, but a right to retain property as security for a debt.[1] " A lien," says Mr. Justice Buller, " is a personal right, and cannot be transferred to another." [2]

It is a general rule that, in the absence of any statutory provision, the assignment of a demand for which the assignor may have by law a specific lien at common law destroys the right of lien; and a reassignment to him before action does not revive the lien.[3] A lien cannot be assigned while the assignor retains possession of the property charged therewith.[4] On the other hand, a transfer of the property while the assignor retains the lien debt, destroys the lien, unless the transfer be merely to an agent of the assignor to hold for him subject to the lien.

983. A lien is a purely personal privilege, and can only be set up by the person to whom it accrued.[5] He cannot assign his claim, so as to enable the assignee to set up the lien as a ground of claim or defence to an action for the property or its value as against the general owner. A manufacturer of starch, having a lien for the price of manufacturing several tons for one

---

[1] Lovett *v.* Brown, 40 N. H. 511; Bradley *v.* Spofford, 23 N. H. 444, 447; Jacobs *v.* Knapp, 50 N. H. 71; Roberts *v.* Jacks, 31 Ark. 597.

[2] Daubigny *v.* Duval, 5 T. R. 604, 606; and see Holly *v.* Huggeford, 8 Pick. (Mass.) 73.

[3] Tewksbury *v.* Bronson, 48 Wis.

581; Caldwell *v.* Lawrence, 10 Wis. 331.

[4] Wing *v.* Griffin, 1 E. D. Smith (N. Y.), 162.

[5] Holly *v.* Huggeford, *supra;* Ruggles *v.* Walker, 34 Vt. 468; Wing *v.* Griffin, *supra.*

who furnished the materials, and the latter not being ready to receive and pay for the starch when it was ready for delivery, obtained from a third person the amount of his claim on the starch, and delivered the stock to him, by placing it in another building near the factory, and marking it with the name of such third person. The latter notified the general owner of the starch that he had purchased the manufacturer's claim, and that the owner could have his property by paying what he had agreed to pay the manufacturer. The owner, however, took possession of the starch without paying the price for manufacturing, and the person who had made advances upon it brought suit against him, declaring in trespass and trover for taking and converting the starch to his own use. It was held that he could not maintain the suit, because the lien was a personal privilege which the original lien-holder could not sell or transfer except with the consent of the general owner of the property.[1]

984. A person having a lien upon goods may transfer the possession of them to a third person to hold subject to the lien, as agent or bailee of the original lien-holder, until the lien shall be satisfied. The lien is not affected in such case because the possession of the property really remains with the lien-holder.

If the lien debt be assigned to such third person with the possession of the property, for the purpose of collection, or otherwise to hold for the original lien-holder as his agent, it would seem that the lien would not be destroyed by the transfer. But though the lien-holder may, under some circumstances, put the property into the hands of another person without forfeiting his lien, yet, inasmuch as the general rule is that the lien is divested by a transfer of the possession, the burden is upon the lien-holder to show that the transfer was of such a nature as to make it lawful. "Although it may be, and no doubt is true, that the holder of goods or chattels subject to a lien may transfer them to third persons under special circumstances, and for purposes consistent with the continuance of the lien, yet it would seem equally plain that the burden of proof and allegation lies on those who aver that such a transfer is rightful, and seek to hold the goods under it against the owner." [2]

[1] Ruggles v. Walker, 34 Vt. 468.   [2] Bean v. Bolton, 3 Phila. (Pa.) 87, 89, per Hare, J.

985. The lien-holder may transfer the lien debt, and with it the possession of the thing as security for the debt, for this amounts merely to an appointment of the assignee as his agent to keep possession and collect the claim in the name and for the account of the assignor.[1]

The rights of the owner remain unchanged. He can demand and receive the property from the assignee on the same terms he could if it still remained in the hands of the original lien-holder. "In the absence of fraud, or removal of the property out of reach, or any other act of abuse of the original relation of bailment, there seems to be no equity in permitting him to recover without doing equity, by paying or tendering the charge which is a lien on the property."[2]

An assignee of the lien debt, accompanied by possession of the property to which the lien attaches, is only an equitable assignee. He cannot enforce the lien in his own name, but must use the name of the original lien-holder for that purpose, unless the assignee be authorized by statute to prosecute the action in his own name.

986. An absolute sale of the property by the lien-holder forfeits the lien, and neither he nor the purchaser can set up the lien as against the owner of the general title. A lien-holder may assign his lien and deliver the property to another if the assignment be in strict subordination to the rights of the owner ; but an absolute sale is in violation of the property rights of the owner, is tortious, and works a forfeiture of the lien.[3] And so, if the assignee of the lien having possession of the property sells it absolutely to a third person, the owner is remitted to his original rights freed from the lien, and may maintain trover against the assignee.[4] The owner cannot maintain trespass or replevin after such absolute sale, because the purchaser has come lawfully into

---

[1] Davis *v.* Bigler, 62 Pa. St. 242; and see Buckner *v.* McIlroy, 31 Ark. 631, per Pindall, J.

[2] Rodgers *v.* Grothe, 58 Pa. St. 414, 419, per Agnew, J. The transfer in this case was an attempted sale under a statute which was ineffectual to pass the title to the property as against the owner, but was a transfer of the claim and of the possession of the property.

[3] Jones *v.* Pearle, 1 Str. 556; Legg *v.* Evans, 6 M. & W. 36; Lickbarrow *v.* Mason, 6 East, 20, 27, note, per Buller, J. ; Coit *v.* Waples, 1 Minn. 134; Doane *v.* Russell, 3 Gray (Mass.), 382; Holly *v.* Huggeford, 8 Pick. (Mass.) 73; Ruggles *v.* Walker, 34 Vt. 468.

[4] Nash *v.* Mosher, 19 Wend. 431.

possession of the property by delivery from a bailee in rightful possession.[1]

987. A wrong-doer cannot set up the lien. A lien which a bailee has, for the price of labor done, cannot be set up by a wrong-doer to defeat the action of the general owner.[2]

A lien will not pass by a tortious act of the party claiming it, such as his selling or pledging the goods without authority.[3] Thus the lien of a master upon a cargo for freight may be asserted by his factor or agent; but if the master, without authority, directs the factor to sell the goods and the latter sells them, the purchaser cannot set up the lien and require it to be discharged before the owner can properly demand possession of the goods or bring suit for them.[4]

988. If a lien-holder sells the property on which he has a lien without due process of law, but subject to the lien, the owner may bring trover or replevin for it freed from the lien; but he cannot bring trespass as the transferee came lawfully into possession by delivery from a lien-holder who was rightfully in possession.[5] If the lien-holder or his assignee wrongfully sells or pledges the property not in subordination to the rights of the general owner, the transfer puts an end to the possession under the lien and destroys it, and the owner may sue in trespass for the property.[6]

989. The interest of one having possession of a chattel by virtue of a lien, is not attachable as personal property, or as a chose in action.[7] The lien cannot be set up by the attaching officer, or other person, in defence of an action by the owner.[8] It is a personal privilege which the person who is entitled to it may avail himself of or not, as he pleases.[9]

[1] Nash v. Mosher, 19 Wend. 431; Coit v. Waples, 1 Minn. 134.

[2] Bradley v. Spofford, 23 N. H. 444; Jones v. Sinclair, 2 N. H. 319.

[3] M'Combie v. Davies, 7 East, 5; Urquhart v. McIver, 4 Johns. (N. Y.) 103; Everett v. Saltus, 15 Wend. (N. Y.) 474; Bean v. Bolton, 3 Phila. (Pa.) 87.

[4] Everett v. Saltus, supra.

[5] Nash v. Mosher, supra; Davis v. Bigler, 62 Pa. St. 242.

[6] Davis v. Bigler, supra, per Sharswood, J.; Rodgers v. Grothe, 58 Pa. St. 414; Ely v. Ehle, 3 N. Y. 506.

[7] Lovett v. Brown, 40 N. H. 511; Kittredge v. Sumner, 11 Pick. (Mass.) 50; Holly v. Huggeford, 8 Ib. 73.

[8] Kittredge v. Sumner, supra.

[9] Holly v. Huggeford, supra; Ruggles v. Walker, 34 Vt. 468.

II. *Of Statutory Liens.*

990. Some statutory liens may be assigned. Statutory liens which are not merely declaratory of the common law do not generally require possession to support them.[1] Such liens without possession have generally the same operation and efficacy as common law liens with possession, and the assignment of the claim may in such cases carry with it the right to the lien, equitably at least. But statutory liens, which are really common law liens declared by statute, and which depend upon possession for their existence in the same way that common law liens depend upon possession, can be assigned only as common law liens can be assigned : the assignment of such a lien debt without a transfer of the property does not carry with it the lien, but on the contrary destroys the lien.[2] But if the existence of the lien does not depend upon possession, it may be assigned.[3]

A lien, though created by statute, is not assignable at law so as to enable the assignee to maintain an action in his own name. Any assignment that can be made is only equitable.[4]

III. *Of Equitable Liens.*

991. An equitable lien reserved by express agreement passes by an assignment of the debt it was created to secure.[5] Such a lien does not depend upon possession as does a common law lien.

An equitable lien not reserved by contract or declared by court will not pass by an assignment of the debt, as for instance by the transfer, in the ordinary course of business, of a note representing the lien debt.[6]

[1] See § 104.

[2] Caldwell *v.* Lawrence, 10 Wis. 331; Tewksbury *v.* Bronson, 48 Wis. 581.

[3] Pearsons *v.* Tincker, 36 Me. 384.

The statutory lien of the laborer, like that of the mechanic upon real property, is assignable, and the assignee may enforce the lien in the same manner and to the same extent as the laborer. Kerr *v.* Moore, 54 Miss. 286.

[4] Cairo & Vincennes R. R. Co. *v.*

Fackney, 78 Ill. 116 ; Pearsons *v.* Tincker, *supra.*

[5] Ober *v.* Gallagher, 93 U. S. 199; Batesville Institute *v.* Kauffman, 18 Wall. 151, 154; Payne *v.* Wilson, 74 N. Y. 348, 354 ; Talieferro *v.* Barnett, 37 Ark. 511; Campbell *v.* Rankin, 28 Ark. 401, overruling to the contrary Sheppard *v.* Thomas, 26 Ark. 617, and Jones *v.* Doss, 27 Ark. 518. See § 28.

[6] Owen *v.* Reed, 27 Ark. 122.

992. An attorney's lien upon a judgment is assignable.[1] In this regard there is no distinction between an attorney's lien and the lien of a mechanic or material-man. There is nothing in public policy, nor in the policy or language of the statutes creating these liens, which forbids the assignment of them. To take away their assignability would be to take away part of their value. An attorney's lien upon a judgment is a lien of an equitable nature, though in many states it is declared by statute.

IV. *By Subrogation.*

993. A lien may be transferred by subrogation to one who pays the lien debt, not as a volunteer, but in the line of his duty. Thus one in charge of a horse, practically as a stable-keeper, upon paying a farrier's bill for shoeing, is entitled to stand in the farrier's shoes and enforce his lien. It being the duty of the keeper of the horse to see that the horse is cared for, he is not a mere volunteer in paying the farrier's bill; and he can retain the horse for the payment of the bill if the farrier could retain him.[2]

A surety upon a tenant's bond for rent may take up the bond, and have it assigned to him, so as to substitute him to all the rights and lien of the landlord.[3]

A surety upon the bond of a collector of taxes, upon answering for his default, is subrogated to a statutory lien of the state upon the collector's land; and the fact that the surety has taken a mortgage to indemnify him against loss, is no waiver of his right of subrogation.[4] A release by such surety of part of the land mortgaged to the surety to indemnify him against loss, without notice of the equitable right of a purchaser of land from the collector which was subject to such statutory lien, will not defeat his right to be subrogated to the lien of the state, after he has

[1] Sibley *v.* County of Pine, 31 Minn. 201, 202, per Mitchell, J. "There being nothing in the lien right in the nature of a personal trust, there is no distinction in this regard between an attorney's lien upon a judgment, and the lien of a mechanic or material-man. Where the lien-holder is intrusted, as a personal trust, with the property bound by the lien, as would be the case where the papers of a client have come into the possession of

his attorney in the course of his professional employment, an entirely different case would be presented, which we do not now consider. But no such element of personal trust existed in the present case."

[2] Hoover *v.* Epler, 52 Pa. St. 522.

[3] Smith *v.* Wells, 4 Bush (Ky.), 92.

[4] Crawford *v.* Richeson, 101 Ill. 351.

paid judgments in a suit on the collector's bond. A surety upon such bond, against whom a judgment has been recovered, may, before paying the judgment, file a bill to require the lands of the collector, subject to the statutory lien, to be first sold for the payment of such judgment. If the surety pays the judgment he is subrogated to the lien of the state, and may have the lands sold for his reimbursement.[1]

The failure of the holder of a lien to enforce or preserve it does not of itself discharge a surety of the lien debt. It is enough if the lien-holder does nothing to impair the lien, or to prevent the surety from being subrogated to his rights.[2]

994. A seller's unpaid lien passes to a surety who pays the purchase-money upon the default of the purchaser. Thus, if a broker who has bought goods for an undisclosed principal, and therefore stands in the relation of surety for his principal, pays the purchase-money upon the insolvency of his principal, he acquires the vendor's lien upon the goods, and may hold them by virtue of such lien as against the purchaser's pledgee of a delivery order for the goods.[3]

995. But there can be no subrogation to a lien until the lien debt is fully satisfied. Therefore, where a groom gave his promissory note to a stable-keeper for the keeping of a horse which the groom had engaged to take charge of for a stipulated sum for a time specified, it was held that he could not claim the right to use the lien of the stable-keeper until he had actually paid the note, or had shown that the note was received as payment.[4]

[1] Crawford v. Richeson, 101 Ill. 351.

[2] Variol v. Doherty, 1 McGloin (La.), 118 ; Parker v. Alexander, 2 La. Ann, 188; Gordon v. Diggs, 9 Ib.

422; Elmore v. Robinson, 18 Ib. 651, 652; Hill v. Bourcier, 29 Ib. 841, 844.

[3] Imperial Bank v. London Docks Co. 5 Ch. D. 195.

[4] Hoover v. Epler, 52 Pa. St. 522.

CHAPTER XXI.

WAIVER OF LIENS.

I. *By Voluntary Surrender of Possession.*

996. Introductory. — The subject of the waiver of liens has been briefly considered in connection with the several kinds of liens treated of in the preceding chapters. In general it was intended to state only those grounds or modes of waiver which are peculiar to the lien under consideration, or which have peculiar application to such lien. Of course waiver by surrender of possession to the general owner has been repeatedly referred to in connection with all the common law liens; for possession is the foundation of such liens, and the necessity of retaining possession in order to preserve the lien has been repeatedly referred to. But there are many other circumstances under which liens are waived, and it has seemed best to treat in the present chapter of all matters of waiver of general application to all liens.

997. A common law lien is founded upon possession, and is dissolved by a voluntary and unconditional surrender of the property to the owner.[1] If a mechanic surrenders an article made or repaired for another without payment, he loses his lien upon it at common law, and under the statutes also, unless these

---

[1] §§ 308, 466, 519, 699, 821; King *v.* Indian Orchard Canal Co. 11 Cush. (Mass.) 231; Stickney *v.* Allen, 10 Gray (Mass.), 352; Sears *v.* Wills, 4 Allen (Mass.), 212; Huckins *v.* Cushing, 36 Me. 423; McFarland *v.* Wheeler, 26 Wend. (N. Y.) 467; Wingard *v.* Banning, 39 Cal. 543; Sensenbrenner *v.* Mathews, 48 Wis. 250; Smith *v.* Scott, 31 Wis. 420.

In **Kansas**, it is provided by statute that the voluntary delivery to the owner or claimant of any personal property, by any person claiming a lien thereon, shall be held to be an abandonment of such lien, and such lien may also be waived by special contract. Comp. Laws 1885, § 3267.

685

expressly provide for the continuance of the lien for a limited time after delivery of the chattel to the owner.[1]

If the owner of a sawmill permits boards sawed by him to be removed from his mill-yard by the owner to the bank of the canal, half a mile distant from the mill, he loses his lien as against third persons; and it does not avail him that the owner expressly stipulated with him that the lien should continue notwithstanding the removal.[2] And so the mill-owner loses his lien for sawing by allowing the owner of the lumber to remove it to a shed belonging to a third person, and over which the mill-owner has no control.[3]

A blacksmith repaired a sled, and refused to give it up until his charges should be paid. Thereupon the owner agreed that the sled should be the property of the blacksmith until the latter should be fully paid, and the former was allowed to take and keep the sled. It was afterwards attached as his property. It was held that the blacksmith had lost his lien by voluntarily parting with the possession of the sled.[4]

998. A lien created by contract is not discharged by permitting the general owner to take possession of the property, if it may be done consistently with the contract, the course of business, and the intention of the parties.[5] Thus, under a provision of a contract for sawing lumber, that the quantity should be determined by the sales or by inspection at the place of shipment, some five miles from the mill, it was held that the removal of the lumber to the place of shipment, and such inchoate and conditional possession as might be taken by the purchaser as the inspection proceeded, would not cut off the lien.[6]

But if the conduct of the lien-holder be inconsistent with the preservation of his lien, it will be presumed that he intended to waive it. Thus, if a person has a lien upon logs for driving them into a boom, and afterwards, with knowledge that the owner has sold them, assists the purchaser to take possession of the logs for the purpose of having them sawed and converted to his own use, without making known that he had any lien or

[1] McDougall v. Crapon, 95 N. C. 292.

[2] McFarland v. Wheeler, 26 Wend. (N. Y.) 467.

[3] Bailey v. Quint, 22 Vt. 474.

[4] Kitteridge v. Freeman, 48 Vt. 62.

[5] Spaulding v. Adams, 32 Me. 211.

[6] Chadwick v. Broadwell, 27 Mich. 6, Campbell, J., dissenting.

claim upon them, he will be regarded as having waived or abandoned his lien.[1]

And so if a lien claimant acquiesces in the action of a third person in taking possession of the property on exception, without notifying him of his own adverse claim, he waives his lien.[2]

999. Intention as affecting waiver. — A common law lien is created by implication, and it may be waived by implication. But it is always competent to negative an implied waiver by showing by other facts that no waiver was intended.[3] An intention to waive a lien will not be presumed, in the absence of evidence clearly tending to show such an intention.[4]

A lien which is not given by operation of law, but created by express contract, can be waived only by acts done with the intention of discharging the lien.[5] A lien expressly reserved is not impliedly waived by giving credit or taking other security.[6]

An agreement to deliver up the property is not in this respect equivalent to an actual delivery of it, unless the agreement be based on a legal consideration, so as to be obligatory.[7]

1000. A lien once lost by parting with possession of the property cannot be restored by regaining possession, unless this be with the consent or agreement of the owner.[8] Thus the lien of a seller is lost by delivering the goods to the purchaser; yet, if the possession be afterwards redelivered to the seller for the express purpose of rendering it subject to the lien, this is revived from that time, and will continue so long as the vendor retains possession.[9]

1001. Delivery of part. — One who has a lien upon goods in his possession does not, by delivering to the owner a part of them, waive his lien for his whole demand upon the remaining part.[10]

---

[1] Spaulding v. Adams, 32 Me. 211.

[2] McMaster v. Merrick, 41 Mich. 505.

[3] Pratt v. Eaton, 65 Mo. 157, 165; Montieth v. Great Western Printing Co. 16 Mo. App. 450.

[4] Muench v. Valley Nat. Bank, 11 Mo. App. 144.

[5] Smith v. Scott, 31 Wis. 420.

[6] Montieth v. Great Western Printing Co. *supra*.

[7] Danforth v. Pratt, 42 Me. 50.

[8] §§ 310, 469; Cowell v. Simpson, 16 Ves. 275; Hewison v. Guthrie, 2 Bing. N. C. 755; Hartley v. Hitchcock, 1 Stark. 408; Holderness v. Shackels, 3 M. & R. 25; *S. C.* 8 B. & C. 612; Au Sable River Boom Co. v. Sanborn, 36 Mich. 358; Nevan v. Roup, 8 Iowa, 207.

[9] Huff v. Earl, 3 Ind. 306.

[10] §§ 320, 411; Palmer v. Tucker,

II. *By Inconsistent Agreements as to Payment.*

1002. There can be no lien, by common law or usage, where the parties make a special agreement inconsistent with a lien, either for a particular mode of payment, or for payment at a future particular time, although without such agreement the right to a lien would be implied or recognized. If such agreement is antecedent to the possession, no lien is created; if it is made afterwards, the lien is waived.[1]

A contract whereby a sawmill was leased without rent for the sawing season, but the lessees were to saw all logs furnished by the lessor at certain prices, and were to season and ship the lumber as ordered, was held to be inconsistent with a lien for the sawing and other work done by the lessees; for the prices at which the work was to be done could not be considered as independent of the use of the mill, and the rental value could not be apportioned on the price of sawing, because it could not be determined how much sawing was to to be done. Moreover, the work was to continue until the end of the lease, when the lessees would be bound to quit, and could not remain on the premises to enforce the lien; and the obligation to ship was unlimited, and might exhaust the whole of the lumber.[2]

A provision in a contract for sawing lumber, that the bill for sawing should be paid " as often as once a month after the lumber is delivered out of the mill," was held not to be inconsistent with a lien. From the whole contract the manufacturer was regarded as entitled to payment before any lumber could be taken from his possession, and, as entitled to monthly payments on inspections to be made at the place of shipment, whether sales were actually made or not.[3]

And so an agreement by a woollen manufacturer to dress what flannels should be furnished him by the other party during the

---

45 Me. 316; McFarland *v.* Wheeler, 26 Wend. (N. Y.) 467.

[1] §§ **322, 325, 522**; Raitt *v.* Mitchell, 4 Campb. 146, 149; Crawshay *v.* Homfray, 4 B. & Ald. 50; Blake *v.* Nicholson, 3 M. & S. 167, 168; Bailey *v.* Adams, 14 Wend. (N. Y.) 201; Dunham *v.* Pettee, 1 Daly (N. Y.), 112; Trust *v.* Pirsson, 1 Hilt. (N. Y.) 292, per Daly, J.; Chandler *v.* Belden, 18 Johns. (N. Y.) 157; Burdict *v.* Murray,

3 Vt. 302; Pinney *v.* Wells, 10 Conn. 104; Darlington *v.* Chamberlain, 20 Bradw. (Ill.) 443; Lee *v.* Gould, 47 Pa. St. 398; Pulis *v.* Sanborn, 52 Pa. St. 368.

[2] McMaster *v.* Merrick, 41 Mich. 505.

[3] Chadwick *v.* Broadwell, 27 Mich. 6, Campbell, J., dissenting. See, also, Cardinal *v.* Edwards, 5 Nev. 36.

year, and to receive his pay quarterly, is a waiver of a lien upon the cloth ; and if some of the cloth remains in the manufacturer's hands at the end of the quarter, he is not entitled to retain it for the price of dressing it.[1]

In case of a statutory lien which exists for only a definite period after it is acquired, unless proceedings be commenced within such period for its enforcement, it follows that if the person claiming a lien has taken his debtor's promissory note, which does not mature till the expiration of the time within which proceedings for enforcing the lien may be commenced, the taking of the note is a waiver of the lien.[2]

1003. A special agreement for a lien, which provides for payment at a future time or in a particular mode, generally excludes an implied lien. If such agreement is made before the claimant acquires possession, the common law right of lien, which otherwise would be implied, does not attach ; and if such agreement be made after the claimant has acquired possession and this lien has attached, it is thereby waived. In such case there is no lien at all, unless it is expressly provided for by the contract.[3] Thus, by agreement one was to have the right to store, repair, and sell pianofortes in a store, without exclusive possession, but in common with the owner, and for the privilege he was to pay the owner a certain sum per month, at the expiration of each month. In a suit to enforce a lien upon the pianos, this agreement was held to exclude any lien for the amount due. " The distinction," said Judge Daly,[4] " that there can be no lien where the day or time for payment is regulated and fixed by the parties, is as old as the Year-Books, and it is manifest that the law could not be otherwise. The right to detain all the property to which the lien attaches, until the charge upon it is paid, is incident to the right of lien. When, then, did the lien in this case attach ? Certainly not when the possession

[1] Stoddard Woollen Manufac. v. Huntley, 8 N. Y. 441. Judge Parker, delivering the judgment, said: " The operation of a lien is to place the property in pledge for the payment of the debt; and where the party agrees to give time for payment, or agrees to receive payment in a particular mode, it is evidence, if nothing appears to the contrary, that he did not intend to rely upon the pledge of the goods, in relation to which the debt arose, to secure the payment."

[2] Peyroux v. Howard, 7 Pet. 324; Green v. Fox, 7 Allen (Mass.), 85.

[3] Trust v. Pirsson, 1 Hilt. (N. Y.) 292; S. C. 3 Abb. Pr. 84.

[4] Trust v. Pirsson, supra.

commenced, for no payment was to be made until a month after. During that time the defendant had a right, under the agreement, to sell any of his pianos that might be there, and of course to deliver them to the buyers, for the plaintiff could set up no claim to action then, nothing being due. The contract, therefore, went into operation with a recognition of rights on the part of the defendant wholly inconsistent with a reservation of a right of lien. It was nothing else but an agreement for the use of the store for a certain period, at so much per month, for the prosecution of a particular business by the defendant, and gave the plaintiff no lien upon the property which the defendant had there in the prosecution of that business, but, by its nature and terms, was wholly inconsistent with the existence of such a right."

1004. This principle has been extended to cases where a credit might be claimed by custom, without any special agreement for it. Thus, in a case where a ship was taken to a dock for repairs, and great expense was incurred by the shipwright, and it was shown that by usage the ship-owner might demand a credit, it was held that there was no lien for the repairs.[1] And so, where a wharfinger was in the habit of receiving goods, upon which he might have had a lien, but the course of business was that he parted with the goods from time to time, receiving payment at the end of every six months, or every year, for all his dues, it was held that this course of business prevented him from maintaining his right of lien.[2]

But where the course of business with an insurance broker was to make out monthly accounts, and to settle the amounts due for each month at the commencement of the following month, the broker meanwhile retaining the policies, it was held that this course of business was not inconsistent with the retention of his lien.[3] Lord Cairns, Lord Chancellor, remarked, in giving judgment, that if it had been the course of business here for the insurance broker not merely to effect these policies, but from time to time to give them up as they were effected, and simply to stand upon his right to be paid at the end of the month, then

---

[1] Raitt v. Mitchell, 4 Campb. 146.   [3] Fisher v. Smith, 39 L. T. 430.
[2] Crawshay v. Homfray, 4 B. & Ald. 50.

I can understand that the case would be like that of Crawshay *v.* Homfray.[1]

1005. An express agreement to give credit has the same effect as a credit given by note or other obligation. Thus where a mechanic made repairs upon certain stage-coaches under an agreement to give four months' credit upon the bill from the time of completion of the repairs, it was held that he had no lien for the repairs though the owner became insolvent before the coaches passed out of the possession of the mechanic.[2]

1006. An agreement for credit by note is conditional upon the giving of the note. An agreement to take the debtor's note, or the independent security of a third person, falling due at a day beyond the period within which the lien must be asserted, is no waiver of the lien, when the agreement is not performed by the debtor. To hold otherwise would be to say that the person entitled to a lien intended to waive it whether the debtor kept his agreement to give his note or collateral security, or not. On the debtor's failure to keep his agreement the creditor ought not to be bound by it, but should be remitted to his rights, independently of the contract.[3] Thus, an agreement to extend the time of payment of a claim beyond the time within which a mechanic's lien should be asserted, provided a mortgage should be given, will not defeat the lien if the mortgage be not given. The giving of the mortgage is a condition precedent.[4]

In like manner, if the parties agree to settle a claim for work upon a steamboat for which there is a right of lien, by the debtor's note extending the time of payment beyond the time

---

[1] 4 B. & Ald. 50.

[2] Fieldings *v.* Mills, 2 Bosw. 489, 498. "There is a marked difference, in some respects," said Bosworth, J., "between the right of stoppage *in transitu,* and that of a mechanic to detain. Insolvency alone creates the right to stop *in transitu.* The common law right of the mechanic to detain, arises as well against a solvent as an insolvent employer. Neither the solvency nor insolvency of the latter can be deemed an element in the creation of the right of lien which exists in favor of the mechanic. No lien exists in favor of the latter, when his services are performed upon an agreement that payment for them is not to be made until after the article which they have improved is to be delivered."

[3] Chicago & Alton R. R. Co. *v.* Union Rolling Mill Co. 109 U. S. 702.

[4] Gardner *v.* Hall, 29 Ill. 277.

allowed for asserting the lien, the lien is not displaced if the note be not given in pursuance of the agreement. The credit is conditional upon the debtor's giving the note. On his neglecting or refusing to give the note, the credit ceases, and the demand becomes immediately due and payable.[1]

1007. An agreement by a mechanic to do certain labor, in consideration of being employed to do other labor, is inconsistent with a right of lien, and is a waiver of it. Thus, a printer who agreed to repair and alter certain stereotype plates, in consideration of being allowed to do the owner's printing for an indefinite time, has no lien on the plates, on account of the repairs and alterations, when, after several years, the owner withdraws the printing from him.[2] In such case it might properly be presumed that the pay received by the printer for the other work performed was a remuneration for his labor done upon the plates; and at any rate, this is the remuneration which the printer agreed to take.

1008. The fact that by a special agreement payment is to be made in advance does not affect the right of lien where the debtor neglects or refuses to make such agreement.[3]

1009. The taking of a debtor's promissory note, or acceptance, for the amount of a debt secured by a lien, is not necessarily a waiver of the lien; for, by the general commercial law, a promissory note or acceptance given for a precedent debt does not operate as payment, unless the parties agree that it shall have this effect.[4]

If, however, the debtor's promissory note or acceptance be payable at a future day, the lien is generally regarded as waived; for it cannot be presumed that the parties intended that the lien should be extended through any considerable period, but, on the contrary, that the goods or other property should be delivered up immediately.[5]

---

[1] The Highlander, 4 Blatch. 55.

[2] Stickney v. Allen, 10 Gray (Mass.), 352.

[3] Ruggles v. Walker, 34 Vt. 468.

[4] § **324**; De Wolf v. Howland, 2 Paine, 356; Kimball v. Ship Anna Kimball, 2 Cliff. 4; affirmed, 3 Wall.

37; The Skillinger, 1 Flip. 436; Lessels v. Farnsworth, 3 How. (N. Y.) Pr. N. S. 73; Myers v. Uptegrove, Ib. 316; Butts v. Cuthbertson, 6 Ga. 166.

[5] Cowell v. Simpson, 16 Ves. 275; East v. Ferguson, 59 Ind. 169; Au

In pleading a waiver by taking the debtor's promissory note payable at a future day, it should be alleged that the note was taken in payment.[1]

If the creditor gives a receipt in full upon taking the debtor's note for the amount of a lien debt, while the receipt is *primâ facie* evidence of payment and a discharge of the lien, it is not necessarily so ; for the receipt is not an estoppel, but is open to explanation. It may be shown that there was no intention of surrendering the lien.[2]

1010. But where a note is regarded as payment, unless a contrary intention be shown, the acceptance of a promissory note for the amount for which a lien is claimed, is a discharge of the lien.[3] The taking of a promissory note for the claim is such a manifestation of intention to rely upon the personal security of the maker of the note that a waiver of the lien is inferred, whether the note be payable on demand or at a future time, and whether negotiated or not.[4] The taking of a note will not have this effect if the parties agree that it shall not be a satisfaction of the debt. It is in such case a mere liquidation or adjustment of the original debt. But if the creditor indorses such note for value, he cannot, while the note is outstanding, enforce his lien against the original debtor.[5]

The taking of a note of a third person, for the amount of a debt secured by a lien, does not discharge the lien if it be expressly agreed, in a receipt for the note, that it should not be regarded as payment until paid. The note in such case is taken conditionally.[6] If, on the other hand, the note be taken in discharge of the lien debt, the lien is lost.[7]

III. *By Taking Security.*

1011. The mere taking of security for the amount of a debt for which a lien is claimed does not ordinarily destroy

Sable River Boom Co. *v.* Sanborn, 36 Mich. 358 ; Murphy *v.* Lippe, 3 J. & S. (N. Y.) 542.

[1] East *v.* Ferguson, 59 Ind. 169.

[2] Sutton *v.* The Albatross, 2 Wall. Jr. 327 ; *S. C.* 1 Phila. 423.

[3] § **324**; Coburn *v.* Kerswell, 35 Me. 126; Green *v.* Fox, 7 Allen (Mass.), 85 ; Hutchins *v.* Olcutt, 4 Vt.

549; Kimball *v.* Ship Anna Kimball, 2 Cliff. 4; affirmed, 3 Wall. 37.

[4] Hutchins *v.* Olcutt, *supra.*

[5] Morton *v.* Austin, 12 Cush. (Mass.) 389.

[6] Prentiss *v.* Garland, 67 Me. 345.

[7] Dutton *v.* N. E. Mut. F. Ins. Co. 29 N. H. 153.

the lien. To have this effect there must be something in the facts of the case, or in the nature of the security taken, which is inconsistent with the existence of the lien, and destructive of it.[1] Some general expressions of Lord Eldon, in his judgment in the case of Cowell v. Simpson,[2] seem to support the view that a special agreement for security, or the taking of security, is of itself a waiver of a lien for the debt secured. " My opinion," he said, " therefore is, that where these special agreements are taken, the lien does not remain ; and whether the securities are due or not makes no difference." But in the case before him the security was taken by a solicitor who had a lien on his client's papers, and the security was in the form of promissory notes which were payable in three years, and it was very properly held that the security was in its nature inconsistent with the retention of a lien. That was the case decided, and it must be presumed that the fact of the long credit given was the reason why Lord Eldon held the lien to have been lost, rather than the fact of the giving of security.[3]

In the case of Angus v. McLachlan above cited, an innkeeper accepted from a guest, as security for his bill, a letter whereby he charged his interest in a certain ship with the payment of any account due or to become due. The innkeeper subsequently locked up the guest's room and detained his goods. It was held that the taking of this security was no waiver of the innkeeper's lien.

1012. **Where an equitable lien has once arisen and there is no express waiver, it is not waived by the subsequent taking of a legal and perfected lien to the same extent and upon the same property, nor is the equitable merged in the legal lien.** Thus, if there be an agreement to give a mortgage, and afterwards a mortgage be delivered which is void as against a purchaser or incumbrancer because not properly executed, the

---

[1] Angus v. McLachlan, 23 Ch. D. 330, per Kay, J.

[2] 16 Ves. 275, 279. In another case, Balch v. Symes, T. & R. 87, 92, Lord Eldon says: " Notwithstanding the Court of King's Bench has expressed a doubt whether my decision was right in the case of Cowell v. Simpson, I still entertain the opinion that an at- torney who takes a security abandons his lien."

[3] That taking a security payable at a distant day is a waiver of a lien, see, also, Hewison v. Guthrie, 3 Scott, 298; S. C. 2 Bing. N. C. 755; Mason v. Morley, 34 Beav. 471; Cood v. Pollard, 10 Price, 109 ; S. C. 9 Ib. 544.

creditor may rely upon the agreement which created an equitable lien, and this will prevail against a mechanic's lien which has intervened between the agreement and the executed mortgage.[1] "The equitable lien has had, in the case in hand, an existence. There has been no express waiver of it. The law is not anxious to imply a waiver. Whether it has ceased to exist, depends upon the rules of equity which determine whether a merger has taken place. It is a general rule that, where an equitable and legal estate meet and vest in the same ownership, the former is merged in the latter. But the doctrine of merger, as applied to mortgages, is founded upon equitable principles, and is only applied where equity requires that it should be. Where the owner of the legal and equitable titles has an interest in keeping those titles distinct, as where there is an intervening incumbrance, he has a right so to keep them, and the equitable title will not be merged and thereby extinguished; so that, even if we should treat the right obtained by the mortgage, after its due acknowledgment and recording, as a legal one, the equitable lien would not have been extinguished thereby. Still less so when we consider that both are liens of the same character, both equitable in their nature, one implied, the other express."[2]

1013. The taking of a mortgage upon the same property upon which the creditor claims a statutory lien may not displace the lien. The mortgage is regarded as a cumulative security; and the creditor may enforce either the lien or the mortgage.[3]

So, also, the taking of the collateral obligation of another person for the payment of the lien debt, does not ordinarily debar the lien-holder from claiming the security of his lien; unless the circumstances are such that an intention to waive the lien may reasonably be inferred.[4]

A futile effort to acquire a lien more specific and exclusive than that provided for by statute in nowise manifests an intention to release the property from the statutory lien, but it shows

---

[1] Payne v. Wilson, 74 N. Y. 348, affirming S. C. 11 Hun, 302.

[2] Folger, J., in Payne v. Wilson, supra.

[3] Roberts v. Wilcoxson, 36 Ark. 355; Franklin v. Meyer, 36 Ark. 96.

[4] §§ 587, 588. In New Mexico Territory, it is provided by statute that no person shall be entitled to a lien who has taken collateral security for the payment of the sum due him. Comp. Laws 1884, § 1538.

the very opposite intention, — an intention to hold the property. if possible, for the payment of the claim.[1]

1014. **An attachment of goods by one who claims a lien upon them, to secure the same debt for which the lien is claimed, is a waiver of the lien.**[2] The attachment is in effect an assertion that the property attached belongs to the defendant. Having made the attachment, he is estopped from afterwards asserting the contrary by claiming a lien upon the property.[3]

In like manner, a person having a lien on goods waives it by causing them to be taken on execution at his own suit, although he purchases the goods under the execution, and they are never removed from his premises; for, in order to sell, the sheriff must have had possession, and after he had possession with the assent of the person claiming the lien, the subsequent possession of the latter must have been acquired under the sale, and not by virtue of his lien.[4] Property in the hands of a person having a lien thereon cannot be taken from him under an attachment against the general owner. He has a right to retain it until discharged of the *onus ;* and if it be wrongfully taken away, he may maintain an action against the seizing officer for the tort. But he may waive his right, and if he does, it does not lie in the mouth of the debtor himself to object.[5]

IV. *By other Inconsistent Agreements and Claims.*

1015. **A lien is waived by making any agreement inconsistent with its existence,** though if the new agreement be not in writing, it will ordinarily be a question of fact for the jury whether the lien was waived or not. Thus, one in possession of a cow belonging to another, and having a lien upon it for keeping it, purchased the cow of the owner, and agreed that the cow should be and remain the property of the seller until paid for. There was no change of possession of the cow. It was held that it was not for the court to decide as a matter of law whether

---

[1] Clark *v.* Moore, 64 Ill. 273.

[2] § **328**; Legg *v.* Willard, 17 Pick. (Mass.) 140 ; Wingard *v.* Banning, 39 Cal. 543. See, however, Roberts *v.* Wilcoxson, 36 Ark. 355.

The lien may, unde rsome circumstances, be retained. Townsend *v.* Newell, 14 Pick. (Mass.) 332.

[3] This is especially the case where an attachment can only be made upon affidavit to the effect that the debt is not secured by lien or mortgage. Wingard *v.* Banning, *supra.*

[4] Jacobs *v.* Latour, 5 Bing. 130.

[5] Meeker *v.* Wilson, 1 Gall. 419, 425, per Story, J.

the lien was waived or not, but that it was a question for the jury whether the lien was intended and understood by the parties to be waived. The jury is to consider the new contract with all its attendant circumstances; and if nothing was said about the lien, the jury must find from all the evidence what the understanding of the parties was concerning the lien.[1]

1016. A special contract that a seller, shall have a lien on goods sold till payment, and that the possession of the purchaser shall be the possession of the seller, is not a waiver of a statutory lien. Thus a statutory lien for rails furnished to a railroad company is not affected by a special agreement that the manufacturer should have a lien on the rails till payment, and that the possession of the railroad should be the possession of the manufacturer.[2] Such a stipulation shows no purpose on the part of the manufacturer to waive his statutory lien. The evident purpose of such a stipulation is to secure a specific lien on the materials furnished, and to require them to be used in the construction of the railroad where they would become subject to the statutory lien. The contract, instead of showing a waiver of the statutory lien, shows a purpose to retain it.

1017. If a lien-holder purchases goods and takes a bill of sale from the general owner, and afterwards claims them solely under such purchase, he cannot, in a suit in regard to the title, set up his lien. Thus, a currier who had a lien upon skins which he was currying purchased them of the owner, partly in payment for the work done upon them, by a contract, though valid between the parties, yet void as against the seller's creditors. Proceedings in insolvency were commenced against the seller, and the messenger of the court of insolvency took possession of the goods. At the time the messenger took the goods away, the currier claimed them only as purchaser, and gave the messenger no notice of his lien, and made no demand for the amount of his lien. It was held that he could not set up his lien in a suit against the messenger for taking away the goods.[3]

---

[1] Pickett v. Bullock, 52 N. H. 354.

[2] Chicago & Alton R. R. Co. v. Union Rolling Mill Co. 109 U. S. 702. And see Clark v. Moore, 64 Ill. 273.

[3] Mexal v. Dearborn, 12 Gray (Mass.), 336, 337. Merrick, J., delivering the judgment of the court, said: "A lien is an incumbrance upon property, a claim upon it, which may be maintained against the general owner. But there is no foundation upon which

1018. A person having a lien waives it by claiming to own the property absolutely, and on that ground refusing to deliver it to the owner. A lien cannot be waived and resumed at pleasure.[1] When one who has a lien sets up a claim to the property hostile to the right of the owner, and wrongfully sells it, he cannot afterwards set up the lien as a bar to an action against him for his illegal act.[2]

A lien may be waived by setting up any claim of right of detention, instead of a claim under the lien.[3]

If one having a lien does not disclose it when the owner demands the property, but claims to be himself the owner, he is estopped from setting up a lien in defence to the owner's action to recover possession.[4]

But a factor does not waive his lien for advances on goods by declining to give information as to the amount of his advances to one claiming the goods who is not the party who placed them in his hands.[5]

1019. Refusal to deliver property on grounds inconsistent

he who owns the whole can create a special right in his own favor to a part. The inferior or partial title to a chattel necessarily merges in that which is absolute and unconditional, when both are united and held by the same individual. This is a general consequence. But in the present instance, it is obvious that the parties extinguished, and intended to extinguish, the lien which had been previously created upon the calfskins; for the value of the work and labor which had previously been bestowed upon them by the vendor was, by their express agreement, made part of the consideration of the sale. After such a transaction the rights of the parties were wholly changed." Upon the point of the waiver of the lien by concealment, the learned judge said: "The law will not allow a party to insist upon and enforce in his own behalf a secret lien upon personal property after he has claimed it unconditionally as his own, and has thereby induced another to act in relation to it, in some manner affecting his own interest, as he would, or might, not have done if he had been openly and fairly notified of the additional ground of claim. It would be fraudulent in him to practise such concealment to the injury of others ; and, to prevent the possibility of attempts so unjust becoming successful, the law implies that an intended concealment of that kind is of itself a waiver of the lien."

[1] Picquet v. M'Kay, 2 Blackford (Ind.), 465; Boardman v. Sill. 1 Campb. N. P. 410, n.; Munson v. Porter, 63 Iowa, 453.

[2] Andrews v. Wade (Pa.), 6 Atl. Rep. 48; Davis v. Bigler, 62 Pa. St. 242, 251.

[3] Boardman v. Sill, supra; Dirks v. Richards, Car. & M. 626. See, however, White v. Gainer, 2 Bing. 23.

[4] Maynard v. Anderson, 54 N. Y. 641; De Bouverie v. Gillespie, 2 Edm. Sel. Cas. 472.

[5] Buckley v. Handy, 2 Miles (Pa.), 449.

with a lien. — When property is demanded of a person who means to claim a lien upon it, but he refuses to surrender it upon a ground which is inconsistent with a lien, he is not allowed afterwards to set up a claim of lien of which the plaintiff was ignorant at the time he brought the action.[1] Retention on a ground inconsistent with a claim by virtue of a specific lien, operates as a waiver of the lien. On the trial the claimant will not be permitted to rest his refusal to deliver the property to the general owner on a different and distinct ground from that on which he claimed to retain the property at the time of the demand and refusal.

1020. A lien may not be waived by the mere omission of the claimant to assert his lien as the ground of his refusal to deliver up the property on the demand of the owner.[2]

A general refusal to surrender the goods, without specifying the ground of the refusal, may not be inconsistent with a subsequent claim of a lien. It is not necessary for the person of whom the demand is made to speak and claim to hold the goods by reason of a lien, if the person making the demand knows, or has reason to know, that the other has a lien, or is doing an act which would entitle him to a lien. But it may be that if the lien, or the ground of the lien, is unknown to the person making the demand, and the person in possession knows, or has reason to know this, it is the duty of the latter to give the former notice of the lien, if he is going to rely upon it.[3]

1021. The fact that a party claims a general lien when he is only entitled to a specific lien is no waiver of the latter lien. If, therefore, the general owner brings an action of trover for the property detained without tendering the amount of the specific lien, he cannot recover.[4] There are some cases, however,

---

[1] Boardman v. Sill, 1 Campb. 410, n.; Judah v. Kemp, 2 Johns. Cas. (N. Y.) 411; Weeks v. Goode, 6 C. B. (N. S.) 367; Jones v. Tarleton, 9 M. & W. 675; Saltus v. Everett, 20 Wend. (N. Y.) 267; Everett v. Saltus, 15 Ib. 474; Louisville & Nashville R. R. v. McGuire, 79 Ala. 395; Bean v. Bolton, 3 Phila. (Pa.) 87; Hanna v. Phelps, 7 Ind. 21; Piquet v. M'Kay, 2 Blackf. (Ind.) 465.

[2] White v. Gainer, 9 Moore, 41; S. C. 2 Bing. 23; 1 C. & P. 324; Everett v. Coffin, 6 Wend. (N. Y.) 603; Avery v. Hackley, 20 Wall. 407, 411; Fowler v. Parsons (Mass.), 9 N. East. Rep. 799, 803, per Field, J.

[3] Fowler v. Parsons (Mass.), 9 N. East. Rep. supra.

[4] § 334. Scarfe v. Morgan, 4 M. & W. 270. Alderson, B., said: "It seems to me you cannot say that, because

in which it is declared that, after one has refused to deliver up property on the ground of having a lien for a general balance of account, he cannot afterwards set up a specific lien, because, it is said, if he holds possession by virtue of a specific lien, it is obligatory upon him to apprise the owner of this ground of his claim at the time of the owner's demand for the property, so that the owner may then have the opportunity of paying or tendering the amount for which the lien exists.

But it is clear that one does not waive a specific lien by claiming not only this, but a general lien as well. Having a specific lien upon property, such as a lien for work upon it, he does not waive it if, at the time of the owner's demand for it, he mentions this ground to justify his right to detain the property, although he at the same time insists upon a right to detain it for a general balance of account, or for any other claim for which he has no right of lien. He need not, in such case, specify the amount of the particular charge for which a lien exists. All that is necessary is, that he should at the time of the demand apprise the owner of his claim to hold the property by virtue of a lien on which he had a legal right to detain it. It does not answer that he had a specific lien, but claimed to detain the property for a general balance of account, or for another claim for which he had no lien. He waives his lien in such case by not insisting upon it as the ground of his right of possession.[1]

A lien-holder does not lose his lien by detaining more property subject to the lien than is necessary to preserve it.[2]

1022. A creditor may have two liens for the same thing.[3] Thus, where the maker of a steam-engine reserved a lien upon it, and at the same time an express lien was created upon the real estate of the debtor upon which the engine was placed, it was held that the taking of the one was no waiver of the other.[4].

1023. The lien is lost or waived if the claim for which

the party claims more than it may be ultimately found he had a right to, he would not have a right to a tender of the sum which the other ought to pay." Munson v. Porter, 63 Iowa, 453.

[1] Thatcher v. Harlan, 2 Houston (Del.), 178; Brown v. Holmes, 21 Kans. 687.

[2] Hall v. Tittabawassee Boom Co. 51 Mich. 377.

[3] Lagow v. Badollet, 1 Blackford (Ind.), 416; contra, McRea v. Creditors, 16 La. Ann. 305.

[4] Lagow v. Badollet, supra.

there is a lien is so mingled and intermixed with other claims, for which the claimant is entitled to no lien, that it is impossible to distinguish between the two.[1] By commingling privileged claims with those for which there is no lien, so that the amount of the lien is not kept ascertainable without restating the accounts, the lien is impliedly waived.[2] But a lien is not waived by merely restating the account, and deducting three small items for which no lien is claimed.[3]

1024. A lien is lost when the claim is merged in a judgment with other claims for which no lien exists; but if a suit is brought upon such claims, the lien may be preserved by amending the writ before judgment by striking out the items for which there is no lien, and taking judgment upon the items for which there is a lien.[4]

A statute exempting household furniture and working tools from execution, provided that such exemption should not extend to any execution issued on a demand for the purchase-money of such furniture or tools. A judgment for an entire sum was recovered upon separate and distinct debts only, one of which was for the purchase-price of property exempt from execution, and the judgment creditor sought to levy this portion of the execution upon property exempt from execution. It was held that he could not levy the execution in this manner. His right as against exempt property is in the nature of a particular lien on specific property, and must be enforced by itself upon that property. He moreover waived his right to follow the property sold by him by taking a judgment which included other debts. By taking such a judgment he is deemed to have elected to abandon his claim to follow the specific property.[5]

1025. Tender of actual indebtedness. — If the demand for which a lien is claimed is deemed excessive, the owner of the property, in order to dissolve it, should tender such a sum as he himself considers reasonable.[6] If one wrongfully claims a lien

---

[1] Kelley v. Kelley, 77 Me. 135 ; see Baker v. Fessenden, 71 Me. 292.

[2] Terry v. McClintock, 41 Mich. 492, 505.

[3] Comstock v. McCracken, 53 Mich. 123.

[4] Sands v. Sands, 74 Me. 239; Spofford v. True, 33 Me. 283, 297.

[5] Hickox v. Fay, 36 Barb. (N. Y.) 9.

[6] Hall v. Tittabawassee Boom Co. 51 Mich. 377; Scarfe v. Morgan, 4 M. & W. 270 ; Munson v. Porter, 63 Iowa, 453.

for a larger indebtedness than that for which he has a lien, he may perhaps be deemed to have waived or forfeited his lien, especially if he fails to disclose the true amount of the lien, and this cannot be presumed to be within the knowledge of the debtor, so that he could tender the true amount for which the lien attached. But if the claimant has rendered an itemized account which shows the nature of his demand and the time for which the charge was made, and if the debtor's knowledge of the true amount of the account for which there is a lien may be presumed, and it does not distinctly appear that the claimant asserts a lien for the whole balance of the account, or for a greater amount than he actually had a lien for, he does not waive his lien. "If, under any circumstances, a lien could be deemed forfeited by the assertion of a claim for a lien for too large an amount, the assertion should be clear and distinct, and operate to interfere in the present with a claimed right on the part of the owner." [1]

The mere demand of an excessive sum by a creditor holding a lien does not dispense with a tender by the debtor of the sum really due, unless the demand be so made that it amounts to a declaration by the creditor that a tender of a smaller sum is useless; for in that case a tender is dispensed with,[2] although it appears that the debtor was unwilling to tender the amount really due.[3] The claim of a general lien may dispense with the tender of the amount of a specific lien to which the creditor is entitled, and the owner may maintain trover without a tender.[4]

1026. **Tender of performance of an agreement** will not operate to extinguish the lien by which the agreement is secured, if it is not unequivocal and reasonably capable of being understood by the other party as a *bonâ fide* tender of the requisite thing, act, or service; and the offer itself should be accompanied by circumstances fairly implying control of the necessary means, and possession of the necessary ability, to fulfil it.[5]

1027. **A lien is not waived** by the lien-holder's giving of

[1] Munson v. Porter, 63 Iowa, 453, per Adams, J.

[2] Dirks v. Richards, 4 M. & G. 574; S. C. 5 Scott N. R. 534; Kerford v. Mondel, 28 L. J. Ex. 303.

[3] The Norway, 3 Moore P. C. (N. S.) 245; S. C. 13 W. R. 1085.

[4] Jones v. Tarleton, 9 M. & W. 675.

[5] Selby v. Hurd, 51 Mich. 1, per Graves, C. J.

a receipt for the property without making a reservation of the lien. The owner of certain barley pledged to a bank as collateral for a loan, wishing to have the barley malted, arranged with the owner of a malt-house, with the concurrence of the bank, for converting the barley into malt. The maltster delivered to the bank a receipt for the barley, which he agreed to hold subject to the written order of the bank ; nothing being said in the receipt about the charges for malting or any lien therefor. It was held that the absence of a reservation of such lien did not deprive the malt man of his lien.[1]

1028. No waiver arises from an unintentional relinquishment of a right not known to exist. Thus, one having a lien on certain cows, being in ignorance of the fact that his lien extends to their offspring, does not waive his lien by telling an attaching officer that the latter did not belong to him.[2] To constitute a waiver, there must be an intentional relinquishment of a known right.

1029. One who has undertaken to perform certain labor and has failed to fulfil his contract, and performed only a part of the service, has no lien for what he has done. The other party is entitled, if he elects, to recover damages for the non-performance of the contract ; and, these damages being of uncertain amount, it is uncertain whether the person who has undertaken to perform the labor will, on final adjustment, receive anything for the labor he has done. Under such circumstances he cannot be permitted to hold possession by virtue of the lien until this matter is settled.[3]

1030. A creditor having a lien does not forfeit it by using the property so far as is necessary for its preservation. Thus, a livery-stable keeper may use a horse left in his care to the extent of giving the horse proper exercise. If he should go beyond this and habitually let the horse to others, he might be guilty of a conversion of the horse to his own use, so that he would not afterwards be allowed to occupy the inconsistent position of claiming a lien upon the same thing. But even if the

---

[1] Hazard v. Manning, 8 Hun (N. Y.), 613.

[2] Boynton v. Braley, 54 Vt. 92.

[3] Hodgdon v. Waldron, 9 N. H. 66; and see Hilger v. Edwards, 5 Nev. 84.

keeper uses the horse beyond the extent of giving it proper exercise, or lets it to others, if the owner knows of such use, and at times when the horse is in use he accepts, without objection, a substituted horse, the owner cannot claim that there is such a conversion of the horse as will defeat the lien.[1]

1031. The waiver of a lien by agreement is a new and original consideration for a promise by a person not personally bound for the debt secured by the lien to pay that debt; and such need not be in writing, as the promise is original and not collateral, and so not within the statute of frauds.[2] A release of a lien under seal, executed on a promise to pay the money for which the lien was claimed, is void for failure of consideration.[3]

1032. The fact that the contract under which a lien is claimed was executed on Sunday does not defeat the lien after the contract has been executed, and a property upon which the lien is claimed has passed into the possession of the person claiming the lien.   Both parties in such case are *in pari delicto*, and the party who has possession is in the better position. The property must remain in the possessor's hands until the lien is discharged by payment.[4]

---

[1] Munson *v.* Porter, 63 Iowa, 453.
[2] Robinson *v.* Springfield Iron Co. 39 Hun (N. Y.), 634; Prime *v.* Koeh-ler, 77 N. Y. 91; Mallory *v.* Gillett, 21 N. Y. 412.
[3] Benson *v.* Mole, 9 Phila. (Pa.) 66.
[4] Scarfe *v.* Morgan, 4 M. & W. 270.

I. *At Law and in Equity.*

1033. A common law lien, as has already been stated, is merely the right of a person in possession of the property of another to detain it until certain demands, either specific or general, are satisfied. In general there is no remedy for enforcing the lien unless it is given by statute.[1] In this respect a lien differs essentially from a pledge; for a pledgee, when the debt has become due and remains unpaid, may, after due notice, sell the thing pledged and reimburse himself from the proceeds.[2]

A sale of the property by the person in possession and claiming a lien, without the consent of the owner, is a conversion of

---

[1] § 335; Pothonier *v.* Dawson, Holt (N. P.), 383; Jones *v.* Pearle, 1 Stra. 557; Lickbarrow *v.* Mason, 6 East, 21, note; Thames Iron Works Co. *v.* Patent Derrick Co. 1 J. & H. 93; Doane *v.* Russell, 3 Gray (Mass.), 382; Busfield *v.* Wheeler, 14 Allen (Mass.), 139; Briggs *v.* Boston & Lowell R. R. Co. 6 Ib. 246; Rodgers *v.* Grothe, 58 Pa. St. 414.

In Doane *v.* Russell, *supra*, which arose before the enactment in Massachusetts of a statute for the enforcement of liens, Chief Justice Shaw observed with reference to the security of a lien-holder: "If it be said that a right to retain the goods, without the right to sell, is of little or no value, it may be answered that it is certainly not so adequate a security as a pledge with a power of sale; still, it is to be considered that both parties have rights which are to be regarded by the law, and the rule must be adapted to general convenience. In the greater number of cases, the lien for work is small in comparison with the value, to the owner, of the article subject to lien; and in most cases it would be for the interest of the owner to satisfy the lien and redeem the goods, as in the case of the tailor, the coach-maker, the innkeeper, the carrier, and others. Whereas, many times, it would cause great loss to the general owner to sell the suit of clothes or other articles of personal property. But further, it is to be considered that the security of this lien, such as it is, is superadded to the holder's right to recover for his services by action."

[2] Jones on Pledges, §§ 2, 720–729.

it. But if the person having a lien does dispose of it, though wrongfully, he may set up his lien as a defence to any action which the owner may bring against him for a conversion.[1]

1034. If one holding goods under a lien sells them without legal proceedings, the sale is a conversion and renders him liable to the owner in an action for such conversion, or the owner may resume possession of the goods wherever he may find them. The lien only gives the holder the right of possession until the debt is paid, and he can do nothing else to enforce payment except in pursuance of some statute providing for the enforcement of liens.

In a suit by the owner of goods against a bailee who has converted the goods on which he has bestowed labor and acquired a lien, the latter may set up his lien claim in reduction of damages.[2]

If, however, he does not set up his claim in that suit, he may afterwards maintain a suit for the debt. In trover for the conversion of the goods, the owner would recover the full value of the goods at the time of the conversion, in case the defendant does not set up his lien claim in reduction of damages; and *primâ facie* the value of the goods at the time of conversion is the measure of damages recovered.[3] " It may be greatly against the interest of the defendant to present his claim in such action, and against his rights to compel him to do so. Cases may readily be supposed where the value of the work and material put upon plaintiff's property would greatly exceed the value of the property in its altered condition. The article, with all the labor put upon it, might entirely fail to meet the purposes which the owner designed it for, and be valueless for any other: if, being left upon the hands of the artisan, he should destroy it, by carelessness or design, to rid himself of it, it would not be just to compel the defendant, in a suit for its conversion, to set up his claim, to be balanced and liquidated by the inferior value of the converted goods. He may prefer to pay the damages and bring suit for his debt, and he has, in his election, the right to do so." [4]

---

[1] §§ **523, 525**; Briggs v. Boston & Lowell R. R. Co. 6 Allen (Mass.), 246; Rodgers v. Grothe, 58 Pa. St. 414.

[2] Longstreet v. Phile, 39 N. J. L. 63.

[3] Edmondson v. Nuttall, 17 C. B. (N. S.) 280.

[4] Longstreet v. Phile, *supra*, per Knapp, J.

1035. A lien confers a special property and the right of possession, and if the holder is unlawfully deprived of the possession, he may maintain an action of replevin for the purpose of reclaiming it, or an action of trespass or trover for damages.

The general owner cannot maintain trespass either against the lien-holder or a third person for the property subject to the lien, so long as the lien-holder remains in either actual or constructive possession; for the gist of the action is an injury to the plaintiff's possession, and, the possession belonging to the lien-holder, he alone can maintain trespass for the property.[1]

When articles subject to a lien are taken from the possession of one entitled to a lien upon them, the general owner may maintain trover for them, and the lien cannot be set up in bar except by the lien-holder or by his express authority. The lien cannot be set up by a wrong-doer to defeat the action of the general owner.[2]

1036. Lien-holder's measure of damages in trover and trespass. — In an action of trespass by a person having a lien upon goods against the owner, or those claiming under him, for the removal or destruction of the goods, the measure of damages is compensation to the plaintiff for his loss, and consequently he can recover damages only to the extent of his lien.[3] There is a distinction to be observed between the measure of damages in an action against the general owner and in an action against a stranger: for, while in the former case he can recover only according to his special interest, in the latter case he may recover the full value, though exceeding the amount of his lien.[4] The amount recovered in excess of the lien claim, or other special interest, he will hold in trust for the general owner.

[1] Wilson v. Martin, 40 Vt. 88; Cowing v. Snow, 11 Mass. 415.

[2] Jones v. Sinclair, 2 N. H. 319; Bradley v. Spofford, 23 N. H. 444.

[3] Outcalt v. Durling, 25 N. J. Eq. 443; Ingersoll v. Van Bokkelin, 7 Cow. (N. Y.) 670; S. C. 5 Wend. 315; Spoor v. Holland, 8 Wend. (N. Y.) 445; Burdict v. Murray, 3 Vt. 302.

[4] Lyle v. Barker, 5 Binn. 457, 460; Heydon and Smith's Case, 13 Coke, 69. "And so is the better opinion in 11 Hen. IV. 23, that he who hath a special property of the goods at a certain time shall have a general action of trespass against him who hath the general property, and upon the evidence damages shall be mitigated; but clearly the bailee, or he who hath a special property, shall have a general action of trespass against a stranger, and shall recover all in damages, because that he is chargeable over."

1037. If the property upon which it is sought to enforce a lien be in the adverse possession of a third person, the lien claimant should first recover possession of the property, or should sue for a wrongful conversion of it. If he brings an action to enforce the lien without making such third person a party defendant and obtains judgment, this is void as to such third person.[1]

1038. Generally a court of equity has no jurisdiction to enforce a common law lien by sale merely because there is no remedy at law, or because the retaining of possession under a passive lien involves expense or inconvenience. Generally a lien at law or by statute can be enforced only under express statutory provisions. An equitable form of procedure may be expressly provided; but in the absence of such provision, a lien cannot be enforced in equity unless jurisdiction is acquired under well established rules.[2]

This subject was ably discussed by Vice-Chancellor Wood in the High Court of Chancery, where it was sought to enforce a ship-builder's common law lien by a bill in equity.[3] "It was argued," he said, "that, to create a mere right of retainer, involving considerable expenditure, and rendering the subject of the lien utterly useless to both parties, would be absurd; and, to a certain extent, there is authority to show that this is not the law. The case referred to, of a horse having eaten its full value, is one instance of a right of sale being held to flow from a lien.[4] In one statement this is said to rest on the local customs of London and Exeter, but elsewhere it is treated as a general

---

[1] Wingard v. Banning, 39 Cal. 543.

[2] See §§ **94, 112**, *supra*,

[3] Thames Iron Works Co. v. Patent Derrick Co. 1 J. & H. 93, 97.

[4] In Bacon's Abr. (Liens, D.) it is said that, "by the custom of London and Exeter, if a man commit a horse to an hostler, and he eat out the price of his head, the hostler may take him as his own, upon the reasonable appraisement of four of his neighbors; which was, it seems, a custom arising from the abundance of traffic with strangers, that could not be known, to charge them with the action. But the innkeeper hath no power to sell

the horse, by the general custom of the whole kingdom." He cites among other cases Jones v. Pearle, 1 Str. 557, where, "in trover for three horses, the defendant pleaded that he kept a public inn at Glastenbury, and that the plaintiff was a carrier and used to set up his horses there, and, £36 being due to him for the keeping horses, which was more than they were worth, he detained and sold them; and on demurrer judgment was given for the plaintiff, an innkeeper having no power to sell horses, except within the city of London."

right. Whatever the law may be, as a matter of fact, it is certainly very common for such a right to be exercised ; for advertisements threatening to sell horses or other chattels, unless removed by a given date, are constantly to be seen. The contention was, that, as a corollary from the case I have referred to, there followed a general rule of law, that wherever the retaining of a chattel under a lien occasions considerable expense, there the right of sale must arise. But no such doctrine has ever been held, and the authorities on the contrary point to the conclusion, that the right of sale cannot be raised on the mere ground of expense of retaining the chattel which is the subject of the lien. If it could, it would arise in every case of a lien on bulky goods, the retaining of which must involve warehousing expenses. It is not material to consider how far such a case as that put by Story, of notice being given that expense is being incurred, and that if the goods are not removed they will be sold, may hereafter be held to justify a sale, because the present case does not raise such a question. If it did, it would be necessary to analyze the right of lien, and consider whether it amounts to anything more than this, — that a person who chooses to insist on the right of retainer which the law gives, and is willing to put up with any inconvenience which may be the consequence, is at liberty to do so, but has no further right. Even though such an arrangement should be most inconvenient for both parties, it does not follow that this is not the law."

1039. A court of equity has jurisdiction to enforce a lien when matters of account are involved, although the lien may not in itself be an equitable lien.[1] Thus, where a landlord reserved in his lease a lien for rent upon the improvements made or to be made by the lessee on the demised premises, and upon the lessee's interest in the lease, and the lien is enforcible against those claiming under the lessee, and the lease has been assigned and the premises sublet, there is such necessity for taking an account as to bring the case within the equitable jurisdiction of the court. If, pending the bill in such case, rents coming to the assignee have been paid into court, on establishing the lien the court may require the money to be applied to the rent due from the assignee. The right to control the income follows as a sequence from the right to enforce the lien.[2]

[1] Story Eq. Jur. §§ 506, 1217.   [2] Webster v. Nichols, 104 Ill. 160.

1040. But the mere fact that after the sale accounts may require adjustment by the court, does not give jurisdiction to a court of equity to decree a sale.[1] There is no right to an account in equity where the debt for which a lien is claimed is a liquidated debt with interest which is a mere matter of calculation. "Even if the lien (in such case) were supposed to be equivalent to a pledge," said Wood, V. C., "it would be only a pledge for an ascertained sum, and no accounts would be necessary. Were this otherwise, I know of no authority for saying that where the pledgor makes no claim to redeem, and the pledgee insists on selling hostilely, this court acquires jurisdiction in respect of the sale, because after a sale there may be some possibility of questions of account arising such as to require the aid of the court. . . . If such a jurisdiction existed, it would arise in all cases of pledges of chattels ; and I am not aware of any case in which relief of this description has been asked."

1041. In a few states it is held that a court of equity has jurisdiction to enforce liens of personal property generally. Thus, it was held in Kentucky that a court of equity may order the sale of a horse belonging to an innkeeper's guest, in satisfaction of the lien upon the horse.[2] In Illinois it is held that liens for the enforcement of which there is no special statutory provision are enforcible only in equity. This is true not only of equitable liens but also of all statutory liens, except when the lien is in the nature of a pledge, and possession accompanies the lien. A court of law does not possess the means of enforcing such liens.[3]

It is a general rule that all persons who claim an interest in property on which a lien is sought to be foreclosed should be made parties to the suit.[4] If the lien be limited in duration to a specified time, it must be shown affirmatively that the proceeding to enforce it was commenced within that time.[5]

1042. The courts of the United States have jurisdiction for the enforcement of statutory liens wherever the citizen-

[1] Thames Iron Works Co. v. Patent Derrick Co. 1 J. & H. 93.

[2] Black v. Brennan, 5 Dana (Ky.), 310.

[3] Cairo & Vincennes R. R. Co. v. Fackney, 78 Ill. 116.

[4] Jones on Chattel Mortg. § 783; Templeman v. Gresham, 61 Tex. 50; Hall v. Hall, 11 Tex. 526, 547; Trittipo v. Edwards, 35 Ind. 467.

[5] Union Slate Co. v. Tilton, 73 Me. 207.

ship of the parties would give jurisdiction in other cases. This jurisdiction, whether at common law or in equity, is not derived from the power of the state, but from the laws of the United States. The United States courts are not necessarily confined to the remedy prescribed by the state law ; but this remedy will be pursued if it be substantially consistent with the ordinary modes of proceeding used on the chancery side of these courts.[1]

1043. A lien valid by the laws of one state is not lost by taking the property to another state. Although the holder of the lien can enforce it only in accordance with the laws of the state under which the lien accrued, yet the owner of the property cannot take it away from the lien-holder.[2] The lien is as perfect in the one state as in the other, so long as the lien-holder retains possession. The title and claim under the lien may be set up in defence of the possession wherever these may be assailed, just as the title under a mortgage may be shown in defence in any state to which the mortgaged property may be taken.[3] Whether the lien-holder could maintain an action in another state against one who had obtained possession of the property wrongfully, is another question.

1044. A lien which has accrued to a partnership is not lost by the dissolution of the firm, and the assignment by one partner to the other of his interest in the claim. All statutory proceedings for the enforcement of the claim must be had in the name of the partnership. It is a general principle that the continuing partner takes all the rights of the firm, and may exercise them in the name of the firm, for all purposes necessary for their enforcement and for closing up the joint business.[4]

1045. A lien-holder who has a lien upon two funds or upon two pieces of property for his debt is not allowed to enforce his lien in such a way as to exclude the lien of another who has a lien upon only one of the funds or pieces of property ; but he may be compelled to resort in the first instance to the fund or property upon which the other has no lien, if that

---

[1] Fitch v. Creighton, 24 How. 159.
[2] Jaquith v. American Express Co. 60 N. H. 61.
[3] Jones on Chattel Mortgages, § 452.
[4] Busfield v. Wheeler, 14 Allen (Mass.), 139.

course be necessary for the satisfaction of the claims of both lien-holders.[1] This principle, however, is only applicable where the lien-holder's right to resort to both funds is clear, and not seriously disputed, and where the remedies available for reaching and applying the funds are reasonably prompt and efficient.[2] Thus, a lien-holder will not be compelled in the first instance to resort to the personal obligation of a third person, who would probably contest his liability and delay the collection of the lien debt.[3]

1046. **This equitable principle has no application as between creditors of different persons.** It is confined to cases where two or more persons are creditors of the same debtor, and have successive demands upon the same property, the creditor prior in right having other securities. Thus, a landlord having a statutory lien for his rent upon the crops raised upon the rented premises, whether raised by the tenant or sub-tenant, cannot be compelled to so exercise his statutory right as to protect or benefit another person who may have a lien on the crop of the under-tenant.[4] A landlord having sued out an attachment to enforce such a lien on the crops, and having afterwards released the attachment on the crops of under-tenants who had paid their rent to their immediate landlord, does not thereby forfeit or impair his right to subject other portions of the crop, or to proceed against a third person who, having notice of the landlord's lien, has received and sold a portion of the crop. The landlord having brought an action against a merchant who had received and sold some of the products raised by under-tenants, on account of advances made to them, the merchant has no right to insist that the landlord's demand shall be credited with the value of the crops so released from attachment by the landlord.[5]

---

[1] Bruner's Appeal, 7 W. & S. (Pa.) 269; Bryant v. Stephens, 58 Ala. 636; Goss v. Lester, 1 Wis. 43.

[2] Kidder v. Page, 28 N. H. 382.

[3] Block v. Latham, 63 Tex. 414.

[4] *Ex parte* Kendal, 17 Ves. 514, 520. "It was never said that, if I have a demand against A and B, that a creditor of B shall compel me to go against A, without more. If I have a demand against both, the creditors of B have no right to compel me to seek payment from A, if not founded in some equity, giving B, for his own sake, as if he were surety, etc., a right to compel me to seek payment of A. It must be established that it is just and equitable that A *ought to pay in the first instance,* or there is no equity to compel a man to go against A." Per Lord Eldon.

[5] Robinson v. Lehman, 72 Ala. 401.

This sale has no application in a proceeding at law. It is enforced only in equity.[1]

1047. The effect of the enforcement of a lien upon the rights of other lien-holders and of bona fide purchasers, depends largely upon the nature of the lien. Possession under a common law lien is notice of the rights of the person in possession, so that any sale of the property by the general owner, or any liens upon it created by him, must be subject to the rights of the lien-holder in possession. Whether such liens take precedence of liens already existing depends upon the circumstances attending the creation of the lien.[2] Equitable liens and liens by contract, where the possession of the property remains with the general owner, cannot be enforced after a sale to a *bonâ fide* purchaser without notice.[3] As between such liens and other liens upon the same property, much depends upon the priority in time at which the liens come into existence.[4] An attorney who has obtained a judgment for his client has priority over an assignee of the judgment; for the attorney is regarded as an equitable assignee of the judgment from the time it was rendered; and under the statutes of many of the states, he is an equitable assignee of the cause of action, so that his lien attaches from the commencement of the suit. Any person taking an assignment of the cause of action, or of the judgment, from the client, must take notice of the attorney's connection with the suit, and can acquire only the rights of the assignor.[5]

The priority of statutory liens depends for the most part upon the terms of the statutes creating them. A landlord's statutory lien generally attaches from the beginning of the tenancy, and any person dealing with the tenant, with respect to the property subject to the lien, must take notice of the effect of the statute.[6] But the lien is generally defeated by a sale made by the tenant to purchaser for value and in good faith.[7] Priorities under statutory liens are also affected by notice arising from the possession of the lien-holder. Thus, the possession of animals by a stable-keeper or agistor is constructive notice to a purchaser of his

---

[1] Hunter *v.* Whitefield, 89 Ill. 229.

[2] See § **744**, *supra.*

[3] See § **95**, *supra.*
  See § **96**, *supra.*

[5] See §§ **226–228**, *supra.*

[6] See §§ **551–560**, *supra.*

[7] See §§ **577–582**, *supra.*

claim to a lien, just as possession under a common law lien is constructive notice of the claim of such lien-holder.[1]

1048. **Rights of bona fide purchasers for value.** — A statutory lien may be given priority by the express terms of the statute. It is a characteristic feature of the statutes giving liens to lumbermen, that they are declared paramount to all other liens or claims against the property.[2] Whether such a statute gives a lumberman priority from the time the labor is performed, as against a subsequent *bonâ fide* purchaser as well as against the holders of other claims and liens, is a question which has been ably discussed and determined in recent cases in Michigan and Wisconsin; and it is held that the lien does not prevail against a *bonâ fide* purchaser who has no notice of it through the claimant's possession of the property, or his filing a claim or petition under the statute, or through actual notice.[3] The language of the statutes — "all other claims or liens" — is not regarded as broad enough, or sufficiently specific, to cover the claim of a subsequent *bonâ fide* purchaser for value without notice.

In the Wisconsin case, Mr. Justice Orton, delivering the opinion of the court, said:[4] "The language would have to be forced beyond its natural meaning to embrace such a case; and we do not think that the legislature intended such a meaning, for it has omitted the use of language to express it as against the well-known policy of the law governing the transfer of personal property, for the protection of *bonâ fide* purchasers, in an open market for value, without notice of prior claims thereon. . . . The paramount importance and incalculable value of personal property in these modern times make its ready and easy transfer from hand to hand, and the protection of *bonâ fide* purchasers thereof, absolutely essential to our modern systems of trade and commerce. Secret trusts, liens, and incumbrances, and unknown and concealed claims and interests, in and upon personal property, and especially that kind of personal property that enters so largely into the general commerce of a country, would,

---

[1] See §§ **691–697**, *supra.*

[2] See §§ **704, 727**, *supra.* ·

[3] Haifley *v.* Haynes, 37 Mich. 535; Au Sable River Boom Co. *v.* Sanborn, 36 Mich. 358; Smith *v.* Shell Lake Lumber Co. (Wis.) 31 N. W. Rep. 694.

[4] Smith *v.* Shell Lake Lumber Co. *supra.* Mr. Justice Taylor delivered a dissenting opinion. The decision of the court, as delivered by Mr. Justice Orton, seems to be in accordance with sound principles and the best precedents.

if enforced by law, work the greatest injustice, and be utterly destructive of the greatest financial interest that any country can have. . . . Logs, timber, lumber, including boards, shingle, and lath, constitute most valuable and important articles of our trade and commerce, and are readily and necessarily, and almost constantly, being transferred and sold, in wholesale and retail, in open market, and carried and scattered over vast distances by land and water. This interest and trade are too vast and important to be clogged, impeded, and incumbered by secret liens, following them into all the distant markets of the land, to be enforced in violation of such a cardinal principle to facilitate and protect the sale of personal property.

"In view of these considerations and authorities, what is the true interpretation of our statutes giving to laborers thereon a lien upon logs, timber, and lumber? What is the object or purpose of filing a claim for such lien in the office of the clerk of the circuit court of the county unless it be for *notice* to somebody? It is called ' the *notice* of such lien.' [1] This constructive notice would in most cases be the only notice a subsequent purchaser would be likely to have. If he has actual notice or knowledge of such facts and circumstances as to imply it, or to put him on inquiry of such liens, then he is not an innocent or *bonâ fide* purchaser as against them, and should not be protected, and will not be by a reasonable construction of the statute. The laborer, while he is working upon the logs, timber, or lumber, is protected by the notice inherent in this very act in connection with the article itself, equivalent to possession of it, as in common law liens. After he has completed his labor upon it, he can at once file his claim, and his protection will continue. It is not necessary that he should delay his remedy until the article has been removed and gone into the markets of the country, and into the hands of many subsequent purchasers for value and in good faith, without any notice whatever of his claim. The proper meaning of the statute would seem to be that the laborer has a statutory lien for the value of his labor upon the logs or lumber from the time of its commencement. But it is a lien that he must claim in the way provided for, or he will be held to have waived it. He has a lien, no doubt,

---

[1] R. S. 1878, § 3341. The statute under which this case arose was §§ 3329–3342 of R. S. 1878, as amended by Laws 1882, ch. 319 ; since amended by Laws 1885, ch. 469.

against all the world having actual or constructive notice of it.
. . . If this peculiar language of our statute can have force without
violating the great principle and clear public policy of the
law that protects *bonâ fide* purchasers in the usual course of
trade for value, without notice of the lien, then such should be
its construction. If one purchase, before the filing of the claim,
with notice that a certain person has worked upon the article to
produce it, and the time has not expired for the filing of his
claim, it would seem proper that he should take notice of such a
laborer's lien upon it. Or if he had been informed that a lien
existed, or had such knowledge as to put him on inquiry of it,
and be bound to so inquire, he could scarcely be called a *bonâ
fide* purchaser without notice. In this way the laborer can have
ample protection of his lien, without any infraction of, or violent
exception to, the general law which protects subsequent *bonâ
fide* purchasers without notice."

II. *By Statute.*

1049. By recent legislation, remedies by sale have been
very generally provided for the common law liens and for
those created by statute. In only a few states, however, has
legislation reached the comprehensive form of a general provision for enforcing all liens, or all similar liens. In the preceding
chapters have been given the statutory provisions applicable to
the enforcement of the different liens; and reference has been
made to the present chapter for the statutory provisions which
are of general application. Much of the legislation on the subject of liens has been fragmentary, uncertain, and apparently
experimental; and it is to be hoped and expected that more
comprehensive and better considered legislation will follow.

1050. Colorado.[1] — If any charges due any ranchman, agistor,
or livery-stable keeper, or to any keeper of a hotel or boarding-
house, or to any common carrier or warehouseman, or to any
mechanic for labor upon personal property for which a lien is
given, be not paid within thirty days after the same becomes due

---

[1] G. S. 1883, ch. 65, §§ 2121–2126.
For a special statute authorizing the
sale of goods received by a common
carrier, commission merchant, or
warehouseman, and not called for by
the consignee, see § 342, *supra*.

And for a special statute authorizing any commission merchant or warehouseman to sell goods on which he
has made advances, see § 482, *supra*.

and payable, the mechanic, innkeeper, agistor, or other person to whom such lien is given, may apply to any justice of the peace of the county wherein he resides to appoint appraisers to appraise the several articles of personal property whereon such lien is claimed. Such justice shall thereupon appoint, by warrant under his hand, three reputable householders of the county, not interested in the matter, to appraise such personal property.

The appraisers shall be sworn by the justice to well and faithfully appraise and value all such personal property, and shall thereupon proceed to view and appraise the same, and shall return their appraisement, wherein shall be set down each article separately, to the justice by whom they were appointed, within ten days after their appointment.

After such appraisement is made, the person to whom such lien is given may, after giving ten days' prior notice of the time and place of such sale, with a description of the property sold, by publication in some newspaper published in the county wherein he resides (or, if there be no such newspaper, then by posting in three public places within such county), and delivering to the owner of such personal property, or, if he do not reside in the county, transmitting by mail to him at his usual place of abode, if known, a copy of such notice, proceed to sell such personal property, or so much thereof as may be necessary, at public auction, for cash in hand, at any public place within such county, between the hours of ten A. M. and four P. M. of the day appointed; and from the proceeds thereof may pay the reasonable costs of such appraisement, notice, and sale, and his reasonable charges for which he has his lien, together with the reasonable cost of keeping such property up to the time of sale. The residue of the proceeds and of the property unsold he shall render to the owner.

No such sale shall be made for less than two thirds of the appraised value of the article sold, nor except upon due notice, as required by preceding section. Every such sale made in violation of the provisions of this section shall be absolutely void.

At such sale the person to whom such lien is given may become the purchaser.

In any case where the property to be sold cannot conveniently be sold in one day, the sale may be continued from day to day by public outcry at the place of sale. Upon the completion of such sale, the person to whom the lien is given hereby shall cause a sale bill thereof to be filed with the justice of the peace before whom such appraisement was had, in which shall be set down the sum for which each separate article of property was sold, and the name of the purchaser. The justice shall record such sale bill in his docket, and preserve the original thereof, together with the appraisement.

1051. **Dakota Territory.**[1] — An action to foreclose a lien upon a chattel may be maintained by an innkeeper, boarding-house keeper, mechanic, workman, bailee, or other person having a lien at common law or under the statutes of this territory. A judgment in favor of the plaintiff must specify the amount of the lien, and direct a sale of the chattel, to satisfy the same and costs, by the sheriff or other officer of the court, in like manner as when the sheriff sells personal property under execution, and the application by him of the sale, less his fees and expenses, to the payment of the judgment and costs. The judgment must also provide for the payment of the surplus to the owner of the chattel, and for the safe keeping of such surplus if necessary, until it is claimed by him.

1052. **Florida.**[2] — Whenever any person shall wish to proceed against any property upon which he shall have a lien, he may commence his suit in the ordinary form, and shall have judgment against the original debtor for the amount that shall be found due to him, and shall have the liberty of taking his

---

[1] Codes 1883, §§ 674, 675 of Code of Civil Procedure.

For a special statute authorizing carriers to sell unclaimed goods, see § 344, *supra.*

For a special statute for the enforcement of an innkeeper's lien, see § 528, *supra.*

As to liens of livery-stable keepers and agistors, see § 652, *supra.*

As to the enforcement of liens of mechanics and artisans for making or repairing any article of personal property, see § 752, *supra.*

A justice of the peace has jurisdiction of such action, where the amount of the lien claimed is less than one hundred dollars, concurrent with the District Court.

Any other existing right or remedy to foreclose or enforce a lien upon a chattel is not affected by these provisions.

[2] Dig. Laws 1881, ch. 143, §§ 11, 12.

As to enforcement of innkeepers' liens, see § 529, *supra.*

Landlords' liens, § 610.

Lumbermen's liens, § 707.

Mechanics' or artisans' liens, § 755.

execution against such a proportional part of the property charged with the lien as his demand bears to the whole amount of liens that are charged upon the said property under this law (which proportional part shall be decided by the court), and also against other property of the defendant; but if a part of the property cannot be separated from the residue and sold without damage to the whole, then the whole may be sold, subject to all other incumbrances under this law; but no execution shall issue against the property charged with such lien unless the defendant shall have owned or possessed the property at the time of the commencement of said suit, or unless a *scire facias* shall first have issued and been served upon the owner or possessor of such property, requiring him to appear and show cause why a judgment should not be entered up and execution had against such property.

In all cases under this law it shall be lawful for the plaintiff to proceed by *scire facias* against the original debtor, and against all and every person or persons owning or possessing the property against which he wishes to proceed; but no judgment to be rendered on the *scire facias* shall authorize the issuing of any execution, except on the property charged with said lien, or such part thereof as the court shall direct.

1053. Georgia.[1] — Liens on personal property not otherwise provided for shall be foreclosed as follows : —

1. There must be a demand on the owner, agent, or lessee of the property for payment, and a refusal to pay, and such demand and refusal must be averred. If, however, no such demand can be made, by reason of the absence from the county of his residence of the party creating the lien on personal property, by reason of removal from the same, absconding from the same, or other reasons, showing an intention to be absent to defeat such demand, then the party holding such lien shall not be obliged to make a demand or affidavit thereof, but may foreclose without such demand, by stating on oath why no such demand was made.[2]

[1] Code 1882, §§ 1991, 1992, 2140.
As to the enforcement of carriers' liens, see § 346.
Factors' liens, § 455.
Landlords' liens, §§ 611, 612.

[2] As to demand and affidavit, see Gilbert v. Marshall, 56 Ga. 148 ; Moore v. Martin, 58 Ga. 411 ; Lindsay v. Lowe, 64 Ga. 438.

2. It must be prosecuted within one year after the debt becomes due.

3. The person prosecuting such lien, either for himself or as guardian, administrator, executor, or trustee, must, by himself, agent or attorney, make affidavit before a judge of the superior court, or the ordinary of the county in which the personal property may be, or the defendant may reside, showing all the facts necessary to constitute a lien under this code, and the amount claimed to be due. If the amount claimed is under one hundred dollars, the application may be made to a justice of the peace, who may take all the other steps hereinafter prescribed, as in other cases in his court. Upon such affidavit being filed, if before a judge of the superior court, or the ordinary, with the clerk of the superior court of said county, it shall be the duty of the clerk of the superior court, or the justice of the peace if in his court, to issue an execution instanter against the person owing the debt, and also against the property on which the lien is claimed, or which is subject to said lien, for the amount sworn to, and the costs; which execution, when issued, shall be levied by any sheriff of this state, or bailiff, if the amount be less than one hundred dollars, on such property subject to said lien, under the same rules and regulations as other levies and sales under execution.

4. If the person defendant in such execution, or any creditor of such defendant, contests the amount or justice of the claim, or the existence of such lien, he may file his affidavit of the fact, setting forth the grounds of such denial, which affidavit shall form an issue to be returned to the court and tried as other causes.

5. If only a part of the amount claimed is denied, the amount admitted to be due must be paid before the affidavit shall be received by the officer.

6. The defendant may replevy the property by giving bond and security in double the amount claimed, for the payment of the eventual condemnation money.

Liens of pawnees, innkeepers, boarding-house keepers, livery-stable men, and attorneys at law, in possession of personal property under a lien for fees, shall be satisfied according to the provisions of the next following paragraph,[1] in cases where there is no notice of conflicting liens; but if there is a conflicting lien,

---

[1] § 2140 of the Code.

the mode of foreclosure pointed out in the preceding paragraphs shall be pursued.

The pawnee may sell the property received in pledge after the debt becomes due and remains unpaid; but he must always give notice for thirty days to the pawnor of his intention to sell, and the sale must be in public, fairly conducted, and to the highest bidder, unless otherwise provided by contract.[1]

1054. Illinois.[2] — All persons other than common carriers having a lien on personal property, by virtue of the act to revise the law of liens,[3] may enforce such lien by a sale of the property, on giving to the owner thereof, if he and his residence be known to the person having such lien, ten days' notice, in writing, of the time and place of such sale; and if said owner or his place of residence be unknown to the person having such lien, then upon his filing his affidavit to that effect with the clerk of the county court in the county where said property is situated; notice of said sale may be given by publishing the same once in each week for three successive weeks in some newspaper of general circulation published in said county, and out of the proceeds of said sale the costs and charges for advertising and making the same, and the amount of said lien shall be paid, and the surplus, if any, shall be paid to the owner of said property.

055. Maine.[4] — Whoever has a lien on any stock, or certificate thereof, bond, note, account, or other chose in action, or any other personal property in his possession, may enforce it by a sale.

The person claiming the lien may file in the Supreme Judicial Court in the county where he resides, or in the office of the clerk thereof, a petition briefly setting forth the nature and amount of

---

[1] This is § 2140 of the Code.

[2] Annot. Stat. 1885, ch. 141, § 3.

As to sales of unclaimed property left with a common carrier, innkeeper, or warehouseman, see § 344, *supra.*

As to landlords' liens, see §§ 613, 614, *supra.*

[3] Ib. ch. 82, approved March 25, 1874.

[4] R. S. 1883, ch. 91, §§ 47–55.

As to sale of unclaimed goods left with carriers, see § 350, *supra.*

Innkeepers' liens, § 531, *supra.*

Landlords' liens, § 621, *supra.*

Livery-stable keepers' liens, § 662, *supra.*

Lumbermen's liens, §§ 710, 711, *supra.*

Mechanics' liens, § 761, *supra.*

his claim, a description of the article possessed, and the name and residence of its owners, if known to him, and a prayer for process to enforce his lien.

After service of notice in the manner provided at the time fixed in the notice, any party interested in the article as owner, mortgagee, or otherwise, may appear, and after appearance the proceedings shall be the same as in an action on the case in which the petitioner is plaintiff and the party appearing is defendant.

If, in the opinion of the court, the article on which the lien is claimed is not of sufficient value to pay the petitioner's claim, with the probable costs of suit, the court may order the persons appearing in defence to give bond to the petitioner, with sufficient sureties approved by the court, to pay such costs as are awarded against him, so far as they are not paid out of the proceeds of the articles on which the lien is claimed.

After trial and final adjudication in favor of the petitioner, the court may order any competent officer to sell the article on which the lien is claimed, as personal property is sold on execution; and out of the proceeds, after deducting his fees and the expenses of sale, to pay to the petitioner the amount and costs awarded him, and the balance to the person entitled to it, if he is known to the court, otherwise into court.

Money paid into court may be paid over to the person legally entitled to it, on petition and order of the court. If it is not called for at the first term after it is paid into court, it shall be paid into the county treasury; and if afterwards the person entitled to it petitions and establishes his claim to it, the court may order the county treasurer to pay it to him.

Liens for less than twenty dollars may be enforced before any trial justice.

1056. **Massachusetts.**[1] — Whoever has a lien (other than those in favor of mechanics upon real property and liens upon vessels) for money due to him on account of work and labor,

---

[1] P. S. 1882, ch. 192, §§ 24–30, 33.

As to the sale of unclaimed goods left with carriers, see § 351, *supra*. As to mechanics' and artisans' liens, see § 762, *supra*.

Until the .adoption of the General

Statutes in 1860, a creditor having a lien could do nothing with the property but hold it, and wait for the debtor to redeem. Busfield *v.* Wheeler, 14 Allen, 139, 143, per Wells, J.; Doane *v.* Russell, 3 Gray, 382.

care and diligence, or money expended[1] on or about personal property by reason of any contract express or implied,[2] if such money is not paid within sixty days after a demand[3] in writing, delivered to the debtor, or left at his usual place of abode, if within this commonwealth, or made by letter addressed to him at his usual place of abode without the commonwealth, and deposited in the post-office to be sent to him, may apply by petition to a police, district, or municipal court, or to a trial justice in the county where the petitioner resides, for an order for the sale of the property in satisfaction of the debt.[4]

The court or justice shall thereupon issue a notice to the owner of the property to appear at a time and place designated, to show cause why the prayer of the petition should not be granted ; which notice shall be served by delivering to the owner, or by leaving at his usual place of abode, if within the commonwealth, a copy thereof fourteen days before the day of hearing; and a return of the service shall be made by some officer authorized to serve civil process, or by some other person with an affidavit to the truth of the return.[5]

If the owner is unknown, the application may be made sixty days after the money becomes due, and a notice may issue " to the unknown owner " describing the property. If the owner resides out of the commonwealth, or is unknown, notice may be given by a publication of the order in the manner prescribed for the publication of notices in section seven.

[1] Such lien may cover the cost of materials. Busfield v. Wheeler, 14 Allen, 139.

[2] It is not necessary that the agreement under which the work is done should be in writing, or that any notice of an intention to claim a lien should be given to the owner or recorded. Busfield v. Wheeler, supra.

[3] The demand is merely a preliminary to the proceedings. It need not set out " a just and true account," nor " a description of the property intended to be covered by the lien," as in the case of a mechanic's lien upon real property. The petition is not defeated by the petitioner's demanding too large a sum. Notice of the claim and a request for payment is a demand. Busfield v. Wheeler, supra.

[4] No time being fixed by the statute for the commencement of proceedings to enforce the lien, a petition may be sustained, though not commenced for more than two years, and though no written demand for payment was made for more than fifteen months, after the completion of the work. The general owner has no occasion to complain of delay; for if he wishes to have the property returned, he can pay the debt and claim the property at any time. Busfield v. Wheeler, supra.

[5] The notice issued on the petition need not set forth a statement in detail of the work done and money expended for which a lien is claimed. Busfield v. Wheeler, supra.

If the owner makes default at the time appointed, or if upon a hearing of the parties it appears that a lien exists upon the property, and that the property ought to be sold for the satisfaction of the debt, the court or justice may make an order for that purpose, and, if no appeal is taken, the property may be sold in conformity·therewith. Any surplus of the proceeds of the sale, after satisfying the debt and all costs and charges, shall be paid to the owner upon demand.

The court or justice may ascertain the amount due up to the time of the entering of the order, and may make a record thereof.

Either party may appeal from the final order of the court or justice in the same manner as in other civil cases, and the case shall be heard and determined in the court above, and such order made as justice may require. If the respondent appeals, he shall recognize for the prosecution of his appeal, and for the payment, if judgment is rendered against him, of any balance of the debt, with costs, which may remain unsatisfied after a sale of the property.

The prevailing party shall recover his costs, and the court or justice may issue execution therefor.

When a lien upon live animals is sought to be enforced, the application by petition may be made at the expiration of ten days after a demand in writing instead of at the expiration of sixty days, as therein required; and the notice issued thereon may be served seven days before the hearing, instead of fourteen days, as required by section twenty-five.[1]

1057. New Hampshire.[2] — Any person having a lien on any personal property, by pledge or otherwise, where no time is limited for the payment of the debt or redemption of the property, may sell the same, or so much thereof as is needful, at auction, notice thereof being given as hereinafter required, and from the proceeds reimburse himself for said debt and the expenses incident to such sale.

If a time is limited for the payment of such debt or the re-

---

[1] It is expressly provided that boarding-house keepers may enforce their liens under the foregoing provisions. P. S. ch. 192, § 31. A lien for pasturing, boarding, or keeping horses or other domestic animals may be enforced in the same manner. Ib. § 32. As to the application of the statute to liens of carriers, see Briggs v. Boston & Lowell R. R. Co. 6 Allen, 246.

[2] G. L. 1878, ch. 139, §§ 3–8.

demption of such property, the property may be sold at any time after the expiration of said time, upon like notice, provided the same shall not be in conflict with the terms of the contract under which it is holden.

Notice of such sale shall be given by posting notices thereof in two or more public places in the town where such property is situate, and, if the value of the property exceeds one hundred dollars, by publishing notice thereof three weeks at least before the sale.

A notice of such sale shall be served upon the pledgor or general owner, if resident in the county, the same number of days before the sale, stating in writing the time and place of sale, the property to be sold, and the amount of the lien thereon.

The balance of the proceeds of such sale, if any, after payment of the amount of such lien or pledge and the reasonable expenses incident to such sale, shall be paid to the pledgor, general owner, or person entitled thereto, on demand.

The holder of such lien shall cause a copy of such notices and affidavits of service, with an account of such sale and the fees and charges thereon, to be recorded in the books of the town where such sale is had, and a certified copy thereof may be used in evidence.

1058. Oregon.[1] — Liens of mechanics and laborers, common carriers, agistors, and warehousemen are enforced as follows : If their just and reasonable charges be not paid within three months after the care, attention, and labor shall have been performed or bestowed, or the materials or food shall have been furnished, the person having such lien may proceed to sell at public auction the property on which a lien is given, or a part thereof sufficient to pay such just and reasonable charges. Before selling, he shall give notice of such sale by advertisement for three weeks in a newspaper published in the county, or by posting up notice of such sale in three of the most public places in the city or precinct, for three weeks before the time of such sale, and the proceeds of such sale shall be applied, first, to the discharge of such

[1] Laws 1878, p. 102, §§ 1–4; 2 Hill's Annotated Laws, 1887, §§ 3685, 3686.

As to sale of property left with forwarding merchant, wharfinger, warehouseman, tavern-keeper, or keeper of any depot for storage, see § **363**, *supra.*

As to lumbermen's liens, see § **716**, *supra*, and 2 Hill's Annotated Laws, 1887, §§ 3687–3689.

lien, and the cost of keeping and selling such property, and the remainder, if any, shall be paid over to the owner thereof; provided, that nothing herein contained shall be so construed as to authorize any warehouseman to sell more of any wool, wheat, oats, or other grain than sufficient to pay charges due said warehouseman on such wool, wheat, oats, or other grain; and provided further, that if any such warehouseman shall sell, loan, or dispose of in any manner, without consent of the owner thereof, of any such wool, wheat, oats, or other grain, he shall, for each and every offence, forfeit and pay to the owner of such wool, wheat, oats, or other grain, a sum equal to the market value thereof, and fifty per cent. of said market value in addition as a penalty, the market value to be the price such article or articles bear at the time the owner thereof determines to sell the same, such value and penalty to be recovered by an action at law.

These provisions shall not interfere with any special agreement of the parties.

1059. Pennsylvania.[1] — A commission merchant, factor, common carrier, or other person having a lien for the expenses of carriage, storage, or labor bestowed upon any goods, wares, merchandise, or other property, may sell the same after the expiration of sixty days from a demand of payment.

1060. Texas.[2] — Liens in favor of the proprietors of hotels and boarding-houses and of livery-stables, and in favor of mechanics' for labor upon personal articles, may be foreclosed as follows: —

When possession of any of the property under either of such liens has continued for sixty days after the charges accrue, and the charges so due have not been paid, it shall be the duty of the persons so holding said property to notify the owner, if in the State and his residence be known, to come forward and pay the charges due, and, on his failure within ten days after such notice has been given him to pay said charges, the persons so

---

[1] See statute, § **364**, *supra*.

As to the enforcement of innkeepers' liens, see § **537**, *supra*.

Landlords' liens, §§ **632, 633**, *supra*.

Livery-stable keepers' liens, § **676**, *supra*.

[2] R. S. 1879, arts. 3186–3189.

As to sale of unclaimed goods left with carriers, see § **368**, *supra*.

As to landlords' liens, see § **638**, *supra*.

As to mechanics' and artisans' liens, see § **772**, *supra*.

holding said property, after twenty days' notice, are authorized to sell said property at public sale and apply the proceeds to the payment of said charges, and shall pay over the balance to the person entitled to the same.

If the owner's residence is beyond the State or is unknown, the person holding said property shall not be required to give the ten days' notice before proceeding to sell. If the person who is legally entitled to receive the balance mentioned is not known, or has removed from the State or from the county in which such repairing was done, or such property was so held, it shall be the duty of the person so holding said property to pay the balance to the county treasurer of the county in which said property is held, and take his receipt therefor.

Whenever any balance shall remain in the possession of the county treasurer for the period of two years unclaimed by the party legally entitled to the same, such balance shall become a part of the county fund of the county in which the property was so sold, and shall be applied as any other county fund or money of such county is applied or used.

Printed in the United States
71758LV00003B/46